AMERICAN SPIRITUALITIES

AMERICAN SPIRITUALITIES

A Reader

EDITED BY
CATHERINE L. ALBANESE

Indiana University Press
BLOOMINGTON | INDIANAPOLIS

This book is a publication of

Indiana University Press
601 North Morton Street
Bloomington, IN 47404-3797 USA

http://www.indiana.edu/~iupress

Telephone orders   800-842-6796
Fax orders   812-855-7931
Orders by e-mail   iuporder@indiana.edu

Library of Congress Cataloging-in-Publication Data

American spiritualities : a reader / edited by Catherine L. Albanese.
    p.   cm.
Includes bibliographical references and index.
ISBN 0-253-33839-5 (cloth : alk. paper)—ISBN 0-253-21432-7 (pbk. :
alk. paper)
    1. Spirituality—United States. 2. United States—Religion—20th
century.   I. Albanese, Catherine L.

BL2525.A545 2001
200'.973—dc21

                                                                00-044825

1   2   3   4   5   06   05   04   03   02   01

For my sister, Lucille,
who is spiritual but not religious.

Contents

ACKNOWLEDGMENTS

This book probably began when my colleague Richard Hecht, then Chair of the Department of Religious Studies here at the University of California, Santa Barbara, discussed with me the possibility of creating a course on spirituality in the United States. I bit; and my course—"Religious Studies 150: American Spiritualities"—was born. The students who enrolled in this course in the winter quarter of 1998 took it against great odds. UCSB was retrofitting buildings for earthquake readiness, and space on campus was at a premium. "Religious Studies 150" was summarily rescheduled to be taught in a different building and at a different time. The students who persevered quickly became a loyal and enthusiastic crew. Our in-class conversations were frank and candid, and the learning curve—for both students and professor—was high. I owe both Richard Hecht and these students a tremendous debt of gratitude.

I owe other debts to Robert J. Sloan, Senior Sponsoring Editor at Indiana University Press. It is he who—when in another context I casually discussed the course I had invented and taught—imagined it into a reader for other students. Again I bit, although this time more slowly; and eventually this reader came to be. At least part of my enthusiasm for its creation came, again, from the influence of a colleague—this time Wade Clark Roof, whose own work in the area of American spirituality among the baby boomers encouraged me in the pursuit of my task. Meanwhile, Erica Hurwitz, a graduate student in the original class, meticulously reproduced selections in photocopy to be keyboarded by Indiana University Press. My parents, Louis and Theresa Albanese, and my sister, Lucille Albanese Santo, were constant supports just by being there. It is time past time that I dedicate a project to my wonderful sister, and so, Lucille, this one is for you!

AMERICAN SPIRITUALITIES

Introduction

"When you look closely into American history and in the minds of those great, courageous and intelligent men who were the founding fathers, you would recognize that they were not religious, but spiritual." So wrote Robert Haake in the February–March 1997 issue of *Information Press,* an ephemeral and informally edited pulp periodical. "Remember," he continued, "religions are only man-made systems. . . . But the spiritual is not man made and is universal. It is true and the same everywhere and at all times. It has neither a doctrine nor a leader and need not be supported by any organization nor by anyone's devotion." Haake's perception about a distinction between spirituality and religion is pervasive in present-day American culture. "How do you define a 'spiritual experience'?" asked the July–August 1999 issue of *Yoga Journal* in a poll of its readers. None of its list of possible answers presupposed an organized religious milieu, and most of them, in fact, suggested a noninstitutional context. "Check all that apply," instructed the magazine: "transcendence, oneness with the universe, connection with others, connection with God, quiet mind, sense of harmony, bliss, sense of grace, suspension of time, being in 'the zone,' energy rising up through my chakras, other."[1]

Undergraduate university students at the University of California, Santa Barbara, where I teach, had for the most part anticipated the built-in *Yoga Journal* message about the nature of things spiritual. "Spirituality is the awareness and recognition of the intangible connections between all things," wrote one student when asked to define spirituality. It is "a personal sense of connectedness to others and/or to a higher power," responded a second. For others, spirituality represented "the source within oneself that can guide one's way of life," "a subjective ideology that both constructs and expresses moral conviction," and "an understanding of a higher essence of oneself through all the capacities of the body." Still other students addressed the rumored distinction between spirituality and religion more directly. One declared that spirituality was "a feeling of heightened inner awareness brought about by outer experiences" and that such experiences "could be anything—church, sports, chanting, meditation, gatherings." Another said spirituality was "an individual's own inner experience" that "might be an experience of transformation caused by faith, prayer, meditation, nature, or intellectual inquiry." A third had no room for church or synagogue or mosque at all, with spirituality representing "a way of thinking not based on conventional religious foundations."

Some students became even more thoughtful and philosophical in their responses. For example, one reflected that spirituality "taps into that part of ourselves that exists outside of space and time" and that the "challenge" of spirituality was "to make this part of ourselves manifest in space and time." He went on to observe that "spirituality relates to the essential, religion to the form" and that forms were "inherently incomplete" and "subject to interpretation and change over time," whereas spirituality, which was "complete and changeless," ideally could use religion with its forms to "act as a medium to realize the spiritual." Another student articulated an understanding in which she saw spirituality as "a force that exists universally between all entities in our world, connecting them all." "Everything," she wrote, "has spirit, including plants, animals, air, earth, stars, water." She declared that she was raised with "no named religion" but was taught to "believe that we are all one, connected in a cycle of life." "I feel a special, magical feeling, a sort of 'connectedness' to nature and animals," she affirmed.

By the late twentieth century, sociologists of religion were corroborating what was more or less a consensus regarding a distinction between spirituality and religion—a consensus that the diverse voices of Robert Haake, the editors of *Yoga Journal,* and UCSB students had all acknowledged in their different ways. Studies by Wade Clark Roof and Robert Wuthnow, for example, have been to a considerable degree predicated on a perceived distinction between spirituality and religion articulated by many in today's culture.[2] Yet despite all of this attention to spirituality and its reiterated distinctiveness from religion, the free-ranging statements about what exactly spirituality was and is remained elusively vague—and different.

Above or elsewhere, spirituality has been called the depth dimension of life or the values at one's core center. It has been linked to artistic creativity and to feelings of beyondness and separation from society or, by contrast, to feelings of close communion with others. It has been associated with stillness, silence, and peace, and, alternately, with ecstatic surges of feeling and exuberant shouts. And significantly, as will be seen, it has been called a vehicle for meeting what is sacred. "When *I* use a word," declared a scornful Humpty Dumpty in Lewis Carroll's classic *Through the Looking-Glass,* "it means just what I choose it to mean—neither more nor less."[3] Clearly, Americans who invoke spirituality without the scorn agree, and Wade Clark Roof has rightly alluded to the "multiple discourses about spirituality" that pervade our culture.[4] Philosophers would no doubt call this definitional subjectivity an egregious case of nominalism, but most enthusiasts for spirituality would hardly object, one way or the other. The question about words, they might retort with Humpty Dumpty, is "which is to be master—that's all."[5]

What is ironic, however, about both the assumed distinction between spirituality and religion, and the elusiveness of its definition, is the historical and cultural markers that supply answers different from the apparent prevailing consensus. While spirituality was surely a buzzword in the nineties to the delight of many publishers and purveyors of spiritual goods and services, it has retained a rather conventional and unassuming presence in standard dictionaries. It is not a neologism. Spirituality, according to the unabridged version of *Webster's Third New International Dictionary*, is, in its first meaning, "something that in ecclesiastical law belongs to the church or to a person as an ecclesiastic or to religion." In its second meaning, it is "the whole body of clergy (as in a nation or country)." Third, and closest to the current usage, it is "sensitivity or attachment to religious values and things of the spirit rather than material or worldly interests." The abridged *Webster's Ninth New Collegiate Dictionary*, beloved of writers and publishers, more or less agrees, if shorter and terser in its statement: spirituality is "something that in ecclesiastical law belongs to the church or to a cleric as such," or it is another word for "clergy," or it means "sensitivity or attachment to religious values." All of these definitions locate spirituality squarely in the realm of religion. More than that, they mostly link it to Christianity in its organized, ecclesiastical form.

Nor does the recent history of the use of the term spirituality yield a different picture. Anchored respectably as spirituality is in dictionaries, it acquired a new life in the United States beginning in the 1950s—and that in Roman Catholic circles. Catholics had long been familiar with language about the "spiritual life," however unexciting they may have found it.[6] The specific word spirituality, translating the Latin noun *spiritualitas*, had become "spiritualty" or "spirituality" in English, "spiritualty" being used in a devotional sense as early as the fourteenth century, and "spirituality" in a philosophical one (in contradistinction to "matter") by the seventeenth. In the twentieth century, the term appeared in English under distinctly Catholic auspices in the book *Christian Spirituality*, translated in 1922, the title of the first volume of a work by Frenchman Pierre Pourrat.[7] The French fondness for spirituality would continue to be apparent.

Meanwhile, the rhetoric of the spiritual was part of the devotional literature available for laypeople, and it was particularly noticeable in writings produced to support the piety of monks and nuns. The life of perfection, as it was called—evoking centuries of monastic and mystical literature—was usually conducted with the guidance of a "spiritual director," a priest in the confessional or a monastic superior. It was a "spiritual life" that involved God, Christ, his mother Mary, and all of the saints but also one's "progress" in meditation or contemplative prayer and in the practice of virtue within the confines of the monastery or convent. In the fifties, however, what had been an unexceptional part of twentieth-century religion as usual in the Catholic subculture became transformed into an occasion for wider cultural yearning—among Catholics themselves, and others, too.

Roman Catholic works on spirituality began to appear noticeably, at first more slowly and then with increasing frequency.[8] And the icon for the new spiritualizing times became Thomas Merton. A cosmopolitan adult convert to Catholicism, Merton entered a Trappist monastery and pursued a contemplative life there, emerging as an American culture hero through his autobiography *Seven Storey Mountain* (1948) and through a steady stream of "spiritual" writings—works about the life of prayer and instructions on how to pursue it.[9] "The scope of his work and its impact on the Catholic community in the United States has yet to be fully comprehended," wrote Joseph P. Chinnici in his Bicentennial history of American Catholic spirituality.[10]

Robert Ellwood, in his wide-ranging study of American religion in the fifties, found Merton appealing to a wider audience. Working through the fifties, said Ellwood, was "something more than sentimental I-and-God religion, or neoorthodox dialectics" (the consensual, largely Anglo-Protestant choices for populist and elite religion respectively). Ellwood called the "more" spirituality and discovered it in the popularity of Merton's works in general. He also located it in "the stream of postulants entering monasteries and convents (Episcopal and even Lutheran, as well as Roman Catholic)" and in "the regular publication of books and articles reprinting or discussing the classics of Christian mysticism." All of this "was an all-right thing to talk about; even *Time,* in its cover story on nuns, wrote knowingly of St. John of the Cross and the dark night of the soul."[11]

The mid-century turn to the spiritual, then, was a turn to religion, but religion in its devotional aspects as pursued under the rubric of Christian contemplation. It was, as Ellwood summarized, "a subtle, deeply-infused, wordless awareness of divine presence more akin to that known by the mystics."[12] Catholics, however, continued to take the lead, using a term that, for them, seemed as comfortable as an old monastic shoe. The Dominican periodical *Cross and Crown,* published from 1949, would rename itself *Spirituality Today* in 1977 and continue to thrive. Meanwhile, as early as the fifties, a *Cross and Crown* series on spirituality began to be produced under Dominican editorship by Herder, a Roman Catholic publishing house. Renowned French Catholic theologian Louis Bouyer's *Introduction to Spirituality* appeared in translation in 1961, published by the Liturgical Press at St. John's Abbey in Collegeville, Minnesota, a press that assumed a leadership role in the liturgical changes associated with Vatican Council II.[13] New works appeared on the spirituality of individuals, on biblical spirituality, on the spirituality of different historical eras and groups, on the spirituality of the Catholic mass and sacraments, and on a growing range of other subjects.

The spirituality industry in the Catholic community was off and running. By the late seventies Paulist Press had brought out the first volume in its extensive and ambitious series The Classics of Western Spirituality. The "classic" was Julian of Norwich's *Showings*, the mystical work of a fourteenth- and early-fifteenth-century English anchoress who pursued a solitary contemplative life in a cell attached to the parish Church of St. Julian in Conisford at Norwich.[14] By this time, too, New York's Roman Catholic Fordham University had established a Spirituality Graduate Program, and Ewert H. Cousins, editorial consultant for the Paulist Press series, was its director. To suggest, with a vengeance, the orthodoxy of the term spirituality in Roman Catholic quarters, Jean LeClercq, who wrote the preface to the Julian of Norwich volume, was listed therein as Professor at the Institute of Spirituality at Gregorian University in Rome.

Other "classics" followed in the Paulist series. Editors did not confine themselves to writings by Catholic authors but included Protestant, Jewish, Muslim, and North and South American Indian works, too. What was clear in all of them, however, was that these volumes were predominately mystical or at least deeply devotional in focus. "For sheer publishing courage and imagination, what can surpass . . . The Classics of Western Spirituality?" *Publishers Weekly* enthused, in an estimate that duly appeared on the back cover of one Classics volume in 1980.[15] And apparently others agreed. Volumes were sold by subscription and also individually. Business seemed good, because more "classics" kept coming. Then, in 1981, Paulist Press published *An American Experience of God*, John Farina's revised Columbia University doctoral dissertation on Isaac Hecker, founder of the Paulists, in which Farina read Hecker as an exponent of the mystical tradition.[16] By 1984, Farina was editing the Sources of American Spirituality series for Paulist Press, a series that continued until 1993 and produced some twenty-three titles.

At almost the same time as Farina's first book, in 1980, Jon Alexander asked in the Dominican periodical *Spirituality Today*, "What do recent writers mean by spirituality?" By now, Alexander could point to a series of understandings of the term that had moved from less particularized to more general understandings.[17] Still, in the Catholic context, spirituality usually meant something related to religion, however broadly conceived, as, for example, in the definition by Catholic moral theologian Hans Urs von Balthazar that Alexander cited in his article. Here spirituality referred to "that basic practical or existential attitude of man which is the consequence and expression of the way in which he understands his religious—or more generally, his ethically committed—existence" and, again, "the way in which he acts and reacts habitually throughout his life according to his objective and ultimate insights and decisions."[18] Later in the decade, Ewert Cousins could pronounce spirituality to be "the experiential dimension of religion in contrast with formal beliefs, external practices, and institutions"; and he could go on to declare that "it deals with the inner depth of the person that is open to the transcendent." "In traditions that affirm the divine," he continued with an older Catholic emphasis, "it is concerned with the relation of the person to the divine, the experience of the divine, and the journey of the person to a more intimate relationship with the divine."[19]

As Cousins's words suggest, even among the Catholic spirituality faithful, traditional ties to religious orthodoxy were loosening. Indeed, as early as 1961, Louis Bouyer's translated *Introduction to Spirituality* had made distinctions between what he called the interior life, the spiritual life, and the religious life. The interior life stood for the world of personal thought and feeling, whatever its object; the spiritual life, for something akin to the "more" that Robert Ellwood would later describe for fifties Americans—some reality beyond the self and its projects; and the religious life, for an explicit reference to a transcendent God with whom one could enter a personal relationship.[20]

Change was clearly afoot in the referential orbit of the language of spirituality. Was the change the result of increasing semantic precision, as Bouyer's distinctions suggest? Or, on an American terrain where the book was received and where other works on spirituality were being published, were there different reasons for the persuasiveness of the transforming usage? Had anything happened in the American cultural world to generate changed ideas about spirituality? The answer, for most U.S. invokers of spirituality, whether Catholic or not, lay in that profoundly transformative decade, the 1960s. "The Sixties wanted spirituality," wrote Robert Ellwood, "but they mistrusted the church on the corner; what was exotic or archaic was better, and what lay behind the most arcane symbols one could find might be best of all."[21]

Catholics had successfully launched the language of spirituality in the cultural discourse of the time, but the language met an era rife with religious change. The term that Catholics had effectively contributed to public rhetoric came back to American Catholics with new and broader inscriptions and meanings, changing Catholics themselves along with others. So Ellwood could notice, for the sixties, that the baby boomer generation liked the term spirituality because of its flexibility.[22] And in so doing, he could echo sociologist Wade Clark Roof, whose searching study of the baby boomers transcribed an understanding of spirituality as loose and diffuse as the boomers had by now made it. By the time that Roof wrote *A Generation of Seekers,* he was quoting then-Roman Catholic Dominican priest Matthew Fox to the effect that spirituality concerned "heart-knowledge": "In its truest sense, spirituality gives expression to the being that is in us; it has to do with feelings, with the power that comes from within, with knowing our deepest selves and what is sacred to us, with, as Matthew Fox says, 'heart-knowledge.'"[23] Significantly, Roof's index listing for "spirituality" referred the reader to "mysticism" as well ("*see also* Mysticism"). Roof was, in fact, echoing a new Catholic understanding that was speaking more in an American dialect than in a traditional one. In Fox's own expanded version, as an advocate he had underlined the centrality of learning "just to be" for his "heart-knowledge" brand of spirituality, and he had gone on to say that spirituality was about "power." More specifically, he had declared spirituality to be "about developing the powers of creativity, justice, and compassion in all persons" and "about unleashing divine powers in us all."[24]

What had happened was that the mystical side of Catholic culture had encountered a series of cultural changes in the sixties that made it strikingly malleable and newly appealing to a much broader audience of Americans, who—as the "spirituality" word made its way into the public square—absorbed it in a context in which its traditional trappings had fallen away. The Vietnam War has surely been one such change, raising probing questions on an unprecedented public scale about the wisdom of authorities and institutions and the integrity of the self in relation to them. The civil rights movement, which challenged long-held notions of status and place—not only for Southerners but for all Americans—was another. Black consciousness and pride, enhanced by legal and congressional victories, helped fuel the consciousness of other groups. A new ethnic awareness swept the land, and an earlier "women's liberation" movement began to speak a renewed language of personal power. The continuing demographic shifts, in which more and more people stayed put less and less of the time, and in which more and more families experienced their fragility and capacity for disintegration, brought their own suspicions of conventional answers and arrangements. The children of the highway and of the divorce court seemed inherently to question what an organized and established order told them.

More than that, baby boomers and fellow travelers who lived through the Vietnam War years and experienced the changes in American society were met by new outsiders, who came bearing messages of their own. These outsiders were Asian religious teachers, who began to achieve critical mass in American society after the immigration law was changed in 1965 to reflect a reformed quota system that was even-handed for all national groups. The Oriental Exclusion Act had been rescinded at last, and Asia could send its religious emissaries to gain a hearing in the American world.

Gordon Melton has documented the most prominent of the Asian teachers who subsequently appeared on these shores: In 1965 alone came A. C. Bhaktivedanta Swami Prabhupada, founder in that year of the International Society for Krishna Consciousness (ISKCON), Sant Keshavadas of the Temple of Cosmic Wisdom, and Thera Bode Vinita of the Buddhist Vihara Society. In 1968, Yogi Bhajan of the Sikh Dharma, founder a year later of the Healthy-Happy-Holy Organization (3HO) and teacher of a new kundalini yoga, likewise arrived. By 1969 Tarthang Tulku was here with Tibetan Nyingmapa, and by 1970 so was Swami Rama of the Himalayan Institute. The following year brought Swami Satchidananda of the Integral Yoga Institute, Gurudev Chitrabhanu of the Meditation International Center, and the Maharaj Ji of the Divine Light

Mission. And in 1972 Sun Myung Moon of the Unification Church and Vesant Paranjpe of the Fivefold Path both arrived, preaching their good news to Americans who would listen.[25]

Missionary Asia was camping in American fields. "Very like the change that came over Christianity in the move from the eighteenth to the nineteenth century," Melton observed, "a dormant zeal to spread their faith emerged among Hindus and Buddhists, who set out to return the compliment paid Asia by the Christian missionaries in the previous century." The new Asian presence and missionary consciousness, wrote Melton, added up to "a large-scale movement of both people and religion from East to West, a movement with the potential to reshape the Western religious scene as significantly as nineteenth-century Christianity reshaped Africa and the Orient."[26] Americans, unsure of conventional institutional authorities because of a traumatizing series of public events and because of social and demographic stresses, saw in Asian teachings answers to age-old questions about meaning, destiny, and purpose. And they saw them to be seemingly unencumbered by traditional organizational structures. It was true, of course, that the Asians had their own organizations and authorities, but the charisma of leaders who spoke with "spiritual" presence and the otherness and unfamiliarity of their institutions made both seem, often, a desirable alternative for individualizing Americans—in search of ultimate answers and wisdom, too, for everyday living.

Still, relatively speaking, the numbers of Americans who turned East in fundamental commitments was small, even minuscule. What the presence of Easterners did that was, in the end, more important was to introduce into the cultural vocabulary new ways to talk and think about the former world of religion. Pluralism multiplied options and paradigms. Those Americans who were alienated from their own traditions, and therefore suspicious of conventional institutional moorings, found through the diffusion of Asian traditions and concepts a new way of understanding their relationship to ultimate values and concerns. More than that, the Asian presence blended comfortably with American religious alternatives that had flourished on a small scale since the nineteenth century.

The Theosophical Society, founded in New York City in 1875 by Russian immigrant Helene P. Blavatsky along with American Colonel Henry Steel Olcott and others, had from 1878 functioned as a vehicle for the introduction of key Asian ideas and concepts to a seeker community of upscale Americans. Indeed, in theosophical and related quarters, there was even a small cottage industry in spirituality in the late nineteenth and early twentieth centuries. As Westerners encountered South Asian religion, through theosophical efforts and through the World's Parliament of Religions—held in conjunction with the Columbian Exposition of 1893—they began to talk about the "spirituality" of modern Hinduism. Contrary to Western materialism, theosophizing students and adepts thought Indian religion should be celebrated for its spiritual superiority.[27] Moreover, it was from Blavatsky and her followers that terms like "karma" and "reincarnation" began to become available. And it was from theosophical lineages, with new spin-off theosophical teachers—such as Alice Bailey and Guy Ballard in the 1920s—that Asia continued to maintain its presence in American quarters, now blended and metamorphosed through contact with the esoteric tradition of the West.

Theosophists were joined in the late nineteenth century by the early proponents of the New Thought or mind-cure tradition. Carrying trails of Swedenborgian mystical teachings about correspondences between the world of spirit and the world of matter, and carrying, too, a legacy of mesmeric or magnetic teaching (an early version of hypnotism) about invisible tides, New Thought gave practical voice and application to these ideas. New Thoughters called themselves metaphysicians, and they denominationalized into groups like the Unity School of Christianity, Religious Science, and Divine Science. But they denominationalized only weakly, and they mostly made their mark on general culture through the language of positive thinking that was spread, not by a New Thought denomination per se, but by Norman Vincent Peale of the Methodist faith and by others.[28]

In the 1960s, the religious vernaculars of the three movements—a newly arrived Asian presence, the theosophical legacy, and the New Thought tradition—were being heard, by a generation of spiritual seekers, in overlapping ways.[29] It was these blended voices that spoke with increasing authority to the American times. And it was these voices that, in the cultural marketplace of the era, linked their once-and-sometime language about spirituality to an articulate Catholic usage, spinning off into new permutations for the spiritual and its cognate terms. Spiritual learners in the culture heard and understood. Spirituality became the encoded sign for elusive metaphysically and mystically oriented turns of mind, for experiential and receptive emotional states of unusual nature and/or intensity—within or outside of Christian circles, for acts of bodily and ritual deliberateness that had little to do with economic imperatives, or for societal commitments toward reform or revolution generated by the towering presence of an ideal. Spirituality, in short, became what Robert Haake and *Yoga Journal* said it was and what Southern California university students said it was; it became what American sociologists of religion alike could agree was, for many, distinct and separate from religion.

Humpty Dumpty was apparently right concerning the meanings of words. Still, if we follow the Alice-in-Wonderland cue, the question is about "whether you *can* make words mean so many different things." And the answer—not just the question—may include something about achieving mastery over word and language, however arbitrarily.[30] Put another way, any study of spirituality must work with usage to find a comfort zone in which the term resides. But such a study must also set limits for the comfort zone and so decide what falls within and outside of it. Consider, for example, Robert Wuthnow's definition of spirituality in *After Heaven*. Wuthnow's book is concerned with a "profound change in our spiritual practices" since the 1950s, a change in which, he argues, "a traditional spirituality of inhabiting sacred places has given way to a new spirituality of seeking." Americans, says Wuthnow, have generally moved away from what he calls a "spirituality of dwelling" and toward a new seeker version. Yet as richly as his work ranges to advance this case, it is clear from Wuthnow's prefatory remarks that not anything under the American sun counts as spiritual. "At its core," writes Wuthnow, "spirituality consists of all the beliefs and activities by which individuals attempt to relate their lives to God or to a divine being or some other conception of a transcendent reality."[31] Meanwhile, Phillip C. Lucas, who studies new religious movements, in an encyclopedia article on New Age spirituality uses language that is strikingly similar—calling spirituality "beliefs and practices that attempt to bring a person into harmonious relationship with a sacred realm or being."[32] Significantly, both of these definitions echo Ewert Cousins and, to a certain extent, Hans Urs von Balthazar. The "expanded" Catholic definition of spirituality, available from at least the eighties, seems in some sense here still operative.

Meanwhile, in his *Spiritual Marketplace*, Wade Clark Roof, returning to boomer culture for a follow-up study of religious and spiritual change among its population, forms his own assessment of what he calls "a quest culture." "*The boundaries of popular religious communities are now being redrawn,*" he writes, "*encouraged by the quests of the large, post–World War II generations, and facilitated by the rise of an expanded spiritual marketplace.*"[33] And what is spirituality in the context of the quest culture at the close of the twentieth century and the beginning of the twenty-first? The "spiritual" is "the experiential face of religion." Spirituality encompasses "a source of values and meaning beyond oneself, a way of understanding, inner awareness, and personal integration." Indeed, Roof tells, "the spiritual comprehends but cannot be contained by intellect, cognition, or institutional structure; it reaches out for unity and the ordering of experience; it abhors fixity in the interest of transformation. Both the notion of ordering experience and that of transformation suggest something deeply existential, directed to connections with ultimate meanings, values, and ethical commitment."[34]

As these definitional forays suggest, the comfort zone for scholars must come to terms with the comfort zone for other Americans. Thus, it is important to notice that contemporary Americans who insist that they are spiritual but not religious are often engaging in a clearly identifiable elision. They conflate all religion with organized religion, and since they would not be caught darkening traditional institutional doors for reasons other than marriage (somebody else's) or death (also somebody else's), they forthrightly declare themselves free of religion. Closer scrutiny, however, often discovers the spiritual-but-not-religious heavily engaged in what any scholar of religion would call religious acts and predicating them on what would equally be called religious beliefs. To be sure, these are often, in cultural terms, unconventional religious acts and beliefs, but they count as religious acts and beliefs nonetheless.

With all of this as horizon for reflection, in the pages that follow the spiritual will be understood to be, indeed, related to the religious. In fact, spirituality will be read and understood as the personal, experiential element in religion—whether the religion in question is organized or of movement status or mostly individual; and whether it involves God, or other-than-human guides and spirits, or the center of the Self, or an almighty Nature, or an Ideal held to be worth living or dying for. In the readings presented here, spirituality will emerge as a kind or quality of "knowledge," with knowledge standing for lived encounters that involve people as whole human beings, often to deeply transformative ends. So the definitional task will become, in large part, a descriptive task, a task of coming to terms with what some Americans have, by their own accounts, seen and sensed of worlds beyond (and sometimes in) the everyday. The task will be to address aspects of experience that, for those involved, signal transcendence, sacrality, ultimacy, and/or a higher and purposive wisdom that empowers by explaining and attesting life's meaning.

This is a large span of territory. But the point here is that there can be—and are—markers. Although, as Jonathan Z. Smith has memorably told, "map is not territory," maps *can* be supplied for an American spiritual terrain.[35] This landscape is neither monotonously vague nor chaotically confused. Indeed, despite the amorphous character of popular commentary on things spiritual, religious studies interpreters, both contemporary and older, have often noticed profound differences in styles of spirituality or personal experiential religiosity among believers. Robert Wuthnow is one example, and others surely can be given, classical sociologists of religion such as Max Weber and Joachim Wach prominent among them.[36]

Like these other charters of the territory, this reader, too, works to move past the vagaries of the spirit in favor of maps. With historical attention to prevalent types of American religious experience as one backdrop and the rumblings of an older faculty psychology (i.e., basic faculties of the human person) as another, the reader is constructed around a typology of sorts. Sections of this text will introduce examples of four kinds of spiritual knowing—through the body, through the heart, through the will, and through the mind. This is distinctly not the classical and received faculty psychology of either Roman Catholicism or orthodox Protestantism, but it is a faculty psychology that, I believe, resonates strongly with what has transpired spiritually on these shores. Here knowing through the body encompasses ritually based forms of spirituality in which gesture and movement, usually in public contexts, are essential. Knowing through the heart, by contrast, foregrounds a spiritual style in which strongly felt emotion is uppermost, with the classic conversion experience seemingly the epitome but other strongly toned experiences prominent as well. Knowing through the will explores the kind of spirituality in which social action inspired by ideals of justice and right becomes a profoundly impelling way of life. Knowing through the mind—the ubiquitous spiritual style of the "spiritual-but-not-religious"—examines some of the many ways in which metaphysical religion uses the mind (as distinct from the brain and its "linear," deductive logic) as a religious tool that leads to states of heightened awareness and sometimes mysticism as well as symbolic forms of action.

However, if these types resonate with a kind of faculty psychology, foregrounding various aspects of a common humanity in their emphases, they also—and here more important—resonate with the lived realities of American religious history. A significant glimpse into these dynamics may be gained through Jon Butler's masterful work *Awash in a Sea of Faith*, a revisionist historical overview of American religiosity from the seventeenth century to the time of the Civil War.[37] Butler's "plot" is the Christianization of the land, as his subtitle indicates. But in the process of telling that tale he demonstrates, in the pre-1865 era, the presence of three major forces that vied for religious control of what became the United States. As first of the three, Butler points to evangelicalism, which virtually all historians know about and emphasize. Second, he pays careful attention to the occult/magical (metaphysical) tradition, which he has done much rigorous work to identify as an important, but until his writing, virtually ignored historical presence. Third, Butler underscores the significance of the mainstream institutional tradition, largely Anglo-Protestant in much of the earlier history of the country, which—he argues vigorously (and this is, indeed, the burden of his book)—has been wrongly downplayed in American religious historiography.

However much one may agree or disagree with Butler's argument regarding the relative explanatory power of each of these three religious "camps," his identification of the three contending forces is valuable for any attempt to explore what counts as American spiritualities. For if one begins to think of the three in terms of spiritual styles, what emerges is a typology that gets us well on the way to the one explored in these pages. Butler's evangelicals, as we will see, can easily be matched to the religion of emotion and feeling, or knowing through the heart. His mainstream tradition points toward the ritual orientation of knowing through the body. And his occult-magical camp becomes the metaphysical forms that privilege knowing through the mind—not simply in mentalistic and meditative ways but also in imagistic ones that lead toward more externalized forms of practice. Here, then, are three "types" of spirituality functioning at or near the center of American religious history.

If we look to the margins, though, and return to the evangelicals—who have played so large a share in shaping the nation's spiritual life—we can easily find a fourth form of spirituality that completes the typology that grounds this book. For the evangelicals were characteristically imbued with an overriding sense of mission, a zeal that could be—and was—expressed in their conviction that the social order needed radical reform. Thus, out of one side of the evangelical impulse as it began to encounter the pluralizing forces that more and more came to mark the nation's life, came the spiritual style that is prophecy, or knowing through the will. It is a minority spiritual style, to be sure, and one that, with pluralism, acquired nonevangelical sources and expressions. But, for any student of American religious history it is a minority style that cannot be overlooked or ignored because of its role in explaining the dynamics of the nation's religious history. Hence, a typology emerges with three players at the center—evangelicals, institutionalists, metaphysicians—and one, comprising the prophets, guarding the boundaries and making periodic forays into the center. So the typology, in the end, arises from what has been the American story. From a historical perspective, it is not arbitrarily imposed.

Still, even though the typology that organizes material in this book is experientially based and historically sensitive, like any typology it is of course an extraction from what David Hall and others would call "lived religion."[38] In the religiously combinative United States, any careful historian would need to conclude that pure types melt into blended religious cosmologies and forms of practice. That fact is surely amply demonstrated in these pages. But to gain clarity about an American range of possibilities for the spiritual, it *is* useful to extract, at least provisionally. The readings offered here will not answer all questions regarding American spirituality and spiritualities. Nor are they intended to; nor should they. What they should help to do, however, is to spur readers to keep asking questions about spiritual styles, to be uneasy with facile statements of disregard for religious connections, and to stay on the trail of following these forms of experiential knowledge and of searching out the differences and distinctions among them.

"I long ago lost a hound, a bay horse, and a turtle-dove, and am still on their trail," wrote a spiritually minded Henry David Thoreau in an elliptical passage in *Walden*. He kept on, he said, asking other travelers about the disappeared speeders on wind and wing but only got elusive reports in reply—answers from "one or two who had heard the hound, and the tramp of the horse, and even seen the dove disappear behind a cloud."[39] The readings here put us on Thoreau's remembered trail and add other information for the quest, a quest with which most of us, at one time or another in our lives, can identify.

NOTES

1. "Sex and the Spirit: A *Yoga Journal* Reader Survey," *Yoga Journal* 147 (July/August 1999): 61.

2. Wade Clark Roof, *A Generation of Seekers: The Spiritual Journeys of the Baby Boom Generation* (San Francisco: Harper, 1993), esp. 76–80, 129–30, and Wade Clark Roof, *Spiritual Marketplace: Baby Boomers and the Remaking of American Religion* (Princeton: Princeton University Press, 1999); Robert Wuthnow, *After Heaven: Spirituality in America since the 1950s* (Berkeley: University of California Press, 1998), esp. 74–80, 182.

3. Lewis Carroll, *Through the Looking-Glass and What Alice Found There* (New York: Harper, 1902), 117.

4. Roof, *Spiritual Marketplace*, 34.

5. Carroll, *Through the Looking-Glass*, 117.

6. Josef Sudbrack, in his essay "Spirituality" in *Sacramentum Mundi: An Encyclopedia of Theology*, ed. Karl Rahner et al., vol. 6 (New York: Herder and Herder, 1970), describes mid-twentieth-century connotations of "banality" and "anaemic unreality" for "spirituality" (Sudbrack, "Spirituality," 149). One would assume that the related "spiritual life" likewise carries the connotations.

7. Pierre Pourrat, *Christian Spirituality*, trans. W. H. Mitchell and S. P. Jacques, vol. 1 (London: Burns, Oates and Washbourne, 1922). See Walter Principe, "Toward Defining Spirituality," *Studies in Religion/Sciences Religieuses* 12, no. 2 (Spring 1983): 131–32 and n. 29, 134 and n. 42.

8. Principe, "Toward Defining Spirituality," 128–29.

9. Thomas Merton, *The Seven Storey Mountain* (New York: Harcourt, Brace, 1948). Joseph P. Chinnici's list of Merton's spiritual writings before 1960 also includes, *Seeds of Contemplation* (1949), *The Waters of Siloe* (1949), *The Ascent to Truth* (1951), *The Sign of Jonas* (1953), and *No Man Is an Island* (1955). See Joseph P. Chinnici, *Living Stones: The History and Structure of Catholic Spiritual Life in the United States*, The Bicentennial History of the Catholic Church in America (New York: Macmillan, 1989), 205.

10. Ibid., 206.

11. Robert S. Ellwood, *The Fifties Spiritual Marketplace: American Religion in a Decade of Conflict* (New Brunswick: Rutgers University Press, 1997), 146.

12. Ibid.

13. Louis Bouyer, *Introduction to Spirituality*, trans. Mary Perkins Ryan (New York: Desclee, 1961). For the transmutation of *Cross and Crown* into *Spirituality Today*, see Principe, "Toward Defining Spirituality," 129.

14. Julian of Norwich, *Showings*, trans. and intro. by Edmund Colledge and James Walsh, The Classics of Western Spirituality (New York: Paulist Press, 1978). For biographical details on Julian's life, see the introduction, 18–19.

15. Miguel Leon-Portilla, ed., *Native Mesoamerican Spirituality: Ancient Myths, Discourses, Stories, Doctrines, Hymns, Poems from the Aztec, Yucatec, Quiche-Maya, and Other Sacred Traditions* (New York: Paulist Press, 1980).

16. John Farina, *An American Experience of God: The Spirituality of Isaac Hecker* (New York: Paulist Press, 1981), 178–79.

17. Jon Alexander, "What Do Recent Writers Mean by Spirituality?" *Spirituality Today* 32, no. 2 (September 1980): 247–54. Alexander's *American Personal Religious Accounts, 1600–1980: Toward an Inner History of America's Faiths* (New York: Edwin Mel-

len Press, 1983) provided an early and comprehensive anthology on spirituality. I owe to Alexander my initial acquaintance with confessional statements by Charles W. Colson, Emma Goldman, Aimee Semple McPherson, and Jerry Rubin, all represented in the pages thaat follow.

18. Hans Urs von Balthazar, quoted in ibid., 251.

19. Ewert Cousins, "Spirituality in Today's World," in *Religion in Today's World: The Religious Situation of the World from 1945 to the Present Day,* ed. Frank Whaling (Edinburgh: T. & T. Clark, 1987), 306.

20. Bouyer, *Introduction to Spirituality,* 1–4.

21. Robert S. Ellwood, *The Sixties Spiritual Awakening: American Religion Moving from Modern to Postmodern* (New Brunswick: Rutgers University Press, 1994), 94.

22. Ibid., 9.

23. Roof, *Generation of Seekers,* 64.

24. Matthew Fox, "A Mystical Cosmology: Toward a Postmodern Spirituality," in *Sacred Interconnections: Postmodern Spirituality, Political Economy, and Art,* ed. David Ray Griffin (Albany: State University of New York Press, 1990), 15–33.

25. J. Gordon Melton, "How New Is New? The Flowering of the 'New' Religious Consciousness since 1965," in *The Future of New Religious Movements,* ed. David G. Bromley and Phillip E. Hammond (Macon, Ga.: Mercer University Press, 1987), 52.

26. Ibid., 52, 53.

27. See Principe, "Toward Defining Spirituality," 133–34.

28. For Peale, see Carol V. R. George, *God's Salesman: Norman Vincent Peale and the Power of Positive Thinking* (New York: Oxford University Press, 1993).

29. See Melton's related assessment in "How New Is New?"

30. Carroll, *Through the Looking-Glass,* 117.

31. Wuthnow, *After Heaven,* 3, viii.

32. Phillip Charles Lucas, "New Age Spirituality," in *Contemporary American Religion,* ed. Wade Clark Roof (New York: Macmillan Reference USA, 2000), 2: 489.

33. Roof, *Spiritual Marketplace,* 10. Italics in original.

34. Roof, *Spiritual Marketplace,* 33, 35, 34. Roof cites, in this context, the work of Protestant theological giant Paul Tillich in his *Systematic Theology* (Chicago: University of Chicago Press, 1963), 3: 24.

35. Jonathan Z. Smith, *Map Is Not Territory: Studies in the History of Religions* (Leiden: E. J. Brill, 1978).

36. See, for example, Max Weber, *The Sociology of Religion,* 4th ed., trans. Ephraim Fischoff (Boston: Beacon Press, 1963); Joachim Wach, *Sociology of Religion* (Chicago: University of Chicago Press, Phoenix Books, 1944), and *Types of Religious Experience: Christian and Non-Christian* (Chicago: University of Chicago Press, 1951). For more recent interpreters, see, for instance, Frederick J. Streng, *Understanding Religious Life,* 3d ed. (Belmont, Calif.: Wadsworth, 1985); and, for the United States, Robert S. Ellwood, Jr., *Alternative Altars: Unconventional and Eastern Spirituality in America* (Chicago: University of Chicago Press, 1979), esp. 1–61.

37. Jon Butler, *Awash in a Sea of Faith: Christianizing the American People* (Cambridge: Harvard University Press, 1990).

38. David D. Hall, ed., *Lived Religion in America: Toward a History of Practice* (Princeton: Princeton University Press, 1997).

39. Henry D. Thoreau, *Walden,* ed. J. Lyndon Shanley, The Writings of Henry David Thoreau (Princeton: Princeton University Press, 1971), 17.

PART ONE

Knowing through the Body

KNOWING THROUGH THE BODY:
THE PATH OF RITUAL

At one time or another, many—if not most—Americans have probably heard the phrase "empty ritual." Indeed, this familiar, almost hackneyed, expression is one that numbers of people nowadays would use to initiate a conversation about religion. Ritual seems "empty" to its critics because of cultural formations that are both historical and contemporary. The sixteenth-century Protestant Reformation brought with it strenuous objection to Catholic ritual displays in the mass and sacraments and to a theory of indulgences that put its premium on earning spiritual rewards through what were usually ritual acts of devotion. American public culture, formed in the Anglo-Protestant shadow of the Reformation with a strong Calvinist component, inherited a suspicion of ritual forms. Rites in religion carried the odor of Catholicism and papal corruption; they emanated Roman dominance and mindless conformance to "superstition."

Protestants, of course, developed their own ritual forms—in traditional services that showcased sermon, hymnody, and congregational participation for low-church adherents and something very like the Catholic mass for high-church advocates. Thus, throughout American religious history and, important here, in the late twentieth century, traditional church forms—Protestant and Catholic alike—could be acknowledged as ritually based. The same was true as well for Judaism, for Eastern Orthodoxy, and for other religious legacies in the United States. It was no wonder, then, that persons who became alienated from organized religion would become alienated, too, from formal religious ritual. Hence, for historic reasons and for more immediate ones, there have been powerful persuaders to encourage people to dismiss ritual.

Not all Americans, past or present, however, have found ritual to be empty. In fact, for countless numbers, in both traditional and heterodox contexts, ritual has been not empty but very full. As discussion above already begins to suggest, Roman Catholicism, high-church Protestantism, Judaism, Eastern Orthodoxy, Islamic and Asian religious forms, Native American ones, and smaller spiritual practice groups, too, have demonstrated a spirituality in which ritual acts and gestures are central. For all of these forms, the term liturgy comes to mind. Etymologically derived from the Greek *leitourgia*—a compound word built from the Greek *laos* (Attic *leos*) for "people" and *ergon* for "work"—liturgy means, literally, the work of the people. In Greek, the term was used to refer to a public service or a divine service. In English, it has come to mean the formal communal worship that characterizes religious groups. Hence, at the very core of ritual spirituality is a sense that knowing through the body is knowing done for the most part in public and in deliberate, prescribed terms.

These markers point, in turn, to a strong sense of the worth of tradition in ritual spirituality. An existing public and a prescribed rubric are fixed anchors for continuity, for historic memory and ties that bind across the years. Moreover, following from the ritual constellation of values is a preference for the organic and evolutionary—a normalization of gradual growth and transformation. Corn may sometimes shoot up in the night, but most organic changes are slow changes. And proponents of ritual spirituality mostly expect and cherish religious gradualism. Here there are no sudden and dramatic conversions and no world-shattering moments of enlightenment and illumination—or very few of them. Instead, there is abiding hope for fullness over time, for maturation in the spirit over the years. Empowerment comes in and through the ritual act itself for believers, and ritual becomes the container that is filled with the deliberateness of intention and aspiration.

Behind ritual acts of spirituality may be one of two worldviews—either the worldview of causality or that of correspondence. In the worldview of causality, God or Nature or some other transcendent force caused our present world to be and continues to provide it with a life energy that enables it to keep on existing. But the transcendent is also separate from the world, and often the separation is felt as rift or interruption between the eternal and the everyday. In this analysis of the human situation, ritual itself becomes the way to overcome the rift or restore the interruption, so that life-force energy may more richly and plentifully flow into the believer's world. Ritual becomes the divine vehicle for reconnection; it enables the acting out of inner work that leads to a reinhabitation of one's space and time.

By contrast, in the worldview of correspondence, our present world is a replica of sorts, modeled on an eternal order that may be transcendent but is also immanent in the world as we know it. Either there are dual worlds that mirror and reflect one another; or there is a macrocosm (great world) that the human microcosm (small world) faithfully replicates in an "as-above-so-below" formula; or there is a manifest reality that arises from the Unmanifest that is its source. Here the present world is made of the same "stuff" or material as that Other One to which it is related, and so, in some sense, it is divine or fully energized or filled with grace. In this worldview, ritual becomes the way to disclose the face of God; it becomes the vehicle to enter into the deep reality already present.

Those who follow the path of ritual spirituality may define their community ethnically or ideologically or in terms of common sentiment. Ritual practice, although most often predicated on a public—a rite that is received and, so, similar to the rite as others have executed it—can sometimes be solitary. Whether fully in the presence of the community or connected to it only by tenuous threads, ritual engagement brings its graduated changes in one of at least three ways. First, ritual can act as the tool for the work of releasing. Here ritual becomes the "prop" individuals use to let go—to surrender to higher power; to melt hardness, forgive, and be reconciled to other individuals and the community as a whole; to dissolve tight bonds of control and go with a ritual "flow"; to stop inner noise through outer gesture and enter a profound silence that is felt to be holy. Second, ritual can act as a tool for the work of focusing. In this second ritual labor, the body becomes the learning device to bring scattered energies together; to unite body, mind, emotion, and resolution so that individuals experience themselves as completely integrated, with a clear sense of identity, purpose, and process. In fact, knowing through the body can bring a person so deeply into the body that the ritual result may be the experience of losing all consciousness of self and separation, and so, paradoxically, moving "outside" body boundaries and barriers. And thus, third, ritual can act as a tool for bonding. Beyond the labors of release and focus, ritual can bring individuals—in the midst of their restoration process— in touch with one another and with what they construe as higher power. Ritual bonding cements the ties of community; reinforces existing social hierarchies or sometimes overturns them; creates enthusiasm for a group and its projects; connects group members as a collective to what they hold to be their source and center. Because of all of this, ritual tends to create established social contributors more than revolutionaries.

Above all, ritual must be seen as the site for *embodied* spirituality. Ritual that is full (and not empty) is characterized by a deliberateness and riveted sense of conscious awareness, in which every bodily act carries serious import. Knowing through the body, in the sense in which the phrase is being employed here, is a knowing that is different—at least in its self-conscious and deliberate beginnings—from the spontaneous and even ecstatic religious uses of the body that have sometimes accompanied the heart-based, evangelical spirituality, to be explored in Part Two. But as already suggested, the unitive power and transformative power of ritual knowing through the body are nonetheless real and noticeable.

Western religious philosophy grew up, in a Christian context, with a strong sense of a spirit-matter distinction. The cultural mantra that the spirit was willing, but the flesh was weak was recited from Pauline times down through the centuries. People were told that their bodies would die but that their souls, or spirits, would continue to exist in an afterlife of reward and/or punishment. The resurrection of the body became a final, very-far-in-the-future event. Knowing through the body provided an experiential dimension to religious life that, in basic ways, countered and overcame the received philosophy. It provided, if you will, a lived dissonance with cognitive beliefs. But the apparent ideological contradiction became a way to achieve religio-cultural balance, so that the same Christendom that expressed alienation from physical reality also supplied the secret path to reconciliation through the liturgical life of the church. For Jews, Muslims, and members of other traditions in America, the dissonance would not be so great. But in a public culture still shaped by the old Christian stories, the ritual work of reconciliation could address lingering issues that came with the times.

For those who follow a spirituality of ritual, their choice brings certain advantages. Ritual is concrete; it carries an energy that is congealed, highly visible, and, so, clear and definitive. Ritual is also sensuous; that is, it employs all five of the senses when it is making full-dress presentations. The wholly occupied body—with all of the senses reinforcing intentional messages—becomes a natural teaching device for the emotions, the will, the mind, the spirit. It becomes, in effect, an instrument for transmutation and translation into the spiritual dimension. And finally, ritual is pragmatic. The ritual work discussed above functions, often superbly, as a social unifier and tension resolver. At its most efficient, ritual work becomes a graphic representation of the spirituality the religious culture seeks to bring.

In what follows, we examine the work of ritual—of knowing through the body—in a variety of cultural contexts on American shores. We survey an American history of ritual presented within a theoretical frame. We examine the labor that occurs in ritual space in seventeenth-century Puritan culture, and—juxtaposed to it—in Latino Catholic and Jewish feminist present-day contexts. We see ritual at work among Native Americans of the Oglala nation; and we observe its empowering function among Wiccans. Discrete ritual communities, we discover, often have more in common than they know, but they also have their differences.

1

Ritual Sites in the Narrative of American Religion

Tamar Frankiel

The earliest comprehensive history of American religion was Robert Baird's *Religion in America*, which first appeared in 1843 and again, in a revised edition, in 1856. There Baird created the grid that functioned for many years as the operating model for how to imagine religion in the nation. What emerged was a series of consensus histories that emphasized and celebrated Anglo-Protestant themes. More than that, these histories, until the late twentieth century, told stories of institutional development and missionary effort, of leaders and the work they left behind. The histories were what might be called "outer" narratives, with little attention paid overall to the symbolic expression of the most deeply felt *inner* thoughts and feelings of religious practitioners. By the late twentieth century, a number of American religious historians were searching for new ways to tell the evolving story of American religiosity. Tamar Frankiel is one of these historical innovators. In her essay reprinted here, she asks the question, What would happen if we looked at American religious history from the point of view of ritual development and change? What sort of story would emerge? What clues to inner realities could it offer? And how could this retelling affect conventional periodizations used by historians to demarcate zones of change in the nation's history? Frankiel's answer constitutes a broad-gauged outline for retelling the religious history of America from the perspective of its symbolic ritual life. It forms an appropriate framework from which to begin to reflect on the spirituality of knowing through the body.

In August 1994, my family and I took an excursion to Watts Cultural Center in south-central Los Angeles, where the current attraction was a series of workshops for children, titled "Healing Violence through Art." It featured sand painting by Tibetan monks. When we arrived, a pleasant "Anglo" woman greeted us, explained the exhibits briefly, and offered to show us the sand painting. In a room all to itself stood a large, about six-by-six-foot square,

From *Retelling U.S. Religious History,* edited by Thomas Tweed. Copyright © 1996 The Regents of the University of California. Reprinted by permission of the publisher.

waist-high table where the painting was emerging. On three sides stood the three monks, each holding a pair of metal funnels that were about ten inches long and smooth except for one serrated strip of metal along their length. Each monk put colored sand in one funnel and then stroked it repeatedly with the other, so that the vibrations created by the metal rubbing on the serration caused grains of sand to drop out in a tiny stream. This flow of sand "painted" an intricate design.

The monks were in the middle of a two-week span of work, spending about six hours a day, five days a week on a four-sided mandala design. We watched for several minutes as they spun tiny lines from their tubes. One monk then stopped painting to offer a commentary for the visitors. The design was, he explained, the Palace of the Four Enlightened Beings of Compassion. The monks were painting from memory, in two dimensions, but the design truly represented a palace, in three dimensions. He described the names of the enlightened beings and showed us rooms, walls, and pillars on the painting.

Our guide took us to another very large room. Along three walls were altars, fashioned by the Watts community on West African models. In the center children sat at a long table, busily coloring mandala outlines on paper. The African American program director welcomed our younger children, explained the drawing project to them, read a poem, and began talking about stories of Africa and slavery. His people were in "exile," he explained, and the Tibetans in the next room were too.

While our younger children busied themselves coloring, my husband, our older children, and I moved into a third room where another mandala sand painting stood on a table. This one was being created by Watts teenagers. It featured in its four lobes a variety of symbols suggestive of Africa and nature, together with a dozen or more names of African Americans (for example, Malcolm X, Rosa Parks, Martin Luther King, Jr.) who, our guide explained, had been identified by the children as heroes whose lives were significant for them. Then she offered us the opportunity to learn and practice the sand painting techniques ourselves at a small table nearby.

After some hours of talking, drawing, painting, and watching, we departed. The intricate sand paintings would be completed in another week. Then, in a traditional ceremony, both the Tibetan monks and the Watts children would sweep up the sand, gather it together, and return it to the sea with a blessing.

Thus, in one of the more violent sectors of the African American community of Los Angeles, an extraordinary event of cultural contact was occurring, focused around learning and adapting a ritual. Both communities explicitly intended to cross geographical and cultural boundaries. The Watts community offered the space; the Tibetans offered the practice, negotiating a ritual setting in which the two groups could, temporarily and partially, share their traditions and enlarge their horizons. The director, who identified himself as a Jewish

Buddhist, had chosen the concept of "exile," which both communities had experienced, to help bridge the gap. In practice, however, the monks and teenagers were not discussing common themes (indeed, only one Tibetan could speak much English at all) but were meeting one another through ritual. The community was constituting itself less by ecumenical dialogue than by common practice.

Creating a new community was, moreover, only part of the story. Watts participants also immersed themselves in a new experience by creating their own sand painting. This meant not merely acquiring the basic skills and discipline of hand necessary for a new art form, but entering into the psychological space of a Buddhist ritual marked by concentration and quietude. They painted in a silence broken only by the pleasant clinking of metal on metal as the tubes were rubbed together. Except for exchanges with visitors, there was no talking. The African American youngsters worked in silence with the same solemn visage as the monks, focusing intently on the work at hand. They were learning a practice that had as its intention "healing violence through art."

This example illustrates two of the fundamental functions of religion—defining a community and effecting inner change. These occur in the ritual act itself. Until recently, however, scholars of American religion would not likely have bothered to study ritual events like this one—and not only because it occurred in an urban ghetto, featured a group (Tibetans) who are quantitatively a small presence in America, and was focused on children. Rather, a scholar who happened on this scene a few decades ago might have admired the skill of the "artists," but then looked for the cognitive content of the adult dialogue—perhaps about exile—that would "explain" the meaning of this cultural exchange. Until very recently, our cultural and scholarly bias toward words, beliefs, leaders, and institutions would have made it difficult to recognize any other significance in the ritual event.

Fortunately, this situation has changed. One of the most exciting developments in American religious and cultural studies in the past decade or so is the proliferation of excellent studies of ritual. Some initial moves in this direction came from scholars of American "civil religion," beginning with Robert Bellah's work in the late 1960s. The field expanded rapidly to include many theoretically sophisticated and historically sensitive monographs on particular rituals, as well as historical studies that include ritual as part of the analysis.[1] The theoretically oriented work of anthropologists and historians of religion helped break new ground in deciphering ritual on its own terms.[2] The result is that we now can imagine narrating American religious history with a focus on ritual, illuminating previously obscure aspects of that history.

The task of this chapter is to illustrate how this end might be accomplished. It is not possible to present in such a brief space a full description of the processes of ritualization, or apply it to every period and movement. I stipulate certain features of ritualization without defending or explaining them at length. Then, to hint at the potential usefulness of writing American religious history from ritual sites, I offer the outlines of a broad-brush historical narrative.

Ritualization and Empowerment

Like other components of culture, ritual actions continually reconstruct the human situation in particular terms. Ritualizations are different from discursive verbalizations, however, in that they rely primarily on the physical embodiment of both actors and things used in the ritual environment. As many scholars have noted, the effect of coordinated ritualizations often resembles that of drama, which relies heavily on body, positioning, and props on a stage.[3] Yet the effects of ritualizations seldom achieve closure (in contrast to drama acted on a stage) and frequently are not even systematic. Ritualizations are sets of interlocking *practices* by which the participants orient themselves to one another, to aspects of their own selves, to outsiders or nonpractitioners, and to the "other" which they often identify in religious terms (for example, divinity or spirit).[4] Ritual practices are frequently repetitive or habitual; they are always strategic. They are bodily actions that dynamically and continually define individual and community space through implicit or explicit contrasts: we stand (instead of sit); we sit in circles (rather than in rows).

Religious ritualization, further, orients the person in "spiritual space," beyond the immediate social context: even the king kneels before God; one washes one's feet before entering the mosque; the priest dons a special robe. Rituals can be very straightforward and "everyday," as when a Jew selects kosher over nonkosher food. Or they can develop into elaborate sets of contrasts and analogies, forming complex and even paradoxical networks of interlocking practices that do not readily yield to analysis. Most important, however, the ritual act itself communicates the "message" of ritual, telling participants what cues to attend to. In church, one is not told "kneel because you are supposed to express humility"; rather, one kneels because this is the way it is done. As we learn the "right way" to perform the ritual, our bodies become ritualized, thus embodying and internalizing the meaning of, for example, humility. In our opening vignette, the Watts students were not taught to "be quiet so you can attain peace of mind," but rather they imitated the monks, painting in silence, and thereby, if the ritual learning was successful, internalized a sense of meditative concentration.[5]

One of the principal accomplishments of ritualization is empowerment. Each strategic move enables individuals or groups to reorient themselves in relation to the powers that be. Imagine, for example, varieties of empowerment in the following actions: taking a seat on the dais next to the visiting lecturer;

wearing flowers in your hair; taking time for personal prayer in the church service; washing your hands on leaving the cemetery; saying the password. These acts respectively enable one to align with the powerful, assert one's distinctiveness, carve out an individual space in the midst of a crowd, purify oneself of contact with the defiling, become an insider and reject the outsider. One can embody different selves by becoming socially "liminal," paradoxically gaining power by identifying with the powerless,[6] or, just as paradoxically, by entering into trance states that empower by separating the self from ordinary bodily experience. In our original example, the Tibetan monk—here the ritual expert teaching students the art of the mandala—empowers ritual apprentices in the art of inward peace and self-integration, offering an alternative to the rough-and-tumble life of the streets. At the same time, as the two groups work together on their own mandalas, designing symbols that help them imagine their historic traditions, they empower themselves as members of a larger community that extends over space and time.[7]

The range of ritualization is immense, limited perhaps only by the number of movements a human body can make or imagine. Nevertheless, it is possible to describe them as patterned strategic practices, responding to other actors' practices, within the immediate cultural context. On the macro level, each act of ritual empowerment opens up a direction that, when successful, can define a subculture or even an era. In the following pages I sketch out this process of orientation for American religious history.

Toward a New Historical Narrative

We can divide American religious history roughly into four periods, each dominated by different patterns of ritualization: independent ritual communities in interaction, 1600–1730; enthusiasm and the ritualization of passion, 1730–1850; national conformity and diversity, 1850–1950; and experiments in embodiment, 1950 to the present. As with all periodizations, these eras overlap. As broad generalizations, they serve heuristically as a framework for narrating the story of dominant trends.

Independent Ritual Communities in Interaction, 1600–1730

When Europeans began their attempts to colonize North America, they met Native Americans as complete strangers, each unprepared for one another's very existence. Yet each culture had standard ritualizations of encounter with the stranger—whether polite bows, presenting gifts, or preparing for war. Despite some early conflicts in the English colonies, including a few incidents in which Indians destroyed entire settlements, war was the last resort before 1689. Both sides explored many other alternatives.

Native Americans recognized potential as well as threat in the new settlements, and therefore attempted to incorporate Europeans in ways familiar from intertribal affairs, where each tribe's separate identity and way of life were respected. Tribal alliances had ensured territorial stability and allowed social, economic, and cultural exchanges (for example, learning the dances and rites of other tribes). Ritually, Indians sealed their alliances at gatherings of representatives from each tribe, meetings where mutual respect was ritually refined to such a degree that a person would never disagree publicly with another. Native Americans also attempted to create these kinds of relations with Europeans, a kind of egalitarian incorporation into new or existing alliances. In the long run, however, Europeans did not treat the indigenous system of relations with respect.

Another alternative was to incorporate Europeans as individuals. When Native Americans brought home captives, they usually adopted them into one of the families of the tribe to replace a lost family member. After an initiatory scenario to ritually eliminate the captive's "whiteness," the person became part of the tribe. So long as the European captive did not betray the group's trust, she or he would have complete freedom and appropriate privileges. Particularly with children, Native Americans invested a great deal of energy in teaching them their ways, treating them with patience and respect. Indeed, the Indians' reputation for kindness and patience spread back to the colonies, making some religious leaders fear the influence of Indians on New England.[8]

Most European settlers saw little value in Native American ways of life and, as Indian settlements became decimated by disease while European immigration increased, the newcomers expanded where they could. This often meant war. Protestant leaders sometimes had genuine concern for the Native Americans, but the best future they could imagine for Indians was for them to become Christian and civilized. But Protestants, as sectarians and separatists, had no group incorporation rites, and the only way for people to join was individually by conversion. Especially in New England and the Middle Colonies where conversion efforts were most intense, Protestants demanded numerous qualifications before admitting Native Americans into their churches. Essentially, the Native American had to be "civilized" before he or she could convert, and this involved a series of social-ritual adjustments ranging from giving up the "wandering" way of life and living in a "praying town" to wearing short hair and attending school. Such acts indicated a willingness to submit to discipline, understood as the "yoke" of Christian life. Notably, the English did not take Indians into their homes as Native Americans did their captives.

After separating American Indians from their traditional way of life, their Christian guides prescribed a more specific and demanding ritual education. In the schools, Indians were "sexually segregated, morally guarded, classically oriented, rigorously disciplined, patriarchally dominated."[9] Protestant ritual reliance on the Word—focusing on preaching and the understanding of preaching, reading and being able to reflect on and converse about the Bible—meant that the process of ritual incorporation could take years. In addition, the New England way required an ability to reflect and speak about one's own spiritual struggles. Puritans oriented themselves to being one of God's elect by means of a ritual language far more familiar to medieval mystics than to Native Americans—the drama of introspection. The construction of the "visible saint," in Edmund Morgan's classic phrase, required imagining God's judgment on oneself as sinner, ritual confession of one's distance from God, intense personal prayer and, eventually, a testimony of hope to the minister or congregation.

The Puritan also had to identify closely with the organic community to which he or she was bound in covenant, as part of the New Israel. The minister in the late seventeenth century frequently led communal introspection, in the form of the "jeremiad," full of warnings and urgings to repentance. Therefore, even to be baptized, a convert had to become fairly fluent in the Word, mastering many verbal ritual formulas of self-examination as well as embodying appropriate emotional responses. This requirement was quite different from most indigenous cultures, where normally only ritual experts such as shamans developed special competence in orienting themselves inwardly. Moreover, for the Native American to feel truly a part of most Protestant communities would ultimately require identifying with the cultural history of the Reformation and the exodus from England—a most difficult transformation.[10]

Until recently, historians interested in Protestant attempts to convert Native Americans usually attributed failures either to the external situation (war, disease, and treaty breaking) or to the difficulty in accepting Christian beliefs. Indeed, Indians sometimes did challenge Christian theology, or listened politely while disagreeing privately. Highlighting ritual shows, however, that the difficulty was not so much understanding new religious concepts as embodying a different practice.

Roman Catholic missions to Native Americans operated with different expectations. While the intellectual framework of Catholic doctrine was as complex as that of Protestant teaching, ritual entry into the community was far simpler. The approach of Catholic regulars in North America (mostly Franciscans or Jesuits), based on centuries of Catholic encounters with pagan cultures, involved contacting prospective converts, learning their languages, and either moving into the community and becoming adopted (as with the Jesuits) or bringing Native Americans into a mission to form a separate community (as with the Franciscans in California and the Southwest). There the friars would instruct them. As Axtell has pointed out vividly in regard to Jesuit missions, this instruction involved all the senses:

> In native hands he put attractive silver and brass medals, rings, crucifixes, and rosaries as mnemonic devices to recall his oral messages. . . . To their noses he

introduced the mysterious fragrances of incense. To their lips he lifted holy wafers. To their eye he offered huge wooden crosses, candle-lit altars rich with silk and silver, long brocaded chasubles, and pictorial images of the major acts in the drama of Christianity. And into their ears he poured sonorous hymns and chants, tinkling bells, and an endless stream of Indian words, haltingly, even laughably pronounced at first, but soon fluent and cadenced in native measures.[11]

The Franciscans in California, with their structured towns or "missions," offer perhaps the closest Catholic parallel to the Puritan "praying towns."[12] An Indian who was willing to separate himself by living in the mission compound had taken one step toward salvation. If he could, at minimum, acknowledge one God and a consciousness of "sin" by recognizing wrongdoing in his earlier life, he could be baptized. Fuller instruction in theology could come later. Meanwhile, the friars could offer additional involvement, such as altar service for the church or, since the missions were total communities, becoming trained in European technologies. For example, some Native Americans became expert in the making of musical instruments. Therefore, it was not difficult, ritually speaking, to have access to some benefits of belonging to the community. In many ways the empowerment might seem considerable. It meant supplies of new kinds of food and clothing, as well as opportunities for learning in music and art, even if one never learned to read.

For these reasons California missions attracted more Native Americans, proportionately, than did the Puritan "praying towns." Yet the missions were not entirely successful because, as the Indians soon learned, the problem with a California Indian becoming a Roman Catholic was not getting into the community, but getting out. The friars seldom converted large groups, so the convert was isolated from familiar social relations. Because the friars feared pollution of the shallow-rooted new faith by contact with the "idolatrous" practices of the native community, they discouraged contact with the tribe. They sometimes used coercive rituals such as whipping, both to make converts work at the missions and to prevent new converts from leaving.[13] A particular source of stress developed when a neophyte or convert wished to attend the funerary ceremonies for a deceased family member. This was a powerful draw to return, at least briefly, to the traditional community for the rites. To many Native Americans, there was no necessary conflict between their ancestral practices and the rituals to the new Christian god, but the friars could not abide the two together. Thus ritual entry was easy, but converts learned, sometimes after the fact, that the exclusivity of Christianity often blocked the paths back to their old ways and relationships. In addition, they had to live under threat of punishment from the Franciscans.

These examples illustrate that patterns of ritualization were as important as modes of belief in the failure of Europeans and Native Americans to relate successfully. Christian missionaries either made ritual competence hard to attain—so that few Indians could experience the empowerment of truly belonging—or failed to accommodate sufficiently the Native Americans' desire to convert gradually, adding new practices and dropping the old little by little. The result was that, from the period of colonial empires in North America down to the mid-eighteenth century (and later in California), largely independent communities struggled to perpetuate themselves and to incorporate or dominate one another.

The struggle of Indian communities to reach working agreements with Europeans, and the Europeans' efforts to convert Native Americans are only two examples. In addition, each transplanted European settlement had, at first, its own dominant religious body that attempted to exclude or dominate others. Getting in and getting out—or being driven out—were regular issues within colonial Protestantism. At the extremes, Congregationalists persecuted and killed Quakers; separatists refused to commune with the impure. With each religious group striving to maintain its own separate patterns of ritualization, its own embodiment of the pure community, religious exchanges functioned mainly to defend the group's boundaries.

Enthusiasm and the Ritualization of Passion, 1730–1850

The patterns of ritualization in Anglo-Protestant tradition itself were gradually changing so that, by 1730, we can speak of a new era in Protestant ritual. Our periodization here coincides roughly with the years from the beginning of the First Great Awakening to the enthusiasm that flooded the Northeast in the 1830s and 1840s. Notable throughout this period is the tendency for towns, cities, and regions to nourish revivalism and revolutionary enthusiasm, each with novel ritualizations.

The First Great Awakening was in part the result of a long process of erosion of the Puritan and early Protestant ritualizations that had empowered people through the practices of an organic, hierarchical community. The church, led by its clergy, stood at the center of a deferential society. These ritualizations had included requirements for proper social behavior such as codes of dress and demeanor, but also, and most specifically in Puritanism, for that complex mode of introspection and imagination known as the conversion experience. Already in 1662, the Halfway Covenant implicitly acknowledged that the ritual process did not always produce the desired experience, as did Solomon Stoddard's admission of the unconverted to the communion table. The jeremiad as a sermon form came to the fore as a kind of communal substitute, presenting current events in terms of God's judgment and proclaiming communal prayer and fast in times of declension.

In this way the community came to ritually mediate divine empowerment for those many who did not have their own personal experiences. This also meant that young people born after, say, 1700 had fewer mentors in the rituals of conversion, which made it even less likely that they would find a way to reaffirm their spiritual status as part of the New Israel. At the same time, power in society at large was shifting away from the "saints" to the newly aggressive merchant community, many of them not defined by their holy demeanor. Gradually the "reform of manners," a ritualization of civility, replaced what the devout believed to be the true foundation of morality, the personal relation to God that developed only through deep introspection. This trend toward an emphasis on civility and manners as attributes of the good person worried the more devout; by 1740, the "Log College" minister Gilbert Tennent could attract approval in many quarters by proclaiming that even many ministers were "unconverted."[14]

The "surprising conversions" of the Great Awakening, sparked by dramatic preachers like the Tennents, Jonathan Edwards, and George Whitefield, were ritual acts that empowered converts and challenged not only the immoral behavior of the larger society, which Whitefield especially attacked, but also the constraints of the local church. Their "enthusiasm" drew much criticism, but in the end religious communities grew stronger. Attention to ritual can illumine how practices challenged traditional community and how revivals strengthened the churches.

The kinds of manifestations found in the Great Awakening were not new: they had appeared long before in the British Isles, also in the context of challenges to the prevailing religious situation. As Leigh Schmidt has shown in his award-winning *Holy Fairs,* revival rituals evolved among Presbyterians in seventeenth-century Scotland during the annual summer and fall communion seasons. In great outdoor gatherings, people fasted, heard preparatory sermons on Saturday, took communion on Sunday, and held thanksgiving services on Monday before departing home. Fasting, confrontational sermons, vivid depictions of the "wondrous" drama of salvation appeared in revivals not only in Scotland but also in America, and continued in Presbyterian contexts until the nineteenth century, as in the work of Scottish preacher James McGready and the famous Cane Ridge revival in Kentucky.[15] Such gatherings in America became, in effect, pilgrimages to the great preachers and implicitly challenged sacred community and, more specifically, the established minister who had been "called" by the local congregation. Pilgrimage to the revival preacher served to create a sacred community beyond the local church, through the act of leaving one's home and engaging in a complex series of rituals designed to empower the individual through direct contact with God.[16]

At the same time, the often extreme bodily manifestations of the revivals transformed the bodily experience itself. They could have been rejected as demonic (as similar manifestations had been in the era of the Salem witch trials); but, when accepted by at least part of the community, they encouraged a radical rejection of prevailing orientations of the self. These strategies of ecstasy defined the participants in direct relationship to God, as different from both the "civil," rational-ethical religious community and those who indulged in the material temptations that were flooding the colonies. In the aftermath, the "enthusiastic" conversions gave individuals their authentic entry into a church, strengthening the churches numerically. The newly converted also insisted on stronger rituals of moral discipline and, thereby, constructed for the enlarged community a bulwark against the temptations of the outside world.[17]

Another unintended consequence was that the creation of a larger revival community softened boundaries between denominations, suggesting that the bonds among Christians who felt the divine power were more significant than their differences. Schisms were, to be sure, as common as ecumenical feelings; but the debates were less over canonical rituals than the ritualization of enthusiasm itself. These debates continued over the next hundred years and more. As Terry Bilhartz has pointed out, still in the early 1800s Episcopalians in Baltimore were castigating those who "instead of controlling their passions . . . are continually expecting visionary attestations of divine favour," while Methodists continued to criticize the lukewarm "formalist" and attested to the reality of "the power."[18]

The diminishing of the significance of boundaries applied also to borders between colonies. The waves of enthusiastic revivals empowered individuals to act beyond their local communities, and their first joint moves were political and military. During the French and Indian War that followed on the heels of the First Awakening (1745–63), the colonists identified themselves as the pure community against France, the "scarlet whore," and Canada, the "North American Babylon." As Sacvan Bercovitch has observed, the ritual of the jeremiad, adapted to this millennial scenario, extended to the Revolution. John Adams could write in traditional ritual formulas (on 3 July 1776) that "Americans shall suffer Calamities still more wasting and Distress yet more dreadful," but later predict that "deliverance be wrought out . . . as it was for the children of Israel." Likewise, one of the first proposals for the Seal of the United States, from Franklin and Jefferson, showed Moses leading the chosen people; in fact, the adopted symbol, the eagle, represented the eagles of the books of Exodus and Revelation.[19] Political "enthusiasm" fell into disfavor after the violence of the French Revolution, but millennial ideas erupted dramatically again after the turn of the century.[20] Moreover, as many observers have noted, when party politics began in earnest in the 1830s, that new "enthusiasm" had similarities with revivals of the period. Here were the beginnings of "civil religion," a grand new ritual drama to be acted out in many variations over the next century and more.

In short, the evangelical revival empowered participants by adapting familiar ritualizations—from the Puritan conversion and the Scottish fair—to
new situations. The unintended results were dramatic. Instead of the Puritan
approach in which divine power was mediated through small communities of
the elect, and ultimately through the "little commonwealth" of the family
where election ideally passed from parent to child, now God empowered individuals directly. At the end of the eighteenth century, the emotional and physical realms became the locus of individual empowerment, even more than in
the First Awakening, while weeping, fainting, and more extreme manifestations characterized even urban revivals.[21] A major issue in the scholarship on
the Second Great Awakening has revolved around whether the awakening was
an "organizing process" or a destabilizing force. A ritual perspective suggests
that the emphasis on empowerment through individual ecstasy, in the open
context of the early 1800s, was likely to be revolutionary.[22] This supports the
contention of some scholars that, while church membership increased, the
Second Awakening undermined traditional authority and gave far more scope
to individuals, sectarian groups, and churches that encouraged lay participation.[23]

Lay participation began to include African Americans. Even the southern
slaves were able to merge their African heritage with evangelical belief in the
ritual setting of the revival, but with a different style of empowerment from
that of whites. As Walter F. Pitts has explained in his analysis of Afro-Baptist
ritual, the structure of African ritual allowed for a rather smooth amalgamation with evangelical practice. The African initiatory structure of chanting
produced a passive-receptive frame of mind, followed by rhythmic drumming
and dancing to induce spirit-possession (in American revivalism called the
"shout"). This was structurally analogous to the preparation period with
prayer and quiet hymn singing, followed by dramatic, rhythmic preaching
which was intended to bring the "sinner" to a religious experience. The difference was that African Americans looked to this experience of being overcome
by the Spirit as a regularly desirable religious experience (although its duration
was much shorter in the New World), while evangelical whites regarded it
as a humbling one-time experience, rather to be feared than welcomed. This
confirms Donald Mathews's interpretation some years ago that "while whites
might rightfully be said to have 'broken down' under preaching, blacks were
lifted up, enabled to celebrate themselves as persons because of their direct
and awful contact with divinity." The black/white divisions did not remain so
clear, however. Some black churches later dropped the ecstatic aspects of ritual,
while some whites later in the century, notably Pentecostals, adopted them for
regular ritual use.[24]

In particular, African Americans contributed to the musical style of the
revivals. A disapproving observer testified to this phenomenon: "We have too,

a growing evil, in the practice of singing in our places of public and society worship, *merry* airs, adapted from old *songs,* to hymns of our own composing: often miserable as poetry, and senseless as matter, and most frequently composed and first sung by the illiterate *blacks* of the society."[25] Methodists had used hymns, particularly those of John Wesley, while Puritans began to introduce Isaac Watts's hymns in the late eighteenth century. Often a testimonial in simple lyric form, the hymn became a new lay cultural form, with tunes frequently adapted directly from popular music. In addition, lay people learned to organize orderly meetings that previously had been in the hands of the clergy alone. They led public prayer and used testimonial, a ritual form evolved from Puritan self-examination, to replace or supplement the sermon (or lay exhortation).[26] All of these elements constituted a new ritual form which transformed evangelical religion.

An increase in negative attitudes toward the clergy undermined the range of their authority. Ritually speaking, authority figures are those who are themselves proficient in ritualization and/or who can teach others. They also may be individuals who can negotiate differences in order to hold the community together. The decline of the covenanted, established church and the cultural demotion of the minister made room for the "prophet." Prophets use information and insights which they access while (presumably) in altered states of consciousness—dreams, visions, and the like—to prescribe and model solutions to a community's problems. The late eighteenth and early nineteenth centuries brought forth, for example, Ann Lee of the Shakers, Alexander Campbell of the Disciples of Christ, Joseph Smith of the Mormons, Ellen G. White of the Seventh-day Adventists, and John Humprey Noyes of the Perfectionists.[27]

These more radical, "prophetic" movements illustrate by their extremes a significant feature of ritualization. The trance manifestations of the revivals had encouraged a spontaneous, "uncontrolled" physical body. The visions of the prophets taught new ways to ritualize the body. They regulated excitement and "enthusiasm" through new social rules, frequently focused on sexuality and the family. Shakers, Adventists, Mormons, and Oneida Perfectionists all regulated relations between men and women. Concurrently but less dramatically, new medical and health alternatives emerged (such as vegetarianism, which the Adventists later adopted) to purify or perfect the physical body.[28]

In the 1840s, as the more radical groups were re-ritualizing the body, especially its sexual aspects, mainstream evangelicals faced the same issues. The greatest threats to evangelical purity were physical acts that "excited" or "over-stimulated" the passions. The leading contenders were alcohol, slavery (believed to encourage violence), and materialism. In addition, as Ann Taves points out . . . , mainstream Protestant culture defined as deviant many forms of sexuality, ranging from too much sexual activity in marriage to Roman

Catholic celibacy. Any such behaviors were a threat to the pure community, many believed, and indulgence in them could drive a person crazy.[29] While the radicals created new versions of family and society, mainstream Protestants put their faith in what they considered the "traditional" home, the still center in the maelstrom of a passionate society. In fact, however, they created a new version of the home where the woman was domestic priestess, who learned (from numerous housekeeping and family manuals) the rituals that would, together with her faith, empower her to create the perfect home and haven for her husband and children.

Yet openings for the laity who were empowered by their direct contact with God meant far greater opportunities for women in the outside world. While women always had been a majority in the churches, as Ann Braude argues . . . , they now began to employ organizational talents and devote their energy to creating a more holy community.[30] Beyond the home, in reform associations comprised largely of women and clergy, northerners created a white Protestant network that aimed to purify the national community of its vices, particularly the passion-exciting practices of drinking, prostitution, and slavery. The reformers' ubiquitous tracts and impassioned lectures promoted an intense concern for social morality within the millennial community. As a corollary to the increasing emphasis on the home and transdenominational reform movements, many churchgoers belittled denominational ritual differences in areas like the church service, baptism, and the Lord's Supper.[31]

In the South, separatists under local leaders tended not to form large denominational movements or reform societies. They differentiated within small communities, as for example the Baptists did. There too, lay people redefined their churches by developing or elaborating, within a biblical-evangelical framework, ritual practices such as the love feast, laying on of hands, anointing the sick, devoting children to Christ, the right hand of fellowship, the kiss of charity, and the washing of feet. The prominence of the body is clear, particularly in crossing established boundaries of intimacy. "Separates," comments Donald Mathews, "touched each other with hands, arms, and lips, actions which were completely at odds with conventions that maintained invidious distinctions among people in part by maintaining social distance." Changes in ritualization undermined the power invested in the South's social class system and replaced it with tight communal bonds.[32]

Thus the long struggle over how to orient self and community in a New World, a struggle marked by the repeated abandonment of established identities in favor of contact with God, seemed to have come to a new consolidation by 1850. What Marilyn Westercamp has called the "triumph of the laity" in the First Great Awakening became even more pronounced. Enthusiasm faded, and the generation born after 1840 would not stir up the same kinds of revivals as their grandparents had. God now worked through the nation as a millennial

instrument, in the meantime counting on woman, home, and family to socialize every individual into the rituals of pure living. Whether living in a Shaker
utopian community or toiling in a reform group, American Protestants were
promoters of a new order.

National Conformity and Diversity, 1850–1950

The revivals of Dwight L. Moody and Ira D. Sankey in the 1870s were a con-
summate expression of the predominant evangelical ritual form. They emphasized lay prayer meetings, Sankey's "gospel hymns," and mothers' weeping for
their wayward sons. Moody saw domesticated, revival Christianity as the bulwark of hope in the stormy sea of urbanizing America. Yet his sense of a national community centered around evangelical religion, family, and home was
necessarily incomplete, and soon it became the ritual practice and ideology of
only one faction, albeit a powerful one.

The nation's new challenge was diversity. By the middle of the nineteenth
century, large numbers of Roman Catholics from Ireland had moved into urban centers, while Mexicans challenged American efforts to control California
and Texas. The Mexican War may have seemed a minor affair, but only because
it was soon overshadowed by the intense national suffering of the Civil War. A
"Yankee" victory heralded new expansion, but also brought new wars—the
Indian Wars, ending in the consolidation of the reservation system, and the
Spanish-American War that made the United States an imperial power. Internal stresses arose from immigration, particularly Jews fleeing from Russian
pogroms and other eastern Europeans from economic and political distress.
World War I brought the United States into collusion with a larger European
community, yet it also brought more immigrants until, in the 1920s, Congress
established strict immigration quotas. Intense antiforeign, racist, and anti-
Semitic sentiments followed, ironically, on the heels of the war to "make the
world safe for democracy." During the same period, class divisions became
more intense, while secular pastimes became more acceptable (for example, in
entertainment, sports, and the arts), diversifying Americans' behavior even
more.

Mainline Protestants, who still dominated numerically and wielded cultural
influence, were sharply aware of the rapid expansion of the power of the
United States westward and internationally. They developed new kinds of ritualizations to orient the expanded community, in what could be called the
commemorative phase of American civil religion. Northerners, by 1900, transformed the horrors of the Civil War into sacrifices that fulfilled a providential
destiny. They saw the succeeding wars of territory and ideology as fulfilling the
promise of the millennial community. These developments took ritual form
in devout observance of Thanksgiving in the home, enabling identification

with the Pilgrims and their mission as the New Israel, while simultaneously connecting the domestic priesthood to civil religion. Self-sacrifice on behalf of that mission was taught in Memorial Day parades in virtually every town, where young children marched, carried American flags, and placed flowers on soldiers' graves at the town cemetery.[33] In the arena of church-religion, missionary work became a highlight of Protestant public relations, with reports of missionaries heavily featured in evangelical magazines. The founding of the new journal entitled, significantly, the *Christian Century,* heralded the glories to come. Unfortunately, there was also a dark side to this aspect of American ritualization: antiblack and anti-Semitic sentiments flourished. Attempts were made to quash Native American dance. Lynchings became communal rituals in the South and, by the 1930s, protofascist groups appeared who equated "America" with "Anglo-Saxon."

The aspiring upper and middle classes initiated new efforts, often outside the religious institutions, to reorient themselves to a larger world. Philanthropy in the late nineteenth and early twentieth centuries made possible the establishment of several major museums, from the American Museum of Natural History to the University of Pennsylvania Archeology Museum to the Southwest Museum in Los Angeles. One of the most popular features of a ritual museum visit, for the cultured American, was the tour through archeological exhibits. These reminded the visitor of the glories of Egypt and Peru and introduced our own "ancient" peoples, the Native Americans, through ancient and contemporary artifacts. Americans could walk through history and see the vanished and supposedly vanishing races and, at the same time, recognize themselves as at the pinnacle of civilization. This period also saw new definitions of society's relationship to nature (often through imitation of Native American culture) in such varied movements as the Sierra Club, Boy Scouts, Campfire Girls, and conservation groups.[34]

Meanwhile, the lower and middle classes became a market for new kinds of entertainment. The circus and vaudeville achieved great popularity with their celebrations (or parodies) of diversity. The "dime novel" offered models of American heroes, the best-known among them being Horatio Alger's self-made man. Baseball and football emerged as popular sports that, in addition to providing diversion, celebrated a manliness and competitiveness that the prevailing evangelicalism had not much encouraged. (Significantly, one of the great revivalists of this era, Billy Sunday, was a former baseball player.) Fraternal societies such as the Masons and Lions Club flourished. What would eventually become a major imaginal ritual by which Americans oriented themselves—the entertainment of the "movies"—emerged in the early twentieth century. That industry was the product of entrepreneurs who were willing, unlike the established wealthy investors, to play to the working classes. Many of the creators of the film studios and movie house empires were immigrants, an unusual proportion of them Jews.[35] Like African Americans in the religious world of the early nineteenth-century revival, such "outsiders," along with their black contemporaries, continued to shape American religion and culture.

"Outsiders" were becoming more important numerically in this period, even as they debated among themselves how to Americanize. The growing Roman Catholic population chose, for the most part, to maintain their ritual distinctiveness through parish and private devotional life. The Catholic Church rapidly developed ecclesiastical organizations to incorporate un-churched individuals through a system of private schools that attracted some liberal Protestants as well. The Jesuits in particular transformed education and founded colleges. Priests, sometimes imitating revivalist techniques, gathered the unchurched in the cities or on the frontiers. The system of ritualizations into which they were incorporated was essentially the traditional one of masses and confession, feasts and fasts, and devotions to the saints, largely uninflu-enced by the Protestant majority. However, as Catherine L. Albanese points out . . . , Catholics argued over acculturation issues such as the school system, the dominant language, the use of alcohol, and the appropriateness of fraternal societies. New immigrations also raised tensions within Catholicism. For ex-ample, the dominant Catholic community, the Irish, found it disturbing when Italians immigrated in large numbers, since the Italian customs brought more dramatic emotional and bodily rituals into public view.[36] But most Catholics accepted the possibility of remaining a practicing Catholic and, at the same time, affirming an American identity through the rituals of the civil religion such as Thanksgiving and the Fourth of July.

Jews were in a somewhat different situation. Those who immigrated in the nineteenth century were mostly from Germany, where the Enlightenment's influence on educated Jews had led many communities to adopt a Reform practice. The Reformers understood themselves not as imitating non-Jews but simply as "modernizing" in the light of reason and in pace with civilization. Their watchword in reforming ritual was "decorum" or, as one congregation described it, "that high standing of respectability which the world has a right to expect." In practice, this meant adopting synagogue ritual styles similar to those in "cultured" Christian churches. In the American case, it meant white northern Protestant styles that were dominant in the major cities. Jewish Re-formers used unison readings instead of individual chanting, adopted more refined hymns, and added choirs. They changed the traditional *d'var Torah* (word of Torah) into an inspirational sermon rather than a discourse on Jew-ish law, moved the reader's desk to the front instead of the center of the syna-gogue, and gave their rabbis titles such as "Lecturer and Preacher." Amid much controversy, they adopted mixed seating (an innovation of late eighteenth cen-tury Protestants).[37] They gradually dropped ritualizations that they judged to be primarily social-cultural (kosher food and distinctive dress) and substituted confirmation for bar mitzvah. In making these choices, they oriented their communities through synagogue services that paralleled those designed by mainline, upper-class Protestants for their churches. They also maintained distinctiveness by recognizing implicitly that their channel of empowerment was not the personal-salvation model of Christianity, but their special communal relationship to God mediated through the holidays they chose to emphasize, particularly Rosh Hashanah, Yom Kippur, and Passover.

Orthodox Jews arrived from eastern Europe in small numbers in midcentury, and by the tens of thousands a few generations later (mostly 1880–1920). It is significant that most of these Jews were from Russian-controlled areas where, even before the pogroms, they had learned about the temptations and the effects of assimilation.[38] In addition, traditional synagogues of eastern Europeans tended to be small gatherings primarily for men. As such, the shuls not only helped to maintain the habits and lifestyle of the home country, but also functioned as communal supports. In their small groups, they strengthened the internally empowering aspects of Jewish life, insisting on the religious value of every element of Jewish distinctiveness. Their sense of election went hand in hand with purity and seclusion, much like Puritans in the early days of the colonies. They made few changes except that, being sensitive to accusations of a lack of "decorum," they often hired cantors.

Still, they rapidly lost ground with the younger generation. Despite attempts by new turn-of-the-century organizations like the Orthodox Union and Young Israel to offer English sermons and classes, Orthodoxy rapidly became the smallest Jewish "denomination." Conservative Judaism, beginning in the 1890s with attempts to strike a balance between Reform and Orthodoxy, was more successful with the younger generations. Conservatives used more English in services, emphasized Hebrew schools, and tried, like many large Protestant churches around 1900, to make the synagogue a versatile community center for many activities ranging from school to recreation. In this respect the Conservatives were more like the immigrant Catholics, insisting on distinctive rituals but Americanizing all the while. Like all Jews of this period, they emphasized family and community rather than the individual in their ritualizations, in this way distinguishing themselves from Protestants.

Within traditional Protestantism, another division was emerging with the movement known as Fundamentalism. Accusing the Protestant denominations of becoming "modernist" to the point of denying the Bible, the Fundamentalists provoked a crisis that pitted the Bible against science and materialism in all forms, demanding that Americans join one of two opposing camps. The public significance of the movement was clear since the crux of the debate centered on the primary issue of education: were children to be taught to imagine themselves as descendants from monkeys or as creations of God? The

1925 Scopes trial of a public school teacher became a national drama that ended in the (temporary) public defeat of Fundamentalism.

Ritually, there was far more diversity than is suggested by the dichotomy assumed by Fundamentalists. In the late nineteenth century, several diverse metaphysical religious movements had emerged, first in the Northeast and later spreading rapidly to urban areas in the Midwest and California. Spiritualism, which began with the famous "rappings" in upstate New York, was one of the first of these. After being scandalized in the post-Civil War era by revelations of fraudulent séances, Spiritualism continued to grow in a low-profile way. Another series of movements emerged from the forging of mesmerist and healing traditions—Christian Science and a variety of New Thought organizations (Church of Divine Science, Church of Religious Science, Unity, and others). Each claimed to harness the power of mind to produce positive effects on the body and the material world.

Notable in the metaphysical movements was a loose relationship to community. In a communal ritual where contact and interaction are significant, the individual makes a bodily connection to other participants and to material reality. Whether the ritual acts are a common meal with prayers or a choreography of kneeling, bowing, and processing, the practices create a shared physical reality. In groups with a more tenuous communal structure, the "spiritual"—with its physical manifestations in various states of consciousness from dream to ecstasy—appears to separate from the material. The Spiritualist séance oriented participants to other realms through its meditative atmosphere. As participants sat in a circle around a table, their community enlarged. It became a heavenly one because it included nonphysical beings who manifested themselves in these rituals. These figures did their part for the community as they advised and consoled those who remained in the material world. Christian Science and New Thought, using the recital of formulas known as "affirmations," oriented people to a world where everything was "Mind" or "Energy." It was not family Bible study, but the private affirmation (a last remnant of the testimonial) and the "reading room" visit that empowered individuals. Despite the apparent isolation from the ordinary world, however, the aim of such practices was mastery of the material world, so that many affirmations spoke of physical strength and bodily health as well as material wealth.[39] Logically enough, both Spiritualists and New Thought proponents proclaimed universalist, nonsectarian messages. As body did not "matter," group membership was not significant either. Thus, these groups attracted occasional Catholics or Jews who broke away from their traditional communities. In addition, American versions of Buddhist and Hindu thought began to appear, particularly among the more educated.[40]

On another track in the same era, the Holiness movement emerged from revival origins and developed into new denominations. Holiness churches emphasized a stricter moral code than the mainstream churches, which they believed had accommodated too much to the customs and fashions of the secular world. They focused on rituals of appropriate dress, emphasized behavioral codes such as avoiding dance halls and sensual entertainment, and separated themselves from the worldliness around them (without forming economically separate communities). In addition, they often had strong "spiritist" inclinations, as appeared in the early Church of the Nazarene. Those who were suspicious of "matter" opened themselves to the presence of "spirit."[41] The search for a deeper connection with the Holy Spirit also came to fruition in another movement, Pentecostalism. This movement flourished both in rural areas, as in its Kansas origins, and in urban enclaves, as in the Azusa Street revival in Los Angeles in 1906. Pentecostalism ritualized altered states of consciousness which resulted in "gifts of the Spirit," most notably glossolalia or speaking in tongues. In ways similar to metaphysical movements, but with a different style and communal context, Pentecostals ritualized individual behavior to promote inner transformation.[42]

The century from 1850 to 1950, then, saw an increasing materialism and elaboration of rituals of the secular sphere, together with an increasing "spiritualism" in religion. The idea of a single nation with a mission in the world promoted outward conformity, often on a military model with successful generals as the heroes. This Protestant and civil-religious orientation remained dominant throughout the period, largely defining the meaning of "American." Yet those who oriented themselves by means of an inward spirituality offered vigorous alternatives for empowerment through intense or unusual experiences. These ranged from infusions of divine energy to possession by the Holy Spirit. These explorations of other realms underwent considerable modification and, in some ways, went underground during the two World Wars and the Great Depression.

Experiments in Embodiment, after 1950

As suggested earlier, dance, music, and film began to transform Americans' bodily orientation as early as the 1920s (the Jazz Age). These popular trends eventually affected religion and spirituality as well. In dance, the flappers of the 1920s gave way to dancer Fred Astaire in the 1930s and 1940s, while the Big Band sound captivated the public. African American culture was the direct source of these cultural phenomena, and it is no accident that African Americans themselves first gained recognition in the field of music, in blues and jazz. The film industry, particularly in promoting the romantic stars of the 1930s, produced imaginal ritualizations of more permissive sexual relationships. Simultaneously, the temperance movement's century-long attempt to control

Americans' passions died with the repeal of the Eighteenth Amendment (Prohibition) in 1933.[43] During the Great Depression and World War II, however, people tended to reaffirm traditional values. In the popular imagination, African Americans and their jazz music came to be associated with degeneracy and drugs, just as Jews became linked with (anti-American) socialism.

The traditional ritualizations that constituted evangelical culture continued to be powerful counterweights to new explorations throughout the 1950s, the era of the "man in the gray flannel suit." Conformity was the watchword in politics and social relations as well as religion. But the emergence of rock music, epitomized in Elvis Presley and expanded by the Beatles, introduced new, less controlling attitudes toward the body, which reflected the influence of both African American and working-class styles. Some intellectuals alienated by the conformity of mainstream America produced the Beat Generation culture which modeled new lifestyles. One of the most critical religious developments, which also deeply affected American society at large, was the practice of nonviolent resistance, adapted by Dr. Martin Luther King, Jr., from Mahatma Gandhi. The combination of African American preaching style and communal energy with influences from India produced revolutionary ritualizations—the sit-in and the protest march. None of these became core elements in new or old church rituals. Even rock music did not enter the churches for two decades or more. But the cumulative effect of these secular and religious practices was twofold: they shifted the focus toward the *integration* of body and soul, rather than toward the spirit/matter distinction that had characterized the previous period, and they connected spiritual pursuits with moral ideals and political action.

One of the most widespread forms of mind-body ritual integration appeared in what was first called the human-potential movement. Springing from psychological practice in the late 1940s and 1950s (especially Gestalt psychology), this movement reached its apotheosis in the famous retreats at Esalen on the Big Sur coast of California. A wide variety of ritualizations attempted to integrate the "whole self" through individual and group psychotherapy, massage, and meditation. This holistic movement, led primarily by psychologists and self-proclaimed spiritual teachers, was one example in a multifaceted exploration of the connections between psychological and physical health. It later inspired a large collection of self-improvement groups, workshops, and literature. At the same time, pastoral counseling became a new ritual practice in some mainstream (particularly Methodist) churches as early as the 1960s, bringing psychological know-how to bear on individual spiritual growth.

Some of the self-improvement movements either claimed religious credentials or advocated spiritual healing. Probably the most widespread in its influence was the network of what came to be called "twelve-step programs." Beginning with Alcoholics Anonymous, which had originated in the 1930s to address the medical problem of alcoholism from a spiritual perspective, this network expanded enormously after the 1960s. It became a multipronged attack on many personal problems labeled as addictions, from drug use and compulsive eating to anger and obsessive gambling. Similar to the New Thought movements in their emphasis on positive thinking and self-directed development, they went beyond their predecessors in offering a structured plan based on abstinence, that is, control of the body in the area of the problem being solved. A full program of social support via telephone and meetings made these twelve-step programs systems of multiple, mutually reinforcing, verbal affirmations.

These movements were just the beginnings of an approach to spirituality that was highly eclectic, using a variety of techniques from different sources to orient the individual in a pluralistic universe where community and family ties were highly unpredictable. The result was a kind of cultural revolution in the 1960s that led to diverse practices in the 1970s and 1980s. Without major changes in traditional religious affiliation, people came to tolerate a wide range of physical expression in body and dress. After the initial shocks of the fifties and early sixties, rock groups and protest marches had become part of American culture. Some Americans accepted a variety of Asian religions, with Buddhist and Hindu forms of meditation becoming a significant feature even for many people who retained loose affiliations with other traditions. In this new atmosphere, the jockeying of various religions for people's allegiance did not necessarily create conflict. A religious person in the 1980s could sit in Buddhist meditation, eat a Japanese macrobiotic diet, practice ta'i chi, attend Alcoholics Anonymous meetings, and elicit no reaction at all from neighbors in the pews of her suburban Methodist church. In a parallel way, a Catholic could practice a much wider variety of ritual—endorsed by the Second Vatican Council in the 1960s—and not be condemned as a heretic.

Earlier movements also reawakened during this period. Some religious groups who had not embraced the ritualizations of emotion and encounter in earlier periods began to do so. The charismatic movements in Catholic and Episcopal churches introduced ecstatic encounters with the Holy Spirit as accompaniments or supplements to the more usual means of grace, the sacraments. The traditional rituals did not disappear, but participants in "charismatic" services now could orient themselves by direct religious experience. Thus traditions that already had emphasized "embodiment" now added another ritual form that allowed a more intense and personal spirituality. Even more telling, many contemporary Pentecostals, whether Catholic or Protestant, made physical-psychological healing prominent among the "spiritual gifts" they celebrated in communal ritual. Indeed, a range of religious leaders, from Pentecostal preachers to psychic healers, emphasized therapeutic practices for mind and body.

Eclecticism for its own sake was not the goal. The aim of most of these movements was to deepen individual spirituality and connect participants to the physical world. In some ways, this effort resembled that of nineteenth-century Evangelicals to harness the energy of the Second Great Awakening to drive efforts for social reform. But the groups acting on new ideals after 1960 had no one framework (such as the domestic model that had united many nineteenth-century reformers). Many "reforms" espoused by the spiritual movements of the late twentieth century were private and personal, such as physical fitness and psychotherapy.

Many movements, nevertheless, looked beyond the individual, the church, and even the nation to a larger sphere of moral responsibility. This was true of those who joined Martin Luther King in the civil rights movement and protested against the Vietnam War. Ecologically oriented movements frequently tried to connect spirituality and political action as they worked to preserve the environment. Some of these adopted a model of human connection to nature inspired by John Muir; others created neopagan groups or borrowed Native American rituals. Implicitly, such ritualizations created an imagined global moral community. But in this view, that moral community should be imagined not as a melting pot, but as one that preserved and celebrated differences. Jews, Native Americans, African Americans, Latino Americans, and others could hope to define a social space in which they could recover their roots, reinterpret their traditions, and negotiate their place in American culture. This orientation was enshrined in two major museums of the era—the Holocaust memorial in Washington, D.C., and its West Coast counterpart, the Museum of Tolerance in Los Angeles. On one level, these sites focused on Jews and other minorities, commemorating people who died at the hands of Nazis; but, as the name of the Los Angeles museum indicates, the more important message was that prejudice of all kinds must disappear.

Changes in Judaism and Catholicism during this period provide an example of how these various trends worked together. On the one hand, for Jews the trauma of the Holocaust resulted in significant disaffection from religious identity and increased inclination toward religious intermarriage. On the other hand, among those who remained formally connected to Judaism, emotional-spiritual emphases showed marked change after World War II. Hasidic teachings that emphasized prayer, music, and joyous service, which were brought to the United States with the twentieth-century waves of Jewish immigration, began to attract attention in mainstream Judaism during the 1950s.[44] One sect in particular, Chabad-Lubavitch, trained rabbis to move out of the traditional study halls into communities and colleges where Jews were highly assimilated

and reintroduce Jews to ritual observance in an energetic, positive, and emotionally satisfying way. Significantly for our understanding of this period, these
same Hasidic traditions emphasized the sanctification of everyday, material,
and bodily life through spiritual intentions. As a result of this and other similar
movements that modeled themselves on this kind of outreach, the number of
Orthodox adherents began to grow rather than decline for the first time in two
hundred years. A Jewish renewal movement, modeled on Hasidic fellowship
but not necessarily Orthodox, began in the late 1960s, attracting many who
had participated in the civil rights and antiwar movements. In the 1980s,
teachers emerged to introduce one or another form of Jewish meditation,
sometimes incorporating Hasidic along with modified Buddhist or Hindu
practices. If we recall that a Jewish program director spearheaded the teaching
of Tibetan Buddhist sand painting to Watts teenagers, we can see an unusual
way in which, for some Jews, the connection between spirituality and political
concerns manifested itself.

As Jews faced disaffiliation, Catholics too lost the loyalty of many members
of the younger generations. Far fewer entered the priesthood, and many of
those who remained officially affiliated abandoned traditional practices such
as devotion to the saints and refused to follow papal injunctions on such issues
as contraception. The Second Vatican Council, however, helped shift the tide
by allowing for greater lay participation, and this encouraged spiritual growth
and liturgical experimentation beginning with the "underground church" of
the late 1960s. Soon after, ferment in many other Roman Catholic populations,
notably in Latin America, brought U.S. Catholics to an intensified moral consciousness. Protests and boycotts on behalf of Spanish-speaking farm workers
brought the message home to the United States. Liberation theology encouraged followers to identify with the poor, making that the criterion for authentic Christianity. Thus spirituality, morality, and changing attitudes toward embodiment marked some forms of Catholicism as well.

In contrast, this also was a period, like the early nineteenth century, of religious experimentation in prophet-led groups. Some groups, such as Sung
Myung Moon's Unification Church and L. Ron Hubbard's Church of Scientology, attracted widespread condemnation from mainstream religions for their
evangelistic techniques or their adherence to prophets. Other groups gradually
have achieved acceptance with less fanfare. Of greatest concern, however, were
those that seemed to threaten violence or terrorism. The 1978 collapse of the
communitarian experiment at Jonestown, Guyana, in a mass suicide was a
shock felt throughout the United States. The experiment had roots in a promising religious development—the People's Temple, which initially had a high
moral purpose and a strong interracial base. The apparent degeneration into
a "cult" focused around the charismatic Jim Jones, who demanded complete
allegiance, was all the more disturbing. Other groups also developed millennial

expectations with doomsday scenarios that sometimes became self-fulfilling prophecies. In 1993 the Branch Davidians, an offshoot of Seventh-day Adventism, died in a blaze provoked by confrontation with federal agents. Parallel events in other countries, together with fundamentalist-inspired international terrorism, made Americans more wary of unusual religious groups even while they were becoming more culturally tolerant.

National identity seemed less important to many Americans in this period than a higher moral purpose and a transcendent religious ideal. Many of these tendencies toward diversity challenged the civil religion and provoked a corresponding response. In the 1960s, protests against the Vietnam War showed that the sacredness of the American government could be challenged: people burned the flag instead of saluting it. While the power of civil religion, and even its "holy days," declined, the great Protestant communal empowerments such as revivals also were losing much of their force. By the 1990s, Billy Graham was, for some, the last nationally respected mass evangelist.

Counterforces emerged to reinstate "American" and "Christian" standards. A family values movement led by conservative Protestants developed in the 1980s and early 1990s. Adherents promoted both true womanhood, along the lines of nineteenth-century domesticity, and true manhood, with male authority and committed fatherhood being the main themes. Whereas in the nineteenth century the advocates of domesticity condemned both excessive arousal and celibacy, in the late twentieth century advocates of family values focused on homosexuality and abortion as their principal foes. People who deviated from prescribed gender roles were the principal sinners. Yet these efforts to reinstate behavioral codes of an earlier, more homogeneous country were themselves far more diverse than before. They rarely involved the ethnic slurs associated with such causes in the nineteenth century (against African Americans and Roman Catholics, for example). They also were religiously pluralistic. Conservative Protestants made common cause with conservative Catholics and Jews, and whenever possible included African Americans prominently in their campaigns. Such campaigns were explicit efforts to resanctify America as a pure community that might also be inclusive—so long as "liberals" were excluded. A strong Fundamentalist current accompanied this movement, advocating school prayer, respect for the Bible, and teaching creationism in the public schools.

In short, religious "liberals" developed practices that minimized group boundaries and maximized individual body-spirit integration, creating what they saw as universal communities supportive of individual spiritual goals. "Conservatives" focused on moral behavior, emphasizing the preservation of traditional American social and family structures as the unifying factor.

All the movements described in this section are still in the process of development as this essay is written, and none is, by itself, representative of American religion. Nevertheless, the distinctive movements of the late twentieth century help us identify certain themes in ritualization. Sometimes they have offered temporary palliatives, an escape into spiritual bliss. Rarely have they attempted to build stable churches or communities, and those that did often have been messianic groups that appeared threatening to the dominant culture. Despite their self-absorption and loose communities, however, most recent religious groupings have been predominantly this-worldly, using practices that orient people to the sacred "other" in direct relationship to this world. Most American Buddhists studied child-rearing methods and engaged in political action rather than joining monasteries. Environmentalists sought a spiritual base in Native American rituals of the earth. Suburban churches adopted psychotherapeutic practices, while support groups prayed to a Higher Power. In many ways, healing became a dominant theme of American religion in this period, which emphasized the body and celebrated supraphysical powers that are efficacious in the world.

I began this essay with an account of Tibetan monks teaching a ritual to Watts teenagers in a program created by a Jewish Buddhist. In retrospect, that story is remarkably apt for understanding the contemporary scene. Its characters were diverse. Its theme, "healing violence through art," championed the ideal of a global moral community and appealed to the therapeutic tone that has predominated in the most recent period of American history. Creating the art was a rite of communal healing through an act of collective remembering. The ritual itself offered participants an intense personal experience in a quiet meditative atmosphere. Its movements were eminently physical, the body constantly engaged in the act of painting. At the same time, the sponsors and participants created a spiritual process whose ultimate aim was to deal with that most physical of activities, violence. As with many other practices of the era, by integrating the physical and the spiritual, emphasizing emotional and physical healing, and exhorting the community to moral and political action, this ritual oriented individuals in a world that seemed larger and more complex than ever before.

In my analysis of this ritual, and the many others I have considered, I also have tried to show that the orientational processes that constitute ritual can be central to understanding individuals and groups. A focus on bodily actions as orientational processes illumines new areas of historical interest and allows new angles of vision. This concern with ritual reflects, of course, our own cultural setting, and particularly the heightened interest during the last forty years in embodiment. Yet it is not merely an expression of cultural trends or an attempt to correct the previous generation's preoccupation with ideas. Ritualization is a central, though still understudied, theme in American religious history.

NOTES

1. Robert Bellah's classic article, "Civil Religion in America," first appeared in *Daedalus* in 1967; for easy access to it see Russell E. Richey and Donald G. Jones, *American Civil Religion* (New York: Harper, 1974), 21–44. Bellah's work was foreshadowed by W. Lloyd Warner in *The Family of God: A Symbolic Study of Christian Life in America* (New Haven: Yale University Press, 1961). Such studies have been amplified by, among others, Conrad Cherry's documentary history *God's New Israel* (Englewood Cliffs, N.J.: Prentice-Hall, 1971), and Catherine L. Albanese's *Sons of the Fathers: The Civil Religion of the American Revolution* (Philadelphia: Temple University Press, 1976). See also the discussion of civil religion in John F. Wilson's *Public Religion in America* (Philadelphia: Temple University Press, 1979). In addition, Charles Reagan Wilson has identified the southern version of civil religion, the "Religion of the Lost Cause," in *Baptized in Blood: The Religion of the Lost Cause 1865–1920* (Athens: University of Georgia Press, 1980); Sean Wilentz has written about working-class versions of the civic rituals in *Chants Democratic: New York City and the Rise of the American Working Class 1788–1850* (New York: Oxford University Press, 1984); see also Roy Rosenzweig, *Eight Hours for What We Will: Workers and Leisure in an Industrial City* (New York: Cambridge University Press, 1983). Monographs on ritual in the American setting go back to Ronald L. Grimes, *Symbol and Conquest: Public Ritual and Drama in Santa Fe, New Mexico* (Ithaca: Cornell University Press, 1976). Studies that feature ritual prominently in historical contexts include Tamar [Sandra S. Sizer] Frankiel, *Gospel Hymns and Social Religion: The Rhetoric of Nineteenth Century Revivalism* (Philadelphia: Temple University Press, 1978); Robert Anthony Orsi, *The Madonna of 115th Street: Faith and Community in Italian Harlem, 1880–1950* (New Haven: Yale University Press, 1985); Susan Davis, *Parades and Power: Street Theater in Nineteenth Century Philadelphia* (Philadelphia: Temple University Press, 1986); Rhys Isaac, *Worlds of Experience: Communities in Colonial Virginia* (Williamsburg, Va.: Colonial Williamsburg Foundation, 1987); David Hall, *Worlds of Wonder, Days of Judgment: Popular Religious Belief in Early New England* (New York: Knopf, 1989); Leigh Schmidt, *Holy Fairs: Scottish Communions and American Revivals in the Early Modern Period* (Princeton: Princeton University Press, 1989); David Glassberg, *American Historical Pageantry: The Uses of Tradition in the Early Twentieth Century* (Chapel Hill: University of North Carolina Press, 1990); and A. Gregory Schneider, *The Way of the Cross Leads Home: The Domestication of American Methodism* (Bloomington: Indiana University Press, 1993).

2. Among anthropologists, Clifford Geertz's "Religion as a Cultural System," in M. Banton, ed., *Anthropological Approaches to the Study of Religion* (London: Tavistock Publications, 1966), and his *Islam Observed: Religious Development in Morocco and Indonesia* (New Haven: Yale University Press, 1968) were highly influential among scholars of religion, as was Victor Turner's *The Ritual Process* (Chicago: Aldine, 1969). Recent theorists have gone considerably beyond these works, however; see, in particular, Jonathan Z. Smith, *To Take Place: Toward Theory in Ritual* (Chicago: University of Chicago Press, 1987); Catherine Bell, *Ritual Theory, Ritual Practice* (New York: Oxford University Press, 1992); and Thomas Csordas, *The Sacred Self: A Cultural Phenomenology of Charismatic Healing* (Berkeley: University of California Press, 1994).

3. Clifford Geertz has been a leading figure among anthropologists who use drama

as a central metaphor for ritual. Since his 1966 article, "Religion as a Cultural System," ritual has been central to his analyses; his fieldwork in Indonesian culture has often used dramatic cultural performances as central foci for analysis. An example in an American setting is Grimes, *Symbol and Conquest*. Bell, however, has launched significant criticisms against using the metaphor of drama, and its extension in performance theory, to understand ritual. See Bell, *Ritual Theory*, 42–43. For our purposes here, the metaphor is meant to suggest the power of embodied action; certainly it should not be taken to mean that rituals require an explicit physical frame such as a stage, but neither does the focus on embodiment exclude verbalizations in ritual. Ritual use of language is distinctive, however. It is often repetitive or rhythmic (for example, repeated "Amens"), takes the form of performative utterances (such as the "I do" in marriage vows), or relies heavily on formulaic frameworks (like the Puritan "jeremiad" as a sermonic form).

4. See especially Bell, *Ritual Theory*, for the emphasis on embodiment and the term *practices* (from Pierre Bourdieu); and Csordas, *Sacred Self* (who also draws on Bourdieu as well as Merleau-Ponty), for the emphasis on orientation and open-ended processes.

5. For an excellent discussion of this point, see Bell, *Ritual Theory*, chap. 5: "The Ritual Body."

6. Liminality was most fully described, with its paradoxical structures of power/powerlessness, by Victor Turner in his important work *The Ritual Process*, adapted from the threefold pattern of initiation outlined by Arnold Van Gennep in his classic book, *The Rites of Passage* (1909; London: Routledge and Kegan Paul, 1960).

7. I use "imagine" here in line with Csordas's interpretation of imagery as a self-process that orients the person in relation to different aspects, or "subselves," that exist in memory (Csordas, *Sacred Self*, chaps. 4–6). The imaginative process behind the African-American mandala may bear some resemblance to the charismatic ritual of "healing of memories," although the latter is more therapeutically inclined.

8. For an excellent discussion, see James Axtell, "The White Indians of Colonial America" and "The Scholastic Philosophy of the Wilderness," in *The European and the Indian: Essays in the Ethnohistory of Colonial North America* (New York: Oxford University Press, 1981). On the latter point Axtell notes, for example, that Cotton Mather complained people were learning three vices from the Indians: idleness, lying, and indulgence toward children, the latter of which he called "an epidemical miscarriage of the country" (ibid., 160, 281). Among scholars of early North American culture contact, Axtell treats religion quite fully; his results, however, have been questioned by some Native American scholars. Therefore, in addition to his work, one should look at Karen O. Kupperman, *Settling with the Indians: The Meeting of English and Indian Cultures in America, 1580–1640* (Totowa, N.J.: Rowman and Littlefield, 1980); Wilbur Jacobs, *Dispossessing the American Indian* (1972; Norman: University of Oklahoma Press, 1985); and Jack D. Forbes, *A World Ruled by Cannibals: The Wetiko Disease of Aggression, Violence, and Imperialism* (Pittsburgh: Duquesne University Press, 1979). Many other scholars have examined Native American and European assumptions; for sources that include vivid examples from primary texts, see Gordon Brotherston, *Image of the New World: The American Continent Portrayed in Native Texts* (London: Thames and Hudson, 1979), and Ronald Wright, *Stolen Continents: The Americas through Indian Eyes since 1492* (Boston: Houghton Mifflin, 1992).

9. Axtell, *European and Indian*, 119.

10. A particularly vivid portrait of the demands on Puritans for constant devotion, beyond the conversion experience, appears in Charles Hambrick-Stowe, *The Practice of Piety: Puritan Devotional Disciplines in Seventeenth Century New England* (Chapel Hill: University of North Carolina Press, 1982); and Hall, *Worlds of Wonder,* particularly chap. 1 on literacy and the Bible, and chap. 4 for a discussion of confession.

11. Axtell, *European and Indian,* 122. Hall, *Worlds of Wonder,* 70. As many commentators have observed in comparing Protestant to Catholic ritual attitudes, focus on the Word reduced the use of the several senses, requiring containment of the body rather than symbolizing or dramatizing emotion and sensation outwardly. "Rational" discourse was presumed to be the model. For an early discussion with reference to America see Warner, *The Family of God,* chap. 3: "The Protestant Revolt and Symbolism."

12. The Jesuits created a few separate communities, called "reserves," but they also worked by developing a Christian faction within the native village, with the intent of getting the Christians into positions of influence. There, baptism was often deferred longer than among the Franciscans, until the convert was believed to be strong in the faith so he or she would be able to resist the contempt of former fellows in the village (Axtell, *European and Indian,* 69–71).

13. Reports suggest that Jesuits used punishment only rarely, whereas Franciscans used it fairly regularly depending on the policy of the senior missionary. The Jesuit model was different, of course, in that the priests frequently lived within the community and sometimes accepted certain Native American customs in order to win converts.

14. On the notion of civility, see Richard P. Gildrie, *The Profane, the Civil, and the Godly: The Reformation of Manners in Orthodox New England, 1679–1749* (University Park: Pennsylvania State University Press, 1994). On these developments see also Hall, *Worlds of Wonder.* For a recent treatment of the eighteenth-century revolution in consumer demand and the public media in relation to revivalism, see Frank Lambert's *"Pedlar in Divinity": George Whitefield and the Transatlantic Revivals, 1737–1770* (Princeton: Princeton University Press, 1994).

15. Schmidt, *Holy Fairs,* 78, 91.

16. This line of thinking suggests several areas of investigation. For example, what were the patterns of ritual in local revivals, where people underwent radical experiences not while "on pilgrimage" but in the familiar space of their own home church? It may be significant that, as Edwards records in his "Narratives of Surprising Conversions," he sometimes has to *go out* to visit a person in his or her home who is fainting, catatonic, or talking wildly. Clearly, as revivals proceed, the Methodist class meeting and the Presbyterian conference meeting are means by which the laity promote the revival outside the realm of the public worship service, often unobserved by the eye of the minister. The nature of the preachers' role in the revival also deserves more investigation. Alan Heimert, in his seminal *Religion and the American Mind* (Cambridge, Mass.: Harvard University Press, 1966), chap. 4, held that changes in preaching to a more straightforward, forceful style full of dramatic images and impressive metaphors were the hinge of the Great Awakening. But more investigation is needed to relate this style to other specific changes in ritualization.

17. For comparison, see Marilyn J. Westerkamp, *Triumph of the Laity: Scots-Irish Piety and the Great Awakening, 1625–1760* (New York: Oxford University Press, 1988),

211. On the strength of localism of colonial society up to the American Revolution, see the classic studies of Michael Zuckerman, *Peaceable Kingdoms: New England Towns in the Eighteenth Century* (New York: Knopf, 1970), and Bernard Bailyn, *The Ideological Origins of the American Revolution* (Cambridge, Mass.: Harvard University Press, 1967). As Heimert pointed out, however, the revivalistic Calvinists were developing a concept of the harmony of different "modes" of religion which eventually allowed them to conceive of an idea of the "common good" or the "general will of the community" (Heimert, *Religion and the American Mind,* 17–18, 402–5). For the strengthening of local churches in the Second Great Awakening, see Terry D. Bilhartz, *Urban Religion and the Second Great Awakening: Church and Society in Early National Baltimore* (Rutherford, N.J.: Fairleigh Dickinson University Press, 1986), 140.

18. Bilhartz, *Urban Religion,* 75.

19. Scholars have long suggested that the First Great Awakening contributed to a heightened white Protestant awareness, tied to an inherited Puritan sense of millennial mission; see especially Heimert, *Religion and the American Mind,* 403–5, and Westerkamp, *Triumph of the Laity,* 212–13. The John and Abigail Adams correspondence is quoted by Sacvan Bercovitch in "The Typology of America's Mission," *American Quarterly* 30, 2 (summer 1978): 150. For further development see Bercovitch's *The American Jeremiad* (Madison: University of Wisconsin Press, 1978). See also Bercovitch's *The Rites of Assent: Transformations in the Symbolic Construction of America* (New York: Routledge, 1993). For further discussion of the definition of new symbols in revolutionary times, see Albanese, *Sons of the Fathers.*

20. Bilhartz, *Urban Religion,* 140.

21. For a sense of the range of experiences of bodily action in the frontier revivals (many familiar from the First Great Awakening), see Paul K. Conkin, *Cane Ridge: America's Pentecost* (Madison: University of Wisconsin Press, 1990), 109–31. Voluntary practices included loud singing, exhorting, hand shaking, engaging in prayer matches and mass confessions, shouting, dancing; involuntary ones included falling, rolling, jerking, barking, "holy laughter," and having visions.

22. Not all ecstasy is revolutionary. If it becomes a criterion for group membership or status, it can be conservative, like the Puritan conversion experience or later Pentecostal "gifts of the Spirit." Emotional experiences in general need a different approach from their usual treatment as catharses. In my view, emotions are aspects of the ritualized body just as much as standing or kneeling, or chanting or singing in prayer. Examples include such varied expressions as family mourning rites, the agony of the mystic, the weeping crowds at the elevation of the host in the Roman Catholic Eucharist, or hymns that bring tears to the eyes. Emotions in such contexts are usually not under voluntary control and may represent some slight degree of dissociation. However, they can become patterned responses through the establishment and repetition of ritual acts that evoke them.

23. See for example Nathan O. Hatch, *The Democratization of American Christianity* (New Haven: Yale University Press, 1989). Meanwhile, as democratic ideology grew in popularity and the idea of church-state separation took hold, most states disestablished their churches. As Roger Finke argues elsewhere . . . , such "deregulation" is a powerful catalyst in opening up new religious possibilities.

24. Walter F. Pitts, *Old Ship of Zion: The Afro-Baptist Ritual in the African Diaspora* (New York: Oxford University Press, 1993), especially chaps. 3 and 4; Donald G. Mathews, *Religion in the Old South* (Chicago: University of Chicago Press, 1977), 215.

25. John F. Watson, quoted in Hatch, *Democratization,* 155.

26. For treatment of hymns and testimonials as ritualized expressions, see Frankiel, *Gospel Hymns.* The power of testimony is still not well understood, but accounts of revivals often witness to the domino effect, so to speak, of testimonials. For example, as Paul Conkin relates, Barton Stone's telling a story of revivals, "as so often before . . . led to an almost immediate eruption of physical exercises roughly similar to those he described" (*Cane Ridge,* 70).

27. An older but still helpful treatment of the "prophet" is Kenelm Burridge's *New Heaven, New Earth* (New York: Schocken, 1969), which discusses millennial movements; his *Mambu: A Study of Melanesian Cargo Movements* (1960; New York: Harper, 1970) is a monograph that describes such a prophet.

28. See, for example, Louis J. Kern, *An Ordered Love* (Chapel Hill: University of North Carolina Press, 1981), and Lawrence Foster, *Religion and Sexuality: Three American Communal Experiments of the Nineteenth Century* (New York: Oxford University Press, 1981). On the Seventh-day Adventists, see in particular Ronald L. Numbers, *Prophetess of Health: A Study of Ellen G. White* (New York: Harper, 1976), and Malcolm Bull and Keith Lockhart, *Seeking a Sanctuary: Seventh-Day Adventism and the American Dream* (San Francisco: Harper and Row, 1989), especially chap. 10. On Mormons, see Klaus J. Hansen, *Mormonism and the American Experience* (Chicago: University of Chicago Press, 1981), especially 104, where he compares Mormons with Shakers and Oneida Perfectionists. On medicine and health, see Robert Fuller, *Alternative Medicine and American Religious Life* (New York: Oxford University Press, 1989).

29. Michael Barkun notes that this same period generated attempts to isolate and rehabilitate social deviants through institutions: the asylum, the penitentiary, the almshouse, the orphanage. Michael Barkun, *Crucible of the Millennium: The Burned-Over District of Western New York in the 1840s* (Syracuse: Syracuse University Press, 1986).

30. A significant study that relates the development of American Methodism to this ideology is Schneider, *The Way of the Cross Leads Home.* An earlier work that connects domesticity to hymnody is Frankiel, *Gospel Hymns* (1978). Among others, see Mary P. Ryan, *Empire of the Mother: American Writing about Domesticity, 1830 to 1860* (New York: Haworth Press, 1982); Colleen McDannell, *The Christian Home in Victorian America, 1840–1900* (Bloomington: Indiana University Press, 1986); Barbara Leslie Epstein, *The Politics of Domesticity: Women, Evangelism, and Temperance in Nineteenth Century America* (Middletown, Conn.: Wesleyan University Press, 1981). For a Roman Catholic comparison, see Ann Taves, *The Household of Faith: Roman Catholic Devotions in Mid-Nineteenth Century America* (Notre Dame, Ind.: Notre Dame University Press, 1986). Studies of Jewish domestic practice and ideology would probably reveal a great deal about assimilation, or resistance to it, among various groups of American Jews. A seminal treatment of "domesticity" as a category for understanding American religion, and particularly the evangelical tradition, is Ann Douglas, *The Feminization of American Culture* (New York: Alfred A. Knopf, 1977), although Douglas has been criticized for seeing "feminization" as a negative development. . . . Mark Carnes has suggested that many upwardly mobile middle-class men reacted against the domestication of American religion by creating their own strictly male rituals and even a perception of deity that was more powerful and less intimate. See Mark Carnes, *Secret Ritual and Manhood in Victorian America* (New Haven: Yale University Press, 1989).

31. Among recent treatments, see John A. Andrew III, *From Revivals to Removal: Jeremiah Evarts, the Cherokee Nation, and the Search for the Soul of America* (Athens:

University of Georgia Press, 1992). Andrew examines the dynamics of revivals and change in sensibility, followed by the move toward reform societies and missionary work as a way of generating proper feeling and behavior.

32. Mathews, *Religion in the Old South*, 26. As Mathews has noted, southern Methodists were somewhat different and perhaps more "northern," with little of the Baptist interest in theological disputations and forming tight, closed communities. More open to communion with other Christians, they focused on intrachurch structure and morality.

33. For an examination of similar rituals in the former Confederate regions, see Wilson, *Baptized in Blood.*

34. Similar movements, particularly in the arts and literature, have been identified as "anti-modernist" by T. J. Jackson Lears in *No Place of Grace: Antimodernism and the Transformation of American Culture, 1880–1920* (New York: Pantheon, 1981). Americans' ambivalent relationship to nature has been discussed in depth by Catherine L. Albanese in *Nature Religion in America: From the Algonkian Indians to the New Age* (Chicago: University of Chicago Press, 1990). The attempt to put a new face on American history is suggested by Rodman Wanamaker's proposal to put an American Indian statue in New York harbor next to the Statue of Liberty. Since the "vanishing race" was no longer a threat to civilization, they could now be honored. The Educational Bureau of Wanamaker's Clothing Store (Philadelphia) also sponsored filming expeditions among Native Americans. See Manfred E. Keune, "An Immodest Proposal: A Memorial to the American Indian," *Journal of American Culture 1* (1978): 788–86.

35. See Neal Gabler, *An Empire of Their Own: How the Jews Invented Hollywood* (New York: Crown, 1988).

36. As Robert Orsi has shown, Italian ritual dramas eventually became involved even in papal politics and opposing "Americanism" within the church. See Orsi, *Madonna of 115th Street.* On related issues, see also R. Laurence Moore, "Managing Catholic Success in a Protestant Empire," in *Religious Outsiders and the Making of Americans* (New York: Oxford University Press, 1986).

37. For example, Isaac Wise's early reforms, which became models for others, included eliminating from the liturgy some medieval poems and using German and English hymns, abolishing the sale of synagogue honors, sitting during the Torah reading, introducing a (mixed) choir and, a little later, the family pew. Wise at first adopted the latter for pragmatic reasons, so that his new congregation would not have to spend money on remodeling the church building they bought in 1851 (and similarly with the first synagogue in New York to have mixed seating in 1854). However, this aspect soon became a mark of "modernity" and equality with Christianity in Judaism's presumed attitudes toward women. For discussion, see Jonathan D. Sarna, "Mixed Seating in the American Synagogue," in Jack Wertheimer, ed., *The American Synagogue: A Sanctuary Transformed* (New York: Cambridge University Press, 1987), 23.

38. Russia's "modernization" program in the mid-nineteenth century had attempted to lure Jews into Jewish, government-supported schools which allowed Jewish education but also taught secular subjects. The bitter struggles between traditional and "enlightened" Jews over this subject, together with the clear trend toward assimilation among students who went to these schools, had established firm attitudes among eastern Europeans about mixing their culture with that of non-Jews.

39. Despite the emphasis on mind, however, it was still necessary to discipline the body to its nonexistence, and certain of the positive thinkers developed exercises for the ear and eye, senses of taste, touch, and smell, as well as for nerves and paying attention.

40. Donald Meyer, in *The Positive Thinkers: Religion as Popular Psychology from Mary Baker Eddy to Oral Roberts* (New York: Pantheon, 1980), 165, cites Frank Haddock's *Power of Will* (1907) as an example. For general treatments of the metaphysical movements, see Stephen Gottschalk, *The Emergence of Christian Science in American Religious Life* (Berkeley: University of California Press, 1973); Robert Peel, *Christian Science: Its Encounter with American Culture* (New York: Holt, 1958); J. Stillson Judah, *History and Philosophy of the Metaphysical Movements in America* (Philadelphia: Westminster, 1967); and Charles Braden, *Spirits in Rebellion* (Dallas: Southern Methodist University Press, 1963). On Buddhism in America, see Thomas A. Tweed, *The American Encounter with Buddhism, 1844–1912: Victorian Culture and the Limits of Dissent* (Bloomington: Indiana University Press, 1992). Another important related movement was Theosophy, which had a few communities in America. See Judah's *History and Philosophy;* Bruce F. Campbell, *Ancient Wisdom Revived: A History of the Theosophical Movement* (Berkeley: University of California Press, 1980); Emmett A. Greenwalt, "The Point Loma Community in California 1897–1942," Ph.D. dissertation, University of California, Los Angeles, 1949; and Robert V. Hine, *California's Utopian Colonies* (San Marino, Calif.: Huntington Library, 1953).

41. For a treatment of this dimension, see the chapter on Nazarene founder Phineas Bresee in Tamar [Sandra S.] Frankiel, *California's Spiritual Frontiers: Religious Alternatives in Anglo-Protestantism 1850–1915* (Berkeley: University of California Press, 1988).

42. A recent work suggests the connection of certain key figures in Pentecostalism to the mesmeric tradition; see McDannell, *Christian Home.*

43. As T. J. Jackson Lears has pointed out in *No Place of Grace,* gender relations had already been changing since the turn of the century. Women were advocating new feminine models from the suffragette to the outdoors type; the diaphragm was invented, which aided birth control. For a summary of the Jazz Age influences, see Itabari Njeri, "Trickle-Down Culture," *Los Angeles Times Magazine,* 28 August 1994, 53–54, citing jazz critic Stanley Crouch. Jill Watts has commented on similar themes in her article on the popular 1936 film *Klondike Annie:* "Constructions of Western Religion on the Screen: Mae West as Sister Annie," presented at the Seminar on American Dreams, Western Images, William Andrews Clark Memorial Library, University of California, Los Angeles, May 1994.

44. Hasidism, a movement within traditional Orthodoxy, had emerged in eastern Europe in the middle and late eighteenth century, and by the nineteenth was a major force in many European towns. Thus it was contemporary with Methodism, and its emphasis on intimate groupings of followers, self-examination, the importance of song and prayer, and joy in worshiping and serving God indeed bears many similarities to Methodism and other Protestant forms of pietism.

2

The Ordinances of Public Worship

Charles E. Hambrick-Stowe

Christian worship services occupy today a prominent place in ritual spirituality. They come in a variety of denominational forms and with a rich range of expressive features. What is easy to forget, however, is that their presence in the land reflects, at least in part, a Christian history that began in the seventeenth century. New England Puritans, in their carefully constructed ordinances of public worship, sought to act out their beliefs about themselves as covenanting communities ready to serve God as one body, as a redeemed people with sacred tasks to be executed. In the material presented here, Charles E. Hambrick-Stowe explores the Puritans' symbolic behavior in classic seventeenth-century services of prayer and worship. Puritans had come to be part of the "covenant of grace" through individual conversion experiences, and they valued introspection. But as important to them were the corporate and performative aspects of their religious lives. Their low-church revolution—distinguishing them from the conventional spirituality of the more Catholic-leaning Church of England—combined aspects of the English church with continental Calvinism and Anabaptism, both of which in different ways sought a heavenly order in a perfected earthly society. As Hambrick-Stowe shows here, in their public demonstrations of worship, New England Puritans aimed to create that order by combining inner spiritual worlds with outward and organized Christian forms. The Puritans Hambrick-Stowe writes about, with their Sabbath ceremonies and days of public worship, provide an especially strong example of ritual that is not empty but very full—ritual that is a nurturing force, a source of security, and a vehicle for the integration of self and society.

The Puritan devotional pilgrimage was a mystical journey in Christ, frequently leading to experiences of union with Him. But New Englanders were not mystics if that term implies abandoning life in society or earthly, historical means for reaching God. Puritans clung to the traditional "means of grace," including ecclesiastical "ordinances," and to the concept of "the Church," through which God mediated Himself. Thomas Shepard preached that "the visible Church of

God . . . is the kingdom of Heaven upon earth." The people of New England were led to find their salvation in the rituals performed in and endorsed by the Church. And whereas most of the seven Roman Catholic sacraments constituted rites de passage, Puritan believers employed ordinances continually.[1]

The means of grace were technically divided into two groups, ordinances of public worship and private devotions. Puritan theologians never canonized a precise number of approved ordinances; so any listing of them remains informal and flexible. By every account they included the sacraments of Baptism and the Lord's Supper, plus other scripturally founded acts of worship. Early manuals generally set forth three public means through which God was expected to act: the ministry of the Word (reading of and preaching on the Bible), the sacraments, and prayer. Sometimes the list included fasting.[2]

New Englanders built upon this foundation through the seventeenth century. One enumeration gave five "principal" public ordinances: Prayer, "the Apostles Doctrine" (Bible reading and the sermon), the sacraments, "Mutual Communion," and "Discipline." At its gathering in 1638 the Dedham Church identified the following as official ordinances: preaching of the Word, administration of Baptism and the Lord's Supper, application of discipline among members, excommunication and absolution, collection for the poor, prophecy by members with "speciall guifts" (exercised when "approved by the Church as fitt for publike edification"), singing of psalms, and Sabbath worship itself. Even this was a preliminary list. Nothing was said about the rituals of covenant making and renewal, key liturgical actions throughout the seventeenth century. Nor did the Dedham Church mention lecture days, fast days, and thanksgivings. These, together with the weekly cycle of Sabbaths, formed the outward religious practice of the inhabitants. New Englanders also understood certain civil events, notably elections and militia training days, as occasions for special worship.[3]

The private devotional life of New Englanders, meanwhile, consisted of exercises that took various forms: "private" prayer meeting, "conference" with another believer, family prayer time, and individual, or "secret," devotion. A complete view of worship and devotional practice in New England must include this wide range of activities and settings.

The maintenance of outward means of grace ran counter to the iconoclastic spiritualizing thrust within Puritanism that renounced sacrament, Scripture, and ministry. The cry of "Christ alone" was heard on the lips of Antinomians, Gortonists, Quakers, and early Baptists. All Puritans, of course, denied the Catholic doctrine of the efficacy of forms in themselves and the Arminian doctrine of human capability of salvation through self-willed use of forms. The spiritualizing impulse in all Puritans was apparent in John Cotton's warning that "it is not the liberty of Gods Ordinances, and the dispensation of them that can secure us; and therefore trust not in them, trust not in this, that you are diligent Hearers, or that you can pray powerfully; trust not in this, though you were Preachers of the Word of God, but trust on him only for life, and salvation, and he will never deceive you." But orthodoxy went on: "There is no life in them further than [God] puts in them." Cotton broke finally with Anne Hutchinson on the matter of immediate revelation and her negation of the need for Scripture and ministry. The New England clergy denied that the "emptiness" of forms mandated their abandonment. They were empty in themselves, but full of grace when God employed them. New England continued to insist that the way to God was through outward forms and exercises.[4]

Orthodox Puritan spirituality would not endorse the mysticism of the fourteenth-century author of *The Cloud of Unknowing*. For him, and for his New England descendants Anne Hutchinson and Samuel Gorton, "creatures" like bread and wine, scriptural Word, and baptismal water came "between you and your God" as a barrier. It was "far better to think about His naked being." Gorton in this spirit denounced sacramental wine as "the juice of a poor, silly grape" and even the simplified liturgical apparatus of New England as a set of "idols." To the orthodox this was unscriptural and unrealistic. Thomas Shepard could long for and experience "Christ with a naked hand, even a naked Christ," but never would he presume to approach the deity except through the scriptural means of grace. Thomas Hooker's diatribe against mystical antinomianism was highly graphic. He warned, "We must not looke for revelations and dreames, as a company of phantastical braines doe; but in common course Gods Spirit goes with the Gospell."[5]

The phrase "in common course" is important. Union with Christ, ecstatic as it might be, always resulted from an orderly set of exercises that centered on the devotional use of the Bible. The Puritan God, Perry Miller proved, was the God of order, and the divine order corresponded with "the order of nature," manifested in the faculty psychology of the day and in the stages of conversion. Just as Bunyan's Christian made his way in orderly (nonetheless suspenseful and dangerous) fashion through Perkins's ten stages, so the New England pilgrim progressed beyond conversion along an orderly devotional way marked by Sabbath worship, personal and family devotions, and pious counsel of clergy and other saints. God could, of course, save without the means of grace but He did not "ordinarily" do so. In Puritan theology the word "ordinarily" carried a stronger meaning than modern usage conveys, for the Puritans believed that since the close of the apostolic age God had ceased to work in "extraordinary" ways. He continued to work in remarkable ways (and the recording of one's own "remarkable providences" was an important part of Puritan devotion), but not in extraordinary ways that defied the order of nature. It was "not that God is tyed to any means, but he tyeth himself to this means." The Lord will indeed eventually come "as a Theefe" in the night, Cotton preached, but in the meantime the believer will find Him "at Supper, he shall finde him at the Ordinances, at every spirituall dutie he shall finde him." The phrases "in ordinary course" and "in common course" were used in conjunction with the practice of devotion to describe both the regularity of devotional exercises and their importance as God's "conduits to convey [the] water of life." As expressed in one popular manual, the godly life was "upholden by means."[6]

Public Worship

Worship in New England revolved around the Sabbath. Much of private devotion during the week was preparation for that special day on which the greatest concentration of spiritual activity occurred. Use of the Sabbath as the devotional point of reference was a major Puritan innovation within Christianity. The Puritans replaced an annual, irregular cycle with a weekly, regular one, a celebration of the salvation drama in which "the mighty acts of God in the creation, redemption and sanctification of man, through the life, death, and resurrection of Christ" were each week completely re-presented and reexperienced. The Puritan Sabbath voiced Old Testament Sabbatarian ideas—especially God's rest on the seventh day of Creation and the Sabbath proclaimed in the Law by Moses—transformed by the Christian revelation of God's new creation at Easter. The Puritan Sabbath was thus a "little Easter" or "a sort of weekly Pascha," the day of Christ's resurrection and the day of believers' redemption.[7]

The nature of the rest prescribed for the Sabbath in New England was not identical with that of traditional England. Winton U. Solberg has suggested that in the Church of England's "ecclesiastical," or "dominical," view, the Sabbath was not based on God's eternal moral law in creation but on Mosaic Law and Jewish ceremonial, which expired with Christ. Sabbath activity was thus to be based on ecclesiastical tradition, rather than directly on biblical injunction. The Church of England "recognized man's compound nature and provided for body as well as the soul," thereby opening the way for merriment and sports. Rest became at least partly human rest and the day a time for recreation as well as worship. Puritans insisted that the Sabbath was a day to attend solely to spiritual realities. "The word Sabbath properly signifies not common, but sacred and holy rest," Shepard wrote. In the same vein *The Practice of Piety* posited two necessary elements for Sabbath keeping: first, "resting from all servile and common business pertaining to our natural life"; and second, "consecrating that rest wholly to the service of God, and the use of those holy means which belong to our spiritual life." It was a day of rest from all secular work and a day for the spiritual work whereby the soul could find rest. The Sabbath was a day for the re-creation of the soul, not the recreation of the body.[8]

The Sabbath was a means of grace. Shepard rejected the radical view that the external Sabbath was abolished with Christ and now existed as a nontemporal element within the individual soul. The best way to achieve a daily personal communion with Christ, Shepard believed, was to assign "a special day" for spiritual things, which would be "a most powerful means to Sabbatize every day." He argued that a spiritualized everyday Sabbath, which the radicals proposed, would soon have the effect of de-sabbatizing every day, including the first day of the week. Shepard's argument encompassed much of the theological and psychological basis for Puritan ritual. Special days, special observances, special things properly used according to biblical precedent, could foster the religious experience Puritans sought. The Sabbath was "the special season of grace" in the cycle of time. "If a mans heart be lost in the necessary cumbers of the weeke, (upon the Sabbath) the Lord is wont to recall it again to him; if any feare that the time of Grace is past, the continuation of the Sabbaths ... confutes him; if a mans soul be wearied with daily griefs and outward troubles, the bosome of Jesus Christ (which is in speciall wise opened every Lords day) may refresh him." On the Sabbath the Lord again called New Englanders "off from all occasions" with the words "Come to me my people, and rest in my bosome of sweetest mercy all this day."⁹

Beyond looking back to the Resurrection, Puritans on the Sabbath looked forward to the perfection of the work of redemption at the Second Coming. Since Old Testament times the Sabbath's dynamic qualities have stemmed from its eschatology; the Lord's Day pointed to the terrible approaching Day of the Lord. Thomas Shepard wrote at the end of his *Theses Sabbaticae* that devotional preparation for the Sabbath each week was a part and a miniature version of the saint's lifelong preparation for glory and eternal rest. "And as the rest of the Day is for the holinesse of it, so is all the labour of the Week for this holy rest; that as the end of all the labour of our lives is for our rest with Christ in Heaven, so also of the six daies of every weeke for the holy Rest of the Sabbath, the twilight and dawning of Heaven." The vignette of Shepard ... shows something of what pre-Sabbath exercises entailed.... The forward-looking nature of the Sabbath suited the progressive qualities of Puritan devotion. The sequence of Sabbath after Sabbath in earthly time marked off stages toward eternity, each one a resting place on the journey. The spiritual pilgrim set himself within the context of just this progress through stages established by God and leading to His heavenly Kingdom.¹⁰

Sabbath neglect, which Puritan diarists and church membership applicants almost invariably confessed as an early sin, was abominable because of the eschatological nature of the day. When John Dane was stung by a wasp on his finger not once but on two separate occasions as he shunned worship, he knew his heart had actually been pierced. The sting forced him to recall the redemption that should have been applied to his soul that day. As with the piercing of Christ on the cross, remarkably, "watter and blod cam out of it!" He recalled his mother's parting words as he embarked on his journeys: "Goe whare you will, god he will finde you out." Her warning referred not only to small judgments such as the stings but to the great and final judgment of which they were emblematic. Thomas Shepard warned that while "the Lord Jesus certainly hath great blessings in his hand to poure out upon his people in giving them better dayes, and brighter and more beautiful Sabbaths, and glorious appearances," neglect of the day would bring God's Judgment on soon. New England had better attend to the means of grace, Shepard preached, "lest the Lord make quick work, and give those things to a remnant to enjoy, which others had no hearts to prize."[11]

New Englanders worshiped publicly in both the morning and the afternoon of the Lord's Day. Services were long, about three hours each, so in effect the day was spent in church. Appraisals of individuals' emotional involvement in worship range from the unsympathetic description by the Labadist Jasper Danckaerts of Boston in 1680—"There was no more devotion than in other churches, and even less than at New York; no respect, no reverence; in a word, nothing but the name of Independents; and that was all"—to the sanguine picture in ministerial and pious lay diaries. Since church members and non-members alike throughout the century were required by law to attend worship, it is not surprising that attitudes varied. But however one felt about being present, Sabbath worship constituted a common experience of the populace. And it seems likely, as Sacvan Bercovitch has suggested, that the themes of public worship infused the entire culture. By granting six hours on the first day of every week for the clergy to rehearse the drama of sin and salvation before the people, New England put the Sabbath at the center of its temporal existence.[12]

Nor was public worship limited to the Sabbath. "Every week in most of our Churches," John Cotton wrote in his survey of New England's worship practices, "lectures are kept on some or other of the weeke days." Boston's lecture, the first established, was held on Thursday throughout the century. Cotton noted that "such as whose hearts God maketh willing, and his hand doth not detaine by bodily infirmitie, or other necessary imployments, (if they dwell in the heart of the Bay) may have opportunitie to heare the Word almost every day of the weeke in one Church or other, not farre distant from them." The emphasis on lecture day was ostensibly on doctrinal teaching complementary to the Sabbath's evangelical preaching; in churches with both a pastor and a teacher, the teacher usually gave the lecture. But this distinction broke down quickly (most churches soon had only one minister in any case), and the faint line between preaching and teaching all but vanished. For the parishioner lecture day was a weekday worship service, with the same type of prayers, psalm singing, and sermons as on the Sabbath, and one could legitimately take time away from work to attend.[13]

Other, more occasional, days of public worship were proclaimed as well. Upon "extraordinary occasions," such as when "notable judgments" and "speciall mercies" from God were evident, days of humiliation and thanksgiving, respectively, were set aside. As John Eliot put it, these "were so many Sabbaths more" in the calendar of New England worship. Such days were sometimes proclaimed by civil authority for the entire populace and sometimes by churches for members. Horton Davies has remarked that in England days of humiliation and thanksgiving differed from previous national special days in two ways: first in their "great solemnity, intensity, and length, . . . with only a minimal concession to the needs of the body"; and second, such days of special providence were observed within the Puritan family as well as in public ceremony. The unity of public and private devotion was indeed characteristic of Puritan spirituality and is seen in the Puritans' approach to fasting and giving thanks. One manual noted that in both private and public fasts the participant "voluntarily undertakes, to make his body and soul the fitter to pray more fervently to God upon some extraordinary occasion." The aim was "more devoutly [to] contemplate Gods holy will, and fervently pour forth our soule unto him by prayer," so that "by our serious humiliation, and judging of our selves, we may escape the judgment of the Lord."[14]

Public fast days were held in response to dire agricultural and meteorological conditions, ecclesiastical, military, political, and social crises both in New England and in Europe, and in preparation for important events such as the ordination of a minister or the militia's embarkation on a campaign. Thanksgiving days, similarly, were proclaimed after a good harvest, military success, or some other evidence of the Lord's favor and mercy. William DeLoss Love cataloged many of these days in a classic work and showed that both fast and thanksgiving days grew in importance in New England over the course of the century. The fast especially became a standard weapon in the arsenal of public rituals available in time of trouble. It was employed regularly in the wake of the major crises of the second half of the century, from general declension in piety to witchcraft. The distinctively American Puritan sermonic style, the jeremiad, which Perry Miller first identified, was based on the mood of the fast.[15]

Love also indicated that a shift occurred in New England's declarations of special days of worship. Originally, the Puritans set aside "occasional days" as events dictated. But a regular pattern of annual spring fasts and autumn thanksgivings soon developed. Diaries indicate that Love's analysis is essentially correct, although irregularly and spontaneously proclaimed special days also continued throughout the century. Given that the Puritans rejected the annual ecclesiastical cycle of saints' and holy days in favor of a more "modern" and "industrious" weekly cycle, one may ask, Why did this regular pattern develop? It seems the Puritans retained, perhaps almost involuntarily, a sense of the annual cycle. The yearly rhythms of life were too deeply ingrained to shake off. Puritans objected to the Catholic calendar, with its roots in pagan agricultural rites, but their annual cycle of special days followed the same traditional seasonal pattern.[16]

Spring has commonly been viewed as the time of new life following the winter of death. . . . We will find that elements of this particular death-rebirth cycle persisted in Puritan devotion even as they rejected the springtime celebration of Easter. But spring is also the time of planting in the agricultural year. In biblical thought seedtime is a time of death. The seed, like the dead Christ and the dead saint, is buried in the ground. And death is the prerequisite of resurrection. "Except a corn of wheat fall into the ground and die, it abideth alone: but if it die, it bringeth forth much fruit" (John 12:24). Puritans, like Paul, insisted that the "old man" of sin must die before the "new man" may be born in Christ (Romans 6:6, Ephesians 4:22–24, Colossians 3:9–12). The old stock of Adam must be cut off and pre-pared before it can be grafted onto the new stock of Christ. New Englanders enacted these themes daily, weekly, and annually. They received special attention in the spring, when seeds were buried in the ground and whole days of humiliation and self-examination seemed natural. Experience reinforced biblical images: quite practically, spring was a time of death, not new life, in that it was a time of hunger as the winter larder was depleted. Although they would never have acknowledged the relationship, the New Englanders' pattern of fasting corresponded with the Catholic observance of Lent. The gradual regularizing of the calendar in New England is a good example of Puritan re-ritualization.[17]

New England most often proclaimed thanksgiving days in the autumn, in association with the harvest. The mythic "First Thanksgiving" at Plymouth was actually a week-long harvest festival, yet before many years had passed, a single day of worship was observed annually in November. John Hull noted in his diary that November 8, 1665 (an unexceptional year), was "kept as a day of solemn thanksgiving that the Lord was pleased to spare so much of the fruits of the earth; that we had not want, but were able to supply other countries; and likewise the continuance of our health and present peace." Ministers connected the autumn thanksgiving not with any ecclesiastical tradition but with the Old Testament Feast of Tabernacles, the final great festival of the Hebrew calendar, when grapes and olives, the fruit of the earth, were offered to God (Exodus 23:16). New Englanders also made use of other harvest references in the Bible. Jesus connected the harvest with conversion when He sent out the seventy as "laborers" and called God "the Lord of the harvest" (Luke 10:2). And the Old Testament prophets and Revelation associated the harvest with the eschaton: "Thrust in thy sickle, and reap; for the time is come for thee to reap; for the harvest of the earth is ripe ... and the earth was reaped" (Revelation 14:15–16). John Eliot used the theme in this manner in his celebrative tract *New Englands First Fruits* (1643). Although on public days of thanksgiving New Englanders expressed joy for divine favors recently granted—thus giving the occasions concrete historical referents—their joy looked forward to God's Kingdom in the same way the Sabbath did. New Englanders thought of themselves as firstfruits and as recipients of the firstfruits of the Holy Spirit, as converted saints and citizens of the Kingdom. As Paul had written, "Ourselves also, which have the firstfruits of the Spirit, even we ourselves groan within ourselves, waiting for the adoption, to wit, the redemption of our body" (Romans 8:23).[18]

The annual appointment of a day of fasting and humiliation in the spring, the time when seeds were buried and larders were empty, and of a day of thanksgiving in the autumn, when the harvest was gathered in, demonstrates the Puritans' re-ritualizing activity. They persisted within the traditional cycle of the agricultural and religious calendar even as they abandoned the saints' and holy days of the Old World. They reconstructed the annual cycle through the use of biblical imagery and Old Testament cultus.

Our understanding of the ways New Englanders worshiped must take in the full scope of their activities: the regularity of the Sabbath as each week the cycle of the salvation drama was re-presented and reexperienced; the supplementary instruction and worship of the weekday lecture; the seasonally regular days of fasting and thanksgiving; and the occasional days of worship designated in connection with special events. Implicit in all these instances was the psychological and spiritual cycle of death and resurrection, or new birth—as in the humiliation and contrition of the soul in preparation for salvation and the soul's implantation into Christ. If the soul truly humbled itself in preparation for the Sabbath or in the fast, occasion for thanksgiving would surely follow in course.

The Holy Ordinances

Two extant contemporary sources illuminate for us exactly what happened in the meetinghouse during worship. One of these was written by the vehement anti-Puritan Anglican Thomas Lechford; the other is from the pen of the arch-Puritan John Cotton. Both men published their descriptions in London in the early 1640s with the intention of influencing official and popular opinion in their respective directions. Lechford's *Plain Dealing, or, News from New England* (1641) is a dispassionate, fair, and highly critical account of the civil and ecclesiastical practices of a society from which he was an outcast. Cotton's *The True Constitution of a Particular Visible Church* (1642) and *The Way of the Churches of Christ in New England* (1645) were paeans of the New England way. The two men agreed remarkably—almost exactly—on the framework of public worship. As outlined by Cotton and Lechford and corroborated by entries in clerical diaries, the order of worship was as follows for both morning and afternoon Sabbath services:

Opening prayer
Scripture reading
Exposition of Scripture
Psalm singing
Sermon
Prayer
Psalm singing
Sacraments, Lord's Supper ideally monthly or
bimonthly in the morning,
Baptism in the afternoon
Collection for needy saints, occasionally, in the afternoon
Admission of new members, occasionally, in the afternoon
Blessing

This general outline describes the activities at public days of fasting and thanksgiving and lecture days as well. Each element of the service was considered an ordinance, a public means of grace, a religious act through which God might work in the worshiper's heart.[19]

Public Prayer

After the people had gathered in the meetinghouse, "men with their heads uncovered the women covered," the pastor opened worship with prayer, which lasted "about a quarter of an houre." This opening prayer was generally based on themes from 1 Timothy 2:1: "prayers and intercessions and thanksgivings for our selves and for all men, not in any prescribed forme of prayer, or studied Liturgie," but freely and extemporaneously. Other prayers during the service were equally spontaneous, though with varying focuses. Before the sermon the preacher prayed briefly for inspiration and power from the Holy Spirit for himself and for the congregation to listen for God's Word. The major prayer of both morning and afternoon services usually came after the sermon, although in some churches it came before. Ministers held it to be almost as important as the sermon itself. Peter Thacher in his diary typically linked the two ordinances as the crux of his work for the Sabbath: "The Lord did much to in large my heart both in prayer and preaching, and draw it forth to himself," and "God did graciously warme my heart in praying and preaching."[20]

The major prayer was also about equal to the sermon in length. Thacher wrote on one occasion that he "stood about three hours in prayer and preaching." On another: "God was pleased graciously to assist mee much beyond my Expectation. Blessed be his holy name for it. I was near an hour and halfe in my first prayer and my heart much drawne out in it and an hour in the sermon." Jasper Danckaerts likewise attested to the length of the prayers. "We went to church, but there was only one minister in the pulpit, who made a prayer an hour long, and preached the same length of time, when some verses were sung. We expected something particular in the afternoon, but there was nothing more than usual." On a fast day he even reported that "a minister made a prayer in the pulpit, of full two hours in length." In the afternoon "three or four hours were consumed with nothing except prayers, three ministers relieving each other alternately." The norm on a common Sabbath seems to have been a major prayer of sixty to ninety minutes, with the sermon about the same.[21]

John Cotton implied that the custom for public prayer may not have been always to bow, though for prayers of confession this penitential posture was assumed. Arguing against the use of a prayer book, he said, "nor will it stand with the holy gesture of Prayer, which is to lift up our eyes to Heaven, to cast downe our eyes upon a Booke." Cotton cited two instances where Jesus "lifted up his eyes" when He prayed. In any case, kneeling in public worship was generally proscribed as papist invention (even though it was recommended for private prayer).[22]

Prayer in New England's public worship was "free" or "conceived" because in the Puritan perception Scripture offered no grounds for "a stinted Liturgie ... by vertue of any Divine precept." Rather, "the primitive patterns of all the Churches of God in their best times" was spontaneous prayer conceived and spoken extemporaneously. Indeed, since the saints had experienced grace and had received the Holy Spirit, why did they need set prayers? God imparted "a spirit of prayer," and of all people ministers, as exemplars of sainthood, must be able to pray freely. In the primitive Church, Thomas Shepard wrote, "they prayed without a Promptour, because from the heart. . . . Their persecutions and dayes of afflictions preserved them from formalitie in prayer, and taught them how to finde their hearts and knees, and tongues, to poure out their soules to God, while under the Altar they were pouring out their blood." Could New Englanders in their pilgrimage through the wilderness do otherwise? Besides, prayer must be responsive to the congregation's immediate situation. Ministers prayed for the conversion of people present, for the spiritual condition of the town and the political situation of the commonwealth, and for the welfare of other spiritual armies on other fronts of the Reformation.[23]

Styles of public prayer varied because they were conceived in the heart of the minister. Thomas Hooker was reputedly more succinct and, as the prayer reached its climax, more emotional than most ministers. As Cotton Mather remarked, "He affected Strength, rather than Length; and though he had not so much variety in Publick Praying, as in his Publick Preaching, yet he alwayes had a seasonable Respect unto Present Conditions. And it was Observed, that his Prayer was usually like Jacobs Ladder, wherein the nearer he came to an End, the nearer he drew towards Heaven; and he grew into such Rapturous Pleadings with God, and Praysings of God, as made some to say, That Like the Master of the Feast, he Reserved the best Wine until the Last." Mather pointed to John Norton as one whose style of relevant and well-organized public prayer younger ministers emulated. Ministers who followed his example prayed "with more Pertinent, more Affecting, more Expanded Enlargements, than any Form could Afford unto them." Mather went on to comment on the state of public prayer at the end of the century. "New England can show, even Young Ministers, who never did in all Things Repeat One Prayer twice over, in that part of their Ministry wherein we are First of All, to make Supplications, Prayers, Intercessions, and Thanksgivings; and yet sometimes, for much more than an Hour together, they pour out their Soules unto the Almighty God in such Fervent, Copious, and yet Proper Manner, that their most Critical Auditors, can complain of Nothing Disagreeable, but profess themselves extreamly Edifyed."[24]

Despite the individuality and the extemporaneity of ministers' prayers, none was entirely unique or distinct in language from those that had gone before. The clergy worked with a common biblical vocabulary and adhered to a formal pattern that followed the stages of the order of redemption. Remnants of public prayers are, of course, exceedingly rare because prayers were delivered orally, without notes. In a few cases, however, ministers copied down what they could remember of their prayers after the service. From these notations we can discover something of the content and form of the prayers. The best examples are portions of particularly efficacious eucharistic prayers by Increase Mather, recorded in his diary and transcribed in his autobiography. Mather's rhetorical style emerges when the prayers are transposed into poetic form. On March 30, 1673, Mather was "much affected in administring the Lords supper, especially in the last prayer."

> Now dearest Lord,
>> If ever there were poor creatures in this world,
>> that had cause to love and bless the Lord,
>> we are they.
>
> Wee have done thee Infinite wrong,
>> but you hast forgiven us all those wrongs,
>> and dealest with us as with thi friends this day.

How can wee but mourn for the wrong wee have done thee?

If wee had wronged though an enemy,
   and that in a small matter,
   wee should grieve for it.

But wee have wronged the son of God our Saviour;
   yea wee have killed him.

Hee had never come to the cross,
   had it not bin for our sins
   as wee are the elect of God.

But this blood which wee have shed has procured our pardon,
   as it did for the Jewes that killed him,
   so many of them as belonged to election.

Also Christ prayed for them, saying,
   Father forgive them,
   And so you knowest hee has done for us.

Christ has sayd before thee concerning us,
   Father, forgive them.

If children offend their Father much,
   yet if any of them come and say,
   I am sory for what I have done,
   I'll do so no more,
   Father be reconciled to me,
   will not a Father then forgive them?

O! our Father, wee have sinned against thee,
   but wee are sory for it,
   and would do iniquity no more;
   Father forgive us.

You knowest our Hearts,
   you knowest that wee could be glad
   if wee might never have so much as one sinfull thought in our hearts,
   nor speake so much as one unprofitable word more whilest wee live.

And there is another thing which wee would beg of thee,
   if ever you wilt hear the cries of poor creatures,
   deny us not that request,
   It is O Lord, that you wouldst sanctify us by thy spirit.

Another prayer during which Mather was "much affected" soared by means of the eschatological imagery of the Sacrament:

Lord, wee shall never perish.

They that beleeve on Christ shall never perish;
    And you knowest that we beleeve on him.

You hast brought us to the blood of sprinkling,
    and therefore you wilt bring us to Jesus
    the Mediator of the new Covenant,
    and wee shall behold his glory.

Wee shall see our Joseph,
    our Jesus in all his glory.

Wee shall behold King Solomon in all his glory.

Yea, Solomon in all his glory
    was not arayed as Christ is;
    wee shall see that glory,
    and shall sit with him on thrones of glory.

A third focused on the hope of those in the Covenant:

O Heavenly Father and our God in Jesus Christ,
    wee have avouched thee to be our God,
    and now wee know that you hast avouched us to be thi people,
    because you hast given us thi son,
    and you wilt with him give us all things.

Father, wee humbly expect from thee,
    that according to thi Covenant, even the new Covenant,
    you wilt forgive us our iniquities.

Such is the grace of thi Covenant
    as that you wilt not impute our infirmities to us,
    if they be our burden,
    and you knowest that they are so.

Wee put the Answer of our prayers upon that,
    and are willing to be denyed if it be not so.

But you that searchest hearts,
    knowest that you hast created such a spirit within us.

Wee are willing to be delivered from all sin,
    and wee are willing to yeild Holy perfect obedience to all thi
        commands,
    tho' how to perform wee find not.

Father Father, deal with us as with thi children![25]

Mather's preeminently biblical phrases tumble over one another in an orderly fashion, according to syllogistic logic, through the stages of the salvific cycle. The first prayer begins in humiliation and confession of sin, moves to forgiveness of sin, and concludes with a prayer for sanctification. The second portion demonstrates how closely bound ministers were to a biblical language. Mather used three passages of Scripture as stepping-stones: John 3:16 ("whosoever believeth in him should not perish"), Hebrews 12:22 and 24 ("ye are come unto mount Sion. . . . And to Jesus the mediator of the new covenant, and to the blood of sprinkling"), and Luke 12:27 ("Consider the lilies. . . . Solomon in all his glory was not arrayed like one of these").

When New Englanders went to prayer, without notes or books, their heads were stocked with a whole Bible full of devotional resources. Puritans relinquished the set phrases of the Book of Common Prayer, as Robert Paul has noted, in exchange for language flowing straight from Scripture, language "now made personal and immediate through the experience and eloquence of the individual pastor." The language of public prayer was formulary even while Puritans rejected printed forms.[26]

The Reading of Scripture

After the opening prayer, the pastor read a biblical passage that established the theme of the entire service. The reading was generally of a chapter chosen by the preacher and containing the text that served as the basis of his sermon. In the case of a sermon series, the same chapter was used for morning and afternoon services, and even for several weeks running. It does not appear that both Old and New Testaments were necessarily included in a given service, as they were in Church of England worship. One reason may have been the Puritan typological reading of Scripture, in which they followed St. Augustine: "What else is the Old Testament but the New foreshadowed? And what other the New than the Old revealed?" The Christian revelation, specifically the work of Christ in redemption, was the prism through which Puritans received the Old Testament. Indeed, both testaments shone through the prism of Christ onto the lives of New Englanders. A second reason for the adequacy of a single reading was that sermons were studded with dozens of direct references to both testaments. Cotton Mather wrote of Samuel Danforth, for example, "The sermons with which he fed his flock were elaborate and substantial; he was a notable text-man, and one who had more than forty or fifty scriptures distinctly quoted in one discourse." And hundreds of indirect references formed the vocabulary of every sermon and prayer. Old Testament types and New Testament antitypes played off one another, and ministers pressed every possible parallel, supporting, and proof text into service. By the end of the day the congregation had heard the equivalent of the "twelve or thirteen chapters and psalms" that Lechford said typified Church of England worship.[27]

The Bible was the Word of God, a means of grace in itself. The Holy Spirit could affect the heart simply through the impact of the words. But simple reading, or "dumb reading," was deemed inadequate for a service of worship. The congregation must be well prepared and listen actively, and the pastor must give a thorough explication after the reading. William Perkins advised, "To the profitable hearing of Gods Word three things are required: Preparation before we heare, a right Disposition in hearing, and Duties to be practised afterward." In preparation individuals must first "disburden" themselves of all "impediments which may hinder the effectuall hearing of the Word" (typically "presumption," arrogance, "troubled affections" such as anger, and "superflu-ity of maliciousnesse, that is, the abundance of evill corruptions and sinnes"). They must "lift up" their hearts "in prayer to God." A "hearing eare" did not come naturally but was "a gift of God, enabling the heart" to understand and submit. And as the worshipers were thus enabled they must "labour to be affected with the Word," so it might "dwell plenteously" in them. Finally, the Spirit continued working through the "opening" of the passage by a skilled exegete. After the minister read the chapter, Cotton wrote, he "expoundeth it, giving the sense, to cause the people to understand the reading." Phrases from the chapter then resounded for more than two hours in the prayer and sermon and carried through the week in the private devotions of the congregation.[28]

The Singing of Psalms

"As wee are to make melody in our hearts, so with our voyces also," wrote John Cotton in his important work *Singing of Psalmes a Gospel-Ordinance.* The congregation sang psalms and sometimes other "spiritual Songs recorded in Scripture" in services both "before [the] Sermon and many times after" as well. A psalm was sung in conjunction with the administration of the Lord's Supper and with other occasional ordinances. The early versions used in New England were those by Sternhold and Hopkins (1562) and Henry Ainsworth (1612). Plymouth continued to use the Ainsworth psalter through most of the century, as did Salem until about 1667. After its publication in 1640 the translation, or more properly the versification, used most commonly, however, was the product of the Massachusetts Bay clergy, *The Whole Booke of Psalmes,* popularly called the *Bay Psalm Book.*[29]

Why should the clergy have toiled to produce a new psalter, the first book to issue from the Cambridge press? At one level, Zoltán Haraszti has suggested, the Ainsworth version was unacceptable because of its association with sepa-ratism. But the primary reason was that New England ministers deemed earlier versions linguistically inadequate. "The former translation of the Psalmes,"

Cotton observed, "doth in many things vary from the originall, and many times paraphraseth rather than translateth." Haraszti has demonstrated that in addition to Sternhold-Hopkins, Ainsworth, and the Geneva Bible, the 1611 version of the Bible exerted considerable influence on the New England translators. The clergy, all of whom read Hebrew, could choose what they considered the best translation of each word and line for English metric verse. The *Bay Psalm Book* was the result of accomplished biblical scholarship. Cotton explained, "Wee have endeavoured a new translation of the Psalmes into English meetre, as neere the originall as wee could expresse it in our English tongue, so farre as for the present the Lord hath been pleased to helpe us, and those Psalmes wee sing, both in our publike Churches, and in private." New England clerical leaders produced a new translation because the advances in Hebrew scholarship evident in the 1611 version of the Bible had left all previous psalters behind. New Englanders wanted the praises they sang to their Lord to be accurate and understandable renderings of Scripture.[30]

The massive undertaking of completing the *Bay Psalm Book* within the first ten years of settlement makes sense only if we recognize Puritanism as a popular devotional movement. Singing was a means of grace, a well-established way that one might communicate with God. As with all means of grace, singing was a natural phenomenon, a human activity through which God chooses to work. Cotton wrote that whereas "singing with Instruments was typicall, and so ceremoniall worship, and therefore ceased . . ., singing with heart and voyce is morall worship, such as is written in the hearts of all men by nature." That is, all persons have within them the duty and the means to sing praises. The act of singing, then, could bring a soul into harmony with God. "The end of singing is not onely to instruct, admonish, and comfort the Church" but also to help those who "are godly, though out of the Church. . . . Nay further, the end of singing is . . . to instruct, and convince, and reprove [the] wicked, as hath been shewed, Deut. 31.19." Singing was what Puritans called a converting ordinance.[31]

Devotional singing, like other means of grace, had to be biblically grounded. Puritans were more cautious about public worship than with private devotion in this regard. "Any private Christian, who hath a gift to frame a spirituall song, may both frame it, and sing it privately, for his own private comfort, and remembrance of some speciall benefit, or deliverance." Saints could even use "an Instrument of Musick therewithall," so long as they did not thereby subordinate the devotional intent to the art of music. But in public worship songs had to be from the Bible and unaccompanied.[32]

Congregational singing was popular singing. Horton Davies has identified the great Puritan contributions to English worship as "firstly, the restoration of the people's rights to sing the Davidic Psalms in the vernacular; secondly, the versification of the psalms, that they might the easier be memorized by congregations and set to repetitive melodies." Everyone was familiar with the ballad cadences of the *Bay Psalm Book*. Everyone sang from it. Women were exempted from the rule of silence, since several scriptural precedents (for example, Miriam in Exodus 15:20–21) sufficiently justified "the lawfull practise of women in singing together with men the Praises of the Lord." The size of the printings of the *Bay Psalm Book* indicates that a large percentage of families owned a copy, but even men and women who could not read were exposed to it weekly. The self-understanding and spiritual lives of few New Englanders would have remained unaffected by the constant use of this worship book.[33]

The poetic style and method of singing furthered the likelihood of memorization. The singsong quality of the *Bay Psalm Book* is as notorious as are some of its grammatical infelicities. But whatever the aesthetic appeal of a given passage, it is evident that this type of versification made memorization easy and even unavoidable.

> The Lord to mee a shepherd is,
> want therefore shall not I,
> Hee in the fold of tender-grasse
> doth cause mee downe to lie . . .

The method of singing also drove the lines home. Since not all churchgoers had books or could read, "one of the ruling Elders" dictated the words "before hand, line after line, or two lines together."[34]

John Cotton defended the regular meter of the version both in his preface to the *Bay Psalm Book* and in his larger work on spiritual singing. He argued that "as all Verses in all Poems doe consist of a certaine number, and measure of Syllables; so doe our English Verses . . . which make the Verses more easie for memory, and fit for melody." The poetic form of the original Hebrew warranted that psalms be translated into English poetry "soe wee may sing Lords songs." The ministers followed popular taste: "In our english tongue . . . such verses as are familiar to an english eare . . . are commonly metricall." Further, since the "the Tunes of the Temple are lost and hidden from us, . . . therefore we must sing such other Tunes, as are suitable to the matter, though invented by men."[35]

All Puritan devotion was ultimately preparation for glory, and this may be said of the public singing of psalms. In the conclusion to his preface Cotton put forth the reason for the new translation. Acts of worship in the "Sion" of New England were not an end in themselves. New England was a resting place on the pilgrim way to the perfect Zion. And Zion, as envisioned by the author of Revelation and almost as clearly by New England Puritans, would be a place of singing.

> And I looked, and, lo, a Lamb stood on the mount Sion, and with him an
> hundred forty and four thousand, having his Father's name written in their fore-
> heads. And I heard a voice from heaven, as the voice of many waters, and as the
> voice of a great thunder: and I heard the voice of harpers harping with their
> harps: And they sung as it were a new song before the throne, and before the
> four beasts, and the elders: and no man could learn that song but the hundred
> and forty and four thousand, which were redeemed from the earth (Revelation
> 14:1–3).

By singing in their churches now (together with the unredeemed, for the final
separation of wheat from tares would not come until Judgment Day), saints
hoped to glimpse that coming glory. In the meanwhile, the Church was called
to be God's Kingdom on earth. It embodied in germ form the Kingdom's glory.
And when the Kingdom comes, as Isaiah had seen, "the redeemed of the Lord
shall return, and come with singing into Zion; and everlasting joy shall be
upon their head . . . and sorrow and mourning shall flee away" (51:11). John
Cotton wrote that the *Bay Psalm Book* was composed

> that soe wee may sing in Sion the Lords
> songs of prayse according to his owne
> will; untill he take us from hence,
> and wipe away all our teares, &
> bid us enter into our masters
> joye to sing eternall
> Halleluiahs.[36]

The Sermon

The preaching and hearing of the sermon were the central acts in the New
England worship service. The minister had spent several days in its preparation, and the congregation, in return, was composed of generally active listeners. In the early years people were so hungry for preaching that they flocked
to every possible service. The midweek lectures were added to accommodate
popular demand. Newcomers such as young John Brock wrote excitedly in
their diaries, "We came all safe to Land, and our first Sermon was by Mr.
Shepard," as though that were the reason for their voyage. Roger Clap and
others were swept into the enthusiasm of faith as "the Lord Jesus Christ was
so plainly held out in the Preaching of the Gospel unto poor lost Sinners." As
the years progressed and zeal waned, people often seemed to become "quite
sermon-proof," but the sermon retained its central place in worship and in
the culture. Ministers found themselves preaching to "larger, less enthusiastic"
congregations from the 1640s on, which suggests that the sermon had become
an established element in the everyday life of the populace. Preachers contin-

ued to place confidence in the sermon. The development of increasingly "jeremiad" characteristics demonstrates not the decline but the vitality of the genre. As the civil law in Connecticut stated, "The preaching of the word by those whom God doth send, is the chiefe ordinary means ordained by God, for the converting, edifying, and saving of the soules of the elect."[37]

The gathering wave of printed sermons from the Cambridge and then Boston presses attests to the popularity of preaching. That many of these sermons were edited for publication from listeners' notes indicates an active auditory. It was not uncommon for New Englanders to keep a personal book of sermon notes. Samuel Sewall used such a notebook in his secret devotions. In clerical diaries and in public relations of faith we see instances of the conversion process being set in motion by sermons. Evangelism fell behind the growth rate of the population but did not cease. As Perry Miller wrote, "Puritan life, in the New England theory, was centered upon a corporate and communal ceremony, upon the oral delivery of a lecture." Miller misunderstood the private devotion that complemented the public gathering, and he underestimated the emotional quality of the sermons, but he was right in placing the sermon at the center of it all.[38]

Recent scholarship employs the idea of "myth," the "cosmic redemptive drama" undergirding New England society, to understand the place of the sermon. Sermons on the stages of conversion linked preaching with New England's salvation history and finally with "God's great plot for humanity's redemption." The preachers, as the culture's spokesmen, "collectively shaped a narrative" that interpreted and defined the culture. A literary approach to the sermons has recently found even "the form of the doctrinal matter to be a narrative, mythic in its repetition and heroics." For modern readers to appreciate "the full impact of the sermons" they must "sound the phrases in the imagination and use the punctuation not so much for semantic clues as for rhythmic markers." Each sermon built from a doctrinal and rational beginning and progressed, in the uses or application, to rhetoric aimed at the affections and will. Typically a crescendo came at the sermon's conclusion, with the most emotionally compelling exhortations.[39]

The key to the power of the preached word in Puritan New England is that the culture, although highly literate by European standards and even bookish in its use of devotional manuals and its attachment to such works as John Foxe's *Acts and Monuments* (first published in London, 1563) was still very much oriented toward oral performance and oral communication. Information was available in print (in almanacs and broadsides), but most ideas and information were transmitted verbally. The society defined itself first of all through spoken means. The *Bay Psalm Book* comes to us as a great translating and publishing achievement, but it was published only so people could sing its verses. Sermons were printed, but none were published that had not first been preached, and a Puritan sermon was normally preached even before it was written down. Usually the sermons that had the greatest impact when preached were selected for publication. At that point, for the first time, a full text would be prepared from notes and memory. The printed sermon must become a means of recovering at least something of the originally preached sermon, opening for us the realm of religious experience.

Puritan rhetoric, known as the "plain style," was intended to produce powerful biblical preaching. Sermons were plain in the sense of being explicit, plain so the "simplest hearer" could follow. As John Cotton taught in his well-known catechism, "Milk for Babes," preaching drew the soul "towards Christ" by "bringing me to know my sin and the wrath of God against me for it," and then "by humbling me yet more and then raising me up out of this estate" by the application of personal redemption in Christ's death and resurrection. Even for children, preaching must be "plain and powerful" in its exposure of sin. "When sin and sinners are set out in their native and natural colours and carry their proper names," when "a Spade is a Spade, and a Drunkard is a Drunkard," when preachers "make sin appear truly odious, and fearful to the open view of all," God may be expected to work on the heart.[40]

The sermon was also "plain" in its strict adherence to accepted homiletical order. Every sermon began with a reading of the text, followed by the opening, or exegesis, of the text, the extraction from the text of the doctrine to be propounded, the discussion of reasons for and refutation of objections against the doctrine, and finally the application of the doctrine to the lives of the listeners. No New England sermon failed to follow this order.

For Thomas Hooker and the other ministers, "plain and powerful preaching" depended first on "soundness of argument," but sermons were not entirely rational expositions of doctrine. It was said of Samuel Danforth, for example, that "though he were a very judicious preacher, yet he was therewithal so affectionate, 'that he rarely, ef ever, ended a sermon without weeping.'" Great passages of emotional exhortation have survived transition to print, most exciting in the work of Hooker and Shepard but evident in others as well. A "spiritual heat in the heart" of the preachers bespoke a personal quality in the exhortations. "When the heart of a Minister goeth home with the words," Hooker said, "then he delivers the word powerfully and profitably to the hearers." The minister must preach "as if he were in the bosome of a man." Affective preaching "shoot[s] home into the hearts and consciences of men like an arrow" and "doth discover the very secrets of a mans soule; together with the vileness and wickedness that is in a mans heart." After the penitent had allowed the preacher to "hew . . . and hack . . . frame and fashion" the heart in preparation, he gently lifted the soul into union with Christ. The immediacy of the sermons was rooted in the doctrine of the means of grace. Now was the time for repentance; now was the season of faith. The Holy Spirit was present in the congregation in the words of the preacher. "Me thinkes your hearts begin to stirre," Hooker preached, "and say, hath the Lord engaged himself to this? *Oh then (Lord) make me humble.*" Again, "If there be a soule here present that it hath pleased God thus to move, oh know and consider that this is thy particular time." And, "God stands this day and knocks. . . . The Lord knocks this day."[41]

The conclusion to many sermons was framed in the quasi-poetic style of the chanted sermon, characterized by repetition, rhyme, alliteration, and rhythmic cadence. Peter Burke has said that the chanted sermon was "exceptional in early modern Europe, although it could be found in Britain" among radical lay preachers on the enthusiastic fringe of Puritanism. He cites late seventeenth-century Dissenters who "were said to 'think they hear a very powerful preacher, if his voice be sharp and quavering, and near to singing; if he draws out some words with a mournful accent.'" New England orthodoxy has never been suspected of such preaching, but one instance at the end of a sermon by Thomas Shepard has already been partially quoted. Shepard repeated similar sounds both at the end of successive lines:

> . . . the time is not long,
> but that we shall feel what now we doe but heare of,
> and see but a little of,
> as we use to doe of things afar off

and within lines:

> let us be scourged, and disgraced,
>   stoned, sawn asunder, and burned;
> let us live in sheep-skins, and goat-skins,
>   destitute, afflicted, tormented.

Here repetition of the "s" sound gradually gives way to hard "t" sounds. Meanwhile, the sequence of seven exhortations in the identical pattern—"let . . . and"—builds to a tension-filled climax broken finally by the ejaculation "Oh glory, glory, / oh welcome glory."[42]

Transposition from printed prose form into verse recaptures something of the original oral qualities of the Puritan sermon. It is possible to imagine the voice of John Cotton at the conclusion of a discourse on "prayer in the Spirit."

> Goe home therefore, and call to remembrance what you have
>   heard,

let it be your care to observe
and lay up daily some fit matters for your prayers,
and lay up the chiefest of these against the times
    of your greatest mournings, and thanksgivings;
Lay them not up for a day or two before,
    but from day to day;
Lay up bulkie passages of Gods waies, and your owne,
    that you may have them in readinesse against speciall occasions,
and then keep your heart in a praying frame
    pure from wronging God or your brethren or neighbours,
and be sensible of what you come before God for,
and keep your hearts in a very reverent and holy awe of God,
and pray for what is according to Gods will for matter,
and according to the Spirit for manner,
and stand upon your watch-Tower, to see what God will answer,
and use the meanes to obtaine your desires,
and come with confidence that your persons and prayers are
    accepted,
and when you are in the lowest case, and make the poorest shifts,
then looke up to God, in the name of Christ,
and then shall you finde your prayers not drosie and dull
but such life in them, as will put a life in your callings,
and in all the duties that ever you perform,
and it will be a matter of much comfort and refreshment to you.

Cotton created the power of the passage by vigorously piling phrase upon phrase, connecting them first by "lay" and then by the conjunction "and." Alliteration and near-rhyme carry the listener along. Cotton followed "heard" with "observe" and "prayers"; and "matter" with "manner," "watch-Tower," and "answer." He combined "mournings" with "thanksgivings"; "persons" with "prayers" and "accepted"; and "drosie" with "dull" and "duties." The most rhetorically effective couplet is composed, save one word, of monosyllables: "Lay them not up for a day or two before, / but from day to day." The last two words even heighten the sense of immediacy with their homonym, "today." Whole phrases repeat for cumulative effect: ". . . according to Gods will for matter / and according to the Spirit for manner." And, perhaps most compelling: "and when you are in the lowest case, and make the poorest shifts, / then looke up to God in the name of Christ." Here Cotton linked two lines with the rhyme of "when" and "then," and the mirroring of the phrases "the lowest case" and "the poorest shifts" with "the name of Christ." The phrase "then looke up to God" breaks the tension, and the final lines form the denouement, a safe and gentle landing at the end of an exciting rhetorical flight.[43]

The most dramatic exhortation to union with Christ that survives in the sermon literature comes at the conclusion of a sermon, "The Soul's Invitation unto Jesus Christ," preached by Thomas Shepard on a text from the Song of Songs. After developing the doctrine that Christ desires to be "an earnest Suitor and a real Speeder, between every poor Soul and himself," Shepard *performed a wedding* and then sternly warned those who had refused to enter the bond. Shepard joined the emotion implicit in the doctrine of mystical marriage with the affective rhetoric of the preached sermon:

> If thou consenteth to match with Christ, he doth so with thee,
> and so I pronounce Christ and you married;
> as he was an earnest suitor, now he is become a real speeder,
> and you are made for ever happy,
> happy that ever you were born,
> happy that ever you saw him in the Ordinances,
> and that ever he came to thee in the way of love,
> that your time was a time of love,
> happy that ever he took delight in thee,
> and that your heart is come unto him
> to close with him,
> and to be his for ever blessed:
> Man or Woman, thou art in a Heavenly condition already,
> and shall enjoy him for ever,
> I say, you are happy if you have him,
> but miserable, and wretched for ever if you want him.
> Poor wretch your condition is lamentable,
> who ever thou art that hast not Christ,
> thou art in an undone condition, who can express it;
> who can make thee understand it, altho' we should declare it
>   unto thee?
> The Lord pity thee, and bow thy heart, and ear
> to attend unto the things that belong
> to thy everlasting peace, *Amen.*

Shepard's techniques in this remarkable passage were again repetition, alliteration, and rhyme. He coupled "thee" with "married," "suitor" with "speeder," "born" with "Ordinances," and "the way of love" with "the time of love." The same short words play off one another in different combinations:

> and you are made for ever happy,
> happy that ever you were born,
> happy that ever you saw him . . .
>
> and that your heart is come unto him
> to close with him,
> and to be his . . .

The crucial moment comes after Shepard has escorted the soul into Christ's bedchamber. One can imagine him lingering over the words, "I say, you are happy if you have him," then suddenly raising his voice: "but miserable, and wretched for ever if you want him!" By the sudden use of terror he caught up those who failed to follow. It was not too late, however, and Shepard ends with yet another gentle plea in the form of a prayer:

> The Lord pity thee, and bow thy heart, and ear
> to attend unto the things that belong
> to thy everlasting peace, *Amen*.[44]

Thomas Shepard's startling line "I pronounce Christ and you married" is unique in New England sermon literature. But the intention of his exhortation, with its strongly liturgical overtones, was identical with that of every sermon: to lead the person through the redemptive drama to the point where the heart and will say "yes" to union with Christ. It was especially in passages such as these that the Spirit was felt to work through the preacher's words. God Himself was present in the meetinghouse as the minister opened his mouth. Then, as Hooker put it, "there is the Concurrence of all Causes putting forth themselves for the work of Conversion."[45]

The Sacraments

The "seals of the Covenant" were administered after the sermon and prayer, the Lord's Supper in the morning (ideally once a month but actually anywhere from six to twelve times annually) and Baptism in the afternoon as occasion required. A subtle but important distinction was made between the sacraments and other ordinances. Like all ordinances, sacraments were outward means through which God worked. But other ordinances were "ordinary" means of grace while the sacraments were "special." Ordinances were ordinary in that they were employed daily or weekly; they were the stuff of regular worship and devotion. They were also ordinary in that they were practiced by every member of the social covenant—all inhabitants of New England without regard to church membership. The sacraments were special because they were administered only on specially designated Sabbaths and were restricted to members of the church covenant.[46]

The sacraments were another sign that the life of faith was an ongoing pilgrimage. The redemptive cycle that pervaded Puritan spirituality was seen at work in the sacraments. Baptism was the sacrament of preparation and implantation, and the Lord's Supper was one means whereby the saint continued to grow in grace after implantation. John Cotton's catechism, "Milk for Babes," asked, "What is done for you in baptism?" The answer that came back was,

"The pardon and cleansing of my sins," since I am washed not only with water but "with the blood and Spirit of Christ." Baptism led to "my ingrafting into Christ" and "my rising out of affliction, and also . . . my resurrection from the dead at the last day." Ministers advised parents to teach children that "a solemn Covenant . . . between the God of heaven and them" is sealed in Baptism. This preparatory sacrament sustained a person through childhood and acted as part of the preparatory stage of conversion. The typological interpretation of the rite of circumcision as the Old Testament precursor of Baptism further strengthened its connection with the preparatory stage: "Hence you may see what circumcision once did, and baptism now seals unto . . . that hereupon [God] will prune, and cut, and dress, and water them." The acts associated with circumcision were precisely God's actions in cutting the soul off from sin and pre-paring it for the graft onto the stock of Christ.[47]

Cotton's reply to the same question concerning the Lord's Supper was that the broken bread and poured wine were "a sign and seal of my receiving the communion of the body of Christ broken for me, and of His blood shed for me, and thereby of my growth in Christ, of the pardon and healing of my sins, of the fellowship of His Spirit, of my strengthening and quickening in grace, and of my sitting together with Christ on His throne of glory at the Last Judgment." Thomas Shepard's adult catechism concurred: Baptism was the sacrament of "our new birth, and ingrafting into Christ," and the Lord's Supper, "given to nourish and strengthen beleevers, renewing their faith unto eternall life," was the sacrament of "our growth in Christ." The rituals of Baptism and Communion as they were performed in New England churches reminded participants and witnesses of the redemptive drama that framed their spiritual existence.[48]

The pastor or teacher performed Baptism "in the Deacons seate, the most eminent place in the Church, next under the Elders seate." In infant baptism (and most, though not all, cases were) the parents presented the child "to the Lord, and his Church." The minister, acting "in Gods roome[,] calleth upon the parent to renew his Covenant with God for himselfe and his seed and calleth upon God as the nature of the Ordinance requireth for the pardon of originall sinne, and for the sin of the parents and for a blessing upon the Sacrament and Infant." The minister "most commonly makes a speech or exhortation to the Church, and parents concerning Baptisme, and then prayeth before and after." After the prayer, "calling the childe by the name which the Parent hath given it, for his owne edification, and the Childes he baptizeth it either by dipping or sprinkling in the name of the Father, the Son, and the Holy Ghost." Sprinkling probably predominated among New England churches.[49]

The Lord's Supper, as the recent work of E. Brooks Holifield and Edward Taylor scholars has shown, became the center of much devotional activity in New England. One thrust of Puritan piety led to sacramental iconoclasm; at the same time the orthodox displayed a burst of "fascination with eucharistic devotional material" and "sacramental piety." The private aspects of this devotion will be discussed. . . . In their public worship New Englanders maintained a doctrine of the real presence that differed little from Calvin. "By the symbols of bread and wine," Calvin had written, "Christ, his body and blood, are truly exhibited to us . . . that being made partakers of his substance, we might feel the result of this fact in the participation of all his blessings." Yet he also warned that "the presence of Christ in the Supper we must hold to be such as neither affixes him to the element of bread, nor encloses him in bread, nor circumscribes him in any way." Thomas Hooker and others wrote in the same vein, that the bread and wine "present Christ neerly and visibly to the soule. They shew Christ's merits and obedience, inflaming our hearts with love to him." And Hooker, like Calvin, warned that we must look "beyond our outward elements, and see the spirit of Christ."[50]

An entry from Samuel Sewall's diary demonstrates the extent to which at least some New Englanders believed in Christ's real presence. Young Sewall, on account of coming to the table without a lively faith, worried that "for the abuse of Christ I should be stricken dead; yet I had some earnest desires that Christ would, before the ordinance were done, though it were *when he was just going away,* give me some glimpse of himself; but I perceived none." Sewall consoled himself with his increased desire "for the next Sacrament day, that I might do better." His startling phrase suggests popular belief in the literal presence of Jesus Christ in the meetinghouse during the Sacrament.[51]

The minister would announce the scheduled celebration two weeks in advance, to remind members to prepare themselves for the Sacrament. Thus, whether or not all worshipers engaged in extensive private preparatory exercises, if administered monthly, the Sacrament was either mentioned or administered on three weeks out of four or five. On Sacrament day, after the sermon, prayer, and psalm, the non-members in the congregation were dismissed with a blessing, and the members remained in their pews. The ministers and "ruling Elders" took their places at the table, in conscious reenactment of Jesus' Last Supper. The words of institution, or solemnization, were the traditional ones from the gospels:

> The Minister taketh the bread and blesseth it, and breaketh it, and giveth it to the brethren with this commandement once for all, to take and eate it, as the body of Christ broken for them, and this doe in remembrance of him; in like manner also he taketh the cup, and having given thanks, he powreth it forth, and giveth it to them, with a commandement to them all, to take and drink it as the bloud of Christ shed for them, and this also to do in Remembrance of him.

The minister took the elements first, then gave them "to all that sit at Table with him, and from the Table is reached by the Deacons to the people sitting in the next seates about them, the Minister sitting in his place at the Table." Deacons distributed the bread in a charger and the wine in a single cup. The elements were blessed and distributed separately, first the bread, until all had eaten, and then the wine. The people received the elements sitting in their pews, not, as in Catholic and Anglican liturgy, kneeling at a rail before an altar. Lechford pointed out, perhaps with some justice, that since all members were seated, some could not see the consecration of the elements.[52]

Through the words of institution, the eucharistic prayer, and the symbolism of the bread and wine the people were led once again through the stages of the redemptive drama revealed in the work of Christ. The Lord's Supper was occasion for renewed repentance followed by the experience of union with Christ. In a visually and verbally explicit way it reminded believers of the order of redemption that sustained their lives. Christ Himself was present offering that salvation to them. After the Sacrament was completed the people sang a psalm of thanksgiving, based on the model in Matthew 26:30, and were dismissed with a blessing.[53]

Mutual Communion

Under the heading of the ordinance of mutual communion we may discuss several communal rituals that acted as public means of grace. These include the ceremony surrounding the gathering of a new church, especially the act of covenant making; the call and ordination of a pastor; covenant renewal; the ceremony admitting new members into the church; catechism of the young; the collection of contributions for needy saints; and the exercise of discipline, excommunication and absolution. All these were marked by the themes already established, so that the celebration of any one ordinance reinforced the whole sense of New England's part in God's plan of salvation. Worship in New England was a system of complementary parts geared to run together. When one element was in danger of malfunctioning, as was Baptism by the end of the 1660s, adjustments were made to preserve the ordinance and the integrity of the system. In the face of social change, covenant renewal, incipient from the beginning, emerged as a key ordinance in the last two decades of the century. Like the Halfway Covenant, the covenant-renewal ceremony was an adjustment, but not a failure, in the Puritan devotional system.

New Englanders were brought into the order of redemption by virtue of the covenant, and that covenant, with God and with one another, supported the ordinances of mutual communion. The making of the church covenant was the primary ordinance upon which the others were built. The gathering of a church was an act of public worship undertaken by a small number of charter members. Richard Mather noted that typically "about eight or nine" men acted as a church's founding members. At Dedham there were ten, "whome we had best hopes of for soundnes of grace and meete guifts for such a worke." These included the man who had been academically trained for the ministry, who had reached a tacit agreement with the other members concerning his pastorate. Even if the minister had been ordained in England, the church founders acted as if he were unordained or at least not fully ordained until they publicly chose and reordained him. In the second half of the century new towns were likely to be settled with fresh Harvard graduates. Managing the gathering of the church would be one of the graduate's first tasks.[54]

The charter members and the minister-to-be prepared for months by attending meetings "lovingly to discourse and consult together." They fasted and prayed among themselves, and each spent an entire day "to open every one his spirituall condicion to the rest, relating the manner of our conversion to god and the lords following proceedings in our soules with present apprehensions of gods love or want thereof." The men presented their spiritual qualifications to the town, then discussed further "the nature of the covenant" before setting a date for the ceremony.[55]

The church covenant was finally consummated on a day devoted to public professions of faith, many prayers and sermons, and the singing of psalms. Although it was a local affair, other churches were invited and gave their consent to the proceedings. The charter members signed, read, and officially "owned" the covenant document that was the product of their labors. Each step was carefully taken, since New Englanders believed that the hope of future purity rested on this "foundation work."[56]

The day for gathering a church was proclaimed "a day of solemn humiliation," of "fasting and prayer," because covenant making entailed subjection to God and thus resembled the mood of the preparatory stages of salvation. The making of a covenant, after all, was the work of preparation to be God's people. Worship began with a prayer of confession of sin. After the regular order of worship was complete, the future minister and the other founding members again related publicly their faith and experiences of grace. The covenanting ceremony then opened with visitors from other churches voicing their assent to the proceedings. Everyone said a prayer "for the presence of the Lord" and for grace to keep the covenant. The minister-to-be "publikly read the covenant whereof they had all agreed before," and the founding members owned it by "lifting up of hands." After the concluding prayer visiting clergy offered each member "the right hand of fellowship, in token of the loving acceptations of us into communion with them in the lord." The following day a thanksgiving service was held at the meetinghouse.[57]

The minister was likely to be ordained several months after the covenanting ceremony. A recent graduate called to an already-gathered church could also expect a waiting period between his arrival and his ordination. The pastor and lay leaders were officially elected "by the joint and free votes of the church," again on a day of fasting. At Dedham, even though the minister, John Allen, had guided the founding members through the making of the covenant, only after they "in ther judgments remaine satisfied" that he was "in some measure guifted and by providence provided for that place," did they "in due time" proceed to "a sollemne election and ordination." Lay ordination with the laying on of hands by the lay "ruling Elders," or "some prime men in the name of the church," was characteristic of the early decades. Visiting clergy participated only by voicing their consent and extending the right hand of fellowship. By the second half of the century, with the rise of professionalism and in defensive response to a changing society, ordination increasingly became a ritual under clerical control. The 1672 ordination of William Adams to the Dedham pulpit represents a transitional stage: a neighboring minister gave "the charge" to Adams, two lay leaders of the church performed the laying on of hands, and another minister "gave the right hand of fellowship." By 1681, when Peter Thacher was ordained in Milton, the shift was complete. The entire cast was made up of clergy: "1 June 1681. This day I was Ordained (though most unworthy) Pastour of the Church in Milton. My Text 2. Tim. 4. 5. Mr. [Increase] Mather Called the votes, Old Mr. Eliot, Mr. Mather, Mr. Torry, Mr. Willard laid On hands. Mr. Torry gave the Charge, Mr. Willard Gave the right hand of fellowshipe. We sung the 24 ps. Then I gave the blessing." Cotton Mather's 1685 ordination before "one of the vastest Congregations that has ever been seen in these parts of the World" was identical, with Mather himself praying and preaching for three hours, and the Boston area ministerium conducting the entire ceremony. Mather commented that his ordination "produc[ed] a greater Number of moved Hearts and weeping Eyes, than perhaps have been at any Time here seen together." As the mirror image of the clergy's taking over the ordination procedure, local congregations became more reluctant to rush into the ordination of a candidate. Trial ministries were stretched out for years and were distressing experiences for young graduates. The ritual of ordination was owned by the clergy, but the call to ordination remained solely in the hands of the laity.[58]

The covenant of the church was the point of reference for other ordinances of mutual communion. The admission of new members, for example, centered not just on the owning of the covenant by the applicants but on a reaffirmation of the covenant by the entire church. Admission of new members was in effect a reenactment of the first founding of the church. Richard Mather said explicitly that "Members are admitted as the church state was first erected, viz., by solemn confession publicly before the whole church and by joining with the church in the covenant, in which the church was joined at her first gathering together." The same kind of preparatory discussion and prayer and confession of faith that preceded the first covenanting typified subsequent owning of the covenant. On the day of their covenanting, at the close of the afternoon service, applicants made "profession of ther faith unto the Church" by reading their spiritual relation. The pastor formally questioned them on their agreement to the terms of the covenant and on their willingness "to submitt themselves to every ordinance of Christ in that church, to walke in spirituall communion with Christ and his people therein, and in a way of Christian love to the Church according to the rule of the gospell." If found acceptable by congregational vote, they formally assented to the covenant. The minister "rehearseth the covenant, on their parts, to them, which they publiquely say, they doe promise, by the helpe of God, to performe." The minister "in the name of the Church, then promiseth the Churches part of the covenant, to the new admitted members" and gave them the right hand of fellowship.[59]

The administration of discipline, including the ultimate act of excommunication, was an occasional but established part of the afternoon service, continuing "sometimes till it be very late." This too was a celebration of the covenant. By judging one another, sometimes quite critically, on the basis of the covenant, New Englanders reaffirmed the bond that held church and society together. The taking up of collections for needy saints, also an irregular part of Sabbath worship, and the catechism of the young in the doctrine and ways of the church were ordinances that further maintained the ecclesial bond. The covenant was, in fact, implicitly renewed on these many occasions.[60]

The sacraments were more explicit renewals of the covenant. In Baptism, as an infant was brought into covenant, the members were reminded of and urged to reaffirm their part in the church covenant and the covenant of grace. Popular eucharistic manuals and Sacrament day sermons encouraged the understanding that "in receiving the Lord's Supper, we renew covenant with God." In receiving the elements the communicants would find grace "to live a new life . . . as having renewed [their] covenant with the Lord for that purpose."[61]

For the clergy, covenant making and covenant renewal were means of reformation in the church. In New England, where a truly new beginning was possible, John Allen and Thomas Shepard wrote, "Reformation is to be sought in the first Constitution" of churches. Covenant renewal was a way "corrupted Churches (such as we conceive the Congregations of England generally to be) are to be reformed." If such congregations could be "called by able Ministers unto repentance for former evills, and confessing and bewayling their sins, renew a solemn Covenant with God to reform themselves, and to submit unto the disciplines of Christ," then the English church could be reformed. Yet even newly covenanted New England churches soon adopted a ritual of covenant renewal. Just as Shepard and Allen urged covenant renewal in England as a way to reform originally pure but long since corrupt churches, the ceremony in New England became a means to recapture original purity after only a few years of perceived declension.[62]

Scholars have associated the covenant-renewal ceremony with the results of the Reforming Synod of 1679–1680 and with the worship practices of the late seventeenth century. As early as the first decade, however, church leaders feared declension and initiated the ceremony. John Winthrop noted in his journal that on February 25, 1636, at the onset of the Antinomian tensions, the Boston Church renewed its covenant. Other concerns, such as Hooker's move to Hartford and "the great scarcity of corn," also led the lay elders to proclaim "a general fast." Winthrop recorded: "The church of Boston renewed their covenant this day, and made a large explanation of that which they had first entered into, and acknowledged such failings as had fallen out, etc." The Reverend John Fiske, who served three churches over the course of his career, introduced a covenant-renewal ceremony at the beginning of his tenure in at least the first and third. At Salem in 1636 he used the ceremony to enlarge the doctrinal content of the original covenant. Salem's enlarged covenant was explicitly intended as a renewal of the first: "Wee whose names are here under written, members of the present Church of Christ in Salem, having found by sad experience how dangerous it is to sitt loose to the Covenant wee make with our God: and how apt wee are to wander into by pathes, even to the looseing of our first aimes in entring into Church fellowship: Doe therefore solemnly in the presence of the Eternall God, both for our own comforts, and those which shall or maye be joyned unto us, renewe that Church Covenant we find this Church bound unto at theire first beginning." Similarly in 1656, within a year of Fiske's settling in Chelmsford, during a "publick general fast," "in the close of the day was the Church Covenant renewed, repeated, and voted by the Brethren." Fiske viewed the start of his ministry as an opportunity for a new beginning—or more correctly, a renewal of the first beginning—for the church. His motivation included a sense of declension and the need for reformation. It was, as John Winthrop said of himself in 1636, "as if the whole work had been to begin anew."[63]

Covenant renewal during the first half of the century was undertaken in conjunction with a fast day, at the end of a day of public repentance. This was utterly characteristic of New England spirituality and reflected the manner of original covenant making. Churches were gathered on a day not of thanksgiving but of fasting. Covenants were entered in a spirit of contrition, not jubilation. A day of thanksgiving was proclaimed later, but making a covenant was preparatory work; in contrition and humiliation believers prepared for union with God in the covenant. The act of covenant renewal thus involved preparation for renewed life in Christ. Self-examination, repentance, and all the stages of preparation that were expounded first in relation to conversion were also the marks of the day of renewal. Reformation of church and society, like the rebirth of an individual, would come only after the painful travail of preparatory contrition and humiliation. And as did the individual, so the congregation had to traverse these stages again and again if progress was to be made. In covenant renewal—and in all the ordinances of mutual communion—the salvation drama found in the Bible and heard from the pulpit was enacted once more.

Worship in Civil Society

Every inhabitant of the New England colonies was by definition a member of the social covenant and hence took part in a number of devotional acts that attended the civil year. Chief among these were election day, militia training days, and civil days of fasting and thanksgiving proclaimed by magistrates. Weddings were civil affairs, and no evidence indicates that ministers participated in them or that they carried religious significance. Funerals, however, took on more religious and ecclesiastical characteristics as the century progressed, with the clergy involved first as fellow mourners and finally as officiating preachers and pastors. Besides these, execution sermons stirred public interest from time to time. But throughout the century election day, training days, and public days of fasting and thanksgiving were regular events on the civil calendar that had spiritual impact on people's lives.[64]

In the capitals of the New England colonies a minister was invited every year on election day to preach a sermon on the general theme of the godly society and the duties of magistrates and citizenry. The sermons, especially those preached in Boston, were frequently printed, thus giving us access to a significant body of New England social thought. The perennial message was New England's special election by God. As Jonathan Mitchel preached in the most powerful of seventeenth-century election sermons, *Nehemiah on the Wall in Troublesom Times* (1667), the people of New England were "the People of the God of Israel." He advised those who had just been elected to the General Court:

> The Concernments of a People framed into a Body Politick, are put into your hands, . . . a part of Gods *Israel,* though but a part, yet no inconsiderable part of the people of God at this day in the world: such a part of Gods people as are retired to these Ends of the Earth, for known ends of Religion and Reformation. . . . You are betrusted with as precious an Interest as is this day upon the Earth, viz. with the Lives, Estates, Liberties, and Religious Enjoyments of some thousands whose Names are written in Heaven, and bound upon the Breast and Heart of Christ Jesus. . . . The eyes of the whole Christian World are upon you; yea which is more, the eyes of God and of his holy Angels are upon you.

The great function of the election sermon, as Mitchel makes clear, was social integration and continuity. The power of his dramatic statement "The eyes of the whole Christian World are upon you" came less from its political realism than from its symbolic value. By echoing Winthrop's original phrase, Mitchel asserted that in spite of social change, in spite of any decline in piety, in spite of the more complex and less significant role of New England after the Restoration, New England was still New England. "The eyes of God" were still fixed on New England. Election sermons imbued civil election with the character of a covenant-renewal ceremony. Through these sermons the themes of Puritan spirituality continued to assert themselves in the culture.[65]

The third public institution (in addition to church and civil government) in which ministers led worship was the militia. Militia companies invited local pastors to pray with and preach to their members throughout the century. In the 1680s, for example, Peter Thacher regularly attended Milton training days, as in November 1681: "Being sent for I went and prayed with our Military Company, then went and dined with Sargant Badcock and Sargant Vose and the rest of the officers." Most of the officers were also leaders of the church, so that the social institutions of the New England town reinforced one another and worship was a major cohesive force in society. The annual election of local company officers called for a sermon, some of which were published. Preachers tended to take one of two approaches. They might follow Urian Oakes in his popular sermon, *The Unconquerable All-Conquering & More-Then-Conquering Souldier* (1674), and spiritualize the figure of the soldier to teach every citizen a lesson. "Every true Believer is a Souldier, and engaged in a Warfare," Oakes preached, elaborating the familiar theme of the saints' "Holy Warre" against the "Enemies of his Soul," sin and Satan. He continued, "I would it were reciprocally true, that every Souldier amongst us is a true Believer." Or the preacher could follow the path of Samuel Nowell's *Abraham in Arms*, which celebrated New England military might as the arm of the Lord. Nowell went so far as to preach that the New England militia was a means of worldly grace: "Our Military Strength is, under God, the appointed means, or in the ordinary way of Providence, is the proper and only means for our preservation; therefore it is a duty to encourage Souldiers." He reached millennialist heights reminiscent of Edward Johnson's *Wonder-Working Providence*. "It will not be long ere the Lord will call out Souldiers" for the final battle. The New England training day was for Nowell preparation for Armageddon.[66]

Sermons preached at public fasts and days of thanksgiving likewise served to integrate New England society along the lines of the original covenant. Public fast-day sermons, like their ecclesiastical counterparts, invariably called the people back to their beginnings, pleading that New England must continue to understand itself as God's own people. Though society was always more complex than the ideal presented in any sermon, to assert that the preaching was ineffectual or anachronistic is to ignore the continuing power of the myth of New England and the pervasiveness of the redemptive drama in the popular mentality. The myth and the drama were not the property of the clergy and a few magistrates but were rooted in the culture. The persistence of these themes in public worship in church and society, and the inhabitants' almost daily contact with them, leads us to infer that the rhythms and content of the rituals shaped ways of thinking and acting.[67]

NOTES

1. Shepard, *Ten Virgins*, 4.

2. Downame, *Guide to Godlynesse*, 479. Bayne, *Briefe Directions*, 113. Dod and Cleaver, *Ten Sermons*, 123. Hooker, *Paterne of Perfection*, 3. [Hooker], *Soules Humiliation*, 82.

3. Cotton, *Practical Commentary upon the First Epistle Generall of John*, 337. *Dedham Church Records*, 4.

4. Hooker, *Application of Redemption, First Eight Books*, 415. Hooker, *Application of Redemption, Ninth and Tenth Books*, 34, 299–300. Cotton, *Christ the Fountaine*, 22. Cotton, *Thirteenth Chapter of Revelation*, 240. David D. Hall, ed., *The Antinomian Controversy, 1636–1638: A Documentary History* (Middletown, Conn., 1968), 14–20.

5. Ira Progoff, trans., *The Cloud of Unknowing: A New Translation of a Classic Guide to Spiritual Experience* (New York, 1957), 71. Samuel Gorton, *Simplicity's Defence against Seven-Headed Policy*, ed. William R. Staples (Rhode Island Historical Society, *Collections*, II [1835]), 263–270, cited in Gura, "Radical Ideology of Gorton," *WMQ*, 3d Ser., XXXVI (1979), 89. Shepard, "Autobiography," in McGiffert, ed., *God's Plot*, 46. H[ooker], *Soules Vocation*, 63. T[homas] H[ooker], *The Unbeleevers Preparing for Christ* (London, 1638), 160.

6. The orderliness of the Puritan universe is a major thesis of Miller's *New England Mind: Seventeenth Century*. See Hall, *Faithful Shepherd*, 59; Stoever, '*Faire and Easie Way*,' 74, 124, 148–150. Hooker, *Application of Redemption, First Eight Books*, 133–134. H[ooker], *Soules Vocation*, 64. [Hooker], *Soules Humiliation*, 82. Cotton, *Seven Vials*, 128. Shepard, *Theses Sabbaticae*, sig. B3. Thomas, ed., *Diary of Samuel Sewall*, I, 89. Bayne, *Briefe Directions*, 113.

7. See generally, Winton U. Solberg, *Redeem the Time: The Puritan Sabbath in Early America* (Cambridge, Mass., 1977). Davies, *Worship of the English Puritans*, 75–76. Dom Gregory Dix, *The Shape of the Liturgy* (London, 1945), 7n. Dix was clearly not thinking of Reformed liturgics when he wrote of "this idea of Sunday as a little weekly Easter" that "in practice there is no evidence that it has ever made very much appeal to popular piety in any part of christendom" (p. 359). Shepard, *Theses Sabbaticae*, 5–6.

8. Solberg, *Redeem the Time*, 2. Shepard, *Theses Sabbaticae*, 77. Bayly, *Practice of Piety*, 222.

9. Shepard, *Theses Sabbaticae*, 65, sig. B1.

10. *Ibid.*, 79. Davies, *Worship and Theology*, II, 245.

11. Dane, "Declaration of Remarkabell Prouedenses," *NEHGR*, VIII (1854), 149–155. Shepard, *Theses Sabbaticae*, 98.

12. Bartlett Burleigh James and J. Franklin Jameson, eds., *Journal of Jasper Danckaerts, 1679–1680* (New York, 1913), 261–262. Sacvan Bercovitch, *The American Jeremiad* (Madison, Wis., 1978).

13. J[ohn] Cotton, *The Way of the Churches of Christ in New England* . . . (London, 1645), 70. Ministers frequently took the opportunity to hear colleagues preach on neighboring lecture days. Peter Thacher, "Diary," MS and typescript, Massachusetts Historical Society, Boston, *passim*.

14. Cotton, *Way of the Churches*, 70. John Eliot, "Sermon," in C. Mather, ed., *Life and Death of J. Eliot* . . . , 20. Davies, *Worship and Theology*, II, 246. Bayly, *Practice of Piety*, 288–301. For the impact of fast days on experience, see Woolley, "Shepard's Cambridge Church Members," 106–107, 138.

15. W. DeLoss Love, Jr., *The Fast and Thanksgiving Days of New England* (Boston, 1895). Horton Davies's belief that these days "were occasional and rare, and were no more than the foothills of their corporate devotion" may have been correct for England but the situation in New England was far different (*Worship and Theology*, I, 268). Miller, *New England Mind: From Colony to Province*, chap. 2.

16. Love, *Fast and Thanksgiving Days*, 79, 239–255. Peter Thacher's "Diary" lists a thanksgiving almost invariably in November.

17. I am indebted to Ellen Smith of the American and New England Studies program, Boston University, for the insight of spring as the time of the empty larder and hence as symbolic of death.

18. Love, *Fast and Thanksgiving Days*, 68–77. Hull, *Diaries*, 219.

19. Thomas Lechford, *Plain Dealing, or, News from New England* (London, 1641), ed. J. Hammond Trumbull (Boston, 1867), 43–50. John Cotton, *The True Constitution of a Particular Visible Church, Proved by Scripture* (London, 1642), 5–8. Cotton, *Way of the Churches*, 66–70. See also, Love, *Fast and Thanksgiving Days*, 88.

20. Cotton, *True Constitution*, 5. Cotton, *Way of the Churches*, 66–67. Lechford, *Plain Dealing*, ed. Trumbull, 44–45. Thacher, "Diary," MS, I, 37, 42, and *passim*.

21. Thacher, "Diary," MS, I, 121–122, 79. James and Jameson, eds., *Journal of Jasper Danckaerts*, 261–262.

22. Cotton, *True Constitution*, 6. John 11:41, 17:1.

23. [Richard Mather], *Church-Government and Church-Covenant Discussed* . . . (London, 1643), 56–57. Shepard, *Treatise of Liturgies*, 64.

24. Cotton Mather, "Piscator Evangelicus," in *Johannes in Eremo. Memoirs Relating to the Lives, of the Ever-Memorable, Mr. John Cotton,* . . . *Mr. John Wilson,* . . . *Mr. John Davenport,* . . . *and Mr. Thomas Hooker* . . . (Boston, 1695), 27–28. C. Mather, "Nortonus Honoratus," *ibid.*, 38.

25. Hall, ed., "Autobiography of Increase Mather," Am. Antiq. Soc., *Procs.*, N. S., LXXI (1961), 316–317.

26. Paul, "Accidence and Essence of Puritan Piety," *Austin Seminary Bulletin*, XCIII, no. 8 (May 1978), 15.

27. Bercovitch, *Typology and Early American Literature*, 2. C. Mather, *Magnalia Christi Americana*, II, 61. Lechford's letter is cited in *Plain Dealing*, ed. Trumbull, 45n.

28. Perkins, *Cases of Conscience*, in *Works*, II, 70–71. Cotton, *True Constitution*, 6. Cotton's description of the reading of Scripture is tied to the wording of Nehemiah 8. In John Davenport's New Haven church, and perhaps others, it seems that, following this text and ancient custom, the people stood for the reading. See Thomas Hooker's 1640 letter to Thomas Shepard, cited in Lechford, *Plain Dealing*, ed. Trumbull, 45n.

29. John Cotton, *Singing of Psalmes a Gospel-Ordinance* . . . (London, 1650 [orig. publ. 1647]), 2. Cotton, *Way of the Churches*, 67, 69. J. H. Dorenkamp, "The *Bay Psalm Book* and the Ainsworth Psalter," *Early Am. Lit.*, VII (1972), 7.

30. Zoltán Haraszti, *The Enigma of the Bay Psalm Book* (Chicago, 1956), 8, chap. 6. *Whole Booke of Psalmes,* sig. **2. Dorenkamp pointed out the many incidences of identical wording with Ainsworth, in "*Bay Psalm Book* and the Ainsworth Psalter," *Early Am. Lit.,* VII (1972), 9–15. Cotton, *Way of the Churches,* 67.

31. Cotton, *Singing of Psalmes,* 5–6, 48.

32. Cotton went so far as to say a gifted person could compose a song and "sing it before the Church, and the rest hearing it, approving it, may goe along with him in Spirit, and say Amen to it." *Ibid.,* 15.

33. Davies, *Worship of the English Puritans,* 162. Cotton, *Singing of Psalmes,* 42–43. Winship, *Cambridge Press,* 34. Harrison T. Meserole, ed., *Seventeenth-Century American Poetry* (New York, 1968), xxiv.

34. Meserole, ed., *Seventeenth-Century American Poetry,* 353. Haraszti, however, has shown the generally high literary quality of the *Bay Psalm Book* (*Enigma of the Bay Psalm Book,* chap. 6). *Whole Booke of Psalmes,* Psalm 23. Lechford, *Plain Dealing,* ed. Trumbull, 45. Significant work on New England's sacred music has been done by Barbara Dailey, a graduate student in the history department, Boston University. Her group has researched and performed the psalms and spiritual songs of meetinghouse and home.

35. Cotton, *Singing of Psalmes,* 55, 58, 62. *Whole Booke of Psalmes,* sig. **2.

36. *Whole Booke of Psalmes,* Introduction, sig. **4.

37. Shipton, ed., "Autobiographical Memoranda of John Brock," Am. Antiq. Soc., Procs., N. S., LIII (1943), 98. *Clap's Memoirs,* 20. Hall, *Faithful Shepherd,* 156–157. See generally, Bercovitch, *American Jeremiad. The Code of 1650, Being a Compilation of the Earliest Laws and Orders of the General Court of Connecticut . . . ,* cited in David Kobrin, "The Expansion of the Visible Church in New England: 1629–1650," *Church History,* XXXVI (1967), 194.

38. Thomas, ed., *Diary of Samuel Sewall,* I, 26. Miller, *New England Mind: Seventeenth Century,* 297–298.

39. Phyllis M. Jones and Nicholas R. Jones, eds., *Salvation in New England: Selections from the Sermons of the First Preachers* (Austin, Tex., 1977), xi, xiii, 12–13.

40. The plain style is discussed by Miller, *New England Mind: Seventeenth Century,* chaps. 11 and 12, and Levy, *Preaching in New England History,* 81–97. John Cotton, "Milk for Babes," in Everett H. Emerson, *John Cotton* (New York, 1965), 128.

41. Hooker, *Application of Redemption, First Eight Books,* 210–212. C. Mather, *Magnalia Christi Americana,* II, 61. Hooker, *Application of Redemption, First Eight Books,* 213, 215. [Hooker], *Soules Implantation,* 66–68, 78. [Hooker], *Soules Humiliation,* 297. H[ooker], *Unbeleevers Preparing,* 180, 27. See Leverenz, *Language of Puritan Feeling,* chap. 6.

42. Burke, *Popular Culture in Early Modern Europe,* 133. Shepard, *Sound Beleever,* 316–317. See above, p. 61.

43. Cotton, *Way of Life,* 420–421.

44. Thomas Shepard, "The Soul's Invitation unto Jesus Christ," in Shepard, *The Saint's Jewel Shewing How to Apply the Promise* (Boston, 1743), 38.

45. A similar use of matrimonial language appears in Cotton Mather, *Ornaments for the Daughters of Zion: Or the Character and Happiness of a Vertuous Woman . . .* (Boston, 1741 [orig. publ. Cambridge, Mass., 1692]), 78–79. [R. Mather], *Church-Government and Church-Covenant,* 79–80. Hooker, *Application of Redemption, First Eight Books,* 432.

46. Cotton, *Way of the Churches*, 68. Lechford, *Plain Dealing*, ed. Trumbull, 45–46.

47. Cotton, "Milk for Babes," in Emerson, *John Cotton*, 130.

48. *Ibid.* Shepard, *First Principles*, 86. Thomas Shepard, *The Church-Membership of Children, and Their Right to Baptisme* . . . (Cambridge, 1693), 8. R. Mather, *Farewel-Exhortation*, 12.

49. Lechford, *Plain Dealing*, ed. Trumbull, 48. Cotton, *True Constitution*, 7.

50. Holifield, *Covenant Sealed*, 74. John Calvin, *Institutes of the Christian Religion*, trans. Henry Beveridge (Grand Rapids, Mich., 1966 [orig. publ. Edinburgh, 1845]), II, 564, 571. Thomas Hooker, *An Exposition of the Principles of Religion* (London, 1645), 28. Hooker, *Paterne of Perfection*, 375.

51. Thomas, ed., *Diary of Samuel Sewall*, I, 40. Italics added.

52. Lechford, *Plain Dealing*, ed. Trumbull, 46. Cotton, *Way of the Churches*, 68–69. Cotton, *True Constitution*, 7.

53. Cotton, *True Constitution*, 7.

54. Perry Miller developed the Puritan idea of the covenant in all its ramifications in *New England Mind: Seventeenth Century*, chaps. 13–16. Richard Mather to William Rathband and Mr. T., June 25, 1636, Emerson, ed., *Letters from New England*, 202. *Dedham Church Records*, 1–13. See Kenneth A. Lockridge, *A New England Town, The First Hundred Years: Dedham, Massachusetts, 1636–1736* (New York, 1970), chap. 2.

55. *Dedham Church Records*, 5–10.

56. On the development of the covenant as a document, see Williston Walker, *The Creeds and Platforms of Congregationalism* (Boston, 1960 [orig. publ. New York, 1893]), 116–117, 131, 154–156.

57. R. Mather to Rathband, Emerson, ed., *Letters from New England*, 202. *Dedham Church Records*, 10–13.

58. R. Mather to Rathband, Emerson, ed., *Letters from New England*, 203. *Dedham Church Records*, 17–20. Hall, *Faithful Shepherd*, 47, 79, 106, 220–222, and chap. 8. "Memoir of the Rev. William Adams," Mass. Hist. Soc., *Colls.*, 4th Ser., I (1852), 20–21. Thacher, "Diary," MS, I, 212. Ford, ed., *Diary of Cotton Mather*, I, 98–99.

59. R. Mather to Rathband, Emerson, ed., *Letters from New England*, 202. *Dedham Church Records*, 20–21. Lechford, *Plain Dealing*, ed. Trumbull, 29.

60. Lechford, *Plain Dealing*, ed. Trumbull, 29–34. See Wilberforce Eames, *Early New England Catechisms: A Bibliographical Account of Some Catechisms Published before the Year 1800, for Use in New England* (New York, 1898); "Rev. John Eliot's Records of the First Church in Roxbury, Mass.," *NEHGR*, XXXIII (1879), 239; and "The Rev. John Fiske's Notebook," Mass. Hist. Soc., *Proceedings*, 2d Ser., XII (1897, 1899), 318–319.

61. Increase Mather, *Renewal of Covenant the Great Duty Incumbent on Decaying or Distressed Churches* . . . (Boston, 1677), 6–7. Francis Roberts, *A Communicant Instructed, or, Practical Instructions for Worthy Receiving of the Lords-Supper* (London, 1651), cited in Wilfred W. Biggs, "Preparation for Communion: A Puritan Manual," *Congregational Quarterly*, XXXII (1954), 17.

62. John Allen and Thomas Shepard, "Preface to the Reader," in Shepard, *Treatise of Liturgies*, 10.

63. Walker, *Creeds and Platforms*, 435. Hall, *Faithful Shepherd*, 242–244. Winthrop, *Journal*, ed. Hosmer, I, 175. "Extracts from Records Kept by the Rev. John Fiske during His Ministry at Salem, Wenham and Chelmsford," Essex Institute, *Historical Collections*, I (1859), 37. "The Rev. John Fiske's Notebook," Mass. Hist. Soc., *Procs.*, 2d Ser., XII (1897, 1899), 325.

64. Stannard, *Puritan Way of Death,* chap. 5. Ford, ed., *Diary of Cotton Mather,* I, 279.

65. Jonathan Mitchel, *Nehemiah on the Wall in Troublesom Times* ... (Cambridge, Mass., 1671), 2, 18–19. See A. W. Plumstead, ed., *The Wall and the Garden: Selected Massachusetts Election Sermons, 1670–1775* (Minneapolis, Minn., 1968). Of special note is Thomas Shepard, [Jr.], *Eye-Salve, or a Watch-Word from Our Lord Jesus Christ unto His Church* ... (Cambridge, Mass., 1673).

66. Thacher, "Diary," MS, II, 237. The Boston, Cambridge, and Charlestown companies followed the same practice of hearing a sermon and prayer, with Cotton Mather as chaplain in the mid-1680s. Thomas, ed., *Diary of Samuel Sewall,* I, 79–80. Urian Oakes, *The Unconquerable All-Conquering & More-Then-Conquering Souldier* ... (Cambridge, Mass., 1674), 4. S[amuel] N[owell], *Abraham in Arms* ... (Boston, 1678), 11, 19. See Darrett B. Rutman, "A Militant New World, 1607–1740: America's First Generation, Its Martial Spirit, Its Militia Organization, Its Wars" (Ph.D. diss., University of Virginia, 1959). It may be significant that Oakes's almost pacifist sermon and Nowell's militarist sermon were preached just before and just after King Philip's War, respectively.

67. The best examples of fast-day sermons are John Davenport, *Gods Call to His People to Turn unto Him* ... (Cambridge, Mass., 1669), and Thomas Thacher, *A Fast of Gods Chusing, for the Help of Those Poor in Spirit, Whose Hearts Are Set to Seek the Lord Their God in New England* ... (Boston, 1678). See Bercovitch, *Puritan Origins,* 132–133, and Bercovitch, *American Jeremiad,* 23–30.

3

Popular Religion as the Core of Cultural Identity Based on the Mexican American Experience in the United States

Virgilio Elizondo

The spirituality that knows through the body knows through a body that has been initiated into a culture. *Any* "body" that engages in ritual does so as an ethnic body—as someone who is part of a distinct people. Seventeenth-century New England Puritans, who were Protestant Christians, were also Anglo-Americans. By the late twentieth century (indeed, by the middle of the previous century), the largest organized religious body in the United States was not Protestant at all but Roman Catholic—and, as important, had been constituted by a series of ethnic communities that inflected their Catholicism in ways that differed from group to group. From the nineteenth century, however, Irish Catholicism had become ascendant and continued to shape the public culture of Catholicism into our own times. Virgilio Elizondo, who is a Roman Catholic priest with an expertise in liberation theology, announces, though, that he is a "native-born Mexican American Tejano from San Antonio." As such, he is one of the well over 22 million Latinos in the United States, who constitute at least 9 percent of the population. And in this context, his essay demonstrates especially clearly that while ritual possesses a "vertical" dimension, it likewise moves "horizontally," capturing and reinforcing the spiritual bonds within each distinctive culture. Elizondo is keenly aware of the way that Mexican American Catholicism stands apart from the official Catholicism of the United States, because of their differences on the horizontal axis. Using the symbols of Mexican identity, he points to their connections with the symbolic life of Catholic piety as practiced in Latino culture. Ritual spirituality, he tells us, is always culture-bound.

Introduction

I am a native-born Mexican American Tejano from San Antonio, Texas. I have always lived and worked among my own people—except for brief periods of

From *The Enduring Flame: Studies on Latino Popular Religiosity,* edited by Anthony M. Stevens-Arroyo and Ana María Díaz Stevens. Published as Volume I in the series produced by the Program for the Analysis of Religion among Latinos/as (PARAL), following a 1993 conference at Princeton University made possible by grants from the Lilly Endowment and the Pew Charitable Trusts. Copyright © 1994 by Anthony M. Stevens-Arroyo and Ana María Díaz Stevens. Reprinted by permission of the editors.

time when I went away to do advanced studies or was on special assignments in different parts of the world. My own family and the people from my barrio have been my basic formation team and it is from them that I have received my most cherished values, beliefs and religious expressions. It is through them and with them that I have experienced God, Jesus and the communion of saints—the extended family of my people.

Today, I am a grass-roots pastor with a doctorate in theology working in the parish where my parents were married, and where the people who nourished me as a child are the senior citizens I minister to every day. I could have left to become a university professor as I have had some very attractive offers from various universities and certainly enjoy going for brief periods as a visiting professor, but I have chosen to do what I can—academically and pastorally—with my people in their daily life and struggles. As I practice and reflect on the popular faith tradition of my own Mexican American people, I become more and more fascinated with its meaning and function in our everyday lives and the enriching contribution that our faith tradition can make to the universal church and to society in general.

Since 1731, my people have been living, transmitting and celebrating our Christian faith in continuity with the ways of our ancestors in the very same spot where I minister today, and we know that future generations will continue to find identity, solidarity and life in these *mestizo* traditions of deeply inculturated faith. The *Benditos* and *Alabados* will continue to be the common songs of the spiritual homeland within us that nobody can abolish, while our processions and fiestas will continue to celebrate ritually the painful and arduous way of the immigrants, undocumented, unjustly condemned, exploited and ridiculed of today's society who refuse to be eliminated or destroyed.

Many have tried to suppress our language, culture and even the religious expressions of our faith. But we have resisted and to the degree that we have resisted, we continue to be *el pueblo . . . la raza . . .* What ultimately makes us who we are? We continue to recreate annually the ancient traditions which are the substance of our collective soul. I became a priest to work with my people; to maintain alive that which had given our lives meaning in an otherwise meaningless and alien cultural world; to animate the struggle for justice, equality and liberty in a world where "law and order"—even in the Church— worked to justify and mask segregation and the exploitation of the poor; to celebrate life despite the many death threats; to transmit to the coming generations the basic elements of our common soul which are the substance of our identity as a people—as a *pueblo*.

Formation of Mexican American Religious Tradition

Religion and religious expression is power—but will it be a power unto life or a power of sacralized and legitimized oppression, margination, exclusion, ethnocide and even genocide? I am involved in the praxis of what theologians and social scientists tend to call "popular religiosity." And from within the praxis of "popular religiosity" I find few authors that seem to know what they are really talking about—they always seem to be speaking about the faith expressions of someone else who does not have the "pure faith" the author seems to presuppose about him/herself. I do not believe that anyone can penetrate the deep mystery of the religious expressions of a people from the outside. Outsiders can describe it and analyze it, but they will never know it for what it truly is. To the outsider, the ways in which people express their faith will always appear as "religiosity," but to the people themselves, their religious practices are the tangible expressions of the ultimately inexpressible: the mystery of God present and acting in our midst.

Our Mexican American religious expressions started with the prodigious *mestizaje* of Iberian Catholicism with the native religions which were already here. This rich and original synthesis did not take place in the theological universities or the councils of the Church, but in the very ordinary crossroads of daily life. This mestizising process started in 1519 and is still going on today. It is in the context of these religious symbols and rituals that the Mexican American experiences the deepest belonging and cultural communion. Our faith expressions need no explanation for those of us for whom they are meaningful, and no explanation will suffice for those who live and operate in a world of different religious symbols. We Mexican Americans do not need or seek explanations about *Our Lady of Guadalupe, Nuestra Señora de los Lagos, el Cristo Negro de Esquipulas, San Martín de Porres* . . . we know them well as living persons. In them, we experience the mystery of our own identity. They are our collective *alter ego.*

The Christian word of God was inculturated deeply within the collective soul of Mexico not by the intention of the missioners, but by the process of symbolic interchange which took place in a very natural way in the *cocinas, mercados, plazas, hogares, tamaladas, panteones, milpas y fiestas del pueblo* . . . Although no one planned or organized it, it was in these places that the free interchange of life and ideas between the Iberians and the Nahuatls took place as naturally as the new flowers blossom in spring time.

The ordinary Spaniards of that period were mostly illiterate and came from a Catholic culture which was rich in imagery, and the native world of the Americas communicated mainly through an image-language, as well. Thus it was much more at the level of the image-word than of the alphabetic spoken word that the new synthesis of Iberian Catholicism and the native religions took place and continues to take place today. This synthesis became flesh in the gastronomic world which produced the new foods for which Mexico is famous today. Our cuisine, rich in contradictory flavors, is the earthly expression of the heavenly banquet referred to in the Scriptures. As Mexican cuisine emerged, so did the Mexican soul. Our mothers struggled to prepare tasty dishes out of the little or nothing they had available. They managed to nourish both our bodies and our spirit out of the same domestic tabernacles of life: *Las cocinas.*[1] Here they were free to talk, discuss, imagine, think, formulate and understand without coercion or control from higher authorities. This interchange at the grass-roots level has gradually given birth to Mexican Christianity.[2]

Ritual, mystery and image might well be called the trinity of the Mexican and Mexican American cultural-religious identity. Dogma and doctrines seem to be so Western, while ritual and mystery seem to be so *mestizo* Mexican. It is only in Our Lady of Guadalupe that the dichotomy is both assumed and transformed into synthesis. It would be the *madrecitas* in the *cocinas* who would gradually unfold and transmit the innermost meaning of this theophany which ushered in the new Christian tradition of the Americas. The male theologians have imposed western Marian categories on Guadalupe and have missed the creative and generative power of Guadalupe which has been articulated, developed and transmitted by the *abuelitas,* story-tellers and artists.[3] This articulation, development, and transmission is the starting point of our own indigenous Christian tradition—or what some people call "popular religiosity."

Function of Religious Tradition

Popular religiosity is simply the religious tradition of the local church (Tillard, 1976). The term "popular religiosity" is also what others call the religious expressions of my people. For us, these expressions are simply ¡nuestra vida de fe! They are our own sacramental life which has arisen out of the common priesthood of the people acting in the power of the Spirit. The Word has become flesh in us in the form of our religious practices and traditions. They are the visible expressions of our collective soul through which we affirm ourselves in our relationship to each other and to God. Others may take everything else away from us, but they cannot destroy our expressions of the divine. Through these practices we not only affirm ourselves as a people, we also resist ultimate assimilation. Thus our religious practices are not only affirmations of faith, but the language of defiance and ultimate resistance. In our collective celebrations, we rise above the forces which oppress us or even seek to destroy us, and we celebrate our survival publicly. But it is much more than survival: through our communal rituals and symbols the new born babies and growing children are initiated into the God-language of our people and thus we are assured that life will continue unto the next generation and generations to come.

By popular expressions of the faith I do not refer to the private or individual devotions of a few people but to the ensemble of beliefs, rituals, ceremonies, devotions and prayers which are publicly practiced by the people at large. It is my contention, which is beyond the scope of this paper to develop but which will be its point of departure, that the deepest identity of the people is expressed in those expressions of faith which are celebrated voluntarily by the majority of the people, transmitted from generation to generation by the people themselves, and go on with the Church, without it, or even in spite of it.

Popular faith expressions function in different ways for various peoples depending on their history and socio-cultural status. For the dominant culture, these expressions serve to legitimize their way of life as God's true way for humanity. They will tranquilize the moral conscience and blind people from seeing the injustices which exist in daily life. For a colonized/oppressed/dominated group, they are the ultimate resistance to the attempts of the dominant culture to destroy them as a distinct group either through annihilation or through absorption and assimilation. They will maintain alive the sense of injustice which the people experience in their daily lives.

These religious practices are the ultimate foundation of the people's innermost being and the common expression of their collective soul. They are supremely meaningful for the people who celebrate them, but often appear meaningless to the outsider. To the people whose very life-source they are, no explanation is necessary, but to the casual or scientific spectator no explanation will ever express or communicate their full meaning. Without them, there might be associations of individuals bound together by common interest (e.g. the corporation, the state, etc . . .), but there will never be the experience of being a people, *un pueblo.*

It is within the context of the group's tradition that one experiences both a sense of selfhood and a sense of belonging. Furthermore, it is within the tradition that one remains in contact both with one's beginnings, the stories of origins and with one's ultimate end. We are born into them and within them we discover our full and ultimate being. I might enjoy and admire other traditions very much, but I will never be fully at home within them. No matter how much I get into them, I will always have a sense of being other.

In the very beginning, those who followed the way of Jesus presented a very unique way of universalizing peoples without destroying their localized identity. This in fact was the genius and grace of the "Good News." People could now become members of the same family without ceasing to be who they were ethnically, even without giving up the symbols which were sacred to them. St. Paul at Athens does not ask the people to tear down their gods, but to recognize the one who was already there but had not yet been named. People would neither have to disappear through assimilation nor be segregated as inferior. The Christian message interwove with the local religious traditions so as to give the people a deeper sense of local identity (a sense of rootedness) while at the same time breaking down the psycho-sociological barriers that kept nationalities separate and apart from each other so as to allow for a truly universal fellowship (a sense of universality).

This process was the very core of the evangelizing process of the various European tribes. In fact that is precisely why today's Europe is so deeply united as Western culture and yet so diversified linguistically, culturally, gastronomically and in so many other exciting ways. Early Christianity affirmed the local identity while providing truly universalizing rites, words and symbols. In other words, it affirmed rootedness while destroying ghettoishness. Christianity changed peoples and cultures not by destroying them, but by re-interpreting their core rituals and myths through the foundational ritual and myth of Christianity. Thus, now a Jew could still be a faithful Jew and yet belong fully to the new universal fellowship and equally a Greek or a Roman could still be fully Greek or Roman and equally belong to the new universal group.

Unfortunately, once Christian Europe went out to conquer and evangelize other peoples, the missioners so identified the Gospel with their own Western culture that for the most part, they ignored the original genius of the Gospel and used it to destroy differences rather than bringing them into the whole of the Christian family which has room for all of the peoples—nations—of the world. It would take hundreds of years before the Second Vatican Council would begin to rectify these historical deviations. Thus, today, the greatest challenge of the Church has become the process of inculturation.

In ways similar to that of early Christians, Christianity without destroying our ancient rootedness, allowed us to enter into a universal family by sharing in a new common faith and in universal religious symbols. The missioners tried desperately to uproot all the ancient religions, but the laity—Spanish and Natives—simply constructed a new synthesis. This synthesis changed our native ancestors and their *mestizo* descendants not by the elimination of our religious ways, but by combining them with the Iberian-Christian ways to the mutual enrichment of both. This has been the basic way of the Christian tradition as it has historically made its way from Galilee, to Jerusalem, through Europe, Asia and North Africa and to the ends of the earth (Aragon, 1976). Without ceasing to be who we had been, we have become part of a broader human group—the Christian family which takes its members from all the nations of the world without destroying their cultural genius.

Two Distinct American Religious Traditions

The beginning of the Americas reflects two radically distinct images/myth representations of the Christian tradition. The United States was born as a secular enterprise with a deep sense of religious mission. The native religions were eliminated and supplanted by a new type of religion. Puritan moralism, Presbyterian righteousness and Methodist social consciousness coupled with deism and the spirit of rugged individualism to provide a sound basis for the new nationalism which would function as the core religion of the land. It was quite different in Latin America where the religion of the old European world clashed with native religious traditions. In their efforts to uproot the native religions, the conquerors found themselves assumed into them. Iberian Catholicism with its emphasis on orthodoxy, rituals and the divinely established monarchical nature of all society conquered physically. But it was absorbed by the pare-Colombian spirituality with its emphasis on the cosmic rituals expressing the harmonious unity of opposing tensions: male and female, suffering and happiness, self-immanence and transcendence, individual and group, sacred and profane, life and death.

In the secular based culture of the United States, it is the one who succeeds materially who appears to be the upright and righteous person—the good and saintly. The myth of Prometheus continues to be the underlying myth through which religions of the United States are reinterpreted and reshaped. In the pare-Colombian/Iberian-Catholic *mestizo* based culture of Mexico it is the one who can endure all of the opposing tensions of life and not lose one's interior harmony who appears to be the upright and righteous one. Our religion and culture is constantly reinterpreted and reshaped through the combined myths of the suffering and crucified Jesus—as Jaime Vidal has stated: *El Señor del Gran Poder*—combined with the myths of Cuatemoc (the young Aztec prince whom the Spaniards killed because he refused to release Aztec gold) and Quetzalcoatl (who sacrificed himself for the good of his people).

Prometheus sacralized the power to conquer for self-gain while *El Señor del Gran Poder* and Quetzalcoatl sacralized the power to endure any and all suffering for the sake of the salvation of others—two very distinct foundations for the main religions of the Americas.

The Catholicism of the United States and the Catholicism of Mexico accept the same creed, ecclesiology, sacraments, commandments and official prayer. But the ways these are interpreted, imaged, and lived are quite different. The use of sacramentals and prayer forms and the relationship of people to the institutional Church is different in Mexican and Mexican American Catholicism than in the United States. For example, in the United States, many Anglo-Americans tend to see the Pope more as the President/CEO of our giant, world-wide Catholic "multinational," while in the Mexican American group, we love and reverence him as the *"papa grande"* of our big family. The implications of this are quite vast! In the United States, the sacraments have been the ordinary way of Church life, while in Mexico it has been the sacramentals. The written and spoken alphabetic-word (dogmas, doctrines and papal documents) are most important in U.S. Catholicism while the ritual and devotional image-word have been the mainstay of Mexican Catholicism. The United States has been parish-centered while the Mexican Church has been home, town and shrine centered.

With the great Western expansion of the United States in the 1800's, the two religious traditions of the Americas came into contact and conflict. During this period, the United States conquered fifty percent of northern Mexico. The

Mexicans living in that vast region spanning a territory of over 3500 kilometers from California to Texas, suddenly became aliens in their own land ... foreigners who never left home. Their entire way of life was despised. The Mexican *mestizo* was abhorred as a mongrel who was good only for cheap labor. Efforts were instituted to suppress everything Mexican: customs, language and Mexican Catholicism. The fair-skinned/blond Mexicans who remained had the choice of assimilating to the White, Anglo-Saxon, Protestant culture of the United States or be ostracized as inferior human beings. The dark-skinned had no choice! They were marked as an inferior race destined to be the servants of the White master race.

Today, social unrest and dire poverty force many people from Mexico to relocate in the former Mexican territories which politically are part of the United States. Newcomers are harassed by the immigration services of the United States as illegal intruders—a curious irony since it was the United States citizens who originally entered this region illegally and stole it from Mexico. Yet the Mexican American descendants of the original European settlers in this region, along with recent Mexican immigrants, continue to feel at home, to resist efforts of destruction through assimilation, and to celebrate their legitimacy as a people.

Religious Symbols of Mexican American Communities

The Mexican Americans living in that vast borderland between the United States and Mexico have not only survived as a people but have even maintained good mental health in spite of the countless insults and put-downs suffered throughout their history and continuing to the present (Acuña, 1972). Anyone who has suffered such a long history of segregation, degradation and exploitation could easily be a mental wreck (Jiménez, 1985). Yet, despite this on-going suffering, not only are the numbers of Mexican Americans increasing, but in general Mexican Americans are prospering, joyful and healthy thanks to our profound faith as lived and expressed through group religious practices. I could explore many of them,[4] but I will limit myself to what I consider to be the three sets of related core expressions which mark the ultimate ground, the perimeters and the final aspirations of the Mexican American people: Guadalupe/Baptism; *polvo/agua bendita;* crucifixion/*los muertos.* They are the symbols in which the apparently destructive forces of life are assumed, transcended and united. In them, we experience the ultimate meaning and destiny of our life pilgrimage.

Guadalupe/Baptism

There is no greater and more persistent symbol of Mexican and Mexican American identity than devotion to Our Lady of Guadalupe. Thousands visit her home at Tepeyac each day and she keeps reappearing daily throughout the Americas in the spontaneous prayers and artistic expressions of the people. In her, the people experience acceptance, dignity, love and protection . . . they dare to affirm life even when all others deny them life. Since her apparition she has been the banner of Mexican and Mexican American movements of independence, reform and liberty.

Were it not for Our Lady of Guadalupe[5] there would be no Mexican or Mexican American people today. The great Mexican nations had been defeated by the Spanish invasion which came to a violent and bloody climax in 1521. The native peoples who had not been killed no longer wanted to live. Everything of value to them, including their gods, had been destroyed. Nothing was worth living for. With this colossal catastrophe, their entire past became irrelevant. New diseases exacerbated the trauma and collective death-wish of the people, and the native population decreased enormously.

It was in the brown Virgin of Guadalupe that Mexicanity was born and through her that the people have survived and developed. At the very moment when the pre-Colombian world had come to a drastic end, a totally unsuspected eruption took place in 1531 when, in the ancient site of the goddess Tonantzin, a dark-skinned woman appeared to announce a new era for "all the inhabitants of this land." Guadalupe provided the spark which allowed the people to arise out of the realm of death like the rising Phoenix arising out of the ashes of the past—not just a return to the past but the emergence of a spectacular newness (Ruffle, 1976:247–252). In sharp contrast to the total rupture with the past which was initiated by the conquest-evangelization enterprise, Guadalupe provided the necessary sense of continuity which is basic to human existence. Since the apparition took place at Tepeyac, the long venerated site of Tonantzin, mother of the Gods, it put people in direct contact with their ancient past and in communion with their own foundational mythology. It validated their ancestry while initiating them into something new. The missioners claimed their ancestors were wrong and that the diabolical past had to be totally eradicated. But the lady who introduced herself as the mother of the true God was now appearing among them and asking that a temple be built on this sacred site. She was one of them, she was clothed with the colors of divinity, but she definitely was not one of their goddesses. In her, there was continuity and newness, rootedness and breakthrough. Out of their own past and in close continuity with it, something truly new and sacred was now emerging.

Furthermore, she was giving meaning to the present moment in several ways for she was promising them love, defense and protection. At a time when the people had experienced the abandonment of their gods, the mother of the true God was now offering them her personal intervention. At a time when new racial and ethnic divisions were emerging, she was offering the basis of a new unity as the mother of all the inhabitants of the land. At a time when the natives were being instructed and told what to do by the Spaniards, she chose a low-class native to be her trusted messenger and to instruct the Spaniards through the person of the Bishop. In her, the conquered, oppressed and crushed begin to liberate and rehabilitate.

Finally, she initiated and proclaimed the new era which was now beginning. Over her womb is the Aztec glyph for the center of the universe. Thus she carries the force that will gradually build up a new civilization—not a simple restoration of the past nor simply New Spain, but the beginning of something new. The flowers, which she provided as a sign of authenticity, were for the indigenous world the sign which guaranteed them that the new life would truly flourish.

Thus in Guadalupe, the ancient beginnings connect with the present moment and signal what is yet to come! The broken pieces of their ancient numinous world are now reconfigured in a new way. Out of the chaos, a new world of ultimate meaning is now emerging. The Phoenix had truly come forth not just as a powerful new life, but also as the numinosum which would allow them to once again experience the awe and reverence of the sacred—not a sacred which was foreign and opposed to them, but one which ultimately legitimized them in their innermost being—both collectively as a people and individually as persons.

The complementary symbol of Guadalupe is the BAPTISM of infants. Our Lady of Guadalupe had sent the native Juan Diego to the Church. Many indigenous people thereafter sought baptism. They were no longer being uprooted from their ancient ways in order to enter into the Church. Sent by their mother, Guadalupe, they were entering as they were—with their customs, their rituals, their songs, their dances and their pilgrimages. The old Franciscan missioners feared this greatly. Many thought it was a devil's trick to subvert their missionary efforts. But the people kept on coming. They were truly building the new temple the Lady had requested: the living temple of Mexican-Christians. It is through baptism that every newborn Mexican and Mexican American enters personally into the temple requested by the Lady.

Through baptism the child becomes part of the continuum and is guaranteed life despite the social forces against life. The physical birth of the child is completed by the spiritual birth and both form an integral part of the biological life of the child. For our people, baptism of infants in not just a Catholic sacrament of initiation, but also a biological-anthropological event which binds the child and the community together in a profound and lasting blood-spiritual relationship.

Through baptism, the community claims the child as its very own and with pride presents it to the entire people—no matter how it was conceived or what might be the social status of the child. In the group, the child will receive great affirmation and tenderness. This will give the child a profound sense of existential security and belonging. Whether others want us around or not is of little consequence because we grow up knowing that we belong. The child will be able to affirm selfhood despite the put-downs and insults of society: Our children will dare to be who they are—and they will be who they are with a great sense of pride! This deep sense of security and belonging will further develop through participation in the multiple religious rituals of the people such as *posadas, rosarios, velorios, peregrinaciones,* and the *vía-crucis.*

For a people who have an historical memory and a contemporary situation of degradation, insults and rejection, baptism signifies that this child, regardless of what the world thinks of it, is of infinite dignity. It is the sacred rite of initiation into the community and the ancestors. Through it, not only are the newborn welcomed into the group, but the continuity of the group's life is assured ... the life of the ancestors will continue in the future generations because of our religious celebrations today.

As the apparitions of Our Lady of Guadalupe at Tepeyac were the beginning of an anthropological resurrection event for the native and *mestizo* peoples of Mexico, so is baptism, the individual entry into the life of these resurrected people. Through baptism a child not only becomes a child of God according to the Christian tradition, but equally a child of our common mother of the Americas, *Nuestra Señora de Guadalupe.*

Cenizas/Agua Bendita

There is no doubt that ashes on Ash Wednesday is one of the most popular rituals of the entire year for Mexicans and Mexican Americans. In my parish of San Fernando in San Antonio, we have a service of ashes every half hour averaging 1200 persons per half hour. By the end of the day, over 30,000 persons celebrate the rite of ashes in our church. The Church does not promote this day as a day of obligation, yet it is one of the most popular rituals of the entire Church year. Why?

For us, the earth is sacred. We come from the earth and in time we return to the earth. The earth, and especially the portion of the earth out of which we originate, is the very source of our life, subsistence and existence. In a survey I conducted a few years ago of Mexican Americans living in the Southwest, the most frequent response to the question "What would you like to leave your children?", was *"una tierrita."* Precisely because we are so bound to the earth, one of the deepest sources of our suffering as a people is that we have been deprived of our own land. Without even having migrated, we have been forced to live as aliens in the very lands of our ancestors. Only the languages, dress, foods, customs and religion of the foreigners who invaded these lands are considered true and legitimate while the ways of earlier inhabitants continue to be despised as pagan, savage and inferior. In our own land, we cannot be at home!

We are treated like squatters without rights to be moved as the powerful see fit. We are moved from one space to another without any regard for our families or cemeteries. Our natural resources are taken away from us and replaced with garbage and toxic wastes. Whatever the rest of society does not want around—jails, public housing, garbage dumps—is conveniently placed in our neighborhoods. What is life without connectedness to our own proper earth? POLVO!

On Ash Wednesday, as the people come up to receive the ashes, they hear the words: *"Polvo eres . . ."* The ashes at the beginning of Lent are a religious expression of the Mexican tradition which finds its full socio-religious meaning when coupled with the holy water which is blessed during the Easter Vigil—when through God's power, justice triumphed over injustice in the resurrection of the innocent victim from the death inflicted upon him by the unjust "justice" of this world. The one whom the world had rejected and killed, God raised and exalted as the Lord of all nations.

For people who have been forced to become foreigners in their own land, who have been driven from their properties and who have been pushed around by the powerful like the mighty wind blows the dust around, ashes are a powerful sign post on the pilgrimage of life. They mark the radical acceptance of the moment—like Jesus accepting the cross. This ritual reflects the burning of Cuatemoc's feet while he refused to give in to the demands of the Spaniards. He endured rather than giving in to the unjust demands of his captors in their lust for gold. But this acceptance does not indicate approval in any way whatsoever. It is the acceptance of an unjust situation without the acceptance of its disastrous consequences: the destruction of our people. The very fact that we are here in growing numbers and walking up to receive the ashes is an act of public and collective defiance of the destructive situation that has been forced upon us.

We will not be eliminated from this earth. We might be dust today, but dust settles down and becomes fertile earth when it receives moisture. The people come not only for ashes, throughout the year they also come for holy water to sprinkle upon themselves, their children, their homes . . . everything. They are aware that our entire world yearns and travails in pain awaiting to be redeemed—a redemption which in Christ has indeed begun but whose rehabilitating power is yet to take effect in the present day escalating injustices of our world. The use of the regenerative waters of baptism in every aspect of life is a constant plea for God to right the wrongs of our present society. If God is truly God, God must intervene. God cannot remain distant and passive in the light of the great misery and suffering of God's people. We know that God hears the cries of the poor and God will come to save us. God will redress this unjust situation which has been imposed upon us. God opened the sea to allow the Hebrew people to escape enslavement, God called the Crucified One to life from the tomb and this same God will convert us from aliens to children in our own land. The present situation will not last forever for the God of justice and mercy will bring about change.

The sprinkling with the waters of the Easter Vigil is a call for the regeneration of all creation. The dust which is sprinkled with the water will be turned into fertile earth and produce in great abundance. As in the reception of ashes, in the sprinkling of holy water there is an unquestioned affirmation: the ashes will again become earth, and the dust-people will once again inherit the earth. The dust-water binomial symbolizes the great suffering of an uprooted people who refuse to give in to despair but live in the unquestioned hope of the new life that is sure to come.

Crucifixion/Muertos

The final set of religious celebrations which express the core identity of the Mexican American people is the crucifixion which is celebrated on Good Friday, and the day of the dead celebrated on November 2. For a people who have consistently been subjected to injustice, cruelty and early death, the image of the Crucified One is the supreme symbol of life despite the multiple daily threats of death. If there was something good and redemptive in the unjust condemnation and crucifixion of the God-man, then, as senseless and useless as our suffering appears to be, there must be something of ultimate goodness and transcendent value in it. We don't understand it, but in Jesus the God-man who became the innocent victim who suffered for our salvation, we affirm it and in this very affirmation receive the power to endure it without it destroying us. Even if we are killed, we cannot be destroyed.

Jesus was assassinated but not eliminated. He is alive and his cross has become the source and symbol of the ultimate triumph of goodness over evil, courage over fear, love over self-righteousness. No wonder that in their faith-filled evangelical intuition, at the moment when the scourged and humiliated Jesus of Nazareth appears to be the most powerless, the people spontaneously acclaim him as *El Señor del Poder . . . El Señor de la Gloria. . . .* He had the incredible power to sustain the most cruel suffering for the sake of our salvation. This, in the minds of our people, is the ultimate power of God—the power to endure for the sake of those we love. The power to conquer might be glamorous and appealing, but only the power to endure for the sake of another is truly divine and life-giving. Animals conquer by force, God conquers by enduring love—enduring even unto death on the cross. The power to conquer diminishes with time and remains only in the dust of unread history books, while the power to endure lives on in those who follow in the way of Jesus. Today, the crucified Jesus still lives, but the conquering Caesars and armies have long been dead, buried and hardly remembered. The Crucified One is alive, but the executioners are all dead and gone.

In the presence of *el Señor del Gran Poder*, we see and celebrate our own inner strength which has allowed us to endure for the sake of our families and our people. What others ridicule as weakness, we see as the divine power alive in us. We are not a fatalistic people who enjoy suffering, but a powerful people who will not allow suffering to destroy our lives or even our joy of living. The radical acceptance of the cross of life is the basis for our festive music, dances and fiestas. We do not celebrate because we suffer; we celebrate because we refuse to allow suffering to control or destroy our lives.

People who only know us from the outside claim that we are so fascinated with suffering and death that we ignore joy and resurrection. Nothing could be further from the truth. Such people see us but they do not know us. Our people accept openly the harshness of suffering and death because we participate already in the beginning of resurrection. We celebrate our collective resurrection on the early morning of December 12 at our sunrise service to our Lady of Guadalupe, and we celebrate resurrection every time we use the *agua bendita* in reaffirming God's power over sickness and death. But at no time do we celebrate the communion of living saints more than on *el día de los muertos* which in effect is the day of the living—the day of those who have defied death and are more alive than ever!

We know the secret mystery of life. Those whom the world takes for dead, we know beyond a doubt are alive not only in God—and God is the fullness of life—but in us who remember them. Because they are no longer limited or imprisoned by "this body", they are now more alive than ever. The final, absolute, definitive death beyond which there is no earthly life left is when there is no one around to remember me or celebrate my life. Thus in remembering—*recordando*—we keep alive our ancestors as much as they keep us alive and continue to guard over us. The pain which we experience when someone we know and love dies is transformed into an inner joy at the annual celebration of those who through death have entered ultimate life. Our memory of their lives becomes a source of life and energy. As we bring them flowers, build altars of remembrance, light candles, share in the common bread and punch of the dead, we enter into the ultimate fiesta. In the mystical moment of celebrating *el día de los muertos,* the veil of time and space is removed and we are all together on earth and in heaven, in time and in eternity singing the same songs, enjoying the same food and drink and sharing in the same life that no earthly power can take away from us.

It should be noted that our *día de los muertos* is the very opposite of Halloween. Our "dead" do not come to spook us, but to visit, comfort and party with us. We do not fear them. We welcome their presence and look forward to having a good time with them. Sometimes we even take music to the cemeteries and share with them their favorite songs. We celebrate together that death does not have the final word over life and that life ultimately triumphs over death. Our family and our *pueblo* is so strong and enduring that not even death can break it apart. Thus what is celebrated as the day of the dead is in effect the celebration of indestructive life—a life which not even death can destroy. Society might take our lands away, marginate us and even kill us, but it cannot destroy us. For we live on in the generations to come and in them the previous generations continue to be alive.

Conclusion

The conquest of ancient Mexico by Spain in 1521 and then the conquest of northwest Mexico by the United States in the 1830s and 1840s forced the native population and their succeeding generations into a split and meaningless existence. It was a mortal collective catastrophe of gigantic death-bearing consequences. Yet the people have survived as a people through the emergence of new religious symbols and the reinterpretation of old ones which have connected the past with the present and projected into the future. The core religious expressions as celebrated and transmitted by the people are the unifying symbols in which the opposing forces of life are brought together into a harmonious tension. This gives the people who participate in them the experience of wholeness. In them and through them, opposites are brought together and pushed towards a resolution and the people who celebrate them experience an overcoming of the split. Where formerly there was opposition, now there is reconciliation and even greater yet, synthesis. This is precisely what gives joy and meaning to life, indeed makes life possible in any meaningful sense, regardless of the situation. It is in the celebration of these festivals of being and memory that the people live on as a people.

I have limited my observations and attempts at interpretation to my own personal Mexican American experience, not because I am not uninterested in all Hispanics, but precisely because I do not dare the arrogance to speak for the others. I have not lived their experience and even though I respect their religious symbols and practices deeply, they are not my own. I am convinced that you can only understand religious symbols correctly from within and not by mere observation—even the best and most critical—from the outside. In seeking to understand religious symbols correctly, the so-called "objective distance" of western scholars is a sure guarantee of falsification and objective error, especially if their research is not done in dialogue with the believers themselves. Only by a patient and prolonged listening to the believers can one begin to understand the real meaning of their practices and rituals. They cannot be judged by criteria of another cosmovision or world-view.

I very much admire what Richard Flores is doing with the *pastorelas* and how he has gone through the process of becoming a *pastorcito* himself, has personally taken part in all the aspects of the process and is gradually beginning to understand them from within. I very much appreciate what Ana María Díaz-Stevens is doing to study the religious thought of Puerto Rican women. Her insights have opened up a whole new field of reflection for me. All of a sudden *las cocineras* were not just the women in the kitchens, but the creative thinkers who were cooking-up new and profound theological thought. We need Hispanic theologians and social scientists who will reflect from within the common experience of our people's faith, not as outsiders but as believers who are seeking to understand, clarify and enrich that life of faith.

I am anxiously awaiting and looking forward for the other Hispanic groups in the United States to speak and write more extensively about the religious expressions of their cultures. To the degree that this takes place, we will be able to begin a fruitful dialogue among ourselves. I long to see deeper studies on the Cuban American devotion to *Nuestra Señora de Caridad del Cobre* and their Afro-Cuban sense of santeria, on the Puerto Rican devotion to *San Juan Bautista* and other religious practices, on the *Cristo Negro de Esquipulas* of Guatemala and other devotions and rituals of the various Hispanic peoples living in the United States. I trust that PARAL will be able to continue encouraging this type of socio-theological reflection and dialogue among the various groups—each from within its own lived experience of inculturated faith with its corresponding religious symbols. These religious symbols and rituals are the keys that will unlock the secret to the deepest and most far-reaching elements of our people's cosmovision and thus provide the ultimate basis for our earthly identity.

NOTES

1. I do not intend to indicate that women should stay in the kitchens, but to bring out a very important aspect of life which has not been properly recognized. It was Ana María Díaz-Stevens during the PARAL symposium who first made me aware of how much more had come out of the kitchens than mere food. They had been the most exciting place where new life in all its aspects had truly blossomed and developed.

2. Orlando Espín has some fine articles on the relation between popular expressions of the faith and the Roman Catholic tradition. In particular, see his "Tradition and Popular Religion: An Understanding of the *Sensus Fidelium*," in *Frontiers of Hispanic Theology in the United States*, ed. Allan Figueroa-Deck (Maryknoll, New York: Orbis, 1992), 62–87; a classical work on this subject is J. M. R. Tillard, et al., *Foi Populaire Foi Savante*, Paris: Editions du Cerf, 1976.

3. For more in-depth studies on Our Lady of Guadalupe I recommend my own book: *La Morenita: Evangelizer of the Americas* (San Antonio Mexican American Cultural Center Press, 1980) and subsequent articles on this subject in *Concilium*. See also Jeanette Rodriguez's 1994 book.

4. For a fuller discussion of other religious symbols, consult my previous works: *Christianity and Culture* (San Antonio: Mexican American Cultural Center Press, 1975); *Galilean Journey: The Mexican American Promise,* (Maryknoll, New York: Orbis, 1983).

5. For other aspects of Guadalupe, consult my previous articles in *Concilium* number 102/1977 and number 188/198.

BIBLIOGRAPHY

Acuña, Rodolfo. 1972. *Occupied America: A History of Chicanos.* San Francisco: Canfield Press.

Aragon, Jean-Louis. 1976. "Le 'Sensus Fidelium' et ses fondaments neotestamentiares," in Tillard, *Foi Populaire.*

Elizondo, Virgilio. 1975. *Christianity and Culture.* San Antonio: Mexican American Cultural Center Press.

———. 1980. *La Morenita: Evangelizer of the Americas.* San Antonio Mexican American Cultural Center Press.

———. 1983. *Galilean Journey: The Mexican American Promise.* Maryknoll, New York: Orbis.

Espín, Orlando. 1992. "Tradition and Popular Religion: An Understanding of the *Sensus Fidelium,*" in *Frontiers of Hispanic Theology in the United States,* ed. Allan Figueroa-Deck. Maryknoll, New York: Orbis.

Jiménez, Roberto. 1985. "Social Changes/Emotional Health", *Medical Gazette of South Texas* VII, 20 June.

Rodríguez, Jeanette. 1994. *Faith and Empowerment Among Mexican American Women.* Austin: The University of Texas Press.

Ruffle, J. 1976. *De La Biologie a la Culture.* Paris: Flammarion.

Tillard, J. M. R. et al. 1976. *Foi Populaire, Foi Savante.* Paris: Edition du Cerf.

4

Thought, Speech, Action: Rhythms of Jewish Life

Tamar Frankiel

An American religious historian with expertise in the study of revivalism and ritual in general, Tamar Frankiel here turns her attention to ritual in the traditional Judaism that shapes her own way of life. By the end of the nineteenth century, three forms of Judaism were present in the United States. Traditional Judaism had been joined, by mid-century, by Reform Judaism from Germany. Later Conservative Judaism would occupy a middle position between traditional practice and the liberal Reform orientation. And as tradition itself became more self-conscious, a deliberate Orthodox Judaism emerged. Throughout the twentieth century, this Orthodoxy, enriched by new immigration from abroad and especially the presence of Hasidic groups, has preserved its legacy of distinct gender roles in religion, with men clearly in their domain in the synagogue and women in theirs in the household. How does a late-twentieth-century American Jewish woman with a professional background and a sophisticated grasp of the feminist agenda bring together her embrace of both tradition and modernity? How does she get the two worlds to interface, to be reconciled to one another? These are the questions that Frankiel answers in her own way in her book *The Voice of Sarah,* from which this reading is taken. She is careful therein to invoke "feminine spirituality," which she reads as richly present in Jewish tradition, and not "femin*ist* spirituality," the late-twentieth-century construction that she eschews. By looking at Jewish tradition in its ritual embodiment from her consciously feminine perspective, Frankiel opens a window into the tradition in its entirety, helping readers to gain a glimpse of the power of the spirituality that traditional Jews uphold.

She turned to call the mists. . . .
She drew a deep breath,
charging herself for the magical act,
knowing she must concentrate all her strength. . . .
Up went her arms into the arch of the sky;

down, with the mists following
the sweep of her trailing sleeves.
*Mist and silence hung dark around them.**
Avalon.

She touched the flame to each light, one by one,
closed her eyes,
focusing inwardly,
gathering her loved ones with her. . . .
She drew a deep breath,
concentrating all her strength. . . .
Raised her hands gently, powerfully,
three circles
bringing the light toward her,
that distant light, essence of light,
hidden since the dawn of time,
its softness suddenly filled her home.
Shabbat.

Rituals have fascinated anthropologists, psychologists, and students of religion for decades. Many explanations have been proposed of their power and endurance. Less than a century ago, many thought that rituals were obsolete in the face of science. Yet today rites and ceremonies are enjoying a renaissance. Rituals of rebirth in psychotherapy, rituals of magic in new cults, rituals of prayer for people who had long ago given up belief in God—these and more one can find among people of any social group or class. In Judaism too individuals who otherwise are alienated from traditional religion find pleasure and satisfaction in attending some kind of Shabbat or holiday celebration; people who will not attend a synagogue form their own informal groups to celebrate the rituals.

The specialness of ritual is twofold: first, it is not mere thought or speech but a concrete, usually tangible, reality that is taken up and consciously transformed in a dramatic context. Lighting Shabbat candles or a Chanukkah menorah is not like other candlelighting. A sukkah is an inhabitable space that is also a fantasy house. In ritual, things of this world are made to be like things from another world, another time and space. Yet at the same time one often feels more attuned to the present when participating in a ritual than in one's normal course of life.

Second, rituals often are connected to a different state of consciousness in those who perform them. Some of this consciousness is created by the person's intention: I intend that my prayer should open my heart to God. Often, in addition, there are specific physical and mental acts that create an unusual state of mind and body: fasting, intense activity, group participation, music, dancing, repetition of movements or words, meditation. The changes are subtle and often untraceable. They work, however, in breaking down the hypnotic force of everyday consciousness and allowing, hopefully, some deeper perception or some more intense energy to break through.

The reason most scholarly explanations of ritual have not been satisfactory is that those explaining do not usually believe that the transformation experienced in ritual is real. The world created, the drama performed, is to the observer simply an aesthetic object. But to the person inside the ritual, whose consciousness is being changed in the very same acts that create the drama, the reality is unquestionable. Acts, thoughts, emotions become possible that were not possible before. It may look like psychological sleight of hand, but no: something from another "world," another level, has indeed slipped in, been allowed into our ordinary world. Once this is experienced, nothing can quite be the same again.

I quoted the passage from *The Mists of Avalon* to suggest that we, like the female heroines of that story, can be vessels—priestesses, so to speak—of these transformations.... Women often steer away from activities that separate them from concrete experience, that are merely abstract. We prefer to stay close to people and things, knowing the details, being involved rather than being observers or manipulators from outside. For this reason ritual is often more congenial than abstract study of spiritual matters. In addition, we saw that women can lose or loosen their ego boundaries to be open to processes that come from other levels of consciousness, other levels of reality. Our receptivity is great, and we are easily affected by practices that shift our consciousness. (This may be the reason that the sages held that women are more spiritual than men, more easily focused inward, and less in need of specific techniques to train their spirituality.)

As women, then, we are in a privileged position in opening the channels of the world to the divine flow. At the beginning we may not see what is the direct benefit to the world of all the rituals we can perform. It is tempting to push aside davening and run to a political action meeting or sign up for a Saturday class on economic theories that will end poverty. These may be valuable actions, but we must learn to think twice before we relegate ritual practice to second priority. What happens through our Jewish practice is nothing less than a realignment of the world, preparing the world to accept goodness and truth that have never before been revealed. Women are spiritual midwives in rebirthing the world. Just how is a mystery; but this too is revealed to us, piece by piece, as we do the work itself.

To everything there is a season.
In the play of love and mourning,

laughter and solemnity,
God hides and reappears,
and so do we.

The life in which we sanctify the world revolves around what in Judaism are called the *mitzvot,* usually translated "commandments." Many of these have to do with rituals, the ceremonial acts by which we consecrate our time, our space, our relationships, our passages through life. The details of the mitzvot, how to do them and whatever explanations may be attached to them, are the subject of much discussion in Torah and rabbinic literature. Yet there is an important dimension of living the *mitzvot* that one does not always encounter on first meeting, namely, what is called the *kavannah,* the "intention" that accompanies the act. Kavannah or intention is, as Rabbi Adin Steinsaltz puts it, the "subjective meaning to the *mitzvah* in the mind of the doer at the moment when he carries it out."[1] This aspect of the work of ritual (or other kinds of mitzvot) is significant because the intention, the thought and general orientation we bring to the mitzvah, can greatly enhance our awareness of God and of our purpose in life, and can affect the quality of the act itself.

Rabbi Steinsaltz points out that there are different kinds of kavannot. First, we perform a mitzvah with the awareness that we are doing just that: doing what God asks of us, with a desire to connect to God. In addition, there are various kinds of "mystical and symbolic" kavannot that, he says, "are essentially forms of communion with the Divine, but are active and affective rather than intellectual or abstract. The meditation [on these] lends the performance of the *mitzvah,* the outward physical act, a depth and warmth of feeling and a spiritual exaltation."[2] As workers in a holy sanctuary, we want to bring such warmth into our lives, not simply perform rote actions. This is how our conscious minds can bring us in touch with the deeper, unconscious significance encoded in the rituals.

When we seek to develop this kind of consciousness in ways that also will connect us with our femininity, we find that Jewish tradition offers great delights. The very fabric of Jewish life, established by the rhythms of seasons and festivals, is richly interwoven with feminine themes. A friend and early teacher once remarked to me, "Judaism is a feminine religion with a patriarchal veneer." Nowhere is this more true than in the round of seasonal rituals. Indeed, one of the most direct ways of deepening our understanding of Jewish life is to look at Shabbat and the holidays and how they incorporate what we might call the feminine principle.

Rituals that have to do with time are one of the most fascinating and mysterious of mitzvot. When we perform, with kavannah, a ritual that inaugurates a festive day, we have the possibility of entering into new dimensions of time. Each time, each season, each year, each period of history has its own quality of energy, its own distinctive subtle traits. As we incorporate even a little of the kavannah associated with the day or season, the effect is twofold: our experience changes, and we become channels for that energy to affect our part of the world. We learn, for example, that God created a special quality of rest, *menuchah,* which is revealed on every seventh day; when we observe Shabbat, we can experience that quality of being.

The same is true of the Yomim Tovim, the holidays—as we read in the prayers, "times for rejoicing, holidays and seasons for happiness." Many of the Jewish holidays partake of two kinds of energy: that of the season of the year where they fall—spring, fall harvest, and so on—and that of the events of Jewish history and tradition they commemmorate. There is an energy associated with spring, and at Pesach that quality is interwoven with the qualities of God that were revealed to the Jewish people during the Exodus from Egypt. (Indeed, all the holidays as well as Shabbat have some taste of the Exodus, in addition to whatever other qualities they have. We say in every kiddush before the celebratory evening meal that it is "in memory of the going out from Egypt.") Shavuot is a harvest holiday, and also the time of the giving of the Torah; and so on through the year. With this in mind, we can follow the days of celebration around the calendar and explore their various dimensions.

The center of Jewish life is, of course, Shabbat. We count our days from Shabbat and to Shabbat and organize our lives around it. An acquaintance once remarked, "Some of these other groups seem so much better organized than we are. But I finally recognized that they have much more time to spend on meetings, telephone, and the rest because their main purpose is political organization. Our main purpose is Shabbat and the holidays—we have to stretch to have time for anything else!" She spoke a great truth: as Jews, we must do in six days what others do in seven; in addition, we spend time doing special things to prepare ourselves for Shabbat.

If one prepares for it and sets the day aside as holy, the blessings of Shabbat pour out in remarkable ways. At the same time, the more complete the preparation, the more one's consciousness changes, and the more receptive one can be. Shabbat is a day of being, not becoming, so we need to put away all those bits of life that involve creating, finishing, planning, in order to have a mind free of past and future. For six days we are active co-creators of the world with God; on the seventh, we enter with God into a receptive frame. And, although God is always masculine and feminine and beyond either of these, we experience God on Shabbat as the feminine, the Queen.[3]

The queen, the *kalla* or bride, enters the home and the synagogue on Friday night, to the sweet and joyous melodies of "L'cha Dodi": "Come, my beloved, to greet the bride, to welcome the face of Shabbat!" The whole Jewish people are urged to rise up, shake off the dust of worry and discontent, and join in rejoicing; for when the Shabbat Queen arrives, we glimpse the promise of messianic times. The legends tell us that a male prophet, Elijah, will announce the coming of a male king, the Mashiach (Messiah), a descendant of David. But the spirit of the times will be like the spirit of Shabbat in its freshness: the joyous feminine represented by the bride.

We read at the Shabbat table—sometimes it is read (or sung) only by the head of the household, sometimes by men, sometimes by all—the famous "woman of valor" passage from the end of the book of Proverbs. It is often taken as a tribute to the woman of the house; but it is also a proclamation of the feminine as Israel itself, the Jewish people with their collective feminine soul, the Shekhinah. The passage invokes many feminine themes:

> *Who can find a woman of excellence?*
> *Her value is far greater than gems.*
> *. . .*
> *Like the merchant ships she brings food from afar.*
> *She rises while it is night,*
> *gives food to her household*
> *and sets out the tasks for her maids.*
> *She considers a field and buys it;*
> *From her earnings she plants a vineyard.*
> *. . . Her lamp does not go out at night.*
> *She holds out her hands to the poor,*
> *and extends her hands to the destitute . . .*
> *She makes her own tapestries;*
> *her garments are of fine linen and purple . . .*
> *Strength and dignity are her garb;*
> *she looks smilingly to the future.*
> *She opens her mouth with wisdom,*
> *and the teaching of kindness is on her tongue.*
> *She watches the conduct of her household*
> *and does not eat the bread of idleness.*
> *Her children rise and acclaim her;*
> *her husband also, and praises her:*
> *Many daughters have done worthily,*
> *but you surpass them all.*
> *Charm is deceptive, beauty is vain—*
> *the Godfearing woman is to be praised.*
> *Give her praise for her accomplishments,*
> *and let her deeds laud her at the gates.*

The woman is praised for her part in the continuing work of creation: providing, planting, caring and nurturing, compassion, and providing for the future.

Deeply involved in the daily life of family, community, and world, she creates bounty and plenitude. Always active, weaving and moving, in a vigorous beauty that comes from inner strength, she also speaks and teaches wisdom to those around her.[4]

Each Shabbat evening we remind ourselves that these forces are what sustain us, have sustained us throughout the week of activity, and now join together in a special quality of rest. In the Shabbat davening according to the Nusach Ari, which includes some of the mystical kavannot of the great Isaac Luria, we say that She, the Shekhinah, the divine force manifest in this world, "unites below into the mystery of oneness." "Her countenance is irradiated with the holy supernal light, and she crowns herself here below with the holy people, all of whom are crowned with new souls."[5] This is the "Shabbat Queen," the divine and deeply feminine forces of the world for whom we, the Jewish people, are the crown. In the Shabbat evening service we pray that "all Israel who sanctify Your name will rest on her [vah]"; and we call the evening meal "the meal of the holy *Chakal Tapuchin*," a feminine divine manifestation, and the masculine forces "come to join her in the meal."[6] Thus, the sense of the feminine, queenly presence continues throughout Shabbat evening.

Although all of Shabbat is considered feminine, it is noteworthy that the prayer in the Amidah referred to above changes as the day progresses. The next morning, in the Shacharit and Musaf services, we pray "may all Israel who sanctify your name rest on him [vo]," while at Mincha we ask that God grant us holy Shabbat days, and "may all Israel who sanctify your Name rest on them [vam]." The second and third meals are offered by the masculine forces, and "she" comes to join them. We have a hint here of a shift of energy, to the masculine in the morning and the union of the two in the afternoon as Shabbat comes to a harmonious close. This dynamic is crucial to a sense of the rhythm of Jewish life, and we will see it again in the cycle of the holiday seasons discussed below.

Shabbat represents the feminine in powerful form, the Shekhinah manifest in her unity. The whole concept of the Shekhinah, the divine Presence in the world, has become very important in Jewish mysticism.[7] It suggests that insofar as we know God's presence in the world—in the forces of nature, in the ordinary course of our own lives—we know it as feminine. The Shekhinah was manifest in the clouds of glory covering the Israelites traveling in the desert; she was the radiance experienced in the Holy Temple in Jerusalem. After the destruction of the Temple and the exile of the Jewish people, the Shekhinah went into exile as well. Fragmented and scattered, she is difficult to perceive; but she is with us, like Rachel yearning and weeping, even in our alienated state. When we reunify the Jewish people, we will once more be able to experience, clearly and powerfully, the Shekhinah in our daily life. In the meantime, we can still experience the powerful impact of her unity on Shabbat. And Shabbat is the direct feminine connection with God.

Another of the strongly feminine holidays is Rosh Chodesh, or the New Moon, which is celebrated one or two days each month. This ancient holy day, on which it was customary to go and hear the teaching of Torah, is considered a holiday special to women. This should not surprise us: in many cultures the moon has often been associated with women, its changing phases analogous to our monthly menstrual cycles. Its diffuse, mysterious light, its harmony with the darkness, and its changes archetypally represent the feminine in the symbolism of the psyche.

In Jewish tradition the midrash tells us that the day was given over to women as a reward for their devotion to God in the episode of the golden calf. According to the story, after Moses had disappeared on Mount Sinai for forty days, the "mixed multitude" who had come out of Egypt with the Hebrew slaves demanded a figure of a god so that they could worship the god who had brought them out of Egypt. The Jewish men, of all the tribes except Moses' own tribe Levi, supported their request and gave over all the gold they had brought out of Egypt to Moses' brother Aaron, the high priest, to be melted down and made into a golden calf. The women refused. They knew that although Moses was gone, his "light" was hidden only temporarily, like the moon in its dark phase. Soon he would return and lead them onward. As a reward for their faith and loyalty, they were given a special holiday, Rosh Chodesh.

The custom has been for women to treat Rosh Chodesh as a kind of half holiday: we do not refrain from all work, but avoid hard labor—classically, doing laundry (which certainly used to be backbreaking) and other difficult chores. Many women have the custom of dressing up for the holiday or preparing some kind of special dish for the evening meal. Women's groups often set aside a Rosh Chodesh evening for a special gathering—to learn together, hear a guest speaker, or sing and dance.

Rosh Chodesh is observed by men too via changes in the Shemoneh Esreh prayers and grace after meals, the singing of half-Hallel, and a special reading from the Torah scroll. Most of all, however, Rosh Chodesh guides the whole Jewish year: we operate on a primarily lunar calendar. This calendar is adjusted to fit the solar cycle by adding a thirteenth lunar month every second or third year, so that the holidays keep their approximate place in the solar seasons (Pesach staying in the spring, Sukkot in the fall, etc.). But the whole structure of the year has a lunar—which is to say a feminine—foundation. We might say that God honored the feminine dimension of the created universe by giving the moon the rulership of our structure of time.

The command to proclaim the appearance of the New Moon was the first command given to the Jewish people in Egypt. They were to announce the New Moon of Nisan, and henceforth that month would be the first of the months. From that day they would be able to count to the tenth, when each family was to take out a lamb from the flock, and the fourteenth, when they were to sacrifice the lamb and eat it—the first Passover meal. The New Moon of Nisan thus inaugurates the counting of months, beginning with the month of the great redemption. Although we also have a new year celebration six months later, we can best see the feminine elements in the structure of the year by starting from Nisan: from this lunar month begins a special cycle of the human-divine relationship.

One of the most important kavannot through which Jewish mystics have grasped Jewish life is to see it as a series of moments in the relationship between God and Israel, on the model of a bride and groom. We have seen already, in discussing Shabbat, that the feminine expression is followed by the masculine, then the union of the two. In the larger scheme, the bride is Israel on the human side; the groom is God, the divine.[8] Their courtship begins in the month of Nisan, when God takes his beloved out from slavery, where her beauty had been hidden from the world. In celebration of this aspect of the Exodus, we sing at Pesach the *Shir HaShirim,* the Song of Songs, as the biblical book that accompanies the holiday. This beautiful love poem speaks of the love between a man and woman, their desire for each other, their separation and union—a moving accompaniment to the betrothal, the first pledge of love, between Israel and God. The images of woman in the book are powerful as well; as Arthur Waskow has noted, the song celebrates "a mode of spirituality that flows from the life-experience of women."[9]

Women are quite prominent in the midrashic stories about Pesach. Tradition tells us that God performed the redemption from Egypt because of the merit of the Jewish women. Their honorable actions proved to him that the people deserved to be redeemed. The chief Hebrew midwives, known in the Bible as Shifrah and Puah (the midrash says that their Hebrew names were Yochoved and Miriam, Moses' mother and sister), refused to assist Pharaoh in his wicked plan to kill all the newborn babies. The Torah reports that they told him, "The Hebrew women are not like the Egyptian women; when they go into labor, they give birth before the midwife can get to them" (Exod. 1:19). Thus they were unable to kill the baby boys immediately as he had commanded. The midrash adds that they hid babies in special caves and other places, and the infants were miraculously fed.

A wonderful story is told about Miriam, Moses' sister, before Moses was born. Her father, Amram, had become very downhearted about the situation of the Jewish slaves. In despair he declared that he would bring no more babies into this world and divorced Yochoved. Miriam went to him and said, "You are worse than Pharaoh! The king is trying to kill only the boys—you want to do away with the girls too!" He recognized the truth of what she was saying and decided to remarry Yochoved. Soon after, Moses was born, who was destined to lead the people to freedom.

Part of the "affliction" of the hard labor in Egypt was its disruption of family life, in particular, relations between husband and wife. But, the midrash says, the women overcame that by stealing quietly out to the fields where the men slept not only to bring them food, but also dressed in their finest clothes and made up to be attractive to them, so that, despite the men's exhaustion, their relations would continue. They polished pieces of copper into mirrors so that they could make themselves attractive. For this God later rewarded them when the Mishkan was built, by having these mirrors made into the washing vessel for the priests. Moses objected to this plan, seeing the mirrors as simply utensils of vanity. But God insisted: these mirrors were used with holy intent, for the very survival of the Jewish people. . . . Part of woman's power is her sexuality, here used also to help save Jewish lives.

These midrashic embellishments to the story of the Exodus emphasize how potent is the motif of the union of man and woman in Jewish tradition. Egypt, which is often taken as a symbol of descent into materialism and hedonism— the "fleshpots" of Egypt, the rich delicacies available there—distracted the Hebrew slaves from what was most holy, the relation of husband and wife. We might say that in Egypt the Jewish women corrected Eve's sin of eating the forbidden fruit: ignoring the temptations of Egypt's rich cuisine, they focused on building families.

In this light too it is clear how the metaphor of male-female union became a mode of understanding the redemption itself: a new relationship between the people and God was formed, the relationship not of father to son ("Jacob is my firstborn son") but of lover to beloved. The midrash reflects the people's experience of the importance of the male-female bond in the family. Thus, from the parent-child stage of the Abrahamitic period, the Jewish people moved to a mature relationship, that of wife to husband.

The next major holiday, Shavuot, becomes another stage in the relationship: the written marriage contract, or ketubah, symbolized in the tablets containing the Ten Commandments given to the Jews on Mount Sinai. The Torah is the binding document, the legal aspect of the relationship. Here the feminine side is rather subdued, as in Jewish legal practice itself: the man gives the ketubah as his promise to the woman, for her security and protection. But in the giving of the Torah at Sinai, the midrash stresses that the women were very significant recipients. The Torah states that Moses was told to "speak to the households of Jacob, and say to the children of Israel." The "households," says the midrash, were the women; the "b'nei Yisroel" the men. The Torah was given first to women, because God knew they had to be the primary guardians of the agreement. Moreover, the difference in the command, "speak" rather than "say," means that God told Moses to use a soft tone and kind voice—for this is how a man should speak to a woman. To the men he should be stricter and more commanding.

We have already mentioned another principal feminine aspect of Shavuot: the book read to accompany the holiday is the book of Ruth. We saw that Ruth, while modest, was a bold and decisive woman, willing to take risks to create the kind of life she believed in. In the context of Shavuot, Ruth represents the total dedication with which a Jew approaches the marriage contract with God. "Where you go, I will go, . . . your people will be my people, and your God, my God." The unquestioning devotion she offered to Naomi, her mother-in-law, is the model here—a woman binding herself to a kind of mother and spiritual guide. The gentleness between them, the sense of respect from younger to older, concern from older to younger, and their absolute mutual support—each doing her part according to her ability—compose a delicate picture of the relation of the Jewish people to God. For, at the time of Shavuot, every Jew dedicates herself again to Torah, becomes in effect a convert, like Ruth, like the whole Jewish people at Sinai thirty-three hundred years ago. The book of Ruth softens the hierarchical, masculine feeling of the giving of commandments or writing of a legal contract, offering us a genuinely feminine perspective on marriage bonds, which are the model for human beings' relationship to God. It is not the relationship between Ruth and Boaz that is the model here, but Ruth's devotion to Naomi. As women bond to each other, so we enter into our marriage commitment to God.

Thus a partnership is established at Shavuot between God and the Jewish people. But before the marriage can be consummated, as it were, trouble appears on the horizon: the wife is unfaithful. The incident is that of the golden calf, described above. Although the women did not support the worshiping of the calf, the Jewish people, as the "woman" betrothed to God, turned aside from their true love to follow an idolatrous temptation. This act of infidelity took place in the month of Tammuz. The next unhappy event, according to tradition, was on the ninth of Av a year later: the spies who had been sent to Canaan brought back a mixed report, and the people, frightened of the difficult wars they might have to fight, backed off from the plan to cross over into the promised land. Subsequently this was the date on which both the First and Second Temple were destroyed and, among other things, the date of the expulsion of the Jews from Spain. Midsummer became a time of tragedy, sadness, heartbreak. We can see here a subtle change in the energies of the universe, in the heat of high summer symbolized by broken relationships, wars, separation, violation of what is holy.[10] Nature reflects that shift, but what we see in nature mirrors spiritual reality on a higher plane. Thus today, because of many tragic events of the season recorded in tradition and history, Jews are warned to be cautious and circumspect during the "three weeks" from the seventeenth of Tammuz to the ninth of Av.

Av is followed by Elul, when Moses ascended the mountain again, begging forgiveness from God on behalf of the Jewish people. God is especially close during this time: the king, according to the mystical teachings, is walking in the field among his people, and we can approach him like a friend. We are preparing our *tshuvah,* our return to God, our return to our deepest selves, which will culminate in Rosh Hashanah. The Hebrew letters for Elul—*aleph, lamed, vav, lamed,* are an acronym for a verse from the Song of Songs: *ani l'dodi v'dodi li*—"I am my beloved's, and my beloved is mine"—again echoing the theme that nearness to God is like the closeness of two lovers.

Rosh Hashanah is known by several names besides the day of the "new year." One is Yom Hazikaron, the day of remembering. On the first day of Rosh Hashanah, we read in the synagogue two passages about God's remembering, and in both cases they are about women. "And God remembered Sarah," and gave her a son, Isaac; and in the Haftarah, "God remembered Channah," answering her prayers by giving her a child, Shmuel the prophet. Many other remembrances are mentioned on Rosh Hashanah, but it is very much to the point that the theme is told first of all in the stories of two women. Originally, Sarah had accepted her childlessness and had given her maid Hagar to Abraham as a concubine. But this had caused trouble in the household, and Hagar was sent away. An angel told her to return and promised her that her son would be the ancestor of a great nation; but at this point God also promised Abraham that Sarah would become pregnant. The entire episode communicates God's continual caring and watching over the events on earth. More particularly, it was in response to Sarah's distress over her changed relationship with Hagar that the promise came to her.

We have not yet met Channah, but, as we will see . . . , her heartfelt prayer also expressed her great distress. Her situation was much like Rachel's: she was greatly loved by her husband, Elkanah, but she was childless. Her co-wife, Pnina, continually reminded her of her troubles. She promised that if she could have a son, she would dedicate him to God as a *nazir* and bring him to the temple to learn with the priests. God remembered Channah, giving her Shmuel, who was to be one of the great judges and prophets of Jewish history, leading the Jewish people himself and then establishing the kingship of Saul and then David.

There are many other times that God is said to have "remembered" the Jewish people or specific individuals. It is not, of course, as if God could literally "forget." Rather, the time of remembering is the time of a shift in destiny. The significance of the examples of the two women is that this came about from a renewed commitment on their part: Sarah had expressed her commitment by offering Hagar to Abraham so that he could have a child, Channah by vowing to give her child to be raised by the Temple priests. God's response was to alter their destiny entirely. In this context it is no accident that in the Haftarah reading for the second day, from the prophet Jeremiah, another woman is mentioned: Rachel, weeping for her children. The promise is that as we renew our commitment, God will fulfill her hopes and prayers, returning us to our land and the life that we yearn for. In a number of ways, then, it is women who signal the renewal of life and hope and the potential shift in our lives that comes with each new year.

Other aspects of Rosh Hashanah should be mentioned briefly here, although they are not particularly feminine. The day is also Yom HaTruah, the day of the sounding of the shofar—an experience powerful and beloved to the people for centuries. The shofar recalls the giving of the Torah, when trumpet sounds were heard on Mount Sinai, and, made from a ram's horn, it recalls Abraham and Isaac. Thus it echoes deep in Jewish history. In the psyche it is like an implement of a shaman, an instrument from the animal world that augurs power and strength, calling us back to our inner depths. The mitzvah of hearing the shofar was not originally obligatory for women, but, because women have universally taken it on, it is now considered a mitzvah for us as well as for men. At the same time, Rosh Hashanah expresses *Malkhut,* "kingship," which is also equivalent to the Shekhinah, the feminine aspect of God. In accepting God as our king, we the Jewish people express our consent to God as ruler of the universe. We acknowledge that the creative energy that transcends the universe, from which everything came, is connected to the depths within ourselves, the inner power that cannot be expressed in words.

Rosh Hashanah also inaugurates the ten Days of Awe, the intense time of introspection and self-evaluation that we call *tshuvah,* returning to God. The culmination is, of course, Yom Kippur. The midrash tells us that it was on Yom Kippur that Moses returned from Mount Sinai with the second set of tablets, announcing God's complete forgiveness. The relationship between God and the Jewish people was restored to its original purity. Thus Yom Kippur, despite its solemn prayers, is also a day of great joy. In an earlier period, the day after Yom Kippur was a great festive day on which the women danced in their fine garments, and many matches were made. Mystically speaking, the "marriage" between God and the Jewish people is reaffirmed, with a rewritten "contract," and then consummated a few days later at Sukkot—which, like Pesach, when the courtship began, falls on a full moon.

The sukkah is a kind of chupah, a marriage canopy, as well as symbolizing the huts the Israelites inhabited in their desert travels. Indeed, when one eats and (as some have the custom) sleeps in a festive sukkah, it becomes a kind of dream house—one brings to it none of the cares and worries of every day, only the joyous feelings of Yom Tov. This holiday is the "season of our rejoicing," so the mood is much like a wedding. The six months from Pesach to Sukkot thus replicate the movements of a love relationship, from romance to betrothal, commitment and alienation, renewed commitment, reconciliation, union and rejoicing.

During the cycle of these major holidays, the feminine is engaged in a kind of dance—the Shekhinah or feminine Presence in the world with the more distant masculine aspect of God. In the next six months the tempo and tone shift somewhat. Major biblical and agricultural holidays are absent, and instead we have two popular rabbinically established holidays, Chanukkah and Purim. One might expect that since these are not rooted in the most ancient layer of Jewish history, where we have seen that women are fairly prominent, these would be masculinized holidays. But the contrary is true. The feminine, which is in so many traditions associated with darkness, winter, and the hidden potential of things, emerged here in Judaism as well. The stories associated with the two holidays involve, historically, both men and women, but in popular tradition they are often considered a "tribute to women."[11] Certainly that is true of Purim, as we have seen already with the story of Esther. In many respects it is true of Chanukkah as well.

Traditionally, Chanukkah celebrates a military victory and a miracle—the "miracle of the oil"—associated with the rededication of the Temple. (Chanukkah literally means "dedication.") But legends surrounding the events that led to the Maccabean revolt involve women—for example, the incident that tradition tells us incited Judas Maccabee to rally his men for war. A daughter of Matthiahu, enraged at the prohibition of circumcision, led a group of mothers of infant boys to the top of the city walls. There, in full view of the people, they circumcised their children then leaped to their deaths. Another famous incident occurred when soldiers, enforcing King Antiochus's religious persecution, rounded up crowds of people and demanded that they bow down to an idol. When the soldiers came to Channah and her family of seven sons, all refused to bow down. The soldiers took the sons, one by one, and killed them right in front of their mother. Each time, they offered to spare the life of the next one if she would bow down; each time she refused. Even the youngest went bravely to his death, and then they killed Channah herself.

The moral of the stories is not merely that the women were willing to sacrifice themselves for the cause but that they led and inspired the whole people to uphold their Jewish faith and practice in the face of persecution. Like Esther and Yehudit in their times, they emerged from their usual private lives into the public domain when the situation called for it—in this case in dramatic self-sacrifice that challenged and inspired the rest of the people to overthrow the hated Hellenistic government. As we have already pointed out, we read the story of Yehudit at Chanukkah, even though the events on which it is based took place long before the Maccabean era, and the story of Esther at Purim. Each story echoes the other: the tales of courageous women whose actions molded the history of the Jewish people.

Other themes of Chanukkah are suggestive of the feminine. The Chanukkah celebration is focused in the home, emphasizing family togetherness and enacting the themes of rededication and renewal. Like most Jewish holidays, it has a seasonal dimension suggesting the natural world: the renewal of the lighting of the menorah in the Temple, symbolized by lighting candles each of the eight nights of the holiday, corresponds to the renewal of light at the winter solstice—suggested by the fact that we light an increasing number of lights each night.

One develops a sense of the winter holidays as different in quality from the cycle from spring to fall. They are oriented more toward home and children; even though there is a public reading of Megillat Esther on Purim, it is done lightly and with much festive entertainment for the children (and the adults, expressing the child within). Chanukkah and Purim both commemorate serious events, but those events have been transformed into strongly positive and even lighthearted remembrances.

At the same time, meaning lies hidden beneath the surface. . . . One meaning of the name "Esther" is "hidden"; and, as is often pointed out, the name of God does not appear at all in the Megillah—God's name, God's hand, is hidden behind the surface events. The sense of secret truths, of mysteries yet to be unveiled, lingers beneath all the frivolity of Chanukkah and Purim.

What are these secrets? In my view, they are the mystery of the feminine. The feminine rules over the winter in a way that expresses darkness but not foreboding—darkness as a natural part of life, like the months when many more hours are spent in the dark than in the light. This is the time of reflection, of long hours by the firelight, telling stories, of gathering together and sharing. The surface lightness of the holidays, the games and frivolity, are a way of entering this realm, especially of teaching children about the seriousness of life without frightening them. Like the kachinas of Southwest Indian tribes, they introduce children to spiritual reality in a comfortable, playful way. And this too is the feminine in action, as in the "woman of valor" passage we examined earlier: "She looks smilingly toward the future. . . . And the teaching of kindness is on her tongue."

The spiritual reality of Chanukkah and Purim is very deep. The sages taught that in the time of Mashiach, Chanukkah and Purim will continue to be celebrated while other holidays will drop away. Like the moon, whose size will increase to that of the sun, these days represent the mysteries that will then be revealed. Now we have hints, pieces of a puzzle that we can assemble only in part. For example, we have games of chance (like spinning the dreidel) that are not particularly favored in Jewish circles at other times. The letters stand for the miracle—*Nes gadol haya sham,* "A great miracle happened there"— which together with the "wheel of fortune" aspect of the game suggests again the hidden workings of God. At Purim we have costumes for changing our identity, revealing hidden dimensions of ourselves. Or, like the kachinas, we take on the masks of our ancestral spirits—Mordecai, Haman, the King, the Queen, the Jester, even the Horse—and act out a classic melodrama.[12]

At the same time, the historical stories of these times reflect the themes of courage and self-sacrifice, particularly with the heroines of the tales. We can see these as interwoven with the themes of change, renewal, hiddenness, and surprise. For surely one of the great mysteries of existence is that the willingness to sacrifice oneself, to take the risks of giving up the ego, enables one to open to one's deeper self and ultimately to God. But here we perceive it in a different way: not the serious, straight path of self-examination, repentance, atonement, nullification of the ego, with their nuances of analysis and intellect. Rather, we see the path the way a jester reveals it, or a child. The many levels of archetypes, from heroes to fools, reflect like a hall of mirrors the hidden and secret dimensions of our personal lives, the miraculous history of the Jewish people, and the mysteries of life itself.

There is a quality to Purim and its festivities, at the end of the winter season, analogous to the opening of Pandora's box, the release of the hidden creative energies that are under the rule of the feminine. Then begins again, with Pesach and springtime, the cycle of the meeting of male and female, the betrothal and marriage. Over and over again the cycle repeats itself. In our personal lives it is like a spiral: every Purim is Purim, but not the same; every Pesach, Pesach, but different. We hope to find ourselves each year on a higher rung, deepening and refining our approach to God.

This deepening happens in many ways. Simply by fuller participation in these holidays as communal events, we are bound more closely to the rhythms of Jewish life. Study of the literature about the holidays and their mitzvot also helps us develop our kavannah and bring a feminine consciousness into what we do. Most of all, the rituals and ceremonies take us on a detour from our usual analytical and practical modes of consciousness. We become actors in a play that moves at a deeper level, engaging us in a script written with the rhythm of life, the dynamics of male and female. What begins as a work of our own conscious mind, relating to Torah and tradition by adding our reflection upon it, takes us below the conscious level to the deeper meanings of our own life and to a growing love of God. The framework of ritual, thoughtfully undertaken, thus speaks to us year by year, from within our own life experience.

NOTES

*Marion Zimmer Bradley, *The Mists of Avalon* (New York: Ballantine Books, 1982), pp. 142–43.

1. Rabbi Adin Steinsaltz, *Teshuvah: A Guide to the Newly Observant Jew* (New York: Free Press, 1982, Eng. trans. 1987), p. 29.

2. Ibid.

3. For a beautiful and moving description of Shabbat, including its feminine aspect as "queen" or "bride," see Abraham Joshua Heschel, *The Sabbath: Its Meaning for Modern Man* (New York: Farrar, Straus and Giroux, 1951). Heschel's work is still unsurpassed as an evocation of the meaning of Shabbat.

4. Some scholars believe the passage from Proverbs may be premonarchical in origin, i.e., from a historical era when women were more prominent. See Carol Meyers, *Discovering Eve: Ancient Israelite Women in Context* (New York: Oxford University Press, 1988), 179.

5. *Siddur Tehillat Hashem,* Nusach Ha-Ari Zal, according to the text of Rabbi Schneur Zalman of Liadi, trans. Nissen Mangel (Brooklyn: Merkos L'Inyonei Chinuch, 1978), pp. 133, 134.

6. Ibid., pp. 140, 146. The translation from the Amidah is usually given as "thereon," so it is not immediately recognizable as the feminine "on her." The special kabbalistic titles used here refer to various manifestations of the divine energies, one feminine and two masculine, respectively.

7. For a history, see Rafael Patai's *The Hebrew Goddess* (New York: Avon Books, 1967). Some feminists have complained that the idea of the Shekhinah is not particularly useful, since it was not originally feminine and, even when it has been, it has not empowered women but has "only supported the male-centered vision." See Marcia Falk, "Notes on Composing New Blessings: Toward a Feminist-Jewish Reconstruction of Prayer," *Visions,* pp. 129–30. I frankly do not find the argument convincing, simply because many women in my experience do find the Shekhinah image viable and inspiring. The hierarchical polarization Falk finds objectionable in the kabbalistic interpretation of the Shekhinah has to do with the transcendent-immanent dichotomy. . . .

8. Some have taken this metaphor as expressing a negative valuation of woman. See, for example, Rosemary Radford Reuther, "Sexism and God-Language," in *Visions,* 152. She claims that God, the "groom," is possessive, jealous, and judgmental; while humankind, the "bride," is his female servant. She takes this to be a reversal of the ancient Near Eastern portrayal of the Queen of Heaven with her male consort. On the level of mythology, this certainly appears to be the same motif with genders reversed. But to portray the Jewish version as wholly negative is unfounded. True, as she notes, the prophet Hosea and others use the motif to accuse Israel of harlotry, being the unfaithful wife, when the people worship other gods. She reads it as carrying a negative stereotype of women, based on a double standard that dominates Bible and rabbinic tradition; but the Queen of Heaven in other traditions accuses her male lovers of similar unfaithfulness. Sexism is not the issue here, but rather the rhetorical use of a metaphor.

In Judaism, other uses of the metaphor are quite positive. God's redemption of his "bride," Israel, from slavery in Egypt in response to their cries echoes Isis's search for

Tammuz in the underworld but with a great sense of compassion added: God performs an act of love not dependent on Israel's merit. And while Israel is often presented as the weaker partner compared to the "king," their love, as in the *Shir HaShirim* (Song of Songs), is profound and moving on both sides. In rabbinic presentations of the "unfaithful wife" motif (e.g., in interpreting the story of the golden calf) the fault on Israel's side is clearly understood as a general human flaw, not a sin of woman. Indeed, women are specifically exempted from complicity in it. The picture, in short, is much more complex than Reuther allows in her brief allusion to this metaphor.

9. Carol Meyers, *Discovering Eve*, pp. 178–79, discusses the powerful female images in the song. For Waskow's comment, see "Feminist Judaism: Restoration of the Moon," in *On Being a Jewish Feminist: A Reader*, ed. Susannah Herschel (New York: Schocken, 1983), p. 264.

10. This was a time of mourning in some of the other traditions of the ancient Near East, particularly those connected with nature deities. Midsummer, when the land begins to dry out and the grass to turn brown, was associated with the disappearance of the forces of fertility. Mythologically, the male consort of the great goddess died, and she went into mourning for him. The pagan idea as such had no place in Judaism: we find a prophet criticizing those "women mourning for Tammuz," the female devotees who identified with the goddess's sadness. But the parallel with the seasonal forces of nature is clear.

11. The phrase is from Masha Zweibel, "Jewish Women Shaped History," in *The Modern Jewish Woman: A Unique Perspective*, ed. Raizel Schnall Friedfertig and Freyda Schapiro (Brooklyn: Lubavitch Educational Foundation, 1981), p. 152.

12. It is no accident either that other cultures mark this same time of year—late winter to early spring—with great costume events, parades, and "calling of the spirits." We need only think of Chinese New Year, or Carnival and Mardi Gras in Roman Catholic regions. The seasonal significance is the emergence of the spirits from their hidden winter habitations, before the trees and crops begin to emerge.

5

Wiwanyag Wachipi: The Sun Dance
Black Elk, edited by Joseph Epes Brown

Along with the sweat lodge ceremony, the Sioux sun dance is probably the most well-known of Native American religious rituals. Indeed, the sun dance has gained notoriety in non-Indian circles because of the self-inflicted pain that participants have sometimes endured by dancing until their flesh pulled away from thongs to which it was attached. Ritual self-sacrifice in this manner alternately fascinates and repels those for whom such spiritual expression is foreign and incomprehensible. The Oglala Sioux (the Lakota) from whom this account comes were one of thirty-one or so Indian nations, hunter-gatherers who roamed the plains in the nineteenth century and were part of the large Sioux family of nations. The sun dance is one of a series of seven rites that traditional Oglala believe was bequeathed to them by a sacred being they call White Buffalo Calf Woman. The renowned Black Elk, who provided the material for the narrative to Joseph Epes Brown at the Pine Ridge Reservation in South Dakota in the late 1940s, was a traditional spiritual leader among the Oglala and also a Roman Catholic catechist. Here his story is one about tradition. In his careful construction of the small and precise details of the sun dance ceremony from its preparatory phases to its conclusion, he demonstrates in clear and compelling terms how much power, for believers, the body and the material order as a whole can generate for the human spirit. If we follow the spiritual logic of knowing through the body, the site and situation of the Oglala—the specificity of place and people—become a means of transport into regions that make the sacrifice of a piece of flesh seem an appropriate spiritual offering, one that is cheerfully given and not problematic in the way that white observers have sometimes made it.

The *wiwanyag wachipi* (dance looking at the sun) is one of our greatest rites and was first held many, many winters after our people received the sacred pipe from the White Buffalo Cow Woman. It is held each year during the Moon of Fattening (June) or the Moon of Cherries Blackening (July), always at the time when the moon is full, for the growing and dying of the moon reminds us of our ignorance which comes and goes; but when the moon is full it is as if the eternal light of the Great Spirit were upon the whole world. But now I will tell you how this holy rite first came to our people and how it was first made.

Our people were once camped in a good place, in a circle, of course, and the old men were sitting having a council, when they noticed that one of our men, Kablaya (Spread), had dropped his robe down around his waist, and was dancing there all alone with his hand raised towards heaven. The old men thought that perhaps he was crazy, so they sent someone to find out what was the matter; but this man who was sent suddenly dropped his robe down around his waist, too, and started dancing with Kablaya. The old men thought this very strange, and so they all went over to see what could be the matter. Kablaya then explained to them:

"Long ago *Wakan-Tanka* told us how to pray with the sacred pipe, but we have now become lax in our prayers, and our people are losing their strength. But I have just been shown, in a vision, a new way of prayer; in this manner *Wakan-Tanka* has sent aid to us."

When they heard this the old men all said, *"How!"* and seemed very pleased. They then had a conference and sent two men to the keeper of the sacred pipe, for he should give advice on all matters of this sort. The keeper told the men that this was certainly a very good thing, for "we were told that we would have seven ways of praying to *Wakan-Tanka,* and this must certainly be one of them, for Kablaya has been taught in a vision, and we were told in the beginning that we should receive our rites in this manner."

The two messengers brought this news back to the old men, who then asked Kablaya to instruct them in what they must do. Kablaya then spoke to the men, saying: "This is to be the sun dance; we cannot make it immediately but must wait four days, and during this time we shall prepare, as I have been instructed in my vision. This dance will be an offering of our bodies and souls to *Wakan-Tanka* and will be very *wakan.* All our old and holy men should gather; a large tipi should be built and sage should be placed all around inside it. You must have a good pipe, and also all the following equipment:

Ree twist tobacco	a tanned buffalo calf hide
bark of the red willow	rabbit skins
Sweet grass	eagle plumes
a bone knife	red earth paint
a flint axe	blue paint
buffalo tallow	rawhide
a buffalo skull	eagle tail feathers
a rawhide bag	whistles from the wing bones of the Spotted Eagle.

After the people had secured all these sacred things, Kablaya then asked all those who could sing to come to him that evening so that he could teach them the holy songs; he said that they should bring with them a large drum made from a buffalo hide, and they should have very stout drum sticks, covered at the end with buffalo hide, the hair side out.

Since the drum is often the only instrument used in our sacred rites, I should perhaps tell you here why it is especially sacred and important to us. It is because the round form of the drum represents the whole universe, and its steady strong beat is the pulse, the heart, throbbing at the center of the universe. It is as the voice of *Wakan-Tanka,* and this sound stirs us and helps us to understand the mystery and power of all things.

That evening the singers, four men and a woman, came to Kablaya, who spoke to them in this manner: "O you, my relatives, for a very long time we have been sending our voices to *Wakan-Tanka.* This He has taught us to do. We have many ways of praying to Him, and through this sacred manner of living our generations have learned to walk the red path with firm steps. The sacred pipe is always at the center of the hoop of our nation, and with it the people have walked and will continue to walk in a holy manner.

"In this new rite which I have just received, one of the standing peoples has been chosen to be at our center; he is the *wagachun* (the rustling tree, or cottonwood); he will be our center and also the people, for the tree represents the way of the people. Does it not stretch from the earth here to heaven there?[1] This new way of sending our voices to *Wakan-Tanka* will be very powerful; its use will spread, and, at this time of year, every year, many people will pray to the Great Spirit. Before I teach you the holy songs, let us first offer the pipe to our Father and Grandfather, *Wakan-Tanka.*"

"O Grandfather, Father, *Wakan-Tanka,* we are about to fulfill Thy will as You have taught us to do in my vision. This we know will be a very sacred way of sending our voices to You; through this, may our people receive wisdom; may it help us to walk the sacred path with all the Powers of the universe! Our prayer will really be the prayer of all things, for all are really one; all this I have seen in my vision. May the four Powers of the universe help us to do this rite correctly; O Great Spirit, have mercy upon us!"

The pipe was smoked by all, and then Kablaya began to teach the songs to the five people. Many other people had gathered around the singers, and to these Kablaya said that while they listen they should frequently cry "O Grandfather, *Wakan-Tanka,* I offer the pipe to You that my people may live!"

There were no words to the first song that Kablaya taught the singers; it was simply a chant, repeated four times, and the fast beat on the drum was used. The words to the second song were:

> *Wakan-Tanka, have mercy on us,*
> *That our people may live!*

And the third song was:

> *They say a herd of buffalo is coming;*
> *It is here now!*
> *Their blessing will come to us.*
> *It is with us now!*

The fourth song was a chant and had no words.

Then Kablaya taught the men who had brought their eagle-bone whistles how they should be used, and he also told the men what equipment they should prepare and explained the meaning of each ritual object.

"You should prepare a necklace of otter skin, and from it there should hang a circle with a cross in the center. At the four places where the cross meets the circle there should hang eagle feathers which represent the four Powers of the universe and the four ages. At the center of the circle you should tie a plume taken from the breast of the eagle, for this is the place which is nearest to the heart and center of the sacred bird. This plume will be for *Wakan-Tanka,* who dwells at the depths of the heavens, and who is the center of all things.

"You all have the eagle-bone whistles, and to the ends of each of these an eagle plume should be tied. When you blow the whistle always remember that it is the voice of the Spotted Eagle; our Grandfather, *Wakan-Tanka,* always hears this, for you see it is really His own voice.

"A *hanhepi wi* [night sun, or moon] should be cut from rawhide in the shape of a crescent, for the moon represents a person and, also, all things, for everything created waxes and wanes, lives and dies. You should also understand that the night represents ignorance, but it is the moon and the stars which bring the Light of *Wakan-Tanka* into this darkness. As you know the moon comes and goes, but *anpetu wi,* the sun, lives on forever; it is the source of light, and because of this it is like *Wakan-Tanka.*

"A five-pointed star should be cut from rawhide. This will be the sacred Morning Star who stands between the darkness and the light, and who represents knowledge.

"A round rawhide circle should be made to represent the sun, and this should be painted red; but at the center there should be a round circle of blue, for this innermost center represents *Wakan-Tanka* as our Grandfather. The light of this sun enlightens the entire universe; and as the flames of the sun come to us in the morning, so comes the grace of *Wakan-Tanka,* by which all creatures are enlightened. It is because of this that the four-leggeds and the wingeds always rejoice at the coming of the light. We can all see in the day, and this seeing is sacred for it represents the sight of that real world which we may have through the eye of the heart. When you wear this sacred sign in the dance, you should remember that you are bringing Light into the universe, and if you concentrate on these meanings you will gain great benefit.

"A round circle should be cut and painted red, and this will represent Earth. She is sacred, for upon Her we place our feet, and from Her we send our voices to *Wakan-Tanka*. She is a relative of ours, and this we should always remember when we call Her "Grandmother" or "Mother." When we pray we raise our hand to the heavens, and afterwards we touch the earth, for is not our Spirit from *Wakan-Tanka,* and are not our bodies from the earth? We are related to all things: the earth and the stars, everything, and with all these together we raise our hand to *Wakan-Tanka* and pray to Him alone.

"You should also cut from rawhide another round circle, and this should be painted blue for the heavens. When you dance you should raise your head and hand up to these heavens, looking at them, for if you do this your Grandfather will see you. It is He who owns everything; there is nothing which does not belong to Him, and thus it is to Him alone that you should pray.

"Finally, you should cut from rawhide the form of *tatanka*, the buffalo. He represents the people and the universe and should always be treated with respect, for was he not here before the two-legged peoples, and is he not generous in that he gives us our homes and our food? The buffalo is wise in many things, and, thus, we should learn from him and should always be as a relative with him.

"Each man should wear one of these sacred symbols on his chest, and he should realize their meanings as I have explained to you here. In this great rite you are to offer your body as a sacrifice in behalf of all the people, and through you the people will gain understanding and strength. Always be conscious of these things which I have told you today; it is all *wakan!*"

The next day it was necessary to locate the sacred rustling tree which was to stand at the center of the great lodge, and so Kablaya told his helper of the type of tree which he should find and mark with sage, that the war party will be able to locate it and bring it back to camp. Kablaya also instructed the helpers how they must mark out the ground where the sacred sun-dance lodge will be set up, around the holy tree, and how they should mark the doorway at the east with green branches.

The following day the scouts, who had been chosen by the spiritual leaders, went out and pretended to scout for the tree. When it was found they returned immediately to camp, and after circling sun-wise around the place where the lodge was to be, they all charged for the doorway, trying to strike a coup on it. These scouts then took up a pipe, and, after offering it to the six directions, they swore that they would tell the truth. When this had been done, Kablaya spoke to the men in this manner:

"You have taken up the holy pipe, and so you must now tell us with truth all that you have seen. You know that running through the stem of the pipe there is a little hole leading straight to the center and heart of the pipe; let your minds be as straight as this Way. May your tongues not be forked. You have been sent out to find a tree that will be of great benefit to the people, so now tell us truthfully what you have found."

Kablaya then turned the pipe around four times, and pointed the stem towards the scout who was to give the report.

"I went over a hill, and there I saw many of the sacred standing peoples."

"In which direction were you facing, and what did you see beyond the first hill?"

"I was facing the west," the scout replied, "and then I went further and looked over a second hill and saw many more of the sacred standing people living there."

In this manner the scout was questioned four times, for as you know with our people all good things are done in fours; and then this is the manner in which we always question our scouts when we are on the warpath, for you see we are here regarding the tree as an enemy who is to be killed.

When the scouts had given their report, they all dressed as if they were going on the warpath; and then they left the camp as if to attack the enemy. Many other people followed behind the scouts. When they came to the chosen tree, they all gathered around it; then, last of all, Kablaya arrived with his pipe, which he held with its stem pointing towards the tree; he spoke in this manner:

"Of all the many standing peoples, you O rustling cottonwood have been chosen in a sacred manner; you are about to go to the center of the people's sacred hoop, and there you will represent the people and will help us to fulfill the will of *Wakan-Tanka*. You are a kind and good-looking tree; upon you the winged peoples have raised their families; from the tip of your lofty branches down to your roots, the winged and four-legged peoples have made their homes. When you stand at the center of the sacred hoop you will be the people, and you will be as the pipe, stretching from heaven to earth. The weak will lean upon you, and for all the people you will be a support. With the tips of your branches you hold the sacred red and blue days. You will stand where the four sacred paths cross—there you will be the center of the great Powers of the universe. May we two-leggeds always follow your sacred example, for we see that you are always looking upwards into the heavens. Soon, and with all the peoples of the world, you will stand at the center; for all beings and all things you will bring that which is good. *Hechetu welo!*"

Kablaya then offered his pipe to Heaven and Earth, and then with the stem he touched the tree on the west, north, east, and south sides; after this he lit and smoked the pipe.

I think it would be good to explain to you here why we consider the cottonwood tree to be so very sacred. I might mention first, that long ago it was the cottonwood who taught us how to make our tipis, for the leaf of the tree is an exact pattern of the tipi, and this we learned when some of our old men were watching little children making play houses from these leaves. This too is a good example of how much grown men may learn from very little children, for the hearts of little children are pure, and, therefore, the Great Spirit may show to them many things which older people miss. Another reason why we choose the cottonwood tree to be at the center of our lodge is that the Great Spirit has shown to us that, if you cut an upper limb of this tree crosswise, there you will see in the grain a perfect five pointed star, which, to us, represents the presence of the Great Spirit. Also perhaps you have noticed that even in the very lightest breeze you can hear the voice of the cottonwood tree; this we understand is its prayer to the Great Spirit,[2] for not only men, but all things and all beings pray to Him continually in differing ways.

The chiefs then did a little victory dance there around the tree, singing their chief's songs, and as they sang and danced they selected the man who was to have the honor of counting coup on the tree; he must always be a man of good character, who has shown himself brave and self-sacrificing on the warpath. Three other men were also chosen by the chiefs, and then each of these four men stood at one of the four sides of the tree—the leader at the west. This leader then told of his great deeds in war, and when he had finished the men cheered and the women gave the tremulo. The brave man then motioned with his axe three times towards the tree, and the fourth time he struck it. Then the other three men in turn told of their exploits in war, and when they finished they also struck the tree in the same manner, and at each blow all the people shouted *"hi! hey!"* When the tree was nearly ready to fall, the chiefs went around and selected a person with a quiet and holy nature, and this person gave the last blow to the tree; as it fell there was much cheering, and all the women gave the tremulo. Great care was taken that the tree did not touch the ground when it fell, and no one was permitted to step over it.

The tree was then carried by six men towards the camp, but before they reached camp they stopped four times, and after the last stop they all howled like coyotes—as do the warriors when returning from the war path; then they all charged into camp and placed the sacred tree up upon poles—for it must not touch the ground—and pointed its base towards the hole which had already been prepared, and its tip faced towards the west. The lodge around the tree had not yet been set up, but all the poles had been prepared, and all the equipment for constructing the *Inipi* had been gathered.

The chief priest, Kablaya, and all those who were to take part in the dance, then went into a large tipi where they were to prepare themselves and receive instructions. The lodge was shut up very tightly, and leaves were even placed all around the base.

Kablaya, who was seated at the west, scraped a bare place on the ground in front of him, and here a coal was placed; as Kablaya burned sweet grass upon the coal, he said: "We burn this sacred herb for *Wakan-Tanka*, so that all the two-legged and winged peoples of the universe will be relatives and close to each other. Through this there shall be much happiness."

A small image of a drying rack was then made from two forked sticks and one straight one, and all were painted blue, for the drying rack represents heaven, and it is our prayer that the racks always be as full as heaven. The pipe was then taken up, and after being purified over the smoke, it was leaned against the rack, for in this way it represents our prayers and is the path leading from earth to heaven.

All the sacred things to be used in the dance were then purified over the smoke of the sweet grass: the hide figures; the sacred paints; the calf skin; and the buckskin bags; and the dancers, also, purified themselves. When this had been done, Kablaya took up his pipe, and, raising it to heaven, he prayed.

"O Grandfather, *Wakan-Tanka,* You are the maker of everything. You have always been and always will be. You have been kind to your people, for You have taught us a way of prayer with the pipe which You have given us; and now through a vision You have shown to me a sacred dance which I must teach to my people. Today we will do Thy will.

"As I stand upon this sacred earth, upon which generations of our people have stood, I send a voice to You by offering this pipe. Behold me, O *Wakan-Tanka,* for I represent all the people. Within this pipe I shall place the four Powers and all the wingeds of the universe; together with all these, who shall become one, I send a voice to You. Behold me! Enlighten my mind with Your never fading Light!

"I offer this pipe to *Wakan-Tanka,* first through You O winged Power of the place where the sun goes down; there is a place for You in this pipe. Help us with those red and blue days which make the people holy!"

Kablaya then held up a pinch of tobacco, and after motioning with it to Heaven, Earth, and the four Powers, he placed it in the bowl of the pipe. Then after the following prayers, he placed pinches of tobacco in the pipe for each of the other directions.

"O winged Power of the place where *Waziah* lives, I am about to offer this pipe to *Wakan-Tanka;* help me with the two good red and blue days which You have—days which are purifying to the people and to the universe. There is a place for You in the pipe, and so help us!

"O You, Power there where the sun comes up; You who give knowledge and who guard the dawn of the day, help us with Your two red and blue days which give understanding and Light to the people. There is a place for You in this pipe which I am about to offer to *Wakan-Tanka;* help us!

"O You, most sacred Power at the place where we always face; You who are the source of life, and who guard the people and the coming generations, help us with Your two red and blue days! There is a place for You in the pipe.

"O You, Spotted Eagle of the heavens! we know that You have sharp eyes with which you see even the smallest object that moves on Grandmother Earth. O You, who are in the depths of the heavens, and who know everything, I am offering this pipe to *Wakan-Tanka!* Help us with Your two good red and blue days!

"O You, Grandmother Earth, who lie outstretched, supporting all things! upon You a two-legged is standing, offering a pipe to the Great Spirit. You are at the center of the two good red and blue days. There will be a place for You in the pipe and so help us!"

Kablaya then placed a small grain of tobacco in the pipe for each of the following birds: the kingbird; the robin; the lark, who sings during the two good days; the woodpecker; the hawk, who makes life so difficult for the other winged peoples; the eagle hawk; the magpie, who knows everything; the blackbird; and many other wingeds. Now all objects of creation and the six directions of space have been placed within the bowl of the pipe. The pipe was sealed with tallow and was leaned against the little blue drying rack.

Kablaya then took up another pipe, filled it, and went to where the sacred tree was resting. A live coal was brought, and the tree and the hole were purified with the smoke from sweet grass.

"O *Wakan-Tanka,*" Kablaya prayed as he held his pipe up with one hand, "behold this holy tree-person who will soon be placed in this hole. He will stand with the sacred pipe. I touch him with the sacred red earth paint from our Grandmother and also with the fat from the four-legged buffalo. By touching this tree-person with the red earth, we remember that the generations of all that move come from our Mother the Earth. With your help, O tree, I shall soon offer my body and soul to *Wakan-Tanka,* and in me I offer all my people and all the generations to come."

Kablaya then took the red paint, offered it to the six directions, and again spoke to the sacred tree: "O tree, you are about to stand up; be merciful to my people, that they may flourish under you."

Kablaya painted stripes of red on the west, north, east, and south sides of the tree, and then he touched a very little paint to the tip of the tree for the Great Spirit, and he also put some at the base of the tree for Mother Earth. Then Kablaya took up the skin of a buffalo calf, saying: "It is from this buffalo person that our people live; he gives to us our homes, our clothing, our food, everything we need. O buffalo calf, I now give to you a sacred place upon the tip of the tree. This tree will hold you in his hand and will raise you up to *Wakan-Tanka.* Behold what I am about to do! Through this, all things that move and fly upon the earth and in the heavens will be happy!"

Kablaya next held up a small cherry tree, and continued to pray: "Behold this, O *Wakan-Tanka,* for it is the tree of the people, which we pray will bear much fruit."

This little tree was then tied upon the sacred cottonwood, just below the buffalo hide, and with it there was tied a buckskin bag in which there was some fat.

Kablaya then took up the hide images of a buffalo and a man, and, offering them to the six directions, he prayed: "Behold this buffalo, O Grandfather, which You have given to us; he is the chief of all the four-leggeds upon our sacred Mother; from him the people live, and with him they walk the sacred path. Behold, too, this two-legged, who represents all the people. These are the two chiefs upon this great island; bestow upon them all the favours that they ask for, O *Wakan-Tanka!*"

These two images were then tied upon the tree, just underneath the place where the tree forks; after this Kablaya held up a bag of fat to be placed underneath the base of the tree, and he prayed in this manner:

"O Grandfather, *Wakan-Tanka*, behold this sacred fat, upon which this tree-person will stand; may the earth always be as fat and fruitful as this. O tree, this is a sacred day for you and for all our people; the earth within this hoop belongs to you, O tree, and it is here underneath you that I shall offer up my body and soul for the sake of the people. Here I shall stand, sending my voice to You, O *Wakan-Tanka*, as I offer the sacred pipe. All this may be difficult to do, yet for the good of the people it must be done. Help me, O Grandfather, and give to me courage and strength to stand the sufferings which I am about to undergo! O tree, you are now admitted to the sacred lodge!"

With much cheering and many shrill tremulos, the tree was raised, very slowly, for the men stopped four times before it was straight and dropped into the hole prepared for it. Now all the people—the two-leggeds, four-leggeds, and the wingeds of the air—were rejoicing, for they would all flourish under the protection of the tree. It helps us all to walk the sacred path; we can lean upon it, and it will always guide us and give us strength.

A little dance was held around the base of the tree, and then the surrounding lodge was made by putting upright, in a large circle, twenty-eight forked sticks, and from the fork of each stick a pole was placed which reached to the holy tree at the center.

I should explain to you here that in setting up the sun dance lodge, we are really making the universe in a likeness; for, you see, each of the posts around the lodge represents some particular object of creation, so that the whole circle is the entire creation, and the one tree at the center, upon which the twenty-eight poles rest, is *Wakan-Tanka*, who is the center of everything. Everything comes from Him, and sooner or later everything returns to Him. And I should also tell you why it is that we use twenty-eight poles. I have already explained why the numbers four and seven are sacred; then if you add four sevens you get twenty-eight. Also the moon lives twenty-eight days, and this is our month; each of these days of the month represents something sacred to us: two of the days represent the Great Spirit; two are for Mother Earth; four are for the four winds; one is for the Spotted Eagle; one for the sun; and one for the moon; one is for the Morning Star; and four for the four ages; seven are for our seven great rites; one is for the buffalo; one for the fire; one for the water; one for the rock; and finally one is for the two-legged people. If you add all these days up you will see that they come to twenty-eight. You should also know that the buffalo has twenty-eight ribs, and that in our war bonnets we usually use twenty-eight feathers. You see, there is a significance for everything, and these are the things that are good for men to know, and to remember. But now we must return to the sun dance.

The warriors all dressed and painted themselves, and after entering the sacred lodge they danced around the center tree, for in this way the ground was purified and made smooth by the dancing feet. The chiefs then gathered and selected braves, one of which was to be the leader of the dancers. These chosen men then danced first towards the west, and then back to the center, then to the north and to the center, to the east and to the center, and finally to the south and then back to the center, and in this way they made a path in the shape of a cross.

Kablaya then entered the *Inipi* lodge, carrying the sacred pipe which had already been filled, and he sat at the west; all the other men who were to take part in the dance also entered, taking care not to pass in front of Kablaya, and then one woman entered last, taking her seat next to the door.

All the buffalo robes to be used in the dance were placed on top of the *Inipi* lodge, for in this way they are purified. The five hot rocks for the five directions were brought in and put in their proper places at the sacred altar, and then a sixth rock was placed upon the sacred path.

Kablaya held that pipe which was to be used in the dance, but a second pipe which was to be used for the rites of the *Inipi* was filled and was handed to Kablaya to bless and to light. This pipe was smoked around the circle in the ritual manner, purified by Kablaya, and was then handed out of the lodge. The door was closed, and now it was the time for Kablaya to explain his vision to the people.

"My relatives all—listen! *Wakan-Tanka* has been kind to us, and has placed us upon a sacred Earth; upon Her we are now sitting. You have just seen the five sacred rocks placed here at the center, and that sixth rock which was placed upon the path represents the people. For the good of you all *Wakan-Tanka* has taught to me in a vision, a way of worship—this I am now teaching to you.

"The heavens are sacred, for it is there that our Grandfather, the Great Spirit, lives; these heavens are as a cloak for the universe—this robe is now upon me as I stand here. O *Wakan-Tanka*, I show to You the sacred hoop of our nation, which is this circle within which there is a cross; this circle one of us wears upon his breast. And I show to You the earth which You have made, and which You are always making; it is represented by this round red circle which we wear. The never-ending Light which turns the night into day, we also wear, that the Light may be amongst our people, that they may see. I show to You also the Morning Star which gives knowledge to us. The four-legged buffalo whom You have placed here before the two-legged people is also here with us. And here is also the sacred woman who came to us in such a holy manner. All these holy peoples and holy things are now hearing what I say!

"Very soon I shall suffer and endure great pain with my relatives here, in behalf of my people. In tears and suffering I shall hold my pipe and raise my voice to You, O *Wakan-Tanka*. I shall offer up my body and soul that my people may live. In sending my voice to You, *Wakan-Tanka*, I shall use that which connects the four Powers, Heaven, and Earth, to You. All that which moves on the universe—the four-leggeds, the insects, and the wingeds—all rejoice and help me and all my people!"

Kablaya then sang his sacred song:

> *The Sun, the Light of the world,*
> *I hear Him coming.*
> *I see His face as He comes.*
> *He makes the beings on earth happy,*
> *And they rejoice.*
> O Wakan-Tanka, *I offer to You this world of Light.*

The pipe to be used in the sacred dance was then wrapped in sage and was taken out of the lodge by the woman; she carried it along the sacred path to the east and placed it upon the buffalo skull, being careful to have its stem point towards the east. This woman then remained outside the little lodge and assisted in opening and closing the door. The *Inipi* then began as I have described before, but after the second time the door was closed, Kablaya made a special prayer in this manner:

"Grandfather, *Wakan-Tanka*, behold us! The sacred pipe which You have given to us, and with which we have raised our children, will soon go to the center of the universe, along with the buffalo, who has helped to make strong the bodies of the people. The sacred woman who once before came to the center of our hoop will again come to our center, and a two-legged who will suffer for his people will also go to the center. O *Wakan-Tanka*, when we are all at the center, may we have only You in our minds and hearts!"

Kablaya then sang another of the sacred songs which he had received in his vision.

> *I hear Him coming; I see His face.*
> *Your day is sacred! I offer it to You.*

> *I hear Him coming; I see His face,*
> *This sacred day You made the buffalo roam.*
> *You have made a happy day for the world;*
> *I offer all to You.*

Water was then put on the rocks as Kablaya prayed: "O *Wakan-Tanka*, we are now purifying ourselves, that we may be worthy to raise our hands to You." Then raising their right hands, all the men sang.

> *Grandfather, I send my voice to You.*
> *Grandfather, I send my voice to You.*
> *With all the universe I send my voice to You,*
> *That I may live.*

When the door was opened the third time, the men were all allowed to drink a little water, but this was the only time during the whole rite that this was permitted. As the men received the water, Kablaya said to them: "I give you water, but remember the One in the west who guards the waters and the sanctity of all things. You are about to drink the water, which is life, and so you should not spill any of it. When you finish you should raise your hands in thanks to the Power of the place where the sun goes down; he will help you to bear the difficulties which you are about to undergo."

The door was closed for the last time, and again all the men sang as the heat and steam purified them. And when the door was finally opened, they all came out, led by Kablaya, and they raised their hands to the six directions, saying: "*Hi ho! Hi ho! Pila-miya!*" (thanks).

Each dancer had a helper, who took a purified buffalo robe from the top of the *Inipi* lodge and put it around the dancer. Kablaya then took his pipe which had been resting on the buffalo skull, and, with all the men, he entered a sacred tipi and placed his pipe against the little drying rack, which had been painted blue to represent the heavens. Sweet grass was put on a coal, and Kablaya and all the men purified themselves in the sacred smoke. After this, the drum and drumsticks were blessed and purified, and as he did this Kablaya said: "This drum is the buffalo and will go to the center. By using these sticks upon the drum, we shall certainly defeat our enemies."

All the clothing and equipment to be used in the dance were then purified; the four buffalo skulls were also purified, for one of the men would soon fasten these to his skin, bearing them in this way until they break loose.

Kablaya then explained to the men that their bodies had been purified and, thus were now sacred and should not even be touched by their own hands. The men must carry little sticks in their hair with which to scratch themselves, should it be necessary, and even when they paint themselves with the red earth paint they must use sticks instead of their hands.

Kablaya put around his neck the round blue hide circle representing the heavens, and each of the other men wore the different symbols: the circle with the cross; the red earth circle; the sun; the moon; and the Morning Star. The seventh man wore the buffalo, and the woman carried the pipe, for she represents the White Buffalo Cow Woman. The men also put rabbit skins on their arms and legs, for the rabbit represents humility, because he is quiet and soft and not self-asserting—a quality which we must all possess when we go to the center of the world. The men also put feathers in their hair, and, after these preparations, Kablaya instructed them in what they must do when they enter the sacred dance lodge.

"When we go to the center of the hoop we shall all cry, for we should know that anything born into this world which you see about you must suffer and bear difficulties. We are now going to suffer at the center of the sacred hoop, and by doing this may we take upon ourselves much of the suffering of our people."

Each of the men then declared which of the sacrifices he would undergo, and Kablaya made his vow first: "I will attach my body to the thongs of the Great Spirit which come down to earth—this shall be my offering."

(I think I should explain to you here, that the flesh represents ignorance, and, thus, as we dance and break the thong loose, it is as if we were being freed from the bonds of the flesh. It is much the same as when you break a young colt; at first a halter is necessary, but later when he has become broken, the rope is no longer necessary. We too are young colts when we start to dance, but soon we become broken and submit to the Great Spirit.)

The second dancer said: "I will tie myself to the four Powers of the world which *Wakan-Tanka* has established."

Here the dancer actually is the center—for standing at the center of four posts, rawhide thongs from these posts are tied into the flesh of his shoulders, his breast, and his back, and in this manner he dances until these thongs have broken out from his flesh.

The third dancer made his vow: "I will bear four of my closest relatives, the ancient buffalo."

By this the dancer means that four thongs will be tied into his back, to which will be attached four buffalo skulls, and these four bonds represent the pull of ignorance which should always be behind us as we face the light of truth which is before us.

The fourth dancer said: "I will leave twelve pieces of my flesh at the foot of the sacred tree. One shall be for *Wakan-Tanka*, our Grandfather, one for *Wakan-Tanka*, our Father, one for the Earth, our Grandmother, and one for the Earth, our Mother. I will leave four pieces of flesh for the Powers of the four directions, and then I will leave one for the Spotted Eagle, one for the Morning Star, one for the moon, and one for the sun."

The fifth dancer said: "I will make an offering of eight pieces of my flesh; two shall be for *Wakan-Tanka,* two for the Earth, and four for the Powers of the four directions."

The sixth dancer said: "I will leave at the sacred tree four pieces of my flesh; one shall be for *Wakan-Tanka,* one for the Earth upon whom we walk, one for the people that they may walk with firm steps, and one for the wingeds of the universe."

The seventh dancer made his vow: "I will leave one piece of my flesh for *Wakan-Tanka* and one for the Earth."

Then the eighth dancer, who was the woman, made her vow: "I will offer one piece of my flesh to *Wakan-Tanka* and for all moving things of the universe, that they may give their powers to the people, that they with their children may walk the red path of life."

When all had finished making their vows, Kablaya told them to purify themselves by rubbing sage on their faces and all over their bodies, "for we are now about to approach a sacred place where the tree stands, as the pipe, stretching from Heaven to Earth. We must be worthy to go to this center!"

All the people of the band had gathered around the outside of the sacred lodge, and within the lodge at the south were the singers, with the women who were their helpers, and all were wearing wreaths around their foreheads and holding little sprigs of some sacred plant.

Then the dancers arrived, being led by the woman, who carried the sacred pipe, and followed by Kablaya, carrying the buffalo skull, and at the end of the line were the helpers who carried all the equipment. They all walked slowly around the outside of the lodge, in a sun-wise direction, and all the time they were crying most pitifully: "O *Wakan-Tanka,* be merciful to me, that my people may live! It is for this that I am sacrificing myself."

And as the dancers chanted this, all the other people cried, for they were the people—the nation—for whom the dancers were to suffer. The dancers entered the lodge at the east and, after moving around the lodge sun-wise, took their places at the west. Then Kablaya placed the buffalo skull between the dancers and the sacred tree, with the nose of the skull facing the east; and just in front of him, he set up the three blue forked sticks, and upon this rack the woman rested the sacred pipe.

The singers then sang one of the sacred songs:

> Wakan-Tanka *be merciful to me. We want to live!*
> *That is why we are doing this.*
> *They say that a herd of buffalo is coming;*
> *Now they are here.*
> *The power of the buffalo is coming upon us;*
> *It is now here!"*

After the chanting of this song the people all cried, and then, for the rest of the day and all that night, they danced. This dance, during the first night, represents the people in the darkness of ignorance; they were not yet worthy to meet the Light of the Great Spirit which would shine upon them with the coming of the next day; first they must suffer and purify themselves before they could be worthy to be with *Wakan-Tanka.*

Just before dawn, the dance stopped, and at this time the dancers, or their relatives, placed offerings outside the sacred lodge at each of the four quarters.

At dawn the dancers again entered the lodge, and with them there was the keeper of the sacred pipe; this holy man had been asked by Kablaya to make the sacred altar, but he had replied, "this is your vision Kablaya, and you should make the altar; but I will be present beside you, and when you have finished I will offer up the prayer."

Thus, it was Kablaya who made the sacred place; he first scraped a round circle in the ground in front of him, and then within this circle he placed a hot coal.[3] Then taking up some sweet grass and holding it above him, he prayed.

"O Grandfather, *Wakan-Tanka*, this is Your sacred grass which I place on the fire; its smoke will spread throughout the world, reaching even to the heavens. The four-leggeds, the wingeds, and all things will know this smoke and will rejoice. May this offering help to make all things and all beings as relatives to us; may they all give to us their powers, so that we may endure the difficulties ahead of us. Behold, O *Wakan-Tanka*, I place this sweet grass on the fire, and the smoke will rise to You."

As Kablaya placed the sacred grass on the fire, he sang this song:

> *I am making sacred smoke;*
> *In this manner I make the smoke;*
> *May all the peoples behold it!*
> *I am making sacred smoke;*
> *May all be attentive and behold!*
> *May the wingeds, and the four-leggeds*
>   *be attentive and behold it!*
> *In this manner I make the smoke;*
> *All over the universe there will be rejoicing!*

The knife which was to be used for piercing the breasts of the dancers was purified over the smoke, as was also a small stone hatchet and a small quantity of earth. Kablaya was then ready to make the sacred altar; but first he prayed.

"O Grandfather, *Wakan-Tanka*, I shall now make this Your sacred place. In making this altar, all the birds of the air and all creatures of the earth will rejoice, and they will come from all directions to behold it! All the generations of my people will rejoice! This place will be the center of the paths of the four great Powers. The dawn of the day will see this holy place! When Your Light approaches, O *Wakan-Tanka*, all that moves in the universe will rejoice!"

A pinch of the purified earth was offered above and to the ground and was then placed at the center of the sacred place. Another pinch of earth was offered to the west, north, east, and south and was placed at the west of the circle. In the same manner, earth was placed at the other three directions, and then it was spread evenly all around within the circle. This earth represents the two-leggeds, the four-leggeds, the wingeds, and really all that moves, and all that is in the universe. Upon this sacred place Kablaya then began to construct the altar. He first took up a stick, pointed it to the six directions, and then, bringing it down, he made a small circle at the center; and this we understand to be the home of *Wakan-Tanka*. Again, after pointing the stick to the six directions, Kablaya made a mark starting from the west and leading to the edge of the circle. In the same manner he drew a line from the east to the edge of the circle, from the north to the circle, and from the south to the circle. By constructing the altar in this manner, we see that everything leads into, or returns to, the center; and this center which is here, but which we know is really everywhere, is *Wakan-Tanka*.

Kablaya then took up a small bundle of sage, and, offering it up to *Wakan-Tanka*, he prayed.

"O *Wakan-Tanka*, behold us! Next to the two-leggeds, the chief of all the four-leggeds is *tatanka*, the buffalo. Behold his dried skull here; by this we know that we, too, shall become skull and bones, and, thus, together we shall all walk the sacred path back to *Wakan-Tanka*. When we arrive at the end of our days, be merciful to us, O *Wakan-Tanka*. Here on earth we live together with the buffalo, and we are grateful to him, for it is he who gives us our food, and who makes the people happy. For this reason I now give grass to our relative the buffalo."

Kablaya then made a little bed of sage to the east of the sacred altar, and, taking up the buffalo skull by the horns, and facing the east, he sang:

> *I give grass to the buffalo;*
> *May the people behold it,*
> *That they may live.*

Then turning, and holding the skull to the west, Kablaya sang:

> *Tobacco I give to the buffalo;*
> *May the people behold it,*
> *That they may live.*

Then turning to the north, Kablaya sang:

> *A robe I give to the buffalo;*
> *May the people behold it,*
> *That they may live.*

And turning to the south he sang:

> *Paint I give to the buffalo;*
> *May the people behold it,*
> *That they may live.*

Then standing over the sage, Kablaya sang:

> *Water I will give to the buffalo;*
> *May the people behold it,*
> *That they may live.*

The buffalo skull was then placed on the bed of sage, facing east, and Kablaya placed little balls of sage in its eyes and tied a little bag of tobacco on the horn which was facing south, and he also tied a piece of deerhide on the horn at the north, for this hide represents the robe for the buffalo. Then Kablaya painted a red line around the head of the buffalo and drew, also, a red line from the forehead to the tip of the nose. As he did this Kablaya said: "You, O buffalo, are the earth! May we understand this, and all that I have done here. *Hechetu welo!* It is good!"

When the offerings to the buffalo had been completed, the dancers walked around the lodge and stood at the doorway facing east, in order to greet the rising sun.

"Behold these men, O *Wakan-Tanka*," Kablaya prayed as he raised his right hand. "The face of the dawn will meet their faces; the coming day will suffer with them. It will be a sacred day, for You, O *Wakan-Tanka*, are present here!"

Then, just as the day-sun peeped over the horizon, the dancers all chanted in a sacred manner, and Kablaya sang one of his *wakan* songs.

> *The light of* Wakan-Tanka *is upon my people;*
> *It is making the whole earth bright.*
> *My people are now happy!*
> *All beings that move are rejoicing!*

As the men chanted, and as Kablaya sang the sacred song, they all danced, and as they danced they moved so that they were facing the south, then the west, the north, and then they stood again at the east; but this time they faced towards the sacred tree at the center.

The singing and drumming stopped, and the dancers sat at the west of the lodge, upon beds of sage which had been prepared for them. With sage the helpers rubbed all the paint off the men, and then upon their heads they placed wreaths of sage and plumes from the eagle, and the women also wore eagle feathers in their hair.

In every sun dance we wear wreaths of sage upon our heads, for it is a sign that our minds and hearts are close to *Wakan-Tanka* and His Powers, for the wreath represents the things of the heavens—the stars and planets, which are very mysterious and *wakan*.

Kablaya then told the dancers how they must paint themselves: the bodies were to be painted red from the waist up; the face, too, must be painted red, for red represents all that is sacred, especially the earth, for we should remember that it is from the earth that our bodies come, and it is to her that they return. A black circle should be painted around the face, for the circle helps us to remember *Wakan-Tanka*, who, like the circle, has no end. There is much power in the circle, as I have often said; the birds know this for they fly in a circle, and build their homes in the form of a circle; this the coyotes know also, for they live in round holes in the ground. Then a black line should be drawn from the forehead to a point between the eyes; and a line should be drawn on each cheek and on the chin, for these four lines represent the Powers of the four directions. Black stripes were painted around the wrists, the elbow, the upper part of the arm, and around the ankles. Black, you see, is the color of ignorance,[4] and, thus, these stripes are as the bonds which tie us to the earth. You should also notice that these stripes start from the earth and go up only as far as the breasts, for this is the place where the thongs fasten into the body, and these thongs are as rays of light from *Wakan-Tanka*. Thus, when we tear ourselves away from the thongs, it is as if the spirit were liberated from our dark bodies. At this first dance all the men were painted in this manner; it is only in recent times that each dancer is painted with a different design, according to some vision which he may have had.

After all the dancers were painted, they purified themselves in the smoke of sweet grass and put on the various symbols which I have described before. The dancer who had vowed to drag the four buffalo skulls wore the form of the buffalo on his chest, and on his head he wore horns made from sage.

When all the preparations were finished, the dancers stood at the foot of the sacred tree, at the west, and, gazing up at the top of the tree, they raised their right hands and blew upon the eagle-bone whistles. As they did this, Kablaya prayed.

"O Grandfather, *Wakan-Tanka*, bend down and look upon me as I raise my hand to You. You see here the faces of my people. You see the four Powers of the universe, and You have now seen us at each of these four directions. You have beheld the sacred place and the sacred center which we have fixed, and where we shall suffer. I offer all my suffering to You in behalf of the people.

"A good day has been set upon my forehead as I stand before You, and this brings me closer to You, O *Wakan-Tanka*. It is Your light which comes with the dawn of the day, and which passes through the heavens. I am standing with my feet upon Your sacred Earth. Be merciful to me, O Great Spirit, that my people may live!"

Then all the singers chanted together:

> O Wakan-Tanka, *be merciful to me!*
> *I am doing this that my people may live!*

The dancers all moved around to the east, looking towards the top of the sacred tree at the west, and, raising up their hands, they sang:

> *Our Grandfather,* Wakan-Tanka,
> *has given to me a path which is sacred!*

Moving now to the south, and looking towards the north, the dancers blew upon their eagle-bone whistles, as the singers chanted:

> *A buffalo is coming they say.*
> *He is here now.*
> *The Power of the buffalo is coming;*
> *It is upon us now!*

As the singers chanted this, the dancers moved around to the west, and faced the east, and all the time they blew upon their shrill eagle-bone whistles. Then they went to the north and faced the south, and, finally, they again went to the west and faced towards the east.

Then the dancers all began to cry, and Kablaya was given a long thong and two wooden pegs, and with these he went to the center, and grasping the sacred tree he cried: "O *Wakan-Tanka,* be merciful to me. I do this that my people may live."

Crying in this manner continually, Kablaya went to the north of the lodge, and from there he walked around the circle of the lodge, stopping at each of the twenty-eight lodge poles, and then returned to the north. Carrying their thongs and pegs, all the dancers then did as Kablaya had done. When they all returned to the north and faced the south, Kablaya once again went to the center and grasped the sacred tree with both hands.

As the singers and drummers increased the speed of their chanting and drumming, the helpers rushed up and, grasping Kablaya roughly, threw him on the ground. The helper then pulled up the skin of Kablaya's left breast, and through this loose skin a sharp stick was thrust; and in the same manner the right breast was pierced. The long rawhide rope had been tied at its middle, around the sacred tree, towards its top, and then the two ends of the rope were tied to the pegs in Kablaya's chest. The helpers stood Kablaya up roughly, and he blew upon his eagle-bone whistle, and, leaning back upon his thongs, he danced, and continued to dance in this manner until the thongs broke loose from his flesh.

I should explain here why we use two thongs, which are really one long thong, for it is tied to the tree at its center, and also it was made from a single buffalo hide, cut in a spiral. This is to help us remember that although there seem to be two thongs, the two are really only one; it is only the ignorant person who sees many where there is really only one. This truth of the oneness of all things we understand a little better by participating in this rite, and by offering ourselves as a sacrifice.

The second dancer then went to the center, and, grasping the sacred tree, he too cried as Kablaya had done. The helpers again rushed up and, after throwing him roughly on the ground, pierced both his breasts and both sides of his back; wooden pegs were thrust through the flesh, and to these pegs four short thongs were attached. This brave dancer was then tied at the center of four poles, so tightly that he could not move in any direction. At first he cried, not as a child from the pain, but because he knew that he was suffering for his people, and he was understanding the sacredness of having the four directions meet in his body, so that he himself was really the center. Raising his hands to heaven, and blowing upon his eagle whistle, this man danced until his thongs broke loose.

The third dancer who was to bear the four buffalo skulls then went to the center, and, after grasping the sacred tree, he was thrown on his face by the helpers, and four sticks were thrust through the flesh of his back. To these were tied the four buffalo skulls. The helpers pulled on the skulls to see that they were firmly attached, and then they gave to the dancer his eagle whistle, and upon this he blew continually as he danced. I think that you can understand that all this was very painful for him, for every time he moved the sharp horns of the skulls cut into his skin, but our men were brave in those days and did not show any signs of suffering; they were really glad to suffer if it was for the good of the people.

Friends or relatives would sometimes go to the dancers and dance beside them, giving encouragement; sometimes a young woman who liked one of the dancers would put a herb which she had been chewing into the mouth of the dancer in order to give him strength and to ease his thirst. And all this time the drumming, singing, and dancing never stopped, and above it all you could hear the shrill call of the eagle-bone whistles.

The fourth man, who had vowed to give twelve pieces of his flesh, then went and sat at the foot of the tree, holding on to it with both hands; the helpers took a bone awl and, raising up little pieces of flesh on the shoulders, cut off six small pieces from each. This flesh was left as an offering at the foot of the tree, and the man then stood up and continued dancing with the others.

In the same manner, the fifth dancer sacrificed eight pieces of his flesh; the sixth dancer gave four pieces of his flesh; and the seventh dancer sacrificed two pieces. Then, finally, the woman grasped the sacred tree, crying as she sat down, and said: "Father, *Wakan-Tanka*, in this one piece of flesh I offer myself to You and to Your heavens and to the sun, the moon, the Morning Star, the four Powers, and to everything."

They all continued to dance, and the people cheered Kablaya, telling him to pull harder upon the thongs, which he did until finally one thong broke loose, and then all the people cried *"hi ye!"* Kablaya fell, but the people helped him up, and he continued to dance until the other thong broke loose. Again he fell, but, rising, he raised both hands to heaven, and all the people cheered loudly. They then helped him to the foot of the sacred tree, where he rested on a bed of sage, and, pulling the loose flesh from his breast, where the bonds had broken loose, he placed twelve pieces of it at the foot of the tree. The medicine men put a healing herb on his wounds, and they carried him to a place in the shade where he rested for a few moments. Then, getting up, he continued to dance with the others.

Finally, the man who had been dancing for a long time with the four skulls lost two of them, and Kablaya gave the order that his skin should be cut so that the other two should break loose. But even though he was free from the four skulls, this brave man still continued to dance.

Then the man who had been dancing at the center of the four posts broke loose from two of his bonds, and Kablaya said that he, too, had had enough, and with a knife the skin was cut, so that he broke loose from the other two bonds. These two men each offered twelve pieces of their flesh to the sacred tree, and then all the men and many of the people continued to dance until the sun was nearly down.

Just before sundown, a pipe was taken to the singers and drummers as an indication that their work had been finished and that they may now smoke. Then the dancers and the keeper of the most sacred pipe sat at the west of the lodge, and the holy woman took up in her two hands the pipe which had been resting in front of her; holding the stem of the pipe up, she walked around the buffalo skull, and, standing in front of the keeper of the pipe, she prayed.

"O holy Father, have pity on me! I offer my pipe to *Wakan-Tanka*. O Grandfather, *Wakan-Tanka,* help me! I do this that my people may live, and that they may increase in a sacred manner."

The woman then offered the pipe to the keeper three times, and the fourth time she gave it to him. *"How!"* the keeper said as he received the pipe; and then he went and stood under the north side of the sacred tree and prayed.

"Hee-ay-hay-ee-ee! [four times] Grandfather, *Wakan-Tanka,* You are closer to us than anything. You have seen everything this day. It is now finished; our work has ended. Today a two-legged person has made a very sacred rite, which You have appointed him to do. These eight people here have offered their bodies and souls to You. In suffering they have sent their voices to You; they have even offered to You a part of their flesh, which is now here at the foot of this sacred tree. The favor that they ask of You is that their people may walk the holy path of life and that they may increase in a sacred manner.

"Behold this pipe which we—with the Earth, the four Powers, and with all things—have offered to You. We know that we are related and are one with all things of the heavens and the earth, and we know that all the things that move are a people as we. We all wish to live and increase in a holy manner. The Morning Star and the dawn which comes with it, the moon of the night, and the stars of the heavens are all brought together here. You have taught us our relationship with all these things and beings, and for this we give thanks, now and always. May we be continually aware of this relationship which exists between the four-leggeds, the two-leggeds, and the wingeds. May we all rejoice and live in peace!

"Behold this pipe which is the one that the four-legged brought to the people; through it we have carried out Thy will. O *Wakan-Tanka,* You have put Your people upon a sacred path; may they walk upon it with firm and sure steps, hand in hand with their children, and may their children's children, too, walk in this sacred manner!

"Have mercy, O *Wakan-Tanka,* on the souls that have roamed the earth and have departed. May these souls be worthy to walk upon that great white path which You have established! We are about to light and smoke the sacred pipe, and we know that this offering is very *wakan.* The smoke that rises will spread throughout the universe, and all beings will rejoice."

The dancers then sat at the west side of the lodge, and the keeper took the tallow from the top of the bowl of the pipe and placed it upon a purified buffalo chip. The pipe was then lit from a coal, and, after offering it to the six directions, and after taking a few puffs himself, the keeper handed it to Kablaya, who cried as he offered the pipe and, after smoking it a little, handed it to the person next to him. After each man had offered and smoked the pipe, he handed it back to Kablaya, who then handed it on to the next man. When all had smoked in this manner, Kabalaya slowly and carefully placed the ashes upon the very middle of the sacred altar and then prayed.

"O *Wakan-Tanka*, this sacred place is Yours. Upon it all has been finished. We rejoice!"

Two helpers then placed upon the altar the ashes from the sacred fire at the east of the lodge; the purified earth was also placed upon the altar, and then all the wreaths, furs, feathers, and symbols which had been used in the dance were all piled up in the center of the sacred place. This was done because these things were too sacred to be kept and should be returned to the earth. Only the buffalo robes and the eagle-bone whistles were kept, and these things will always be regarded as especially sacred, for they were used in this first great rite of the sun dance. On top of the pile of sacred things the buffalo skull was placed, for this skull reminds us of death and also helps us to remember that a cycle has here been completed.

The people all rejoiced, and the little children were allowed to play tricks on the old people, at this time, but nobody cared; and they were not punished, for everybody was very happy.

The dancers, however, had not yet finished, for they now took their buffalo robes and returned to the preparation tipi. Here they took off their clothes, except for the breech cloth, and they all entered the *Inipi* lodge, except the woman who guarded the door for the men. The five rocks were brought in, and the pipe was smoked around the circle; but, as each man took the pipe, he first touched one of the rocks with it. The door of the lodge was closed, and Kablaya spoke.

"My relatives, I wish to say something. Listen closely! This day you have done a sacred thing, for you have given your bodies to the Great Spirit. When you return to your people always remember that through this act you have been made holy. In the future you will be the leaders of your people, and you should be worthy of this sacred duty. Be merciful to your people, be good to them and love them! But always remember this, that your closest relative is your Grandfather and your Father, *Wakan-Tanka*, and next to Him is your Grandmother and your Mother, the Earth."

Water was put on the hot rocks, and, after a short time, when the little lodge was filled with steam and was very hot, the door was opened and water was handed in. Sweet grass was put in the water and was then touched to the mouths of the dancers, but this was all the water that was allowed at this time. The pipe was passed around; the door was closed; and again Kablaya spoke to the men.

"By your actions today you have strengthened the sacred hoop of our nation. You have made a sacred center which will always be with you, and you have created a closer relationship with all things of the universe."

Water was again put on the rocks, and as the steam rose the men chanted a sacred song. When the door was opened this third time the men were allowed to drink one mouthful of water; after this the pipe was passed around as before. Again the door was closed, and as the steam rose from the rocks, all the men sang.

> *I am sending a voice to my Grandfather!*
> *I am sending a voice to my Grandfather!*
> *Hear me!*
> *Together with all things of the universe,*
> *I am sending a voice to* Wakan-Tanka.

Then Kablaya said: "The four paths of the four Powers are your close relatives. The dawn and the sun of the day are your relatives. The Morning Star and all the stars of the sacred heavens are your relatives; always remember this!"

The door was then opened for the fourth and last time, and the men drank all the water they wished; and when they had finished drinking and had smoked, Kablaya said to them: "You have now seen the Light of *Wakan-Tanka* four times. This Light will be with you always. Remember that it is four steps to the end of the sacred path.[5] But you shall get there. It is good! It is finished! *Hechetu welo!*"

The men then went back to the sacred tipi, where much food was brought to them, and all the people were happy and rejoicing, for a great thing had been done, and in the winters to come much strength would be given to the life of the nation through this great rite.

NOTES

1. In the *Atharva Veda Samhita* of the Hindu scriptures, we find a description of the significance of their World Tree, which is quite identical to the symbolism of the tree for the Lakota: "The World Tree in which the trunk, which is also the sun pillar, sacrificial post, and *axis mundi*, rising from the altar at the navel of the earth, penetrates the world door and branches out above the roof of the world (A. V. X. 7. 3.); as the 'nonexistent (unmanifested) branch that yonder kindreds know as the Supernal' (A. V. X. 7. 21)." (Translated by A. K. Coomaraswamy, Svayamatrna: Janua Coeli," *Zalmoxis.*)

For a full explanation of the symbolism of the tree, see René Guénon, *Le Symbolisme de la Croix*, Les Editions Vega (Paris, 1931); especially Chap. IX, "L'Arbre du Milieu."

2. An interesting parallel to this attitude towards trees is found in an Islamic source: "[Holy] men dance and wheel on the [spiritual] battlefield: From within them musicians strike the tambourine: at their ecstacy the seas burst into foam. You see it not, but for *their* ears the leaves too on the boughs are clapping hands . . . one must have the spiritual ear, not the ear of the body." (Jalaluddin Rumi, *The Mathnawi* [R. A. Nicholson translation, 8 vols., Cambridge University Press, Cambridge, 1926], III 9.)

3. This coal was taken from a fire which had been kept burning all through the previous night, and which will burn every night during the dance. It is located to the east, out-

side the lodge, and, according to Black Elk, it is kept in order to remind the people of the eternal presence of *Wakan-Tanka*. During the day this fire is not necessary because the sun is then present as a reminder.

4. The Sioux also paint their faces black for the dance which is held when they return from the warpath, for, as Black Elk has said, "By going on the warpath, we know that we have done something bad, and we wish to hide our faces from *Wakan-Tanka*."

5. The four steps represent, to the Sioux, the four ages or phases of a cycle: the rock age, the bow age, the fire age, and the pipe age. The rock, bow, fire, or pipe constitutes the main ritual support for each age. The four ages may also refer, microcosmically, to the four phases of a man's life, from birth to death.

6

The Coven

Starhawk

Probably the best-known practitioner of witchcraft in the United States today is Starhawk: and certainly the best-known of her books is *The Spiral Dance,* from which the reading here is taken. A feminist psychotherapist, frequent workshop leader and lecturer, and antinuclear activist, Starhawk carries contemporary feminist and general political concerns to her practice of the Craft. She uses witchcraft as a way especially to empower women, aiming to bring the support of the group to bear on the plights and problems of individual participants. Witchcraft, as Starhawk explains it, is clearly a religion of nature, centering on the worship of the Goddess and her horned consort, with careful attention to the directions and the seasons and cycles of the year. Indeed, the spiral of her book's title is what she calls the "double spiral, . . . whirling into being, and whirling out again." It is the fundamental motion found in all natural forms, including the structure of deoxyribonucleic acid or DNA. Contemporary witchcraft in the United States is of British and American provenance, and against this backdrop the coven—ideally a group of thirteen—is the ritual assembly, the sacred circle created by the ceremonial invocations of witchcraft practitioners as they perform their work. Many who engage in the Craft do so alone, of course. Still, in the coven the circle is cast, as Wiccans, or witches, say. Wiccans also say that the presence of the group raises a "cone" of energy and power. As their ritual ends, witches pray that their circle be open yet unbroken—that the power of the group's knowing through the body go with them as they engage, like other Americans, in life's ordinary tasks.

Between the Worlds
New Moon

"We met tonight in the rented storefront. For a long time, we just talked—about our fears and doubts about magic and ourselves: that it isn't real, that it is real, that it will stop, that it's an ego-trip, that we're crazy, that what we really want is power, that we'll lose our sense of humor and become pompous about it, that we won't be able to take it seriously, that it won't work, that it will work. . . .

At one point, we all took hands, and started breathing together. Suddenly we realized that a circle had been cast. We passed around the oil, for anointing, and kissed. Someone began a low humming, and Pat started tapping out a rhythm on the drum. And we were all chanting, interweaving voices and melodies, as if different words were coming through each of us:

> Isis . . . Astarte . . . Ishtar . . .
> Dawn and darkness . . . dawn and darkness . . .
> Moo-oo-oon, Crescent Moo-oo-oon . . .
> Pour out your light and your radiance upon us. . . .
> Shine! Shine! Shine! Shine! Shine!

and through it and behind it all, Beth was wailing on her kazoo, and it sounded like some strange, Arabian oud, or a sobbing jazz saxophone, but we were smiling at the humor of it . . .

At the same moment, we all fell silent. Then we shared fruit, laughed, and talked about humor. We were thinking about a coven name, and someone suggested Compost. It was perfect! Earthy, organic, nurturing—and discouraging to self-inflation.

We are now the Compost coven!

The ritual worked. Whatever magic brings, it will not take away our ability to laugh at ourselves. And those fears grow less and less all the time."

From my Book of Shadows

The coven is a Witch's support group, consciousness-raising group, psychic study center, clergy-training program, College of Mysteries, surrogate clan, and religious congregation all rolled into one. In a strong coven, the bond is, by tradition, "closer than family": a sharing of spirits, emotions, imaginations. "Perfect love and perfect trust" is the goal.

The coven structure makes the organization of Witchcraft very different from that of most other religions. The Craft is not based on large, amorphous masses who are only superficially acquainted; nor is it based on individual gurus with their devotees and disciples. There is no hierarchical authority, no Dalai Lama, no Pope. The structure of Witchcraft is cellular, based on small circles whose members share a deep commitment to each other and the Craft.

Witchcraft tends to attract people who, by nature, do not like to join groups. The coven structure makes it possible for rabid individualists to experience a deep sense of community without losing their independence of spirit. The secret is its small size. A coven (usually pronounced so as to rhyme with oven), by tradition, never contains more than thirteen members. In such a small group, each person's presence or absence affects the rest. The group is colored by every individual's likes, dislikes, beliefs, and tastes.

At the same time, the coven becomes an entity in itself, with a personality of its own. It generates a *raith* form, an energy swirl that exists over and beyond its membership. There is a quality of synergy about a strong coven. It is more than the sum of its parts; it is an energy pool on which its members can draw.

To become a member of a coven, a Witch must be initiated, must undergo a ritual of commitment, in which the inner teachings and secrets of the group are revealed. Initiation follows a long training period, during which trust and group security are slowly built. When properly timed, the ritual also becomes a rite of passage, that marks a new stage in personal growth. Witchcraft grows slowly; it can never be a mass-market religion, peddled on streetcorners or between flights at the airport. Witches do not proselytize. Prospective members are expected to seek out covens and demonstrate a deep level of interest. The strength of the Craft is felt to be in quality, not quantity.

Originally, coveners were the teachers and priestesses/priests of a large pagan population of noninitiates. They were the councils of elders within each clan, the wise women and wise men who delved beneath the surface of their rites and sought the deeper meanings. At the large solar festivals, the Sabbats, they led the rituals, organized the gatherings, and expounded the meanings of the ceremonies. Each coven had its own territory, which by tradition extended for a league. Neighboring covens might join for the great Sabbats, in order to share knowledge, herbs, spells, and, of course, gossip. Federations of covens were sometimes linked together under a Witch "Queen," or Grandmaster. On full moons, covens met alone for Esbats, when they studied the inner teachings and practiced magic.

During the Burning Times, the great festivals were stamped out or Christianized. Persecution was most strongly directed against coven members, because they were seen as the true perpetuators of the religion. The strictest secrecy became necessary. Any member of a coven could betray the rest to torture and death, so "perfect love and perfect trust" were more than empty words. Covens were isolated from one another, and traditions became fragmented, teachings forgotten.

Today, there is a growing effort throughout the Craft to reestablish communication between covens and share knowledge. But many individual Witches still cannot afford to "come out of the broom closet." Public recognition may mean the loss of their jobs and livelihoods. Known Witches are easy targets for violent crackpots: A Southern California couple were firebombed out of their home after appearing on a television talk show. Other Witches face harassment by the authorities for traditional practices such as divination, or become scapegoats for local crimes. Unfortunately, prejudice is still widespread. Sensitive people never identify anyone as a Witch without first asking permission privately. In this book, my own friends and coveners have generally been referred to by coven names in order to protect their privacy.

Every coven is autonomous. Each functions as its own authority in matters of ritual, theology, and training. Groups of covens who follow the same rites may consider themselves part of the same tradition. To ensure legal protection for their members, many covens band together and incorporate as a church, but the rights of separate covens are always jealously guarded.

Covens usually develop a specific orientation and focus. There are covens that concentrate on healing or teaching; others may lean toward psychic work, trance states, social action, or creativity and inspiration. Some simply seem to throw good parties; after all, "all acts of love and pleasure" are rituals of the Goddess. Covens may include both men and women or be limited to women only. (There are very few all-male covens. . . .)

A coven is a group of peers, but it is not a "leaderless group." Authority and power, however, are based on a very different principle from that which holds sway in the world at large. Power, in a coven, is never power *over* another. It is the power that comes from within.

In Witchcraft, power is another word for energy, the subtle current of forces that shape reality. A powerful person is one who draws energy into the group. The ability to channel power depends on personal integrity, courage, and wholeness. It cannot be assumed, inherited, appointed, or taken for granted, and it does not confer the right to control another. Power-from-within develops from the ability to control ourselves, to face our own fears and limitations, to keep commitments, and to be honest. The sources of inner power are unlimited. One person's power does not diminish another's; instead, as each covener comes into her own power, the power of the group grows stronger.

Ideally, a coven serves as the training ground in which each member develops her or his personal power. The support and security of the group reinforces each member's belief in herself. Psychic training opens new awarenesses and abilities, and feedback from the group becomes the ever-present mirror in which we "see ourselves as others see us." The goal of a coven is not to do away with leaders, but to train every Witch to be a leader, a Priestess, or a Priest.

The issue of leadership has plagued the feminist movement and the New Left. Exemplars of power-from-within are sadly lacking on the American political scene. Power-over-others is correctly seen to be oppressive, but too often the "collective ideal" is misused, to tear down the strong instead of to build strength in the weak. Powerful women are attacked instead of supported: "Am I a traitor? They ought to shoot me. Made me into a leader. We're not supposed to have leaders. I will be executed in some underground paper, my character assassinated subterraneously."[1]

The concept of power-from-within encourages healthy pride, not self-effacing anonymity; joy in one's strength, not shame and guilt. In Witchcraft, authority means responsibility. The coven leader must have the inner power and sensitivity to channel the group's energy, to start and stop each phase of the ritual, adjusting the timing to the mood of the circle. A ritual, like a theater production, needs a director.

In practice, leadership is passed from one covener to another in a fully developed group. The wand representing the authority of the leader may be passed to each covener in turn. Different sections of the ritual may be led by different people.

For example, our last Fall Equinox Ritual was inspired by Alan, who is an apprentice but not yet an initiate of Compost Coven. Alan is very much involved with the men's liberation movement and wanted a ritual centered around changing the sex-role conditioning we have each received. Eight of us, from Compost, from Honeysuckle, my women's coven, and from Alan's men's group, planned the ritual together. Here is my account:

Fall Equinox, 1978

A hot night. Seventeen of us met at Guidot's, nine women and eight men. After some socializing, we went upstairs to the ritual room.

Alan, aided by Guidot and Paul, cast the circle, using beautiful invocations, which I think he improvised on the spot. Three or four of us had explained the ritual to the rest, so they were ready. I led the invocation to the Goddess, using the Kore Chant. I began speaking it, and as I switched into the sung chant, it was as if something came in from behind and lifted me out of myself. My voice physically changed, became a low, deep throbbing, with power pouring through into the circle, and then, as everyone picked up the chant, pouring through all of us—the dark moaning wail of summer's passing, sad but beautiful. . . .

Change is . . . touch is . . .
Touch us . . . change us . . .

Alan, Paul, and Guidot invoked the God, Alan calling Him as the Gentle Brother, the Rape Fighter. He wrote a powerful invocation. . . .

We began a banishing dance, widdershins around the circle. As we moved, one person would throw out a phrase—the group took it up and repeated it, chanted it rhythmically, building it, shrieking it, then letting it die away until its power to control us faded with it. Alan began it:

"You must be successful!"

"You must be successful!" "You must be successful!" "Must be! Must be! Must be!" "Must!"

"Nice girls don't *do* that!" "Nice girls don't *do* that!" "Big boys don't cry!" "You're not a real woman!" "Sissy! Sissy! Sissy!"

Sixteen howling echoes took up every cry, frenzied, mocking voices that became, in the dim light, the pursuing Furies of our own minds, taunting, laughing, screaming—then vanishing, like wisps of smoke. By the end we were stamping, shouting—seventeen stark-naked adults, jumping up and down, yelling "No! No! No! No! No!"

Younger Self was awake in its full, primal glory, all right.

Val has come into her own, her power as the Crone. She performed the Mystery (which is secret), aided, I think, by Alan and Paul. I never saw. Laurel, Brook, and I led the trance, a soft, whispered, three-voiced induction:

> Your fingers are dissolving into. . . .
> Dream deep, and sleep the magic sleep. . . .
> Dissolving into water, and your toes are. . . .

Valerie awakened us. We formed into two groups, for the male and female Mysteries. The men took a long time—I think they got involved in a historical discussion of the rites of Dionysus. When they finished, we one by one moved back into the circle, sitting man and woman alternately. We went around the circle, each saying how we become strong.

"I become strong through facing my fears."
"I become strong through my friends."
"I become strong through making mistakes."
"I become strong through taking a stand."
"I become strong through dreaming."

Then we chanted, raising power to actualize the visions we had seen in trance, of our true, free selves. The chant went on and on, it was so physically pleasurable, feeling the flow of power, the low resonance of the deep male voices, the high, bell-like notes of the women—it swirled around us like a great, warm wave.

After, Alan and I blessed the wine and cakes. As the cup went around the circle, we each said what we were thankful for. The cup went around many times. Then we relaxed, ate, laughed, talked as usual. Alan ended the ritual and opened the circle.

Afterward, I was amazed at how smoothly it all went, with everyone taking different parts. It feels good to be able to step back and let other people take the center, to see them developing their power.

At the present time, both Compost and the women's coven, called Honeysuckle, are covens of elders. Each initiate is capable of leading rituals, directing the energy, and training newcomers. The process of development in each group, however, was very different.

Compost was typical of many of the new, self-initiatory covens that are springing up today without benefit of formal Craft training. I had been taught by Witches many years previously, when I was a college student, but never actually initiated. Most of my knowledge came from dream figures and trance experiences. I had been unable to find a coven I felt was right for me, and for many years I had worked alone. Finally, I decided to see if I could start my own coven, whether or not I was "authorized" to do so. I began teaching a class in Witchcraft through the Bay Area Center for Alternative Education.

Within a few weeks, a group of interested individuals began meeting weekly. Our rituals were collective and spontaneous, like the one described at the opening of this chapter. We resisted set forms and set words.

After a few months had passed, a strong core group developed, and we performed a formal initiation. Our rituals had also taken on a regular pattern, and we decided to set the structure of the rites so that we would have a collective framework, within which we could all be spontaneous and open. Before, the leader—usually me—had decided what was going to happen at any given moment, and everyone else had followed along.

We met many Witches from other covens, and I began studying with a teacher from the Faery Tradition. I began to come into a sense of my own power. As a group, we also realized that the energies we were raising were *real*, not merely symbolic. The group felt a need for an acknowledged leader; at the same time, I felt the need to have my newfound inner power recognized. The coven confirmed me as High Priestess.

Like most people whose sense of inner strength is developing quickly, I occasionally went to extremes. From being a collectivist nonleader, I became a rather heavy-handed High Priestess at times. There are days when my records of rituals read quite differently from either of the two presented in this chapter: "I cast the circle . . . I invoked the Goddess . . . I led the chant . . . I directed the Cone of Power . . ." Fortunately, my coveners were both tolerant enough to let me make mistakes and honest enough to tell me when they didn't like what I was doing. We began sharing responsibilities: One covener would bring the salt and water and purify the circle, another would bring the incense and charge the space. The men invoked the Horned God, and we took turns invoking the Goddess and directing the cone of power. I became more relaxed in the role of leader.

As other coveners developed their own strengths, we decided to "pass the wand." Diane, a tremendously warm individual, who radiates a sense of caring, was our unanimous choice. She had always liked our simple, spontaneous rituals best, and under her leadership we let go of a lot of structure and experimented. "I don't feel like formally casting the circle tonight," she might say, "let's just tap the four walls, and chant. Why don't we chant each other's names?" And so we would chant—sometimes for hours, in the process developing one of the simplest and most beautiful rituals we use today.

Diane left for the summer, and we passed the wand to Amber, the youngest member of our coven. Diane warmed the circle with a steady glow, Amber lit it up with skyrockets, fireworks, and colored flames. Talented, charming, lovable, and unsteady, she is a fine musician with an operatic singing voice and a flair for drama. She inspired us to the creation of more theatrical rituals. . . . But Amber had difficulty functioning at the high level of responsibility that coven leadership demands. She was going through a tense period in her personal life, and, while she usually carried through her commitments, doing so caused her a lot of anxiety and stress. In retrospect, we did her a disservice by not allowing her a longer period of training.

Honeysuckle underwent a different process of formation. It began as a class in the Great Goddess, at a time when I had been High Priestess of Compost for many months, and was already an initiate of the Faery Tradition. I was coming from a much stronger position as a leader, and it took a much longer time before anyone questioned my authority. I was determined not to rush the training of this group, and it was almost a year before I so much as mentioned the word *initiation*. When each woman in turn felt ready to take on more responsibility, was able to question my authority, and was willing to move out from the role of student, she was initiated. A new ritual was created for each member, and each rite crystallized a period of growth.

Finding a coven to join can be difficult. Witches are not listed in the Yellow Pages and rarely place classified ads. Often, however, they do give classes through Open Universities or metaphysical bookstores. Some universities are beginning to offer courses in Witchcraft in their religious studies departments. Occult shops sometimes also furnish leads. The best route, of course, is through personal contacts. Witches feel that when a person is internally ready to join the Craft she will be drawn to the right people.

Unfortunately, a lot of people claim to be Witches who are merely unsavory characters. When you meet someone who calls herself a Witch, listen carefully to your underlying feelings and intuitions. The rituals of many covens are secret, but you should be told or shown enough about them to form a fairly clear picture of what goes on. A true coven will never ask you to do something you feel is wrong for you. Any form of force, coercion, or high-pressure sales tactics are contrary to the spirit of Witchcraft. Real Witches will let you take the initiative in seeking them out.

Witchcraft is not for sale. There are no fees for initiation, and it is considered a breach of ethics to charge money for coven training. Of course, Witches who teach public classes or work as psychic counselors are allowed to charge a fair fee for their time and labor. They will not, however, sell you "blessed" candles for large sums of money or ask you to hand over your life savings in order to remove a curse: Those are favorite dodges of the con artists who prey on the gullible public. A coven may charge dues to cover candles, incense, and other expenses: but the High Priestess will *not* be driving a Mercedes bought by the contributions of her faithful followers.

In a strong coven, members will feel close to each other and turn naturally to each other in times of stress. They generally spend time together socially outside of group meetings and enjoy each other's company. But they also have varied and interesting outside friends and lives and do not spend all of their time together. A coven should not be a retreat from the world, but a supportive structure that helps each member function in the world more fully.

At the present time, there are far more people who want to join covens than there are groups capable of taking in newcomers. If you cannot find a congenial coven, you can either practice the Craft alone or start your own coven.

Working alone is not ideal. Opening up the starlight vision is much more difficult without the support of a group. Those who travel the uncharted pathways of the mind alone run more risk of being caught in subjectivity. Also, working with other people is much more fun.

But, as one Witch who has practiced the Craft by herself for many years says, "Working alone has its good points as well as bad. Your training is rather erratic—but then it is in a lot of covens, anyway. The advantage is that you learn to depend on yourself and learn your limitations. When you do join a coven, you know what you want and what works best for you."

Solitary meditation and visualization practice is part of every Witch's training. . . . Solitary worship is far preferable to joining the wrong group.

You do not have to be an hereditary or even an initiated Witch in order to start your own coven. Naturally, training helps. But the school of trial and error is also a very fine one.

When a group of interested but inexperienced people come together, the first task is to establish a feeling of security. Openness and trust develop slowly, through both verbal and nonverbal sharing. People need time to socialize, as well as work magic. I often start groups with a pot luck dinner, so that everyone can share a very tangible form of energy: food. Consciousness-raising techniques can also be very effective. We may go around the circle, letting each person tell why she or he came to the group and what she or he hopes to get out of it. Everyone is allowed to speak for a limited period of time without interruptions, so that quieter people are encouraged to express themselves and more voluble individuals do not dominate the conversation. Questions and comments come after everyone has had a turn to speak.

Nonverbal sharing is also important in creating group trust. The following exercises teach the sensing and sharing of energy, which is the basis of Craft rituals. They can be done singly or flow into a smooth sequence. I have written down what I say when leading a group through the exercise. In guiding a group, the actual words spoken are less important than the rhythm of your voice and the timing of pauses. The only way to learn this is by practice. Read through the exercises, become familiar with them, and then improvise in your own natural speech patterns.

Exercise . . . : Sensing Group Energy

"The energy we talk about in Witchcraft is real, a subtle force that we can all learn to perceive. Right now, as we are sitting in the circle, be aware of the energy level in the group. Do you feel alert? Aware? Excited? Calm or anxious? Tense, or relaxed? (Pause.)

"Energy travels up and down your spine. Now sit up, as erect as you can without straining. Good. Notice how the energy level has changed. Do you feel more alert? More aware? Good. (Pause.)

"Your breath moves energy in and out of your body. It wakens your body's centers of power. So take a deep breath. Breathe deep . . . breathe all the way down. Breathe from your diaphragm . . . from your belly . . . from your womb. Your stomach should push in and out as you breathe . . . loosen your pants if you need to. Fill your belly with breath. Feel yourself relaxing, recharging. Now notice how the energy of the group has changed. (Pause.)

"Now let's reach out and take hands, linking ourselves together around the circle. Continue to breathe deeply. Feel the energy move around the circle. It may seem like a subtle tingling, or a low heat, or even a sensation of cold. We may all perceive it differently. Some of us may see it—dancing like sparks in the center of the circle. (Long pause.)

(To end here:) "Now take a deep breath, and suck in the power, as if you were sucking through a straw. Feel it travel down your spine, and flow into the earth. Relax."

(Or go on to the next exercise.)

Exercise . . . : Group Breath

(To begin here, say:) "Let's take hands around the circle and sit (or stand) up straight.

"And now, closing your eyes, let's breathe together—breathing the deep breath of the belly, of the womb. Inhale . . . (slowly), exhale . . . inhale . . . exhale . . . inhale . . . exhale . . . feel yourself relax, as you breathe. Feel yourself become strong . . . with each breath . . . become refreshed . . . with each breath . . . feel your worries floating away . . . with each breath . . . become revitalized . . . as we breathe together . . . inhale . . . exhale . . . inhale . . . exhale . . .

"And feel our breath as it meets in the center of the circle . . . as we breathe as one . . . breathing one breath . . . inhale . . . exhale . . . breathing one circle . . . breathing one, living organism . . . with each breath . . . becoming one circle . . . with each breath . . . becoming one . . ." (long pause).

(End [as in first exercise], or go on.)

Exercise . . . : The Tree of Life

(This is one of the most important meditations, which is practiced individually, as well as in the group. In solitary practice, begin by sitting or standing erect, and breathing deeply and rhythmically.)

"And as we breathe, remember to sit erect, and as your spine straightens, feel the energy rising . . . (pause).

"Now imagine that your spine is the trunk of a tree . . . and from its base roots extend deep into the earth . . . into the center of the earth Herself . . . (pause).

"And you can draw up power from the earth, with each breath . . . feel the energy rising . . . like sap rising through a tree trunk . . .

"And feel the power rise up your spine . . . feel yourself becoming more alive . . . with each breath . . .

"And from the crown of your head, you have branches, that sweep up and back down to touch the earth . . . and feel the power burst from the crown of your head . . . and feel it sweep through the branches until it touches the earth again . . . making a circle . . . making a circuit . . . returning to its source . . .

(In a group:) "And breathing deeply, feel how all our branches intertwine . . . and the power weaves through them . . . and dances among them, like the wind . . . feel it moving . . ." (long pause).

(End [as in first exercise], or go on.)

Exercise . . . : Power Chant

(This should always begin with a Group Breath. . . .)

"Now let your breath become sound . . . any sound that you like . . . a moan . . . a sigh . . . a giggle . . . a low hum . . . a howl . . . a melody . . . chant the wordless sounds of the vowels. . . ."

(Wait. In a new group, there may be silence for a moment. Slowly, someone will begin to sigh, or hum very quietly. Others will gradually join in. The chant may develop into a strong hum, or a swelling wave of open-throated notes. People may begin to chortle, bark, or howl like animals, if they feel so inclined. The chant may peak suddenly, and drop to silence, or it may rise and fall in several tides of power. Let it direct itself.

When everyone is silent, allow a quiet time of relaxation. Before the group has time to get restless, earth the power as in Exercise [below].)

Exercise . . . : Earthing Power

(Also called *grounding,* earthing power is one of the basic techniques of magic. Power must be earthed every time it is raised. Otherwise, the force we feel as vitalizing energy degenerates into nervous tension and irritability. In the earlier exercises, we grounded the energy by sucking it in and letting it flow through us into the earth. That technique is often useful when working alone.)

"Now sink to the ground and relax. Place your palms flat on the ground, or lie flat. Let the power sink through you into the earth." (Even if you are meeting in a penthouse fifteen floors above the earth, visualize the energy flowing down to the actual ground.) "Relax, and let the force flow through you . . . let it flow deep into the earth . . . where it will be cleansed and renewed. Relax and let yourself drift peacefully."

These five exercises contain the essence of a Craft ritual. The circle is cast by taking hands; power is raised, shared, and earthed. Sharing of wine and food generally follows—magic is hungry work! As the wine cup is passed around, toasts are made and people express thanks to the Goddess for good things that have come to them. This part of the meeting is relaxed and informal, a good time for sharing impressions and discussing what has gone on. People may move out of the circle at this time, but the meeting *must* be formally ended before anyone goes home. Meetings that dribble off at the end leave people without a sense of closure and completion. If magic has been worked, the energy absorbed then tends to turn into anxiety and irritation, instead of peace and vitality. A meeting can be ended quite simply by having everyone take hands and say together:

> The circle is open, but unbroken,
> May the peace of the Goddess go in our hearts;
> Merry meet, and merry part.
> And merry meet again. Blessed be.

A kiss is then passed around the circle (clockwise).

Sharing poems, songs, stories, pictures, and creative work in the circle also helps build a feeling of closeness. In Honeysuckle, when we are taking in a group of new members we devote an evening to sharing our life stories in the circle. We also jog together regularly and have gone backpacking as a group. Compost occasionally makes "excursions"—for example, to the Chinese Moon Festival parade. We devoted one meeting to watching *The Wizard of Oz* on television and to skipping down the street singing "Follow the Yellow Brick Road."

As the group grows more unified, certain interpersonal conflicts will inevitably arise. The very cohesiveness of the group itself will make some members feel left out. Each person is part of the whole, but also an individual, partly separated from the rest. Some people tend to see the group as a solid entity that completely enfolds everyone else, while they alone are partly left out. Sexual attraction often arises between coveners, and, while the first bright flush of love will draw power into the group, a quarreling couple will cause disruption. If the two break up, and no longer feel they can work in the group together, a real problem arises. A coven leader who is strong and charismatic often becomes the focus of other member's projections. She may be seen as the all-giving earth mother, the eternally-desirable-yet-unattainable woman, or the all-wise prophetess. It is always tempting for her to believe these flattering images and psychically feed on the energy charge they contain; but if she does she stunts her own growth as a real human being. Sooner or later, she will fumble and the image will be shattered; the results can be explosive.

A certain amount of group time and energy spent on resolving interpersonal conflicts is necessary and desirable, part of the growth process that goes on in a healthy coven. But it is all too easy for a group to degenerate into a sort of amateur encounter session or shouting match. A coven cannot function as a therapy group. Problems between members can often be solved more effectively by using magic than by endless discussion. For example, instead of verbally reassuring an insecure covener, place her in the center of the circle and chant her name. If two members cannot work together, but neither wants to leave, the group may need to cast lots, leaving the decision up to the Goddess. And if a High Priestess seems in danger of being seduced by her own public relations campaign, the less star-struck members of the group should gently tell her so. Objective, constructive criticism is one of the great benefits of the coven structure.

A coven becomes a safe space in which members feel free to release their inhibitions: laugh, dance, act silly, burst into song, chant spontaneous poetry, make bad puns, and let Younger Self come out and play. Only then can the higher states of awareness be reached. Many techniques have been developed to drop the "censor" of Talking Self and to let the inner voice speak freely.

Nudity is one such technique. When we take off our clothes, we drop our social masks, our carefully groomed self-images. We become open. The mystical meaning of the naked human body is "truth." Different people need different levels of private space; while some romp happily on nude beaches, others cannot feel comfortable naked until trust has been built over a long period of time. In our covens, public rituals are always clothed. If guests invited to private "sky-clad" ceremonies feel uncomfortable disrobing, they are welcome to wear whatever they like. Vulnerability cannot be forced on anyone, except destructively.

Here is one of the exercises we use to begin opening the inner voice and releasing the blocks to expression:

Exercise . . . : Word Association Trance

(Everyone should lie down and position themselves comfortably. Turn off the lights. Begin with a Group Breath—Exercise [above]. When everyone is relaxed, proceed:)

"Now we're going to go around the circle, clockwise. I'll start by saying a word, and the next person will say the first word that pops into her mind. Then the person after that will respond to her word, and so on, around the circle. Don't think about the word, just relax, breathe deep, and let it come."

(Start. The sequence might go like this:)

"Green/Pea/Soup/Hot/Cold/Ice/Snow/White/Black/Bird/Fly/Sky/Starry/Night/Dark."

(After a few rounds:)

"Now we're each going to repeat the last person's word before we add our own."

(The sequence might go like this:)

"Dark Cave/Cave Bury/Bury Deep/Deep Sea/Sea Wave/Wave Flag/Flag Star/Star Light/Light Ray/Ray Sun."

(After a few rounds:)

"Now we're each going to repeat the last two words before adding our own."

(Now the sequence might run like this:)

"Ray Sun Shine/Sun Shine Day/Shine Day Forever/Day Forever Night/Forever Night Sky/Night Sky Star/Sky Star Light."

(This is an actual invocation we use, which was created by a group during this exercise. As the trance continues, words become entities in themselves. The combinations form constantly shifting scenes, which flash vividly before the inner eye. Gradually, the cycle may die away, and people simply describe what they see:)

"I see a dark sky, dotted with a million stars—one of them shoots across the sky . . ."

"I see a blazing comet, with a golden tail trailing behind . . ."

"I see a trailing peacock's tail with iridescent eyes . . ."

"I see an eye looking at me . . ."

"I see a face, the dark face of a beautiful woman . . ."

(Descriptions may be elaborate or simple. Some may obtain striking visions, others hear sounds or voices, or feel new sensations. A few people may drift off to sleep. After a time, the group will fall silent, each member floating in her own vision. Allow time for everyone to fully experience her inner world, then say:)

"Now breathe deeply and say farewell to your visions. In a moment, we're going to open our eyes and awaken, fully and completely, feeling refreshed and renewed. When I count to three, we will open our eyes and wake up. Now take a deep breath . . . inhale . . . exhale . . . one . . . two . . . three. . . . Open your eyes, and awaken, refreshed and renewed."

It is extremely important to bring everyone fully back into ordinary consciousness. Turn on the lights and change the atmosphere completely. Share food and drink (but not alcohol); move around and talk. Otherwise, participants may remain slightly entranced, a condition that becomes draining and depressing.

This is especially good for opening up the creative imagination and could be used in art or writing classes as well as in covens.

Ritual is partly a matter of performance, of theater. Some people delight in this aspect of Witchcraft; others become shy and frozen in front of a group. The quieter coveners, however, may channel power in other ways. Brook, for example, rarely wants to cast the circle or invoke the Goddess, but when she chants, her voice, ordinarily pleasant but unremarkable, becomes an eerie, more-than-human channel for power.

Magical training varies greatly from coven to coven, but its purpose is always the same: to open up the starlight consciousness, the other-way-of-knowing that belongs to the right hemisphere and allows us to make contact with the Divine within. The beginner must develop four basic abilities: relaxation, concentration, visualization, and projection.

Relaxation is important because any form of tension blocks energy. Muscular tension is felt as mental and emotional stress, and emotional stresses cause physical and muscular tension and *dis*-ease. Power trying to move through a tense body is like an electric current trying to force its way through a line of resistors. Most of the juice is lost along the way. Physical relaxation also seems to change brain wave patterns and activate centers that aren't ordinarily used.

Exercise . . . : Relaxation

(This can be done in a group, alone, or with a partner. Begin by lying down on your back. Do not cross your limbs. Loosen any tight clothing.)

"In order to know how relaxation feels, we must first experience tension. We are going to tense all the muscles of the body, one by one, and keep them tense until we relax our entire bodies with one breath. Don't clench the muscles so they cramp, just tense them lightly.

"Start with your toes. Tense the toes in your right foot . . . and now your left foot. Tense your right foot . . . and your left foot. Your right ankle . . . and your left ankle. . . .

(Continue throughout the whole body, part by part. From time to time, remind the group to tense any muscles that they have let slack.)

"Now tense your scalp. Your whole body is tense . . . feel the tension in every part. Tense any muscles that have gone slack. Now take a deep breath . . . inhale . . . (pause) . . . exhale . . . and relax!"

"Relax completely. You are completely and totally relaxed." (In a sing-song tone:) "Your fingers are relaxed, and your toes are relaxed. Your hands are relaxed, and your feet are relaxed. Your wrists are relaxed, and your ankles are relaxed."

(And so on, throughout the entire body. Periodically pause and say:)

"You are completely and totally relaxed. Completely and totally relaxed. Your body is light, it feels like water, like it is melting into the earth."

"Allow yourself to drift and float peacefully in your state of relaxation. If any worries or anxieties disturb your peace, imagine they drain from your body like water and melt into the earth. Feel yourself being healed and renewed."

(Remain in deep relaxation for ten to fifteen minutes. It is good to practice this exercise daily, until you can relax completely simply by lying down and letting go, without needing to go through the entire process. People who have difficulty sleeping will find this extremely helpful. However, do not allow yourself to drift off into sleep. You are training your mind to remain in a relaxed but alert state. Later, you will use this state for trance work, which will be much more difficult if you are not in the habit of staying awake. If you practice this at night before sleeping, sit up, open your eyes and consciously end the exercise before dozing.

Many of the other exercises can be most effectively practiced in a state of deep relaxation. Experiment to find what works best for you.)

Visualization is the ability to see, hear, feel, touch, and taste with the inner senses. Our physical eyes do not *see*, they merely transmit nerve impulses touched off by light stimuli to the brain. It is the brain that *sees*, and it can see inner images as clearly as those in the outer world. In dreams, all five senses are vivid. With practice, most people can develop the ability to use the inner senses vividly while awake.

Some people naturally see images, others may hear or feel impressions. A few people find it difficult or impossible to visualize, but most find the facility will improve with exercise.

Visualization is important because it is through internal images and sensations that we communicate with Younger Self and the High Self. When the inner senses are fully awake, we may see visions of extraordinary beauty, smell the blossoms of the Isle of Apples, taste ambrosia, and hear the songs of the Gods.

Exercise . . . : Grounding and Centering

Before beginning visualization practice, we should ground and center ourselves. This is again one of the basic techniques of magical work. *Grounding* means to establish an energy connection with the earth. The Tree of Life exercise is one method of grounding. Another is to visualize a cord or pole extending from the base of your spine into the center of the earth. Center yourself by aligning your body along its center of gravity. Breathe from your center—from your diaphragm and abdomen. Feel energy flow up from the earth and fill you.

Grounding is important because it allows you to draw on the earth's vitality, rather than depleting your own. When channeling energy, it serves as a psychic lightning rod—forces run through you into the earth, rather than "burning out" your mind and body.

Exercise . . . : Simple Visualizations:

This exercise is for those of you who have difficulty visualizing. Ground and center. Close your eyes, and imagine that you are looking at a white wall or a blank screen. Practice visualizing simple geometric forms: a line, a dot, a circle, a triangle, an ellipse, and so on.

When you are able to see the forms clearly, visualize the screen in color: red, yellow, blue, orange, green, violet, and black in turn. It may help to look at a colored object with your eyes open, first—then close your eyes and mentally see the color.

Finally, practice visualizing the geometric forms in various colors. Change the colors and forms until you can mentally picture them at will.

Exercise . . . : The Apple

Visualize an apple. Hold it in your hands; turn it around; feel it. Feel the shape, the size, the weight, the texture. Notice the color, the reflection of light on its skin. Bring it up to your nose and smell it. Bite into it, taste it; hear the crunch as your teeth sink in. Eat the apple; feel it slide down your throat. See it grow smaller. When you have eaten it down to the core, let it disappear.

Repeat with other foods. Ice cream cones are also excellent subjects.

Exercise . . . : The Pentacle

Visualize a line of flickering blue flame, like a gas flame from a Bunsen burner. Now mentally draw a pentacle, a five-pointed star with one point up, in the invoking direction: starting at the top and moving down to the left. . . . Watch it form out of the blue flame. Hold the image in your mind for a few moments.

Now retrace it in the banishing direction, starting at the lower left-hand corner and moving up. As you do so, watch it disappear.

Practice until it comes to you easily. This visualization is part of casting a circle.

Exercise . . . : The Knot

Visualize yourself tying a knot—any knot you can tie easily in reality. Try not to see a mental picture of yourself from outside; instead, put yourself in the picture. See your hands moving, and feel the string. Feel every movement you would make, then draw the knot closed, and feel the string pull taut.

This visualization is used to bind spells.

. . . Concentration is the ability to focus on an image, thought, or task, to narrow one's field of awareness and shut out distractions. Like a muscle, it grows stronger with exercise.

Many people today practice forms of Eastern meditation—yoga, Zen, Transcendental Meditation—which are excellent for developing concentration. The more you practice the visualizations, the easier it is to concentrate on the images. The following three exercises will help improve your inner focus:

Exercise . . . : Candle Gazing

In a quiet, darkened room, light a candle. Ground and center, and gaze quietly at the candle. Breathe deeply, and let yourself feel warmed by the light of the candle. Let its peaceful radiance fill you completely. As thoughts surface in your mind, experience them as if they came from outside. Do not let the flame split into a double image: keep your eyes focused. Remain for at least five or ten minutes, then relax.

Exercise . . . : The Diamond

Again, light a candle in a dim quiet room. Ground and center. Gaze at the candle, and visualize a diamond in the center of your forehead, between and just above your eyebrows. The diamond reflects the light of the candle, and the candle reflects the light of the diamond. Feel the reverberation of energy. Hold for at least five or ten minutes, then relax.

Exercise . . . : Mirror, Mirror

Ground and center. In a mirror, gaze into your own eyes. Focus your attention on the space between them. Repeat your own name to yourself, over and over. Again, as thoughts surface, experience them as if they were out-side you. After five or ten minutes, relax.

Projection is the ability to send out energy. It comes quite naturally to most people, once they are aware of its "feel." Projection is also used in another sense to mean the ability to travel "out-of-body". . . . In the Tree of Life exercise and during the Group Breath and Power Chant, we have already experienced what it feels like to send out energy. Here are two other exercises:

Exercise . . . : The Rock

Ground and center. Imagine that you are standing on the seashore, looking out over the waves. In your strongest hand, you hold a heavy rock. Pick it up, inhale, and as you exhale, let it fly! Watch it splash into the sea just below the horizon.

Now look up again. Realize that you can see a horizon twice as far away. Mentally stretch to see it. In your hand, you hold a rock twice as large as the first. Again, take a deep breath, and, as you exhale, throw with all your might. Watch it splash into the far waves.

Once again, look up and realize that you can see a horizon twice as far away again. In your hand, you hold a rock twice as heavy. Take one more deep breath, and as you exhale, throw hard! Watch it splash.

Practice this exercise until you can feel the release of power that goes with the rock.

Exercise . . . : The Hammer

Ground and center. Visualize a heavy hammer in your hand. A stubborn nail is sticking out of a board in front of you. With all your strength, drive the nail into the board. Repeat, doing it three times in all.

Covens have many different ways of taking on new members. Some hold open classes or study groups. We prefer to have initiates take on individual apprentices. Each newcomer gets individualized instruction, tailored to her particular needs. And each coven member has a chance to be an authority, and is forced to conceptualize her own knowledge of the Craft in order to teach it. Apprentices and their teachers develop a strong bond, so each newcomer feels she has a special relationship to one group member. Apprentices also develop a bond with each other as a group. They attend rituals together, so that nobody has to be the "only new kid on the block."

When I train an apprentice, I think of myself as being somewhat like a dance teacher. I suggest a regular discipline, including many of the exercises in this chapter, the "basic barre-work" of magic. Also, I try to identify areas of weakness and imbalance, and prescribe corrective exercises. For example, for one student whose mind continually wanders I might suggest concentration practice. For Paul, on the other hand, who studied for years with a sect of Buddhists and can, in his own words, "bore holes through walls," I suggested daily jogging. During rituals, apprentices have a chance to combine skills learned in solitary practice into an intricate dance of power with the coven and each other.

As a basic, daily discipline, I recommend three things. The first is regular physical exercise. The importance of this cannot be overstressed. Unfortunately, it is one of the hardest things to get people to do. The Craft tends to attract mental and spiritual types rather than brawny athletes. But magic and psychic work requires tremendous vitality—literally, the energy of the *raith*, of Younger Self. That vitality is replenished and renewed by physical activity—much as the motion of an automobile's wheels turns the generator, which re-charges the batteries. Too much mental and spiritual work that is not balanced by physical exercise drains our etheric batteries. Yoga is sometimes good, but it is usually taught as a spiritual discipline that opens the psychic centers, rather than increasing physical vitality. For our purposes, jogging, swimming, bicycling, tennis, or roller-skating are better—something active and enjoyable that gets us out into the elements. Witches who are physically disabled, of course, may be limited to sedentary exercises such as isometrics. If they can spend some time each day outdoors, on the grass or under a tree where they can soak up elemental energies, they will reap many of the same benefits as the marathon runners.

The second thing I recommend for students is daily relaxation practice and a daily meditation, visualization, or concentration exercise. These often change as the student develops. Some people practice several at once, but one is enough. Too many are cumbersome. At one point in my own training, I woke up in the morning and did a trance exercise at my typewriter for up to an hour, then twenty minutes of yoga, including meditations on the four elements and the Circle Visualization; . . . Later in the day I practiced deep relaxation and a lying-down trance. At night, I did a candle-gazing, a water purifica-tion, and a variety of personal spells. Unfortunately, I had very little time left for actually *living*. After a few weeks, I decided that moderation was the essence of wisdom, in magic, as in other things.

The third practice I suggest is the keeping of a magical diary, called a Book of Shadows. Traditionally, this was the "recipe book" of rituals, spells, chants and incantations, hand-copied by each Witch from her teacher. Today, al-though I blush to admit it, such information is generally xeroxed for coven distribution. The Book of Shadows is more of a personal journal. It may in-clude descriptions of rituals, records of dreams, reactions to exercises, poems, stories, and trance journeys. Solitary Witches can use their Book of Shadows to develop some of the objectivity that generally comes from working in a coven. Trances and meditations can be written out in the journal. Tristine Rainer, in *The New Diary,* even describes techniques for using journal writing to remember past lives.[2]

Womb, support group, magical training college, and community of friends—the coven is the heart of the Craft. Within the circle, each Witch is trained to develop her inner power, her integrity of mind, body and spirit. Like families, covens sometimes have their squabbles. But whenever the circle is cast, whenever they raise the cone and call on the Gods together, they recognize in each other the Goddess, the God, the life spirit of all. And so, when every initiate is challenged at the gate to the circle, she speaks the only password: "Perfect love and perfect trust."

Notes

1. Kate Millett, *Flying* (New York: Ballantine Books, 1974), p. 14.
2. Tristine Rainer, *The New Diary* (Los Angeles: Tarcher, 1978), pp. 259–261.

PART TWO

Knowing through the Heart

KNOWING THROUGH THE HEART:
THE PATH OF FEELING AND EMOTION

Here in the United States, the spirituality of feeling and emotion is probably the best-known of all the spiritual forms. Stereotypical images of the evangelical preacher and spirit-filled convert are staples of American literature and even film. This is so much the case that, in fact, both religious sincerity and its converse, religious fraud, are often hung on stick figures labeled "preacher" and "convert"—images of truth and glory, on the one hand, and hypocrisy and deceit, on the other, that attest to the public historical dominance of evangelical piety. From the time of the British North Atlantic colonies to the growing years of the new United States, through the nineteenth and twentieth centuries and into our own day, versions of Protestant Christianity have actively promoted the spirituality of the heart. Indeed, evangelical religion, born out of a series of American awakenings and revivals from the eighteenth century, has been hailed by later historians and religion scholars as *the* classic form of American religious experience.

Already within seventeenth-century Puritanism, the familiar pattern of the "born-again" experience could be traced. In a Christian theological universe governed by concepts of God and the world, of grace and sin, and of heaven and hell, even individuals raised in devout homes amid a righteous society were expected to undergo a deeply personal and emotionally toned experience of sin and salvation, through the power of Jesus Christ. Typically, the would-be convert began by growing "heavier" under the weight of realized sin, went through a time of spiritual desolation and often despair when prayer and contact with higher power seemed blocked and thwarted, and then—often suddenly and inexplicably—broke through to glory. The convert felt—profoundly and intensely—a sense of being grasped and taken over by an Other Power. Sometimes there were fits and starts and faintings; sometimes a sense of loving Presence and forgiveness. The convert had "got religion." The spirituality of the heart had won.

What the convert had won, too, was entry into the religious form that came to be called evangelicalism. Here was a species of heartfelt religion in which a new birth in the spirit was predicated on the words of the Christian Bible, understood as divine revelation with authority to judge and measure individuals, societies, and historical eras. More than that, the new birth in the spirit was experienced as impelling the convert to declare the good news of salvation to all hearers, willing and unwilling, in a process in which the heart feeling of the convert transmuted into the passion and zeal of the missionary. "Go tell it on the mountain," the title and refrain of a well-known black spiritual, became a summary phrase for the spiritual trajectory of those who knew through the heart. And thus, individual experience led to social investment and became the bond of communal joining.

In the Puritan-dominated society of seventeenth-century New England, this felt bond between convert and community was expressed in the notion of the covenant—a pact or agreement between God and his people understood as a collectivity, and also between the people themselves united in the church and in political society. Later religious groupings in American society would have their own terms and their own understandings of the spiritual ties they felt with one another. But the model of the love of things of the spirit overflowing into a love for one another remained as a basic intuition and idea that had measurable social consequences. Paradoxically, what began as sentiment and attention to feeling generated processes of social control that tempered the life of emotion and decidedly curtailed its spontaneity. In American society, the legacy of the revivals was not simply a sensationalized spirituality of strong feeling but, as important, rationalized ends in churches and denominations, in schools and colleges, and in political formations that legislated an identifiable moral order in society.

Closer scrutiny of the religion of the heart suggests that there has often (but not always) been at its center an experience of extreme dualism that, initially, is as destabilizing as ritual spirituality is stabilizing and solidifying. In this version of the heart path, before one can sense empowerment there must be moments—or longer periods—dominated by feelings of utter powerlessness. The news for believers is to give up and let go, in a form of release that is unmediated by the comfort and assurance that ritual brings. Almost, it seems, the seeker comes to the end of an imaginary rope and finds him- or herself hanging. But juxtaposed to the experience of extreme powerlessness stands the strikingly different experience of power. Taken over by a power felt as completely beyond the ordinary self, the individual on the heart path moves from this totalizing image of death to an explosion of divine life, from the depths to the heights. And in this form of spirituality, it is precisely by giving up that, to switch metaphors, the floodgates are opened and the source of power becomes available in ways and capacities not glimpsed or internalized before.

It is this dualism of experience—powerlessness/power, despair/glory, sin/grace, and so forth—that shapes the time dimension of this form of heart spirituality as well. For the temporal signature of those who know through the heart is often "instantism." Whereas the ritualist dwells in an organic nursery of the spirit, mostly content with slowly growing the forms that will lead to next-level life, the evangelical tends to savor the split second of time and its miraculous power of transformation. Spiritual change in this kind of spirituality is prototypically sudden, dramatic, seemingly unpremeditated or explained. Almost, for the outsider, it looks as if the worse off you have been, the better off you will be. Believers cannot experience the split-second shift to glory unless they have been immersed in a seemingly bottomless pit of the spirit.

Given all of this, it should already be obvious that the worldview that dominates the spirituality of those who know through the heart is that of causality. Theirs is a world formed by a creator who, after the generative moment, has in major ways left the creation on its own. The earth plane, on its natural terms, is experienced as seriously deficient and lacking, and at the core of cosmology there is need for a *super*natural order—a plane of existence that can rescue and transform the order of nature, which in its unredeemed state can only limp along. Like world, so individual: weakness and helplessness are almost normative as initial feelings; indeed, they are spiritual triggers for the powers that reside in the causal plane, able to rescue the spiritual seeker if the right formula, the right disposition, can be found.

Much of this description, if not most, is predicated on historical descriptions of Anglo-Protestant and African-American piety in the United States. In the twentieth and twenty-first centuries, however, when pluralism prevails, we can well ask what variations can be found in the classic model. Moreover, even earlier in American religious history and in distinctly Protestant contexts, it is relatively easy to find variations on the heart theme, with these implying a spirituality that is softer, easier, more mildly drawn. Historians, for example, talk about the feminization of American religion in the nineteenth century, a process that—as one consequence—helped nudge many men out of the churches and into men's clubs, lodges, and secret societies. The feminization yielded, in emotional terms, a more and more sentimentalized brand of religiosity, so that the depths and dramas of the classic convert spirituality were neither approached nor experienced. Instead, for many, spirituality came to dwell on a lighter, more pleasurable plane, one on which good feelings were augmented and good spiritual times encountered without a haunting sense of sin and disgrace. Older-style guilt yielded before walks in spiritual gardens with a Jesus who existed to hearten, comfort, and console.

Even with men's clubs and men's movements, however, the feminized model hardly read "for women only." The main evangelical players in Protestant America, by the late nineteenth century, were encouraging for both men and women a brand of sentimentalized religion in which spiritual change was internalized more than acted out in strong emotional displays. Converts and devotees surely continued to feel their religion, but they felt in ways that were polite and decorous more than uninhibited and uncontrolled. The altar call and, by the mid-twentieth century, the decision for Christ, became new signs of the transformed heart. This is so much the case, that a psychologized reading of the rise and continuing popularity of pentecostalism would point to the more permissive space the new religious form offered for exuberant and unrestrained emotional display.

Beyond the Christian orbit, however, the spirituality of the heart was thriving in the twentieth century and on into the twenty-first. Jewish devotionalism on the Hasidic model actively encouraged it; so did the Sufi tradition in Islam, as it came to be adopted in a variety of combinative contexts by non-Islamic American seekers. Hinduism, with its tradition of the *bhakti* spiritual path—the path of love and devotion—fit easily into the evangelical model; so, for example, did Nichiren Buddhism and a variety of other spiritual paths—all of them paths of the heart. As fascinating, a variety of so-called "secular" modalities—movements for self-improvement and the growth of one's human potential—worked on a structural grid that suggested, in the background, evangelical piety and the spirituality of the heart.

For all of these heart devotees, new and old, emotional expressivity in a spiritualizing context has brought its own rewards. When inner equals outer, people experience themselves as strong and self-actualizing, even in the midst of weakness. When they let go to "be themselves" at any given moment, they often feel a sense of integrity and integration, of being in "their truth." The further payoff is that in a sympathetic community of like-minded believers and experiencers, they are likely to receive the kind of acceptance and support that most humans strongly desire, and even require, to live at their best. Moreover, feeling enhances and encourages further feelings—so that individuals who feel together grow closer to one another. Strangers become friends; the ice of alienation and separation is broken, usually—believers say—for the better.

The readings offered here explore the spirituality of the heart in a variety of American contexts. We look first at the classic expression in nineteenth-century evangelicalism in a discursive and descriptive summary. Thereafter, we look at the first-person accounts that come from five very different narrators. We hear the proto-holiness female voice of a nineteenth-century African-American woman who followed, in paradigmatic fashion, the storyline from conversion to missionary labor; and we listen to a not-so-different female voice from a white, originally Canadian woman who founded her own pentecostal denomination. In the late twentieth century, we see a Watergate defendant turn to Jesus and confess unashamedly what the experience has meant to him, even as a secularized Jew and political activist recalls his emotional transformation through the human potential movement in the heavily psychologized est of Werner Erhard. Finally, we meet a Krishna devotee who tells her own compelling story of emotional heights and depths as she strives for a *bhakti* surrender. Once again, as with ritual spirituality, we find threads of commonality in all of these experiences, but we also find distinctive differences.

7

The Second Birth

Curtis D. Johnson

Being "born again" is a verbal formula that many, if not most, Americans have probably heard before. What they may or may not know as well is the spiritual style that accompanies the phrase. As early as the seventeenth century, New England's Puritans insisted on the need for personal conversion before one could enter the church covenant. And after the initial experience of second birth—as conversion came to be called—the devotion of the heart could, and did, continue. As the great eighteenth-century Puritan theologian Jonathan Edwards recalled his own childhood, for example, he wrote in his autobiographical "Personal Narrative" that his sense of "divine things" would "often of a sudden kindle up, as it were, a sweet burning in my heart." By the nineteenth century, Anglo-American evangelicalism had inherited much of the Puritan spiritual agenda and began to modify it, bringing to heart religion a new expressivity and demonstrativeness. In the reading here, from his book *Redeeming America*, Curtis D. Johnson charts what became the classic American evangelical spirituality of knowing through the heart. Departing from a formalist Calvinism in the activist and ideologically democratic early national period, heart religion became personal-choice religion, with personal choice not a private affair of one's solitude but something that one did in public. These changes were institutionalized in the new techniques that came to characterize the emotionally toned religiosity of the revivals that swept the nation in resurgent waves. They were largely a Protestant affair for both whites and African Americans, but they had their Catholic equivalent, too. And they set a pattern that would continue in the United States into the twentieth and twenty-first centuries.

The preaching of the Word was central to the lives of nineteenth-century evangelicals. But this preaching had a greater purpose—to encourage individuals to seek God and experience the Second Birth. Like most Protestants, evangelicals believed in the Reformation principle of *Sola Fides,* or justification by faith alone. This doctrine viewed human beings as inherently sinful and incapable of earning their way to heaven through good works. God, being just, was obligated to punish those who violated his holy law. Fortunately, for humankind, God mercifully sent his son in the form of a human, Jesus Christ, to live a perfect life and then to die by crucifixion as a substitute for sinful humanity. Humans who had faith in Jesus Christ (i.e., who gave up all attempts to save themselves by doing good works, repented of their wrongdoing, and placed all hope for salvation on Christ's atonement for their sins) would receive eternal life after their earthly sojourn had ended. Although Martin Luther was most responsible for bringing the principle of *Sola Fides* to modern Christianity, evangelicals gave the Lutheran principle of justification by faith a subtle shift in emphasis. Evangelicals contended that true faith was more than belief or trust and required a life-changing experience coming from God himself.

The process of religious conversion followed a distinct pattern. Evangelicals went through a five-step process as they moved from unbelief to a full-fledged member of a Christian community. In the first stage of conversion—conviction—souls were awakened to their sinful condition. In the second stage—struggle—anguished seekers tentatively turned to God as an escape from eternal doom. These attempts at salvation were faltering and inconclusive. Frequently individuals confessed sins, only to repeat them later. By the end of the second stage, most seekers were in a state of despair as the old self sought to maintain itself and a new self struggled to be born.

In the third stage—conversion—convicted sinners finally gave up trying to save themselves. Instead they abandoned themselves to the mercy of God, accepted Christ's death as full pardon for their sins, and in the process received emotional reassurance that God included them among the redeemed. In the nineteenth century the type of internal release that came varied widely. Some testified to experiencing a deep, penetrating sense of peace; others claimed to see Jesus, or to being bathed in light. Outside behavior also varied greatly. In some circles converts were "struck down by the power of God" and laid perfectly still on the ground. Others shouted, yelped, or danced as they were "seized by the Spirit."

In the fourth stage—recognition—converts came to grips with the newness of their lives. Many of the redeemed professed to have new hands and new feet; others claimed new powers. Those who had been plagued by unfortunate habits occasionally related that God had destroyed the appeal of vices that previously had tempted them. In the final stage—reintegration—the life of the convert began to coalesce around the new, revitalized evangelical personality. The initial step into the evangelical life-style usually was formal church membership, which included participation in the two Protestant sacraments—baptism, if they had not been baptized as children, and Communion (or the Lord's Supper).

While evangelicals agreed on the necessity of the Second Birth, social location affected how particular groups perceived and experienced this pivotal event. Although the five-step pattern was common to formal, antiformal, and black evangelicals, the farther a group was from the center of society, the more dramatic and tumultuous were its conversion experiences.

Calvinism influenced formalist theories of conversion. Because God was all-powerful and humans were hopelessly flawed, there was nothing people could do to bring about their own salvation. If redemption was to occur, it would happen only by the grace of God.

By the early nineteenth century traditional Calvinists developed a method by which people could, in a limited way, seek their own conversion. The strategy was to "wait upon the Lord," a wise decision in light of conversion being exclusively in the divine realm. While one waited, some useful activities were possible. Many prayed for divine intervention in their souls. Others read the Bible. Some even wrote extensive diaries as they sought to understand the ways of God. Eventually, however, such exercises led to intense frustration and a sense of helplessness. Although they were ready for God's intervention in their lives, only when they knew they could do nothing and were totally dependent upon God's mercy would God act.

The accompanying transformation experienced by traditional Calvinists was remarkably quiet. The entire personality, both mind and emotions, was reorganized around God's divine and eternal plan as the convert internalized the Calvinist understanding of the Christian faith. No longer did the individual question the nature of God or the justice of his laws. Instead the affections focused on God, the soul sought greater understanding, and the self submitted to divine authority. After conversion, new believers fit themselves into the religious social order. Formal evangelicals believed that only "visible saints," those fortunate enough to experience God's intervention in their lives, should be granted full church membership. Thus the first step for new believers was to testify to their conversion before the church so that they could receive full membership. The focus of the testimony and interrogation that followed was not on the experience of conversion but on doctrine. The truly converted would be able to discuss correctly all points of faith.

By the 1820s the so-called "New School" theologians, led by Nathaniel Taylor, Lyman Beecher, and Charles Finney, found the traditionalist formula inadequate. Waiting for conversion seemed antiquated in an activist, democratic America. White Americans were free to choose their occupation, their residence, and their social relationships. With the coming of universal white manhood suffrage, adult white males involved themselves in politics as never before. Everywhere self-determination beckoned, at least until one entered a Calvinist church. There parishioners had no choice, no control over their salvation, but were forced to wait for a distant, omnipotent God to determine their fate. The common frustration over election was revealed in a popular song:

> You can and you can't,
> You shall and you shan't;
> You will and you won't.
> You're damned if you do,
> And damned if you don't.

The New School theologians reworked formalist theology to bring it in line with a society that held personal freedom and self-determination in high esteem. A professor of theology at the Yale Divinity School, Nathaniel Taylor began the modification of Calvinism with the New Haven Theology. By arguing that mankind had the moral ability to choose good or evil, Taylor shifted the source of human sinfulness from a divine plan to the human will. The problem was not that people could not obey God, according to Taylor, but that "Man will not do what he can do." This being the case, the role of the minister was to appeal to the heart so that sinners would choose the salvation freely offered by Jesus Christ.

While Lyman Beecher spread the New Haven Theology throughout New England, Presbyterian evangelist Charles Finney went even further in reshaping traditional Calvinism. Whereas the New Haven theologians sought to save Calvinism by supporting qualified free will, Finney abandoned Calvinism and adapted Methodist techniques and doctrine to a formalist audience. In accepting the Methodist position that humans were free to accept the grace of God, Finney discarded the doctrine of election altogether. Finney believed that human beings, not God, had the final word on whether they would spend eternity in heaven or hell. In portraying this decision for his audiences, Finney used the most powerful democratic imagery at his disposal—the American political election. "The world is divided into two great political parties," Finney argued. "The difference between them is that one party choose Satan as the god of this world [and] the other party choose Jehovah for their governor." Each individual had a choice, and salvation came when sinners decided to yield their lives to God, thus joining Jehovah's party. Election still was a key term in the language of conversion; but in Finney's view, individual sinners, not God, cast the crucial ballot which determined salvation or damnation.

Finney realized that the key to conversion was forcing his audience to choose, which meant overcoming the tendency of many to defer the decision. The sermon, he believed, was the key to mass evangelism. He argued, "We must have exciting, powerful preaching, or the devil will have the people, except what the Methodists can save." Getting effective preaching meant discarding traditional Presbyterian conventions such as writing out sermons according to laws of classical rhetoric and using illustrations from ancient history. Instead Finney, who was a lawyer before his religious conversion, delivered his sermons as though he was arguing a case before a jury. He used everyday examples to illustrate his point, used "you" when speaking of sinners rather than the more abstract and less offensive "they," and spoke extemporaneously, using gestures to increase the emotional power of his presentation. When he described the fall of sinners, for example, he pointed to the ceiling, and as his finger dropped downward, people in the rear seats stood up so they could see the final entry into the flames of damnation.

But powerful sermons alone could not bring fence-straddlers to the point of decision: Finney used a number of New Measures to create an environment that would maximize the beneficial effects of good preaching. The central element of the New Measures was the "protracted meeting." In western New York protracted meetings were held for three or four days at the beginning or end of a series of revival meetings. During that time pious businessmen, craftsmen, and farmers and their families would stop their everyday activities and attend dawn-till-dusk religious services at the local church. In the Eastern cities, asking businesses to suspend operations was out of the question, so the protracted meeting was extended to three- or four-week series of nightly meetings. Inevitably the curious, scoffers, and the religiously uncommitted went to the revival services. Once they were within the church walls, Finney was able to spin his magic. The beauty of the protracted meeting was that should a sinner delay deciding for Christ one night, Finney could urge that soul to choose Jesus on a later evening.

Numerous other New Measures were employed within each revival meeting. Many Christians spent the entire time during services in a separate room where they prayed for the salvation of souls, sometimes out loud and by name. Popular religious music was used to set the mood early in the service. At the end of the revival meeting Finney invited those concerned about their souls to come forward to sit on the "anxious seat," usually the front benches or pews, where they could be spoken to or prayed for individually. Altogether the combination of emotional music, powerful sermons, the anxious seat, the inquiry room, extended prayer meetings, and personal testimonies all extended over a period of days or weeks brought the desired impact for Finney and formalists who copied his methods: thousands were converted and joined Presbyterian, Congregational, and evangelical Episcopalian churches.

Finney and evangelists who used similar methods not only made religious conversion immediate, they also made it public. In moving the experience of the Second Birth from the private to the public sphere, the revivalists simultaneously expanded and diminished the religious role of women. On the one hand revivalism gave middle-class women opportunities to break out of the woman's sphere. Women were central to evangelism, with one observer noting that "in all instances, where they were most active, revivals were most powerful." Traditionally women were active in prayer meetings that preceded revivals. During the 1820s this role increased as men and women joined together to pray in "small circles" for the conversion of individuals, first in Finney's revivals and then throughout the North. Women were also formidable fundraisers and organizers for formalist revivals. On the other hand the rise of professional evangelists, who among formal evangelicals were always men, removed the act of conversion from divine to male hands. Male authority was further enhanced by formalist desires to keep women out of the public sphere. As the revivals progressed it became increasingly clear that while women sowed the seeds of salvation, men reaped the harvest.

Finney's greatest success was among the well-to-do, because his message and his methods paralleled those of the emerging commercial economy. From the moment they laid eyes on him, professionals, merchants, and prosperous artisans rightly suspected that Finney was a man who spoke their language. Unlike most formalist clergy, he forsook the usual elaborate clerical garb for "an unclerical suit of gray." In short, Finney looked like a businessman, and his listeners soon realized that he couched his theology in the language of the commercial center.

Four middle-class values—self-discipline, self-determination, systemization, and order—were prominent in the evangelist's message and ministry. Finney's promotion of self-discipline was particularly evident after 1830 when he toned down the emotional excesses of his early meetings and emphasized order and decorum in the sanctuary even during the emotional intensity of a revival. In the Rochester crusade of 1830–1831, Finney paired personal conversion with temperance, making the abstention from intoxicating drink proof that an individual's experience with God was genuine. Self-determination was prominent as Finney argued that salvation was available not just to a preordained elect but to whomever would choose to join the Lord's army. Finney's love of systemization became clear in 1835 when he published his *Lectures on Revivals of Religion.* Finney argued that a revival was "not a miracle or dependent on a miracle in any sense" but was rather based on scientific laws as was physics or engineering. All any evangelist, or revival engineer, had to do was to employ Finney's scientific means and he would convert dozens, if not hundreds, of souls. While Finney borrowed many of the techniques of such antiformalists as the Methodists, his love of order kept them from offending middle-class sensibilities. The evangelist would not permit the "loud praying and pounding on benches" that accompanied antiformalist religious rallies, noting that "inquirers needed more opportunity to think than they had when there was so much noise."

Despite the success of Taylor, Beecher, and Finney's New School innovations, traditionalists retained enormous power in formalist circles. Taylor managed to escape censure, but Beecher was tried for heresy by the Presbytery of Cincinnati in 1835. Finney found the confines of Presbyterianism too constricting, left the denomination, and became an independent Congregationalist in the mid-1830s. But the New School movement had grown too large to be stopped by removing its leaders. In 1837 the traditionalist majority expelled the New School faction (almost half of total membership) from the Presbyterian church. The New School faction promptly organized its own General Assembly and competed against the Old School until after the Civil War.

Even as Finney was reaching the peak of his influence, a new form of formalist religion—devotionalism—gained power after 1830. Devotionalism was particularly attractive to urban middle-class women because it gave them a social role that was in theory equal to, but not equivalent to, that of their husbands. With their husbands "winning the bread" away from the house, women assumed nearly exclusive responsibility for raising the children. Not only were women supposed to teach their offspring the values of hard work, honesty, thrift, and obedience, all of which would ensure future success in the business world, but they were to bring their children to saving faith. This latter role received national validation in 1847 when Horace Bushnell published *Christian Nurture.* Bushnell rejected the revivalist ethos outright, arguing that a life-changing conversion experience was unnecessary. Instead of waiting for children to receive Christ during an adolescent crisis, Bushnell maintained "that the child is to grow up a Christian, and never know himself as being otherwise." With this statement Bushnell removed the mantle of evangelistic responsibility from the professional revivalist and placed it on the shoulders of the Victorian mother.

By the 1850s devotionalism had made significant inroads into areas once dominated by traditionalists and New School theologians. Religion no longer focused on God the Father, a deity who may or may not have given people free will regarding salvation, but rather on a loving Jesus who exhibited the feminine virtues of obedience, submission, gentleness, and long-suffering faithfulness. Instead of emphasizing correct doctrine or saving grace, devotionalists sought a closer walk with Jesus, a Savior who not only atoned for the sins of all but who befriended and solved the personal problems of those who loved him. With the success of devotionalism, formal evangelicalism was barely distinguishable from nonevangelical forms of Christianity. Devotionalists believed that a personal commitment to Christ was necessary for salvation, but they also maintained that conversion need not be internally disruptive in any way. Instead children could grow in their knowledge of God and commit themselves to Jesus at a very early age.

While the conversions of formal evangelicals were relatively orderly, antiformalists understood the Second Birth to be both democratic and emotional.

The religious populism characteristic of Methodists and Baptists extended to conversion, as these two groups headed for the frontier and brought tens of thousands of ordinary folk into their folds. Religious fervor, cried the populists, was the only thing God respected. Formalist wealth, prestige, and education meant nothing to the Almighty—only a life dedicated to Him mattered. Antiformalists believed that the emotions could not stand idle while people passed from death unto life; they expected conversions to be emotional and were suspicious of claimed transformations that did not have the requisite drama.

The most prominent antiformal group, the Methodists, preached a democratic theory of conversion known as Arminianism. This doctrine maintained that God did not choose who would be saved or damned; that Christ died for all sinners, not just an elect few; and that individuals could determine their own eternal fate by accepting Jesus or continuing to follow the devil. Evangelical Arminianism in the United States appealed most to social outsiders who believed that elites used Calvinism as a way to monopolize religion. Antiformalists identified Calvinism as the faith of the comfortable and privileged few while less prestigious groups did the true work of God. Peter Cartwright, the Methodist circuit rider, boasted how "the illiterate Methodist preachers actually set the world on fire, (the American world at least,) while [the Calvinists] were lighting their matches!"

Antiformalists were not surprised that Calvinists promoted predestination, as they suspected the Calvinists assumed that they, not the poor, were God's chosen few. Methodists attacked the Calvinist theory of election as not only undemocratic (by negating the human will and restricting salvation to a few) but as unscriptural and a violation of common sense. Perhaps the greatest criticism that Methodists leveled against predestination was that it kept people from seeking salvation. When James Finley was a young man his father asked him why he did not pray. The young Finley responded, "Because I do not see any use in it. If I am one of the elect, I will be saved in God's good time; and if I am one of the non-elect, praying will do me no good, as Christ did not die for them."

Officially Baptists were Calvinists, but for the most part they operated as Arminians when it came to saving souls. One Baptist missionary noted the similarity between Western Baptist and Methodist preaching in that both were "very controversial and most bitter against Calvinists." Baptists were able to slip away from their Calvinist origins because they placed ultimate ecclesiastical authority in the hands of the local congregation. Recognizing no authority but the Bible, local congregations avoided the conundrums of Calvinism by downplaying doctrine, emphasizing the human role in conversion, and trying to convert as many sinners as the Methodists.

Unlike the formalists, Methodists and Baptists did not try to "restrain the

Spirit." Powerful emotions were proof of conversion, not a hindrance to understanding doctrine. Antiformalists wanted spontaneous worship that was free to move whichever way God might lead. The camp meeting embraced both democracy and emotionalism and dominated antiformal evangelism in the early nineteenth century. While Presbyterians created the essential elements of the camp meeting in their eighteenth-century sacramental meetings, the camp meeting did not become a staple of nineteenth-century life until it was adopted by the Methodists. The white population was widely dispersed in the new states of Kentucky and Tennessee. Usually Methodists dealt with this problem by having their ministers "ride the circuit" by periodically visiting homes and class meetings. The problem with this approach was that it could take a circuit rider six weeks to make one trip around the five-hundred-mile circuit, making it impossible for the minister to preach regularly to any group of people. In 1800 a group of Methodist, Baptist, and Presbyterian ministers decided to preach to thousands of people for an extended period of time. Instead of sending the minister to the people, they had the people come to the minister. The eighteen clerics planned a four-day meeting, sent fliers across two states, and cleared a site near Gasper River, Kentucky, so that people coming from forty to a hundred miles away could camp out in tents overnight between the day-long preaching services. The meeting was successful in the eyes of its promoters, and additional meetings were held in the summer and fall of 1800.

The Cane Ridge revival in 1801 further popularized the camp meeting as an antiformal evangelistic tool. The Cane Ridge meeting was spectacular both in terms of its size and its activities. Observers estimated that between 10,000 and 25,000 people attended. At any given moment as many as seven preachers—speaking separately—each had huge crowds hanging on their every word. The masses that attended Cane Ridge were both emotional and vocal; the audience laughed, cried, shouted, and sang in response to the minister's message. One participant described the resulting noise to be "like the roar of Niagara." Cane Ridge was so noted for its physical expressions of religiosity that cynics referred to the events there as "acrobatic Christianity." Saints, seekers, and sinners frequently experienced what one observer called "the jerks," in which "hundreds of men and women would commence jerking backward and forward with great rapidity and violence, so much so that their bodies would bend so as to bring their heads near to the floor, and the hair of the women would crack like the lash of the driver's whip." When a preacher was driving home the horror of hell and the glories of heaven, many in his audience sometimes stiffened, toppled over, and laid in a semiconscious state from a few minutes to twenty-four hours. "At one time," a witness related, "I saw at least five hundred swept down in a moment, as if a battery of a thousand guns had been opened upon them, and then immediately followed shrieks and shouts that rent the very heavens. My hair rose up on my head, my whole frame trembled, the blood ran cold in my veins . . ."

By 1820 the camp meeting was the central feature of Methodist evangelism. In that year alone almost one thousand encampments were held across the United States. No longer restricted to the frontier, camp meetings were held on the east coast near urban areas. As camp meetings grew in popularity, they lost some of the bizarre behavior that characterized Cane Ridge. Jerking and falling largely disappeared as the newly redeemed now expressed their joy through the more understandable means of leaping and shouting. In its mature phase the camp meeting had a predictable format whereby the five-step process of conversion, an event that could take months or years according to traditional Calvinists, was often compressed into a four-day period. In the ideal case, seekers, scoffers, and the merely curious would be convicted, experience great emotional discomfort, receive an emotional release upon conversion, testify to saving grace, and finally integrate their lives with fellow believers by joining a church and participating in Communion by meeting's end.

During the encampment clergy and laity each played specific roles in encouraging conversions. The first stage, conviction, was the responsibility of the preacher. Religious services were held throughout the day, with ministers taking turns on the elevated platform. Preachers began by quoting a specific scriptural text but used it as a launching pad rather than as an organizing device. Once into the sermon, ministers emphasized the sinfulness of mankind, the horrors of hell, the glories of heaven, and the necessity of seeking God immediately. Homey examples and folk illustrations elaborated each point. Should anyone doubt their sinfulness, preachers attacked a wide variety of frontier vices. Should all else fail, there was always the Methodist "trinity of devils to fight, namely superfluous dress, whisky, and slavery." The goal of each sermon was to "strike fire" or bring a powerful emotional response from the preacher's listeners.

Once the preacher had struck fire and many appeared to be under conviction, he stepped down from the platform and joined a host of believers who had sprung into action to exhort the awakened. At this point struggling sinners exhibited great emotion as they wrestled with a sense of guilt. Crying, wailing, and other signs of emotional distress appeared as the convicted struggled to separate themselves from their past "sinful" lives. The symbolic step of separation was to leave their place in the crowd and move forward to seats (called mourners' benches) directly in front of the speaker's stand. The decision to go forward was difficult because conversion meant rejecting secular life, abandoning old pleasures, and joining a church that had extremely strict behavioral codes. Realizing that those in distress needed encouragement, numerous lay people (including women and children) and clergy served as exhorters who milled around the audience and pleaded with the convicted to step forward.

One by one, mourners experienced emotional release, assurance of God's acceptance, and a belief they had attained eternal life.

Both the convert and the church community recognized the individual's new status after the experience of grace. New believers went to instructional sessions where they were told what was expected of those who professed saving faith. Converts also attended the love feast, a communal gathering usually held toward the end of the camp meeting, where they shared bread and water and told everyone what they had experienced. In Baptist camp meetings the newly redeemed were led down to a nearby river where they were baptized by immersion and were granted church membership. Methodists usually had acceptance ceremonies toward the end of their encampments as well. New confessors were welcomed into a local class (a fellowship group of approximately fifteen people), were placed on probation (usually for six months), and were admitted as full members if they lived a strict, moral life during the probationary period. Camp meetings ended with "closing exercises" where converts joined other believers in a march around the campsite, once again demonstrating the new believer's status within the community of saints.

Camp meetings were not only religious meetings, they were social gatherings for the whole community. Geographically, saints and seekers occupied the worship and encampment areas in the center of the meeting area. Socializers and scoffers pitched their tents in an outer ring where they could pursue their own activities without being disturbed by enthusiastic preachers and their emotionally wrought audiences. While those in the center focused on religious conversion, the out-dwellers were most interested in selling and consuming whiskey, gambling, fornicating, and brawling. Frequently the two groups came into conflict. On more than one occasion Peter Cartwright left the preacher's stand to battle rowdies intent on breaking up his meeting. Prosperous women often saw the camp meeting as an opportunity to find prospective mates and to show off their finery, while prostitutes saw the encampment, with its many thousands of men in a relatively confined area, as an unusual opportunity to make money. Emotional religion and sexual license both flourished in the camp environment. Many encampments set up patrols which monitored the borders between the religious and the irreligious, but problems of violence and illicit sex were never fully eradicated.

Protracted meetings were a variation of camp meetings, and they eventually replaced the encampments as an evangelistic tool. Baptists preferred protracted meetings from the early nineteenth century, and Methodists (and New School Calvinists) came to prefer them as well. Protracted meetings were held inside a church building and continued every evening for several weeks. They were particularly useful in regions that had left the frontier stage of development and were part of a commercial network. Everyday economic activities were not interrupted as participants could perform their normal business functions by day and attend services at night. In addition, the protracted meetings were much easier to police as the walls of the church building were a natural barrier between religionists and town rowdies.

Despite the importance of camp and protracted meetings, many antiformalist conversions occurred away from mass gatherings. One such instance occurred in central New York, after George Peck, a local circuit rider, visited James Andrews, a young, recently married farmer. Peck counseled Andrews regarding his soul, then left the field where they spoke and returned to the farmhouse. Moments later Andrews's mother found the young farmer lying in a field, and she shouted, "O dear me, the horse has kicked James!" After Peck rushed back to the field he found Andrews and his parents "with their arms around each other, reeling this way and that, James shouting, 'Glory to God!' and all three weeping, praising the Lord, and acting as if they were wild with joy."

By the 1840s and 1850s antiformalist religion was less emotional and conversions occurred less frequently than in earlier years. A major factor in this change was that Methodists and Baptists prospered, gained influence and status, and moved toward the political and economic center of American society. They also adopted some of the formalist religious patterns that characterized evangelical Episcopalians, Presbyterians, and Congregationalists. The tendency to formalize was strongest in the urban North. Well-to-do New York City Methodists found an important ally in Nathan Bangs, a prominent minister who stressed orderly worship and believed that "clapping of the hands, screaming, and even jumping . . . marred and disgraced the work of God."

Generational change was another factor that undercut emotional religion during the 1840s and 1850s. This decline occurred partly because the religion's adherents generally grew up in the faith rather than having consciously chosen it, and tended to take their religion for granted. Although camp meetings continued after 1820, more and more Methodists and Baptists grew up in the faith than were converted to it. As a result they were also less enthusiastic about their Christianity and found it difficult to experience dramatic conversions that sharply differentiated between their life in "the world" and their life after redemption.

But Methodists did not simply mimic the formalists and move toward the relatively tranquil childhood conversions of maternal Christian Nurture. Instead some Methodists maintained emotional religion by transferring the climactic event in a Christian's life from conversion to "the second blessing," an event in which the Holy Spirit brought the Christian purity of heart. Phoebe Palmer, the principal figure in the holiness movement that promoted the second blessing, grew up in the home of devout New York City Methodists. Palmer experienced giving her heart to Jesus at such an early age that she could not point to the moment of her conversion. Throughout her twenties and thirties Palmer wondered if she was a true Christian because she did not have the dramatic conversion experience considered necessary for salvation. In the course of her struggle Palmer accepted John Wesley's doctrine of entire sanctification, also known as evangelical perfection or the second blessing, which stated that personal holiness came as a gift from God, that Christians could overcome the "inbred sin" that remained in their lives even after conversion, and that total submission to Jesus would result in sinless perfection. Individuals who were sanctified, according to Palmer, received the witness of the Holy Spirit in the emotions, thus producing an experience in many ways similar to conversion. Palmer's experience of entire sanctification in 1837 finally gave her the emotional proof she needed to be convinced she was truly a Christian. In 1843 she published *The Way of Holiness* which spread her teachings among second- and third-generation urban Methodists whose conversions came too early to remember but whose tradition demanded that God touch their hearts in a remarkable manner.

Black Americans experienced the most tumultuous conversions among antebellum evangelicals. Being "struck dead" by the power of God was the norm for African American conversions long after the Civil War. Even more than white antiformalists, blacks believed such otherworldly experiences as dreams and visions to be an integral part of the Christian life.

In order to understand African American conversion experiences, it is necessary to look at West African religion, which was a rich source of slave culture. In African religions, humans lived in the physical world but had to deal successfully with two kinds of spiritual beings immediately above them if they were to prosper. The living dead (those who had died relatively recently and who were still remembered by name) were directly above humans. Like kinfolk within a specific community, they were closely tied to their descendants. Africans were expected to venerate the living dead; the departed would reciprocate by rewarding faithful descendants with longevity and prosperity, and by punishing the neglectful with disease or other personal disasters. The divinities (mythic leaders, founders of clans, and the spirits of ordinary folk who died in the distant past) often had greater powers than the living dead and could direct natural elements such as weather and animals, as well as intervene directly in the lives of human beings. Both the living dead and the divinities were unpredictable and dangerous, and priests and mediums were needed to discern their wishes and appease them. The High God, by far the most powerful figure in the sacred cosmos, operated far above humans, the living dead, and the divinities. The High God created the world, combated evil and worked for good, and presided over all other beings, but did not actively influence the affairs of humankind.

Africans believed that spirits (the divinities and living dead) communicated their desires to humans through sacred ceremonies. Typically tribesfolk danced in a circle using the whole body, including hands, feet, belly, and hips. The circle moved counterclockwise and was driven by beating drums which set the pace of the dance and called up the spirits. The community supported the dancers by encouraging them through hand-clapping, foot-tapping, and antiphonal (call-and-response) exhortation and singing. The song and dance were continuously repeated, steadily increasing in speed and intensity, until the emotions of the dancers and their observers were at fever pitch. At this point the dancers had fully opened themselves to the spirits, and the lesser gods and/or divinities responded by "mounting" the participants and dancing them in front of the community. The spirit had now totally absorbed the individual personalities of the dancers, and each possessed person, in a trance, paraded in the spirit's emblems and colors, and sampled the spirit's favorite foods.

Once slaves were Christianized, many African religious practices were given a new meaning. Rhythmic singing, preaching, and shouting were continued but in praise of a Christian God. Blacks still sought ecstatic experience, but the experience of the Holy Spirit was qualitatively different from possession by a tribal spirit. In the Christian context the enraptured believer's personality was not replaced by another being. Rather, the Holy Spirit filled the believer with happiness and power, and the believer had no choice but to sing, shout, and dance in response to the spirit's acting on his or her soul. The "ring shout" or "running spirituals" were central to slave worship, and black evangelicals used the "ring shout" to call on the Holy Spirit. The shout was so central to slave worship that when white missionaries and free urban blacks (whose religion was more acculturated) tried to suppress it, slaves invariably resisted, protesting that "without a ring sinners won't get converted."

Unlike white evangelicals, African American evangelicals were not obsessed with doctrinal quarrels over the nature of conversion. Predestination had little appeal to slaves, as it implied that God intended their involuntary servitude. Concern for theological abstractions paled beside the more practical question of how to obtain eternal life. While African American evangelicals agreed that having a conversion experience was essential to gaining salvation, what they thought important was the fact of conversion, not theories about how the process of conversion occurred.

Interviews in the late 1920s show that African American slaves typically fell into a deep trance where they visited the eternal realms of heaven and hell. By contrast, European American dreams and visions were usually limited to a single phenomenon such as a visit by a warm and compassionate Jesus or the presence of a light that caused all objects within a room to glow. Whites, unlike blacks, were not transported to a different reality but saw only an alteration of ordinary experience.

Black conversions occurred in a variety of places and circumstances, in groups and in private. Many blacks were already under conviction and sought release in church. Many others experienced grace at camp meetings (which usually were segregated until the last day), at revival meetings, or at the hush harbors. Slave worship reinforced community solidarity and the communal rite of conversion; still, many slaves experienced conversion alone as they underwent a period of "striving." The African precedent for this approach was the initiation ceremony into the cult of the gods, when individuals went into the bush first for a period of self-purification. Baptists in the Sea Islands of South Carolina encouraged those under conviction to undergo a long process of prayer and self-examination "in the bush" as they sought personal conversion.

Many African Americans who had no conscious desire to get right with God experienced sudden conversion while working in the cotton fields, chopping wood in a forest, piling lumber, or playing "in a crap game out on the Harding pike." Those who experienced unexpected conversion often expressed amazement that they were among the chosen: "I don't know why it was I got converted because I had been doing nearly everything they told me I ought not to do."

Whether conversion was sought or totally unexpected, narratives inevitably began with a voice speaking to the future convert. Sometimes the voice was inward; other times it came from the environment and the hearer looked for a human source. A slave named Morte said he "jumped because I thought it was my master coming to scold and whip me for plowing up some more corn." Sometimes the voice brought a comforting message, but more often it conveyed the warning, "You got to die and can't live."

Shortly after hearing the voice, the convert was immobilized and entered a trance often described as a form of death. One convert recalled, "I was in my house alone and I declare unto you when His power struck me I died. I fell out on the floor flat on my back. I could neither speak nor move for my tongue stuck to the roof of my mouth; my jaws were locked and my limbs were stiff." Others claimed to have become "weak and faint" or "just heavy" immediately before having a divine vision.

Once in the conversion trance, individuals usually traveled to hell where they saw the horrors of damnation and struggled over the state of their souls. The portrayal of hell was graphic. One convert insisted he "saw old Satan chained about his chest and legs in a square pit. He just stood staring at me and moving his club-foot." Another saw "a deep chasm filled with ravenous beasts and old satan was there with a ball and chain on his leg. He had a great ball in his hand and threw this at me but it missed." To compound the horror, those in the trance frequently saw those they had known in life who were "were just roaming and staggering along" and "saying, 'Oh, how long?'" The horror reached a climax when travelers saw their own condition. Frequently they saw themselves dangling over the flames of hell or split in two, with a smaller self looking over the old dead self that was perched "on the very brinks of hell." This idea of two selves appears to have been carried over from West Africa, as many tribes believed in an inner self or soul that was distinct and could be removed from the outer self or the body.

At this point the convert invariably cried out for God's mercy. In every case the Lord responded quickly by providing a visible means of escape, demonstrating to the traveler that his or her soul had been spared and salvation had been accomplished. Sometimes hell's visitors escaped by using God-given angel wings, a heavenly chariot, a divine ladder, or by following a comforting voice. Most often help came in the form of "a little man, very small and with waxen hair." Invariably the little man (who was usually white) gave words of comfort, urged the convert to follow him, and led the way eastward to the gates of heaven. Paradise was described in a number of ways but most often as a huge beautiful city, as a huge room where all God's children sat eating around a table, or as "a beautiful green pasture [where] there were thousands of sheep and they turned towards me and all in one bleat cried out, 'Welcome! Welcome! to the House of God.'" In most accounts God was a dominating personal force who had at last set things in proper order and rewarded the righteous with everlasting life.

Individual slaves experienced in different ways the final two stages of the conversion process. Sometimes recognition and reintegration occurred while the convert was still in the trance. After one man was lifted over the gulf of hell, he reported, "I looked at my hands and they looked new. I looked at my feet and they looked new too." He went on to experience divine acceptance, as "there was the heavenly host of angels and they all said, Welcome! Welcome!" At other times the last two stages of conversion occurred directly after the trance. One woman professed that "When I came to I looked at myself and I was all new. . . . I began shouting and praising God." An ex-slave named Mary reported that within a week after she regained consciousness, she "went to church . . . having been directed in the spirit to an old preacher named Rev. Mason who, after hearing my testimony, reached me among his flock."

The conversion trance allowed slaves to go through the redemptive process in a specifically African manner. While traditional Calvinists saw conversion as taking months or years, and Methodists compressed the period of conversion into the camp meeting's four days, African Americans had trances that moved them through all five stages in a matter of hours. The rapidity of the process appears to be linked to the perceived closeness of God. Groups that believed God to be very near, rather than simply transcendent, tended to have dramatic, quick conversions, and Americans who drew inspiration from their

African heritage, which drew no sharp distinction between the secular and the sacred, had the most stunning, rapid transformations of all. Just as African worship went beyond "head" and "heart" to involve the body, African American conversion was not just an intellectual or an emotional event but a totally soul-stunning experience, physically felt.

For many slaves the conversion trance was only the first step in the world of the supernatural. Many reported having dreams, visions, and premonitions for years afterward. Believers reporting these phenomena maintained that these experiences were part of the way their Heavenly Father spoke to his children. Most ongoing accounts tell of angels, heavenly ladders, or celestial objects appearing to give the faithful direction or confidence. A few believed God revealed the future through such experiences. One woman claimed she saw Jesus in a vision and "this time it was a warning of death. I saw in the west one evening, a cloud and in it I first saw a man's foot but as I looked I saw the head exposed at another point in the cloud. . . . About a month after this a very dear uncle of mine died and I think that this vision was a warning." In Africa the power to see the future belonged to the priest-king; among black Southern evangelicals such powers were claimed by those whom God especially touched.

The stunning nature of slave conversion narratives suggests that conversion played a different emotional role for black slaves than it did for whites. Formalists and antiformalists looked to conversion as proof of their salvation; African Americans saw conversion as proof that God recognized them in a society that gave them so little recognition. One ex-slave testified that as a result of her dramatic conversion, "I say that a child that has been truly born of God knows it . . . the law is written in my heart and I don't need no book." Another regarded his conversion as God's "spiritual answer of approval" that gave him confidence. Shortly before he attempted his escape from slavery, he heard "a voice like thunder" that told him "though wicked men hunt you, trust in me, for I am the Rock of your Defense."

While this portrayal of religious conversion fits most antebellum black evangelicals, some blacks experienced conversion and worshiped God in ways that deviated from the African American norm. Just as white antiformalists lost some of their exuberance when they rose in social status, some black evangelicals downplayed African aspects of worship when they moved beyond the status of bondsmen. The tendency toward acculturation was strongest in the North where blacks were heavily outnumbered by whites and where African Americans had some chance at vocational and educational advancement. Thus some Northern free blacks experienced conversion and preferred worship styles that were less overtly African than those in the South. But the dominant influence in shaping antebellum black religion was the overwhelming power of the Southern, African-oriented majority.

The impact of emotional, revivalist religion was felt far beyond the evangelical community. Christians from other traditions began to mirror evangelicalism and to stress conversion experiences. By mid-century, when a number of evangelicals deemphasized revivalism in favor of feminine, devotional, and domestic religion, American culture was moving in a parallel, feminized direction.

Although American revivalism was an evangelical invention, it spread beyond evangelical circles between 1820 and 1860. Its use can be seen in three traditionally nonevangelical groups—the Quakers, Lutherans, and Roman Catholics.

By the 1820s evangelical ideas had become controversial among Quakers. While country Friends were more successful in continuing the traditional Quaker life-style which emphasized plain speech, dress, and homes, city Friends reflected the larger commercial culture, wearing "plain" clothes made of the finest fabric and living in well-furnished, luxurious houses. In addition, country Friends maintained the traditional emphasis on the "inner light" while city Friends often adopted the evangelical themes of *Sola Scriptura,* social reform, and the need for a saving, inner experience of grace. The "evangelicalization" of Quakerism alienated traditionalists, and the two groups battled for control of the movement. In 1827 the Friends split permanently into two, both sides claiming to be the true heirs of the Quaker tradition. Some Friends gravitated toward Elias Hicks, who denied that the Bible had any unique authority, rejected original sin, and saw Jesus as being unimportant, except as an example of one who was "wholly given over to following the Inner Light." The "evangelical" Friends called the Hicksites heretics (even though Hicksite teaching was closer to traditional Quakerism than was their own), renamed themselves the Orthodox Friends, and in essence became another evangelical denomination.

In central Pennsylvania a similar controversy emerged among German-speaking Lutherans. Traditionally Lutherans were critical of American revivalists, particularly the Methodists, calling them "fanatics," "head-hangers," "knee-sliders," and "foot-stampers." But as later generations of Lutherans came to have greater contact with American culture, their English-speaking leaders began to advocate revivalist methods. Among Lutherans the leading "evangelical" figure was Samuel Schmucker, founder of Gettysburg Seminary. Schmucker's followers, known as "American Lutherans" or "New Measure Lutherans," often held protracted meetings which they renamed "special conferences" to pacify their more traditionalist brethren. The special conferences included altar-calls, exhorting, shouting, and Lutherans "falling as dead" when convicted of sin.

Nor did American Catholics escape revivalist practices. Although the "parish mission" was imported from Europe, by the 1850s it was remarkably similar to evangelical revivalism. The goal of the mission was to reclaim sinners and encourage the faithful. One mission manual, a Catholic equivalent to Finney's *Lectures on Revivals of Religion,* declared that "a true mission is that which, after restoring the grace of God to those who have fallen, renews the people in their belief in Christ and the Church, teaches sound principles of morality, and reestablishes the pious frequentation of the Sacraments." In order to restore faith among lukewarm Catholics, the parish mission employed many tactics similar to those of the Protestants. Missions lasted from eight days to two weeks, with brief services in the morning, teaching sessions during the day, and the main attraction at night. At the evening service, a priest-evangelist, usually a specially trained Redemptorist or Jesuit, began worship with music, song, and prayers, and then delivered an hour-long sermon. At the end of the mission the preacher held up a white baptismal robe to remind people of their baptismal vows. According to one priest, this tactic "set the people almost frantic; all the preacher said after this was drowned in the uproar." Catholics streamed forward to confess their sins, lining up to enter a vast array of confessionals set up for the occasion. When the evening's work was done the priest-evangelist, like the circuit rider who counted converts, measured his success by the number of confessions and communions that had taken place that night.

By the time American Catholics implemented the parish mission, enthusiastic revivalism was beginning to wane and devotionalism was growing in many evangelical circles. With men absent because of business, women became the spiritual directors of their households, and they preferred intense, private, and personal devotion to rambunctious and tumultuous conversions. The assumption was that if housewives performed their spiritual duties properly, their children would grow gradually in the faith and would never need to undergo the "trauma" of conversion. Part of this strategy was to emphasize Jesus, the children's friend, the ever faithful confidant, the sacrificial victim, the female alter ego, rather than the more powerful and demanding figure of God the Father. By getting their children to bond to Jesus, evangelical females also tied their offspring closer to themselves. The end result of the domestication of religion was a feminized and sentimentalized faith.

The feminization of evangelicalism was part of a broader feminization of American culture. As urban men became more and more concerned with commercial activity, middle- and upper-class women became the stewards of the culture. Book venders catered to female desires, and as a result published literature changed. The essay continued to be a popular literary form, but fiction and poetry, especially the romantic and sentimental variety, absorbed a growing share of the book market. Sir Walter Scott and Charles Dickens undercut critics' attacks on the novel by writing works that even Lyman Beecher could appreciate. Most novels, however, were not written by British men but by, to use Hawthorne's caustic words, "a damned mob of scribbling women." Female authors produced scores of moralistic and sentimental novels which portrayed life in domestic settings. Together these novels emphasized the joys of self-sacrifice, the nobility of suffering, the correctness of conventional morality, and the need for women to be connected to family, home, and church. Besides providing an imaginary "sisterhood" with whom readers could identify and storylines with an underlying eroticism, the novels gave women suggestions on how to handle difficulties in their daily lives. Should fiction fail to provide guidelines for handling life's problems, a great many ladies' magazines and self-improvement books were available to answer remaining questions. By mid-century religion and culture were so domesticated that religious eclectic and writer Orestes Brownson grumbled, "The curse of our age is its feminity [and] its lack, not of barbarism, but of virility."

8

The Life and Religious Experience of Jarena Lee

Jarena Lee

Jarena Lee (1783–ca. 1850) was an African Methodist Episcopal (AME) exhorter and preacher, converted under the well-known Richard Allen, whose separatist Methodist movement later became the denomination. Rebuffed by Allen when she thought she heard a call to preach, Lee at first simply exhorted. She married and bore six children. But when four of them died and her husband died too, she pursued her desire to preach with Allen, now a bishop, and—with his agreement—began an itinerant preaching career and a ministry lasting more than thirty years. Lee's articulation of the major themes of her own life makes it clear that knowing through the heart could encompass a holiness orientation. In nineteenth-century America and later, holiness meant a second intense experience of the divine presence after the work of conversion. Also known as sanctification, holiness was understood to be the special work of the Holy Spirit, the third (divine) person acknowledged as part of the orthodox Christian Trinity, and it carried implications of perfection, although different holiness believers interpreted their "perfection" in different ways. For Lee, the experience of sanctification soon brought a strong desire for missionary service, a theme familiar in some versions of holiness religion. More than that, however, Lee's knowing through the heart also meant a protofeminist knowing. She challenged Allen, however respectfully, and left her sickly child in order to preach; did editing work; and joined the American Antislavery Society in 1840. She was active as well in the movement for women's full access to the pulpit. Lee's story gives us a glimpse of how African American religiosity could blend with holiness and feminism in the spirituality of the heart.

And it shall come to pass . . . that I will pour out my Spirit upon all flesh; and your sons, and your *daughters* shall prophecy.

Joel ii. 28

I was born February 11th, 1783, at Cape May, state of New Jersey. At the age of seven years I was parted from my parents, and went to live as a servant maid, with a Mr. Sharp, at the distance of about sixty miles from the place of my birth.

My parents being wholly ignorant of the knowledge of God, had not therefore instructed me in any degree in this great matter. Not long after the commencement of my attendance on this lady, she had bid me do something respecting my work, which in a little while after, she asked me if I had done, when I replied, Yes—but this was not true.

At this awful point, in my early history, the spirit of God moved in power through my conscience, and told me I was a wretched sinner. On this account so great was the impression, and so strong were the feelings of guilt, that I promised in my heart that I would not tell another lie.

But notwithstanding this promise my heart grew harder, after a while, yet the spirit of the Lord never entirely forsook me, but continued mercifully striving with me, until his gracious power converted my soul.

The manner of this great accomplishment was as follows: In the year 1804, it so happened that I went with others to hear a missionary of the Presbyterian order preach. It was an afternoon meeting, but few were there, the place was a school room; but the preacher was solemn, and in his countenance the earnestness of his master's business appeared equally strong, as though he were about to speak to a multitude.

At the reading of the Psalms, a ray of renewed conviction darted into my soul. These were the words, composing the first verse of the Psalms for the service:

> Lord, I am vile, conceived in sin,
> Born unholy and unclean.
> Sprung from man, whose guilty fall
> Corrupts the race, and taints us all.

This description of my condition struck me to the heart, and made me to feel in some measure, the weight of my sins, and sinful nature. But not knowing how to run immediately to the Lord for help, I was driven of Satan, in the course of a few days, and tempted to destroy myself.

There was a brook about a quarter of a mile from the house, in which there was a deep hole, where the water whirled about among the rocks; to this place it was suggested, I must go and drown myself.

At the time I had a book in my hand; it was on a Sabbath morning, about ten o'clock; to this place I resorted, where on coming to the water I sat down on the bank, and on my looking into it; it was suggested, that drowning would be an easy death. It seemed as if some one was speaking to me, saying put your head under, it will not distress you. But by some means, of which I can give no account, my thoughts were taken entirely from this purpose, when I went from the place to the house again. It was the unseen arm of God which saved me from self murder.

But notwithstanding this escape from death, my mind was not at rest—but so great was the labour of my spirit and the fearful oppressions of a judgment to come, that I was reduced as one extremely ill. On which account a physician was called to attend me, from which illness I recovered in about three months.

But as yet I had not found him of whom Moses and the prophets did write, being extremely ignorant: there being no one to instruct me in the way of life and salvation as yet. After my recovery, I left the lady, who during my sickness, was exceedingly kind, and went to Philadelphia. From this place I soon went a few miles into the country, where I resided in the family of a Roman Catholic. But my anxiety still continued respecting my poor soul, on which account I used to watch my opportunity to read in the Bible; and this lady observing this, took the Bible from me and hid it, giving me a novel in its stead—which when I perceived, I refused to read.

Soon after this I again went to the city of Philadelphia; and commenced going to the English Church, the pastor of which was an Englishman, by the name of Pilmore, one of the number, who at first preached Methodism in America, in the city of New York.[1]

But while sitting under the ministration of this man, which was about three months, and at the last time, it appeared that there was a wall between me and a communion with that people, which was higher than I could possibly see over, and seemed to make this impression upon my mind, *this is not the people for you.*

But on returning home at noon I inquired of the head cook of the house respecting the rules of the Methodists, as I knew she belonged to that society, who told me what they were; on which account I replied, that I should not be able to abide by such strict rules not even one year;—however, I told her that I would go with her and hear what they had to say.

The man who was to speak in the afternoon of that day, was the Rev. Richard Allen, since bishop of the African Episcopal Methodists in America.[2] During the labors of this man that afternoon, I had come to the conclusion, that this is the people to which my heart unites, and it so happened, that as soon as the service closed he invited such as felt a desire to flee the wrath to come, to unite on trial with them—I embraced the opportunity. Three weeks from that day, my soul was gloriously converted to God, under preaching, at the very outset of the sermon. The text was barely pronounced, which was: "I perceive thy heart is not right in the sight of God" [Acts 8:21], when there appeared to *my* view, in the centre of the heart *one* sin; and this was *malice*, against one particular individual, who had strove deeply to injure me, which I resented. At this discovery I said, *Lord* I forgive *every* creature. That instant, it appeared to me, as if a garment, which had entirely enveloped my whole person, even to my fingers ends, split at the crown of my head, and was stripped away from me, passing like a shadow, from my sight—when the glory of God seemed to cover me in its stead.

That moment, though hundreds were present, I did leap to my feet, and declare that God, for Christ's sake, had pardoned the sins of my soul. Great was the ecstasy of my mind, for I felt that not only the sin of *malice* was pardoned, but all other sins were swept away together. That day was the first when my heart had believed, and my tongue had made confession unto salvation— the first words uttered, a part of that song, which shall fill eternity with its sound, was *glory to God.* For a few moments I had power to exhort sinners, and to tell of the wonders and of the goodness of him who had clothed me with *his* salvation. During this, the minister was silent, until my soul felt its duty had been performed, when he declared another witness of the power of Christ to forgive sins on earth, was manifest in my conversion.

From the day on which I first went to the Methodist church, until the hour of my deliverance, I was strangely buffetted by that enemy of all righteousness—the devil.

I was naturally of a lively turn of disposition; and during the space of time from my first awakening until I knew my peace was made with God, I rejoiced in the vanities of this life, and then again sunk back into sorrow.

For four years I had continued in this way, frequently labouring under the awful apprehension, that I could never be happy in this life. This persuasion was greatly strengthened, during the three weeks, which was the last of Satan's power over me, in this peculiar manner: on which account, I had come to the conclusion that I had better be dead than alive. Here I was again tempted to destroy my life by drowning; but suddenly this mode was changed, and while in the dusk of the evening, as I was walking to and fro in the yard of the house, I was beset to hang myself, with a cord suspended from the wall enclosing the secluded spot.

But no sooner was the intention resolved on in my mind, than an awful dread came over me, when I ran into the house; still the tempter pursued me. There was standing a vessel of water—into this I was strongly impressed to plunge my head, so as to extinguish the life which God had given me. Had I have done this, I have been always of the opinion that I should have been unable to have released myself; although the vessel was scarcely large enough to hold a gallon of water. Of me may it not be said, as written by Isaiah, (chap. 65, verses 1, 2.) "I am sought of them that asked not for me; I am found of them that sought me not." Glory be to God for his redeeming power, which saved me from the violence of my own hands, from the malice of Satan, and from eternal death; for had I have killed myself, a great ransom could not have delivered me; for it is written—"No murderer hath eternal life abiding in him" [1 John 3:15]. How appropriately can I sing—

> "Jesus sought me, when a stranger,
> Wandering from the fold of God;
> He to rescue me from danger,
> Interposed his precious blood."[3]

But notwithstanding the terror which seized upon me, when about to end my life, I had no view of the precipice on the edge of which I was tottering, until it was over, and my eyes were opened. Then the awful gulf of hell seemed to be open beneath me, covered only, as it were, by a spider's web, on which I stood. I seemed to hear the howling of the damned, to see the smoke of the bottomless pit, and to hear the rattling of those chains, which hold the impenitent under clouds of darkness to the judgment of the great day.

I trembled like Belshazzar,[4] and cried out in the horror of my spirit, "God be merciful to me a sinner." That night I formed a resolution to pray; which, when resolved upon, there appeared, sitting in one corner of the room, Satan, in the form of a monstrous dog, and in a rage, as if in pursuit, his tongue protruding from his mouth to a great length, and his eyes looked like two balls of fire; it soon, however, vanished out of my sight. From this state of terror and dismay, I was happily delivered under the preaching of the Gospel as before related.

This view, which I was permitted to have of Satan, in the form of a dog, is evidence, which corroborates in my estimation, the Bible account of a hell of fire, which burneth with brimstone, called in Scripture the bottomless pit; the place where all liars, who repent not, shall have their portion; as also the Sabbath breaker, the adulterer, the fornicator, with the fearful, the abominable, and the unbelieving, this shall be the portion of their cup.

This language is too strong and expressive to be applied to any state of suffering in *time*. Were it to be thus applied, the reality could no where be found in human life; the consequence would be, that *this* scripture would be found a false testimony. But when made to apply to an endless state of perdition, in eternity, beyond the bounds of human life, then this language is found not to exceed our views of a state of eternal damnation.

During the latter part of my state of conviction, I can now apply to my case, as it then was, the beautiful words of the poet:

> "The more I strove against its power,
> I felt its weight and guilt the more;
> 'Till late I hear'd my Saviour say,
> Come hither soul, I am the way."

This I found to be true, to the joy of my disconsolate and despairing heart, in the hour of my conversion to God.

During this state of mind, while sitting near the fire one evening, after I had heard Rev. Richard Allen, as before related, a view of my distressed condition so affected my heart, that I could not refrain from weeping and crying aloud; which caused the lady with whom I then lived, to inquire, with surprise, what ailed me; to which I answered, that I knew not what ailed me. She replied that I ought to pray. I arose from where I was sitting, being in an agony, and weeping convulsively, requested her to pray for me; but at the very moment when she would have done so, some person rapped heavily at the door for admittance; it was but a person of the house, but this occurrence was sufficient to interrupt us in our intentions; and I believe to this day, I should then have found salvation to my soul. This interruption was, doubtless, also the work of Satan.

Although at this time, when my conviction was so great, yet I knew not that Jesus Christ was the Son of God, the second person in the adorable trinity. I knew him not in the pardon of my sins, yet I felt a consciousness that if I died without pardon, that my lot must inevitably be damnation. If I would pray— I knew not how. I could form no connexion of ideas into words; but I knew the Lord's prayer; this I uttered with a loud voice, and with all my might and strength. I was the most ignorant creature in the world; I did not even know that Christ had died for the sins of the world, and to save sinners. Every circumstance, however, was so directed as still to continue and increase the sorrows of my heart, which I now know to have been a godly sorrow which wrought repentance, which is not to be repented of. Even the falling of the dead leaves from the forests, and the dried spires of the mown grass, showed me that I too must die, in like manner. But my case was awfully different from that of the grass of the field, or the wide spread decay of a thousand forests, as I felt within me a living principle, an immortal spirit, which cannot die, and must forever either enjoy the smiles of its Creator, or feel the pangs of ceaseless damnation.

But the Lord led me on; being gracious, he took pity on my ignorance; he heard my wailings, which had entered into the ear of the Lord of Sabaoth. Circumstances so transpired that I soon came to a knowledge of the being and character of the Son of God, of whom I knew nothing.

My strength had left me. I had become feverish and sickly through the violence of my feelings, on which account I left my place of service to spend a week with a coloured physician, who was a member of the Methodist society, and also to spend this week in going to places where prayer and supplication was statedly made for such as me.

Through this means I had learned much, so as to be able in some degree to comprehend the spiritual meaning of the text, which the minister took on the

Sabbath morning, as before related, which was, "I perceive thy heart is not right in the sight of God." Acts, chap. 8, verse 21.

This text, as already related, became the power of God unto salvation to me, because I believed. I was baptized according to the direction of our Lord, who said, as he was about to ascend from the mount, to his disciples, "Go ye into all the world and preach my gospel to every creature, he that believeth and is baptized shall be saved" [Mark 16:15–16].

I have now passed through the account of my conviction, and also of my conversion to God; and shall next speak of the blessing of sanctification.

A time after I had received forgiveness flowed sweetly on; day and night my joy was full, no temptation was permitted to molest me. I could say continually with the psalmist, that "God had separated my sins from me, as far as the east is from the west" [Ps. 103:12]. I was ready continually to cry,

> "Come all the world, come sinner thou,
> All things in Christ are ready now."

I continued in this happy state of mind for almost three months, when a certain coloured man, by name William Scott, came to pay me a religious visit. He had been for many years a faithful follower of the Lamb; and he had also taken much time in visiting the sick and distressed of our colour, and understood well the great things belonging to a man of full stature in Christ Jesus.

In the course of our conversation, he inquired if the Lord had justified my soul. I answered, yes. He then asked me if he had sanctified me. I answered, no; and that I did not know what that was. He then undertook to instruct me further in the knowledge of the Lord respecting this blessing.

He told me the progress of the soul from a state of darkness, or of nature, was threefold; or consisted in three degrees, as follows:—First, conviction for sin. Second, justification from sin. Third, the entire sanctification of the soul to God. I thought this description was beautiful, and immediately believed in it. He then inquired if I would promise to pray for this in my secret devotions. I told him, yes. Very soon I began to call upon the Lord to show me all that was in my heart, which was not according to his will. Now there appeared to be a new struggle commencing in my soul, not accompanied with fear, guilt, and bitter distress, as while under my first conviction for sin; but a labouring of the mind to know more of the right way of the Lord. I began now to feel that my heart was not clean in his sight; that there yet remained the roots of bitterness, which if not destroyed, would ere long sprout up from these roots, and overwhelm me in a new growth of the brambles and brushwood of sin.

By the increasing light of the Spirit, I had found there yet remained the root of pride, anger, self-will, with many evils, the result of fallen nature. I now became alarmed at this discovery, and began to fear that I had been deceived in my experience. I was now greatly alarmed, lest I should fall away from what I knew I had enjoyed; and to guard against this I prayed almost incessantly, without acting faith on the power and promises of God to keep me from falling. I had not yet learned how to war against temptation of this kind. Satan well knew that if he could succeed in making me disbelieve my conversion, that he would catch me either on the ground of complete despair, or on the ground of infidelity. For if all I had passed through was to go for nothing, and was but a fiction, the mere ravings of a disordered mind, then I would naturally be led to believe that there is nothing in religion at all.

From this snare I was mercifully preserved, and led to believe that there was yet a greater work than that of pardon to be wrought in me. I retired to a secret place (after having sought this blessing, as well as I could, for nearly three months, from the time brother Scott had instructed me respecting it) for prayer, about four o'clock in the afternoon. I had struggled long and hard, but found not the desire of my heart. When I rose from my knees, there seemed a voice speaking to me, as I yet stood in a leaning posture—"Ask for sanctification." When to my surprise, I recollected that I had not even thought of it in my whole prayer. It would seem Satan had hidden the very object from my mind, for which I had purposely kneeled to pray. But when this voice whispered in my heart, saying, "Pray for sanctification," I again bowed in the same place, at the same time, and said, "Lord *sanctify* my soul for Christ's sake?" That very instant, as if lightning had darted through me, I sprang to my feet, and cried, "The Lord has sanctified my soul!" There was none to hear this but the angels who stood around to witness my joy—and Satan, whose malice raged the more. That Satan was there, I knew; for no sooner had I cried out, "The Lord has sanctified my soul," than there seemed another voice behind me, saying, "No, it is too great a work to be done." But another spirit said, "Bow down for the witness—I received it—*thou art sanctified!*" The first I knew of myself after that, I was standing in the yard with my hands spread out, and looking with my face toward heaven.

I now ran into the house and told them what had happened to me, when, as it were, a new rush of the same ecstasy came upon me, and caused me to feel as if I were in an ocean of light and bliss.

During this, I stood perfectly still, the tears rolling in a flood from my eyes. So great was the joy, that it is past description. There is no language that can describe it, except that which was heard by St. Paul, when he was caught up to the third heaven, and heard words which it was not lawful to utter.[5]

My Call to Preach the Gospel

Between four and five years after my sanctification, on a certain time, an impressive silence fell upon me, and I stood as if some one was about to speak to me, yet I had no such thought in my heart. But to my utter surprise there seemed to sound a voice which I thought I distinctly heard, and most certainly understood, which said to me, "Go preach the Gospel!" I immediately replied aloud, "No one will believe me." Again I listened, and again the same voice seemed to say, "Preach the Gospel; I will put words in your mouth, and will turn your enemies to become your friends."[6]

At first I supposed that Satan had spoken to me, for I had read that he could transform himself into an angel of light, for the purpose of deception. Immediately I went into a secret place, and called upon the Lord to know if he had called me to preach, and whether I was deceived or not; when there appeared to my view the form and figure of a pulpit, with a Bible lying thereon, the back of which was presented to me as plainly as if it had been a literal fact.

In consequence of this, my mind became so exercised that during the night following, I took a text, and preached in my sleep. I thought there stood before me a great multitude, while I expounded to them the things of religion. So violent were my exertions, and so loud were my exclamations, that I awoke from the sound of my own voice, which also awoke the family of the house where I resided. Two days after, I went to see the preacher in charge of the African Society,[7] who was the Rev. Richard Allen, the same before named in these pages, to tell him that I felt it my duty to preach the gospel. But as I drew near the street in which his house was, which was in the city of Philadelphia, my courage began to fail me; so terrible did the cross appear, it seemed that I should not be able to bear it. Previous to my setting out to go to see him, so agitated was my mind, that my appetite for my daily food failed me entirely. Several times on my way there, I turned back again; but as often I felt my strength again renewed, and I soon found that the nearer I approached to the house of the minister, the less was my fear. Accordingly, as soon as I came to the door, my fears subsided, the cross was removed, all things appeared pleasant—I was tranquil.

I now told him, that the Lord had revealed it to me, that I must preach the gospel. He replied by asking, in what sphere I wished to move in? I said, among the Methodists. He then replied, that a Mrs. Cook, a Methodist lady, had also some time before requested the same privilege; who it was believed, had done much good in the way of exhortation, and holding prayer meetings; and who had been permitted to do so by the verbal license of the preacher in charge at the time. But as to women preaching, he said that our Discipline knew nothing at all about it—that it did not call for women preachers.[8] This I was glad to hear, because it removed the fear of the cross—but not no sooner did this feeling cross my mind, than I found that a love of souls had in a measure departed from me; that holy energy which burned within me, as a fire, began to be smothered. This I soon perceived.

O how careful ought we to be, lest through our by-laws of church government and discipline, we bring into disrepute even the word of life. For as unseemly as it may appear now-a-days for a woman to preach, it should be remembered that nothing is impossible with God. And why should it be thought impossible, heterodox, or improper, for a woman to preach? seeing the Saviour died for the woman as well as the man.

If a man may preach, because the Saviour died for him, why not the woman? seeing he died for her also. Is he not a whole Saviour, instead of a half one? as those who hold it wrong for a woman to preach, would seem to make it appear.

Did not Mary *first* preach the risen Saviour, and is not the doctrine of the resurrection the very climax of Christianity—hangs not all our hope on this, as argued by St. Paul? Then did not Mary, a woman, preach the gospel? for she preached the resurrection of the crucified Son of God.[9]

But some will say, that Mary did not expound the Scripture, therefore, she did not preach, in the proper sense of the term. To this I reply, it may be that the term *preach*, in those primitive times, did not mean exactly what it is now *made* to mean; perhaps it was a great deal more simple then, than it is now:— if it were not, the unlearned fishermen could not have preached the gospel at all, as they had no learning.

To this it may be replied, by those who are determined not to believe that it is right for a woman to preach, that the disciples, though they were fishermen, and ignorant of letters too, were inspired so to do. To which I would reply, that though they were inspired, yet that inspiration did not save them from showing their ignorance of letters, and of man's wisdom; this the multitude soon found out, by listening to the remarks of the envious Jewish priests. If then, to preach the gospel, by the gift of heaven, comes by inspiration solely, is God straitened; must he take the man exclusively? May he not, did he not, and can he not inspire a female to preach the simple story of the birth, life, death, and resurrection of our Lord, and accompany it too, with power to the sinner's heart. As for me, I am fully persuaded that the Lord called me to labour according to what I have received, in his vineyard. If he has not, how could he consistently bear testimony in favour of my poor labours, in awakening and converting sinners?

In my wanderings up and down among men, preaching according to my ability, I have frequently found families who told me that they had not for several years been to a meeting, and yet, while listening to hear what God would say by his poor coloured female instrument, have believed with trembling—tears rolling down their cheeks, the signs of contrition and repentance towards God. I firmly believe that I have sown seed, in the name of the Lord, which shall appear with its increase at the great day of accounts, when Christ shall come to make up his jewels.

At a certain time, I was beset with the idea, that soon or late I should fall from grace, and lose my soul at last. I was frequently called to the throne of grace about this matter, but found no relief; the temptation pursued me still. Being more and more afflicted with it, till at a certain time when the spirit strongly impressed it on my mind to enter into my closet, and carry my case once more to the Lord; the Lord enabled me to draw nigh to him, and to his mercy seat, at this time, in an extraordinary manner; for while I wrestled with him for the victory over this disposition to doubt whether I should persevere, there appeared a form of fire, about the size of a man's hand, as I was on my knees; at the same moment, there appeared to the eye of faith a man robed in a white garment, from the shoulders down to the feet; from him a voice proceeded, saying: "Thou shalt never return from the cross." Since that time I have never doubted, but believe that god will keep me until the day of redemption. Now I could adopt the very language of St. Paul, and say that nothing could have separated my soul from the love of god, which is in Christ Jesus [Rom. 8:35–39]. From that time, 1807, until the present, 1833, I have not yet doubted the power and goodness of God to keep me from falling, through sanctification of the spirit and belief of the truth.

My Marriage

In the year 1811, I changed my situation in life, having married Mr. Joseph Lee, Pastor of a Coloured Society at Snow Hill, about six miles from the city of Philadelphia. It became necessary therefore for me to remove. This was a great trial at first, as I knew no person at Snow Hill, except my husband; and to leave my associates in the society, and especially those who composed the *band* of which I was one. Not but those who have been in sweet fellowship with such as really love God, and have together drank bliss and happiness from the same fountain, can tell how dear such company is, and how hard it is to part from them.

At Snow Hill, as was feared, I never found that agreement and closeness in communion and fellowship, that I had in Philadelphia, among my young companions, nor ought I to have expected it. The manners and customs at this place were somewhat different, on which account I became discontented in the course of a year, and began to importune my husband to remove to the city. But this plan did not suit him, as he was the Pastor of the Society; he could not bring his mind to leave them. This afflicted me a little. But the Lord soon showed me in a dream what his will was concerning this matter.

I dreamed that as I was walking on the summit of a beautiful hill, that I saw near me a flock of sheep, fair and white, as if but newly washed; when there came walking toward me, a man of a grave and dignified countenance, dressed entirely in white, as it were in a robe, and looking at me, said emphatically, "Joseph Lee must take care of these sheep, or the wolf will come and devour them." When I awoke, I was convinced of my error, and immediately, with a glad heart, yielded to the right way of the Lord. This also greatly strengthened my husband in his care over them, for fear the wolf should by some means take any of them away. The following verse was beautifully suited to our condition, as well as to all the little flocks of God scattered up and down this land:

> "Us into Thy protection take,
> And gather with Thine arm;
> Unless the fold we first forsake,
> The wolf can never harm."

After this, I fell into a state of general debility, and in an ill state of health, so much so, that I could not sit up; but a desire to warn sinners to flee the wrath to come, burned vehemently in my heart, when the Lord would send sinners into the house to see me. Such opportunities I embraced to press home on their consciences the things of eternity, and so effectual was the word of exhortation made through the Spirit, that I have seen them fall to the floor crying aloud for mercy.

From this sickness I did not expect to recover, and there was but one thing which bound me to earth, and this was, that I had not as yet preached the gospel to the fallen sons and daughters of Adam's race, to the satisfaction of my mind. I wished to go from one end of the earth to the other, crying, Behold, behold the Lamb! To this end I earnestly prayed the Lord to raise me up, if consistent with his will. He condescended to hear my prayer, and to give me a token in a dream, that in due time I should recover my health. The dream was as follows: I thought I saw the sun rise in the morning, and ascend to an altitude of about half an hour high, and then become obscured by a dense black cloud, which continued to hide its rays for about one third part of the day, and then it burst forth again with renewed splendour.

This dream I interpreted to signify my early life, my conversion to God, and this sickness, which was a great affliction, as it hindered me, and I feared would forever hinder me from preaching the gospel, was signified by the cloud; and the bursting forth of the sun, again, was the recovery of my health, and being permitted to preach.

I went to the throne of grace on this subject, where the Lord made this impressive reply in my heart, while on my knees: "Ye shall be restored to thy health again, and worship God in full purpose of heart."

This manifestation was so impressive, that I could but hide my face, as if someone was gazing upon me, to think of the great goodness of the Almighty God to my poor soul and body. From that very time I began to gain strength of body and mind, glory to God in the highest, until my health was fully recovered.

For six years from this time I continued to receive from above, such baptisms of the Spirit as mortality could scarcely bear. About that time I was called to suffer in my family, by death—five, in the course of about six years, fell by his hand; my husband being one of the number, which was the greatest affliction of all.[10]

I was now left alone in the world, with two infant children, one of the age of about two years, the other six months, with no other dependance than the promise of Him who hath said—"I will be the widow's God, and a father to the fatherless" [Ps. 68:5]. Accordingly, he raised me up friends, whose liberality comforted and solaced me in my state of widowhood and sorrows. I could sing with the greatest propriety the words of the poet.

> "He helps the stranger in distress,
> The widow and the fatherless,
> And grants the prisoner sweet release."

I can say even now, with the Psalmist, "Once I was young, but now I am old, yet I have never seen the righteous forsaken, nor his seed begging bread" [Ps. 37:25]. I have ever been fed by his bounty, clothed by his mercy, comforted and healed when sick, succoured when tempted, and every where upheld by his hand.

The Subject of My Call to Preach Renewed

It was now eight years since I had made application to be permitted to preach the gospel, during which time I had only been allowed to exhort, and even this privilege but seldom.[11] This subject now was renewed afresh in my mind; it was as a fire shut up in my bones. About thirteen months passed on, while under this renewed impression. During this time, I had solicited of the Rev. Bishop Richard Allen, who at this time had become Bishop of the African Episcopal Methodists in America, to be permitted the liberty of holding prayer meetings in my own hired house, and of exhorting as I found liberty, which was granted me. By this means, my mind was relieved, as the house was soon filled when the hour appointed for prayer had arrived.

I cannot but relate in this place, before I proceed further with the above subject, the singular conversion of a very wicked young man. He was a coloured man, who had generally attended our meetings, but not for any good purpose; but rather to disturb and to ridicule our denomination. He openly and uniformly declared that he neither believed in religion, nor wanted anything to do with it. He was of a Gallio disposition,[12] and took the lead among the young people of colour. But after a while he fell sick, and lay about three months in a state of ill health; his disease was consumption. Toward the close of his days, his sister who was a member of the society, came and desired me to go and see her brother, as she had no hopes of his recovery; perhaps the Lord might break into his mind. I went alone, and found him very low. I soon commenced to inquire respecting his state of feeling, and how he found his mind. His answer was, "O tolerable well," with an air of great indifference. I asked him if I should pray for him. He answered in a sluggish and careless manner, "O yes, if you have time." I then sung a hymn, kneeled down and prayed for him, and then went my way.

Three days after this, I went again to visit the young man. At this time there went with me two of the sisters in Christ. We found the Rev. Mr. Cornish, of our denomination, labouring with him.[13] But he said he received but little satisfaction from him. Pretty soon, however, brother Cornish took his leave; when myself, with the other two sisters, one of which was an elderly woman named Jane Hutt, the other was younger, both coloured, commenced conversing with him, respecting his eternal interest, and of his hopes of a happy eternity, if any he had. He said but little; we then kneeled down together and besought the Lord in his behalf, praying that if mercy were not clear gone forever, to shed a ray of softening grace upon the hardness of his heart. He appeared now to be somewhat more tender, and we thought we could perceive some tokens of conviction, as he wished us to visit him again, in a tone of voice not quite as indifferent as he had hitherto manifested.

But two days had elapsed after this visit, when his sister came for me in haste, saying, that she believed her brother was then dying, and that he had *sent* for me. I immediately called on Jane Hutt, who was still among us as a mother in Israel, to go with me. When we arrived there, we found him sitting up in his bed, very restless and uneasy, but he soon laid down again. He now wished me to come to him, by the side of his bed. I asked him how he was. He said, "Very ill;" and added, "Pray for me, quick?" We now perceived his time in this world to be short. I took up the hymn-book and opened to a hymn suitable to his case, and commenced to sing. But there seemed to be a *horror* in the room—a darkness of a mental kind, which was felt by us all; there being five persons, except the sick young man and his nurse. We had sung but one verse, when they all gave over singing, on account of this unearthly sensation, but myself. I continued to sing on alone, but in a dull and heavy manner, though looking up to God all the while for help. Suddenly, I felt a spring of energy awake in my heart, when darkness gave way in some degree. It was but a glimmer from above. When the hymn was finished, we all kneeled down to pray for him. While calling on the name of the Lord, to have mercy on his soul, and to grant him repentance unto life, it came suddenly into my mind never to rise from my knees until God should hear prayer in his behalf, until he should convert and save his soul.

Now, while I thus continued importuning heaven, as I felt I was led, a ray of light, more abundant, broke forth among us. There appeared to my view, though my eyes were closed, the Saviour in full stature, nailed to the cross, just over the head of the young man, against the ceiling of the room. I cried out, brother look up, the Saviour is come, he will pardon you, your sins he will forgive. My sorrow for the soul of the young man was gone; I could no longer pray—joy and rapture made it impossible. We rose up from our knees, when lo, his eyes were gazing with ecstasy upward; over his face there was an expression of joy; his lips were clothed in a sweet and holy smile; but no sound came from his tongue; it was heard in its stillness of bliss, full of hope and immortality. Thus, as I held him by the hand his happy and purified soul soared away, without a sign or a groan, to its eternal rest.

I now closed his eyes, straightened out his limbs, and left him to be dressed for the grave. But as for me, I was filled with the power of the Holy Ghost—the very room seemed filled with glory. His sister and all that were in the room rejoiced, nothing doubting but he had entered into Paradise; and I believe I shall see him at the last and great day, safe on the shores of salvation.

But to return to the subject of my call to preach. Soon after this, as above related, the Rev. Richard Williams was to preach at Bethel Church, where I with others were assembled.[14] He entered the pulpit, gave out the hymn, which was sung, and then addressed the throne of grace; took his text, passed through the exordium, and commenced to expound it. The text he took is in Jonah, 2d chap. 9th verse,—"Salvation is of the Lord." But as he proceeded to explain, he seemed to have lost the spirit; when in the same instant, I sprang, as by an altogether supernatural impulse, to my feet, when I was aided from above to give an exhortation on the very text which my brother Williams had taken.

I told them that I was like Jonah; for it had been then nearly eight years since the Lord had called me to preach his gospel to the fallen sons and daughters of Adam's race, but that I had lingered like him, and delayed to go at the bidding of the Lord, and warn those who are as deeply guilty as were the people of Ninevah.

During the exhortation, God made manifest his power in a manner sufficient to show the world that I was called to labour according to my ability, and the grace given unto me, in the vineyard of the good husbandman.

I now sat down, scarcely knowing what I had done, being frightened. I imagined, that for this indecorum, as I feared it might be called, I should be expelled from the church. But instead of this, the Bishop rose up in the assembly, and related that I had called upon him eight years before, asking to be permitted to preach, and that he had put me off; but that he now as much believed that I was called to that work, as any of the preachers present. These remarks greatly strengthened me, so that my fears of having given an offence, and made myself liable as an offender, subsided, giving place to a sweet serenity, a holy joy of a peculiar kind, untasted in my bosom until then.

The next Sabbath day, while sitting under the word of the gospel, I felt moved to attempt to speak to the people in a public manner, but I could not bring my mind to attempt it in the church. I said, Lord, anywhere but here. Accordingly, there was a house not far off which was pointed out to me, to this I went. It was the house of a sister belonging to the same society with myself. Her name was Anderson. I told her I had come to hold a meeting in her house, if she would call in her neighbours. With this request she immediately complied. My congregation consisted of but five persons. I commenced by reading and singing a hymn, when I dropped to my knees by the side of a table to pray. When I arose I found my hand resting on the Bible, which I had not noticed till that moment. It now occurred to me to take a text. I opened the Scripture, as it happened, at the 141st Psalm, fixing my eye on the 3d verse, which reads: "Set a watch, O Lord, before my mouth, keep the door of my lips." My sermon, such as it was, I applied wholly to myself, and added an exhortation. Two of my congregation wept much, as the fruit of my labour this time. In closing I said to the few, that if any one would open a door, I would hold a meeting the next sixth-day evening; when one answered that her house was at my service. Accordingly I went, and God made manifest his power among the people. Some wept, while others shouted for joy. One whole seat of females, by the power of God, as the rushing of a wind, were all bowed to the floor at once, and screamed out. Also a sick man and woman in one house, the Lord convicted them both; one lived, and the other died. God wrought a judgment— some were well at night, and died in the morning. At this place I continued to hold meetings about six months. During that time I kept house with my little son, who was very sickly. About this time I had a call to preach at a place about thirty miles distant, among the Methodists, with whom I remained one week, and during the whole time, not a thought of my little son came into my mind; it was hid from me, lest I should have been diverted from the work I had to, to look after my son. Here by the instrumentality of a poor coloured woman, the Lord poured forth his spirit among the people. Though, as I was told, there were lawyers, doctors, and magistrates present, to hear me speak, yet there was mourning and crying among sinners, for the Lord scattered fire among them of his own kindling. The Lord gave his handmaiden power to speak for his great name, for he arrested the hearts of the people, and caused a shaking amongst the multitude, for God was in the midst.

I now returned home, found all well; no harm had come to my child, although I left it very sick. Friends had taken care of it which was of the Lord. I now began to think seriously of breaking up housekeeping, and forsaking all to preach the everlasting Gospel. I felt a strong desire to return to the place of my nativity, at Cape May, after an absence of about fourteen years. To this place, where the heaviest cross was to be met with, the Lord sent me, as Saul of Tarsus was sent to Jerusalem,[15] to preach the same gospel which he had neglected and despised before his conversion. I went by water, and on my passage was much distressed by sea sickness, so much so that I expected to have died, but such was not the will of the Lord respecting me. After I had disembarked, I proceeded on as opportunities offered, toward where my mother lived. When within ten miles of that place, I appointed an evening meeting. There were a goodly number came out to hear. The Lord was pleased to give me light and liberty among the people. After meeting, there came an elderly lady to me and said, she believed the Lord had sent me among them; she then appointed me another meeting there two weeks from that night. The next day I hastened forward to the place of my mother, who was happy to see me, and the happiness was mutual between us. With her I left my poor sickly boy, while I departed to do my Master's will. In this neighborhood I had an uncle, who was a Methodist, and who gladly threw open his door for meetings to be held there. At the first meeting which I held at my uncle's house, there was, with others who had come from curiosity to hear the coloured woman preacher, an old man, who was a deist, and who said he did not believe the coloured people had any souls—he was sure they had none. He took a seat very near where I was standing, and boldly tried to look me out of countenance. But as I laboured on in the best manner I was able, looking to God all the while, though it seemed to me I had but little liberty, yet there went an arrow from the bent bow of the gospel, and fastened in his till then obdurate heart. After I had done speaking, he went out, and called the people around him, said that my preaching might seem a small thing, yet he believed I had the worth of souls at heart. This language was different from what it was a little time before, as he now seemed to admit that coloured people had souls, whose good I had in view, his remark must have been without meaning. He now came into the house, and in the most friendly manner shook hands with me, saying, he hoped God had spared him to some good purpose. This man was a great slave holder, and had been very cruel; thinking nothing of knocking down a slave with a fence stake, or whatever might come to hand. From this time it was said of him that he became greatly altered in his ways for the better. At that time he was about seventy years old, his head as white as snow; but whether he became a converted man or not, I never heard.

The week following, I had an invitation to hold a meeting at the Court House of the County, when I spoke from the 53d chap. of Isaiah, 3d verse. It was a solemn time, and the Lord attended the word; I had life and liberty, though there were people there of various denominations. Here again I saw the aged slaveholder, who notwithstanding his age, walked about three miles to hear me. This day I spoke twice, and walked six miles to the place appointed. There was a magistrate present, who showed his friendship, by saying in a friendly manner, that he had heard of me: he handed me a hymn-book, pointing to a hymn which he had selected. When the meeting was over, he invited me to preach in a schoolhouse in his neighbourhood, about three miles distant from where I then was. During this meeting one backslider was reclaimed. This day I walked six miles, and preached twice to large congregations, both in the morning and evening. The Lord was with me, glory be to his holy name. I next went six miles and held a meeting in a coloured friend's house, at eleven o'clock in the morning, and preached to a well behaved congregation of both coloured and white. After service I again walked back, which was in all twelve miles in the same day. This was on Sabbath, or as I sometimes call it, seventh-day; for after my conversion I preferred the plain language of the quakers: On fourth-day, after this, in compliance with an invitation received by note, from the same magistrate who had heard me at the above place, I preached to a large congregation, where we had a precious time: much weeping was heard among the people. The same gentleman, now at the close of the meeting, gave out another appointment at the same place, that day week. Here again I had liberty, there was a move among the people. Ten years from that time, in the neighbourhood of Cape May, I held a prayer meeting in a school house, which was then the regular place of preaching for the Episcopal Methodists; after service, there came a white lady of the first distinction, a member of the Methodist Society, and told me that at the same school house, ten years before, under my preaching, the Lord first awakened her. She rejoiced much to see me, and invited me home with her, where I staid till the next day. This was bread cast on the waters, seen after many days.

From this place I next went to Dennis Creek meeting house, where at the invitation of an elder, I spoke to a large congregation of various and conflicting sentiments, when a wonderful shock of God's power was felt, shown everywhere by groans, by sighs, and loud and happy amens. I felt as if aided from above. My tongue was cut loose, the stammerer spoke freely; the love of God, and of his service, burned with a vehement flame within me—his name was glorified among the people.

But here I feel myself constrained to give over, as from the smallness of this pamphlet I cannot go through with the whole of my journal, as it would probably make a volume of two hundred pages; which, if the Lord be willing, may at some future day be published. But for the satisfaction of such as may follow after me, when I am no more, I have recorded how the Lord called me to his work, and how he has kept me from falling from grace, as I feared I should. In all things he has proved himself a God of truth to me; and in his service I am now as much determined to spend and be spent, as at the very first. My ardour for the progress of his cause abates not a whit, so far as I am able to judge, though I am now something more than fifty years of age.

As to the nature of uncommon impressions, which the reader cannot but have noticed, and possibly sneered at in the course of these pages, they may be accounted for in this way: It is known that the blind have the sense of hearing in a manner much more acute than those who can see: also their sense of feeling is exceedingly fine, and is found to detect any roughness on the smoothest surface, where those who can see can find none. So it may be with such as [I] am, who has never had more than three months schooling; and wishing to know much of the way and law of God, have therefore watched the more closely the operations of the Spirit, and have in consequence been led thereby. But let it be remarked that [I] have never found that Spirit to lead me contrary to the Scriptures of truth, as I understand them. "For as many as are led by the Spirit of God are the sons of God."—Rom. viii. 14.

I have now only to say, May the blessing of the Father, and of the Son, and of the Holy Ghost, accompany the reading of this poor effort to speak well of his name, wherever it may be read. AMEN.

NOTES

1. Joseph Pilmore (1739–1825) accepted John Wesley's call for volunteers to evangelize the American colonies and in 1769 became the first Methodist preacher in Philadelphia. . . .

2. Richard Allen (1760–1831), born a slave in Philadelphia, was converted to Christianity and purchased his freedom at the age of seventeen, whereupon he became a wagon driver during the Revolutionary War and began an itinerant preaching career. Discrimination against blacks in the St. George's Methodist Episcopal Church in Philadelphia moved Allen, with the help of Absalom Jones, to organize in protest the Free African Society, on April 12, 1787. Seven years later, the society's first church, the Bethel African Methodist Episcopal Church, was dedicated into service under the preaching leadership of Allen. In 1799 Bishop Francis Asbury ordained Allen a deacon, making him the first black to receive ordination in the Methodist Episcopal church in America. During the next fifteen years other A.M.E. congregations were established in Delaware, Maryland, New York, and neighboring states. On April 9, 1816, Allen and the leaders of these more recent black churches founded the first independent Afro-American denomination in the United States, the African Methodist Episcopal church. Allen was consecrated as the first bishop of the A.M.E. church on April 11, 1816. See Charles H. Wesley's *Richard Allen: Apostle of Freedom,* 2d ed. (Washington, D.C.: Associated Publishers, 1969) and Allen's narrative, *The Life, Experience and Gospel Labors of the Rt. Rev. Richard Allen* (1833).

3. In her narrative, Lee often quotes verses from popular hymns of the day. Her sources include *A Collection of Hymns, for the Use of the Methodist Episcopal Church* (1823) and *The African Methodist Episcopal Church Hymn Book* (1818, rev. 1836).

4. Belshazzar, king of Babylon after Nebuchadnezzar, is the subject of the fifth chapter of the Book of Daniel.

5. Lee alludes to 2 Cor. 12:2–4, although it was not Paul but an unnamed acquaintance of Paul who was "caught up to the third heaven."

6. Lee's commissioning experience echoes that of several biblical prophets and missionaries. See Jer. 1:9; Exod. 4:1, 12; and Luke 21:15.

7. By this time the Free African Society had become the Bethel African Methodist Episcopal Church.

8. Before 1817, when the A.M.E. church adopted its own *Doctrines and Discipline,* the black Methodists under Allen's leadership accepted the rules of church government and the Articles of Faith that John Wesley selected for the Methodist Episcopal church. Wesleyan Methodists did not allow the formal ordination of women as preachers, although Wesley himself was willing to admit unofficially of "exceptions" to this rule of church polity. See Earl Kent Brown, "Women of the Word," in Hilah F. Thomas and Rosemary Skinner Keller, eds., *Women in New Worlds* (Nashville: Abingdon, 1981), pp. 69–87.

9. Lee refers to Mary Magdalene, who was the first to inform Jesus' disciples of his resurrection in John 20:11–18.

10. At the 1818 Annual Conference of the A.M.E. church, the death of "Joseph Lea, a man of God, who has labored for many years in the ministry" was noted for church records, after which time the Snow Hill church's trustee applied to the conference "to take charge of the spiritual concerns of their church." Daniel A. Payne, *History of the African Methodist Episcopal Church* (Nashville: A.M.E. Sunday-School Union, 1891), I, 26.

11. Among the Methodists, both white and black, exhortation was regularly distinguished from true preaching and usually followed it during a worship service. Exhorters were not licensed to speak from or interpret a biblical text. They were expected to limit themselves to pleas for close attention to the message preached, repentance, and acceptance of the present opportunity for salvation.

12. As Roman proconsul of Achaia in Southern Greece, Gallio refused to arbitrate a dispute between a group of Corinthian Jews and Paul the Apostle. Instead he dismissed the Jewish leaders who wanted Paul tried for breaking religious laws. His indifference to religious issues placed before him seems to be the characteristic that Lee alludes to. See Acts 18:12–17.

13. Lee refers to William Cornish, an early A.M.E. minister and deacon, not the more famous Samuel E. Cornish, the black abolitionist, newspaper editor, and Presbyterian minister.

14. Rev. Richard Williams of Baltimore was a delegate to the first General Convention of the A.M.E. church in 1816, when the Ecclesiastic Compact of the new denomination was written. His leadership in the church was rewarded by his ordination as elder in 1824.

15. Paul, formerly Saul, of Tarsus traveled to Jerusalem to preach the evangelization of the gentiles in Acts 15:2–12. He had formerly persecuted Christians in Jerusalem according to Acts 8:1–3.

9

Girlhood AND Salvation and the Baptism of the Holy Spirit

Aimee Semple McPherson

Pentecostal evangelist and founder of the International Church of the Foursquare Gospel, Aimee Semple McPherson (1890–1944) was born Aimee Kennedy, in Ontario, Canada. In 1908 she became pentecostal and then married Robert James Semple, the evangelist who converted her. An outgrowth in part of holiness religion, pentecostalism incorporated the millennialist message of the imminent Second Coming of Christ and an emphasis on faith healing. Especially, though, it became known for its congregational practice of speaking in tongues, an ecstatic form of speech believed to be the work of the Holy Spirit. As such, the words—not in any language known to the speaker—were understood as a new gift of the Spirit, and their interpretation—often by another congregant—was regarded as prophecy and again the Spirit's gift. McPherson herself was ordained and subsequently traveled to China with Semple as a missionary. But three months after the couple's arrival, Robert Semple was dead. Back in the United States, the young widow married again, this time to Harold McPherson. Later, she became an itinerant evangelist, eventually divorced McPherson (after leaving him twice), and later achieved notoriety for a kidnapping scandal and four-year marriage to David Hutton. Aimee McPherson, meanwhile, performed her way through a spectacular career as dramatic and unpredictable preacher in tent crusades, theaters, and auditoriums throughout the nation. Finally, on New Year's Day in 1923, she opened Angelus Temple in Los Angeles—the beginning of what became the International Church of the Foursquare Gospel. The drama of her life—including her conversion told here—point, in a strong and even provocative way, to the power of passion and emotion in spiritual life.

Girlhood

"Foolishness is bound in the heart of a child." Prov. 22:15.

Then came the days of study in the little white school-house that stood on the corner a mile from our home. I was the only Salvationist [Salvation Army]

From *This Is That: Personal Experiences, Sermons, and Writings of Aimee Semple McPherson, Evangelist* [1923].

child there, the other scholars being church members. At first they teased me about the Army with their shouting, their marching and their drum, for they were still a despised people in those days. I finally won over the hearts of the children, however, when I invented a drum from a round cheese box and with a ruler for a drum-stick and a "Blood and Fire" banner made from a red table-cloth we marched round the school and played "Army."

Everything went well until it was learned that I had some little talent for elocution. The distance to the barracks being great, and the churches seeming much more popular, I began going to the Methodist church, where my father had formerly been a choir leader. Once invited to take part in their entertainments, I was soon received in other churches and appearing on the programs the country round. We received great help and teaching along the lines of elocution, dialogues and plays by the church instructors in this art. After competing with others in the W.C.T.U. [Women's Christian Temperance Union] work, a silver and later a gold medal was awarded me.

Except for the temperance work, however, very few of the selections or plays were anything but comic. Upon asking preachers whether they would prefer something sacred they would invariably answer:

"Oh, give us something humorous; something comical to make the people laugh. That last Irish recitation was grand. Give us something like that."

As I recited, the audience would laugh and clap and laugh again until the tears came to their eyes, and I was very popular indeed with the churches in those days,—a great deal more so than I am now, mayhap.

As years went by I passed from grammar school to high, and became still more interested in the entertainments of the church. There were the oyster suppers, the strawberry festivals, the Christmas trees, and always the concerts to follow, for which tickets were sold—"to help God pay His debts and help support the church," I supposed then. But I have learned now that our God is so richly able to supply the funds for His work that He need not resort to any such methods.

The praise and applause of the people was very alluring to some of us younger ones, and we often talked together of going on the stage, arguing that the church was giving us a good training on this line and that anyway there was not much difference whether a play or a concert was given in the church or at the theatre.

My next step on the downward path was when I began reading novels from the Sunday School library (for a novel is a novel whether in a paper or a cloth-bound cover). And when I had devoured them I learned where more could be obtained.

The next luring of the tempter came when I was asked by a member of the choir as to whether I had been to the moving-picture theatre that week. I told her:

"No," that I had never seen any motion pictures outside of the church. She looked at me in such a condescending, pitying way that my pride was stung and I decided to go. I did not tell my Mother, however, and felt very guilty in entering until I saw several church members and a Sunday School teacher there; then I felt better (it surely must be all right if they were there), and settled down to enjoy the pictures.

Athletic, and fond of out-door sports, next in line came costume skating carnivals and then my first "college ball"—I was now well advanced in the high school. When I brought home the engraved invitation card, Mother flatly refused her permission for me to go and it took a great deal of pleading and coaxing to gain an unwilling consent. My dress and slippers were purchased and I went to my first dance radiantly happy on the exterior, but a little heavy and conscience-stricken on the interior, for I knew that Mother was sad and praying alone at home.

It seemed to be a very proper affair, however. My first dancing partner was the Presbyterian preacher. Other good (?) church members were there—surely Mother must be mistaken or a little old-fashioned in her ideas. How lovely it all seemed, the orchestra, the flowers, the attention paid me, the fine clothes, and the well-appointed luncheon!

Ah, sin, with what dazzling beauty, with what refinement and velvet dost thou cover thy claws! How alluring are the fair promises with which thou enticest the feet of youth! How cunning are the devices of the enemy! How smoothly and craftily he lays his plans and weaves the net which he draws ever tighter and tighter, illumining the future and its prospects with rose colors and fair painted promises, the fruit of which, once plucked, crumbles into gray ashes in the hand of him who runneth after it.

My future and educational prospects looked promising. No effort or labor was counted too great upon the part of my parents to send me to school, and indeed it was no little matter for them—ten miles must be covered each day, five in the morning and five at night, on the train or with horse and carriage, despite country roads, with their mud or rain or snow.

There was introduced into our class room at this time, a text-book entitled "High School Physical Geography," which delved into the problems of earth formation, rock strata, etc., and learnedly described the origin of life and the process of evolution. There were quotations from Darwin and other authorities on these weighty subjects. Explaining the origin of life upon this planet, it taught us that from the sea, with its slime, seaweed and fungus growth, insect life appeared. From insect life came animal life, and through continuous processes of evolution at last man appeared, who, of course, was higher than the monkeys or any other creature.

How these theories or teachings impressed other students I cannot say, but they had a remarkable effect upon me.

"Man?—a process of evolution?

—Why, then God had not created him at all, as the Bible said He did—preachers were true when they said there were errors and mistakes in the Bible." On and on raced the thoughts in my young mind until I reached the point:

"Well, then, if the Bible is mistaken in one place it is very apt to be mistaken in others. Its information is not reliable, and I guess there's no God at all, and that's why Christians act so pious in church on Sundays and do as they please through the week."

"No, I guess there *is* no God." Even the existence of the big moon and the twinkling stars had been explained by science. The sun, once a great mass of molten lava, had acquired a whirling motion and thrown off all these other planets, earth, moon and stars. Nothing about God, just science and a logical outcome of conditions now revealed by wise astronomers who had studied it all out through great telescopes (which had cost fabulous sums of money and taken many years to invent); and therefore they knew all about it.

This book raised so many questions in my mind that I delved deeper into other infidelistic theories. So interested did I become that I wrote an article to the "Family Herald and Weekly Star," published at Montreal, then Canada's leading paper. My inquiries were answered by Archbishop Hamilton and many others. Arguments both for and against the book and its teachings were brought out.

Is it any wonder that our pulpits are filled with infidels and *higher critics* today?

Out of the letters that poured in for months from England, New Zealand, Australia, and all parts of America, as well as from my own land, each containing a different explanation, not one said:

"Child, the Bible is true. Take the simple Word of God and believe it just as it reads."

The more I read and observed the lives of Christians, the more skeptical of the reality of God I became. (How I could ever have doubted is today a puzzle and a shame to me). The devil must have blinded my eyes for a time to the genuine Christians about me. All that I could see was empty profession. I saw men singing in the choir or sitting in the pews on Sunday and attending all sorts of worldly functions during the week. I began reading my Bible, to see whether it contradicted itself and how it compared with the books which I had read. Oh, I must know the truth—was there anything in religion?

Every time I had an opportunity I questioned and cross-questioned each Christian that I could get hold of. But I did not seem to get far. My first attempt was made upon my Mother. I had been thinking earnestly upon the subject, and just as she was coming up the steep cellar steps with a pan of milk in her hands, I met her with the question:

"Mother, how do you know there is a God?"

Poor dear, she was so surprised that she nearly fell backwards, down the steps. She explained things the best she knew how, bringing forth Scriptures, and pointing to creation with all its wonders as proving the handiwork of a Creator.

Each attempt at explanation I met with the learned words of those books and the superior (?) twentieth-century wisdom of my seventeen summers—books and wisdom which left mothers and Bibles far behind. Her arguments seemed to shrink to nothing, and her eyes opened with astonishment as she sat down suddenly on the kitchen chair, unable to get a word in edgeways.

My next attempt was made upon the minister when he came to our house to tea. Mother was out in the kitchen preparing the proverbial ministerial chicken dinner, but I had business in the parlor, ostensibly displaying the family album, but in reality endeavoring to probe him with the questions upon my mind.

"Does the Lord ever perform any miracles or heal any sick folks now?" I asked.

"Why no, child, the day of miracles is over," was his surprised reply. "People are expected to use the intelligence and wisdom the Lord has given them along medical and surgical lines—these are really miraculous, you know."

"But doesn't it say, over here in James 5:14, if any are sick among you to *'let him call for the elders of the church; and let them pray over him, anointing him with oil in the name of the Lord: And the prayer of faith shall save the sick, and they shall recover?'*"

"And is there not a scripture that says, *'Jesus Christ is the same yesterday, and today, and forever'?* and *'He that believeth on Me, the works that I do shall he do also; and greater works than these shall he do; because I go unto my Father'?*

"How do you reconcile the fact that the Lord no longer does such miraculous things, with these scriptures?"

My questions were evaded, and I was made to feel that I was but a mere child, and therefore could not understand these matters. They were never explained to my satisfaction.

Alarmed over my attitude and questions, my Mother asked me to join some church. When I made excuses she offered to take me to all the different churches, asking me to study the teachings of each of them and to join the one that seemed best. I replied that I felt I was doing enough church work now, with the entertainments and concerts, and added, in a self-righteous way, that I thought I was just as good as any of the others—I didn't see any particular difference in our lives, whether I was a member of the church or not did not matter.

"Well, let us go to the Salvation Army special meetings tonight. It is a long time since we have been there together."

Poor Mother! Will I ever forget her face when she found they were having an entertainment there that night, and the first selection rendered after we entered was:

"High diddle, diddle,
The cat and the fiddle,
The cow jumped over the moon!"

acted out by one of the local officers, amid the applause of the laughing audience. He was dressed to represent a colored minstrel.

Later we attended the special services being conducted by the Brigadier, his wife and daughter, who invited me very sweetly to give my heart to Jesus. I argued with her that there was no God, nothing in the Bible. She seemed to get into deep waters and went for her mother, who also begged me to come to the altar. Then they sent for the father, and before long I was the center of a group, my Mother on the outskirts, listening with blushing face while I set forth, in my ignorance, my opinion regarding evolution.

Oh, dear Jesus, how could I ever have doubted You when You have been so good, so merciful and so true to me all the days of my life!

Mother cried bitterly all the long drive home, and all the reproach she laid upon me was:

"Oh, Aimee, I never dreamed that I should bring up a daughter who would talk as you have before those people tonight! After all my years as a Christian, after my prayers and my work in that corps, *you* of all people, to talk like this! Oh, where have I failed? Oh! OH!! O-H!!!"

Conscience-stricken, and shamed before her grief, I fled to my room, as soon as we arrived, to think things over. I certainly loved my Mother; to cause her grief and sorrow was the last thing in this wide world which I wished to do—"and yet—and yet."

Not pausing to light the lamp, I went over to my bedroom window, threw it open wide and sat down on the floor with my elbows on the window-sill, my chin propped on my hands, and gazed reflectively up at the starry floors of heaven and at the great white silvery moon sailing majestically toward me from the eastern sky, before I finished my broken sentence—"I wonder if there really is a God? Who is right? What is the truth?"

The white mantle of snow which covered the fields and the trees, glistened in the clear, frosty air, and—

My! how big that moon looked up there, and how ten million stars seemed to wink and blink and twinkle! I drew a comforter round me and sat on and on, unmindful of the cold, looking up at the milky way, the big dipper, and other familiar luminaries.

—Surely, there m-u-s-t be a God up there back of them all. They seemed to breathe and emanate from His very presence and nearness.

At school we had studied the planets and how each rotated and revolved upon its own axis, and in its own orbit without friction or confusion. It was all so big, so high, so above the reach and ken of mortal man—surely a DIVINE hand must hold and control this wonderful solar system—

Why! how near God seemed—right now!

Suddenly, without stopping to think, I threw both arms impulsively out of the window and, reaching toward heaven, cried:

"Oh God!—If there be a God—reveal Yourself to me!"

The cry came from my very heart. In reality, a whisper was all that came from my lips—but just that whisper from an honest, longing heart, was enough to echo through the stars and reach the Father's throne. Up there, He whose ear is ever open to the cries of His little children, heard me and answered. Bless His Name.

Oh, if every doubter and professed infidel would just breathe that one sincere prayer to God, He would reveal Himself to them as He did to me, for He is no respecter of persons. Hallelujah!

Salvation and the Baptism of the Holy Spirit

"And it shall come to pass, that before they call, I will answer; and while they are yet speaking, I will hear." Isa. 65:24.

Our prayer-answering God who sitteth upon the throne, whose ear is ever open to our cry, and whose heart is touched by our infirmities, was already answering the cry of this poor, unworthy child. He had set on foot a chain of events which was to lead not only to the salvation and baptism of my own soul, but which was to lead me out into His vineyard and make me a worker in His dear service.

It was just a few days after my prayer at the open window of my bedroom that (my Father having come into school for me) we were driving along Main Street on the way home, eagerly talking over and planning my parts in the grand Christmas affairs and concerts in the various churches and halls then looming above us. How pretty the store windows were in their Christmas dress of green and red and tinsel!

But look! Over there on the left hand side of the street there was a new sign on a window, which we had not seen before. It advertised a "Holy Ghost Revival" with old time "Pentecostal Power," and announced meetings every night and all day Sunday.

Turning to my father, I said:

"Daddy, I would like to go to that meeting tomorrow night. I believe this is the place, that I have heard about, where the congregation says "Amen" right out loud, and where sometimes the power of God falls upon the people, as it used to fall upon the old time Methodists. It would be loads of fun to go and see them."

"All right, daughter, we can go tomorrow night before your rehearsal in the town hall," he replied.

And thus it was that the next evening found us in the back seat, (where we could see all) in the little Mission which had recently been opened for the revival.

The congregation seemed to be largely composed of the middle classes. None of the wealthy or well known citizens of the town were there. Dressed as I was in worldly attire with my foolish little heart filled with unbelief and egotism, I felt just a little bit above the status of those round about me and looked on with an amused air as they sang, shouted, testified and prayed.

True to the reports which I had heard they had an "Amen Corner" with a Hallelujah echo. Bright testimonies and earnest zeal left not a dull moment. There was something strange about these people, they seemed to be so in earnest.

Then a tall young man, six feet two inches in height rose to his feet on the platform and taking his Bible in his hand opened it and began to read. His was a frank, kindly face, with Irish blue eyes that had the light of heaven in them, chestnut brown hair, with one rebellious brown curl which would insist in falling down close to his eye no matter how often he brushed it back.

Without a moment's hesitation he opened his Bible at the second chapter of Acts and read the 38th and 39th verses. (There is one thing about these Holy Ghost meetings where the Power of Pentecost is preached, one cannot attend them very long without learning that there is a second chapter to the Book of Acts. I learned this in my first meeting.)

The evangelist—Robert Semple—began his discourse with the first word of his text:

"Repent." Oh, how he did repeat that word—Repent! REPENT!! R-E-P-E-N-T!!! over and over again. How I did wish he would stop and say some other. It seemed to pierce like an arrow through my heart, for he was preaching under divine inspiration and in power and demonstration of the Holy Spirit. He really spoke as though he believed there was a Jesus and a Holy Spirit, not some vague, mythical, intangible shadow, something away off yonder in the clouds, but a real, living, vital, tangible, moving reality dwelling in our hearts and lives—making us His temple—causing us to walk in Godliness, holiness and adoration in His presence.

There were no announcements of oyster suppers or Christmas entertainments or sewing circles made—no appeal for money. Not even a collection was taken. It was just God, God, God from one end to the other, and his words seemed to rain down upon me, and every one of them hurt some particular part of my spirit and life until I could not tell where I was hurt the worst.

"Repent!" The evangelist went on to say that if the love of the world was in us the love of the Father was not there: theatres, moving pictures, dancing, novels, fancy-dress skating rinks (why, it just looked as if somebody had told him I was there, so vividly did he picture my own life and walk), worldly and rag-time music, etc., he condemned wholesale, and declared that all the people who were wrapped up in this sort of thing were of the devil, and were on their way to hell, and that unless they repented and that right speedily, renouncing the world, the flesh and the devil, they would be lost—eternally damned forever.

I did not do any more laughing, I assure you. I sat up straight in my seat. With eyes and ears wide open I drank in every word he said. After he had finished with the word "Repent," and explained what true salvation meant— the death, burial and resurrection that we would know as we were identified with our Lord, he began to preach on the next verse—

"And ye shall receive the gift of the Holy Ghost. For the promise is unto you, and to your children, and to all that are afar off, even as many as the Lord our God shall call."

Here he began to preach the baptism of the Holy Spirit, declaring that the message of salvation and the incoming of the Spirit should be preached side by side and hand in hand, and that for a Christian to live without the baptism of the Holy Spirit was to live in an abnormal condition not in accordance with God's wishes. He told how the Holy Spirit was received in Bible days and how the recipients of the Spirit had spoken in other tongues—languages they had never learned—as the Spirit gave them utterance.

Suddenly, in the midst of his sermon, the Evangelist closed his eyes and with radiant face began to speak in a language that was not his own—but the words of the Holy Spirit.

To me it was the voice of God thundering into my soul awful words of conviction and condemnation, and though the message was spoken in tongues it seemed as though God had said to me—

"YOU are a poor, lost, miserable, hell-deserving sinner!" I want to say right here that I *knew* this was God speaking by His Spirit through the lips of clay. There is a verse in the 14th chapter of I Corinthians which says the speaking in tongues is a sign to the unbeliever. This was certainly true in my case. From the moment I heard that young man speak with tongues to this day I have never doubted for the shadow of a second that there was a God, and that He had shown me my true condition as a poor, lost, miserable, hell-deserving sinner.

No one had ever spoken to me like this before. I had been petted, loved and perhaps a little spoiled: told how smart and good I was. But thank God that He tells the truth. He does not varnish us nor pat us on the back or give us any little sugar-coated pills, but shows us just where we stand, vile and sinful and undone, outside of Jesus and His precious blood.

All my amusement and haughty pride had gone. My very soul had been stripped before God—there was a God, and I was not ready to meet Him. Oh, how could I have looked down upon these dear people and felt that I was better than they? Why, I was not even worthy to black their shoes. They were saints and I was a sinner.

We had to slip out early, before the service was over, and how I got through the rehearsal I cannot say, but one thing I knew, and that is that during the next seventy-two hours I lived through the most miserable three days I had ever known up to that time.

Conviction! Oh! I could scarcely eat or rest or sleep. Study was out of the question. "Poor, lost, miserable, hell-deserving sinner" rang in my ears over and over again. I could see those closed eyes and that outstretched hand that pointed to my shrinking, sinful soul that was bared before the eyes of my Maker.

I began enumerating the many things which I would have to give up in order to become a Christian—there was the dancing. I was willing to part with that,—the novels, the theatre, my worldly instrumental music. I asked myself about each of them and found that I did not count them dear as compared with the joy of salvation and knowing my sins forgiven.

There was just one thing, however, that I found myself unwilling and seemingly unable to do. I knew that I could not be a Christian and recite those foolish Irish recitations and go through those plays and dialogues. A child of God must be holy and consecrated, with a conversation covered with the blood of Jesus. My Bible said that even for one idle word (let alone foolish words), we should have to give an account before the judgment throne of God. Yet it was too late now to cancel my promises for Christmas, too late to get others to fill my place. Evidently there was nothing to do but wait until after Christmas in order to become a Christian.

But how could I wait? I was desperately afraid. I trembled with conviction. It seemed as though every moment which I lived outside of God and without repentance toward Him was lived in the most awful peril and gravest danger of being cast into hell without mercy. Oh, that every sinner who reads these words might feel the same awful conviction upon his soul!

The second and third day I fell to praying something like this:

"Oh, God, I do want to be a Christian. I want to ever love and serve You. I want to confess my sin and be washed in the blood of Jesus Christ. But oh, please just let me live until after Christmas, and then I will give my heart to You. Have mercy on me, Lord. Oh, don't, don't let me die until after Christmas."

Many people smile now as I testify of that awful terror that seized upon my soul, but the eternal welfare of my soul was at stake—for me it was going to be life or death, heaven or hell forever.

At the end of the third day, while driving home from school, I could stand it no longer. The lowering skies above, the trees, the fields, the very road beneath me seemed to look down upon me with displeasure, and I could see written everywhere—

"Poor, lost, miserable, hell-deserving sinner!"

Utterly at the end of myself—not stopping to think what preachers or entertainment committees or anyone else would think—I threw up my hands, and all alone in that country road, I screamed aloud toward the heavens:

"Oh, Lord God, be merciful to me, a sinner!" Immediately the most wonderful change took place in my soul. Darkness passed away and light entered. The sky was filled with brightness, the trees, the fields, and the little snow birds flitting to and fro were praising the Lord and smiling upon me.

So conscious was I of the pardoning blood of Jesus that I seemed to feel it flowing over me. I discovered that my face was bathed in tears, which dropped on my hands as I held the reins. And without effort or apparent thought on my part I was singing that old, familiar hymn:

> "Take my life and let it be
> Consecrated, Lord, to Thee;
> Take my moments and my days,
> Let them flow in ceaseless praise."

I was singing brokenly between my sobs:

> "Take my life and let it be
> Consecrated, Lord, to Thee."

My whole soul was flowing out toward God, my Father.

"M-Y F-A-T-H-E-R !" Oh, glory to Jesus! I had a heavenly Father! No more need for fear, but His love and kindness and protection were now for me.

When I came to the part in the song that said

> "Take my hands and let them move
> At the impulse of Thy love"

I knew there would be no more worldly music for me, and it has been hymns from that time forth. And when I sang—

> "Take my feet and let them be
> Swift and beautiful for Thee"

I knew that did not mean at the dance hall nor the skating rink. Bless the Lord.

> "Take my lips and let them sing
> Always, only, for my King."

No more foolish recitations and rag-time songs.

> "Oh, Jesus, I love Thee,
> I know Thou art mine;
> For Thee all the follies
> Of sin I resign."

Song after song burst from my lips. I shouted aloud and praised God all the way home. I had been redeemed!

Needless to say I did not take part in the entertainments, and many in our town thought me fanatical and very foolish. Nevertheless the succeeding days were brimful of joy and happiness. How dearly I loved God's Word! I wanted it under my pillow when I went to sleep, and in my hands when my eyes opened in the morning. At school, where I used to have a novel hidden away inside of my Algebra and Geometry, there was now a little New Testament, and I was studying each passage that referred to the baptism of the Holy Spirit.

Of all the promises in which I found comfort there was none, I believe, that compared with the simple promises of Matthew 7:7 to 11.

"Ask, and it shall be given you; seek, and ye shall find; knock, and it shall be opened unto you:

"For everyone that asketh receiveth and he that seeketh findeth; and to him that knocketh it shall be opened." Here He assured me that if I asked bread He would not give me a stone, also that He was more willing to give me the Holy Spirit than earthly parents were to give good gifts to their children.

I would get about so far with my reading, and oh, the Bible seemed to me all so new, so living and speaking, (and it was God speaking to me), that unable to wait another moment, I would excuse myself from the room, go down to the basement, fall upon my knees and begin to pray:

"Oh, Lord, baptize me with the Holy Spirit. Lord, you said the promise was unto even as many as were afar off, even as many as the Lord our God should call. Now, Lord, you've called me, the promise is unto me; fill me just now."

The girls found me thus praying and did not know what to make of me so utterly was I changed. No more putting glue in teacher's chair or helping to lock him in the gymnasium, or practicing dance steps in the corridors at noon hour. A wonderful change had taken place—all old things had passed away and all things had become new. I had been born again and was a new creature in Christ Jesus.

Each day the hunger for the baptism of the Holy Spirit became stronger and stronger, more and more intense until, no longer contented to stay in school, my mind no longer on my studies, I would slip away to the tarrying meetings where the dear saints met to pray for those who were seeking the baptism of the Holy Spirit.

What wonderful hours those were! What a revelation to my soul! It was as though heaven had come down to earth. So much of the time was I away from school that I began to fall behind in my studies for the first time, and although the final examinations were near, I could not make myself take any interest in Algebra or Geometry or Chemistry, or anything but the baptism of the Holy Spirit and preparing to meet my soon-coming Savior in the air.

Then came the day when the principal of the High School sent a letter to my Mother which told her that unless I paid more attention to my studies I was certainly going to fail.

And to make matters worse, the same day one of the S. A. officers came to call upon Mother, saying:

"We really are surprised and think you do wrong in letting your daughter go to that Mission. You being connected with the work for so many years, it sets a bad example to other people for you to allow her to be in any way associated with them."

When I went home that night Mother was waiting for me. She gave me a very serious talking to, and wound up by issuing the ultimatum:

"Now, if I ever hear of your leaving school and going down to that Mission again, or to the tarrying meetings, I will have to keep you home altogether. I will not have you talked about in this way."

I went to school on the train the next morning as the roads were banked high with snow, and all the way in I was looking out of the window at the falling flakes of snow and praying for the Lord to fix it all some way so that I should be able to knock until He opened or else to baptize me at once.

Walking from the train to High School it was necessary to pass both the Mission and the Sister's home where I often went to tarry for the baptism. As I went past the latter I looked longingly at the windows, hoping that she might be there and that I could speak to her from the sidewalk without going in and thus disobeying Mother's command, but not a sign of her did I see.

I walked slowly past, looking sadly and hungrily back all the way; then finally came to a halt on the sidewalk and said to myself:

"Well, here now, Jesus is coming soon and you know it is more important for you to receive the Holy Spirit than to pass all the examinations in the world. You need the Holy Spirit—oil in your vessel with your lamp—in order to be ready for His appearing.

"As you have to make a choice between going to school and seeking the baptism I guess you won't go to school at all today, but will just go back to the sister's house and make a whole day of seeking the baptism."

With this I turned and walked quickly back to the house, rang the door bell and went in. I told the sister my dilemma, and she said quietly:

"Let's tell Father all about it." So we got down and began to pray. She asked the Lord in her prayer either to baptize me then and there or to arrange it some way that I could stay until I received my baptism.

The Lord heard this prayer, and outside the window the snow which had been falling in light flakes, began to come down like a blinding blizzard. My heavenly Father sent out His angels to stir up some of those big, old, fleecy clouds of His, and down came the snow and—causing the window-panes to rattle, and one of our old-fashioned Canadian blizzards was on.

The entire day was spent in prayer and at night on going to the depot to see about my train home, the ticket agent said, through the window:

"Sorry, Miss, but the train is not running tonight. The roads are blocked with snow. We are not able to get through." Oh, Hallelujah! I was not sorry a bit.

Then the thought came—"This will not do you much good, for you will have to call Mother on the telephone and she will ask you to go to her friend's home to stay, and warn you not to go near the Mission." But when I went to the telephone and gave the number, Central said:

"Sorry, wires all down on account of the storm." This time I did shout "Glory" and ran almost all the way back to the sister's home.

The storm increased, and as fast as the men endeavored to open a pathway, the Lord filled it in with mountains of white snow, until at last all thought of getting through while the storm lasted was abandoned.

Oh, how earnestly I sought the baptism of the Spirit. Sometimes when people come to the altar now and sit themselves down in a comfortable position, prop their heads up on one hand, and begin to ask God in a languid, indifferent way for the Spirit, it seems to me that they do not know what real seeking is.

Time was precious, for while man was working so hard to shovel out the snow, and God had His big clouds all working to shovel it in, I must do my part in seeking with all my heart.

Friday I waited before the Lord until midnight. Saturday morning, rising at the break of day, before anyone was astir in the house, and going into the parlor, I kneeled down by the big Morris chair in the corner, with a real determination in my heart.

My Bible had told me *"the kingdom of heaven suffereth violence, and the violent take it by force."* Matt. 11:12. I read the parable again of the man who had knocked for bread and found that it was not because he was his friend, but because of his importunity, that the good man within the house had risen up and given him as many loaves as he had need of. Now Jesus *was* my friend; He had bidden me knock, and assured me that He *would* open unto me. He had invited me to ask, promising that I should receive, and that the empty He would not turn hungry away. I began to seek in desperate earnest, and remember saying:

"Oh, Lord, I am so hungry for your Holy Spirit. You have told me that in the day when I seek with my whole heart you will be found of me. Now, Lord, I am going to stay right here until you pour out upon me the promise of the Holy Spirit for whom you commanded me to tarry, if I die of starvation. I am so hungry for Him I can't wait another day. I will not eat another meal until you baptize me."

You ask if I was not afraid of getting a wrong spirit, or being hypnotized, as my parents feared. There was no such fear in my heart. I trusted my heavenly Father implicitly according to Luke 11:11, wherein He assured me that if I asked for bread He would not give me a stone. I knew that my Lord was not bestowing serpents and scorpions on His blood-washed children when they asked for bread. Had He not said, if your earthly fathers know how to bestow good gifts upon their children, *"how much more shall your heavenly Father give the Holy Spirit to them that ask Him!"* Lu. 11:13.

After praying thus earnestly,—storming heaven, as it were, with my pleadings for the Holy Spirit, a quietness seemed to steal over me, the holy presence of the Lord to envelop me. The Voice of the Lord spoke tenderly:

"Now, child, cease your strivings and your begging; just begin to praise Me, and in simple, child-like faith, receive ye the Holy Ghost."

Oh, it was not hard to praise Him. He had become so near and so inexpressibly dear to my heart. Hallelujah! Without effort on my part I began to say:

"Glory to Jesus! Glory to Jesus!! GLORY TO JESUS!!!" Each time that I said "Glory to Jesus!" it seemed to come from a deeper place in my being than the last, and in a deeper voice, until great waves of "Glory to Jesus" were rolling from my toes up; such adoration and praise I had never known possible.

All at once my hands and arms began to tremble gently at first, then more and more, until my whole body was atremble with the power of the Holy Spirit. I did not consider this at all strange, as I knew how the batteries we experimented with in the laboratory at college hummed and shook and trembled under the power of electricity, and there was the Third Person of the Trinity coming into my body in all His fulness, making me His dwelling, "the temple of the Holy Ghost." Was it any wonder that this poor human frame of mine should quake beneath the mighty movings of His power?

How happy I was, Oh, how happy! happy just to feel His wonderful power taking control of my being. Oh, Glory! That sacred hour is so sweet to me, the remembrance of its sacredness thrills me as I write.

Almost without my notice my body slipped gently to the floor, and I was lying under the power of God, but felt as though caught up and floating upon the billowy clouds of glory. Do not understand by this that I was unconscious of my surroundings, for I was not, but Jesus was more real and near than the things of earth round about me. The desire to praise and worship and adore Him flamed up within my soul. He was so wonderful, so glorious, and this poor tongue of mine so utterly incapable of finding words with which to praise Him.

My lungs began to fill and heave under the power as the Comforter came in. The cords of my throat began to twitch—my chin began to quiver, and then to shake violently, but Oh, so sweetly! My tongue began to move up and down and sideways in my mouth. Unintelligible sounds as of stammering lips and another tongue, spoken of in Isaiah 28:11, began to issue from my lips. This stammering of different syllables, then words, then connected sentences, was continued for some time as the Spirit was teaching me to yield to Him. Then suddenly, out of my innermost being flowed rivers of praise in other tongues as the Spirit gave utterance (Acts 2:4), and Oh, I knew that He was praising Jesus with glorious language, clothing Him with honor and glory which I felt but never could have put into words.

How wonderful that I, even I, away down here in 1908, was speaking in an unknown tongue, just as the believers had in Bible days at Ephesus and Caesarea, and that now He had come of whom Jesus had said— *"He will glorify Me."*

I shouted and sang and laughed and talked in tongues until it seemed that I was too full to hold another bit of blessing lest I should burst with the glory. The Word of God was true. The promise was really to them that were afar off, even as many as the Lord our God should call. The Comforter had come, lifting my soul in ecstatic praises to Jesus in a language I had never learned. I remember having said:

"Oh, Lord, can you not take me right on up to heaven now? I am so near anyway. Do I have to go back to that old world again?

"Hypnotism," you say? If so, it is a remarkably long spell and an exceedingly delightful one which has lasted for fourteen years, making me love Jesus with all my heart and long for His appearing. Besides this you must take into consideration that there was no one in the room to hypnotize me. I was all alone when I was saved, and all alone when I received the baptism of the Holy Spirit.

"Demon power"—"all of the devil," someone may say. If so the devil must have recently gotten soundly converted, for that which entered into my soul makes me to love and obey my Lord and Savior Jesus Christ, to exalt the blood and honor the Holy Ghost.

"Excitement," you say? Never! It has stood the test too long, dear unbeliever. In sickness, in sorrow, even in the gates of death He has proved Himself to be the Comforter whom Jesus said He would send.

Hearing me speaking in the tongues and praising the Lord, the dear Sister of the home in which I stayed, came down stairs and into the parlor, weeping and praising the Lord with me. Soon Brother Semple and other saints gathered in. What shouting and rejoicing! Oh, hallelujah! And yet with all the joy and glory, there was a stillness and a solemn hush pervading my whole being.

Walking down the street, I kept saying to myself:

"Now you must walk very softly and carefully, with unshod feet, in the presence of the King lest you grieve this tender, gentle dove who has come into your being to make you His temple and to abide with you forever."

The next day was Sunday. The storm had cleared away; the sun was shining down in its melting warmth. Attending the morning services at the Mission, we partook of the Lord's Supper, and as we meditated upon His wonderful love, His blood that was shed for us, His body that was broken on the tree, it was more than I could bear.

Oh, who can describe that exceeding weight of glory as He revealed Himself, my crucified Savior, my resurrected Lord, my coming King!

School-mates and friends were standing up to look over the seats to see what had happened to me, but I was lost again with Jesus, whom my soul loved.

A friend of our family left the meeting, and going to the telephone called my Mother. (The wires which had been down during the storm, unknown to me, had been repaired). He said:

"You had better come into town and see to your daughter, for she is again disobeying your orders. She is at those meetings, shouting more than any of them."

Poor Mother! She was frantic to think her daughter should so far forget her dignity and disgrace herself in such a manner. She called me to the phone and I heard her dear voice saying:

"What in the world is this I hear about you? What does this all mean?"

I tried to answer, but the Holy Spirit began speaking through me again.

"What's that?" she demanded. I tried to explain. Then came her voice stern and forbidding:

"You just wait till I get there, my lady; I will attend to you."

(Just to relieve the tension of your mind, I will run a little ahead of my story and tell you that since then my dear Mother has also received the Baptism of the Holy Spirit just as they did in Bible days).

Returning to the sister's home, I sat down at the organ, awaiting in some trepidation and fear, I confess, the coming of my Mother. To keep my courage up I sang over and over that old, familiar hymn:

> "I will never leave thee nor forsake thee;
> In my hands I'll hold thee;
> In my arms I'll fold thee;
> I am thy Redeemer; I will care for thee!"

What would Mother say? Would she understand? Why, it had not been so very long since the power of God used to come down in the dear old Salvation Army. Had I not heard her tell how Brother Kitchen (whom they used to call "the Kitchen that God lived in") had shaken as he knelt in prayer, until he had gone clear across the platform and had lain stretched out under the power at the other side? Had I not heard my Father tell how the old-time Methodist Church used to have this same power? Praying God for strength and wisdom, I sang on—

> "E'en though the night
> Be dark within the valley,
> Just beyond is shining,
> An eternal light."

Six o'clock arrived—so did Mother! I heard the jingle of the sleigh-bells suddenly stop in response to my Mother's "whoa!" Then an imperious ring of the bell shivered the tense silence within the house. Slipping down from the organ stool I caught my coat and hat in my hand as I hastened to the door. Mother met me, and with:

"My lady, you come right out and get in here this minute," lost no time in bundling me into the cutter. The Sister and Brother both tried to get a word in edgeways, to reason with and explain to her, but she would hear none of it, and in a moment we were off.

All the way home Mother scolded and cried and almost broke her heart over her daughter who had, as she supposed, been cast under some dire spell by those "awful" people. Oh, praise the Lord! No matter what the devil called them he had to admit that they were holy anyway, and that's more than he could have said of many professing denominations, now, isn't it?

Being an only child, loved and petted, it needed only a word of scolding or remonstrance to bring the tears, but now, when she was scolding me more severely and saying more harsh things than she ever had in my life, for some mysterious reason I couldn't shed a tear. I felt duty bound to squeeze out a few tears, out of respect to her feelings, but I could not do it to help myself. All I could do was sing and sing and sing—all the way—

> "Joys are flowing like a river,
> Since the Comforter has come;

He abides with me forever,
Makes the trusting heart His home."

The Spirit within rose up and filled me with joy unspeakable and full of glory. Poor Mother would turn to me and say:

"Oh, Aimee! do stop that singing. I can't understand how you can sing; you know your Mother's heart is breaking. Surely you don't call that a fruit of the Spirit." But it did not seem as if I were singing at all: it just seemed to sing itself and came out without any effort.

"Blessed quietness, holy quietness,
What assurance in my soul;
On the stormy sea, Jesus speaks to me,
And the billows cease to roll."

Upon our arrival home we found my Father sitting by the dining-room fire, with his head in his hands, saying:

"Humph! Humph! Humph!" He always did that when he felt very badly over something. Leading me up to him, Mother said:

"Now I want you to tell your Father all about it. Tell the way you acted out before those people." Well, it certainly did sound dreadful to tell it, but Oh, that something kept whispering and echoing in my heart:

"E'en though the night
Be dark within the valley,
Just beyond is shining
An eternal day."

When at last they sent me to my room, I kneeled down quickly and began to pray. It happened that I was kneeling beside the stove-pipe hole and could not help overhearing a part of the conversation between my parents. It was something like this:

"Oh, what shall we do? Those people have got our girl under their influence, hypnotized her, mesmerized her or something."

"It is perfectly useless to argue with her, for no matter what we say, she only thinks she is being persecuted and will hold to it all the more tenaciously."

"Oh, what shall we do?" With this the door closed and I heard no more.

Oh, how can I describe the joy and the glory that had come within my soul? that deep-settled peace, that knowledge that He would lead and guide and would bring all things out right.

When next my Mother permitted me to go to school she told me of the decision which they had come to, namely, that if I went near those Pentecostal people once more they would take me away from school for good, education or no education. As she told me this the Holy Spirit gave me wisdom to make this reply:

"Mother, the Bible says that children are to obey their parents in the Lord, and if you can show me by the Word of God that what I have received is not in accordance with Bible teaching, or show me any place where we are told that the baptism of the Holy Spirit, with the Bible evidence, speaking in tongues, is not for today, I will never go to the Mission again." I staked my all on the Word.

"Why certainly I can prove it to you," she replied. "Those things were only for the Apostolic days. I will look up the scriptures and prove it to you when you get home tonight."

Dear Mother—she had been a student of the Bible and had taught Sunday School and Bible class for years. Oh, would she be able to prove that all these manifestations of the Holy Spirit's power and presence were only for by-gone days? I was not very well acquainted with the Bible on this subject, yet knew that what I had received was from God.

Assured that Mother would search the Bible honestly, I had pledged myself to stand by the consequences: Whatever the Bible said should stand. Thus it was that we both turned to the Word of God as the final court of appeal to settle the whole matter.

Mother got out her Bible, concordance, pencil and pad, and with heart and mind full of this one thing, immediately sat herself down at the breakfast table, spreading her books out before her, without pausing even long enough to gather up the breakfast dishes for washing—the lamps were not cleaned, and the beds were unmade.

(Oh, if any unbeliever will sit down with an open Bible and an unprejudiced heart, there is no need for us to defend our position, so clear is the Word of God on this subject).

It was half past eight in the morning when I left home for school. At five-thirty, when I returned, Mother was still seated at the breakfast table, with her Bible and paper before her, and—would you believe it?—the breakfast dishes were still unwashed, the lamps uncleaned, the beds unmade, an unheard-of state of affairs for Mother, ever an excellent housekeeper.

I waited with bated breath for her decision. My heart softened within me as I saw by her reddened eyes that she had been weeping. Oh, what would her answer be? The smile upon her face encouraged me to ask—

"Oh, Mother, what is it?"

Now, dear reader, what do you suppose she said? With shining face she replied—

"Well, dear, I must admit that of a truth, *this is that which was spoken of by the prophet Joel, which should come to pass in the last days!*"

She had found that, away back in Isaiah 28:11, He had said—"*With stam-*

mering lips and another tongue will I speak to this people"—that the prophet Joel had clearly prophesied that in these last days there should be a wonderful outpouring of the Holy Spirit, likened unto the latter rain, wherein the sons and daughters, the servants and the maids were alike to rejoice in this glorious downpour.

With one spring across the room, I threw my arms about my Mother's neck, squeezing her till she declared I had almost broken her neck. How happy we were as we danced around the table—laughing, crying and singing together—

> "'Tis the old time religion,
> And it's good enough for me—"

If everyone who is skeptical of the reality of the baptism of the Holy Spirit would take the Word of God and search from cover to cover, he too, would be convinced without the shadow of a doubt that "This Is That."

10

An Unforgettable Night

Charles W. Colson

Charles W. Colson (b. 1931) came under public scrutiny during the
Watergate scandal of the 1960s, when he served as special counsel to
President Richard M. Nixon. A Bostonian by birth, Colson served in
the military, went to law school, and entered private practice but also
alternately worked in government and displayed political interests.
Watergate, with its intense pressure and disruption of his career, brought
with it a period of internal searching and an emotional vulnerability he
had not known before. In many ways, Colson found himself in the classic posture of the nineteenth-century would-be evangelical convert—
feeling heavy and down-burdened by a life that was not working and,
behind it, a pervasive sense of what Christians call sin. In the episode
reprinted here from his autobiography, significantly titled *Born Again,*
Colson recounts the emotion-tinged events leading up to his conversion and radical change of life. Colson's friend Thomas L. Phillips becomes the angel of conversion as he uses a spiritual reading on pride to
noticeable effect; and the former Watergate counsel views his entire life
in retrospect, seeing what now seems to him painful pretentiousness
and arrogance. The spiritual pressure mounts: there is conversation,
prayer together, and then, for Colson, the breakthrough to what he experiences as the presence of God. The tears to which he candidly admits
suggest the deep passional tenor of the entire episode. Although many
among the American public who heard the later news of Colson's evangelical conversion were cynical, Colson himself demonstrated the new
convictions that guided him by serving, as a lay person, in a Christian
ministry to prisoners. The tough and worldly politico had become a
compelling late-twentieth-century example of the spirituality of knowing through the heart.

It was eight P.M., a gray overcast evening, when I turned off the country road
connecting two of Boston's most affluent suburbs, Wellesley and Weston. The
towering gentle pines brought sudden darkness and quiet to the narrow mac-
adam street. Another turn a few hundred yards later brought me into a long
driveway leading to the Phillipses' big white clapboard Colonial home. As I

parked the car I felt a touch of guilt at not telling Patty the truth when I had left her alone with my mother and dad in nearby Dover.

"Just business, honey," had been my explanation. Patty was used to my working at odd times, even on this Sunday night at the start of a week's vacation.

The Phillipses' home is long and rambling. I made the mistake of going to the door nearest the driveway, which turned out to be the entrance to the kitchen. It didn't bother Gert Phillips, a tall smiling woman who greeted me like a long-lost relative even though we had never met before. "Come in. I'm just cleaning up after supper."

Supper. Such an unpretentious New England word. Gert escorted me into a large modern kitchen. "I'll call Tom," she said. "He's playing tennis with the children."

Tom arrived a minute later along with son Tommy, sixteen, and daughter Debby, nineteen, two tanned, handsome young people. Gert fixed us all iced tea while Tom mopped himself dry with a towel. If Gert was aware of the importance of her husband's position as president of the state's biggest company, she certainly did not show it. In fact, she reminded me of a favorite aunt we used to visit in the country when I was a boy, who always wore an apron, smelled of freshly made bread and cookies, and had the gift of making everyone feel at home in her kitchen.

"You men have things to talk about and I've got work to do," Gert said as she handed us tall glasses of iced tea. Tom, towel draped around his neck, led me through the comfortably furnished dining and living rooms to a screened-in porch at the far end of the house. It was an unusually hot night for New England, the humidity like a heavy blanket wrapped around me. At Tom's insistence, first the dark gray business-suit jacket, then my tie came off. He pulled a wrought-iron ottoman close to the comfortable outdoor settee I sat on.

"Tell me, Chuck," he began, "are you okay?" It was the same question he had asked in March.

As the President's confidant and so-called big-shot Washington lawyer I was still keeping my guard up. "I'm not doing too badly, I guess. All of this Watergate business, all the accusations—I suppose it's wearing me down some. But I'd rather talk about you, Tom. You've changed and I'd like to know what happened."

Tom drank from his glass and sat back reflectively. Briefly he reviewed his past, the rapid rise to power at Raytheon: executive vice-president at thirty-seven, president when he was only forty. He had done it with hard work, day and night, nonstop.

"The success came, all right, but something was missing," he mused. "I felt a terrible emptiness. Sometimes I would get up in the middle of the night and pace the floor of my bedroom or stare out into the darkness for hours at a time."

"I don't understand it," I interrupted. "I knew you in those days, Tom. You were a straight arrow, good family life, successful, everything in fact going your way."

"All that may be true, Chuck, but my life wasn't complete. I would go to the office each day and do my job, striving all the time to make the company succeed, but there was a big hole in my life. I began to read the Scriptures, looking for answers. Something made me realize I needed a personal relationship with God, forced me to search."

A prickly feeling ran down my spine. Maybe what I had gone through in the past several months wasn't so unusual after all—except I had not sought spiritual answers. I had not even been aware that finding a personal relationship with God was possible. I pressed him to explain the apparent contradiction between the emptiness inside while seeming to enjoy the affluent life.

"It may be hard to understand," Tom chuckled. "But I didn't seem to have anything that mattered. It was all on the surface. All the material things in life are meaningless if a man hasn't discovered what's underneath them."

We were both silent for a while as I groped for understanding. Outside, the first fireflies punctuated the mauve dusk. Tom got up and switched on two small lamps on end tables in the corners of the porch.

"One night I was in New York on business and noticed that Billy Graham was having a Crusade in Madison Square Garden," Tom continued. "I went—curious, I guess—hoping maybe I'd find some answers. What Graham said that night put it all into place for me. I saw what was missing, the personal relationship with Jesus Christ, the fact that I hadn't ever asked Him into my life, hadn't turned my life over to Him. So I did it—that very night at the Crusade."

Tom's tall, gangling frame leaned toward me, silhouetted by the yellow light behind him. Though his face was shaded, I could see his eyes begin to glisten and his voice became softer. "I asked Christ to come into my life and I could feel His presence with me, His peace within me. I could sense His Spirit there with me. Then I went out for a walk alone on the streets of New York. I never liked New York before, but this night it was beautiful. I walked for blocks and blocks, I guess. Everything seemed different to me. It was raining softly and the city lights created a golden glow. Something had happened to me and I knew it."

"That's what you mean by accepting Christ—you just ask?" I was more puzzled than ever.

"That's it, as simple as that," Tom replied. "Of course, you have to want Jesus in your life, really want Him. That's the way it starts. And let me tell you, things then begin to change. Since then I have found a satisfaction and a joy about living that I simply never knew was possible."

To me Jesus had always been an historical figure, but Tom explained that you could hardly invite Him into your life if you didn't believe that He is alive today and that His Spirit is a part of today's scene. I was moved by Tom's story even though I couldn't imagine how such a miraculous change could take place in such a simple way. Yet the excitement in Tom's voice as he described his experience was convincing and Tom was indeed different. More alive.

Then Tom turned the conversation again to my plight. I described some of the agonies of Watergate, the pressures I was under, how unfairly I thought the press was treating me. I was being defensive and when I ran out of explanations, Tom spoke gently but firmly.

"You know that I supported Nixon in this past election, but you guys made a serious mistake. You would have won the election without any of the hanky-panky. Watergate and the dirty tricks were so unnecessary. And it was wrong, just plain wrong. You didn't have to do it."

Tom was leaning forward, elbows on his knees, his hands stretched forward almost as if he was trying to reach out for me. There was an urgent appeal in his eyes. "Don't you understand that?" he asked with such genuine feeling that I couldn't take offense.

"If only you had believed in the rightness of your cause, none of this would have been necessary. None of this would have happened. The problem with all of you, including you, Chuck—you simply had to go for the other guy's jugular. You had to try to destroy your enemies. You had to destroy them because you couldn't trust in yourselves."

The heat at that moment seemed unbearable as I wiped away drops of perspiration over my lip. The iced tea was soothing as I sipped it, although with Tom's points hitting home so painfully, I longed for a Scotch and soda. To myself I admitted that Tom was on target: the world of *us* against *them* as we saw it from our insulated White House enclave—the Nixon White House against the world. Insecure about our cause, our overkill approach was a way to play it safe. And yet. . . .

"Tom, one thing you don't understand. In politics it's dog-eat-dog; you simply can't survive otherwise. I've been in the political business for twenty years, including several campaigns right here in Massachusetts. I know how things are done. Politics is like war. If you don't keep the enemy on the defensive, you'll be on the defensive yourself. Tom, this man Nixon has been under constant attack all of his life. The only way he could make it was to fight back. Look at the criticism he took over Vietnam. Yet he was right. We never would have made it if we hadn't fought the way we did, hitting our critics, never letting them get the best of us. We didn't have any choice."

Even as I talked, the words sounded more and more empty to me. Tired old lines, I realized. I was describing the ways of the political world, all right, while suddenly wondering if there could be a better way.

Tom believed so, anyway. He was so gentle I couldn't resent what he said as he cut right through it all: "Chuck, I hate to say this, but you guys brought it on yourselves. If you had put your faith in God, and if your cause were just, He would have guided you. And His help would have been a thousand times more powerful than all your phony ads and shady schemes put together."

With any other man the notion of relying on God would have seemed to me pure Pollyanna. Yet I had to be impressed with the way this man ran his company in the equally competitive world of business: ignoring his enemies, trying to follow God's ways. Since his conversion Raytheon had never done better, sales and profits soaring. Maybe there was something to it; anyway it's tough to argue with success.

"Chuck, I don't think you will understand what I'm saying about God until you are willing to face yourself honestly and squarely. This is the first step." Tom reached to the corner table and picked up a small paperback book. I read the title: *Mere Christianity* by C. S. Lewis.

"I suggest you take this with you and read it while you are on vacation." Tom started to hand it to me, then paused. "Let me read you one chapter."

I leaned back, still on the defensive, my mind and emotions whirling.

There is one vice of which no man in the world is free; which every one in the world loathes when he sees it in someone else; and of which hardly any people, except Christians, ever imagine that they are guilty themselves. I have heard people admit that they are bad-tempered, or that they cannot keep their heads about girls or drink, or even that they are cowards. I do not think I have ever heard anyone who was not a Christian accuse himself of this vice. . . . There is no fault . . . which we are more unconscious of in ourselves. And the more we have it ourselves, the more we dislike it in others.

The vice I am talking of is Pride or Self-Conceit. . . . Pride leads to every other vice: it is the complete anti-God state of mind.

As he read, I could feel a flush coming into my face and a curious burning sensation that made the night seem even warmer. Lewis's words seemed to pound straight at me.

. . . it is Pride which has been the chief cause of misery in every nation and every family since the world began. Other vices may sometimes bring people together: you may find good fellowship and jokes and friendliness among drunken people or unchaste people. But Pride always means enmity—it *is* enmity. And not only enmity between man and man, but enmity to God.

In God you come up against something which is in every respect immeasurably superior to yourself. Unless you know God as that—and, therefore, know yourself as nothing in comparison—you do not know God at all. As long as you are proud you cannot know God. A proud man is always looking down on things and people: and, of course, as long as you are looking down, you cannot see something that is above you.

Suddenly I felt naked and unclean, my bravado defenses gone. I was exposed, unprotected, for Lewis's words were describing me. As he continued, one passage in particular seemed to sum up what had happened to all of us at the White House:

For Pride is spiritual cancer: it eats up the very possibility of love, or contentment, or even common sense.

Just as a man about to die is supposed to see flash before him, sequence by sequence, the high points of his life, so, as Tom's voice read on that August evening, key events in my life paraded before me as if projected on a screen. Things I hadn't thought about in years—my graduation speech at prep school—being "good enough" for the Marines—my first marriage, into the "right" family—sitting on the Jaycees' dais while civic leader after civic leader praised me as the outstanding young man of Boston—then to the White House—the clawing and straining for status and position—"Mr. Colson, the President is calling—Mr. Colson, the President wants to see you right away."

For some reason I thought of an incident after the 1972 election when a reporter, an old Nixon nemesis, came by my office and contritely asked what he could do to get in the good graces of the White House. I suggested that he try "slashing his wrists." I meant it as a joke, of course, but also to make him squirm. It was the arrogance of the victor over an enemy brought to submission.

Now, sitting there on the dimly lit porch, my self-centered past was washing over me in waves. It was painful. Agony. Desperately I tried to defend myself. What about my sacrifices for government service, the giving up of a big income, putting my stocks into a blind trust? The truth, I saw in an instant, was that I'd wanted the position in the White House more than I'd wanted money. There was no sacrifice. And the more I had talked about my own sacrifices, the more I was really trying to build myself up in the eyes of others. I would eagerly have given up everything I'd ever earned to prove myself at the mountaintop of government. It was pride—Lewis's "great sin"—that had propelled me through life.

Tom finished the chapter on pride and shut the book. I mumbled something noncommittal to the effect that "I'll look forward to reading that." But

Lewis's torpedo had hit me amidships. I think Phillips knew it as he stared into my eyes. That one chapter ripped through the protective armor in which I had unknowingly encased myself for forty-two years. Of course, I had not known God. *How could I?* I had been concerned with myself. *I* had done this and that, *I* had achieved, *I* had succeeded and *I* had given God none of the credit, never once thanking Him for any of His gifts to me. I had never thought of anything being "immeasurably superior" to myself, or if I had in fleeting moments thought about the infinite power of God, I had not related Him to my life. In those brief moments while Tom read, I saw myself as I never had before. And the picture was ugly.

"How about it, Chuck?" Tom's question jarred me out of my trance. I knew precisely what he meant. Was I ready to make the leap of faith as he had in New York, to "accept" Christ?

"Tom, you've shaken me up. I'll admit that. That chapter describes me. But I can't tell you I'm ready to make the kind of commitment you did. I've got to be certain. I've got to learn a lot more, be sure all my reservations are satisfied. I've got a lot of intellectual hang-ups to get past."

For a moment Tom looked disappointed, then he smiled. "I understand, I understand."

"You see," I continued, "I saw men turn to God in the Marine Corps; I did once myself. Then afterwards it's all forgotten and everything is back to normal. Foxhole religion is just a way of using God. How can I make a commitment now? My whole world is crashing down around me. How can I be sure I'm not just running for shelter and that when the crisis is over I'll forget it? I've got to answer all the intellectual arguments first and if I can do that, I'll be sure."

"I understand," Tom repeated quietly.

I was relieved he did, yet deep inside of me something wanted to tell Tom to press on. He was making so much sense, the first time anyone ever had in talking about God.

But Tom did not press on. He handed me his copy of *Mere Christianity.* "Once you've read this, you might want to read the Book of John in the Bible." I scribbled notes of the key passages he quoted. "Also there's a man in Washington you should meet," he continued, "name of Doug Coe. He gets people together for Christian fellowship—prayer breakfasts and things like that. I'll ask him to contact you."

Tom then reached for his Bible and read a few of his favorite psalms. The comforting words were like a cold soothing ointment. For the first time in my life, familiar verses I'd heard chanted lifelessly in church came alive. "Trust in the Lord," I remember Tom reading, and I wanted to, right that moment I wanted to—if only I knew how, if only I could be sure.

"Would you like to pray together, Chuck?" Tom asked, closing his Bible and putting it on the table beside him.

Startled, I emerged from my deep thoughts. "Sure—I guess I would—Fine." I'd never prayed with anyone before except when someone said grace before a meal. Tom bowed his head, folded his hands, and leaned forward on the edge of his seat. "Lord," he began, "we pray for Chuck and his family, that You might open his heart and show him the light and the way. . . ."

As Tom prayed, something began to flow into me—a kind of energy. Then came a wave of emotion which nearly brought tears. I fought them back. It sounded as if Tom were speaking directly and personally to God, almost as if He were sitting beside us. The only prayers I'd ever heard were formal and stereotyped, sprinkled with *Thees* and *Thous*.

When he finished, there was a long silence. I knew he expected me to pray but I didn't know what to say and was too self-conscious to try. We walked to the kitchen together where Gert was still at the big table, reading. I thanked her and Tom for their hospitality.

"Come back, won't you?" she said. Her smile convinced me she meant it.

"Take care of yourself, Chuck, and let me know what you think of that book, will you?" With that, Tom put his hand on my shoulder and grinned. "I'll see you soon."

I didn't say much; I was afraid my voice would crack, but I had the strong feeling that I *would* see him soon. And I couldn't wait to read his little book.

Outside in the darkness, the iron grip I'd kept on my emotions began to relax. Tears welled up in my eyes as I groped in the darkness for the right key to start my car. Angrily I brushed them away and started the engine. "What kind of weakness is this?" I said to nobody.

The tears spilled over and suddenly I knew I had to go back into the house and pray with Tom. I turned off the motor, got out of the car. As I did, the kitchen light went out, then the light in the dining room. Through the hall window I saw Tom stand aside as Gert started up the stairs ahead of him. Now the hall was in darkness. It was too late. I stood for a moment staring at the darkened house, only one light burning now in an upstairs bedroom. Why hadn't I prayed when he gave me the chance? I wanted to so badly. Now I was alone, really alone.

As I drove out of Tom's driveway, the tears were flowing uncontrollably. There were no streetlights, no moonlight. The car headlights were flooding illumination before my eyes, but I was crying so hard it was like trying to swim underwater. I pulled to the side of the road not more than a hundred yards from the entrance to Tom's driveway, the tires sinking into soft mounds of pine needles.

I remember hoping that Tom and Gert wouldn't hear my sobbing, the only sound other than the chirping of crickets that penetrated the still of the night. With my face cupped in my hands, head leaning forward against the wheel, I forgot about machismo, about pretenses, about fears of being weak. And as I did, I began to experience a wonderful feeling of being released. Then came the strange sensation that water was not only running down my cheeks, but surging through my whole body as well, cleansing and cooling as it went. They weren't tears of sadness and remorse, nor of joy—but somehow, tears of relief.

And then I prayed my first real prayer. "God, I don't know how to find You, but I'm going to try! I'm not much the way I am now, but somehow I want to give myself to You." I didn't know how to say more, so I repeated over and over the words: *Take me.*

I had not "accepted" Christ—I still didn't know who He was. My mind told me it was important to find that out first, to be sure that I knew what I was doing, that I meant it and would stay with it. Only, that night, something inside me was urging me to surrender—to what or to whom I did not know.

I stayed there in the car, wet-eyed, praying, thinking, for perhaps half an hour, perhaps longer, alone in the quiet of the dark night. Yet for the first time in my life I was not alone at all.

11

est

Jerry Rubin

Jerry Rubin (b. 1938) gained notoriety in the 1960s as co-founder of the Youth International Party (the Yippies) and as defendant at the highly publicized Chicago Seven Trial of the era. An Ohioan with solidly Jewish roots, after receiving his baccalaureate he attended Hebrew University and later returned to Israel to spend a year there with his brother. In between, Rubin spent time in Berkeley, at first as a student at the University of California and later as a writer, lecturer, and activist with a bent toward involvement in protest movements. By a decade later, however, it was clear that Rubin was changing and that he was embarked on what many in the 1990s would call a spiritual quest. Rubin's quest led him eventually to the then-controversial Erhard Seminars Training (est). The creation of Werner Erhard (b. 1935 as Jack Rosenberg), est—or the Forum as it later reconstituted itself in a less intense version—offered culturally combinative and decidedly high-pressure workshops to push, startle, or even explode a person into a form of enlightenment outside of any recognizable spiritual tradition. Erhard himself had experimented with a variety of religious paths from Zen Buddhism to Scientology. His seminars took from the "shock" aspect of such traditions to structure an abruptly confrontational format for personal growth and change. Here workshop leaders gave participants a transformed version of accountability, no longer in the rhetoric of the accusing evangelical preacher, who called hearers to task for sinful ways, but now in the language of "getting it"—of seeing one's complicity in the creation of one's world. The deep emotionality of knowing through the heart can surely be recognized here—inflected, however, in a new and different key and with results as different.

Werner Erhard stood in the front of the room and shouted at us, "You spend your entire life trying to cover up the fact that you are assholes!" He was attacking the personality we present to the world, our "acts." I sat in est and held on to my act, furious at Werner for raking in money by calling us names. Where would he have been in mid-1960's when the United States was defoliating Vietnam? He would have been calling the protesters "assholes"!

I felt like leaping out of my seat and strangling the motherfucker, and then making a grand exit. But if I stood up and attacked Werner, two hundred and fifty other people would look at me and say, "There's Jerry Rubin doing his Jerry Rubin number." Werner had me trapped. I'd be damned if I would be the example to prove his point that we go through our lives *playing* ourselves rather than *being* ourselves.

In mere description est (Erhard Seminars Training) sounds absurd. About two hundred people are packed into a hotel room on hard chairs for four eighteen-hour days. Everyone agrees in advance not to eat, leave their seats, or talk unless called on. From the front of the room the trainer barrages people with an attack on their egos, roles, and life-styles, while at the same time giving academic lectures on the nature of reality, the meaning of life, and the process of perception. Then people go to the microphone to share from their hearts and souls the secrets they rarely tell their friends. At the end everyone is enlightened.

Now Werner is teaching me that I control my body; my body does not control me. I am one of fifty thousand people who have been through est. But I sit there feeling like an absolute ass. "Rubin," I think to myself, "you'd fall for anything that promised you the moon."

I figured "Werner Erhard" was a Nazi from Germany. All my Jewish anti-German feelings bubbled to the surface. But Werner is actually a Jew whose real name is Jack Rosenberg, and he's from Philadelphia. He ran away from home at the age of twenty-two and renamed himself after Ludwig Erhard and Werner Von Braun. I decided to leave quietly.

This was another of my acts: to hide or withdraw, the reverse side of my activist act. I play the superior one who looks down on others, the person who can't be conned. I wasn't going to fall for Werner's double talk. I was thinking all these things but was scared to go up to the microphone where, one by one, people were telling their life stories. I worried that I might not have something brilliant to say. What if people thought, "Gee, Jerry Rubin is boring." I'm a great orator when a thousand people are applauding, but in est I'd have to make it on my own. So, instead I sat quietly, putting down all the assholes who went to the microphone to tell their dull inner dramas. Werner was right. These people *were* assholes. I couldn't wait to leave.

Then I remembered: "I paid $200 to sit through this shit! I know what to do! I'll run to the bank early Monday morning and cancel my check. That'll screw Werner's ass!" That night I went home to sleep. The next morning I woke up at 6 A.M. feeling refreshed. My conscious mind had quit est training, but my unconscious mind had other plans for me. I found myself zooming over to the hotel to beat the other assholes to a front-row seat.

Something theatrically revolutionary was happening at est. In the 1960's we had used political guerrilla theater to get people to see beyond their roles.

Now Werner was creating a psychological theater provoking people into self-confrontation. Whenever people discover themselves, they grow and learn—and that has to be revolutionary. (My act is liking something *only* if I can call it "revolutionary.")

The key to the 1970's is the consciousness revolution. External events are important in determining consciousness, but in the end we decide exactly *how* to respond to any event that takes place in our lives. The current consciousness changes reflect the growing awareness by people of their own power: "I control my consciousness, my inner reality."

Throughout history only a minority have dropped out of society to reach higher states of consciousness. Today thousands of people are going through spiritual and psychological transformations. Est is spreading throughout the middle class—to professionals, intellectuals, businessmen, housewives, students, right-wingers, left-wingers.

The consciousness movement is a direct descendant of the grass-acid movement of the 1960's. Grass and acid are tools for altering consciousness, but direct control of consciousness through internal discipline is the goal. All the consciousness movements use various forms of psychic healing, returning the responsibility of health to the people.

Back in the est hotel room for the second day, I was lapsing again into a conscious sleep, feeling superior and contemptuous, ripped off and conned, shy and scared. There was nowhere to go, no one to call, no distraction. I was alone with myself—something that seldom occurs in my life since I am usually too busy doing my act. Doing est we could not talk to each other or leave our seats or read or take notes. If someone left his seat, two est staff members sent him back.

My body felt itchy, my mind bored. Werner kept saying that we create everything that happens to us. Had I created my itchy body and bored mind? *How often* is my body itchy and my mind bored?

The people at the microphone telling their personal dramas were about as interesting as afternoon TV soap operas, but I heard my own in everybody else's story. Listening to these straight housewives and button-down businessmen, I realized that I was just like them. Once we got past our acts, our costumes, we all had the same experiences. Suddenly I felt sympathy for Richard Nixon, Nelson Rockefeller, Gerald Ford. Strip away the mask and the role, and there hides a scared human being behind our acts.

As a child I believed that underneath we were all the same. I believed in God. When you died you would relive your life again, but this time experiencing the feelings of everyone who had interacted with you. Heaven was a big movie theater. One day sitting in the library in high school I had a cosmic realization. What if at this very moment I am simultaneously living my life in the body and consciousness of everyone else on the planet?

Later, my political activities were motivated by basic feelings of equality: a Vietnamese peasant is equal to a Wall Street executive. Everything that makes us different from one another is artificial: all human beings basically want and need the same things—security, love, energy.

Unconsciously I had accepted my environment's definition of the differences between human beings: "We are Americans and they are not; we are free and they are Communists; we are Jewish and they are goyim; we are white and they are black; we are good and they are criminals." Then, when I was in jail with a guard who sadistically brutalized the prisoners, I realized that underneath his act and his scared macho personality—he was me and I was him.

Snapping back to the present, I heard Werner screaming that we create everything that happens to us in our lives. Like a yippie, he took his point to an absurd extreme. He said that Vietnamese babies created the napalm that fell on their heads, that Jews constructed Auschwitz, that rape victims desired to be raped. The audience went crazy, screaming, turning off, throwing up their hands in outrage. Werner ran around the room arguing his theory of self-responsibility with each person, obviously trying to offend, shock, scare, create a mood. He listened to people's miseries—their parents' deaths, broken marriages, financial tragedies—and then laughed in their faces and screamed: "YOU ASSHOLE, YOU CAUSED IT!"

Werner was telling a young woman that she *wanted* to be beaten, raped, robbed. He offered not one iota of sympathy; he certainly is no Jewish Mother. He hears about a tragedy and shrugs his shoulders. "So what!" he says. "So what!"

The room lightened up a bit. People considered what he was saying. Maybe I did create my auto accident. Maybe I did create my cancer. Maybe I did kill my mother. Maybe I'm not a helpless victim. A huge sigh echoed across the room. One woman took the microphone and said, "I had polio as a kid. I see now I wanted polio, I chose my polio." People took a look at the worst thing in their lives, took full responsibility for it, and then realized, "So what?" Nothing makes a difference. Romantic breakups, sickness, death—so what? I caused it all, accepted or resisted it. I created everything that happened to me, even my parents. Do I want to feel sad about it, happy, or what?

"It is up to you!" screams Werner.

I thought of my life, the loneliness, pain, rejection; and I heard Werner's voice inside me shouting at me, "What a big soap opera, you fool! You brought it all on yourself! You wanted it! You plan your colds, your headaches, your insomnia—everything! Now dig it!"

Werner's sheer intensity kept me in the room. He reminded me of Lenny Bruce provoking people. Suddenly I flashed on what Werner was doing. He was a Zen master trying to shock people out of their minds. Werner screams:

"Do you get it? Do you get it? The moment you get it, you'll lose it. The truth is an experience, not a belief!"

Next, Werner went to the blackboard and in an abstract lecture tried to convince us that we had never made a *free* choice in our lives. We had chosen all that happened to us, but we were mere robots playing out our childhood programming. More objections!

"Whattaymean! I chose my career! I chose my wife! I chose my philosophy! I chose my personality!"

"No! No!" screamed Werner, "you are all machines, you have never made a decision in your life." This time people started getting "it" quickly. "The truth is an experience, a Zen koan. It makes no sense to the mind," said Werner.

Is there a consciousness beyond my mind? Around the room people's eyes were lighting up as they screamed: "I got it! I got it!" I wanted to get it too. What if everyone got it but me? I'd miss out on my $200, and feel inferior besides. Werner had created a group atmosphere in which everyone now wanted to "get it."

To get it I would have to give up my identity, beliefs; my feelings of being ripped-off, my repulsion at being part of group pressure, my rationality, my logical mind, my individuality; my ego, my role, my name. Me! I'd have to give up control to someone I didn't even trust. I'd have to relinquish my rebel role and all my resistance. Worst of all, I'd have to give up my freedom.

A lot of things exist between me and the world. I am all the things that define and defend me. Sitting there in est I admitted for a second to myself how much I play the "I'm right-you're wrong" game. That was my approach to life. I peeked outside myself and saw my personality, my games, my trip— The Whole Jerry Rubin Show—and it hurt to look.

I saw that I had created every part of the story to the last detail. It hurt to see so clearly, and it scared me. What if I could see myself so clearly all the time? I set up everything in my life to happen just the way it happens. I felt totally free! Totally powerful—and totally scared to death! I would never be able to lie to myself again.

Werner had permanently altered my consciousness. *I am responsible* for everything that happens to me. If I am miserable, I choose to be miserable. It is up to me: To like it or hate it. To choose. To become the center of my life.

Every condition in the body is determined by the nervous system. When we suffer with a headache, for example, we do not experience the headache, but the past pictures in our minds of headaches. Our eagerness to give our condition a conceptual name, like a "headache" or "cold"—with all the memories the word conjures up—strengthens the condition. Our feeling that we are victims and can do nothing gives the condition power over us.

Like a faith healer, Werner brought people with headaches to the front of the room. He had them experience directly the sensations, naming the location, size, shape, and color of the pain. He had them relate those sensations to pictures and emotional experiences in the past. "Do you want those sensations?" Deciding they did not, focusing directly on the sensations, people began losing the headaches, backaches, and nervous conditions that had plagued them for years.

Next Werner attacked the "seekers" of the 1970's, the growth trippers who go from rolfing to bioenergetics to yoga to tai chi to est to natural foods to gestalt to TM to swamis in search of the "answer." I recognized myself. "Goddamnit, Jerry, you're a guru whore," Sam Keen once ribbed me, after hearing I did Arica after psychic therapy after est. In two years in the growth movement I had tried everything, looking, looking, looking. Werner shouted at us: "WHAT THE HELL ARE YOU LOOKING FOR? THIS IS IT! THERE IS NOTHING TO FIND! YOU'VE FOUND IT! THERE IS NOTHING IN LIFE BUT THIS! YOU'RE HERE! YOU'VE ARRIVED! LOOK AND SEE IT!"

The truth jarred me. All my life I've been obsessed with the idea of seeking, searching, working for some mythical tomorrow. Life is a ladder: climb, climb, climb. To get where?

I have had money and I know its emptiness. I've eaten expensive meals and when they are over I'm full. I've experienced good sex—and gotten used to it. I've gone up and come down from LSD. I've felt myself in the center of history and it's passed. I've traveled—and it's all the same place. I've met the very rich and powerful and discovered that it's the same at the bottom as it is at the top.

When I wasn't at the top, I was trying to get there. When I got there I was trying to stay there. In neither place did I experience "there." It was always tomorrow that I worried about. Now I see that there is no tomorrow, only right now.

"THERE IS NOTHING TO FIND! THERE IS NO TOMORROW! TOMORROW IS TODAY! THERE IS NOTHING NOTHING NOTHING! THIS IS IT! And it doesn't matter! When you are dead, you will be dead," said Werner, "and not one second sooner."

This is it? What I have been hoping for, looking for? Nowhere to go but here? People in the room began screaming at the discovery that there is nowhere to go. I could literally feel the tension disappear. I saw faces lighten. My shoulders relaxed and I felt a full feeling in my stomach. Time slowed down. I felt like the richest man on earth. Because I had everything. I had The Moment, my life in my hands.

Est had sent me inside myself. I've spent time feeling sorry for myself because I did not get what I wanted. But inside, a voice beyond my normal consciousness whispered, "Jerry, if you'd pay attention to what actually happened, rather than what you wanted, you'd be happy." In est I was again hearing that intuitive psychic insight. Werner was telling me: "Your mind never knows what's going on. Your mind lives in its own world of self-justifying need. Pay attention to what is actually happening and be there. Stop living in the pictures of your head. You cause pain for yourself with your expectations and preconceptions."

Throughout the activism of the 1960's I aimed for a goal, but never achieved the precise goal in my mind. As long as I kept my attention on the goal, I always felt disappointed. But if I paid attention to the process, to what *actually happened to me,* then I could never be dissatisfied!

In the 1960's we were demonstrating and holding meetings to make political changes tomorrow. But through it all a psychic part of me knew the truth: We were demonstrating and meeting not for tomorrow, but for today. We were doing what we were doing for the doing of it. While doing, we were *being* our doing.

I saw that I had a scarcity approach to life—there is not enough, I better get mine! "Stop looking for what you've already got," said Werner. The room at that point was high as a balloon. Everybody was digging the moment. We were out of our minds.

But my mind kept fighting back. "Will living in the moment destroy my desire to create and change?" My behavior will not necessarily change but my *awareness* will change. Instead of seeking with the expectation of finding, I experience my seeking as an end in itself. I become one with my seeking, and merge with the moment.

I kept getting this insight, then losing it. It wouldn't stick. I don't experience life because I keep wanting life to come out a certain way. If I keep it up, I'll be laying on my death bed and wondering what happened. Where'd my life go?

But living totally in the moment is scary. It goes against years of conditioning. Still, it works. When I put my awareness completely in what I am doing, I make whatever I do work.

"You can't change anything by complaining about it," said Werner, "so why complain? You change something when you change it, not one second before. And if you complain about it, experience yourself complaining about it. Enjoy your complaining!"

Even though I make decisions every day, on the deepest level I don't have a damn thing to do with my life. I flow with events and do not consciously know what is going on. I have to accept this confusion, because I cannot be in control. I can take responsibility for what happens, but in the end self-responsibility is an illusion too.

As soon as I learn to give up and stop trying to understand-control-plan-direct everything, I feel in tune with the energy of life. "I don't know" turns out to be three high words.

Werner Erhard is taking the mystery out of the spiritual experience. The spiritual movement has always been represented by swamis speaking foreign languages, meditation with strange-sounding foreign mantras, and uncomfortable yoga positions. Spirituality has been for the select few, techniques passed down by word-of-mouth, deliberately kept from the masses. Est is an attempt to Americanize Eastern consciousness—to make it available to the majority of people.

In an instant I flashed on the truth. Everything is process. The spiritual movement of the 1970's, from Zen to Don Juan, is driving home the same point: *see* the moment. Werner said by experiencing the moment *as it is,* I automatically receive pleasure from it, therefore automatically experience my life changing for the better.

12

Surrendering to Krishna: Devi's Story

E. Burke Rochford, Jr.

The story recounted here is that of a young American woman who leaves her Anglo-Protestant cultural moorings to become a devotee of Krishna through the International Society for Krishna Consciousness (ISKCON). Founded in 1965 by the South Asian Indian A. C. Bhaktivedanta Swami Prabhupada (1896–1977), Krishna Consciousness is based on the much earlier teachings of Chaitanya Mahaprabhu (1486–1533) as institutionalized in a sixteenth-century sect. Central to both the earlier movement and its late-twentieth-century relative is Krishna, who is worshiped as supreme God by his followers. Thus, adherents to Krishna Consciousness are Krishna monotheists—different from other Hindus who consider Krishna an incarnation of the God Vishnu, one of the major deities in popular Hindu belief. In ISKCON's years of greatest intensity, the monastic lifestyle of devotees was cultivated assiduously, as Devi's story tells. And at the core of that lifestyle was the Hare Krishna chant, sounded and repeated over and over again as Krishna Consciousness people with fervor and passion danced out their prayer and devotion. Their practice expressed the Hindu spiritual path of *bhakti*, the popular religious orientation that stressed the overriding importance of personal feeling, of a deep and intense attachment to one of the Gods or Goddesses of India. Through love for the chosen deity, it was thought, one tapped into universal power, and one's life was accordingly blessed and transformed. These ideas can be seen in Devi's narrative about her years in Krishna Consciousness and in her continuing commitment to it. In the context of Devi's history of drug abuse and her series of later interpersonal struggles, devotion to Krishna becomes a source, for her, of spiritual transformation and emotional well-being.

The description I have so far given of the devotees and of the circumstances leading up to their joining in Hare Krishna has been to this point largely static in character; it has not allowed for a detailed understanding of the processes leading people to become Krishna devotees. While the survey data . . . provide useful descriptive statistics, which allow us to paint a broad and comprehensive picture of the devotees, such abstract findings inevitably gloss over the interactive processes that have influenced any particular individual's decision to join the movement. Yet recruitment and the processes involved in a person's becoming a member of a movement ultimately are outcomes of social interactions, rather than the result of some specific configuration of demographic and/or social psychological variables that might be interpreted as predisposing individuals toward collective action.

In this chapter, I take a very different approach, both methodologically and analytically, to the issue of recruitment into Hare Krishna. I will make use of a first person narrative to describe the experience of one devotee's surrender to Krishna. The life history method, because it is openly subjective in character and relies upon and respects a person's own story and analysis of his or her life, provides for a rich and detailed research strategy. The life history method may involve telling a person's life story in full, or it may involve telling simply a portion of that story, depending upon the theoretical interests and concerns of the investigator. While a life history is usually not viewed as conventional social science "data," which leads to the development of theoretical propositions, this method has the virtue of providing us with a wealth of richly detailed information about particular substantive topics from the perspective of the person under study. Becker thus explains the distinctive advantages of the life history, in particular its ability to gain a member's own perspective:

> This perspective differs from that of some other social scientists in assigning major importance to the interpretations people place on their experience as an explanation for behavior. To understand why someone behaves as he does, you must understand how it looked to him, what he thought he had to contend with, what alternatives he saw open to him; you can only understand the effects of opportunity structures, delinquent subcultures, social norms, and other commonly invoked explanations of behavior by seeing them *from the actor's point of view* [emphasis added] (1970:64).

This chapter tells the story of one woman who has chosen to dedicate her life to Krishna Consciousness. I have selected Devi's life history for a number of theoretical reasons. Like most ISKCON members, Devi was raised in a middle-class family where religion, particularly in her early childhood years, was an important part of her life. As she grew older, however, her involvements with the church lessened, as she became increasingly involved with the drug culture, men, and Eastern philosophy. In this sense, she comes from a quite typical background. In addition, Devi, like a number of other women recruits to ISKCON, first made contact with the movement through a social relationship, in her case as a result of her knowing a boyfriend who was himself interested in Krishna Consciousness. As it turned out, the two of them ultimately joined the movement together. Finally, Devi's career within ISKCON demonstrates the often problematical character of the recruitment and membership process: On two occasions Devi defected from ISKCON, largely as a result of outside ties that acted to compromise her full commitment to a Krishna-conscious lifestyle. In the end, however, her friendships within the movement, combined with her commitment to the Krishna beliefs, resulted in her rejoining the movement, in which she has now resided for some three years.[1]

Devi's Life History

Devi was born in 1958 in Saulte Saint Marie, Ontario, Canada. At the time of her birth, her parents had only recently moved to Canada from Michigan, where they had met as students. Devi's mother wanted her new child to be born in Canada, where she had been born and raised before coming to the States. Her mother came from a large Canadian family of four brothers and a sister. After spending a year in Canada, Devi moved with her parents to Birmingham, Alabama, the homeplace of her father. Her father was well-educated and the only child of a well-to-do Southern family. His mother, according to Devi, was a typical Southern belle from South Carolina.

For the next six years, the family lived in Birmingham. Devi remembers herself as a spirited child during these early years. When she was aged four, Devi's brother was born. Soon after, her sister was born. In Birmingham, Devi completed her first years of school, completing the second grade before her family once again relocated. The family moved to Baltimore, Maryland, where her father took a government job.

In Baltimore, Devi attended the public schools, where she was a good student and very popular among her peers. She was an avid reader, her favorite books including the Nancy Drew stories and *Little Women,* which Devi remembers reading "about a thousand times." A Walt Disney fan, she watched all of the early Disney films on TV and at the movies. Devi also loved music and dancing. She took ballet lessons beginning in the second grade.

Religion was always important to Devi and to her parents. She was raised as a Protestant Anglican, attending church weekly with the family. Devi's father had been an altar boy in his youth, and although his church involvement had waned since college, he resumed going to church again after Devi's birth. Devi's mother, in her eyes, was always more religious than her father. She was humble and always active in the church where she sang in the church choir every week. Devi remembers her early church involvement in the following terms:

> I always had a very big attachment at this time to Bible stories. I learned to read at a very young age. I was a very avid reader. . . . When I was between about

seven and twelve, I wanted to be a prophet when I grew up. I always thought that I had somehow been born in the wrong time and place though: Why wasn't I born when Jesus was born? I really wanted to be a prophet. I always had a very deep feeling that that was what I was going to grow up and be—a prophet. I believed in Jesus. I believed in God. I believed everything the Bible had to say.

During her early years, Devi matured very quickly and in the sixth grade she began to be aware of the development of her own sense of identity.

In the sixth grade is when my ego really began to take over. I really wanted to develop my own identity. You naturally wonder what other people are thinking about you and you want to develop your image.

As she entered her teenage years, Devi found herself being viewed as both attractive and very popular by her classmates and friends. She was significantly clever at her studies, so that she was an "A" and "B" student despite little effort.

Then senior high school came and I got involved with boys and girls. Little clubs of various sorts and cliques, all that kind of thing. . . . This is when I really started to become a rascal. I started not wanting to attend my classes and not being serious about my studies.

But while her interest in school began to decline in her high school years, she remained committed to and involved in her church.

I still believed in God and I still went to church. I was an active member of the choir. I loved to sing and I so much enjoyed singing hymns in church every Sunday. Even during these years, it was no problem for me to go to church. I really liked it.

Even though she was active in the church, Devi looks back now on her involvement then as ultimately a shallow expression of her spirituality.

I can look back now and say it wasn't that deep a realization that I was experiencing at that time. Church was more like a social, extra-curricular activity. I enjoyed it, but it wasn't really fulfilling me spiritually.

Devi's first experience with drugs came at the age of twelve. On a visit to her father's parents in Florida, she was introduced to marijuana by some young people she met there. From this point forward, Devi became increasingly involved in the drug culture and the music and good times she associated with it. Her involvement in the drug scene ultimately took her still further away from school and from her parents. She desperately wanted to experience the excitement associated with this lifestyle, even if it created problems in other ways:

> I was always a big music fan. I liked music a lot and played the radio every night and danced. I was smoking pot and going to parties. I would stay the night at a girlfriend's house, and Saturday nights we would go to the teen center and dance. Oh, how I loved to dance.

In the tenth grade, Devi became a cheerleader at her high school. She also became more and more involved in the drug scene, a situation which played havoc with her studies:

> By this time I was very knowledgeable in the whole drug scene. I'd been going with a boy who was very rich and by now I had tried pot, cocaine, and some downers. I guess my first experience with LSD was in the ninth or tenth grade. I did [LSD] a total of maybe five times in my life. I didn't like it. . . . It was in the tenth grade that I really started cutting classes regularly. What I would do was go to the park and get high with my friends. We were getting high on a lot of good dope, and that was where my life was at.

By this time Devi's parents had begun to suspect her involvement with drugs, and they suspected that it was linked with her recent performance at school. As Devi remembers:

> I started seeing little pamphlets on the coffee table about marijuana and LSD. They must have been in touch with school groups—the PTA or something. They were trying to fight the problem, but they didn't really know what to do or how to effectively deal with it.

Devi's new lifestyle not only took her away from her studies and antagonized her parents, it also led her to become less and less interested in attending church and keeping up with her religious activities.

> I wasn't reading the Bible anymore. I had finally stopped going to church by about the tenth grade. I still believed in God and at night I would pray to God, but I had lost my sense of direction spiritually. I wasn't thinking of being a prophet anymore, instead there was the pressure of the material world and I was definitely trying to take advantage of it. I was definitely in the fast lane, you might say.

At the age of sixteen, her boyfriend proposed marriage. His family was very successful; they owned a local jewelry store. Devi's parents approved of the marriage and at first she accepted his proposal. Within a few months, however,

Devi decided that she was too young to be married and broke off the engagement. This was during the Christmas season of 1975. Soon after this relationship dissolved, Devi became involved in another that would prove important to her spiritual reawakening and ultimately to her coming to Krishna Consciousness.

After breaking off the engagement, Devi initially felt a need to avoid any involvement with men. She wanted to spend at least a few months by herself, unencumbered by the presence of a man in her life. As it happened, however, she visited an acquaintance whom she knew from buying drugs with her previous boyfriend. The dealer, Aaron, became a major influence on her life during the years that followed. He was five years older than the seventeen-year-old Devi, and as she describes it:

> He was a very far-out person. To me he was a major force in my life. Aaron had a lot of experience about spiritual things, and he actually began my whole reinterest in spiritual life. He had been to India many times, because he was a dealer. He had been to Afghanistan and Nepal, bringing back all of these things like pictures and books and his whole house was like India. He had all these neat artifacts and he was into antiques. I couldn't help but be really impressed by that. So I fell in love with this person. I saw him every night. He really brought about a drastic change in my life.

Devi recalls the first evening she spent with Aaron and how she quickly became deeply influenced by him:

> I went to his house one night and we were doing drugs. I remember being immediately captured by this person. He was attracted to me also, so we got involved. Within a few weeks time, I quit smoking cigarettes because he didn't like it. . . . Within two weeks after that I wanted to become a vegetarian like him. Aaron was such a neat person. He impressed me very deeply.

Aaron took a great interest in Devi and encouraged her to become a vegetarian. He taught her about health foods and how to cook various vegetarian dishes. Aaron was instrumental in teaching Devi about Eastern philosophy as well:

> I had already been exposed to reincarnation. My father read many books by people who believed in witchcraft and ghosts. I believed in God. I believed in witchcraft. I believed in reincarnation. But this boy made it more understandable for me—reincarnation, karma, all these kinds of spiritual ideas which I knew so little about. He would talk to me for hours about these types of things. It was all so far out to me and I just was completely attached to him.

It was during these early days with Aaron that Devi first came upon Krishna Consciousness and Srila Prabhupada. Aaron had a number of books on Eastern philosophy, among them a copy of Prabhupada's translation of the *Bhaga-vad Gita.* Initially she took no special interest in the book and had no idea that there even was a movement in America that followed these teachings. Al-though she had been introduced to Krishna Consciousness, she had no knowl-edge of the Hare Krishna movement.

As Devi became more and more involved with Aaron, she became even less interested in school. In an effort to finish high school early—in the eleventh grade—she began attending a local college part-time. By this time she had fulfilled all her high school requirements and lacked only a few credits towards graduation. As she said: "At this point I just wanted to finish, get out of school and be done with it."

During Devi's final year in school, Aaron was arrested for dealing drugs. After receiving a light sentence involving probation, Aaron, Devi, and their friend Dwight decided to open a health food store in Ocean City, Maryland. When Devi explained to her parents their plan for starting a business and moving away, both parents were outspoken in their disagreement. They were already upset by Devi's involvement with drugs and by her decision to become a vegetarian, but now she wanted to move away with a man whom they dis-liked. When Devi broke the news to her father, he was furious:

> He didn't want me moving out. He didn't like this boy anyway and so I remem-ber sitting around the kitchen table telling my father I'm going to Ocean City, and he was so upset. I wasn't even going to my high school graduation. I didn't care about my diploma; I disliked County High School. I mean there I was, their first child giving up everything and it just blew their minds. . . . The next week Aaron was at my parent's house and my father just said to him, 'If anything happens to her I swear to God, I'll kill you.'

Despite her parents' protest, Devi moved to Ocean City with Aaron and Dwight. With money from Dwight's savings and money contributed by Aar-on's mother, they opened their health food store on the boardwalk. The three of them shared a large house in the woods and they enjoyed that first sum-mer together.

Dwight was also interested in Eastern philosophy and both Devi and Aaron learned various yoga practices from him.

> Dwight was involved in a spiritual practice called *kriya* yoga. He practiced a kind of yoga called *agnihotra.* At sunrise and sunset, you recite mantras and meditate. There was also a pact you had to follow. You had to be a vegetarian, practice nonviolence, practice celibacy, and some other things I can't remember, but we were all doing these yoga exercises, basically deep breathing exercises and follow-ing the pact. It was an impersonal philosophy. The ideal goal was to merge into the absolute light situated between the eyes. I mean I was really into it. I believed

it. There was this little copper pot where you would burn wood and say a mantra and meditate. So we were all doing it.

While life in Ocean City involved practicing yoga, it involved a number of other things as well. Devi describes that first summer and her feelings about it:

> We had our business going and we worked very hard. We were doing yoga and by this time I was a strict vegetarian. I didn't eat any meat, fish, or eggs. I didn't eat any cooked food at all. So we were practicing yoga every morning and night, smoking pot, doing cocaine now and then and laying on the beach. We were into jazz music and we would go to concerts all the time. I was young and free and it was really great.

During this time Devi also continued reading various Eastern spiritual texts. She had read the *Bhagavad Gita,* not realizing that Krishna was God. Even so, she was impressed by the continual search for truth that was embodied in the literature she read. She too was looking for truth, though she wasn't sure where to find it. While reading these texts brought her closer to spiritual matters, she also felt a sense of disappointment in them:

> I felt very disappointed from my readings because I thought that here again I had been born too late. I was born at the wrong time and missed it. It was the same experience I felt from reading the Bible. After reading the *Bhagavad Gita,* I said to myself, 'Well there are no people that live like this, or if there are, they are all in India.'

One day Devi expressed her sense of disappointment to Aaron. She wanted to meet people like those in the *Bhagavad Gita,* but felt sure she would have to go to India. It was then that he told her about the Hare Krishna movement:

> So he told me about the Hare Krishna people. He had seen them in India while he was there, but also in Baltimore. That's how he had gotten all the books about Krishna. He had gone to the temple there. I mean here he had already been there and he hadn't told me! So he told me about them, how they lived and everything and about their Sunday feasts. I just kept asking him why he hadn't ever told me before. He just said that it never occurred to him. The funny thing was that he had given me the Hare Krishna album George Harrison produced and I would play it all the time, even before we moved to Ocean City. I was playing it and singing Hare Krishna every morning when I got up. Even my mother was walking around the house chanting Hare Krishna. There I was chanting this Hare Krishna and I didn't even know there was a group of people with shaved heads and with women wearing saris that were called Hare Krishnas.

It wasn't until the following summer that Devi finally met the devotees firsthand. After spending the winter in Baltimore, they returned to Ocean City to start the business again. One day Aaron walked into the store and announced that the Krishna devotees were giving out magazines on the boardwalk.

> I said 'Really. I've got to go and meet them.' I ran out and up to the boardwalk. There were all of these [Krishna] women and I ran up to them. I said: 'Hello who are you? I've read these books about you, I want to talk.' So this one mother started talking to me and they could all see that I was enthusiastic and very favorable toward Krishna Consciousness. I was ripe. So they were preaching to me. I was like the big attraction for them that day. I was a ripe person and all the mothers [Krishna women] were coming and talking to me. Now, as it turns out, I am very close with all these women. So they were offering the books, telling me to come to the temple. I was so excited. They came to the store and met Aaron. Everyone was so excited. They parked their van just outside the store and I stayed in the van talking with them all day. They gave me some *prasadam* [vegetarian food] and while it was only cashews and almonds with raisins I will never forget it. It was the best food that I had ever tasted in my entire life.

Devi's initial attraction to the movement was based largely upon her immediate feelings for the Krishna women.

> These women had real understanding and foresight. I appreciated that immediately. They knew what they are doing in life and knew what the purpose of life was. They were not afraid of death; they weren't afraid of anything in the material world. Nothing could affect them, it seemed. I just felt like I wanted to be like that too.

Over the next two days Devi spent most of her time with the devotee women. Aaron was also enthusiastic toward them and they decided to invite the women to stay at their house. After calling the temple president to gain permission, the Krishna women stayed over the weekend and nearly every other one that summer. Both Devi and Aaron avoided smoking pot on the weekends when the devotee women stayed at their house. Under the devotees' influence, they began offering their food to Krishna before each meal. One weekend the devotee women returned from Baltimore with japa beads for each of them to chant on, and they took to chanting "Hare Krishna." The women also gave Devi a sari to wear, which she liked very much.

In the coming months, Devi and Aaron both became increasingly involved with the devotees and with the devotional practices of Krishna Consciousness. Not only would they get up early every morning to chant with the devotees, but they also walked on the beach every night, chanting the mantra on their beads. As Devi explains:

We knew by the end of the summer that we wanted to be devotees. As the summer went by, we were very much involved with the chanting. We were into it and realized it would only be a matter of time. We were ready.

But while Devi and Aaron were attracted to the devotees and Krishna Consciousness, Dwight was entirely disinterested. Devi felt hurt by Dwight's lack of interest, since she had always considered him a spiritual teacher in his own right. She wanted him to become involved in the movement with them. But he continued practicing *agnihotra* yoga. Before the summer was over, Dwight decided he wanted to get out of the business and finally he left Ocean City altogether.

In contrast to the previous two years, Devi and Aaron decided to stay in Ocean City for the winter. Devi had already made plans to attend a local college to study art and music. As it turned out, these plans were never realized. Devi's attraction to the movement grew throughout the summer and she became more and more convinced that she wanted to become a Krishna devotee. On a number of occasions over the course of the summer, Devi and Aaron visited the temple in Baltimore, when they would travel there to pick up supplies for the store. They usually stayed overnight at the temple and participated in the movement's religious practices and rituals. Devi describes her first experience of the temple that summer:

> I walked into the temple and the moment that the incense entered my nostrils I was completely attracted. It smelled so good and so clean. The atmosphere was so mystical. The devotees were chanting and I was wearing my sari and Aaron was wearing his yoga pants and it was just wonderful. The whole morning was so wonderful.

Devi's involvement with the movement intensified later that summer when she visited ISKCON's New Vrindaban community, in West Virginia, to celebrate Krishna's birthday. She had decided to go because several of her women friends at the Baltimore temple were to receive initiation into Krishna Consciousness as disciples of Srila Prabhupada. Since Aaron was unable to attend, she traveled to New Vrindaban with the devotees from the Baltimore temple.

> I went to see their initiation. It was going to be a really big thing and I didn't want to miss it. I remember we had to sleep in a barn and it was so different from anything I had been used to; it smelled like a barn and there were children running all over the place. I remember thinking how could anyone get any sleep in this situation. I was so excited, I couldn't sleep anyway. I couldn't eat any of the food either because I had been eating nothing but raw food all summer. . . . That was the first time I ever chanted a full sixteen rounds and it was very heavy for me. After finishing chanting I was so high. I couldn't believe it. It wasn't like

any drug high. It was all such a new experience for me. When you chant Hare Krishna you become purified. Your awareness is acutely intensified. Your awareness of everything: your spiritual awareness, your physical awareness, your awareness of everything around you. It was almost more than my senses could take.

The remainder of Devi's stay at New Vrindaban was no less memorable.

Here I was in the hills of West Virginia chanting Hare Krishna dressed in a sari. I helped decorate the temple for the initiation and it was so beautiful. I had never seen anything like this. The whole thing was just heaven and I remember before the actual fire sacrifice [initiation ceremony] I danced [to the kirtan music] so much I couldn't stop. I was eighteen and full of life. I danced so much that I was feeling a spiritual high, a high that I had never experienced before.

These religious experiences were much more profound than anything Devi had ever felt from practicing other forms of yoga.

When I practiced *agnihotra* yoga I would sit there and meditate, do the breathing exercises, waiting for something to happen, but nothing really ever did.

In addition to her religious experiences, Devi also became very attracted to many of the devotees she met and talked with during her stay at New Vrindaban. They were helping her understand Krishna Consciousness and she felt a sense of belonging.

It was all very attractive to me. The devotees were preaching to me and I was really understanding what they were saying. . . . I believed in them right away because I could see that they were truthful people and knew what they were talking about. It all made sense to me. Krishna Consciousness somehow just seemed like a natural, logical, spiritual progression for me. I had been reading all the books and I could understand that I wasn't my body, reincarnation, birth, death, chanting the Lord's name. I knew God was a person, he wasn't just a light (like in some other forms of yoga). I wanted a loving relationship with God, whoever he was. Ever since I was a little girl, I wanted to find God. Now here he was.

After the festivities at New Vrindaban, Devi returned to Ocean City to help Aaron close the business for the winter. She excitedly told Aaron about her experiences and it was then that they both decided to join ISKCON and become Krishna devotees.

We had made a conscious decision to move into the temple. It was just the right thing to do and we both realized it. . . . I remember the first day of school. My girlfriend knocked on the door and said 'It's time to go' [to school] and I said, 'I'm not going; we're moving into the Hare Krishna temple.'

On September 7, 1977, Devi and Aaron moved into the ISKCON community in Baltimore. For Devi the decision to join was not a difficult one.

Joining was a real natural sequence for me. It wasn't a situation where we sat down and were thinking should we do this or not. What about our lives? What are we giving up? It wasn't like that. It was a real easy decision based on a natural progression that we both understood. We liked the devotees. We agreed with the philosophy. There was nothing we disagreed with in the whole philosophy— nothing. It made perfect sense to us. We were ripe. We were ready. We were on a path and the next attainable level spiritually was before us. So we just moved in. . . . I had no personal crisis. I had plenty to do, I had a lot going for me. I was no misfit. I was very much what a lot of people wanted to be at the time I joined.

Even though they had become ISKCON devotees, Devi and Aaron had decided not to tell their parents immediately of their decision. Only after several weeks did they finally break the news. Aaron's mother, although she was somewhat shocked at first, became more accepting when Aaron and Devi explained what the movement was about. Devi's parents, however, were another matter altogether. Devi called her mother and then went to visit her to break the news of their change in lifestyle. Devi explains what happened:

I went over to my parent's house with this [devotee] girl. I should have gone with Aaron I suppose. I really shouldn't have gone with this devotee girl. We went over in the afternoon, since I knew my father wouldn't be home on a Friday afternoon. I walked in wearing my sari and said 'Hi.' Mother hugged me then said, 'What do you have on?' I said, 'Mom, its a sari. I joined the Hare Krishna movement and it's really far out. Wait until you hear all about it.' And she just freaked out immediately. What it was, was actually a communication gap created by my garb. Just because of my dress, she couldn't relate to me anymore. She didn't know what to say. She just freaked out, went off the deep end. She acted like an insane person, no logic, no sanity at all. Her reaction was so extreme . . . like total anger. . . . First she yelled at the [devotee] girl, 'What have you done to my daughter?' I tried to tell her that she hadn't done anything. But my mother was totally against us. It just blew her away. She ran next door and told the neighbors. I went after her and told her to come and talk with me. . . . That night I went back to the temple really shaken.

Upon returning to the temple, she sought out the temple president for his advice. He persuaded Devi to call her parents. Devi thought that perhaps her father would be more understanding and reasonable.

He is very well read in everything. I knew already that he believed in reincarnation. I just thought, well my father will understand this. He'll be proud and I thought he would think it was neat.

As it turned out, her father's reaction was not unlike her mother's.

I said, 'Daddy. I guess Mom told you I joined the Hare Krishnas.' He said, 'Yes. She told me.' I couldn't tell from his voice where he was at, but the more we talked, the more apparent it was that he was really just mad. He, in the end, couldn't control himself he was so mad. . . . He had traveled all over the world, in and out of airports, and he had seen a lot of Krishna devotees. He had been approached by them, so his image was really shaped by that. He said, 'So you think you're going to save the world by standing on the street corner and passing out magazines?' I actually didn't even know he knew that they did that. So he took it in a very bad way. He was very emotional. He said, 'You are causing us to get a divorce. How can you do this to us?' I kept trying to tell him that I had just chosen a new way of life. I asked him over and over, 'Aren't you interested? Why don't you want to know what this is about?' But neither one of them wanted to hear what it was about, and that just crushed my image of what parents were about. I mean why didn't they respect what I thought? . . . After awhile I was over it and it made no big difference to me. I would call and say, 'Well you know where I am. You know what I am doing. If you want to find out more about what I am doing, please come and see.' They never came. I gave them books, but they would just throw them away. So I just decided to let them be. I didn't want to have anymore contact, if they didn't want to be fair. I wasn't going to let their feelings hamper my spiritual development.

Even Aaron's mother called Devi's parents in an effort to help them understand their daughter's involvement with the movement. This attempt at persuasion didn't help, and Devi's parents remained firmly against Devi's decision to become an ISKCON devotee. In the months ahead, however, as it became more and more clear that Devi was going to stay in the movement, her parents began to be at least more tolerant toward her involvement in the movement.

They were not happy, but they finally decided they weren't going to change me. If that's what I was going to do, OK. They couldn't help but think how I had so much potential and capability to make a success in the material world. They just couldn't understand why I was willing to throw it all away.

While Devi's parents were upset and confused, so too were her brother and sister. Being the oldest, Devi was looked up to and admired by her siblings. She had always been an important role model to them. Her decision to join the movement, however, left them both in a state of confusion.

My brother thought I had deserted him. Here I had set the example of how to make a big material life. And then suddenly I just cut it all off. My sister was also upset. They both looked up to me, since I was the eldest. When I became a devotee, they didn't know what to make of it. They felt like, 'My sister has left material life to become a devotee. What does this mean? What do we think now? What do we do now?'

Despite the reactions of her family, Devi remained committed to her spiritual quest. She was convinced that Krishna Consciousness was a true spiritual path, which would lead her to spiritual realization. In the months ahead, she continued to work towards that goal even though she was only a neophyte devotee.

When Devi and Aaron joined the Baltimore temple, they moved into separate residences: she in the women's ashram and he in an ashram with other men. Because the movement's philosophy stressed a separation between men and women, Devi visited Aaron only infrequently. After being in the movement less than two months, it dawned on her one day that she had not seen Aaron over a period of several days. After making several inquiries, someone told Devi that Aaron had recently taken to going to his mother's house. Devi called Aaron at his mother's. She asked when he was coming back to the temple and why he had been leaving the community. Aaron explained that he was unhappy in the movement and that he was uncertain whether he was coming back to the temple at all. He was seriously considering leaving the movement altogether. In the weeks following that call, Aaron visited the temple now and then, but finally, just before Christmas of 1977, he quit the movement completely. Devi explained his reasons for leaving and her reaction to them this way:

I think he left because he felt I was Krishna's devotee. There was that restriction on our association. He didn't want us to be separated. Our relationship had really gone in different ways since joining the movement. Plus at that time in Baltimore it wasn't so easy for a man. There were a lot of women living at the temple at that time and there were very few men. The women were gone a lot on *sankirtana*. . . . Aaron was helping the temple treasurer, but it was plain to everyone that the temple president really liked me. I was the new girl who was doing really well in spiritual life. The devotees liked me and I was making a real good adjustment. I was getting a lot of attention and instruction in spiritual life, a lot more than Aaron was. That, coupled with the fact that he was getting a whole lot less of my attention, made it really difficult for him. He was really hurt by the situation. He was definitely hurt, so he left because of that. . . . I was upset that he left, but I was so into what I was doing that it didn't really make that much difference to me. I was going on to do my service. I knew I wanted to be a devotee, whether he was there or not.

As Devi suggests, she was now committed to the extent that her relationship with Aaron had become secondary to pursuing Krishna Consciousness. She had readily adjusted to the devotee's lifestyle and was committed to her spiritual goals and to the possibility that they would be realized as a Krishna devotee:

> By this time I was already doing full-time *sankirtana* [literature distribution]. I was getting up for the morning [worship] program, chanting my rounds, eating breakfast, and then going out to distribute books. . . . That was my whole life. But I was developing spiritually very quickly. In the temple I had responsibilities for specific duties, so my [devotional] service was going well. I learned all of the [Sanskrit] songs really quickly. I had nice relationships with the other devotees and everything was going really well for me.

Devi worked hard in spiritual life, looking forward to the day when she would take initiation from Srila Prabhupada. She worshipped Prabhupada as the spiritual master every day and felt that she was already gaining a close relationship to him.

Even as Devi was entering the movement, Prabhupada's health was failing. Finally, after Devi had been in the movement for little more than two months, news came that Prabhupada had passed away in Vrndavana, India, on November 14, 1977. Like the other devotees, Devi was stunned and heartbroken. Devi recalls the day of Prabhupada's passing and her feelings:

> All the devotees knew that Prabhupada was sick. We'd been praying for him regularly. Special prayers were being sung and kirtans [singing and dancing] were always going on for Prabhupada's health. While we knew of his condition there was still talk that he was going to come to America one last time. I was thinking I'm going to get to see him; take initiation from Prabhupada. . . . Then I came home from *sankirtana* one day and there was this guy and he came running out saying 'Did you hear? Did you hear? Srila Prabhupada has left his body.' I had never experienced anything like this before at all. My heart just went to my stomach. It was such a weird thing. I was numb; I couldn't believe it. I didn't even know Prabhupada. I was so upset I was crying. It was a very traumatic experience because here I had joined his movement and Prabhupada was going to be my spiritual master. I had already cultivated a little attachment from worshipping him every day. So when it happened, I thought, 'Oh no, oh no.' I was crying and it was like being in a dream. I walked into the temple and I was watching. I was watching myself walk inside the temple and all the devotees were there. It was like there was a film in front of me and everything had a yellow cast. All the devotees were crying and everybody's eyes were red and everyone was taking the pictures off the walls. We stayed up all night dusting and cleaning the temple. We were all thinking, 'What is going to happen now? What are we going to do without Prabhupada?' It was just so heavy and everybody was crying.

Though she experienced tremendous grief and disappointment over Prabhupada's death, this event did not shatter Devi's growing commitment to Krishna Consciousness. Even though the months ahead were uncertain for the movement, she continued her devotional efforts, and she was now looking forward to the day when she would take initiation from one of the newly appointed gurus. Within months after Prabhupada's death, Devi had decided who would be her spiritual master. She describes her first encounters with the man who would later become her guru:

> The devotees from Baltimore went to Washington, D.C. to see North East Guru. He gave us class and it was then that I came to see him as the true spiritual master. . . . In February [1978], or thereabouts, he came to the Baltimore temple and I asked him a question during class. He liked my question and I knew then in my mind that this person was going to be my spiritual master. I had a lot of faith in the movement. I believed in it and my faith was strong. I believed in the authorities when they said that the movement would go on. And North East Guru was going to be my spiritual master.

Devi continued to work hard, looking forward to the day when she would become North East Guru's disciple. But on Memorial Day of 1978, after she had been in the movement for nine months, Devi's spiritual advancement came to a sudden halt. On this day she had traveled to Ocean City with a number of other women from the temple to distribute literature on Krishna Consciousness:

> We went to Ocean City on *sankirtana*. It was summer and Aaron was there. He had gone back to do the business again. So the situation was kind of like a test for me. When we arrived we all went to see him, to get free juice and stuff. I sat down and talked with him.

After talking with Aaron, Devi found herself making plans to leave the movement, at least for a while. She felt overworked, but her decision to leave the movement was more spontaneous than planned. It was only at that moment, as she sat in Ocean City with Aaron, that the thought of leaving the movement occurred to her.

> It was really whimsical. I wasn't even meditating about leaving. I hadn't even thought about it until that weekend in Ocean City. It wasn't like I wanted to leave. I wasn't feeling dissatisfied with the movement or anything like that. I wasn't being mistreated, or feeling separation from Aaron, nothing like that. It was more like, here I am with all my old friends and I thought, 'Oh this is far out, I don't think I'm going back today.' So I asked Aaron if I could stay with him for a little while. He said, 'Sure you can stay at my house for a while.' But

he asked, 'Are you sure this is what you want to do? You really want to leave?' I just talked myself into it, I guess. It was really weird. I knew it was wrong, but when you get in *maya* [materially minded and contaminated] you just shut out your intelligence. I knew what was right and what was wrong. Just like a little child does something when his mother tells him not to. He knows not to do it, but he does it anyway. So I was like that. . . . But I was at the same time scared to death. I knew that I was going out from the protection of Krishna. If I do this [discontinue practicing Krishna Consciousness] and a car hits me, and I die, I'm in trouble. Whereas if I'm in the movement and I go out and a car hits me and I die, I'm saved.

Devi went back to the devotees' van to pick up her belongings. She then went with Aaron to his apartment on the bay. Aaron was smoking marijuana again and Devi somewhat hesitantly decided to try some. She explains what happened:

It was so heavy it flipped me out. I was tripping from one puff. My body was so clean that I took just one hit and my body was flipping out. I was actually hallucinating. . . . So I was sitting there looking out at the bay and I was praying to Krishna. I was saying, 'Krishna, Krishna just let me come down.' I was so scared—'just let me come down.' I was thinking the police were going to catch me and throw me in the crazy house. I was scared. I was so scared.

But being at Aaron's house meant more than just being around marijuana again. It also involved being around all the temptations of the outside world that she had left behind when she joined the movement. Here she was staying in an apartment with men for the first time in many months.

I had not had any association with men for nine months. I was living a completely celibate life and you actually become shy and chaste. It's like the process reverses itself. You actually develop these qualities after a while. So that night I wouldn't stay inside the house. I didn't want to stay where men were staying. So I slept outside on the porch. The whole time I was so scared to death, because I knew I wasn't under the protection of Krishna. I slept that night with the *Bhagavad Gita* over my head. I was thinking, you are contradicting yourself. You're living outside the movement, thinking you can somehow maintain a devotee way of life. But you can't have both. But I was thinking I could have it all I guess. Here I was, I couldn't sleep and I had this *Bhagavad Gita* over my head and I was feeling horrible.

The next morning her adjustment problems continued.

I didn't want to take a shower in the same bath where the men had been taking theirs. I told Aaron, 'Men have been in this bathroom. I don't want to use this bathroom because I have been living such a pure existence.' Of course I later forced myself because I stayed at the ocean for two weeks.

Even though she was staying with Aaron, it was clear to Devi that their relationship had changed from the early days of their romantic involvement.

Nothing happened between us while I stayed at the beach. We were just friends. I didn't have any rights to this person anymore, because here I had been living a spiritual life and he had been living a *karmic* life. We didn't have anything in common anymore.

Even though she was now out of the movement, Devi continued to have ambivalent feelings about her decision to re-enter the outside world. She constantly thought about her commitment to Krishna Consciousness, not least of all when her parents found out that she had left the movement.

Then I called my mother to tell her that I was living outside the temple. She was so happy, to the point that it made me so mad. I finally just hung up on her. She was so happy that she started crying and I said, 'Mother if you don't stop crying right now I'm going to hang up the phone' because I knew in my heart that I was a devotee. . . . My sister later told me that my parents went out and got a bottle of champagne that night to celebrate. I couldn't believe that. I couldn't believe that they would be celebrating my leaving the spiritual life to come to a life of meat-eaters, intoxication, and illicit sex. They were celebrating these things; I couldn't believe that.

Despite Devi's feelings about her parents' reaction, she moved back to Baltimore and spent the next several months living with them.

I went back to my parents' house and I thought that I would get a job and work; just check out material life for a while. I was a young girl and I wasn't ready to make that lifelong commitment to Krishna Consciousness. . . . I knew that I was a devotee though. I knew that I was going back one day. I was going back and I always knew that. I just wanted to give the material life one more last good try.

During that first summer, Devi divided her time between her parent's house and Ocean City. Her parents supported her financially through the summer months until she finally started working in the fall in a shoe store. Even though she spent time with her parents, she couldn't help feeling distant from them emotionally.

I was mostly only there to sleep. I ate at health food stores or cooked my own food. I didn't eat dinner with them because I was still a strict vegetarian. . . . I cared about my mother and father and I was very kind to them, but I didn't have a deep attachment. . . . I didn't do any activities with my parents. I mean we had a pool in our back yard and I would go swimming and they would go swimming, but that would be about as far as it would go.

During the whole time of her stay with her parents, Devi constantly thought about returning to ISKCON. She often expressed this desire to her parents.

They knew after a while that I might go back [to the movement]. I told them, 'Don't get attached to me being here, because I'm going to be moving back to the temple.' . . . I had my saris and I had my [Krishna] books on my bookshelf. I didn't hide them and they knew that one day I'd go back.

In the fall of 1978, however, Devi became involved in a relationship, which made it extremely difficult for her to decide between Krishna Consciousness and the lifestyle she had been living since she had left ISKCON. After Aaron had asked her to marry him—an offer she refused—he introduced her to a man with whom Devi would soon become deeply involved and who was to become a major influence in her life in the years to come.

Aaron introduced me to this person and he was the one who really got me entangled into the material life. I fell completely in *maya* [entangled in material life] over this person. Ben was very successful, a very successful musician and very handsome.

In a short time, Devi and Ben fell in love. Even though Devi was firmly committed to her relationship with Ben, she continued to believe that some day she would return to the Krishna movement. Her hope at this point, however, was that Ben would join her in her spiritual life and that the two of them would become ISKCON devotees together. In the months to come, she tried over and over again to interest Ben in Krishna Consciousness.

I wanted Ben to become a devotee. I wanted him to visit the temple and I told him all about Krishna Consciousness the very first time we met. . . . I took him to the temple and we would sometimes go to the Sunday feast. He loved *prasadam* [spiritual vegetarian foodstuffs]. But he didn't want to shave his head and move into the temple. He was very attractive and very vain. He didn't want to shave his hair . . . that would be a final surrender and he wasn't ready for that.

Under Devi's influence, Ben did become a vegetarian, and the two of them also avoided marijuana and other intoxicants. As it turned out, however, this was as far as Ben was willing to go. Despite Devi's preaching, Ben refused to consider participating in ISKCON as a real possibility. He was far more interested in continuing his already successful musical career.

Meanwhile, Devi continued to maintain her friendships with the devotees at the Baltimore temple. She frequently visited the temple to talk with them and to take part in the Sunday feast and other religious activities. The new temple president, in particular, played an important role in Devi's life during this period.

> Prabhu used to preach to me whenever I visited the temple. He is a very potent preacher. . . . So one day I went to the temple and he was preaching to me. I realized that everything he was saying to me was true and I couldn't turn him down. I couldn't defeat him philosophically. He just stood there and said finally, 'When are you going to move in?' And because I was a devotee in my heart, I couldn't fight him. I didn't know what to say.

At about this time, Ben was getting ready to leave for Los Angeles where he and his brother were going to produce their first record album. While they were gone, Devi decided to move back to the ISKCON community in Baltimore. This was in May of 1979, a year after Devi had left the movement in Ocean City. Devi was torn between her love for Ben and her belief in Krishna Consciousness. She had chosen once again to commit herself to a spiritual path, despite the grief she was feeling at the loss of Ben.

> I knew I couldn't go on in the material world any more. I was unhappy and I had insomnia. Every night I kept thinking, 'Oh Krishna, Krishna, what if I get hit by a car tomorrow and I'm not a devotee?' I was aware that death could come at any moment and even though I was enjoying the material life I still believed in Krishna. I still knew that North East Guru was my spiritual master.

While determined once again to become an ISKCON devotee, Devi's commitment to the movement was no more than provisional this time around, since Ben continued to be an emotional force in her life.

> Every single day the temple president would preach to me. I would cry because I was so attached to Ben. I just kept saying, 'I can't give up this attachment.' And he would preach and preach every single day to me. His preaching was the only thing that kept me there. . . . I knew he was telling the truth, but my heart and emotions were all tied up with Ben and our relationship.

As the days went by, Devi began to feel more at ease being back in the devotee community and she was feeling less sorrow about Ben and their failed relationship. After several weeks, she was back into her spiritual routine again and was beginning to return to her old devotee self. Then Ben returned from his trip to Los Angeles. His return proved to be a major test of Devi's commitment to the movement.

> I told Prabhu, the temple president, that I wanted to visit my mother for Mother's Day. But really I wanted to go because I knew that Ben was coming home. The temple president knew me very well and told me that if I went I wouldn't come back. But I promised, 'I'll come back.' And he said, 'If you don't come back I'll be upset.'

Devi describes what happened when she saw Ben:

> It was very traumatic for both of us . . . We were both crying. I kept saying that we could live here [ISKCON community] and do so much in the movement. He could still have his music. But he said, 'No, I just can't do it.'

As it turned out, Devi did not return to the temple that night. She had decided to remain with Ben and give up her membership in ISKCON. Once again she felt the pain of being caught between two worlds. She was in love and was committed to her relationship with Ben, but even so, she wanted to maintain her ties to ISKCON and Krishna Consciousness.

> So we went through the whole thing again, for another two years. And of course, I couldn't stay away from the devotees. Even as embarrassed as I was, I would go back to the temple for the Sunday feast and see the devotees.

At the same time, Devi lived with Ben and thought about the day when they would marry. She got a job and the two of them resumed their previous lifestyle together. Unlike the last time, however, Ben now refused to attend the Sunday feast with her at the temple. Although Ben continued to resist Krishna Consciousness, Devi continued to hope and to lay plans for the day when he too would join the movement as her husband.

> I knew that if I married him and had his child, that he too would come to the movement. That was my whole goal. I'll have his child and he'll be attached. That's how he is, and he'll come if we only have a child. But he knew what I was thinking and he wouldn't marry me. He knew I wanted to move into the temple again. He knew that I was just waiting for Krishna to work with him.

For the next two years, Devi and Ben struggled to work out their relationship. Always the issue that divided them was Devi's desire to return to the movement. As Devi reflected:

Krishna came in between us always. Always I knew that I was a devotee and he knew that I was a devotee too.

In January of 1980, Devi traveled with Ben to Las Vegas and Los Angeles where he was performing. While in Los Angeles, she persuaded Ben to visit the ISKCON temple. The movement's recording studio was located in Los Angeles, and she thought his interest in ISKCON might be aroused if he saw the possibilities for music making that existed within the movement. She tried to explain to Ben that his musical life could continue as a devotee. He could work for Krishna through his musical abilities.

> But he wouldn't do it. He wouldn't join. He would say, 'I believe in the spiritual life and I believe that God should be the center of my life, but I don't want to give up everything.' . . . He was attracted to the idea that he was the source of his musical ability. I mean he was a musical genius. In the end, he had a stronger attachment to his music than he did to me.

Upon returning from Los Angeles with Ben, Devi again sought out her friends at the Baltimore temple. Ben was going to leave for Japan in the days ahead and, as before, she sought out the support of the devotees. On one of these visits to the temple her long-time friend, Radha, who had also joined ISKCON in 1977, gave her a tape recording of a conversation that had taken place between Devi, several other devotees, the temple president, and North East Guru. The conversation had taken place during her last abbreviated return to the movement some two years ago. The tape reminded her of North East Guru's words that morning.

> He said, 'What's the matter? Why can't you give up these material attachments?' He was preaching to me about Krishna Consciousness. Later the tape was entitled, 'Yes to Krishna, No to Maya,' and the whole tape was about me!

Radha also gave Devi a picture that had been taken that morning as she walked alongside North East Guru. Devi took both the tape and picture that day when she left the temple.

During this period, Devi was working for Ben's brother, who had recently opened a hair shop. She was working at the shop cutting hair. She began taking the tape of her conversation with North East Guru to the shop every day and she would listen to it while she worked. With Ben in Japan, and with the words of North East Guru in her mind, she began to feel more and more pulled toward returning to the movement.

> I was ripe now. I was again really ripe. I started listening to the tape and I thought, wow, that's what he means, yea. I knew it was just a matter of time, so

I decided to give myself a permanent. . . . I knew I was going back. I was finally going to graduate and leave all these things I was attracted to behind. I told myself then, 'You're going to start chanting and you're going to cooperate with Krishna Consciousness.'

Before Ben returned from Japan, Devi had already made up her mind to return to the movement. To her surprise, however, she then learned that the authorities at the Baltimore temple were in India and that when they returned to the States, they would be transferring to Philadelphia to help manage the ISKCON community there. At first she thought this would disrupt her planned return to the movement. However, the temple president, Prabhu, asked her to join them when they moved to Philadelphia. Devi was relieved for more than one reason.

I needed to get away from Baltimore. I needed to get away from Ben. I felt like if I didn't get away, I'd never make it away from him and back to Krishna.

When Ben returned from his trip, Devi informed him of her decision to rejoin the movement. While the decision was certainly painful, they both had realized this had been coming for some time. Devi's commitment to Krishna had finally won out.

It was strange because, as I was preparing to go back, Ben and I tried not to get emotional about it. I said, 'O.K. here are a few things I need. Can you buy them for me?' He took me out and bought me a tape recorder, socks, tee-shirts, a sleeping bag, all the things I would need. I was real organized and thoughtful about what I needed. He helped me put my suitcase in the car. By then the situation was real heavy as I left.

While he was sad to see Devi go, Ben did not try to dissuade her from joining the movement again. He understood by this time that Devi was seriously committed to Krishna Consciousness, even if he wasn't. Nor did her parents react negatively toward her decision. By this time, all those people who were close to her had come to realize that Devi's faith in Krishna and her commitment to the movement were real and were the most important forces in her life.

With my parents, through all these years in and out, they had come to accept that they couldn't do anything to get me out of Krishna Consciousness. They understood that mentally I was going to be into Krishna Consciousness forever. So when I decided to move back in, they just said 'O.K. if that's what you want, we won't stand in your way.'

So on April 5, 1981, after two years away from the movement, Devi once again turned her back on the material world to resume her spiritual journey. With little difficulty, Devi resumed her life as a devotee. Within a month after her return, she had reestablished her bond with North East Guru and was once again looking forward to her initiation as his disciple.

> I developed a really close and wonderful relationship with North East Guru and he wrote me letters. I wrote him letters about various things and I was asking him, 'How can you guide me back to God?'

Even though she was back in the movement, Devi was not able simply to put Ben out of her life altogether. She often called Ben in those first days, encouraging him to visit her in Philadelphia. North East Guru, however, advised Devi no longer to see Ben because he could only interfere with her spiritual advancement. Reluctantly, but determinedly, she agreed no longer to see or to talk with Ben.

Not long after rejoining the movement in Philadelphia, Devi was asked to return to the Baltimore temple to act as temple secretary. Although she avoided seeking out Ben, she felt sure that just being in Baltimore again would mean that their paths would naturally cross, especially since Ben continued to visit and be friendly with her parents.

> It was Krishna's arrangement that I move to Baltimore at that point. I went to all the same places where Ben and I used to drive around as part of my work. But I never saw him. I kept waiting for the day I was going to run into him. But I guess it was Krishna's plan that I never ran into Ben. It was a confrontation that in many ways I dreaded.

Only weeks after moving to the Baltimore temple, Devi was made the temple treasurer. While she lacked formal training in accounting, she nevertheless learned quickly. Because of her treasury work, she became involved with a number of the leading devotees in the movement, including North East Guru, with whom she began to communicate regularly regarding matters related to her work as well as her own spiritual progress. Because of this growing relationship with her guru and her growing dedication to the spiritual life, she became less and less concerned about Ben.

> Because I was serving the spiritual master through my service [work] and because I was putting my whole heart and mind into Krishna, my attachments outside the movement began to wane. I was chanting sincerely and doing a lot of service. Plus I had the association of the devotees who were preaching to me all the time. My friend Radha and I were very very close and she was such a big help. She was my crutch for a while and I leaned on her as a friend.

Devi's growing skills as temple treasurer led to her being sent to the Washington, D.C. temple to help establish a movement business. While she was there, however, the Baltimore temple received word that they were to be audited by the Internal Revenue Service. Devi quickly returned to Baltimore and took over the responsibility for handling the audit.

> I had this whole audit thing on my shoulders and it was up to me. Everyone was looking to me, this woman, to make this audit come out right. Everything was very heavy, very tense, and I was definitely praying. But the audit went well.

Because of her success with the IRS audit, Devi was sent back to Philadelphia to serve as temple treasurer for the ISKCON community there. She became informally involved in learning business and corporate law in an effort to help the movement gain effective management strategies and overall financial planning for the future.

In February of 1982, Devi took her first initiation from North East Guru. She had finally made the step she had been seeking in spiritual life for nearly five years, ever since the day she had met the devotees on the boardwalk in Ocean City. Finally, after leaving ISKCON twice, she had become initiated into Krishna Consciousness as a disciple of North East Guru. In December of that year, Devi took her second initiation. She described her feelings about being initiated this way:

> Taking initiation from a bonafide spiritual master is the perfection of spiritual life. By accepting instruction from a self-realized soul and serving him, all the imports and meanings of the Vedic scriptures are revealed. So this was a wonderful occasion to formally accept a spiritual master. 'You are my teacher and I'm your student. Please guide me on this path back to the spiritual world.' It is very rare to find a living example of one who has actually understood that serving God—Krishna—is the highest goal and has practically attained that steady platform of performing wonderful devotional service without any tinge of personal motivation.

Even though she was now a committed and valued member of the movement, Devi continued in her struggle to maintain a spiritually pure life. From time to time, she still thought of Ben, continuing to believe that the day would come when he would join her in the movement as a Krishna devotee:

> Time has made a lot of difference, of course. I still wish that Ben had become a devotee and I still have hope that he will in the future. I have faith that he will become a devotee because he ate so much *prasadam* [spiritual food], worshiped the deities, sang the *kirtans,* and took to chanting. So in my mind there is no doubt, he is going to come to Krishna Consciousness one day. . . . I told Ben just

before I left him, 'You must promise me that every time you see a devotee in an airport that you will give ... [him or her] a dollar.' And he promised that he would, so he will continue to gain some advancement in Krishna Consciousness.

As she looks to the future, Devi sees her life as continuing in Krishna Consciousness. She plans to do whatever she can to help advance the movement's message. Her immediate plans include going back to school to become a Certified Public Accountant or perhaps a corporate lawyer. By becoming a professional, she not only hopes to provide the movement with needed skills, but she also plans to use this training as a way to preach Krishna Consciousness:

> I think it is such an important step for the movement to begin preaching to the professional people in America. It is really needed by our movement, since these are the people who have the money and power in society. They are controlling the government and the laws. We need to reach these people and I hope that we can.

While it is not in her immediate plans, Devi also looks forward to the day when she will be married and raise a Krishna-conscious family.

> I'm pretty sure that I'll get married. I'm still a young girl and my guru has told me that I will get married. I'm not real anxious right now. When you are married, it isn't so easy to do a lot of service. I'm doing a lot of service right now and I feel if I was married I wouldn't be able to do as much as I want. I really want to dedicate myself to my service for the movement, for North East Guru, right now.[2]

In terms of her spiritual future in Krishna Consciousness, Devi explains:

> I want to learn to perfect the chanting of the Hare Krishna mantra. That's a main goal. I want to learn to chant Hare Krishna and actually become pure. I've been making spiritual advancement, so I want to make more progress. I want to actually realize that Krishna is God and that everyone won't be happy until they are situated back into the practice of serving God, serving Krishna.

NOTES

1. This life history of Devi is based on a six-hour taped interview conducted in Philadelphia in April 1983. Devi read and made corrections in the initial draft of the chapter in the spring of 1984. All quoted materials in this chapter come from this interview with Devi.

2. Devi married in the fall of 1983; she and her devotee husband moved to Washington, D.C., to assist in running the ISKCON community there.

PART THREE

Knowing through the Will

KNOWING THROUGH THE WILL: THE PATH OF
PROPHECY AND SOCIAL ACTION

Prophets are hardly majority figures in any culture. Even in the United States, and the British North Atlantic colonies from which this country grew—where there was a historical and rhetorical tradition honoring rebels and revolutionaries—in actual practice, prophets were few and far between. This is because, by definition, prophets are people who stand at the boundaries of a given social community, calling into question received ways of operating and directing hearers to a harder, sterner message that, prophets say, is a return to cultural and religious roots. To speak of a prophet in this sense is, of course, to brush to one side the meaning of prophecy that connects it primarily and intrinsically with prediction and futuristic speech. It is much more to hark back to traditional Western understandings of prophecy arising from the literature of the Jewish and Christian Bible, in which prophetic figures emerged as God's messengers to a wayward people, calling them back to the inherited religion of Israel.

The etymological derivation of the word prophet is a clue to the vocation of inspired proclamation to which the term points. Prophet comes from the Greek *prophetes*, meaning variously "one who speaks forth," "one who proclaims," "one who speaks before," and only then "one who speaks for the future." And even here, speaking for the future is to be understood in the context of a strongly visionary sense of history that sees the future in concert with a sacred past and, especially, a deviant present—a future in which the misguided energies of the present unravel and the trajectory of decline prevails. Hence, the prophet speaks out of a sense of connection with an authentic past and a fierce concern for the downwardly spiraling motion of the present. The sociologist Max Weber, who probably more than any other twentieth-century figure has shaped scholarly conceptions of prophecy, saw the prophet as a charismatic individual who felt a sense of personal call to proclaim as divine command a particular religious teaching. In the West, especially, the divine commands that the prophet felt impelled to share were not free messages that one could take or leave. Rather, they demanded obedience from hearers, an obedience that meant changed behavior, altered lifeways predicated on a transformation of heart and mind. So the prophet was, above all, an "ethical" prophet, one whose words carried moral weight and authority—and the sting of divine rebuke for their rejection.

Such an absolute stance on the part of an individual seems to fly in the face of the compromises, meanderings, and moral relativisms of any people's history. The American story has borne the general description out in abundant ways, and it has also disclosed in the prophetic sense of righteousness and privileged access to truth something that other, nonprophetic listeners have at times read as arrogance and fanaticism. The John Browns of American religious history have earned at best mixed reports. And the white supremacists in the tapestry have surely been roundly and rightly condemned. But this is to get ahead of the story. The minority report from American prophets needs to be seen, first, in its own terms, with each prophet's sure sense of connection to an authentic spiritual center and the empowerment that comes from it.

In fact, that sense of empowerment demands closer scrutiny. For the felt experience of divine connection *by itself* is not what empowers. Instead, in this form of spirituality the connection needs to be acted out through a committed sequence of words and deeds. The prophetic brand of spirituality is, in one sense, totalistic. There is within it the mysticism that can also be found in much of metaphysical spirituality, the passional, strongly emotional sense of attachment to a divine source who speaks, and the body behaviors that act out the message in the world, sometimes to the point of sacrificing life itself to advance the message. In the Vietnam War, for example, some antiwar protesters set fire to the American flag, and some set fire to themselves. But unlike the soldiers who gave their lives in this war, as in other of the nation's wars, prophetic protesters engaging in acts of self-immolation sacrificed themselves from the edge—from the boundary of the social structure in acts of radical moral criticism rather than from the center with its affirmation of the conventional order and establishment. Prophetic protesters had heard other voices that called into question the nation's moral choices; their response to the voices literally consumed them.

The traditional faculty psychology of the West identifies the human power or ability that can generate such all-encompassing spirituality with the will. If the intellect represents the power of vision, and the heart the power of feeling, the will here becomes the power of executing and doing—but a power predicated on prior knowledge and passional commitment. Executing is not an automatic activity or a disconnected series of motions; it is a mental act, a choice with "fiber" and with social consequences. Prophetic spirituality can never remain hidden, nor can it flourish without a continuing and impelling sense of alienation that leads, often enough, to some form of punitive action against the prophet. Thus, in the last third of the twentieth century, American prophets of both the left and the right have felt the sting of social rebuke. Antiwar protesters like Roman Catholic priests Daniel and Philip Berrigan, on the left, went to jail for their plans and deeds to protest the Vietnam War and the use of nuclear weaponry. Meanwhile, on the right, other Americans who were protesting abortion, some of them clearly also Catholic, incurred legal consequences when they engaged in forms of personal harassment and even in assaults on people and property.

How do individuals come to so unquestioned a sense of absolute right and privileged status as messengers of God or a sacred world that they turn radically against the morality of the center? How do they become willing to flaunt social convention and esteem by their words and, even more, to defy fundamental injunctions of respect and reverence for life and property that govern social organization in any group? Is the religious change that transforms a person into a prophet a slow or sudden phenomenon? Set beside the routine gradualism that usually marks the path of ritual and, by contrast, the lightning-like transformation that frequently accompanies the spirituality of the heart, the shaping of a prophet is more mixed and various. Some prophets seem to emerge out of evangelical spirituality; their particular conversion experience makes the mission clause primary, and they feel impelled to witness to the divine command they are convinced they have heard. Other prophets, however, have grown into their roles through a gradual transformation of thought and life patterns over an extended period of time. Theirs has been a process of re-education that has convinced them that the received wisdom of the present is false and supremely faulty and that the inner light is directing them to throw themselves into the task of societal warning and transformation.

Whether suddenly or gradually convinced that they should assume the mantle of prophecy, however, American prophets tend to share the worldview of causality. For them, God may have created the world, but, if so, the divine light continues to shine in it only imperfectly. Indeed, in their view some things are terribly wrong with the world, and so it cannot be the unimpeded manifestation of the divine. Rather, the prophetic world is one in which evil is rampant; its ravages are seemingly everywhere, and—in the midst of a bleak landscape of death and destruction—for many American prophets grace is a miraculous gift. It is a world in which the natural requires something more to make it theologically intelligible, in which the structure of reality must include a second tier to make the first-level life of the present meaningful and, so, endurable.

Standing in this prophetic universe, the individual bearer of charisma—the prophet—leads a life committed to criticism in an attempt to bring the reform of society. The path can be lonely, but it can also yield its social rewards. Prophets, with their magnetic gift of charisma, typically attract followers and may function as part of a committed group, either at the center receiving the admiration of disciples or in the midst of others who share a like vision and dream. Moreover, prophets who dedicate their lives to social change can experience a strong sense of fulfillment if, after years of labor, the changes for which they have worked to convince others begin to come about. The history of Supreme Court decisions in twentieth-century America, for example, bears clear witness to decades of challenge regarding conscientious objection to the nation's wars with results that have made the nation more sensitive to issues of individual autonomy and personal ethical choice. The development of organic farming and the growing availability of alternative health choices for millions point to the influence of early voices from the 1960s, like the leaders of the small macrobiotic movement, who urged change and helped to make it happen on a larger scale.

Hence, prophecy brings its rewards, and those who choose to follow the spirituality of prophecy and social action lead lives that, for them, are deeply meaningful. Their willingness to challenge social expectations and norms gives them a measure of personal freedom that often eludes others in society. Prophets are people who are self-starters and whistle-blowers—who, by their example, remind others of the dangers of mindless conformity and unthinking acquiescence to social evil. If their weaknesses are the risk of self-righteousness and judgmentalism and the self-delusion of believing they are hearing divine voices when they are hearing only their own, their strengths lie in their independence and their willingness to throw all of their gifts and energies into making positive change. Prophets point to the importance of standing up and being counted, and they demonstrate in significant ways that individual lives do count and make a difference.

The following pages explore the legacy of various kinds of prophets from the American past and present. First we scrutinize the persona of the reformer and the prophet more closely. Then we turn to the American heritage of civil disobedience in nineteenth- and twentieth-century forms, as we encounter protests of collective social behavior from the Mexican War to Jim Crow laws in the American South to the nuclearism of an American military-industrial machine bent on manufacturing weapons of mass destruction. We look at a tradition of American anarchism in the early twentieth century, here cast in an agnostic and even atheistic mold; and, by contrast, we enter the world of an evangelical who takes up cudgels, literally, against saloon and barroom in a holiness mode that has become transformed into prophecy. In all of the cases, we search for the connecting signs—and different expressions—of the prophetic spirituality that marks the willingness to act so startlingly and decisively in the social world.

13

The Reformer AND The Prophet

Joachim Wach

Joachim Wach (1898–1955) taught at Brown University and the University of Chicago after Nazi pressure in 1935 forced the termination of his university appointment in Leipzig, Germany, because of his Jewish ancestry. As a historian of religions his approach to the discipline foregrounded religious experience and followed it into expression in theoretical, practical, and sociological (group) dimensions. These interests led Wach to the task of distinguishing types of religious authority as they were lived out in various spiritual communities past and present throughout the world. In his classic *Sociology of Religion* (1944), from which this excerpt is taken, he ranges widely through Christian and Jewish history and makes a few forays into prophetic concerns in other traditions as well. Wach's "reformer" leads with easy transition to the work of the "prophet," a figure whom he delineates in terms that echo the German sociologist of religion Max Weber. In a larger sense, though, standing behind the figure of the prophet is the burden of the Jewish Torah and the Christian Bible with their message of the significance of history and of ethical action in the world. Prophecy here means not so much foretelling as "forthtelling." And so Jewish and Christian leaders, inspired by their scriptures and the weight of their tradition, have appeared in every age risking what they cherished in favor of an ideal of right and justice, as they understood it, that they cherished more. Always accompanying prophet and prophecy was the conviction of a divine call to speak up and speak out. The ultimate message from them, and for believers who agreed, was that God was a God of history and that spirit was most at work when human words and deeds were actively aligned with divine will.

The Reformer

In times of threatening decay or disintegration leaders arise in religious groups who are difficult to classify in the traditional historical schemes. They are not on one level with the founders; their creative religious power does not match that of the originator of a great faith. They somewhat resemble the founders in the power, and possibly even in the magnetism, of their personality, in their energy and endurance; but the sociological effect of their activity cannot be compared to that resulting in the emergence of the great faiths. Moreover, their self-interpretation and the role with which these reformers are credited by their followers differ from those of the founder. In some of these leaders the "prophetic" element is strong, and, therefore, not a few of them have been called "prophets," though with doubtful propriety. Reformers differ from prophets psychologically, sociologically, and theologically.

The specific charisma of the reformer varies. With some, it will be the gift of vision or ecstasy, with others pre-excellent virtues of head or heart, an eminent talent for organization or ascetic vigor—all of which are to serve a characteristic basic religious experience. We note a marked difference in the depth and comprehensiveness of this experience, in missionary effort and ability and in the appeal of different reformers. They vary in creative power and breadth of vision, in drive and persuasiveness. Some are great leaders in worship and devotion; others excel as intellectual or moral guides; others, again, magnetically draw their fellow-man in the company they organize. To illustrate these three types of reformers, we may think of Moses, Ezra, and Sabbatai Zebi, the false messiah of the seventeenth century, in Judaism; of Francis, Dominicus, and Ignatius Loyola in Western Christianity; of Basilius, John of Damascus, and Seraphim of Sarov, the modern Russian saint, in Eastern Catholicism; of Luther, Zwingli, and Calvin or of Fox, Penn, and Wesley in Protestantism. Some of these influential figures have lived retired and secluded lives, radiating as it were a power which generates changes and transformations in the religious community of their time. Others were the quiet center of an intimately related group of followers and may be hardly known beyond it. Again, others sought and found contact with larger groups and even masses upon which their immediate influence can be noted. It would not be difficult to enumerate examples. Great mystics like Eckhart, Ruysbroeck, Jacob Böhme, great scholars like Colet, Erasmus, Thomas Cartwright, and Pusey . . . may be classified in the first group; the second would include religious leaders like Gerhard Groote, Lodensteyn, and Schwenckfeld; the third type is represented by John Hus, John Wycliffe, and John Wesley. Different as their personalities may be, they have in common profound religious experiences of some originality and the gift of communicating them directly or indirectly to others, thus becoming sociologically important centers of religious life and activity. We can, furthermore, among the reformers distinguish between the inaugurator and the organizer, as in the case of George Fox and William Penn, of P. J. Spener and von Zinzendorf, of John Wesley and Francis Asbury, of Joseph Smith and Brigham Young. There are the originators such as Luther and the systematizers such as Melanchthon, or as Lelio and Fausto Sozzini, or Kabir and Nanak in India. And we may group together secondary reformers like Knox in Scotland, Olaus

Petri in Sweden, and Agricola in Finland. In some reformers the prophetical element prevails: Montanus in the early, Joachim of Floris in the medieval, and Joseph Smith in the modern phase of Christianity illustrate this point. There are significant differences in the methods and the means selected by the reformers for the realization of their ideals. One way is indicated by the work of theological critics—different as their attitude may be—like Castellio and Erasmus, Newman and Kierkegaard. Whereas their immediate sociological effect may be small, the indirect effect has been enormous. Inversely, some revolutionary reformers like Melchior Hofmann, Thomas Münzer, or Gerard Winstanley have had a wide but short-lived appeal. There will be great differences in character between reformers of equal sociological importance. We can observe this in contrasting personalities like Menno Simons, Robert Browne, and David Joris, all living at the time of the great Reformation, or of Philip Neri, Ignatius Loyola, and Pierre de Bérulle in a later age. Here the psychologist, by applying to character and temperament the categories which he has developed, will prove helpful to the sociologist.

. . . Some of the reformers have been geniuses of devotion; some, great scholars or profound thinkers; some, powerful directors of religious fervor and emotion; some, great teachers and preachers. All these elements we find isolated or in some combination with other types of outstanding religious personalities. Quantitatively, the reformer is characterized by the extent and degree of his activity; qualitatively, by his creative and constructive power, which, however, will always be inferior to that of the founder. Inside and outside of Christianity the history of religion records the work of a great number of outstanding theologians, teachers, interpreters, and leaders in religious life. Less original than the founder, yet more original than the just-mentioned bearers of authority, the reformers in all religions represent an epoch in the life and action of their group and thus a type of religious charisma of great sociological consequence. The historian of church and religion will be more interested in the historical context in which the lifework of these personalities will have to be seen and in the content of their message; the sociologist may aid him by examining and comparing sociological types of reforming activity and resulting group life.

The Prophet

The question arises: Should not the term "prophet" be reserved for a geographically, ethnically, and historically limited group of personalities; in other words, to the best known of all, the "written" prophets of the Old Testament? Such a definition would have the advantage of a rather clear-cut circumscription, but studies of the prophets of the Old Testament in recent years have shown that the "written prophecy," beginning in Israel in the eighth century

B.C., was by no means something entirely new. The content is new, as has been said rightly, but not the form. The latter had a long history in the religion of the Old Testament itself. Balaam, Micah ben Imlah, Nathan, Elijah, Elisha, and others are identified as "predecessors of the later prophets" whose writings happened to come down to us. Moreover, psychological studies have indicated a resemblance, if not an affinity, between Hebrew prophecy and that of other Semitic civilizations, principally the Arabic, but also the Phoenician and Canaanite. Certain priestly groups in Egypt are often styled "prophetic." The term "prophet" is not Semitic but Greek, and an examination of the usage of this designation in the Hellenic world, carefully executed by Erich Fascher, has proved to be of great value for the understanding of similarities as well as differences in the "prophecy" of Israel and of Greece. Meanwhile, ethnologists had become accustomed to speak of "primitive prophets," with reference to American Indians and, to a lesser degree, to Africa. The study of northeastern and southeastern Asiatic and Iranian shamanism was added recently in the hope that it may throw additional light on the subject of "prophecy." The increase of material, however, was likely to increase also the difficulty of interpretation.

We will follow Max Weber's example again. He considered the "prophecy" a special category in his systematic outline of types of religious authorities. As we have indicated above, there is a transition from prophecy to other types of religious authority. That explains to some extent the lack of agreement in terminology. Some founders, such as Mohammed, Zoroaster, and even Mani have been designated as "prophets." Some also would call reformers, teachers, and sectarian leaders like Moses, Pythagoras, and Simon Magus prophets. What, then, is the characteristic of a prophet? The prophetical charisma seems to be the chief religious gift. It implies immediate communion with the deity, the intensity of which is more characteristic than its continuance. The mandate which the prophet receives is essential; usually there is a distinct "call." The mandate may be limited, in which case the authority which goes with it is also limited; it may be repeated, possibly with qualifications; and it may be permanent. The consciousness of being the organ, instrument, or mouthpiece of the divine will is characteristic of the self-interpretation of the prophet. The prophetic authority is distinctly secondary, a derived authority, more distinctly so than the authority of the founder. Furthermore, a certain natural disposition, which many consider to be the basic psychological characteristic of prophecy, belongs to the prophet who is distinguished by an unusual sensitiveness and an intense emotional life. Visions, dreams, trances, or ecstasies are not infrequently encountered, and by these the prophet is prepared to receive and interpret manifestations of the divine. He shares this privilege with other types of religious leaders like the seer, etc. His interpretation, however, is "authorized," a fact which distinguishes him and the seer from the magician and the augur. It is characteristic of prophetic revelations that they are usually not induced by methodical or casual manipulation but arise spontaneously and are received passively. This differentiates prophecy and divination. There is something elemental about the prophet, which can be discerned in his uncompromising attitude and conduct and in the archaism of his manner and language. Frequently the prophet appears as a renewer of lost contacts with the hidden powers of life, and here he resembles the "medicine man" and the physician. He is credited with the power of transcending the limitations of time and space. The prophet illuminates and interprets the past, but he also anticipates the future. The *kairos* (moment) is interpreted by the prophet in this dual light.

It is interesting to note that prophets do not usually come from the aristocracy, the learned, or the refined; they frequently emerge from the simpler folk and remain true to their origin even in a changed environment. Frugality and simplicity mark the life of the prophet, and these features link him with the ascetic and the "saint" (cf. the Russian *staretz*). Since his inspiration means the revelation of hidden truths, the prophet may also be regarded as one who "knows." As one who possesses knowledge and information as to the most essential that man wants to know—the nature, will, and manifestations of God—the prophet has features in common with the teacher, philosopher, and theologian.

The political, national, and social activities of prophets have always attracted the attention of the students of prophecy. In these fields they played so outstanding a part in old Hebrew history (Balaam, Samuel, Nathan, Elijah, Elisha, and most of the great prophets) that some scholars are inclined to regard this side of prophetical activity as the central one. That is not correct, because his moral, social, and political ideas, the prophet's function as the "conscience" of the group, tribe, nation, or state, are caused, conditioned, and determined by his basic religious experience. Owing to his contact with the deepest sources of life, the prophet reacts vigorously against all disturbance or perversion of the civic or moral order which is meant to reflect the divine will. He feels danger and seizes crucial moments to interpret present situations in the light of the past and the future. Hence we have the modern use of the term "prophet" to designate one who anticipates what is to come and advises his people or their representatives according to his intuition. This often results in concrete advice on ways and means to establish or reestablish the divinely ordained state of things and in warning the people and individuals about punishments and rewards. The blunt expression of moral judgment which we are accustomed to associate with prophetic activity, particularly with the messages of Nathan, Amos, Micah, and Jeremiah, is not inspired by personal resentment but is a result of the strong emotion and the profound intuition evoked by basic religious experiences. Such pronouncements and judgments confirm the prophet's charisma. The moral and social *restitutio in integrum* here and now, in this world, will have only a preliminary and preparatory value in the eyes of the prophet. Helped by his deeper perception and surer anticipation of the future, the prophet views the things of the world in the light of its final destiny. Hence eschatology usually plays an important part in all genuine prophecy.

In harmony with the peculiar psychological organization of the prophet, the expression of his experience is characterized by its vigor and directness. The prophet speaks by means of words, signs, gestures, and diverse acts of a common or unusual nature. We find abrupt and sententious utterances often cryptic in nature, but there are also elaborate and systematic sermons and addresses. Images and metaphors abound. The prophet may or may not utilize the traditional theoretical and practical language of his coreligionists. Frequently, he will alter and transform customary ideas and conceptions.

Frequently his attitude in matters of worship will be critical, nonconformist, "protestant." This protest may be directed against the nature and character of a specific illegitimate or falsified cultic practice or may be of a more general character. Accordingly, the prophetic charisma frequently leads to clashes with the powers that be in existing religious institutions. But the authority of a prophet may also help to reintegrate individuals or groups into the religious community and restore the lost balance in its social and political life between ruler and subject and subject and subject. It may act as a new center of sociological crystallization within the religious group, or it may bring about eventual secession, thus causing the formation of a new and independent cultic unit. Thus the transition from the prophet to the founder, the reformer, and the sectarian leader is indicated. History shows that the revolutionary character of prophecy prevails over conservative features, which, however, are not entirely absent from the prophetic character and activity.

One type of prophecy—we may think of Ezekiel, al-Ghazzali, or Chaitanya—is more closely connected with the cultus than others and is associated with ritus: sacrifice, liturgy, and the dance, often in connection with certain cultic centers. This fact is not difficult to explain. Religious rites represent objectified and stereotyped expressions of spontaneous religious experience, which may produce in turn new creative experiences in a mind which is susceptible to it. We know of semi-prophetical and mystical experiences connected with the cult in Christianity, Judaism, Mohammedanism, Buddhism, and Hinduism.

Although the prophetic revelation is obtained in individual experiences which tend to isolate their recipient, it frequently engenders a strong urge to extend the message of the deity to all men (the prophetical mandate). This has important sociological consequences. Groups of listeners, followers, and disciples gather. Their attitude may be passive or active. In the latter case prophecy will operate collectively through disciples and disciple groups. Such group prophecy is found in the "bands," guilds, and "schools" of early Hebrew and Mohammedan ecstatics and in the associations of Iranian, northeastern Asiatic pagan, and Buddhistic shamans. The nucleus of what later develops into an institutional and professional association like some priestly and shamanistic American Indian societies probably has often been originally an organization of disciples of a prophetic leader. Be this as it may, we can trace the transition from purely personal charismatic prophecy to an institution with professional training, habits, and rewards. History shows that the priest, in addition to being the successor, is frequently also the antagonist of the prophet. Since all organizations pass through an initial stage of spirituality, the institution of the priesthood necessarily presupposes the existence of personal charismatic leaders. On the other hand, the emergence of new prophetic charisma will evoke the opposition of those who either reject the prophetic principle or oppose the claims of some individual prophet. The history of Judaism and Christianity in all their phases is most revealing in this respect. Elijah and the priests of Baal; Amos and the court priests; the recession of the charismatic gifts in the early Christian church; the renewal of "prophecy" in the thirteenth, fourteenth, and fifteenth centuries and its conflicts with the Church of Rome; independent and "sectarian" beginnings and movements in Protestantism; Starzestvo in all its forms in Russian Orthodox Christianity—all are examples of this type of antagonism.

One essential element of prophetic activity is the extraordinary spiritual power with which the prophets are credited and which is symbolized in records of their miracles. These are supposedly not performed by the prophet's own energy but by the divine power with which his intimate communion with the deity or the spirits endows him. . . .

. . . Prophecy more than any other type of religious authority has been confused, by contemporary and later generations, with other forms of religious leadership. Where the historian of religion follows developments, the sociologist is bound to discriminate between types which occur and reoccur in various places and at various times.

14

Civil Disobedience

Henry David Thoreau

This essay originated when Henry David Thoreau (1817–1862) decided
to answer the questions that people in his town, Concord, were asking
after he spent a night in jail in July 1846 for tax refusal. An American
Transcendentalist who found in nature a source of authority and an
emblem of spirit, Thoreau had earlier demanded to have his name removed from tax rolls generating revenue for the support of public worship. He managed that successfully, and later, for six years, refused to
pay his poll tax to a slave-holding government. This time, in the context
of the Mexican War, he was jailed and released only when his aunt,
without consulting him, paid the tax for him. Thoreau gave an account
of his conscience in two public lectures at the Concord lyceum in January and February 1848. When the sympathetic Elizabeth Palmer Pea-
body decided to begin publishing a periodical called *Aesthetic Papers,*
she asked for the material of his lectures; and so in 1849 "Resistance to
Civil Government" appeared in its first and only issue. Four years after
Thoreau's death, the essay appeared again in a collection of his writings,
this time under the better-known title *Civil Disobedience.* Whatever it
was called, it was clear that Thoreau's essay proclaimed spirituality to be
a political act with external consequences. He argued that the proper
place for a just person was prison, and he pitted the state and the masses
on one side against the principled individual on the other. If, according
to his Transcendental faith, nature stood outside human society as an
authoritative voice, within each individual lay a corresponding source
of authority in conscience and intuition. Thus, the command that Thoreau heard was a command to follow an organic instead of mechanistic
life—to act as a "counter friction to stop the machine."

I heartily accept the motto, "That government is best which governs least;"
and I should like to see it acted up to more rapidly and systematically. Carried
out, it finally amounts to this, which also I believe,—"That government is best
which governs not at all;" and when men are prepared for it, that will be the
kind of government which they will have. Government is at best but an expedi-

From "Civil Disobedience," in *The Writings of Henry David Thoreau* by Henry David Thoreau [1906].

ent; but most governments are usually, and all governments are sometimes, inexpedient. The objections which have been brought against a standing army, and they are many and weighty, and deserve to prevail, may also at last be brought against a standing government. The standing army is only an arm of the standing government. The government itself, which is only the mode which the people have chosen to execute their will, is equally liable to be abused and perverted before the people can act through it. Witness the present Mexican war, the work of comparatively a few individuals using the standing government as their tool; for, in the outset, the people would not have consented to this measure.

This American government,—what is it but a tradition, though a recent one, endeavoring to transmit itself unimpaired to posterity, but each instant losing some of its integrity? It has not the vitality and force of a single living man; for a single man can bend it to his will. It is a sort of wooden gun to the people themselves. But it is not the less necessary for this; for the people must have some complicated machinery or other, and hear its din, to satisfy that idea of government which they have. Governments show thus how successfully men can be imposed on, even impose on themselves, for their own advantage. It is excellent, we must all allow. Yet this government never of itself furthered any enterprise, but by the alacrity with which it got out of its way. *It* does not keep the country free. *It* does not settle the West. *It* does not educate. The character inherent in the American people has done all that has been accomplished; and it would have done somewhat more, if the government had not sometimes got in its way. For government is an expedient by which men would fain succeed in letting one another alone; and, as has been said, when it is most expedient, the governed are most let alone by it. Trade and commerce, if they were not made of india-rubber, would never manage to bounce over the obstacles which legislators are continually putting in their way; and, if one were to judge these men wholly by the effects of their actions and not partly by their intentions, they would deserve to be classed and punished with those mischievous persons who put obstructions on the railroads.

But, to speak practically and as a citizen, unlike those who call themselves no-government men, I ask for, not at once no government, but *at once* a better government. Let every man make known what kind of government would command his respect, and that will be one step toward obtaining it.

After all, the practical reason why, when the power is once in the hands of the people, a majority are permitted, and for a long period continue, to rule is not because they are most likely to be in the right, nor because this seems fairest to the minority, but because they are physically the strongest. But a government in which the majority rule in all cases cannot be based on justice, even as far as men understand it. Can there not be a government in which majorities do not virtually decide right and wrong, but conscience?—in which majorities decide only those questions to which the rule of expediency is applicable? Must the citizen ever for a moment, or in the least degree, resign his conscience to the legislator? Why has every man a conscience, then? I think that we should be men first, and subjects afterward. It is not desirable to cultivate a respect for the law, so much as for the right. The only obligation which I have a right to assume is to do at any time what I think right. It is truly enough said that a corporation has no conscience; but a corporation of conscientious men is a corporation *with* a conscience. Law never made men a whit more just; and, by means of their respect for it, even the well-disposed are daily made the agents of injustice. A common and natural result of an undue respect for law is, that you may see a file of soldiers, colonel, captain, corporal, privates, powder-monkeys, and all, marching in admirable order over hill and dale to the wars, against their wills, ay, against their common sense and consciences, which makes it very steep marching indeed, and produces a palpitation of the heart. They have no doubt that it is a damnable business in which they are concerned; they are all peaceably inclined. Now, what are they? Men at all? or small movable forts and magazines, at the service of some unscrupulous man in power? Visit the Navy-Yard, and behold a marine, such a man as an American government can make, or such as it can make a man with its black arts,—a mere shadow and reminiscence of humanity, a man laid out alive and standing, and already, as one may say, buried under arms with funeral accompaniments, though it may be,—

> "Not a drum was heard, not a funeral note,
>   As his corse to the rampart we hurried;
> Not a soldier discharged his farewell shot
>   O'er the grave where our hero we buried."

The mass of men serve the state thus, not as men mainly, but as machines, with their bodies. They are the standing army, and the militia, jailers, constables, *posse comitatus,* etc. In most cases there is no free exercise whatever of the judgment or of the moral sense; but they put themselves on a level with wood and earth and stones; and wooden men can perhaps be manufactured that will serve the purpose as well. Such command no more respect than men of straw or a lump of dirt. They have the same sort of worth only as horses and dogs. Yet such as these even are commonly esteemed good citizens. Others—as most legislators, politicians, lawyers, ministers, and office-holders—serve the state chiefly with their heads; and, as they rarely make any moral distinctions, they are as likely to serve the devil, without *intending* it, as God. A very few— as heroes, patriots, martyrs, reformers in the great sense, and *men*—serve the state with their consciences also, and so necessarily resist it for the most part; and they are commonly treated as enemies by it. A wise man will only be useful as a man, and will not submit to be "clay," and "stop a hole to keep the wind away," but leave that office to his dust at least:—

> "I am too high-born to be propertied,
> To be a secondary at control,
> Or useful serving-man and instrument
> To any sovereign state throughout the world."

He who gives himself entirely to his fellow-men appears to them useless and selfish; but he who gives himself partially to them is pronounced a benefactor and philanthropist.

How does it become a man to behave toward this American government to-day? I answer, that he cannot without disgrace be associated with it. I cannot for an instant recognize that political organization as *my* government which is the *slave's* government also.

All men recognize the right of revolution; that is, the right to refuse allegiance to, and to resist, the government, when its tyranny or its inefficiency are great and unendurable. But almost all say that such is not the case now. But such was the case, they think, in the Revolution of '75. If one were to tell me that this was a bad government because it taxed certain foreign commodities brought to its ports, it is most probable that I should not make an ado about it, for I can do without them. All machines have their friction; and possibly this does enough good to counterbalance the evil. At any rate, it is a great evil to make a stir about it. But when the friction comes to have its machine, and oppression and robbery are organized, I say, let us not have such a machine any longer. In other words, when a sixth of the population of a nation which has undertaken to be the refuge of liberty are slaves, and a whole country is unjustly overrun and conquered by a foreign army, and subjected to military law, I think that it is not too soon for honest men to rebel and revolutionize. What makes this duty the more urgent is the fact that the country so overrun is not our own, but ours is the invading army.

Paley, a common authority with many on moral questions, in his chapter on the "Duty of Submission to Civil Government," resolves all civil obligation into expediency; and he proceeds to say that "so long as the interest of the whole society requires it, that is, so long as the established government cannot be resisted or changed without public inconveniency, it is the will of God . . . that the established government be obeyed,—and no longer. This principle being admitted, the justice of every particular case of resistance is reduced to a computation of the quantity of the danger and grievance on the one side, and of the probability and expense of redressing it on the other." Of this, he says, every man shall judge for himself. But Paley appears never to have contemplated those cases to which the rule of expediency does not apply, in which a people, as well as an individual, must do justice, cost what it may. If I have unjustly wrested a plank from a drowning man, I must restore it to him though I drown myself. This, according to Paley, would be inconvenient. But he that would save his life, in such a case, shall lose it. This people must cease to hold slaves, and to make war on Mexico, though it cost them their existence as a people.

In their practice, nations agree with Paley; but does any one think that Massachusetts does exactly what is right at the present crisis?

"A drab of state, a cloth-o'-silver slut,
    To have her train borne up, and her soul trail in the dirt."

Practically speaking, the opponents to a reform in Massachusetts are not a hundred thousand politicians at the South, but a hundred thousand merchants and farmers here, who are more interested in commerce and agriculture than they are in humanity, and are not prepared to do justice to the slave and to Mexico, *cost what it may.* I quarrel not with far-off foes, but with those who, near at home, co-öperate with, and do the bidding of, those far away, and without whom the latter would be harmless. We are accustomed to say, that the mass of men are unprepared; but improvement is slow, because the few are not materially wiser or better than the many. It is not so important that many should be as good as you, as that there be some absolute goodness some-where; for that will leaven the whole lump. There are thousands who are *in opinion* opposed to slavery and to the war, who yet in effect do nothing to put an end to them; who, esteeming themselves children of Washington and Franklin, sit down with their hands in their pockets, and say that they know not what to do, and do nothing; who even postpone the question of freedom to the question of free trade, and quietly read the prices-current along with the latest advices from Mexico, after dinner, and, it may be, fall asleep over them both. What is the price-current of an honest man and patriot to-day? They hesitate, and they regret, and sometimes they petition; but they do noth-ing in earnest and with effect. They will wait, well disposed, for others to rem-edy the evil, that they may no longer have it to regret. At most, they give only a cheap vote, and a feeble countenance and God-speed, to the right, as it goes by them. There are nine hundred and ninety-nine patrons of virtue to one virtuous man. But it is easier to deal with the real possessor of a thing than with the temporary guardian of it.

All voting is a sort of gaming, like checkers or backgammon, with a slight moral tinge to it, a playing with right and wrong, with moral questions; and betting naturally accompanies it. The character of the voters is not staked. I cast my vote, perchance, as I think right; but I am not vitally concerned that that right should prevail. I am willing to leave it to the majority. Its obligation, therefore, never exceeds that of expediency. Even voting *for the right* is *doing* nothing for it. It is only expressing to men feebly your desire that it should prevail. A wise man will not leave the right to the mercy of chance, nor wish it to prevail through the power of the majority. There is but little virtue in the action of masses of men. When the majority shall at length vote for the abolition of slavery, it will be because they are indifferent to slavery, or because there is but little slavery left to be abolished by their vote. *They* will then be the only slaves. Only *his* vote can hasten the abolition of slavery who asserts his own freedom by his vote.

I hear of a convention to be held at Baltimore, or elsewhere, for the selection of a candidate for the Presidency, made up chiefly of editors, and men who are politicians by profession; but I think, what is it to any independent, intelligent, and respectable man what decision they may come to? Shall we not have the advantage of his wisdom and honesty, nevertheless? Can we not count upon some independent votes? Are there not many individuals in the country who do not attend conventions? But no: I find that the respectable man, so called, has immediately drifted from his position, and despairs of his country, when his country has more reason to despair of him. He forthwith adopts one of the candidates thus selected as the only *available* one, thus proving that he is himself *available* for any purposes of the demagogue. His vote is of no more worth than that of any unprincipled foreigner or hireling native, who may have been bought. O for a man who is a *man,* and, as my neighbor says, has a bone in his back which you cannot pass your hand through! Our statistics are at fault: the population has been returned too large. How many *men* are there to a square thousand miles in this country? Hardly one. Does not America offer any inducement for men to settle here? The American has dwindled into an Odd Fellow,—one who may be known by the development of his organ of gregariousness, and a manifest lack of intellect and cheerful self-reliance; whose first and chief concern, on coming into the world, is to see that the almshouses are in good repair; and, before yet he has lawfully donned the virile garb, to collect a fund for the support of the widows and orphans that may be; who, in short, ventures to live only by the aid of the Mutual Insurance company, which has promised to bury him decently.

It is not a man's duty, as a matter of course, to devote himself to the eradication of any, even the most enormous, wrong; he may still properly have other concerns to engage him; but it is his duty, at least, to wash his hands of it, and, if he gives it no thought longer, not to give it practically his support. If I devote myself to other pursuits and contemplations, I must first see, at least, that I do not pursue them sitting upon another man's shoulders. I must get off him first, that he may pursue his contemplations too. See what gross inconsistency is tolerated. I have heard some of my townsmen say, "I should like to have them order me out to help put down an insurrection of the slaves, or to march to

Mexico;—see if I would go;" and yet these very men have each, directly by their allegiance, and so indirectly, at least, by their money, furnished a substitute. The soldier is applauded who refuses to serve in an unjust war by those who do not refuse to sustain the unjust government which makes the war; is applauded by those whose own act and authority he disregards and sets at naught; as if the state were penitent to that degree that it hired one to scourge it while it sinned, but not to that degree that it left off sinning for a moment. Thus, under the name of Order and Civil Government, we are all made at last to pay homage to and support our own meanness. After the first blush of sin comes its indifference; and from immoral it becomes, as it were, *un*moral, and not quite unnecessary to that life which we have made.

The broadest and most prevalent error requires the most disinterested virtue to sustain it. The slight reproach to which the virtue of patriotism is commonly liable, the noble are most likely to incur. Those who, while they disapprove of the character and measures of a government, yield to it their allegiance and support are undoubtedly its most conscientious supporters, and so frequently the most serious obstacles to reform. Some are petitioning the State to dissolve the Union, to disregard the requisitions of the President. Why do they not dissolve it themselves,—the union between themselves and the State,—and refuse to pay their quota into its treasury? Do not they stand in the same relation to the State, that the State does to the Union? And have not the same reasons prevented the State from resisting the Union, which have prevented them from resisting the State?

How can a man be satisfied to entertain an opinion merely, and enjoy *it?* Is there any enjoyment in it, if his opinion is that he is aggrieved? If you are cheated out of a single dollar by your neighbor, you do not rest satisfied with knowing that you are cheated, or with saying that you are cheated, or even with petitioning him to pay you your due; but you take effectual steps at once to obtain the full amount, and see that you are never cheated again. Action from principle, the perception and the performance of right, changes things and relations; it is essentially revolutionary, and does not consist wholly with anything which was. It not only divides States and churches, it divides families; ay, it divides the *individual,* separating the diabolical in him from the divine.

Unjust laws exist: shall we be content to obey them, or shall we endeavor to amend them, and obey them until we have succeeded, or shall we transgress them at once? Men generally, under such a government as this, think that they ought to wait until they have persuaded the majority to alter them. They think that, if they should resist, the remedy would be worse than the evil. But it is the fault of the government itself that the remedy *is* worse than the evil. *It* makes it worse. Why is it not more apt to anticipate and provide for reform? Why does it not cherish its wise minority? Why does it cry and resist before it is hurt? Why does it not encourage its citizens to be on the alert to point out its faults, and *do* better than it would have them? Why does it always crucify Christ, and excommunicate Copernicus and Luther, and pronounce Washington and Franklin rebels?

One would think, that a deliberate and practical denial of its authority was the only offence never contemplated by government; else, why has it not assigned its definite, its suitable and proportionate, penalty? If a man who has no property refuses but once to earn nine shillings for the State, he is put in prison for a period unlimited by any law that I know, and determined only by the discretion of those who placed him there; but if he should steal ninety times nine shillings from the State, he is soon permitted to go at large again.

If the injustice is part of the necessary friction of the machine of government, let it go, let it go: perchance it will wear smooth,—certainly the machine will wear out. If the injustice has a spring, or a pulley, or a rope, or a crank, exclusively for itself, then perhaps you may consider whether the remedy will not be worse than the evil; but if it is of such a nature that it requires you to be the agent of injustice to another, then, I say, break the law. Let your life be a counter-friction to stop the machine. What I have to do is to see, at any rate, that I do not lend myself to the wrong which I condemn.

As for adopting the ways which the State has provided for remedying the evil, I know not of such ways. They take too much time, and a man's life will be gone. I have other affairs to attend to. I came into this world, not chiefly to make this a good place to live in, but to live in it, be it good or bad. A man has not everything to do, but something; and because he cannot do *everything*, it is not necessary that he should do *something* wrong. It is not my business to be petitioning the Governor or the Legislature any more than it is theirs to petition me; and if they should not hear my petition, what should I do then? But in this case the State has provided no way: its very Constitution is the evil. This may seem to be harsh and stubborn and unconciliatory; but it is to treat with the utmost kindness and consideration the only spirit that can appreciate or deserves it. So is all change for the better, like birth and death, which convulse the body.

I do not hesitate to say, that those who call themselves Abolitionists should at once effectually withdraw their support, both in person and property, from the government of Massachusetts, and not wait till they constitute a majority of one, before they suffer the right to prevail through them. I think that it is enough if they have God on their side, without waiting for that other one. Moreover, any man more right than his neighbors constitutes a majority of one already.

I meet this American government, or its representative, the State government, directly, and face to face, once a year—no more—in the person of its tax-gatherer; this is the only mode in which a man situated as I am necessarily meets it; and it then says distinctly, Recognize me; and the simplest, the most effectual, and, in the present posture of affairs, the indispensablest mode of treating with it on this head, of expressing your little satisfaction with and love for it, is to deny it then. My civil neighbor, the tax-gatherer, is the very man I have to deal with,—for it is, after all, with men and not with parchment that I quarrel,—and he has voluntarily chosen to be an agent of the government. How shall he ever know well what he is and does as an officer of the government, or as a man, until he is obliged to consider whether he shall treat me, his neighbor, for whom he has respect, as a neighbor and well-disposed man, or as a maniac and disturber of the peace, and see if he can get over this obstruction to his neighborliness without a ruder and more impetuous thought or speech corresponding with his action. I know this well, that if one thousand, if one hundred, if ten men whom I could name,—if ten *honest* men only,— ay, if *one* HONEST man, in this State of Massachusetts, *ceasing to hold slaves,* were actually to withdraw from this copartnership, and be locked up in the county jail therefor, it would be the abolition of slavery in America. For it matters not how small the beginning may seem to be: what is once well done is done forever. But we love better to talk about it: that we say is our mission. Reform keeps many scores of newspapers in its service, but not one man. If my esteemed neighbor, the State's ambassador, who will devote his days to the settlement of the question of human rights in the Council Chamber, instead of being threatened with the prisons of Carolina, were to sit down the prisoner of Massachusetts, that State which is so anxious to foist the sin of slavery upon her sister,—though at present she can discover only an act of inhospitality to be the ground of a quarrel with her,—the Legislature would not wholly waive the subject the following winter.

Under a government which imprisons any unjustly, the true place for a just man is also a prison. The proper place to-day, the only place which Massachusetts has provided for her freer and less desponding spirits, is in her prisons, to be put out and locked out of the State by her own act, as they have already put themselves out by their principles. It is there that the fugitive slave, and the Mexican prisoner on parole, and the Indian come to plead the wrongs of his race should find them; on that separate, but more free and honorable, ground, where the State places those who are not *with* her, but *against* her,— the only house in a slave State in which a free man can abide with honor. If any think that their influence would be lost there, and their voices no longer afflict the ear of the State, that they would not be as an enemy within its walls, they do not know by how much truth is stronger than error, nor how much more eloquently and effectively he can combat injustice who has experienced a little in his own person. Cast your whole vote, not a strip of paper merely, but your whole influence. A minority is powerless while it conforms to the majority; it is not even a minority then; but it is irresistible when it clogs by its whole weight. If the alternative is to keep all just men in prison, or give up war and slavery, the State will not hesitate which to choose. If a thousand men were not to pay their tax-bills this year, that would not be a violent and bloody measure, as it would be to pay them, and enable the State to commit violence and shed innocent blood. This is, in fact, the definition of a peaceable revolution, if any such is possible. If the tax-gatherer, or any other public officer, asks me, as one has done, "But what shall I do?" my answer is, "If you really wish to do anything, resign your office." When the subject has refused allegiance, and the officer has resigned his office, then the revolution is accomplished. But even suppose blood should flow. Is there not a sort of blood shed when the conscience is wounded? Through this wound a man's real manhood and immortality flow out, and he bleeds to an everlasting death. I see this blood flowing now.

I have contemplated the imprisonment of the offender, rather than the seizure of his goods,—though both will serve the same purpose,—because they who assert the purest right, and consequently are most dangerous to a corrupt State, commonly have not spent much time in accumulating property. To such the State renders comparatively small service, and a slight tax is wont to appear exorbitant, particularly if they are obliged to earn it by special labor with their hands. If there were one who lived wholly without the use of money, the State itself would hesitate to demand it of him. But the rich man—not to make any invidious comparison—is always sold to the institution which makes him rich. Absolutely speaking, the more money, the less virtue; for money comes between a man and his objects, and obtains them for him; and it was certainly no great virtue to obtain it. It puts to rest many questions which he would otherwise be taxed to answer; while the only new question which it puts is the hard but superfluous one, how to spend it. Thus his moral ground is taken from under his feet. The opportunities of living are diminished in proportion as what are called the "means" are increased. The best thing a man can do for his culture when he is rich is to endeavor to carry out those schemes which he entertained when he was poor. Christ answered the Herodians according to their condition. "Show me the tribute-money," said he;—and one took a penny out of his pocket;—if you use money which has the image of Caesar on it, and which he has made current and valuable, that is, *if you are men of the State,* and gladly enjoy the advantages of Caesar's government, then pay him back some of his own when he demands it; "Render therefore to Caesar that which is Caesar's, and to God those things which are God's,"—leaving them no wiser than before as to which was which; for they did not wish to know.

When I converse with the freest of my neighbors, I perceive that, whatever they may say about the magnitude and seriousness of the question, and their regard for the public tranquillity, the long and the short of the matter is, that they cannot spare the protection of the existing government, and they dread the consequences to their property and families of disobedience to it. For my own part, I should not like to think that I ever rely on the protection of the State. But, if I deny the authority of the State when it presents its tax-bill, it will soon take and waste all my property, and so harass me and my children without end. This is hard. This makes it impossible for a man to live honestly, and at the same time comfortably, in outward respects. It will not be worth the while to accumulate property; that would be sure to go again. You must hire or squat somewhere, and raise but a small crop, and eat that soon. You must live within yourself, and depend upon yourself always tucked up and ready for a start, and not have many affairs. A man may grow rich in Turkey even, if he will be in all respects a good subject of the Turkish government. Confucius said: "If a state is governed by the principles of reason, poverty and misery are subjects of shame; if a state is not governed by the principles of reason, riches and honors are the subjects of shame." No: until I want the protection of Massachusetts to be extended to me in some distant Southern port, where my liberty is endangered, or until I am bent solely on building up an estate at home by peaceful enterprise, I can afford to refuse allegiance to Massachusetts, and her right to my property and life. It costs me less in every sense to incur the penalty of disobedience to the State than it would to obey. I should feel as if I were worth less in that case.

Some years ago, the State met me in behalf of the Church, and commanded me to pay a certain sum toward the support of a clergyman whose preaching my father attended, but never I myself. "Pay," it said, "or be locked up in the jail." I declined to pay. But, unfortunately, another man saw fit to pay it. I did not see why the schoolmaster should be taxed to support the priest, and not the priest the schoolmaster; for I was not the State's schoolmaster, but I supported myself by voluntary subscription. I did not see why the lyceum should not present its tax-bill, and have the State to back its demand, as well as the Church. However, at the request of the selectmen, I condescended to make some such statement as this in writing:—"Know all men by these presents, that I, Henry Thoreau, do not wish to be regarded as a member of any incorporated society which I have not joined." This I gave to the town clerk; and he has it. The State, having thus learned that I did not wish to be regarded as a member of that church, has never made a like demand on me since; though it said that it must adhere to its original presumption that time. If I had known how to name them, I should then have signed off in detail from all the societies which I never signed on to; but I did not know where to find a complete list.

I have paid no poll-tax for six years. I was put into a jail once on this account, for one night; and, as I stood considering the walls of solid stone, two or three feet thick, the door of wood and iron, a foot thick, and the iron grating which strained the light, I could not help being struck with the foolishness of that institution which treated me as if I were mere flesh and blood and bones, to be locked up. I wondered that it should have concluded at length that this was the best use it could put me to, and had never thought to avail itself of my services in some way. I saw that, if there was a wall of stone between me and my townsmen, there was a still more difficult one to climb or break through before they could get to be as free as I was. I did not for a moment feel confined, and the walls seemed a great waste of stone and mortar. I felt as if I alone of all my townsmen had paid my tax. They plainly did not know how to treat me, but behaved like persons who are underbred. In every threat and in every compliment there was a blunder; for they thought that my chief desire was to stand the other side of that stone wall. I could not but smile to see how industriously they locked the door on my meditations, which followed them out again without let or hindrance, and *they* were really all that was dangerous. As they could not reach me, they had resolved to punish my body; just as boys, if they cannot come at some person against whom they have a spite, will abuse his dog. I saw that the State was half-witted, that it was timid as a lone woman with her silver spoons, and that it did not know its friends from its foes, and I lost all my remaining respect for it, and pitied it.

Thus the State never intentionally confronts a man's sense, intellectual or moral, but only his body, his senses. It is not armed with superior wit or honesty, but with superior physical strength. I was not born to be forced. I will breathe after my own fashion. Let us see who is the strongest. What force has a multitude? They only can force me who obey a higher law than I. They force me to become like themselves. I do not hear of *men* being *forced* to live this way or that by masses of men. What sort of life were that to live? When I meet a government which says to me, "Your money or your life," why should I be in haste to give it my money? It may be in a great strait, and not know what to do: I cannot help that. It must help itself; do as I do. It is not worth the while to snivel about it. I am not responsible for the successful working of the machinery of society. I am not the son of the engineer. I perceive that, when an acorn and a chestnut fall side by side, the one does not remain inert to make way for the other, but both obey their own laws, and spring and grow and flourish as best they can, till one, perchance, overshadows and destroys the other. If a plant cannot live according to its nature, it dies; and so a man.

The night in prison was novel and interesting enough. The prisoners in their shirt-sleeves were enjoying a chat and the evening air in the doorway, when I entered. But the jailer said, "Come, boys, it is time to lock up;" and so they dispersed, and I heard the sound of their steps returning into the hollow apartments. My room-mate was introduced to me by the jailer, as "a first-rate fellow and a clever man." When the door was locked, he showed me where to hang my hat, and how he managed matters there. The rooms were whitewashed once a month; and this one, at least, was the whitest, most simply furnished, and probably the neatest apartment in the town. He naturally wanted to know where I came from, and what brought me there; and, when I had told him, I asked him in my turn how he came there, presuming him to be an honest man, of course; and, as the world goes, I believe he was. "Why," said he, "they accuse me of burning a barn; but I never did it." As near as I could discover, he had probably gone to bed in a barn when drunk, and smoked his pipe there; and so a barn was burnt. He had the reputation of being a clever man, had been there some three months waiting for his trial to come on, and would have to wait as much longer; but he was quite domesticated and contented, since he got his board for nothing, and thought that he was well treated.

He occupied one window, and I the other; and I saw that if one stayed there long, his principal business would be to look out the window. I had soon read all the tracts that were left there, and examined where former prisoners had broken out, and where a grate had been sawed off, and heard the history of the various occupants of that room; for I found that even here there was a history and a gossip which never circulated beyond the walls of the jail. Probably this is the only house in the town where verses are composed, which are afterward printed in a circular form, but not published. I was shown quite a long list of verses which were composed by some young men who had been detected in an attempt to escape, who avenged themselves by singing them.

I pumped my fellow-prisoner as dry as I could, for fear I should never see him again; but at length he showed me which was my bed, and left me to blow out the lamp.

It was like traveling into a far country, such as I had never expected to behold, to lie there for one night. It seemed to me that I never had heard the town clock strike before, nor the evening sounds of the village; for we slept with the windows open, which were inside the grating. It was to see my native village in the light of the Middle Ages, and our Concord was turned into a Rhine stream, and visions of knights and castles passed before me. They were the voices of old burghers that I heard in the streets. I was an involuntary spectator and auditor of whatever was done and said in the kitchen of the adjacent village-inn,—a wholly new and rare experience to me. It was a closer view of my native town. I was fairly inside of it. I never had seen its institutions before. This is one of its peculiar institutions; for it is a shire town. I began to comprehend what its inhabitants were about.

In the morning, our breakfasts were put through the hole in the door, in small oblong-square tin pans, made to fit, and holding a pint of chocolate, with brown bread, and an iron spoon. When they called for the vessels again, I was green enough to return what bread I had left; but my comrade seized it, and said that I should lay that up for lunch or dinner. Soon after he was let out to work at haying in a neighboring field, whither he went every day, and would not be back till noon; so he bade me good-day, saying that he doubted if he should see me again.

When I came out of prison,—for some one interfered, and paid that tax,—I did not perceive that great changes had taken place on the common, such as he observed who went in a youth and emerged a tottering and gray-headed man; and yet a change had to my eyes come over the scene,—the town, and State, and country,—greater than any that mere time could effect. I saw yet more distinctly the State in which I lived. I saw to what extent the people among whom I lived could be trusted as good neighbors and friends; that their friendship was for summer weather only; that they did not greatly propose to do right; that they were a distinct race from me by their prejudices and superstitions, as the Chinamen and Malays are; that in their sacrifices to humanity they ran no risks, not even to their property; that after all they were not so noble but they treated the thief as he had treated them, and hoped, by a certain outward observance and a few prayers, and by walking in a particular straight though useless path from time to time, to save their souls. This may be to judge my neighbors harshly; for I believe that many of them are not aware that they have such an institution as the jail in their village.

It was formerly the custom in our village, when a poor debtor came out of jail, for his acquaintances to salute him, looking through their fingers, which were crossed to represent the grating of a jail window, "How do ye do?" My neighbors did not thus salute me, but first looked at me, and then at one another, as if I had returned from a long journey. I was put into jail as I was going to the shoemaker's to get a shoe which was mended. When I was let out the next morning, I proceeded to finish my errand, and having put on my mended shoe, joined a huckleberry party, who were impatient to put themselves under my conduct; and in half an hour,—for the horse was soon tackled,—was in the midst of a huckleberry field, on one of our highest hills, two miles off, and then the State was nowhere to be seen.

This is the whole history of "My Prisons."

I have never declined paying the highway tax, because I am as desirous of being a good neighbor as I am of being a bad subject; and as for supporting schools, I am doing my part to educate my fellow-countrymen now. It is for no particular item in the tax-bill that I refuse to pay it. I simply wish to refuse allegiance to the State, to withdraw and stand aloof from it effectually. I do not care to trace the course of my dollar, if I could, till it buys a man or a musket to shoot one with,—the dollar is innocent,—but I am concerned to trace the effects of my allegiance. In fact, I quietly declare war with the State, after my fashion, though I will still make what use and get what advantage of her I can, as is usual in such cases.

If others pay the tax which is demanded of me, from a sympathy with the State, they do but what they have already done in their own case, or rather they abet injustice to a greater extent than the State requires. If they pay the tax from a mistaken interest in the individual taxed, to save his property, or prevent his going to jail, it is because they have not considered wisely how far they let their private feelings interfere with the public good.

This, then, is my position at present. But one cannot be too much on his guard in such a case, lest his action be biased by obstinacy or an undue regard for the opinions of men. Let him see that he does only what belongs to himself and to the hour.

I think sometimes, Why, this people mean well, they are only ignorant; they would do better if they knew how: why give your neighbors this pain to treat you as they are not inclined to? But I think again, This is no reason why I should do as they do, or permit others to suffer much greater pain of a different kind. Again, I sometimes say to myself, When many millions of men, without heat, without ill will, without personal feeling of any kind, demand of you a few shillings only, without the possibility, such is their constitution, of retracting or altering their present demand, and without the possibility, on your side, of appeal to any other millions, why expose yourself to this overwhelming brute force? You do not resist cold and hunger, the winds and the waves, thus obstinately; you quietly submit to a thousand similar necessities. You do not put your head into the fire. But just in proportion as I regard this as not wholly a brute force, but partly a human force, and consider that I have relations to those millions as to so many millions of men, and not of mere brute or inanimate things, I see that appeal is possible, first and instantaneously, from them to the Maker of them, and, secondly, from them to themselves. But if I put my head deliberately into the fire, there is no appeal to fire or to the Maker of fire, and I have only myself to blame. If I could convince myself that I have any right to be satisfied with men as they are, and to treat them accordingly, and not according, in some respects, to my requisitions and expectations of what they and I ought to be, then, like a good Mussulman and fatalist, I should endeavor to be satisfied with things as they are, and say it is the will of God. And, above all, there is this difference between resisting this and a purely brute or natural force, that I can resist this with some effect; but I cannot expect, like Orpheus, to change the nature of the rocks and trees and beasts.

I do not wish to quarrel with any man or nation. I do not wish to split hairs, to make fine distinctions, or set myself up as better than my neighbors. I seek rather, I may say, even an excuse for conforming to the laws of the land. I am but too ready to conform to them. Indeed, I have reason to suspect myself on this head; and each year, as the tax-gatherer comes round, I find myself disposed to review the acts and position of the general and State governments, and the spirit of the people, to discover a pretext for conformity.

"We must affect our country as our parents,
And if at any time we alienate
Our love or industry from doing it honor,
We must respect effects and teach the soul
Matter of conscience and religion,
And not desire of rule or benefit."

I believe that the State will soon be able to take all my work of this sort out of my hands, and then I shall be no better a patriot than my fellow-countrymen. Seen from a lower point of view, the Constitution, with all its faults, is very good; the law and the courts are very respectable; even this State and this American government are, in many respects, very admirable, and rare things, to be thankful for, such as a great many have described them; but seen from a point of view a little higher, they are what I have described them; seen from a higher still, and the highest, who shall say what they are, or that they are worth looking at or thinking of at all?

However, the government does not concern me much, and I shall bestow the fewest possible thoughts on it. It is not many moments that I live under a government, even in this world. If a man is thought-free, fancy-free, imagination-free, that which *is not* never for a long time appearing *to be* to him, unwise rulers or reformers cannot fatally interrupt him.

I know that most men think differently from myself; but those whose lives are by profession devoted to the study of these or kindred subjects content me as little as any. Statesmen and legislators, standing so completely within the institution, never distinctly and nakedly behold it. They speak of moving society, but have no resting-place without it. They may be men of a certain experience and discrimination, and have no doubt invented ingenious and even useful systems, for which we sincerely thank them; but all their wit and usefulness lie within certain not very wide limits. They are wont to forget that the world is not governed by policy and expediency. Webster never goes behind government, and so cannot speak with authority about it. His words are wisdom to those legislators who contemplate no essential reform in the existing government; but for thinkers, and those who legislate for all time, he never once glances at the subject. I know of those whose serene and wise speculations on this theme would soon reveal the limits of his mind's range and hospitality. Yet, compared with the cheap professions of most reformers, and the still cheaper wisdom and eloquence of politicians in general, his are almost the only sensible and valuable words, and we thank Heaven for him. Comparatively, he is always strong, original, and, above all, practical. Still, his quality is not wisdom, but prudence. The lawyer's truth is not Truth, but consistency or a consistent expediency. Truth is always in harmony with herself, and is not concerned chiefly to reveal the justice that may consist with wrong-doing. He well deserves to be called, as he has been called, the Defender of the Constitution. There are really no blows to be given by him but defensive ones. He is not a leader, but a follower. His leaders are the men of '87. "I have never made an effort," he says, "and never propose to make an effort; I have never countenanced an effort, and never mean to countenance an effort, to disturb the arrangement as originally made, by which the various States came into the Union." Still thinking of the sanction which the Constitution gives to slavery, he says, "Because it was a part of the original compact,—let it stand." Notwithstanding his special acuteness and ability, he is unable to take a fact out of its merely political relations, and behold it as it lies absolutely to be disposed of by the intellect,—what, for instance, it behooves a man to do here in America to-day with regard to slavery,—but ventures, or is driven, to make some such desperate answer as the following, while professing to speak absolutely, and as a private man,—from which what new and singular code of social duties might be inferred? "The manner," says he, "in which the governments of those States where slavery exists are to regulate it is for their own consideration, under their responsibility to their constituents, to the general laws of propriety, humanity, and justice, and to God. Associations formed elsewhere, springing from a feeling of humanity, or any other cause, have nothing whatever to do with it. They have never received any encouragement from me, and they never will."[1]

They who know of no purer sources of truth, who have traced up its stream no higher, stand, and wisely stand, by the Bible and the Constitution, and drink at it there with reverence and humility; but they who behold where it comes trickling into this lake or that pool, gird up their loins once more, and continue their pilgrimage toward its fountain-head.

No man with a genius for legislation has appeared in America. They are rare in the history of the world. There are orators, politicians, and eloquent men, by the thousand; but the speaker has not yet opened his mouth to speak who is capable of settling the much-vexed questions of the day. We love eloquence for its own sake, and not for any truth which it may utter, or any heroism it may inspire. Our legislators have not yet learned the comparative value of free trade and of freedom, of union, and of rectitude, to a nation. They have no genius or talent for comparatively humble questions of taxation and finance, commerce and manufactures and agriculture. If we were left solely to the wordy wit of legislators in Congress for our guidance, uncorrected by the seasonable experience and the effectual complaints of the people, America would not long retain her rank among the nations. For eighteen hundred years, though perchance I have no right to say it, the New Testament has been written; yet where is the legislator who has wisdom and practical talent enough to avail himself of the light which it sheds on the science of legislation?

The authority of government, even such as I am willing to submit to,—for

I will cheerfully obey those who know and can do better than I, and in many things even those who neither know nor can do so well,—is still an impure one: to be strictly just, it must have the sanction and consent of the governed. It can have no pure right over my person and property but what I concede to it. The progress from an absolute to a limited monarchy, from a limited monarchy to a democracy, is a progress toward a true respect for the individual. Even the Chinese philosopher was wise enough to regard the individual as the basis of the empire. Is a democracy, such as we know it, the last improvement possible in government? Is it not possible to take a step further towards recognizing and organizing the rights of man? There will never be a really free and enlightened State until the State comes to recognize the individual as a higher and independent power, from which all its own power and authority are derived, and treats him accordingly. I please myself with imagining a State at last which can afford to be just to all men, and to treat the individual with respect as a neighbor; which even would not think it inconsistent with its own repose if a few were to live aloof from it, not meddling with it, nor embraced by it, who fulfilled all the duties of neighbors and fellow-men. A State which bore this kind of fruit, and suffered it to drop off as fast as it ripened, would prepare the way for a still more perfect and glorious State, which also I have imagined, but not yet anywhere seen.

NOTE

1. These extracts have been inserted since the lecture was read.

15

The Divine Call

Carry A. Nation

Carry Amelia Nation (1846–1911) became a public figure in the Midwest and throughout the nation as a result of her saloon "hatchetations." Wielding an ax with a sense that she was a new Deborah (the ancient Hebrew judge of the Bible), in the 1890s she began—as a Women's Christian Temperance Union activist—to smash saloon property in Kansas and to interfere with the liquor trade, which was there illegal. She spent time in jail—more than thirty times in and out of Kansas—and she endured brutal mob violence and other forms of legal harassment. Married twice (she left her alcoholic first husband, who later died, after half a year, and her second husband divorced her on grounds of desertion after twenty-seven years) and an outspoken feminist, she argued that women needed the right to vote in order to help reform the nation. Although many have dismissed her as a postmenopausal virago and a woman mentally disturbed, new scholarship demonstrates that she needs to be taken seriously in human and religious terms. She grew up in a household that followed Alexander Campbell, whose movement generated the Disciples of Christ and, later, the Churches of Christ. She was early exposed to African-American slave religion; later experienced a holiness spirit baptism that gave her a personal sense of conviction regarding sanctification; and incorporated throughout her life aspects of Free Methodism, the Salvation Army, and Roman Catholic devotionalism. What brought all of this into unified religious expression, however, was the spirituality of the prophetic path. Although her actions were not without midwestern precedent, as her letters, diaries, and autobiography (excerpted here) show, Carry Nation was firmly convinced that she was God's instrument.

At the time these dives were open, contrary to the statutes of our state, the officers were really in league with this lawless element. I was heavily burdened and could see "the wicked walking on every side, and the vilest men exalted." (Ps. 12:8.) I was ridiculed, was called "meddler," "crazy," was pointed to as a fanatic. I spent much time in tears, prayer and fasting. I would fast days at a time. One day I was so sad; I opened the Bible with a prayer for light, and saw these words: "Arise, shine, for thy light is come and the glory of the Lord is risen upon thee." (Isa. 60:1.) These words gave me unbounded delight.

From *The Use and Need of the Life of Carry A. Nation* written by herself [1909].

I ran to a sister and said: "There is to be a change in my life."

As Jail Evangelist for the W.C.T.U. in Medicine Lodge, I would ask the men in prison, young and old, why are you here? The answer was, it was "drink," "drink." I said, why do you get drunk in Kansas where we have no saloons? They told me that they got their drink in Kiowa. This town was in Barber county, a county right on the border of Oklahoma. I went to Mr. Sam Griffin, the County Attorney, time after time, telling him of these men being in jail from drink. He would put the matter off and seem very much annoyed because I asked him to do what he swore he would do, for he was oath bound to get out a warrant and put this in the hands of the sheriff who was oath bound to arrest these dive-keepers, and put them in jail and the place or dive was to be publicly abated or destroyed. Mr. Griffin was determined that these dive-keepers should not be arrested. I even went down to Kiowa myself and went into these places and came back asking this County Attorney to take my evidence and he would not do it. Then I wrote to Mr. A. A. Godard of Topeka, the State's Attorney, whose duty it was to see that all the County Attorneys did their duties. I saw he did not intend to do anything, then I went to William Stanley the Governor at Topeka. I told him of the prisoners in jail in our county from the sale of liquor in the dives of Kiowa, told him of the broken families and trouble of all kinds in the county, told him of two murders that had been committed in the county, one alone costing the tax payers $8,000.00, told him of the broken hearted women and the worse than fatherless children as the result. I found out that he would not do his duty. I had gone from the lowest to the chief-executive of the state, and after appealing to the governor in vain I found that I could go to no other authority on earth.

Now I saw that Kansas was in the power of the bitter foe to the constitution, and that they had accomplished what the whiskey men and their tools, the Republican party and politicians had schemed and worked for. When two thirds of the voters of Kansas said at the ballot box—about 1880, I think it was—"We will not have a saloon in our state." This was made constitutional by the two-thirds majority. Nothing could change this or take it out of the constitution except by having the amendment re-submitted and two-thirds of the people voting to bring the saloons back. They intended then with their bribes and otherwise to buy votes. The first act was to organize the state into what they called the "Mystic Order of Brotherhood." Of course this was kept very quiet and few of the people in the towns knew of this order and organization. When the Devil wants to carry out his deepest plots he must do, through a secret order, what he cannot otherwise do. He does his work through, by, and in, the kingdom of darkness. For this one reason he must hoodwink the people to make them his tools.

God has given me a mean fight, a dirty and dangerous fight; for it is a war on the hidden things of darkness. I am, in this book throwing all the light I can on the dangerous foe to liberty, free speech and Christianity, the Masonic Lodge, which is the father of all the other secret orders. Through this Mystic Order of Brotherhood managing the primaries and elections, they got into office from constable up to the governor, the tools of the liquor power. The great question that was then discussed was "re-submission." Every representative to congress at Topeka was in favor of the re-submission without an exception. Money was sent into Kansas by the thousands from brewers and distillers to be used by politicians for the purpose of bringing about re-submission. Kansas was the storm center. If the liquor men could bring back saloons into Kansas then a great blow would be struck against prohibition in all the states. This would discourage the people all over. Their great word was, "you can't," "prohibition will not prohibit." I do not belong to the "can't" family. When I was born my father wrote my name Carry A. Moore, then later it was Nation, which is more still. C. A. N. are the initials of my name, then C. (see) A. Nation! And all together Carry A. Nation! This is no accident but Providence. This does not mean that I will carry a nation, but that the roused heart and conscience will, as I am the roused heart and conscience of the people. There are just two crowds, God's crowd and the Devil's crowd. One gains the battle by can, and the other loses it by can't.

My Christian experience will give you the secret of my life, it is God indwelling. When I found I could effect nothing through the officials, I was sad, indeed. I saw that Kansas homes, hearts and souls were to be sacrificed. I had lost all the hopes of my young life through drink, I saw the terrible butchery that would follow. I felt that I had rather die than to see the saloons come back into Kansas. I felt desperate. I took this to God daily, feeling that he only could rescue. On the 5th of June, 1899 before retiring, I threw myself face downward at the foot of my bed at my home in Medicine Lodge. I poured out my grief and agony to God, in about this strain: "Oh Lord you see the treason in Kansas, they are going to break the mothers' hearts, they are going to send the boys to drunkards' graves and a drunkard's hell. I have exhausted all my means, Oh Lord, you have plenty of ways. You have used the base things and the weak things, use me to save Kansas. I have but one life to give you, If I had a thousand, I would give them all, please show me something to do." The next morning I was awakened by a voice which seemed to be speaking in my heart, these words, "Go to Kiowa," and my hands were lifted and thrown down and the words, "I'll stand by you." The words, "Go to Kiowa," were spoken in a murmuring, musical tone, low and soft, but, "I'll stand by you," was very clear, positive and emphatic. I was impressed with a great inspiration, the interpretation was very plain, it was this: "Take something in your hands, and throw at these places in Kiowa and smash them." I was very much relieved and overjoyed and was determined to be, "obedient to the heavenly vision." (Acts 26:19.) I told no one what I heard or what I intended to do.

I was a busy home keeper, did all my house work, was superintendent of two Sunday schools, one in the country, was jail evangelist, and president of the W.C.T.U. and kept open house for all of God's people, where all the Christian workers were welcome to abide at my house.

When no one was looking I would walk out in the yard and pick up brick bats and rocks, would hide them under my kitchen apron, would take them in my room, would wrap them up in newspapers one by one. I did this until I got quite a pile. A very sneaking degenerate druggist in Medicine Lodge named Southworth, had for years been selling intoxicating liquors on the sly. I had gotten in his drug store four bottles of Schlitz Malt. I was going to use them as evidence to convict this wiley dive keeper.

One of the bottles I took to a W.C.T.U. meeting and in the presence of the ladies I opened it and drank the contents. Then I had two of them to take me down to a Doctor's office. I fell limp on the sofa and said: "Doctor, what is the matter with me?"

He looked at my eyes, felt my heart and pulse, shook his head and looked grave.

I said: "Am I poisoned?" "Yes, said the Doctor."

I said: "What poisoned me is that beer you recommended Bro. ——— to take as a tonic." I resorted to this stratagem, to show the effect that beer has upon the system. This Doctor was a kind man and meant well, but it must have been ignorance that made him say beer could ever be used as a medicine.

There was another, Dr. Kocile, in Medicine Lodge who used to sell all the whiskey he could. He made a drunkard of a very prominent woman of the town, who took the Keeley cure. She told the W.C.T.U. of the villainy of this doctor and she could not have hated any one more. Oh! the drunkards the doctors are making! No physician, who is worthy of the name will prescribe it as a medicine, for there is not one medical quality in alcohol. It kills the living and preserves the dead. Never preserves anything but death. It is made by a rotting process and it rots the brain, body and soul; it paralyzes the vascular circulation and increases the action of the heart. This is friction and friction in any machinery is dangerous, and the cure is not hastened but delayed.

Any physician that will prescribe whiskey or alcohol as a medicine is either a fool or a knave. A fool because he does not understand his business, for even saying that alcohol does arouse the action of the heart, there are medicines that will do that and will not produce the fatal results of alcoholism, which is the worst of all diseases. He is a knave because his practice is a matter of getting a case, and a fee at the same time, like a machine agent who breaks the machine to get the job of mending it. Alcohol destroys the normal condition of all the functions of the body. The stomach is thrown out of fix, and the patient goes to the doctor for a stomach pill, the heart, liver, kidneys, and in fact, the whole body is in a deranged condition, and the doctor has a perpetual patient. I sincerely believe this to be the reason why many physicians prescribe it.

At half past three that day I was ready to start, hitched up the buggy myself, drove out of the stable, rode down a hill and over a bridge that was just outside the limits of Medicine Lodge. I saw in the middle of the road perhaps a dozen or so creatures in the forms of men leaning towards the buggy as if against a rope which prevented them from coming nearer. Their faces were those of demons and the gestures of their hands as if they would tear me up. I did not know what to do, but I lifted my hands, and my eyes to God, saying: "Oh! Lord, help me, help me." When I looked down these diabolical creatures were not in front of the buggy, but they were off to the right fleeing as if they were terrified. I did not know or think what this meant. My life was so full of strange, peculiar things at that time that I could not understand the meaning. Not for years did I interpret the meaning of this vision. I know now what those creatures were. They were real devils that knew more of what I was going to do than I did. The devil is a prophet, he reads scripture, he knew Jesus when He was here, and he knew that I came to fulfill prophecy, and that this was a death blow to his kingdom.

The peoples' consciences were asleep while these dreadful burglars of saloons were robbing the homes and God had to shock them to rouse them up. God cannot work with a people whose conscience is dead. The devil cannot continue with an awakened conscience. I expected to stay all night with a dear friend, Sister Springer, who lived about half way to Kiowa. When I arrived near her home the sun was almost down, but I was very eager to go to Kiowa and I said: "Oh, Lord, if it is Thy will for me to go to Kiowa tonight, have Price, (my horse,) pass this open gate," which I knew he would never do unless God ordered it. I gave him the reins and when I got opposite the open gate my horse jumped forward as if some one had struck him a blow. I got to Kiowa at half past eight, stayed all night. Next morning I had my horse hitched and drove to the first dive kept by a Mr. Dobson, whose brother was then sheriff of the county. I stacked up these smashers on my left arm, all I could hold. They looked like packages wrapped in paper. I stood before the counter and said: "Mr. Dobson, I told you last spring to close this place, you did not do it, now I have come down with another remonstrance, get out of the way, I do not want to strike you, but I am going to break this place up." I threw as hard, and as fast as I could, smashing mirrors and bottles and glasses and it was astonishing how quickly this was done. These men seemed terrified, threw up their hands and backed up in the corner. My strength was that of a giant. I felt invincible. God was certainly standing by me.

I will tell you of a very strange thing. As the stones were flying against this "wonderful and horrible" thing, I saw Mr. McKinley, the President, sitting in an old fashion arm chair and as the stones would strike I saw them hit the chair and the chair fell to pieces, and I saw Mr. McKinley fall over. I did not understand this until very recently, now I know that the smashing in Kansas was intended to strike the head of this nation the hardest blow, for every saloon I smashed in Kansas had a license from the head of this government which made the head of the government more responsible than the dive-keeper. I broke up three of these dives that day, broke the windows on the outside to prove that the man who rents his house is a partner also with the man who sells. The party who licenses and the paper that advertises, all have a hand in this and are *particeps criminis*. I smashed five saloons with rocks, before I ever took a hatchet.

In the last place, kept by Lewis, there was quite a young man behind the bar. I said to him: "Young man, come from behind that bar, your mother did not raise you for such a place." I threw a brick at the mirror, which was a very heavy one, and it did not break, but the brick fell and broke everything in its way. I began to look around for something that would break it. I was standing by a billiard table on which there was one ball. I said: "Thank God," and picked it up, threw it, and it made a hole in the mirror.

By this time, the streets were crowded with people; most of them seemed to look puzzled. There was one boy about fifteen years old who seemed perfectly wild with joy, and he jumped, skipped and yelled with delight. I have since thought of that as being a significant sign. For to smash saloons will save the boy.

I stood in the middle of the street and spoke in this way: "I have destroyed three of your places of business, and if I have broken a statute of Kansas, put me in jail; if I am not a law-breaker your mayor and councilmen are. You must arrest one of us, for if I am not a criminal, they are."

One of the councilmen, who was a butcher, said: "Don't you think we can attend to our business."

"Yes," I said, "You can, but you won't. As Jail Evangelist of Medicine Lodge, I know you have manufactured many criminals and this county is burdened down with taxes to prosecute the results of these dives. Two murders have been committed in the last five years in this county, one in a dive I have just destroyed. You are a butcher of hogs and cattle, but they are butchering men, women and children, positively contrary to the laws of God and man, and the mayor and councilmen are more to blame than the jointist, and now if I have done wrong in any particular arrest me." When I was through with my speech I got into my buggy and said: "I'll go home."

The marshal held my horse and said: "Not yet; the mayor wishes to see you."

I drove up to where he was, and the man who owned one of the dive buildings I had smashed was standing by Dr. Korn, the mayor, and said: "I want you to pay for the front windows you broke of my building."

I said: "No, you are a partner of the dive-keeper and the statutes hold your building responsible. The man that rents the building for any business is no better than the man who carries on the business, and you are party to the crime." They ran back and forward to the city attorney several times. At last they came and told me I could go. As I drove through the streets the reins fell out of my hands and I, standing up in my buggy; lifted my hands twice, saying: ("Peace on earth, good will to men.") This action I know was done through the inspiration of the Holy Spirit. "Peace on earth, good will to men," being the result of the destruction of saloons and the motive for destroying them.

When I reached Medicine Lodge the town was in quite an excitement, the news having been telegraphed ahead. I drove through the streets and told the people I would be at the postoffice corner to tell them of my work in the jail here, and the young men's lives that had been ruined, and the broken hearted mothers, the taxation that had been brought on the county, and other wrongs of the dives of Kiowa; of how I had been to the sheriff, Mr. Gano, and the prosecuting attorney, Mr. Griffin; how I had written to the state's attorney general, Mr. Godard, and I saw there was a conspiracy with the party in power to violate their oaths, and refuse to enforce the constitution of Kansas, and I did only what they swore they would do. I had a letter from a Mr. Long, of Kiowa, saying that Mr. Griffin, the prosecuting attorney, was taking bribes, and that he and the sheriff were drinking and gambling in the dives at Kiowa.

This smashing aroused the people of the county to this outrage and these dive-keepers were arrested, although we did not ask the prosecuting attorney to get out a warrant, or sheriff to make an arrest. Neither did we take the case before any justice of the peace in Kiowa or Medicine Lodge, for they belong to the republican party and would prevent the prosecution. The cases were taken out in the country several miles from Kiowa before Moses E. Wright, a Free Methodist and a justice of the peace of Moore township.

The men were found guilty, and for the first time in the history of Barber county, all dives were closed. Of course it took two or three months to accomplish this and not a word was said about suing me for slander, until after the dives were closed. Then I began to hear that Sam Griffin was going to sue me for slander, because I said he took bribes. The papers were served on me, but I was not at all alarmed, for I thought it would give me an opportunity to bring out the facts of the case. I knew little about the tricks of lawyers, and the unfair ruling of judges.

I will here speak of the attitude of some of the W.C.T.U. concerning the smashing. Most of this grand body of women endorsed me from the first. A few weeks after the Kiowa raid, I held a convention in Medicine Lodge. I got letters from various W.C.T.U. workers of the state, that they would hold my convention for me. I said: "No, I will hold my own convention."

Up to this time, no one had ever offered to hold my convention, and I fully understood, that the W.C.T.U. did not want it to go out that they endorsed me in my work at Kiowa. The state president came to my home the first day of the convention. I believe this was done, thinking I would ask her to preside at the meeting, or convention. I was glad to see her and asked her to conduct a parliamentary drill. She came to me privately and asked me to state to the convention that the W.C.T.U. knew nothing about the smashing at Kiowa and was not responsible for this act of mine. I did so, saying the "honor of smashing the saloons at Kiowa would have to be ascribed to me alone, as the W.C.T.U. did not wish any of it." So far as Sister Hutchinson, who is, and has been the president for some time, is concerned, I believe her to be a conscientious woman, and whose heart is in the right place. She and I have been the best of friends and love each other, and she has often defended me and spoken well of my work. But I think the W.C.T.U. would be much more effective under her management, if she had understood that Stanley, the republican governor, wished to handicap her in her prohibition work when he appointed her husband as physician in the reformatory at Hutchinson, Kansas. Be it said to the credit of this Christian physician he never used alcohol in his practice. And perhaps other bearings have prevented her from seeing that the republican pressure has injured our work more than anything else in Kansas. Many of the wives of these political wirepullers are prominent in the Union. A W.C.T.U. [worker] must of necessity be a prohibitionist, for her pledge is a prohibition pledge, not a temperance one.

The Free Methodists although few in number, and considered a church of but small influence, have been a great power in reform. They were the abolitionists of negro slavery to a man, and now they are the abolitionists of the liquor curse. They were also my friends in this smashing. Father Wright and Bro. Atwood were at the convention I speak of. Father Wright, who has been an old soldier for the defence of Truth for many years said to me: "Never mind, Sister Nation, when they see the way the cat jumps, you will have plenty of friends." The ministers were also my friends and approved of the smashing. Bro. McClain, of the Christian church, was at the convention, and he was trying to apologize for the smashing and defend me at the same time, [and] he said: "We all make mistakes and crooked paths, and Sister Nation we all know, tries to do right, and even if she did some crooked things, all the rest of us do the same thing."

I appreciated his motive, but for the sake of others, I replied: "I could not see that the term 'crooked' should be used. I rolled up the rocks as *straight* as I could, I placed them *straight* in the box, hitched up my horse *straight*, drove *straight* to Kiowa, walked *straight* in the saloon, threw *straight*, and broke them up in the *straightest* manner, drove home *straight*, and I did not make a *crooked* step in smashing." This of course was pleasantry, but it was the way I took to justify myself, as but few seemed to see the merit or result of this crusade.

I never explained to the people that God told me to do this for some months, for I tried to shield myself from the almost universal opinion that I was partially insane.

I will now speak of my persecution for so-called slandering the prosecuting attorney. As I said, no one mentioned such a thing until the dives were closed. Closing the joints, called attention to the perjury of the county officials, for it was proven to be their fault, that we have dives in Kansas. In order to direct the attention from themselves, as perjurers, and to me, and to be avenged, they put their heads together to bring this suit against me. Mr. Griffin was no more to blame in this matter than the rest of the republicans. A. L. Noble, Polly Tincher, Ed. Sample and Mr. Herr, the city attorney of Kiowa, were all employed by Sam Griffin. This practically took all the legal ability, leaving one, G. A. Martin, whom I retained. I had witnesses enough to prove gambling and drinking in these dives by Mr. Griffin and the sheriff; had sufficient testimony to justify me in saying what I did. The republican judge of Kingman, Gillette, ruled out my testimony right through. If my case had been conducted properly by my lawyer, and proper exceptions taken, I could have taken the case to the supreme court, and had it reversed on several rulings. Judge Stevens and Judge Lacey, who were at the trial, told me they never saw such determination on the part of any judge to cut out the defense as the rulings of Judge Gillette. It was evident that everything was cut and dried before going into court. Judge Gillette had several pages of instructions to the jury, telling them their duty was to convict and that the damages should be a large sum. I had these instructions examined by a good lawyer, Mr. Duminel, of Topeka, and he said the judge overleaped his prerogative. He should have told the jury the facts and the statute governing slander, but his instructions were an appeal and command to convict me. This Judge Gillette has a reputation for being a respectable citizen, but his zeal to save from disgrace his republican colleagues led him to thus persecute a loyal woman Home Defender of Kansas, and protect the rum defenders, and republican schemers, who have done more to injure prohibition in Kansas than any other party. If a democrat wanted to carry on a dive, republicans would grant him the permit to do so.

The jury brought in a verdict of guilty; but the damages to the character of this republican county attorney was one dollar, and of course I sent him the dollar, but the cost which was, including all, about two hundred dollars was assessed to me and a judgment put on a piece of property, which I paid off, by the sale of my little hatchets, and lectures. Strange these trials never caused me to become discouraged, rather the reverse. I knew I was right, and God in his own time would come to my help. The more injustice I suffered, the more cause I had to resent the wrongs. I always felt that I was keeping others out of trouble, when I was in. I had resolved that at the first opportunity I would go to Wichita and break up some of the bold outlawed murder-mills there. I thought perhaps it was God's will to make me a sacrifice as he did John Brown, and I knew this was a defiance of the national intrigue of both republican and democratic parties, when I destroyed this malicious property, which afforded them a means of enslaving the people, taxing them to gather a revenue they could squander, and giving them political jobs, thus creating a force to manage the interest and take care of the results of a business where the advantage was in the graft it gave to them and the brewers and distillers.

In two weeks from the close of this trial, on the 27th of December, 1900, I went to Wichita, almost seven months after the raid in Kiowa. Mr. Nation went to see his brother, Mr. Seth Nation, in eastern Kansas, and I was free to leave home. Monday was the 26th, the day I started. The Sunday before, the 25th, I went to the Baptist Sunday school, then to the Presbyterian for preaching, and at the close walked over to the Methodist church for class meeting. I could not keep from weeping, but I controlled myself the best I could. I did not know but that it would be the last time I would ever see my dear friends again, and could not tell them why. I gave my testimony at the class meeting; spoke particularly to members of the choir about their extravagant dress; told them that a poor sinner coming there for relief would be driven away, to see such a vanity fair in front. I begged them to dress neither in gold, silver or costly array, and spoke of the sin of wearing the corpses of dead birds and plumage of birds, and closed by saying: "These may be my dying words." At the close Sister Shell, a W.C.T.U. said to me: "What do you mean by 'my dying words?' for you never looked better in your life." I said: "You will know later."

I took a valise with me, and in that valise I put a rod of iron, perhaps a foot long, and as large around as my thumb. I also took a cane with me. I found out by smashing in Kiowa that I could use a rock but once, so I took the cane with me. I got down to Wichita about seven o'clock in the evening, that day, and went to the hotel near the Santa Fe depot and left my valise. I went up town to select the place I would begin at first. I went into about fourteen places, where men were drinking at bars, the same as they do in licensed places. The police standing with the others. This outrage of law and decency was in violation of the oaths taken by every city officer, including mayor and councilmen, and they were as much bound to destroy these joints as they would be to arrest a murderer, or break up a den of thieves, but many of these so-called officers encouraged the violation of the law and patronized these places. I have often explained that this was the scheme of politicians and brewers to make prohibition a failure, by encouraging in every way the violation of the constitution. I felt the outrage deeply, and would gladly have given my life to redress the wrongs of the people. As Esther said: "How can I see the desolation of my people? If I perish, I perish." (Esther 4:16.) As Patrick Henry said: "Give me liberty or give me death."

I finally came to the "Carey Hotel," next to which was called the Carey Annex or Bar. The first thing that struck me was the life-size picture of a naked woman, opposite the mirror. This was an oil painting with a glass over it, and was a very fine painting hired from the artist who painted it, to be put in that place for a vile purpose. I called to the bartender; told him he was insulting his own mother by having her form stripped naked and hung up in a place where it was not even decent for a woman to be in when she had her clothes on. I told him he was a law-breaker and that he should be behind prison bars, instead of saloon bars. He said nothing to me but walked to the back of his saloon. It is very significant that the pictures of naked women are in saloons. Women are stripped of everything by them. Her husband is torn from her, she is robbed of her sons, her home, her food and her virtue, and then they strip her clothes off and hang her up bare in these dens of robbery and murder. Truly does a saloon make a woman bare of all things! The motive for doing this is to suggest vice, animating the animal in man and degrading the respect he should have for the sex to whom he owes his being, yes, his Savior also!

I decided to go to the Carey for several reasons. It was the most dangerous, being the finest. The low doggery will take the low and keep them low, but these so-called respectable ones will take the respectable, make them low, then kick them out. A poor vagabond applied to a bar-tender in one of these hells glittering with crystalized tears and fine fixtures. The man behind the bar said: "You get out, you disgrace my place." The poor creature, who had been his mother's greatest treasure, shuffled out toward the door. Another customer came in, a nice looking young man, with a good suit, a white collar, and look-ing as if he had plenty of money. The smiling bar-tender mixed a drink and was handing it to him. The poor vagabond from the door called out. "Five years ago, I came into your place, looking just like that young man. You have made me what you see me now. Give that drink to me and finish your work. Don't begin on him."

I went back to the hotel and bound the rod and cane together, then wrapped paper around the top of it. I slept but little that night, spending most of the night in prayer. I wore a large cape. I took the cane and walked down the back stairs the next morning, and out into the alley, I picked up as many rocks as I could carry under my cape. I walked into the Carey barroom, and threw two rocks at the picture; then turned and smashed the mirror that cov-ered almost the entire side of the large room. Some men drinking at the bar ran out; the bar-tender was wiping a glass and he seemed transfixed to the spot and never moved. I took the cane and broke up the sideboard, which had on it all kinds of intoxicating drinks. Then I ran out across the street to destroy another one. I was arrested at 8:30 A.M., my rocks and cane taken from me, and I was taken to the police headquarters, where I was treated very nicely by

330 | THE DIVINE CALL

the Chief of Police, Mr. Cubbin, who seemed to be amused at what I had done. This man was not very popular with the administration, and was soon put out. I was kept in the office until 6:30 P.M. Gov. Stanley was in town at that time, and I telephoned to several places for him. I saw that he was dodging me, so I called a messenger boy and sent a note to Gov. Stanley, telling him that I was unlawfully restrained of my liberty; that I wished him to call and see me, or try to relieve me in some way. The messenger told me, when he came back, that he caught him at his home, that he read the message over three times, then said: "I have nothing to say," and went in, and closed the door. This is the man who taught Sunday school in Wichita for twenty years, where they were letting these murder shops run in violation of the law. Strange that this man should pull wool over the eyes of the voters of Kansas. I never did have any confidence in him.

Kansas has learned some dear lessons, and she will be wise indeed when she learns that only Prohibitionists will enforce prohibition laws.

At 6:30 P.M., I was tried and taken to Wichita jail; found guilty of malicious mischief, Sam Amidon being the prosecuting attorney, and the friend of every joint keeper in the city. He called me a "spotter," when I wanted to give evidence against the jointists.

The legislature was to convene in a few days and it was understood that the question of re-submitting the Prohibition Amendment would come up. Being a part of the constitution, the people had to vote on it, and it was frustrating their plans to have such agitation at this time, and these republican leaders were determined to put a quietus upon me, if possible. The scheme was to get me in an insane asylum, and they wished to increase my insanity, as they called my zeal, so as to have me out of their way, for I was calling too much attention to their lawlessness, at this time, when it might prove disastrous to their plots. Two sheriffs conducted me to my cell. The sensation of being locked in such a place for the first time is not like any other, and never occurs the second time. These men watched me after the door was locked. I tried to be brave, but the tears were running down my face. I took hold of the iron bars of my door, and tried to shake them and said: "Never mind, you put me in here a cub, but I will go out a roaring lion and I will make all hell howl." I wanted to let them know that I was going to grow while in there.

Three days after, on the 30th, there was brought in and put next to my cell an old man named Isaiah Cooper, a lunatic, who raved, cursed and tore his clothes and bedding. There were some cigarette smokers in the jail and the fumes came in my cell, for I had nothing but a barred door. I begged that I might not be compelled to smell this poison, but, instead of diminishing, the smoke increased. Two prisoners from another part of the jail were put in cells next to mine.

What an outrage, to tax the citizens of Sedgwick county to build such a jail as that in Wichita. It holds one hundred and sixty prisoners. There were thirteen there when I was put in. I have been in many jails, but in none other did I ever see a rotary, a large iron cage, with one door, the little cells the shape of a piece of pie. Perhaps there were a dozen in this one. The cage rotated within a cylinder. This was for the worst criminals, and the cells were only large enough for a small cot, a chair and a table about a foot square.

Mr. Simmons was the sheriff and he told the prisoners to "smoke all they pleased," that he would keep them in material, and he kept his word. Tobacco smoke is poison to me and cigarettes are worse. The health board belonged to this republican whiskey ring, and was in conspiracy to make me insane, so they put a quarantine on the jail for three weeks, and I was a lone woman in there, with two cigarette smokers, and a maniac, next to my cell. John, the Trusty, smoked a horrid strong pipe, and he was next to my cell. Strange to say, when that jail had so many apartments, and so few in them, that four inmates shuld have been put next to me; but there was "a cause." Mr. Dick Dodd was the jailer, and for three weeks he was the only one who came in my cell and I was not allowed to see anyone in that time, but Dr. Jordan who called once. I cried and begged to be relieved of the smoke, for I do not think Mr. Dodd realized how poisonous it was to me. I would have to keep my windows up in the cold January weather, and the fire would go down at night. I had two blankets, no pillow and a bed, that the criminals had slept on for years perhaps. I would shiver with cold, and often would lay on the cement floor with my head in my hands to keep out of the draught. Oh! the physical agony! I had a strong voice for singing, which I lost, and have never been able to sing, much since. Hour after hour I would lay on the floor, listening to the ravings of this poor old man, who would fall on his iron bed and hard floor, cursing and calling out names. One night I thought I could not live to see day. I had in my cell sweetest of all companions, my Bible. I read and studied it, and this particular night I told the Lord he must come to my aid. As I often do, I opened my Bible at random and read the first place I opened to, the 144th Psalm. I have often read the book through, but this chapter seemed entirely new. It reads, Verse 1: "Blessed be the Lord my strength, which teacheth my hands to war and my fingers to fight. 2. My God and my fortress my high tower and my deliverer; my shield and He in whom I trust; who subdueth my people under me."

God told me in this chapter that He led me to "fight with my fingers and war with my hands;" that He would be my *refuge* and *deliverer;* that He would use me to bring the people to Him.

David had just such enemies as these when he says in this chapter: 6. "Cast forth thy lightnings and scatter them; shoot out thine arrows and destroy them."

7. "Send thine hand from above; rid me and deliver me out of great waters from the hand of strange children."

8. "Whose mouth speaketh vanity; and their right hand is a right hand of falsehood."

12. "That our sons may be plants grown up in their youth; that our daughters may be as corner-stones polished after the similitude of a palace."

Here is the motive: The drink murders our sons, and do not allow them to grow to be healthy, brave, strong men. The greatest enemy of woman and her offspring and her virtue is the licensed hell-holes or saloons.

13. "That our garners may be full affording all manner of store."

Our grain is used to poison; our bread-stuff is turned to the venom of asps and the bread winner is burdened with disease of drunkenness, where health should be the result, of raising that which, when rotted and made into alcohol, perpetrates ruin and death; our garners or grain houses are spoiled or robbed.

14. "That there be no breaking in or going out; that there be no complaining in our street."

What is it causing the breaking into jails, prisons, asylums, penitentiaries, alms-houses? The going out of the homes, of hearts; going out into the cold; going into drunkards' graves and a drunkards' hell?

"Complaining in our streets." Oh! the cold and hungry little children! Oh! the weeping wives and mothers! Oh! the misery and desolation of the drunkards! All from this drink of sorrow and death.

15. "Happy is that people that is in such a case; yea, happy is that people whose God is the Lord."

"People whose God is the Lord," will not allow this evil. They will smash it out in one way or another. This blessed word was a "lamp to my feet and light to my pathway." (Ps. 119.) I rejoiced for the comfort it gave me; for the Lord truly talked to my soul while I read and reread this. I must say that "Little Dodds," the turnkey as I called him, was often kind to me, but he was completely the servant of Simmons and his wife.

John, the Dutch trusty, said to me one day: "There is something in the wind; people are coming and going and talking to Dodds." Mr. Dodds was supposed to be quarantined in the jail, but he went in and out of the office and he would also go to his home; the prisoners saw him from the window time and time again.

One night the poor old man fell so hard on the floor, or bed that he lay as one dead, for some time. The jailer and others were aroused and before they dare have a physician come in, they had to scrub and clean the cell. Then Dr. Jordan came, and the old man was finally brought to life. This doctor was in the conspiracy to have me adjudged insane. A woman fifty-five years old, who never broke a statute of Kansas.

Mr. Dodds told me that Sam Amidon, county attorney, would have a cab at the back door of the jail and would take me out. I consented. John, the Trusty, said to me, "Don't you leave this jail, there is some plotting going on, and they mean mischief." I asked him to get me a wire to fasten my door, which he did, and I wound it around the open places in the door and to the iron beam it shut on, and then John brought me the leg of a cot. I watched all night, listening for some one to come in my cell to drag me out. With the cot leg I was going to strike their hands if they attempted to open the door. I know what it is to expect murder in my cell. God said: "He would stand by me, and who but He, has."

I got so many letters from poor, distracted mothers, who wrote so often: "For God's sake come here." In some letters there was money. One letter from a United Brethren church in Winfield, Kansas; the minister, Brother Hendershot, wrote me that he took up a collection in their church for me of $7.38. How I cried over that letter and kissed it! I knew that I had some friends who understood me; and just after this letter, one from a Catholic priest came, which was a great comfort. The many letters I got from all kinds of vicious people was a great encouragement to me. I must say: "All hell got hit, when I smashed the saloons." For I never, until then, knew that people thought, or could write such vile things; letter after letter, of the most horrible infidelity, cursing God, calling me every vile name, and threatening me.

I was not allowed a pillow; I begged for one, for I had La Grippe, and my head was very sore, my body was filled with excruciating pains. Mr. Dodd frequently brought me the papers, and nearly every time the *Wichita Eagle* would have some falsehoods concerning me, always giving out that I "was crazy," "was in a padded cell," "only a matter of time when I would be in the insane asylum;" that I used "obscene language" and "was raving." The Bible says: "All liars shall have their part in the lake that burns with fire." (Rev. 21:8); so the Murdocks of Wichita ought to tremble. I associate the name "Murdock" with murder. The real depravity of such people was shown, when a lone old woman with a love of humanity, was in a cell suffering so unjustly, that these people should have left nothing undone to prejudice the people against her. Even when my brother died, this Murdock paper spoke of me "raving in jail," and I was not privileged to go to him in his dying hours. Such people drove the nails in the hands and the spear in the side of Jesus.

This *Wichita Eagle* is the rum-bought sheet that has made Wichita one of the most lawless places in Kansas.

When first arrested in Wichita, in violation of the Constitution, I was denied bail and compelled to bring a habeas corpus proceeding in the supreme court to get a trial or bail. Sam Amidon, as attorney for Simmons proposed a return of the writ, and filed a false certificate from Dr. Shults, president of the board of health, stating that the board had quarantined the jail. Rather than face the supreme court with a false return, the case was dismissed. I do not believe that history ever recorded a quarantine of a jail before, for public buildings, such as postoffices, court houses or jails cannot be made pest houses, and such buildings are cleansed. There was not a meeting of the health board. This was a conspiracy, signed by Dr. Shults and the sheriff, for the purpose of keeping me in jail, preventing me from seeing my friends or lawyers, and by persecution to get me in an insane asylum. Below is a copy of this fraudulent notice:

ORIGINAL NOTICE TO O. D. KIRK, JUDGE, HARDEN EBEY, CLERK, CHAS. W. SIMMONS, SHERIFF.

Served Tuesday, January 15, 1901.

To O. D. Kirk, Judge; Harden Ebey, Clerk; and Charles W. Simmons, Sheriff: You, and each of you, are hereby notified that the following is a copy of a paper purporting to be a statement made by J. W. Shults, President of the Board of Health, of Wichita, Kansas, and attached to the return of Charles W. Simmons in the matter of the application of CARRIE NATION for a Writ of Habeas Corpus now pending in the Supreme Court of the State of Kansas, viz:

"WICHITA, KANSAS, December 29, 1900.
"At special meeting of the Board of Health, held in the City of Wichita, Kansas, on the 29th day of December, 1900, at the office of Dr. J. W. Shults, president of the board of Health, the following resolution was adopted and ordered spread upon the minutes kept by the said board. 'Whereas it has come to the knowledge of the board of health that the inhabitants of the jail of Sedgwick county, Kansas, have been exposed to small pox and that one Isaiah Cooper confined therein has been exposed to smallpox and is infected with said disease and that the said Isaiah Cooper is a violently insane man and it is impossible to move him from said jail and that all of the said jail have been exposed to the same and that one W. A. Jordan, who as county physician of Sedgwick county and city physician of the city of Wichita, Kansas, asked and desired and demanded that said jail be quarantined or that said Isaiah Cooper be removed therefrom and that said jail be fumigated, and whereas it is impossible to remove the said Isaiah Cooper therefrom, the action of said W. A. Jordan in recommending the quarantine of the said county jail and in quarantining the same is hereby approved and the said county jail is hereby declared quarantined and ordered quarantined for the space of twenty-one days from this date and all persons in charge of said jail and the health officer of said city are hereby directed to enforce this said quarantine and the order of the said W. A. Jordan.'

J. W. SHULTS, M. D.,
President of Board of Health."

and that the above statement is not true; that there was no meeting of the Board of Health on the 29th day of December, 1900, and that the said jail has never been quarantined by the said Board of Health on the said 29th day of December or at any other time.

Dated at Wichita, Kansas, January 14, 1901.

W. S. ALLEN,

RAY & KEITH,

ROBT. BROWN,

Attorneys for Carrie Nation, an inmate

of said jail.

Served on O. B. Kirk, 9:20 a. m., Tuesday, January 15, 1901;

Harden Ebey, 9:20 a. m., Tuesday, January 15, 1901;

Chas. W. Simmons, 9:35 a. m., Tuesday, January 15, 1901.

I could tell of many interesting incidents in jail. There were five singers, one a graduate of the Conservatory of Music in Boston, and Mr. Dodd was a fine singer himself; he would often sing with the prisoners, and it was a great pleasure to me. One song he would have the boys sing was: "My Old Kentucky Home." We had a genuine poet there, and I here give you a poem he sent up to me one day, by the trusty:

SOLEMN THOUGHTS.

'Twas an aged and Christian martyr,
Sat alone in a prison cell,
Where the law of state had brought her,
For wrecking an earthly hell.

Day by day, and night she dwelt there,
Singing songs of Christ's dear love;
At His cross she pray'd and knelt there,
As an angel from above.

In the cells and 'round about her,
Prisoners stood, deep stained in sin;
Listening to the prayers she'd offer,
Looking for her Christ within.

Some who'd never known a mother,
Ne'er had learned to kneel and pray,
Raised their hands, their face to cover,
Till her words had died away.

In the silent midnight hours,
Came a voice in heavenly strain,
Floating o'er in peaceful showers,
Bringing sunshine after rain.

Each one rose from out his slumber,
Listening to her songs of cheer,

Then the stillness rent asunder,
With their praises loud and clear.

Praise from those whose crimes had led them,
O'er a dark and stormy sea,
Where its waves had lashed and tossed them
Into "hell's" captivity.

Wine it was, the drink that led them,
From the tender Shepherd's fold,
Now they hear His voice that calls them,
With His precious words of gold.

Like the sheep that went astray,
Twice we've heard the story told,
They heard His voice, they saw the way,
That leads into His pastured fold.

The first time I was put in jail, after everything was quiet, I heard some prisoner down below, swearing, and I called out: "What do you mean boys by asking God to damn this place? I think he has done so and we don't want any more damns here. Get down on your knees and ask God to bless you." And all the rest of the time I never heard an oath. In a week or so I heard them singing hymns; and I called to them: "How are you boys?"

"We have all been converted since the first of January," was their reply.

One of those young men got out while I was there, and came to my cell and told me that it was true about their conversion.

Oh! the sad hearts behind the bars! Oh! the injustice! I am glad I have been a prisoner for one thing, I never see a face behind the bars that my heart does not pity. I have heard so many tales of ruined lives; have seen men with muscles and brain, bowed into tears. Oh! if we would only love each other more; if we would feel as Paul: "To owe love" to all we meet, and pay the debt. 'Tis the most pleasant debt to pay and the indebtedness blesses both parties, especially the one who pays. I used to think that birth and other circumstances made one person better than another. I do not see it that way now. The man with many opportunities is not entitled to as much consideration as one with fewer. I am the defender of the one who needs help most. The great need of the world is Love.

16

(From) *Living My Life*

Emma Goldman

Lithuanian-born Emma Goldman (1869–1940) emigrated to the
United States in the 1880s, settling in Rochester, New York, and working
in clothing factories there. After the Chicago Haymarket Riot of 1886,
which brought the trial and conviction of seven men accused of throwing a bomb in the context of police violence over labor strikes for an
eight-hour workday, she experienced a kind of spiritual conversion to
the anarchist cause. The fiery Goldman lectured widely, spending time
in jail in 1893 for inciting listeners to riot, in 1916 for publicly endors-
ing birth control, and again the next year for obstructing the draft. An
outspoken journalist as well, from 1906 she edited *Mother Earth* with
fellow anarchist Alexander Berkman. By 1919, she found herself in such
poor graces with American public authorities that she was deported to
Russia—although she left two years later and eventually returned to the
United States for a brief period in 1934. Like numbers of other immigrants of the time with Jewish roots, Goldman lived out the ethical
commands of the Torah through the nonbiblical embrace of a radical
social program. As these excerpts from her autobiography demonstrate,
she had a quality of total ardor and engagement about her. Radically
transformed through the prophetic stance of others, Goldman understood conversion to the revolutionary anarchist cause to mean commitment to the itinerant life of a prophet—without the overt religious
ideology that had compelled the prophets of old in the biblical tradition
and in other world religions. For Goldman, the divine call came
through the impassioned voice of conscience and love, ignited by the
anarchist passion for right and justice, as these anarchists understood
them; and for her, the divine call could encompass violence.

It was the 15th of August 1889, the day of my arrival in New York City. I was
twenty years old. All that had happened in my life until that time was now left
behind me, cast off like a worn-out garment. A new world was before me,
strange and terrifying. But I had youth, good health, and a passionate ideal.
Whatever the new held in store for me I was determined to meet unflinchingly.

How well I remember that day! It was a Sunday. The West Shore train, the

From *Living My Life* by Emma Goldman [1931].

cheapest, which was all I could afford, had brought me from Rochester, New York, reaching Weehawken at eight o'clock in the morning. Thence I came by ferry to New York City. I had no friends there, but I carried three addresses, one of a married aunt, one of a young medical student I had met in New Haven a year before, while working in a corset factory there, and one of the *Freiheit*, a German anarchist paper published by Johann Most.

My entire possessions consisted of five dollars and a small hand-bag. My sewing-machine, which was to help me to independence, I had checked as baggage. Ignorant of the distance from West Forty-second Street to the Bowery, where my aunt lived, and unaware of the enervating heat of a New York day in August, I started out on foot. How confusing and endless a large city seems to the new-comer, how cold and unfriendly!

After receiving many directions and misdirections and making frequent stops at bewildering intersections, I landed in three hours at the photographic gallery of my aunt and uncle. Tired and hot, I did not at first notice the consternation of my relatives at my unexpected arrival. They asked me to make myself at home, gave me breakfast, and then plied me with questions. Why did I come to New York? Had I definitely broken with my husband? Did I have money? What did I intend to do? I was told that I could, of course, stay with them. "Where else could you go, a young woman alone in New York?" Certainly, but I would have to look for a job immediately. Business was bad, and the cost of living high.

I heard it all as if in a stupor. I was too exhausted from my wakeful night's journey, the long walk, and the heat of the sun, which was already pouring down fiercely. The voices of my relatives sounded distant, like the buzzing of flies, and they made me drowsy. With an effort I pulled myself together. I assured them I did not come to impose myself on them; a friend living on Henry Street was expecting me and would put me up. I had but one desire— to get out, away from the prattling, chilling voices. I left my bag and departed.

The friend I had invented in order to escape the "hospitality" of my relatives was only a slight acquaintance, a young anarchist by the name of A. Solotaroff, whom I had once heard lecture in New Haven. Now I started out to find him. After a long search I discovered the house, but the tenant had left. The janitor, at first very brusque, must have noticed my despair. He said he would look for the address that the family left when they moved. Presently he came back with the name of the street, but there was no number. What was I to do? How to find Solotaroff in the vast city? I decided to stop at every house, first on one side of the street, and then on the other. Up and down, six flights of stairs, I tramped, my head throbbing, my feet weary. The oppressive day was drawing to a close. At last, when I was about to give up the search, I discovered him on Montgomery Street, on the fifth floor of a tenement house seething with humanity.

A year had passed since our first meeting, but Solotaroff had not forgotten me. His greeting was genial and warm, as of an old friend. He told me that he shared his small apartment with his parents and little brother, but that I could have his room; he would stay with a fellow-student for a few nights. He assured me that I would have no difficulty in finding a place; in fact, he knew two sisters who were living with their father in a two-room flat. They were looking for another girl to join them. After my new friend had fed me tea and some delicious Jewish cake his mother had baked, he told me about the different people I might meet, the activities of the Yiddish anarchists, and other interesting matters. I was grateful to my host, much more for his friendly concern and *camaraderie* than for the tea and cake. I forgot the bitterness that had filled my soul over the cruel reception given me by my own kin. New York no longer seemed the monster it had appeared in the endless hours of my painful walk on the Bowery.

Later Solotaroff took me to Sachs's café on Suffolk Street, which, as he informed me, was the headquarters of the East Side radicals, socialists, and anarchists, as well as of the young Yiddish writers and poets. "Everybody forgathers there," he remarked; "the Minkin sisters will no doubt also be there."

For one who had just come away from the monotony of a provincial town like Rochester and whose nerves were on edge from a night's trip in a stuffy car, the noise and turmoil that greeted us at Sachs's were certainly not very soothing. The place consisted of two rooms and was packed. Everybody talked, gesticulated, and argued, in Yiddish and Russian, each competing with the other. I was almost overcome in this strange human medley. My escort discovered two girls at a table. He introduced them as Anna and Helen Minkin.

They were Russian Jewish working girls. Anna, the older, was about my own age; Helen perhaps eighteen. Soon we came to an understanding about my living with them, and my anxiety and uncertainty were over. I had a roof over my head; I had found friends. The bedlam at Sachs's no longer mattered. I began to breathe freer, to feel less of an alien.

While the four of us were having our dinner, and Solotaroff was pointing out to me the different people in the café, I suddenly heard a powerful voice call: "Extra-large steak! Extra cup of coffee!" My own capital was so small and the need for economy so great that I was startled by such apparent extravagance. Besides, Solotaroff had told me that only poor students, writers, and workers were the clients of Sachs. I wondered who that reckless person could be and how he could afford such food. "Who is that glutton?" I asked. Solotaroff laughed aloud. "That is Alexander Berkman. He can eat for three. But he rarely has enough money for much food. When he has, he eats Sachs out of his supplies. I'll introduce him to you."

We had finished our meal, and several people came to our table to talk to Solotaroff. The man of the extra-large steak was still packing it away as if he had gone hungry for weeks. Just as we were about to depart, he approached us, and Solotaroff introduced him. He was no more than a boy, hardly eighteen, but with the neck and chest of a giant. His jaw was strong, made more pronounced by his thick lips. His face was almost severe, but for his high, studious forehead and intelligent eyes. A determined youngster, I thought. Presently Berkman remarked to me: "Johann Most is speaking tonight. Do you want to come to hear him?"

How extraordinary, I thought, that on my very first day in New York I should have the chance to behold with my own eyes and hear the fiery man whom the Rochester press used to portray as the personification of the devil, a criminal, a bloodthirsty demon! I had planned to visit Most in the office of his newspaper some time later, but that the opportunity should present itself in such an unexpected manner gave me the feeling that something wonderful was about to happen, something that would decide the whole course of my life.

On the way to the hall I was too absorbed in my thoughts to hear much of the conversation that was going on between Berkman and the Minkin sisters. Suddenly I stumbled. I should have fallen had not Berkman gripped my arm and held me up. "I have saved your life," he said jestingly. "I hope I may be able to save yours some day," I quickly replied.

The meeting-place was a small hall behind a saloon, through which one had to pass. It was crowded with Germans, drinking, smoking, and talking. Before long, Johann Most entered. My first impression of him was one of revulsion. He was of medium height, with a large head crowned with greyish bushy hair; but his face was twisted out of form by an apparent dislocation of the left jaw. Only his eyes were soothing; they were blue and sympathetic.

His speech was a scorching denunciation of American conditions, a biting satire on the injustice and brutality of the dominant powers, a passionate tirade against those responsible for the Haymarket tragedy and the execution of the Chicago anarchists in November 1887. He spoke eloquently and picturesquely. As if by magic, his disfigurement disappeared, his lack of physical distinction was forgotten. He seemed transformed into some primitive power, radiating hatred and love, strength and inspiration. The rapid current of his speech, the music of his voice, and his sparkling wit, all combined to produce an effect almost overwhelming. He stirred me to my depths.

Caught in the crowd that surged towards the platform, I found myself before Most. Berkman was near me and introduced me. But I was dumb with excitement and nervousness, full of the tumult of emotions Most's speech had aroused in me.

That night I could not sleep. Again I lived through the events of 1887. Twenty-one months had passed since the Black Friday of November 11, when the Chicago men had suffered their martyrdom, yet every detail stood out clear before my vision and affected me as if it had happened but yesterday. My sister Helena and I had become interested in the fate of the men during the period of their trial. The reports in the Rochester newspapers irritated, confused, and upset us by their evident prejudice. The violence of the press, the bitter denunciation of the accused, the attacks on all foreigners, turned our sympathies to the Haymarket victims.

We had learned of the existence in Rochester of a German socialist group that held sessions on Sunday in Germania Hall. We began to attend the meetings, my older sister, Helena, on a few occasions only, and I regularly. The gatherings were generally uninteresting, but they offered an escape from the grey dullness of my Rochester existence. There one heard, at least, something different from the everlasting talk about money and business, and one met people of spirit and ideas.

One Sunday it was announced that a famous socialist speaker from New York, Johanna Greie, would lecture on the case then being tried in Chicago. On the appointed day I was the first in the hall. The huge place was crowded from top to bottom by eager men and women, while the walls were lined with police. I had never before been at such a large meeting. I had seen *gendarmes* in St. Petersburg disperse small student gatherings. But that in the country which guaranteed free speech, officers armed with long clubs should invade an orderly assembly filled me with consternation and protest.

Soon the chairman announced the speaker. She was a woman in her thirties, pale and ascetic-looking, with large luminous eyes. She spoke with great earnestness, in a voice vibrating with intensity. Her manner engrossed me. I forgot the police, the audience, and everything else about me. I was aware only of the frail woman in black crying out her passionate indictment against the forces that were about to destroy eight human lives.

The entire speech concerned the stirring events in Chicago. She began by relating the historical background of the case. She told of the labour strikes that broke out throughout the country in 1886, for the demand of an eight-hour workday. The centre of the movement was Chicago, and there the struggle between the toilers and their bosses became intense and bitter. A meeting of the striking employees of the McCormick Harvester Company in that city was attacked by police; men and women were beaten and several persons killed. To protest against the outrage a mass meeting was called in Haymarket Square on May 4. It was addressed by Albert Parsons, August Spies, Adolph Fischer, and others, and was quiet and orderly. This was attested to by Carter Harrison, Mayor of Chicago, who had attended the meeting to see what was going on. The Mayor left, satisfied that everything was all right, and he informed the captain of the district to that effect. It was getting cloudy, a light rain began to fall, and the people started to disperse, only a few remaining while one of the last speakers was addressing the audience. Then Captain Ward, accompanied by a strong force of police, suddenly appeared on the square. He ordered the meeting to disperse forthwith. "This is an orderly assembly," the chairman replied, whereupon the police fell upon the people, clubbing them unmercifully. Then something flashed through the air and exploded, killing a number of police officers and wounding a score of others. It was never ascertained who the actual culprit was, and the authorities apparently made little effort to discover him. Instead orders were immediately issued for the arrest of all the speakers at the Haymarket meeting and other prominent anarchists. The entire press and *bourgeoisie* of Chicago and of the whole country began shouting for the blood of the prisoners. A veritable campaign of terror was carried on by the police, who were given moral and financial encouragement by the Citizens' Association to further their murderous plan to get the anarchists out of the way. The public mind was so inflamed by the atrocious stories circulated by the press against the leaders of the strike that a fair trial for them became an impossibility. In fact, the trial proved the worst frame-up in the history of the United States. The jury was picked for conviction; the District Attorney announced in open court that it was not only the arrested men who were the accused, but that "anarchy was on trial" and that it was to be exterminated. The judge repeatedly denounced the prisoners from the bench, influencing the jury against them. The witnesses were terrorized or bribed, with the result that eight men, innocent of the crime and in no way connected with it, were convicted. The incited state of the public mind, and the general prejudice against anarchists, coupled with the employers' bitter opposition to the eight-hour movement, constituted the atmosphere that favoured the judicial murder of the Chicago anarchists. Five of them—Albert Parsons, August Spies, Louis Lingg, Adolph Fischer, and George Engel—were sentenced to die by hanging; Michael Schwab and Samuel Fielden were doomed to life imprisonment; Neebe received fifteen years' sentence. The innocent blood of the Haymarket martyrs was calling for revenge.

At the end of Greie's speech I knew what I had surmised all along: the Chicago men were innocent. They were to be put to death for their ideal. But what was their ideal? Johanna Greie spoke of Parsons, Spies, Lingg, and the others as socialists, but I was ignorant of the real meaning of socialism. What I had heard from the local speakers had impressed me as colourless and mechanistic. On the other hand, the papers called these men anarchists, bombthrowers. What was anarchism? It was all very puzzling. But I had no time for further contemplation. The people were filing out, and I got up to leave. Greie, the chairman, and a group of friends were still on the platform. As I turned towards them, I saw Greie motioning to me. I was startled, my heart beat violently, and my feet felt leaden. When I approached her, she took me by the hand and said: "I never saw a face that reflected such a tumult of emotions as yours. You must be feeling the impending tragedy intensely. Do you know the men?" In a trembling voice I replied: "Unfortunately not, but I do feel the case with every fibre, and when I heard you speak, it seemed to me as if I knew them." She put her hand on my shoulder. "I have a feeling that you will know them better as you learn their ideal, and that you will make their cause your own."

I walked home in a dream. Sister Helena was already asleep, but I had to share my experience with her. I woke her up and recited to her the whole story, giving almost a verbatim account of the speech. I must have been very dramatic, because Helena exclaimed: "The next thing I'll hear about my little sister is that she, too, is a dangerous anarchist."

Some weeks later I had occasion to visit a German family I knew. I found them very much excited. Somebody from New York had sent them a German paper, *Die Freiheit*, edited by Johann Most. It was filled with news about the events in Chicago. The language fairly took my breath away, it was so different from what I had heard at the socialist meetings and even from Johanna Greie's talk. It seemed lava shooting forth flames of ridicule, scorn, and defiance; it breathed deep hatred of the powers that were preparing the crime in Chicago. I began to read *Die Freiheit* regularly. I sent for the literature advertised in the paper and I devoured every line on anarchism I could get, every word about the men, their lives, their work. I read about their heroic stand while on trial and their marvellous defence. I saw a new world opening before me.

The terrible thing everyone feared, yet hoped would not happen, actually occurred. Extra editions of the Rochester papers carried the news: the Chicago anarchists had been hanged!

We were crushed, Helena and I. The shock completely unnerved my sister; she could only wring her hands and weep silently. I was in a stupor; a feeling of numbness came over me, something too horrible even for tears. In the evening we went to our father's house. Everybody talked about the Chicago events. I was entirely absorbed in what I felt as my own loss. Then I heard the coarse laugh of a woman. In a shrill voice she sneered: "What's all this lament about? The men were murderers. It is well they were hanged." With one leap I was at the woman's throat. Then I felt myself torn back. Someone said: "The child has gone crazy." I wrenched myself free, grabbed a pitcher of water from a table, and threw it with all my force into the woman's face. "Out, out," I cried, "or I will kill you!" The terrified woman made for the door and I dropped to the ground in a fit of crying. I was put to bed, and soon I fell into a deep sleep. The next morning I woke as from a long illness, but free from the numbness and the depression of those harrowing weeks of waiting, ending with the final shock. I had a distinct sensation that something new and wonderful had been born in my soul. A great ideal, a burning faith, a determination to dedicate myself to the memory of my martyred comrades, to make their cause my own, to make known to the world their beautiful lives and heroic deaths. Johanna Greie was more prophetic than she had probably realized.

My mind was made up. I would go to New York, to Johann Most. He would help me prepare myself for my new task. . . .

It was May 1892. News from Pittsburgh announced that trouble had broken out between the Carnegie Steel Company and its employees organized in the Amalgamated Association of Iron and Steel Workers. It was one of the biggest and most efficient labour bodies of the country, consisting mostly of Americans, men of decision and grit, who would assert their rights. The Carnegie Company, on the other hand, was a powerful corporation, known as a hard master. It was particularly significant that Andrew Carnegie, its president, had temporarily turned over the entire management to the company's chairman, Henry Clay Frick, a man known for his enmity to labour. Frick was also the owner of extensive coke-fields, where unions were prohibited and the workers were ruled with an iron hand.

The high tariff on imported steel had greatly boomed the American steel industry. The Carnegie Company had practically a monopoly of it and enjoyed unprecedented prosperity. Its largest mills were in Homestead, near Pittsburgh, where thousands of workers were employed, their tasks requiring long training and high skill. Wages were arranged between the company and the union, according to a sliding scale based on the prevailing market price of steel products. The current agreement was about to expire, and the workers presented a new wage schedule, calling for an increase because of the higher market prices and enlarged output of the mills.

The philanthropic Andrew Carnegie conveniently retired to his castle in Scotland, and Frick took full charge of the situation. He declared that henceforth the sliding scale would be abolished. The company would make no more agreements with the Amalgamated Association; it would itself determine the wages to be paid. In fact, he would not recognize the union at all. He would not treat with the employees collectively, as before. He would close the mills, and the men might consider themselves discharged. Thereafter they would have to apply for work individually, and the pay would be arranged with every worker separately. Frick curtly refused the peace advances of the workers' organization, declaring that there was "nothing to arbitrate." Presently the mills were closed. "Not a strike, but a lockout," Frick announced. It was an open declaration of war.

Feeling ran high in Homestead and vicinity. The sympathy of the entire country was with the men. Even the most conservative part of the press condemned Frick for his arbitrary and drastic methods. They charged him with deliberately provoking a crisis that might assume national proportions, in view of the great numbers of men locked out by Frick's action, and the probable effect upon affiliated unions and on related industries.

Labour throughout the country was aroused. The steel-workers declared that they were ready to take up the challenge of Frick: they would insist on their right to organize and to deal collectively with their employers. Their tone was manly, ringing with the spirit of their rebellious forebears of the Revolutionary War.

Far away from the scene of the impending struggle, in our little ice-cream parlour in the city of Worcester, we eagerly followed developments. To us it sounded the awakening of the American worker, the long-awaited day of his resurrection. The native toiler had risen, he was beginning to feel his mighty strength, he was determined to break the chains that had held him in bondage so long, we thought. Our hearts were fired with admiration for the men of Homestead.

We continued our daily work, waiting on customers, frying pancakes, serving tea and ice-cream; but our thoughts were in Homestead, with the brave steel-workers. We became so absorbed in the news that we would not permit ourselves enough time even for sleep. At daybreak one of the boys would be off to get the first editions of the papers. We saturated ourselves with the events in Homestead to the exclusion of everything else. Entire nights we would sit up discussing the various phases of the situation, almost engulfed by the possibilities of the gigantic struggle.

One afternoon a customer came in for an ice-cream, while I was alone in the store. As I set the dish down before him, I caught the large headlines of his paper: "LATEST DEVELOPMENTS IN HOMESTEAD—FAMILIES OF STRIKERS EVICTED FROM THE COMPANY HOUSES—WOMAN IN CONFINEMENT CARRIED OUT INTO STREET BY SHERIFFS." I read over the man's shoulder Frick's dictum to the workers: he would rather see them dead than concede to their demands, and he threatened to import Pinkerton detectives. The brutal bluntness of the account, the inhumanity of Frick towards the evicted mother, inflamed my mind. Indignation swept my whole being. I heard the man at the table ask: "Are you sick, young lady? Can I do anything for you?" "Yes, you can let me have your paper," I blurted out. "You won't have to pay me for the ice-cream. But I must ask you to leave. I must close the store." The man looked at me as if I had gone crazy.

I locked up the store and ran full speed the three blocks to our little flat. It was Homestead, not Russia; I knew it now. We belonged in Homestead. The boys, resting for the evening shift, sat up as I rushed into the room, newspaper clutched in my hand. "What has happened, Emma? You look terrible!" I could not speak. I handed them the paper.

Sasha was the first on his feet. "Homestead!" he exclaimed. "I must go to Homestead!" I flung my arms around him, crying out his name. I, too, would go. "We must go tonight," he said; "the great moment has come at last!" Being internationalists, he added, it mattered not to us where the blow was struck by the workers; we must be with them. We must bring them our great message and help them see that it was not only for the moment that they must strike, but for all time, for a free life, for anarchism. Russia had many heroic men and women, but who was there in America? Yes, we must go to Homestead, tonight!

I had never heard Sasha so eloquent. He seemed to have grown in stature. He looked strong and defiant, an inner light on his face making him beautiful, as he had never appeared to me before.

We immediately went to our landlord and informed him of our decision to leave. He replied that we were mad; we were doing so well, we were on the way to fortune. If we would hold out to the end of the summer, we would be able to clear at least a thousand dollars. But he argued in vain—we were not to be moved. We invented the story that a very dear relative was in a dying condition, and that therefore we must depart. We would turn the store over to him; all we wanted was the evening's receipts. We would remain until closing-hours, leave everything in order, and give him the keys.

That evening we were especially busy. We had never before had so many customers. By one o'clock we had sold out everything. Our receipts were seventy-five dollars. We left on an early morning train.

On the way we discussed our immediate plans. First of all, we would print a manifesto to the steel-workers. We would have to find somebody to translate it into English, as we were still unable to express our thoughts correctly in that tongue. We would have the German and English texts printed in New York and take them with us to Pittsburgh. With the help of the German comrades there, meetings could be organized for me to address. Fedya was to remain in New York till further developments.

From the station we went straight to the flat of Mollock, an Austrian comrade we had met in the *Autonomie* group. He was a baker who worked at night; but Peppie, his wife, with her two children was at home. We were sure she could put us up.

She was surprised to see the three of us march in, bag and baggage, but she made us welcome, fed us, and suggested that we go to bed. But we had other things to do.

Sasha and I went in search of Claus Timmermann, an ardent German anarchist we knew. He had considerable poetic talent and wrote forceful propaganda. In fact, he had been the editor of an anarchist paper in St. Louis before coming to New York. He was a likable fellow and entirely trustworthy, though a considerable drinker. We felt that Claus was the only person we could safely draw into our plan. He caught our spirit at once. The manifesto was written that afternoon. It was a flaming call to the men of Homestead to throw off the yoke of capitalism, to use their present struggle as a stepping-stone to the destruction of the wage system, and to continue towards social revolution and anarchism.

A few days after our return to New York the news was flashed across the country of the slaughter of steel-workers by Pinkertons. Frick had fortified the Homestead mills, built a high fence around them. Then, in the dead of night, a barge packed with strike-breakers, under protection of heavily armed Pinkerton thugs, quietly stole up the Monongahela River. The steel-men had learned of Frick's move. They stationed themselves along the shore, determined to drive back Frick's hirelings. When the barge got within range, the Pinkertons had opened fire, without warning, killing a number of Homestead men on the shore, among them a little boy, and wounding scores of others.

The wanton murders aroused even the daily papers. Several came out in strong editorials, severely criticizing Frick. He had gone too far; he had added fuel to the fire in the labour ranks and would have himself to blame for any desperate acts that might come.

We were stunned. We saw at once that the time for our manifesto had passed. Words had lost their meaning in the face of the innocent blood spilled on the banks of the Monongahela. Intuitively each felt what was surging in the heart of the others. Sasha broke the silence. "Frick is the responsible factor in this crime," he said; "he must be made to stand the consequences." It was the psychological moment for an *Attentat;* the whole country was aroused, everybody was considering Frick the perpetrator of a coldblooded murder. A blow aimed at Frick would re-echo in the poorest hovel, would call the attention of the whole world to the real cause behind the Homestead struggle. It would also strike terror in the enemy's ranks and make them realize that the proletariat of America had its avengers.

Sasha had never made bombs before, but Most's *Science of Revolutionary Warfare* was a good text-book. He would procure dynamite from a comrade he knew on Staten Island. He had waited for this sublime moment to serve the Cause, to give his life for the people. He would go to Pittsburgh.

"We will go with you!" Fedya and I cried together. But Sasha would not listen to it. He insisted that it was unnecessary and criminal to waste three lives on one man.

We sat down, Sasha between us, holding our hands. In a quiet and even tone he began to unfold to us his plan. He would perfect a time regulator for the bomb that would enable him to kill Frick, yet save himself. Not because he wanted to escape. No; he wanted to live long enough to justify his act in court, so that the American people might know that he was not a criminal, but an idealist.

"I will kill Frick," Sasha said, "and of course I shall be condemned to death. I will die proudly in the assurance that I gave my life for the people. But I will die by my own hand, like Lingg. Never will I permit our enemies to kill me."

I hung on his lips. His clarity, his calmness and force, the sacred fire of his ideal, enthralled me, held me spellbound. Turning to me, he continued in his deep voice. I was the born speaker, the propagandist, he said. I could do a great deal for his act. I could articulate its meaning to the workers. I could explain that he had had no personal grievance against Frick, that as a human being Frick was no less to him than anyone else. Frick was the symbol of wealth and power, of the injustice and wrong of the capitalistic class, as well as personally responsible for the shedding of the workers' blood. Sasha's act would be directed against Frick, not as a man, but as the enemy of labour. Surely I must see how important it was that I remain behind to plead the meaning of his deed and its message throughout the country.

Every word he said beat upon my brain like a sledge-hammer. The longer he talked, the more conscious I became of the terrible fact that he had no need of me in his last great hour. The realization swept away everything else— message, Cause, duty, propaganda. What meaning could these things have compared with the force that had made Sasha flesh of my flesh and blood of my blood from the moment that I had heard his voice and felt the grip of his hand at our first meeting? Had our three years together shown him so little of my soul that he could tell me calmly to go on living after he had been blown to pieces or strangled to death? Is not true love—not ordinary love, but the love that longs to share to the uttermost with the beloved—is it not more compelling than aught else? Those Russians had known it, Jessie Helfmann and Sophia Perovskaya; they had gone with their men in life and in death. I could do no less.

"I will go with you, Sasha," I cried; "I must go with you! I know that as a woman I can be of help. I could gain access to Frick easier than you. I could pave the way for your act. Besides, I simply must go with you. Do you understand, Sasha?"

17

Letter from Birmingham Jail

Martin Luther King, Jr.

African American Baptist minister and civil rights leader Martin Luther King, Jr. (1929–1968), was born and raised in Atlanta, Georgia, where he experienced the segregation characteristic of the time. King received degrees from Morehouse College, Crozier Theological Seminary, and Boston University, and in 1954 began to pastor the Dexter Avenue Baptist Church in Montgomery, Alabama. A year later he was receiving national acclaim as leader of the Montgomery bus boycott that sparked the civil rights movement. King had instituted the strategy of nonviolent confrontation to deal with racism, and he authoritatively articulated the philosophical underpinnings to support the tactic. He looked with high esteem to the civil disobedience of South Asian Indian nationalist Mohandas Gandhi, even as behind the Gandhian model he recognized the word and example of Henry David Thoreau. King eventually became associate pastor at his father's church in Atlanta, and, in 1957, president of the Southern Christian Leadership Conference with its coordination of local protests across the South. His major campaigns contributed to the passage of the Civil Rights Act of 1964 and the Voting Rights Act of 1965. The recipient of the Nobel Peace Prize in 1964, after 1965 King became increasingly disturbed by economic inequities in northern cities and then by the Vietnam War. His assassination in 1968 occurred while he was assisting the garbage workers' strike in that city. King wrote his "Letter from Birmingham Jail" in response to a charge by several white southern ministers that agitation over civil rights in that city was "unwise and untimely." In announcing to white Americans that blacks, as remnant of the New Israel, were called to redeem America, he proclaimed to all who listened his own prophetic spirituality.

April 16, 1963

MY DEAR FELLOW CLERGYMEN:

While confined here in the Birmingham city jail, I came across your recent statement calling my present activities "unwise and untimely." Seldom do I pause to answer criticism of my work and ideas. If I sought to answer all the criticisms that cross my desk, my secretaries would have little time for anything other than such correspondence in the course of the day, and I would have no time for constructive work. But since I feel that you are men of genuine good will and that your criticisms are sincerely set forth, I want to try to answer your statement in what I hope will be patient and reasonable terms.

I think I should indicate why I am here in Birmingham, since you have been influenced by the view which argues against "outsiders coming in." I have the honor of serving as president of the Southern Christian Leadership Conference, an organization operating in every southern state, with headquarters in Atlanta, Georgia. We have some eighty-five affiliated organizations across the South, and one of them is the Alabama Christian Movement for Human Rights. Frequently we share staff, educational and financial resources with our affiliates. Several months ago the affiliate here in Birmingham asked us to be on call to engage in a nonviolent direct-action program if such were deemed necessary. We readily consented, and when the hour came we lived up to our promise. So I, along with several members of my staff, am here because I was invited here. I am here because I have organizational ties here.

But more basically, I am in Birmingham because injustice is here. Just as the prophets of the eighth century B.C. left their villages and carried their "thus saith the Lord" far beyond the boundaries of their home towns, and just as the Apostle Paul left his village of Tarsus and carried the gospel of Jesus Christ to the far corners of the Greco-Roman world, so am I compelled to carry the gospel of freedom beyond my own home town. Like Paul, I must constantly respond to the Macedonian call for aid.

Moreover, I am cognizant of the interrelatedness of all communities and states. I cannot sit idly by in Atlanta and not be concerned about what happens in Birmingham. Injustice anywhere is a threat to justice everywhere. We are caught in an inescapable network of mutuality, tied in a single garment of destiny. Whatever affects one directly, affects all indirectly. Never again can we afford to live with the narrow, provincial "outside agitator" idea. Anyone who lives inside the United States can never be considered an outsider anywhere within its bounds.

You deplore the demonstrations taking place in Birmingham. But your statement, I am sorry to say, fails to express a similar concern for the conditions that brought about the demonstrations. I am sure that none of you would want to rest content with the superficial kind of social analysis that deals merely with effects and does not grapple with underlying causes. It is unfortunate that demonstrations are taking place in Birmingham, but it is even more unfortunate that the city's white power structure left the Negro community with no alternative.

In any nonviolent campaign there are four basic steps: collection of the facts to determine whether injustices exist; negotiation; self-purification; and direct action. We have gone through all these steps in Birmingham. There can be no gainsaying the fact that racial injustice engulfs this community. Birmingham is probably the most thoroughly segregated city in the United States. Its ugly record of brutality is widely known. Negroes have experienced grossly unjust treatment in the courts. There have been more unsolved bombings of Negro homes and churches in Birmingham than in any other city in the nation. These are the hard, brutal facts of the case. On the basis of these conditions, Negro leaders sought to negotiate with the city fathers. But the latter consistently refused to engage in good-faith negotiation.

Then, last September, came the opportunity to talk with leaders of Birmingham's economic community. In the course of the negotiations, certain promises were made by the merchants—for example, to remove the stores' humiliating racial signs. On the basis of these promises, the Reverend Fred Shuttlesworth and the leaders of the Alabama Christian Movement for Human Rights agreed to a moratorium on all demonstrations. As the weeks and months went by, we realized that we were the victims of a broken promise. A few signs, briefly removed, returned; the others remained.

As in so many past experiences, our hopes had been blasted, and the shadow of deep disappointment settled upon us. We had no alternative except to prepare for direct action, whereby we would present our very bodies as a means of laying our case before the conscience of the local and the national community. Mindful of the difficulties involved, we decided to undertake a process of self-purification. We began a series of workshops on nonviolence, and we repeatedly asked ourselves: "Are you able to accept blows without retaliating?" "Are you able to endure the ordeal of jail?" We decided to schedule our direct-action program for the Easter season, realizing that except for Christmas, this is the main shopping period of the year. Knowing that a strong economic-withdrawal program would be the by-product of direct action, we felt that this would be the best time to bring pressure to bear on the merchants for the needed change.

Then it occurred to us that Birmingham's mayoral election was coming up in March, and we speedily decided to postpone action until after election day. When we discovered that the Commissioner of Public Safety, Eugene "Bull" Connor, had piled up enough votes to be in the run-off, we decided again to postpone action until the day after the run-off so that the demonstrations could not be used to cloud the issues. Like many others, we waited to see Mr. Connor defeated, and to this end we endured postponement after postponement. Having aided in this community need, we felt that our direct-action program could be delayed no longer.

You may well ask: "Why direct action? Why sit-ins, marches and so forth? Isn't negotiation a better path?" You are quite right in calling for negotiation. Indeed, this is the very purpose of direct action. Nonviolent direct action seeks to create such a crisis and foster such a tension that a community which has constantly refused to negotiate is forced to confront the issue. It seeks so to dramatize the issue that it can no longer be ignored. My citing the creation of tension as part of the work of the nonviolent-resister may sound rather shocking. But I must confess that I am not afraid of the word "tension." I have earnestly opposed violent tension, but there is a type of constructive, nonviolent tension which is necessary for growth. Just as Socrates felt that it was necessary to create a tension in the mind so that individuals could rise from the bondage of myths and half-truths to the unfettered realm of creative analysis and objective appraisal, so must we see the need for nonviolent gadflies to create the kind of tension in society that will help men rise from the dark depths of prejudice and racism to the majestic heights of understanding and brotherhood.

The purpose of our direct-action program is to create a situation so crisis-packed that it will inevitably open the door to negotiation. I therefore concur with you in your call for negotiation. Too long has our beloved Southland been bogged down in a tragic effort to live in monologue rather than dialogue.

One of the basic points in your statement is that the action that I and my associates have taken in Birmingham is untimely. Some have asked: "Why didn't you give the new city administration time to act?" The only answer that I can give to this query is that the new Birmingham administration must be prodded about as much as the outgoing one, before it will act. We are sadly mistaken if we feel that the election of Albert Boutwell as mayor will bring the millennium to Birmingham. While Mr. Boutwell is a much more gentle person than Mr. Connor, they are both segregationists, dedicated to maintenance of the status quo. I have hope that Mr. Boutwell will be reasonable enough to see the futility of massive resistance to desegregation. But he will not see this without pressure from devotees of civil rights. My friends, I must say to you that we have not made a single gain in civil rights without determined legal and nonviolent pressure. Lamentably, it is an historical fact that privileged groups seldom give up their privileges voluntarily. Individuals may see the moral light and voluntarily give up their unjust posture; but, as Reinhold Niebuhr has reminded us, groups tend to be more immoral than individuals.

We know through painful experience that freedom is never voluntarily given by the oppressor; it must be demanded by the oppressed. Frankly, I have yet to engage in a direct-action campaign that was "well timed" in the view of those who have not suffered unduly from the disease of segregation. For years now I have heard the word "Wait!" It rings in the ear of every Negro with piercing familiarity. This "Wait" has almost always meant "Never." We must come to see, with one of our distinguished jurists, that "justice too long delayed is justice denied."

We have waited for more than 340 years for our constitutional and God-given rights. The nations of Asia and Africa are moving with jetlike speed toward gaining political independence, but we still creep at horse-and-buggy pace toward gaining a cup of coffee at a lunch counter. Perhaps it is easy for those who have never felt the stinging darts of segregation to say, "Wait." But when you have seen vicious mobs lynch your mothers and fathers at will and drown your sisters and brothers at whim; when you have seen hate-filled policemen curse, kick and even kill your black brothers and sisters; when you see the vast majority of your twenty million Negro brothers smothering in an airtight cage of poverty in the midst of an affluent society; when you suddenly find your tongue twisted and your speech stammering as you seek to explain to your six-year-old daughter why she can't go to the public amusement park that has just been advertised on television, and see tears welling up in her eyes when she is told that Funtown is closed to colored children, and see ominous clouds of inferiority beginning to form in her little mental sky, and see her beginning to distort her personality by developing an unconscious bitterness toward white people; when you have to concoct an answer for a five-year-old son who is asking: "Daddy, why do white people treat colored people so mean?"; when you take a cross-country drive and find it necessary to sleep night after night in the uncomfortable corners of your automobile because no motel will accept you; when you are humiliated day in and day out by nagging signs reading "white" and "colored"; when your first name becomes "nigger," your middle name becomes "boy" (however old you are) and your last name becomes "John," and your wife and mother are never given the respected title "Mrs."; when you are harried by day and haunted by night by the fact that you are a Negro, living constantly at tiptoe stance, never quite knowing what to expect next, and are plagued with inner fears and outer resentments; when you are forever fighting a degenerating sense of "nobodiness"—then you will understand why we find it difficult to wait. There comes a time when the cup of endurance runs over, and men are no longer willing to be plunged into the abyss of despair. I hope, sirs, you can understand our legitimate and unavoidable impatience.

You express a great deal of anxiety over our willingness to break laws. This is certainly a legitimate concern. Since we so diligently urge people to obey the Supreme Court's decision of 1954 outlawing segregation in the public schools, at first glance it may seem rather paradoxical for us consciously to break laws. One may well ask: "How can you advocate breaking some laws and obeying others?" The answer lies in the fact that there are two types of laws: just and unjust. I would be the first to advocate obeying just laws. One has not only a legal but a moral responsibility to obey just laws. Conversely, one has a moral responsibility to disobey unjust laws. I would agree with St. Augustine that "an unjust law is no law at all."

Now, what is the difference between the two? How does one determine whether a law is just or unjust? A just law is a man-made code that squares with the moral law or the law of God. An unjust law is a code that is out of harmony with the moral law. To put it in the terms of St. Thomas Aquinas:

An unjust law is a human law that is not rooted in eternal law and natural law. Any law that uplifts human personality is just. Any law that degrades human personality is unjust. All segregation statutes are unjust because segregation distorts the soul and damages the personality. It gives the segregator a false sense of superiority and the segregated a false sense of inferiority. Segregation, to use the terminology of the Jewish philosopher Martin Buber, substitutes an "I–it" relationship for an "I–thou" relationship and ends up relegating persons to the status of things. Hence segregation is not only politically, economically and sociologically unsound, it is morally wrong and sinful. Paul Tillich has said that sin is separation. Is not segregation an existential expression of man's tragic separation, his awful estrangement, his terrible sinfulness? Thus it is that I can urge men to obey the 1954 decision of the Supreme Court, for it is morally right; and I can urge them to disobey segregation ordinances, for they are morally wrong.

Let us consider a more concrete example of just and unjust laws. An unjust law is a code that a numerical or power majority group compels a minority group to obey but does not make binding on itself. This is *difference* made legal. By the same token, a just law is a code that a majority compels a minority to follow and that it is willing to follow itself. This is *sameness* made legal.

Let me give another explanation. A law is unjust if it is inflicted on a minority that, as a result of being denied the right to vote, had no part in enacting or devising the law. Who can say that the legislature of Alabama which set up that state's segregation laws was democratically elected? Throughout Alabama all sorts of devious methods are used to prevent Negroes from becoming registered voters, and there are some counties in which, even though Negroes constitute a majority of the population, not a single Negro is registered. Can any law enacted under such circumstances be considered democratically structured?

Sometimes a law is just on its face and unjust in its application. For instance, I have been arrested on a charge of parading without a permit. Now, there is nothing wrong in having an ordinance which requires a permit for a parade. But such an ordinance becomes unjust when it is used to maintain segregation and to deny citizens the First-Amendment privilege of peaceful assembly and protest.

I hope you are able to see the distinction I am trying to point out. In no sense do I advocate evading or defying the law, as would the rabid segregationist. That would lead to anarchy. One who breaks an unjust law must do so openly, lovingly, and with a willingness to accept the penalty. I submit that an individual who breaks a law that conscience tells him is unjust, and who willingly accepts the penalty of imprisonment in order to arouse the conscience of the community over its injustice, is in reality expressing the highest respect for law.

Of course, there is nothing new about this kind of civil disobedience. It was evidenced sublimely in the refusal of Shadrach, Meshach and Abednego to obey the laws of Nebuchadnezzar, on the ground that a higher moral law was at stake. It was practiced superbly by the early Christians, who were willing to face hungry lions and the excruciating pain of chopping blocks rather than submit to certain unjust laws of the Roman Empire. To a degree, academic freedom is a reality today because Socrates practiced civil disobedience. In our own nation, the Boston Tea Party represented a massive act of civil disobedience.

We should never forget that everything Adolf Hitler did in Germany was "legal" and everything the Hungarian freedom fighters did in Hungary was "illegal." It was "illegal" to aid and comfort a Jew in Hitler's Germany. Even so, I am sure that, had I lived in Germany at the time, I would have aided and comforted my Jewish brothers. If today I lived in a Communist country where certain principles dear to the Christian faith are suppressed, I would openly advocate disobeying that country's antireligious laws.

I must make two honest confessions to you, my Christian and Jewish brothers. First, I must confess that over the past few years I have been gravely disappointed with the white moderate. I have almost reached the regrettable conclusion that the Negro's great stumbling block in his stride toward freedom is not the White Citizen's Counciler or the Ku Klux Klanner, but the white moderate, who is more devoted to "order" than to justice; who prefers a negative peace which is the absence of tension to a positive peace which is the presence of justice; who constantly says: "I agree with you in the goal you seek, but I cannot agree with your methods of direct action"; who paternalistically believes he can set the timetable for another man's freedom; who lives by a mythical concept of time and who constantly advises the Negro to wait for a "more convenient season." Shallow understanding from people of good will is more frustrating than absolute misunderstanding from people of ill will. Lukewarm acceptance is much more bewildering than outright rejection.

I had hoped that the white moderate would understand that law and order exist for the purpose of establishing justice and that when they fail in this purpose they become the dangerously structured dams that block the flow of social progress. I had hoped that the white moderate would understand that the present tension in the South is a necessary phase of the transition from an obnoxious negative peace, in which the Negro passively accepted his unjust plight, to a substantive and positive peace, in which all men will respect the dignity and worth of human personality. Actually, we who engage in nonviolent direct action are not the creators of tension. We merely bring to the surface the hidden tension that is already alive. We bring it out in the open, where it can be seen and dealt with. Like a boil that can never be cured so long as it is covered up but must be opened with all its ugliness to the natural medicines of air and light, injustice must be exposed, with all the tension its exposure creates, to the light of human conscience and the air of national opinion before it can be cured.

In your statement you assert that our actions, even though peaceful, must be condemned because they precipitate violence. But is this a logical assertion? Isn't this like condemning a robbed man because his possession of money precipitated the evil act of robbery? Isn't this like condemning Socrates because his unswerving commitment to truth and his philosophical inquiries precipitated the act by the misguided populace in which they made him drink hemlock? Isn't this like condemning Jesus because his unique God-consciousness and never-ceasing devotion to God's will precipitated the evil act of crucifixion? We must come to see that, as the federal courts have consistently affirmed, it is wrong to urge an individual to cease his efforts to gain his basic constitutional rights because the quest may precipitate violence. Society must protect the robbed and punish the robber.

I had also hoped that the white moderate would reject the myth concerning time in relation to the struggle for freedom. I have just received a letter from a white brother in Texas. He writes: "All Christians know that the colored people will receive equal rights eventually, but it is possible that you are in too great a religious hurry. It has taken Christianity almost two thousand years to accomplish what it has. The teachings of Christ take time to come to earth." Such an attitude stems from a tragic misconception of time, from the strangely irrational notion that there is something in the very flow of time that will inevitably cure all ills. Actually, time itself is neutral; it can be used either destructively or constructively. More and more I feel that the people of ill will have used time much more effectively than have the people of good will. We will have to repent in this generation not merely for the hateful words and actions of the bad people but for the appalling silence of the good people. Human progress never rolls in on wheels of inevitability; it comes through the tireless efforts of men willing to be co-workers with God, and without this hard work, time itself becomes an ally of the forces of social stagnation. We must use time creatively, in the knowledge that the time is always ripe to do right. Now is the time to make real the promise of democracy and transform our pending national elegy into a creative psalm of brotherhood. Now is the time to lift our national policy from the quicksand of racial injustice to the solid rock of human dignity.

You speak of our activity in Birmingham as extreme. At first I was rather disappointed that fellow clergymen would see my nonviolent efforts as those of an extremist. I began thinking about the fact that I stand in the middle of two opposing forces in the Negro community. One is a force of complacency, made up in part of Negroes who, as a result of long years of oppression, are so drained of self-respect and a sense of "somebodiness" that they have adjusted to segregation; and in part of a few middle-class Negroes who, because of a degree of academic and economic security and because in some ways they profit by segregation, have become insensitive to the problems of the masses. The other force is one of bitterness and hatred, and it comes perilously close to advocating violence. It is expressed in the various black nationalist groups that are springing up across the nation, the largest and best-known being Elijah Muhammad's Muslim movement. Nourished by the Negro's frustration over the continued existence of racial discrimination, this movement is made up of people who have lost faith in America, who have absolutely repudiated Christianity, and who have concluded that the white man is an incorrigible "devil."

I have tried to stand between these two forces, saying that we need emulate neither the "do-nothingism" of the complacent nor the hatred and despair of the black nationalist. For there is the more excellent way of love and nonviolent protest. I am grateful to God that, through the influence of the Negro church, the way of nonviolence became an integral part of our struggle.

If this philosophy had not emerged, by now many streets of the South would, I am convinced, be flowing with blood. And I am further convinced that if our white brothers dismiss as "rabble-rousers" and "outside agitators" those of us who employ nonviolent direct action, and if they refuse to support our nonviolent efforts, millions of Negroes will, out of frustration and despair, seek solace and security in black-nationalist ideologies—a development that would inevitably lead to a frightening racial nightmare.

Oppressed people cannot remain oppressed forever. The yearning for freedom eventually manifests itself, and that is what has happened to the American Negro. Something within has reminded him of his birthright of freedom, and something without has reminded him that it can be gained. Consciously or unconsciously, he has been caught up by the *Zeitgeist,* and with his black brothers of Africa and his brown and yellow brothers of Asia, South America and the Caribbean, the United States Negro is moving with a sense of great urgency toward the promised land of racial justice. If one recognizes this vital urge that has engulfed the Negro community, one should readily understand why public demonstrations are taking place. The Negro has many pent-up resentments and latent frustrations, and he must release them. So let him march; let him make prayer pilgrimages to the city hall; let him go on freedom rides—and try to understand why he must do so. If his repressed emotions are not released in nonviolent ways, they will seek expression through violence; this is not a threat but a fact of history. So I have not said to my people: "Get rid of your discontent." Rather, I have tried to say that this normal and healthy discontent can be channeled into the creative outlet of nonviolent direct action. And now this approach is being termed extremist.

But though I was initially disappointed at being categorized as an extremist, as I continued to think about the matter I gradually gained a measure of satisfaction from the label. Was not Jesus an extremist for love: "Love your enemies, bless them that curse you, do good to them that hate you, and pray for them which despitefully use you, and persecute you." Was not Amos an extremist for justice: "Let justice roll down like waters and righteousness like an ever-flowing stream." Was not Paul an extremist for the Christian gospel: "I bear in my body the marks of the Lord Jesus." Was not Martin Luther an extremist: "Here I stand; I cannot do otherwise, so help me God." And John Bunyan: "I will stay in jail to the end of my days before I make a butchery of my conscience." And Abraham Lincoln: "This nation cannot survive half slave and half free." And Thomas Jefferson: "We hold these truths to be self-evident, that all men are created equal . . ." So the question is not whether we will be extremists, but what kind of extremists we will be. Will we be extremists for hate or for love? Will we be extremists for the preservation of injustice or for the extension of justice? In that dramatic scene on Calvary's hill three men were crucified. We must never forget that all three were crucified for the same crime—the crime of extremism. Two were extremists for immorality, and thus fell below their environment. The other, Jesus Christ, was an extremist for love, truth and goodness, and thereby rose above his environment. Perhaps the South, the nation and the world are in dire need of creative extremists.

I had hoped that the white moderate would see this need. Perhaps I was too optimistic; perhaps I expected too much. I suppose I should have realized that few members of the oppressor race can understand the deep groans and passionate yearnings of the oppressed race, and still fewer have the vision to see that injustice must be rooted out by strong, persistent and determined action. I am thankful, however, that some of our white brothers in the South have grasped the meaning of this social revolution and committed themselves to it. They are still all too few in quantity, but they are big in quality. Some—such as Ralph McGill, Lillian Smith, Harry Golden, James McBride Dabbs, Ann Braden and Sarah Patton Boyle—have written about our struggle in eloquent and prophetic terms. Others have marched with us down nameless streets of the South. They have languished in filthy, roach-infested jails, suffering the abuse and brutality of policemen who view them as "dirty nigger-lovers." Unlike so many of their moderate brothers and sisters, they have recognized the urgency of the moment and sensed the need for powerful "action" antidotes to combat the disease of segregation.

Let me take note of my other major disappointment. I have been so greatly disappointed with the white church and its leadership. Of course, there are some notable exceptions. I am not unmindful of the fact that each of you has taken some significant stands on this issue. I commend you, Reverend Stallings, for your Christian stand on this past Sunday, in welcoming Negroes to your worship service on a nonsegregated basis. I commend the Catholic leaders of this state for integrating Spring Hill College several years ago.

But despite these notable exceptions, I must honestly reiterate that I have been disappointed with the church. I do not say this as one of those negative critics who can always find something wrong with the church. I say this as a minister of the gospel, who loves the church; who was nurtured in its bosom; who has been sustained by its spiritual blessings and who will remain true to it as long as the cord of life shall lengthen.

When I was suddenly catapulted into the leadership of the bus protest in Montgomery, Alabama, a few years ago, I felt we would be supported by the white church. I felt that the white ministers, priests and rabbis of the South would be among our strongest allies. Instead, some have been outright opponents, refusing to understand the freedom movement and misrepresenting its leaders; all too many others have been more cautious than courageous and have remained silent behind the anesthetizing security of stained-glass windows.

In spite of my shattered dreams, I came to Birmingham with the hope that the white religious leadership of this community would see the justice of our cause and, with deep moral concern, would serve as the channel through which our just grievances could reach the power structure. I had hoped that each of you would understand. But again I have been disappointed.

I have heard numerous southern religious leaders admonish their worshipers to comply with a desegregation decision because it is the law, but I have longed to hear white ministers declare: "Follow this decree because integration is morally right and because the Negro is your brother." In the midst of blatant injustices inflicted upon the Negro, I have watched white churchmen stand on the sideline and mouth pious irrelevancies and sanctimonious trivialities. In the midst of a mighty struggle to rid our nation of racial and economic injustice, I have heard many ministers say: "Those are social issues, with which the gospel has no real concern." And I have watched many churches commit themselves to a completely otherworldly religion which makes a strange, un-Biblical distinction between body and soul, between the sacred and the secular.

I have traveled the length and breadth of Alabama, Mississippi and all the other southern states. On sweltering summer days and crisp autumn mornings I have looked at the South's beautiful churches with their lofty spires pointing heavenward. I have beheld the impressive outlines of her massive religious-education buildings. Over and over I have found myself asking: "What kind of people worship here? Who is their God? Where were their voices when the lips of Governor Barnett dripped with words of interposition and nullification? Where were they when Governor Wallace gave a clarion call for defiance and hatred? Where were their voices of support when bruised and weary Negro men and women decided to rise from the dark dungeons of complacency to the bright hills of creative protest?"

Yes, these questions are still in my mind. In deep disappointment I have wept over the laxity of the church. But be assured that my tears have been tears of love. There can be no deep disappointment where there is not deep love. Yes, I love the church. How could I do otherwise? I am in the rather unique position of being the son, the grandson and the great-grandson of preachers. Yes, I see the church as the body of Christ. But, oh! How we have blemished and scarred that body through social neglect and through fear of being non-conformists.

There was a time when the church was very powerful—in the time when the early Christians rejoiced at being deemed worthy to suffer for what they believed. In those days the church was not merely a thermometer that recorded the ideas and principles of popular opinion; it was a thermostat that transformed the mores of society. Whenever the early Christians entered a town, the people in power became disturbed and immediately sought to convict the Christians for being "disturbers of the peace" and "outside agitators." But the Christians pressed on, in the conviction that they were "a colony of heaven," called to obey God rather than man. Small in number, they were big in commitment. They were too God-intoxicated to be "astronomically intimidated." By their effort and example they brought an end to such ancient evils as infanticide and gladiatorial contests.

Things are different now. So often the contemporary church is a weak, ineffectual voice with an uncertain sound. So often it is an archdefender of the status quo. Far from being disturbed by the presence of the church, the power structure of the average community is consoled by the church's silent—and often even vocal—sanction of things as they are.

But the judgment of God is upon the church as never before. If today's church does not recapture the sacrificial spirit of the early church, it will lose its authenticity, forfeit the loyalty of millions, and be dismissed as an irrelevant social club with no meaning for the twentieth century. Every day I meet young people whose disappointment with the church has turned into outright disgust.

Perhaps I have once again been too optimistic. Is organized religion too inextricably bound to the status quo to save our nation and the world? Perhaps I must turn my faith to the inner spiritual church, the church within the church, as the true *ekklesia* and the hope of the world. But again I am thankful to God that some noble souls from the ranks of organized religion have broken loose from the paralyzing chains of conformity and joined us as active partners in the struggle for freedom. They have left their secure congregations and walked the streets of Albany, Georgia, with us. They have gone down the highways of the South on tortuous rides for freedom. Yes, they have gone to jail with us. Some have been dismissed from their churches, have lost the support of their bishops and fellow ministers. But they have acted in the faith that right defeated is stronger than evil triumphant. Their witness has been the spiritual salt that has preserved the true meaning of the gospel in these troubled times. They have carved a tunnel of hope through the dark mountain of disappointment.

I hope the church as a whole will meet the challenge of this decisive hour. But even if the church does not come to the aid of justice, I have no despair about the future. I have no fear about the outcome of our struggle in Birmingham, even if our motives are at present misunderstood. We will reach the goal of freedom in Birmingham and all over the nation, because the goal of America is freedom. Abused and scorned though we may be, our destiny is tied up with America's destiny. Before the pilgrims landed at Plymouth, we were here. Before the pen of Jefferson etched the majestic words of the Declaration of Independence across the pages of history, we were here. For more than two centuries our forebears labored in this country without wages; they made cotton king; they built the homes of their masters while suffering gross injustice and shameful humiliation—and yet out of a bottomless vitality they continued to thrive and develop. If the inexpressible cruelties of slavery could not stop us, the opposition we now face will surely fail. We will win our freedom because the sacred heritage of our nation and the eternal will of God are embodied in our echoing demands.

Before closing I feel impelled to mention one other point in your statement that has troubled me profoundly. You warmly commended the Birmingham police force for keeping "order" and "preventing violence." I doubt that you would have so warmly commended the police force if you had seen its dogs sinking their teeth into unarmed, nonviolent Negroes. I doubt that you would so quickly commend the policemen if you were to observe their ugly and inhumane treatment of Negroes here in the city jail; if you were to watch them push and curse old Negro women and young Negro girls; if you were to see them slap and kick old Negro men and young boys; if you were to observe them, as they did on two occasions, refuse to give us food because we wanted to sing our grace together. I cannot join you in your praise of the Birmingham police department.

It is true that the police have exercised a degree of discipline in handling the demonstrators. In this sense they have conducted themselves rather "nonviolently" in public. But for what purpose? To preserve the evil system of segregation. Over the past few years I have consistently preached that nonviolence demands that the means we use must be as pure as the ends we seek. I have tried to make clear that it is wrong to use immoral means to attain moral ends. But now I must affirm that it is just as wrong, or perhaps even more so, to use moral means to preserve immoral ends. Perhaps Mr. Connor and his policemen have been rather nonviolent in public, as was Chief Pritchett in Albany, Georgia, but they have used the moral means of nonviolence to maintain the immoral end of racial injustice. As T. S. Eliot has said: "The last temptation is the greatest treason: To do the right deed for the wrong reason."

I wish you had commended the Negro sit-inners and demonstrators of Birmingham for their sublime courage, their willingness to suffer and their amazing discipline in the midst of great provocation. One day the South will recognize its real heroes. They will be the James Merediths, with the noble sense of purpose that enables them to face jeering and hostile mobs, and with the agonizing loneliness that characterizes the life of the pioneer. They will be old, oppressed, battered Negro women, symbolized in a seventy-two-year-old woman in Montgomery, Alabama, who rose up with a sense of dignity and with her people decided not to ride segregated buses, and who responded with ungrammatical profundity to one who inquired about her weariness: "My feets is tired, but my soul is at rest." They will be the young high school and college students, the young ministers of the gospel and a host of their elders, courageously and nonviolently sitting in at lunch counters and willingly going to jail for conscience' sake. One day the South will know that when these disinherited children of God sat down at lunch counters, they were in reality standing up for what is best in the American dream and for the most sacred values in our Judaeo-Christian heritage, thereby bringing our nation back to those great wells of democracy which were dug deep by the founding fathers in their formulation of the Constitution and the Declaration of Independence.

Never before have I written so long a letter. I'm afraid it is much too long to take your precious time. I can assure you that it would have been much shorter if I had been writing from a comfortable desk, but what else can one do when he is alone in a narrow jail cell, other than write long letters, think long thoughts and pray long prayers?

If I have said anything in this letter that overstates the truth and indicates an unreasonable impatience, I beg you to forgive me. If I have said anything that understates the truth and indicates my having a patience that allows me to settle for anything less than brotherhood, I beg God to forgive me.

I hope this letter finds you strong in the faith. I also hope that circumstances will soon make it possible for me to meet each of you, not as an integrationist or a civil-rights leader but as a fellow clergyman and a Christian brother. Let us all hope that the dark clouds of racial prejudice will soon pass away and the deep fog of misunderstanding will be lifted from our fear-drenched communities, and in some not too distant tomorrow the radiant stars of love and brotherhood will shine over our great nation with all their scintillating beauty.

Yours for the cause of Peace and Brotherhood,

MARTIN LUTHER KING, JR.

18

Testimonies

Janet and Robert Aldridge, Molly Rush, and Daniel Berrigan

Antinuclear activism in the United States grew in the wake of the Vietnam War. As American presidents and Pentagon leaders planned smarter and more sophisticated bombs and delivery systems and fueled the American economy through the production of weapons of mass destruction, some citizens saw their conviction mount that the nation's course was wrong and immoral. By the 1970s and early 1980s, that conviction had taken a radical turn. No longer content to work for their livelihoods in jobs that supported the military-industrial complex, nor to engage in conventional political tactics in support of their vision, antinuclear prophets turned their backs on America as usual. They questioned as well the rubric of nonviolent protest that had dominated the career of Martin Luther King, Jr. In the new ethic they set themselves, some antinuclear Americans began to challenge the sanctity of government property when that property was weaponry or was used for the production of nuclear weaponry and delivery systems. In the testimonies reprinted here, four Americans—all of them Roman Catholic—explain why they broke with social expectation or written law to engage in radical antinuclearism. Members of a church that had elaborated the historic just-war theory, they believed that in the nuclear age no war could be just and that the nuclear stakes were too high. They were convinced, with Daniel Berrigan, that *not* to protest was tantamount to actively killing, and they announced to others that they were "not allowed to be complicit in murder." As Roman Catholics protesting the American nuclear age, they were a particularly large and noticeable minority among antinuclearists from a series of Protestant denominations, evangelicals and members of peace churches among them.

Janet and Robert Aldridge

A Nuclear Engineer's Family

In 1956 Lockheed Aircraft Corporation moved its missile division to the San Francisco Bay Area. The plant they built in Sunnyvale was later to become

Lockheed Missiles and Space Company. Wanting to get back into aeronautics, Bob hired on in the engineering department and we bought our present home in Santa Clara. Our sixth and youngest child was not quite a year old at the time.

Before we accepted work at Lockheed, and before we moved to the Bay Area, we did some serious thinking about the function of money in our lives. We were not living in poverty but we had plenty of bills, mainly doctor bills. But we were happy. We could see that that was not always the case when people had lots of money. What if this new job should become a huge financial success? How would we react?

We finally made an agreement between ourselves and with God that if we ever received an abundant income we would not seek material excess. Instead we would use our resources to raise good children and to do God's will as we saw it. At that time we didn't foresee the ramifications of that pact, but it was the beginning of our responsiveness to opportunities that unfolded.

After starting the engineering job, Bob went back to school at San Jose State University. Sputnik was launched shortly after and the Russians flew their first intercontinental missile. The later-to-be-proved-false missile gap sparked national paranoia. Operational dates for the new Polaris submarines were moved ahead. Bob was working on the submarine-launched missiles and his engineering department went on a ten-hour-day, six-day-week schedule. In spite of this exhausting pace, Bob continued part time with college courses and, after five grueling years, managed to graduate with highest honors in his aeronautical engineering class.

Bob took a keen interest in his new engineering job and advanced rapidly. But other forces entered our lives shortly after we moved to Santa Clara. New acquaintances invited us to join the Christian Family Movement, a lay Christian movement that started in the United States and has now spread throughout the world to become a strong force for social change. It emphasizes the importance of the family. Meanwhile our own family continued to grow, until we had ten healthy children entrusted to our care. We were well blessed.

CFM had a strong formative effect on our spiritual life during the 11 years we were active, and in the years since. We worked with other couples in a close community spirit, sharing work projects and recreation. Eventually we saw beyond our own comfort and desired it for all people.

Another important jump in awareness came in 1963 when we made our Cursillo. The Cursillo (a little course in Christianity started in Spain) is an intense three-day experience in Christian love. It forced us to scrutinize ourselves and our commitment to God and humanity.

During his first eight years at Lockheed Bob helped design three generations of Polaris missiles. He worked mostly on wind tunnel testing and underwater launch development. During that time he was convinced that building weapons to deter war was his most important contribution to peace. Once a fellow worker engaged him in a philosophical discussion about religion in daily life and asked, "What do you think God wants you to do most of all?"

"Just what I am doing," Bob responded without hesitation. "To help design this missile to protect our country." Although the conversation died at that point, the question bothered him for time to come. But Bob had not yet learned to pay attention when disturbed.

In 1965 Lockheed cornered the Poseidon missile contract and Bob transferred to reentry systems. That is the part of the missile which carries the hydrogen bomb to its destination. He helped design the multiple individually targeted reentry vehicles (more commonly called MIRVs). MIRVs allow one missile to destroy many targets. Working on these, Bob saw what happens at the other end of the missile's flight.

It bothered him to hear how the Poseidon missile-submarine weapon was evaluated: that system has an "effectiveness" of killing one-quarter of Russia's population. Helping to prepare for such incineration was disquieting. Bob subconsciously resorted to moral self-deception: he dismissed that uncomfortable fact by simply not thinking about it. He did not visualize the killing, maiming, orphaning, and widowing that would take place if Poseidon were ever used, pursuing his work with the superficial awareness that one acquires through the daily newspaper.

Bob's real questioning of nuclear weapons started about 1968. After dinner one evening our oldest daughter, Janie, a sophomore at Santa Clara University at the time, was telling us about some campus demonstrations. Students were protesting against Dow Chemical because it made napalm to use in Vietnam. The discussion went into the wee hours of the morning. Janie expressed her concern that when the Vietnam issue was settled, the protest would turn to the building of nuclear weapons. Bob defended his position: these weapons were needed to prevent Russia from taking over the world: At the least, they were needed until a meaningful treaty could be negotiated. But Janie insisted that people must summon the courage to change their destructive behavior.

Bob was shaken. He had worked hard to complete college. His future was promising. We had a large family to support and it just wasn't realistic to think about starting over. But we were not reckoning on how God would present his desires and how we would respond. The obstacles seemed insurmountable at the time. They forced Bob to another form of self-deception: rationalizing. When troubling thoughts become too persistent to be repressed we often justify immoral activity with faulty logic.

A new consciousness did dawn on us, however. Bob became more aware of what was happening about him at work. He noticed that most of his fellow workers did not really seem convinced that they were defending their country. Patriotic feelings and good intentions took second place to winning contracts and keeping the business going. Lockheed puts much effort on future business—developing new weapons concepts with which to entice the military. The real motive behind the arms race gradually surfaced in our understanding: profits for the company and job security for the workers.

Bob describes how his work environment contributed to his growing uneasiness:

> I observed very little joy within the guarded gates of Lockheed. Only the intellectual surfaced, and that was strictly along the lines of "me and my project." That sterile attitude, accompanied by tough competition to gain more responsibility, was the general rule. Why people wanted to gather more and more work under their control always amazed me. I finally diagnosed this "empire building" as groping for security—a need to become indispensable. But I knew of very few who achieved any degree of permanency. A budget cut or administrative reshuffle could result in being squeezed out of line in the pecking order.
>
> I did not realize it at the time, but my interior attitude was shifting from a "thing-relationship" to concern for others—a change which tolled the death knell for my engineering career in the defense industry.

Bob became involved in subterfuge at Lockheed in 1970, involving the use of secret classifications to deceive the public. The first strategic arms limitation talks (SALT) were just getting under way. Simultaneously, a public outcry to ban the MIRV was gaining momentum. Lockheed and the Navy realized that such a ban could lead to cancellation of the Poseidon missile contract which would mean a profit loss for Lockheed, to say nothing of depriving the Navy of its newest weapon. A task force was set up to investigate other types of warheads which could be used on Poseidon in case MIRVs were outlawed.

At first this effort was openly called SALT Studies. But as the cry to ban the MIRV grew louder, it became apparent that this would be a sensitive issue if people found out that Lockheed and the Navy were trying to evade arms limitation. The task force was moved behind secret doors and given the code name of CAFE; the relationship between SALT negotiations and CAFE became secret information. It was clear that secrecy was being used only to prevent the American people from discerning the government's lack of sincerity in the area of disarmament.

It was about this time that design studies were started on the new Trident missile. Bob was then a leader of an advanced reentry system design group. He was given design responsibility for the maneuvering reentry vehicle (MARV) for Trident. To acquaint himself with maneuvering technology he reviewed many secret reports which revealed the Pentagon's interest in greater accuracy for missile warheads. Such precision was not needed according to our long-standing deterrent policy, which threatens massive retaliation only if attacked. Increased accuracy is only necessary if the Pentagon is planning to destroy targets, such as missile silos. To do that means shooting first; it doesn't make sense to retaliate against empty silos.

Bob saw this policy switch over three years before it was finally revealed to the American public. It had actually started about 1965 when the United States finished its buildup of intercontinental ballistic missiles and missile-launching submarines. Robert McNamara, Secretary of Defense at the time, said that U.S. emphasis would thereafter be on quality improvements. This led to a more aggressive military policy. Because of the overkill in deterrent capability, it was becoming harder to justify more weapons. But improving the quality still sounded reasonable—and that touched off a new sprint in the arms race.

We now read quite openly in the papers that the U.S. might use nuclear weapons first under some circumstances, but such brazen proclamations would not have been accepted at the beginning of this decade. In 1970 it had a traumatic effect on Bob to find them shrouded in secrecy.

No longer could he repress sinister facts from his thoughts, nor was rationalization effective. Another means was needed to salve his conscience. We became active as peace information coordinators for the National Association of Laity, a Catholic lay organization working for church renewal and social reform. In that work we were exposed to more international study and research.

The new knowledge of how multinational corporations' behavior, the substance of our own livelihood, was oppressing poor people at home and abroad made Bob's position even more untenable. We could see that our superficial involvement in peace work had no real roots. But we also tried to convince ourselves that if we were not enjoying the lush salary and ample fringe benefits from this macabre livelihood, they would only go to someone else. Yet I could see that Bob was being torn apart inside because of the work he was performing. I prepared myself psychologically for the impending change.

For slightly over a year we depended on bomb-building for our survival and worked for peace as a hobby. Eventually this hypocritical existence became unbearable. Early in 1972 we agreed that, regardless of the effect our action would have, we had to follow our consciences. We started planning our escape from the military-industrial complex. Bob would have to give up engineering, as it would be practically impossible to find such a job in our area not tied to a military contract.

It was important to us that the children should share in our decisions insofar as they were capable. We talked our plans over with them and answered their questions. At family meetings we let their fears and ours be heard.

We learned from the example of Jim and Shelley Douglass, whom we met in the first months of our "liberation plan." Jim's book, *Resistance and Contemplation: The Way of Liberation,* revealed their struggle to give up security and accept suffering for the whole family.

We had voiced the same fears and asked the same questions, but we hadn't listened well enough to understand the answers. We had to see someone actually try the road before we could venture on it. We had leaned too much on precedents, which were nothing more than crutches for our weak determination. Our subjective morality had to yield. We had to act on our own convictions.

We set the date for January of 1973. Immediately after the Christmas holidays Bob would tell Lockheed he was leaving. We would start the new year with a new life.

Having spent the past quarter-century caring for home and children, I started looking for a job immediately. I wanted to work with handicapped children and had been taking courses in vision therapy. But when I found an instructional aide opening in the school system, I took it. My job reflected our desire to deepen our marriage relationship by abolishing the traditional roles of husband and wife, and by sharing all the chores, joys, trials and responsibilities equally. The first overt step toward the transition was made.

During his last month on the job Bob discussed our decision with co-workers. Some were sympathetic and one even congratulated him for making the move. But they could not imagine taking similar action themselves. The need for financial security was too deeply ingrained. That singular fear is probably the greatest obstacle to moral action in today's society.

When the guarded gates of Lockheed clanged shut behind Bob for the last time, we started cutting expenses as an economical necessity. We ate less meat and experimented with new recipes that give a balanced diet at less expense. Second-hand shops became our source of clothing. We discovered ways to reduce spending and new approaches to pleasure without having to "buy" entertainment.

For us, simple living began by revising our work pattern. Work in the traditional sense usually occupied about half of our waking hours; we tended to center our lives around it, which prevented us from seeing our labor in proper context. It had become an end in itself, rather than the means of living; occupational success outshone all other values.

Living on a large salary, measuring success by income, does violence to the 94 percent of the world's population who must survive on only half the global wealth. We sometimes attempted to alleviate that disparity by donations to "charity," but that type of giving merely numbed our consciences, and in no way approached charity in its gospel sense. Ambrose, bishop of Milan during the fourth century, said about token giving: "You are not making a gift of your possessions to the poor man. You are handing over to him what is his. For what has been given in common for the use of all, you have arrogated to yourself."

There are arguments that one can live simply on a large salary while using the excess for good works, but we have never seen them lived out. Voluntary poverty is not a comfortable thought for the affluent and thus their judgment of simplicity becomes distorted. Too often worldly excesses are rationalized away by willingness to be "poor in spirit."

But a spirit of poverty amid wealth is impossible. That's why Jesus suggested selling all. Voluntary poverty does not mean destitution, but it does require putting our whole being into it. Our family has only scratched the surface of simple living. And the overall effort of trying to live a nonviolent life—wife, husband, and children together—is difficult, because affluence has become so deeply ingrained. But the main thing as we see it is that our family is feeling its way. To us that means really believing Jesus' teachings—saying we are Christians and trying to live it, saying we are nonviolent and trying to act nonviolently. We are trying to be less greedy as we search for ways to reduce our own needs so there will be enough to go around. Life is still scary, but we attempt to follow our consciences and rely on faith.

Molly Rush
A Grandmother and Activist

The bare bones are these, in reverse order of occurrence: grandmother; convicted felon awaiting appeal on a two- to five-year jail sentence; director of a peace and justice ministry since 1973; mother of four sons and two daughters, aged twenty-seven to fourteen; wife of Bill for twenty-eight years; eldest of eight children of Dave and Mary Moore.

In looking back, I see continuity and struggle, a struggle that continues as I ponder the future in terms of responsibility and, especially, of hope. Today I know hope as a lived experience, not as a choice or a false optimism. For that I am deeply grateful.

The crimes for which I was convicted are defined differently by the courts than by me and my friends, now called the Plowshares Eight. In choosing to call forth hope by disarming two Mark 12A nuclear warheads which, when armed, could each cause more innocent deaths and suffering than a Dachau or a Buchenwald, we believe we were acting both legally and morally. It was a response to a legal system that serves to protect the production of genocidal weapons and thereby threatens the life of each child now living and generations not yet born.

As I await the birth of my second grandchild, I know that today the world is a more dangerous place than it was on September 9, 1980, when we walked into that General Electric plant in King of Prussia, Pennsylvania, where these warheads are produced on an assembly line. In taking hammers to the lovingly constructed cones of death, then pouring our blood on them, we were engaged in an old biblical task: smashing idols, symbolically turning swords into plowshares.

My desire in taking this action was to break free of the paralyzing power over our lives that these seemingly invulnerable weapons have held, freeing up the possibility for hope in a seemingly hopeless situation. It allowed me to look forward to this child of my child with a sure knowledge that life itself is a miracle and that it is only by letting go of the illusion of control over my life and trusting in the Creator, and not in the bomb, that I can live in hope.

People sometimes look at me in disbelief when I talk of hope as the central reality in my life. With the bomb over all of our heads and a jail sentence over mine, I know that a few years ago I couldn't have talked this way of faith or miracles. I was at best an optimistic pessimist, a somewhat cynical pragmatist, a "realist," I would have said. I had experienced firsthand the injustice of the system and wanted to change it.

Thirty years ago, after hearing my mother talk of trust in God, accepting our cross as God's will, I had decided that attitude was too passive for me. I thought that to accept it meant to accept a fate that should be struggled against. My family had had to go on welfare when my father's drinking had led to the loss of his last job when I was sixteen. I was angry with him and with my mother for putting up with him. I was even angrier at the intrusive questions put to me by a caseworker a few years older than myself, who in different circumstances might have been my friend.

In later years, Mother humorously taped a tiny snapshot of Dad on the back of a pendant that said, "When life gives you lemons, make lemonade." One of her favorite sayings was that we all have a cross to bear. She was no martyr, but a serene and patient woman whose quiet faith sustained her. But I didn't want to hear about crosses.

She would put a good-morning prayer on the bathroom mirror. Above the kitchen sink was a more homey one, "Dear Lord of the pots and pans. . . ." For years I was allergic to pious talk. Yet any vision I had of church was filtered through the example I saw in my mother's life, just as my sense of being Irish was connected to my dad's storytelling, his sense of humor, and his fine Irish tenor voice.

He loved to argue politics, and years later, when I was involved in the civil rights struggle, he would make an outrageous comment just to get me shouting. Then he would tilt back in his chair, laughing delightedly. He had won; a good lesson for a self-righteous new activist.

I inherited his Irish temper. Any patience I've gained was learned from my mother. She always found time to read a story or play a game with the little ones, her joy. The fact that my father didn't work much meant that he had more time for us than most fathers. After I married at nineteen, my brothers and sisters took their turn supporting the younger ones.

I just wanted a husband, home, and children, with a measure of economic stability. By the time I was twenty-six, we had four children, two boys and two girls.

I joined Christian Mothers in the parish where I'd attended grade school and where my mother had once been a member. A black priest came to speak to us about civil rights, my first direct contact with this issue. I had read about the civil rights movement and watched on television the lunch counter sit-ins in which young black people responded nonviolently to having ketchup poured on their heads. I was outraged that a country that guaranteed liberty and justice for all could allow Jim Crow to exist. I wanted a better world and wanted to be part of the movement for change.

When a few people came to my parish to leaflet for Catholic Interracial Council (CIC), I decided to join. I didn't know a single political activist and was timid about joining the NAACP, but this was a step I could take. On my first picket line, in support of the struggle to open craft unions to blacks, a dignified lady approached me as I carried my CIC sign nervously aloft: "Young woman, I'm ashamed to be a Catholic!"

It was not hard to get cynical about the Church when CIC encountered wide opposition in its attempts to desegregate Catholic schools and encourage fair hiring practices within institutions and parishes. The response of the Church to the widening war in Vietnam was also disillusioning. Dr. King had risked broad support for civil rights when he criticized the war, but with the exception of a few priest friends in CIC, the local Catholic church remained silent.

One Sunday, a few people from a group then called Clergy and Laymen Concerned About Vietnam decided to leaflet my parish church. I joined them, four or five people with a poster and some leaflets questioning the morality of the war. My pastor called the local police, and we were faced with arrest if we did not leave. Unprepared for this stunning response, we left.

By this time, my oldest son Gary was entering his teens. My brother Ed, sent to Vietnam as an army cook, had found himself guarding an ammunition dump his first week there. I had written him to say I was marching against the war and to tell him why. He understood. As the war continued, I worried that Gary would reach eighteen and be drafted. I had not raised him to be a soldier.

My husband supported my protests, but devoted most of his energy to soft-ball. He managed a team as a sideline, and it was taking more and more of his time. I continued to work for civil rights. Two sons, Bob and Greg, were born in 1966 and 1968. With the older children in school, the little ones often accompanied me to meetings or marches. I also shared childcare with a friend.

As the war dragged on, several of us formed a group called CEASE in order to raise the issue as Catholics. Shortly afterwards, in 1972, Larry Kessler, Father Jack O'Malley, and I attended a major antiwar conference in Ann Arbor. It was my first overnight stay away from my family except to have a baby. While there, we met Vietnam Veterans Against the War who graphically described their experiences, including their participation in atrocities. We came home with a greater sense of urgency than ever about the need for a full-time peace center. With a few others, we made calls and raised enough pledges of monthly donations to begin.

The Thomas Merton Center opened its doors in March 1973. Larry quit his job to work as director. By the following year, three sisters had been released by their communities to work full time in our justice and peace ministry. Larry was leaving for Boston, and he asked me to take over. Greg was in kindergarten by now, so I became part-time director. We felt it was important to have lay leadership. I expected it to be a short-term commitment, thinking that once the war was over, support would evaporate.

My work with the center was an intense learning experience for me. I began to study world hunger and its causes in order to help develop a slideshow. As I learned of the links between corporate policies of growing export crops on peasant lands and of support for military dictatorships to maintain control of land and resources, and of food aid being sent to Vietnam in order to support the war, I began to understand that hunger and war and other issues such as racism and sexism were linked.

I was meeting people in liberation struggles in Latin America and Africa. Concerns that had once seemed remote became immediate and personal. I was also gaining information on the arms race, learning about MIRVs and MARVs and ICBMs and about the relentless development of weapons systems and policies that were bringing us to the brink of nuclear war. I began to take my concerns home. Would my children even have a future?

I was also learning how to educate and involve people. I saw the church mainly as a vehicle for reaching the people in the pews and helping them to become aware and active. When I read Thomas Merton, I was most likely to choose his writings on peace and social justice. I was inspired by the witness of people such as Daniel and Philip Berrigan, whose nonviolent resistance to the war seemed to come from the same wellsprings of inspiration as had Martin Luther King, Jr.'s. I began to read Gandhi and, later, James Douglass's *The Nonviolent Cross*. Now I was beginning to link my unspoken faith much more directly to my work for justice.

I had friends who had been arrested, but I didn't see myself as ready or able to take such a step. With six kids? Yet, as early as 1973, I remember talking with a nun friend, Marcia Snowden, who spent a week in jail during the Harrisburg conspiracy trial. I remember saying that it shouldn't be only priests and nuns who took these risks, or young men facing the draft. I felt I had all the more reason to protest what I saw as threats to my children's lives, and all the more responsibility. Yet I held back.

For one thing, my mother was operated on and found to have pancreatic cancer about two years after my father's death in 1971. For the next five years, until her death in April 1978, I watched her struggle with a disease I dreaded. I watched her go down to less than half her previous weight, enduring pain, treatments, and operations with quiet grace and courage. I'd bring the children to visit and ask how she was doing. She would say, "Fine," her eyes dancing. She remained herself throughout her five-year illness. I felt she had conquered cancer even as she died in her own bed, holding my hand.

She had never held a job until she was in her late fifties. Raising children was her life. Yet she encouraged and supported my work, no matter how controversial. She was an obedient daughter of the church, yet she gave the final blessing at a prayer service sponsored by our group which supported the ordination of women. Her entire life was a prayer; pain and suffering were accepted in that spirit, simply and without pretense.

During the years of my mother's illness, I continued to work at the center. We were both reading Merton. I was finding his writings on prayer and contemplation to be increasingly meaningful to me. My children were growing up.

With the end of the war, my attention shifted to the new strategies of counterforce coming out of the Nixon White House. The White House plumbers were getting all the publicity, as were detente and the opening of China. It wasn't yet known that Nixon's secret plan to end the war involved the threat to use the bomb. But the "humane" decision to target Soviet missile silos was awakening a few to a supposed "deterrence" policy which makes nuclear war much more likely.

The center began to organize an active campaign against the B-1 bomber. Its prime contractor, Rockwell International, was headquartered in Pittsburgh. We leafleted, demonstrated, lobbied, and finally decided to stage a sit-in in Rockwell's reception area on the 50th floor of the US Steel Building. Fourteen of us stayed for 25 hours before we were led away to an injunction hearing. We had a lot to learn about nonviolence, but the action generated publicity and was, we felt, "successful."

We later decided to challenge the B-1 bomber in court and spent time researching international law. I learned that these weapons of mass destruction were a violation of international treaties designed to limit the harm done to civilians. King and Gandhi had obeyed a higher law in their disobedience of unjust laws. Do not nuclear weapons result in injustice on a massive scale, involving the threat of extinction to all, including future generations?

Before our case could be heard, President Carter cancelled the B-1. The cruise missile would replace the B-1, creating an even more dangerous situation. Our "victory" turned to ashes.

I read *The Day Before Doomsday*, in which Sidney Lens outlined the developments in the arms race that were making nuclear war all but inevitable.

Earlier I'd met and argued with Phil Berrigan, thinking his vision too harsh, but I was coming to see that his call for civil disobedience in the face of this kind of reality was really rather modest.

What might I have hoped to do to oppose Hitler's death camps had I lived at that time in Germany? The threat today is that the entire planet will become a death camp. As I pondered the fate of Franz Jagerstatter, a family man who refused to go along then, the threat of jail had to be weighed against the danger that my younger children might not live to grow up.

By the summer of 1979, when I was invited to participate in a retreat with Dan Berrigan on these questions, I summoned up my courage and went. I could evade no longer. As we reflected together on the Epistle of James, I realized that what was at stake was not only my life and that of my children, but my faith. If fear of the consequences were to prevent me from following the conclusions of my conscience, then what had I to give to my children that could measure up to my mother's gift to me? The transparency of her faith that shone throughout her life was precious inheritance.

After the retreat, I went home and prayed some more. I was ready to take a first step. In September I carried a photo of a child who had been injured by the bomb in Hiroshima and, with twenty others, I walked up the driveway of a Washington hotel where arms merchants had nuclear weapons on display at an "arms bazaar." Refused entry by the police, we knelt and prayed until we were arrested and charged with unlawful entry.

After agonizing for years, I felt a burden had been lifted. The experience of jail can be extremely dehumanizing, but for me it was an experience of freedom, freedom from the fears that had immobilized me and shackled my conscience.

As for jail, I prefer to think of it as an unpleasant task, such as cleaning the cellar, rather than a dramatic experience that is all too often an everyday reality for the very poor. The women I met in jail shared the little they had, looking out for the weakest among us. I had much to learn from them.

Once home, I continued to be involved in protests, including a nine-day fast for peace with a few friends. The experience deepened my own understanding of the centrality of prayer to all my actions. Soon afterwards, I learned of plans to attempt a direct act of disarmament against first-strike weapons. The consequences would be serious, perhaps years of separation from my family. Months of struggle followed. Was I trying to be a martyr? The complete relief I felt when told the project was off told me that a martyr complex was clearly not one of my characteristics. When plans resumed, I realized that, in Dan Berrigan's words, it was something that I could not *not* do.

Our passive acceptance of the bomb, which means our children's deaths, kills off our feelings. We shut out the reality, refusing to deal with it, experiencing a sort of death in life. In a terrible way we have already succumbed to the bomb, accepting it not only for ourselves, but for those we love. We narrow our sights and tacitly give up on the future, giving silent consent, then "forgetting."

More than anything, the generation growing up today, numbed by a world which offers them the bomb as inheritance, mesmerizing all of us into a sense of helplessness, needs the light of faith in a loving and powerful God, a God of hope who can stand in vulnerable counterforce to this idol of death. The past two years of jail, trial, appeals have not been without tension or continuing struggles within the family regarding ongoing resistance. I am deeply grateful for the words of my son, Gary, before I went to GE. Once he'd asked all the hard questions about my leaving his younger brothers, he said, "I guess you have to follow your conscience." In one way or another all of my children have come to that understanding. And, slowly, so have I.

Daniel Berrigan

A Poet and Priest

On September 9, 1980, Father Daniel Berrigan took part in a civil disobedience action at a General Electric Plant in King of Prussia, Pennsylvania, where Mark 12A Missile components are made. Six months later, he and seven others—all representing themselves at their trial—were convicted on eight of thirteen counts. An appeal was finally resolved in 1990 when they were sentenced to time served in prison plus twenty-three months' probation. What follows is excerpted from the trial; it is Daniel Berrigan's response to the direct examination of Sister Anne Montgomery.

Anne Montgomery: Father Berrigan, I'd like to ask you a simple question: Why did you do what you did?

Daniel Berrigan: I would like to answer that question as simply as I can. It brings up immediately words that have been used again and again in the courtroom—like conscience, justification. The question takes me back to those years when my conscience was being formed, back to a family that was poor, and to a father and mother who taught, quite simply, by living what they taught. And if I could put their message very shortly, it would go something like this:

In a thousand ways they showed that you do what is right because it is right, that your conscience is a matter between you and God, that nobody owns you.

If I have a precious memory of my mother and father that lasts to this day, it is simply that they lived as though nobody owned them. They cheated no one. They worked hard for a living.

They were poor; and, perhaps most precious of all, they shared what they had. And that was enough, because in the life of a young child, the first steps of conscience are as important as the first steps of one's feet. They set the direction where life will go.

And I feel that direction was set for my brothers and myself. There is a direct line between the way my parents turned our steps and this action. That is no crooked line.

That was the first influence. The second one has to do with my religious order. When I was eighteen I left home for the Jesuit order. I reflect that I am sixty years old, and I have never been anything but a Jesuit, a Jesuit priest, in my whole life.

We have Jesuits throughout Latin America today, my own brothers, who are in prison, who have been under torture; many of them have been murdered.

On the walls of our religious communities both here and in Latin America are photos of murdered priests, priests who have been imprisoned, priests under torture, priests who stood somewhere because they believed in something. Those faces haunt my days. And I ask myself how I can be wishy-washy in face of such example, example of my own lifetime, my own age.

This is a powerful thing, to be in a common bond of vows with people who have given their lives because they did not believe in mass murder, because such crimes could not go on in their name.

Dear friends of the jury, you have been called the conscience of the community. Each of us eight comes from a community. I don't mean just a biological family. I mean that every one of us has brothers and sisters with whom we live, with whom we pray, with whom we offer the Eucharist, with whom we share income, and in some cases, the care of children. Our conscience, in other words, comes from somewhere. We have not come from outer space or from chaos or from madhouses to King of Prussia.

We have come from years of prayer, years of life together, years of testing— testing of who we are in the church and in the world. We would like to speak to you, each of us in a different way, about our communities; because, you see, it is our conviction that nobody in the world can form his or her conscience alone.

Now, perhaps I don't even have to dwell on that. Most of you who have children know the importance of others—not just parents, but friends, relatives, those who are loved and who love, in helping us come to understand who we are.

What are we to do in bad times? I am trying to say that we come as a community of conscience before your community of conscience to ask you: Are our consciences to act differently than yours in regard to the lives and deaths of children? A very simple question, but one that cuts to the bone.

We would like you to see that we come from where you come. We come from churches. We come from neighborhoods. We come from years of work.

We come from America. And we come to this, a trial, of conscience and motive. And the statement of conscience we would like to present to you is this.

We could not not do this. We could not not do this! We were pushed to this by all our lives. Do you see what I mean? All our lives.

I would speak about myself, the others will speak for themselves. When I say I could not not do this, I mean, among other things, that with every cowardly bone in my body I wished I hadn't had to enter the GE plant. I wish I hadn't had to do it. And that has been true every time I have been arrested, all those years. My stomach turns over. I feel sick. I feel afraid. I don't want to go through this again.

I hate jail. I don't do well there physically. But I cannot not go on, because I have learned that we must not kill if we are Christians. I have learned that children, above all, are threatened by these weapons. I have read that Christ our Lord underwent death rather than inflict it. And I am supposed to be a disciple. All kinds of things like that. The push, the push of conscience is a terrible thing.

So at some point your cowardly bones get moving, and you say, "Here it goes again," and you do it. And you have a certain peace because you did it, as I do this morning in speaking with you.

That phrase about not being able not to do something, maybe it is a little clumsy. But for those who raise children, who go to work every day, who must make decisions in their families, I think there is a certain knowledge of what I am trying to say. Children at times must be disciplined. We would rather not do it.

There are choices on jobs about honesty. There are things to be gained if we are dishonest. And it is hard not to be.

Yet one remains honest because one has a sense, "Well, if I cheat, I'm really giving over my humanity, my conscience." Then we think of these horrible Mark 12A missiles, something in us says, "We cannot live with such crimes." Or, our consciences turn in another direction. And by a thousand pressures, a thousand silences, people can begin to say to themselves, "We can live with that. We can live with that. We know it's there. We know what it is for. We know that many thousands will die if only one of these is exploded."

And yet we act like those employees, guards, experts we heard speak here; they close their eyes, close their hearts, close their briefcases, take their paycheck—and go home. It's called living with death. And it puts us to death before the missile falls.

We believe, according to the law, the law of the state of Pennsylvania, that we were justified in saying, "We cannot live with that"; justified in saying it publicly, saying it dramatically, saying it with blood and hammers, as you have heard; because that weapon, the hundreds and hundreds more being produced in our country, are the greatest evil conceivable on this earth.

There is no evil to compare with that. Multiply murder. Multiply desolation. The mind boggles.

So we went into that death factory, and in a modest, self-contained, careful way we put a few dents in two missiles, awaited arrest, came willingly into court to talk to you. We believe with all our hearts that our action was justified.

Montgomery: You mentioned work. Could you say something about how your work in the cancer hospital in New York influenced your decision?

Berrigan: Sure. I wouldn't want the jury to get the impression we are always going around banging on nose cones. We also earn a living. I have been doing, among other things, a kind of service to the dying for about three years now in New York. And I would like to speak shortly about that, because I come to you from an experience of death—not just any death, but the death of the poor, death by cancer.

I don't know whether you have ever smelled cancer. Cancer of the nose, cancer of the face, which is the most terrible to look upon and to smell, cancer of the brain, cancer of the lungs: We see it all, smell it all, hold it all in our arms.

This is not just a lecture on cancer. It is a lecture on those Mark 12A missiles, which make cancer the destiny of humanity, as is amply shown. This is another aspect of our justification.

We know now that in Hiroshima and Nagasaki, those who did not die at the flash point are still dying of cancer. Nuclear weapons carry a universal plague of cancer. As the Book of Revelation implies, after one of these missiles is launched, the living will envy the dead.

I could not understand cancer until I was arrested at the Pentagon, because there I smelled death by cancer, in my very soul. I smelled the death of everyone, everyone, across the board: black, brown, red, all of us, death by cancer.

So I talk to the dying. I take a chance on the dying, those that are still able to talk. And I say, "Do you know where my friends and I go from here?" Some of the patients know; and some of them don't. Some had read of our act in the papers. Some hadn't. I would talk about what I can only call the politics of cancer. The service the dying were rendering me was this: With their last days, their last breath, they helped me understand why I had to continue this struggle; because in them I was seeing up close the fate of everyone, and especially the children.

I have seen children dying of cancer. And we will see more and more of that as these bombs are built.

Justification and conscience. Could I mention briefly also that for two semesters I have been teaching at a college in the South Bronx, a college for poor people? It's a unique place, because only poor people who cannot pay are admitted. We have some one thousand students who are finishing degrees. You have undoubtedly seen pictures of the South Bronx; Carter and President Reagan have visited there. It's a required campaign stop by now; and when pictures appear one thinks of a president stepping on the moon, a lunar landscape, a landscape of utter desolation and misery and poverty and neglect.

This is also to our point of justification, because I have been led to ask,

"Why are people condemned to live this way in a wealthy country?" Where is the money going? Why is there a culture of poverty? Why are people born into it? Why do they live outside the economy, never have a job, have no future, live and die that way, hundreds of thousands in the South Bronx?

I don't know what to call our college. It is like a center for survivors. I look at the faces of these marvelous people, my students. And I think with sorrow in my heart that for every one who sits in that room, twenty have died on the way, or are in prison or are on drugs or are suicides, have given up.

And I was led to ask, "Why must this be?" So the cancer hospital and the college lead me to the Pentagon. I discussed freely in class, why are we so poor? Where is the money? General Electric costs the poor three million dollars a day, not for housing, not for schooling, not for neighborhood rehabilitation, not for medical care—for Mark 12A; three million dollars a day stolen from the poor. A larceny of worldwide proportions. This is our justification. We could not be indefinitely silent.

The hospital, the college, and the Pentagon, this is the circuit of my life.

In each of these places I learn more about the other two. At the Pentagon I understand why cancer will befall everyone, and why so many are destitute now. Among the poor, I understand why the poor die in such numbers of cancer. And at the hospital I smell the death that is planned for all.

Montgomery: Getting to the King of Prussia action itself, would you describe something of the preparation for it?

Berrigan: I'm sure, dear friends, that others will speak of the great import to us of the spiritual life, our lives in God. I want to tell you a little about the immediate days preceding this action; indeed, about days that have preceded every arrest we have undergone.

We have never taken actions such as these, perilous, crucial, difficult as they are, without the most careful preparation of our hearts, our motivation, our common sense, our sense of one another. We have never admitted any person to our groups whom we could not trust to be nonviolent under pressure of crises.

This is simply a rule of our lives; we don't go from the street to do something like the King of Prussia action. We go from prayer. We go from reflection. We go from worship, always. And since we realized that this action was perhaps the most difficult of all our lives, we spent more time in prayer this time than before.

We passed three days together in a country place. We prayed, and read the Bible, and shared our fears, shared our second and third thoughts.

And in time we drew closer. We were able to say, "Yes. We can do this. We can take the consequences. We can undergo whatever is required." All of that.

During those days we sweated out the question of families and children— the question of a long separation if we were convicted and jailed.

I talked openly with Jesuit friends and superiors. They respected my conscience and said, "Do what you are called to."

That was the immediate preparation. And what it issued in was a sense that, with great peacefulness, with calm of spirit, even though with a butterfly in our being, we could go ahead. And so we did.

This enters into my understanding of conscience and justification, a towering question, which has faced so many good people in history, in difficult times, now, in the time of the bomb. What helps people? What helps people understand who they are in the world, who they are in their families, who they are with their children, with their work? What helps?

That was a haunting question for me. Will this action be helpful? Legally, we could say that this was our effort to put the question of justification. Will our action help? Will people understand that this "lesser evil," done to this so-called "property," was helping turn things around in the church, in the nation?

Will the action help us be more reflective, about life and death and children and children and all life?

We have spent years and years of our adult lives keeping the law. We have tried everything, every access, every means to get to public authorities within the law. We come from within the law, from within.

We are deeply respectful of a law that is in favor of human life. And as we know, at least some of our laws are. We are very respectful of those laws. We want you to know that.

Years and years we spent writing letters, trying to talk to authorities, vigiling in public places, holding candles at night, holding placards by day, trying, trying, fasting, trying to clarify things to ourselves as we were trying to speak to others; all of that within the law, years of it.

And then I had to say, I could not not break the law and remain human. That was what was in jeopardy: what I call my conscience, my humanity, that which is recognizable to children, to friends, to good people, when we say, "There is someone I can trust and love, someone who will not betray."

We spent years within the law, trying to be that kind of person, a non-betrayer.

Then we found we couldn't. And if we kept forever on this side of the line, we would die within, ourselves. We couldn't look in the mirror, couldn't face those we love, had no Christian message in the world, nothing to say if we went on that way.

I might just as well wander off and go the way pointed to by a low-grade American case of despair: getting used to the way things are. That is what I mean by dying. That is what we have to oppose. I speak for myself.

The Jesuit order accepted me as a member. The Catholic Church ordained me as a priest. I took all that with great seriousness. I still do, with all my heart. And then Vietnam came along, and then the nukes came along. And I had to continue to ask myself at prayer, with my friends, with my family, with all kinds of people, with my own soul, "Do you have anything to say today?" I mean, beyond a lot of prattling religious talk.

Do you have anything to say about life today, about the lives of people today? Do you have a word, a word of hope to offer, a Christian word? That's a very important question for anyone who takes being a priest, being a Christian, being a human being seriously, "Do you have anything to offer human life today?"

It is a terribly difficult question for me. And I am not at all sure that I do have something to offer. But I did want to say this. I am quite certain that I had September 9th, 1980, to say.

And I will never deny, whether here or in jail, to my family, or friends, or to the Russians, or the Chinese, or anyone in the world, I will never deny what I did.

More than that. Our act is all I have to say. The only message I have to the world is: We are not allowed to kill innocent people. We are not allowed to be complicit in murder. We are not allowed to be silent while preparations for mass murder proceed in our name, with our money, secretly.

I have nothing else to say in the world. At other times one could talk about family life and divorce and birth control and abortion and many other questions. But this Mark 12A is here. And it renders all other questions null and void. Nothing, nothing can be settled until this is settled. Or this will settle us, once and for all.

It's terrible for me to live in a time where I have nothing to say to human beings except, "Stop killing." There are other beautiful things that I would love to be saying to people. There are other projects I could be very helpful at. And I can't do them. I cannot.

Because everything is endangered. Everything is up for grabs. Ours is a kind of primitive situation, even though we would call ourselves sophisticated. Our plight is very primitive from a Christian point of view. We are back where we started. Thou shall not kill; we are not allowed to kill. Everything today comes down to that—everything.

I thank you with all my heart for listening.

PART FOUR

Knowing through the Mind

KNOWING THROUGH THE MIND:
THE PATH OF METAPHYSICS

Metaphysics may seem a strange name for a form of American spirituality that puts its premium on experience more than on philosophical theory. Metaphysics, after all, is the time-honored name for a particular form of philosophy. As ontology, or the philosophy of "being" (i.e., existing entity) as being, metaphysics enjoyed high cultural status in the medieval West and has continued to find its place in philosophy, particularly in Roman Catholic quarters. When American metaphysicians without learned backgrounds speak about their journey into metaphysics, however, except for occasional vague allusions to Platonism and Neoplatonism, they usually intend little reference to the philosophical tradition of the West. Moreover, the popular metaphysical tradition in the United States arose in the mid-nineteenth century without serious and sustained contact with European philosophy. Rather, it emerged from a combinative context that included an Anglo-Puritan past, inherited popular European esotericism, English country witchcraft and magic, similar traditions in other ethnic groups—notably Indians and African Americans, new American religious movements such as Mormonism, and an evolving Protestant theological liberalism that fostered popular inquiry and experiment.

Manifesting itself in movements such as spiritualism, theosophy, New Thought, and, most recently, the New Age, the metaphysical tradition has achieved a certain prominence in the United States as a distinct and identifiable cultural formation. But beyond this self-identified metaphysical subculture, the wider world of metaphysics also includes numbers of individuals and groups who do not identify with the United States metaphysical tradition in its historic formations. In fact, metaphysics may be found in circles ranging from Jewish devotionalists to Roman Catholic monastics and mystical devotees, and from Asian immigrants to American converts to Eastern forms of spirituality including even martial arts.

In all of these forms, metaphysics has promoted a spirituality of knowing through the mind, of moving beyond the physical in order to make sense of the physical, as the etymology of the term suggests (from the Greek *meta*, "beyond," and *physis*, "the natural order"). And just as the term metaphysics needs to be construed in a certain way in order to make sense of the American tradition, so does the term mind. The nation's metaphysicians draw from Euro-American romanticism and sometimes from Western mysticism and

Eastern spiritual forms when they invoke "mind" as a spiritual tool. The mind they proclaim is surely an expanded version, a seat of consciousness not exclusively or even primarily identified with the brain and a mode of experience that has little to do with logic, analysis, and syllogistic thought. Instead, the "mind" of metaphysics celebrates intuition and suprasensory perception, exploring varieties of mentalistic activity that move beyond words and thoughts, that can manifest in nonlocal ways for distant effects, and that can include states like clairvoyance, clairaudience, and telekinesis.

Here the mind is understood as a nonmanifest reality that comes to manifest itself through creative expression in the material world, so that—in one imagistic way of saying this—the universe becomes the body of God or the Gods. But there are other ways of speaking, and metaphysical formulations and variations are so numerous that they frequently seem to defy categorization. There are, however, noticeable themes that pervade the metaphysical world, and a basic commonality can be found.

First, the human "mind" acknowledged in metaphysical spirituality points beyond itself to some transcendent Mind that is also immanent in the world. This may be the divine Mind, or the Mind of Nature, or pure Consciousness in Itself, or the Higher Self, or the Universe, or a similar metaphysical absolute. Second, the human mind is understood to correspond in key and controlling ways to this Other Mind, to exist in its undisturbed and natural form in connection with It. Often summarized in the old adage "As above, so below," this conceptualization sees everywhere an "implicate order," to cite the phrase of David Bohm, in which spheres replicate other spheres. Here the human mind is seen as enfolded in a larger, all-embracing Order of Mind; and the human mind is also seen as reflecting the larger order, mirroring it back in faithful ways. Third, the correspondence of human to Other Mind/Larger Mind may be expressed in terms of energy. In other words, for this form of spirituality there is a continuing metaphysical influx into the natural order, a constant inflowing stream that carries and communicates the life quality enabling persons, animals, plants, and all material forms to be something rather than nothing. And fourth, for metaphysical spirituality the mind quality that is manifest in matter—in what Bohm has called the "explicate unfolded order"—is manifest everywhere. Cells and molecules are constellations of intelligent life; but so are rocks and rivers. Matter, in short, is seen as an intelligent form of energy corresponding to other intelligent energetic forms. Matter may be malleable to them, may change, shift, and transform because of them, and is ultimately enfolded into them to be part of these forms.

In theological terms, the belief system that grounds metaphysical spirituality might be termed panentheism. For this form of thought all things exist as part of a single Reality, and in metaphysical thinking that Reality is Mind. The dualistic world of causality, so basic for evangelical spirituality, is banished here, and the traditional worldview of correspondence reigns supreme. Clearly then, for metaphysicians empowerment comes through the use of the mind, and so does control of self and society. It is no surprise, then, that the active form that metaphysical spirituality takes involves, above all, meditation. Indeed, in a plethora of forms—some of them very broadly conceived—the meditative disciplines mark metaphysics with a kind of signature, and seemingly everywhere in the metaphysical world the traces of the meditative work may be found.

In classic American spiritualism, in the nineteenth century and thereafter, the meditative work occurred most notably in the communal setting of the séance, where the medium attempted a form of awareness that was believed to bring communication with spirits of the dead. We can intuit that, in the darkened séance room, those gathered around the table with the medium were focusing strongly, too—meditating to bring the spirits they yearned to contact into communication. In American New Thought, in denominations like Unity, Religious Science, and Divine Science—and in New Thought's relative Christian Science—the meditation was transmuted into an affirmation of a person as existing in a state of perfection, the Idea of the person in the Mind of a Creator God. Here, disease was banished, and health became full and complete. Here, too, scarcity was gone, and the divine Supply met every human material need so that prosperity could be abundant.

Meanwhile, in the theosophical tradition and in its contemporary and combinative version in the New Age movement, meditation calls in the powers of the imagination ever more strongly. If the phrase "Create your own reality" is a mantra for the New Age, this is because of a theosophical heritage with roots in occultism and meditative ritual designed to make the visions of mind manifest by incarnating them in the material world. Nature here is seen as ever pliable to spirit, to energy, to Mind. In fact, in the New Age and in parallel forms that exist alongside it and sometimes interact with it, the task people set themselves is constantly to put the "mind" into the "body." This can be seen, for example, in forms of meditation that became popular in the America of the late twentieth century. Thus, Theravada Buddhist vipassana meditation stresses states of complete attention and awareness in which past and future fall away, while Taoist forms work to raise the chi (qi), or life-force energy, experiencing it as heat in the abdominal center that is said to exist below the navel. Taoist martial arts traditions aim to bring mind to body through sets of "shadow-boxing" forms as in t'ai chi (taiji) and related practices of qi gong, and South Asian hatha yoga is meant to bring mind to body through the concentration needed to assume a yogic pose. Indeed, even activities such as walking and eating have been singled out as the sites for meditative acts, as in Zen Buddhist walking meditations and Japanese-American macrobiotics.

Such meditative work, at its base, must be the province of the individual, and metaphysical spirituality, more than the other forms examined in this book, lends itself to solitary expression. Thus, while it is relatively easy to find within organized religion strong evangelical groups and strong traditions that are heavily committed to ritual, metaphysicians resemble prophets in the looseness of their institutional connections. Metaphysicians do not institutionalize well, if the strongly centralized and rationalized denomination is the norm. The organizational histories of spiritualism, theosophy, and New Thought all bear this observation out. But the observation should not end in stereotype, for metaphysical practitioners do come together as groups and, like all or most humans, do seek public demonstration and expression of private commitments. In fact, this combination of a spirituality that is of its nature personal and individual *and* a need to find other people who are fellow travelers on a path has fostered the growth of new ways of joining.

More specifically, what metaphysical practitioners exemplify strongly is forms of networking. Metaphysical spirituality—for example, as epitomized in the New Age and related new spirituality movements—weaves itself into seemingly endless fluid and overlapping formations. Groups arise and disappear like waves in the ocean; group members are connected to other group members in a series of contexts—people know one another in an often extended number of ways. Not all participants are the same in all groups, and not all metaphysicians believe and practice in the same cultural worlds. But enough carries over to provide a sense of familiarity and at-homeness in any group, to give a sense of continuity in one larger endeavor that exhibits any number of expressions appropriate to moment and mood. Networking is itself facilitated in a variety of ways—by businesses that are frequented, periodicals and books that are published, workshop and educational events that many attend. This easy, nondemanding form of organization is, in fact, the choice for many in the contemporary United States who feel themselves alienated from traditional religious institutions. Often enough to be typical, those who say they are "spiritual but not religious" end up being practitioners of some form of metaphysical spirituality.

Spiritual or religious or both, those on a metaphysical path may have reached it through a sudden change of focus and orientation, perhaps brought on by a health or life crisis and similar in some ways to the conversion experiences of those who know through the heart. Or they may have readjusted their vision and their point of view through stages of gradual change in much the same way as those who follow ritual traditions. Either way, their personal choice usually remains just that—personal. Metaphysicians do not normally understand themselves as emissaries and ambassadors to the world at large in the same essentialist way that evangelicals and their relatives do. Instead, if they achieve notice it is as exemplars—representative specimens whose lifestyle and cultural practice may be emulated by other seekers. With goals of fullness, completion, tranquility, and the like, metaphysicians are concerned about saving the planet, but they understand the nature of salvation differently from evangelicals and prophets. They may engage in active work for social reform as prophets do, but for them the real and essential work remains inner. If the inner work is not accomplished, metaphysicians say, the outer work will fail.

The rewards of metaphysics appear to be intrinsic to the path. Practitioners claim that meditative states, if achieved with facility, carry built-in satisfactions. The language of harmony, bliss, connection, flow, and unity pervades metaphysical spirituality, and metaphysical homesteads of the mind can provide sure ports in time of storm. The sense of personal empowerment that comes with metaphysical practice can make those who know through the mind quietly confident and poised. The sense of an "other" world in which the outer one is enfolded can provide a sense of balance and perspective for the vicissitudes that personal or social history brings. The concentration of focus that meditation requires can provide focus and attention in everyday life and so an ease in accomplishing vocational tasks. Putting the mind in the body can bring greater sensitivity and can often lead to greater health and material success. In short, like the other forms of spirituality examined in this book, metaphysics earns high praise from its practitioners.

On the following pages, we examine American metaphysics in a variety of contexts. After some further introduction to metaphysical belief and history, we see it expressed in a classic New Thought statement and a Roman Catholic one as classic. We observe its expression in one version of nature religion, and we trace its presence in an American Buddhist articulation of the meditation of mindfulness. We look at a Native American metaphysical declaration in the words of one modern-day Cherokee woman, and we find a New Age manifestation in the words of another, this time Anglo-American, woman. Finally, we follow the accounts of those who seek to put mind into body through forms of yoga and martial art. Throughout, we look for the major themes that mark metaphysical spirituality, and we notice, too, the signposts of difference on the many-faceted path of knowing through the mind.

19

The Subtle Energies of Spirit: Explorations in Metaphysical and New Age Spirituality

Catherine L. Albanese

What does it mean to hold to a metaphysical form of spirituality in America at the dawn of the twenty-first century? If the term metaphysical means, literally, "beyond the physical," are those who practice metaphysical spirituality in the United States individuals who have separated themselves from American culture? Does knowing through the mind mean that the everyday world is forgotten or that its shaping contours somehow fail to leave their impression on metaphysical practitioners? The essay reprinted here begins to address these questions by raising some questions of its own. Older readings of metaphysical spirituality have stressed its emphasis on themes of permanence and changelessness—how the spirit life of Mind is a life untroubled by the pain of transition and ephemerality. Closer scrutiny of the language that permeates metaphysical spirituality, however, suggests otherwise. In the United States past and present, the essay argues, those who have practiced various forms of knowing through the mind have been keenly aware of movement and transformation. They are acutely interested in energy phenomena as sources of spiritual empowerment, and they have characterized the world of spirit as a world of subtle but effective energies. Such understandings need to be set in the context of the American culture that has produced them. And even when the ideas arrive on these shores imported from Asian and other cultures, their attractiveness to mainstream Americans needs to be explained in terms of the values they already cherish. In place of the uninterrupted peace and harmony of transcendental realms, American culture offers variation and change. Metaphysicians, like other Americans, live in the midst of American changes that have spiritually shaped them.

I

If a quintessential metaphysical catechism were to be named, one of the major textual candidates would be H. Emilie Cady's *Lessons in Truth*—a basic for the Unity School of Christianity, a staple in its bookstores, and an often-cited work

Originally published in *The Journal of the American Academy of Religion*, 67, no. 2, (June 1999). Reprinted by permission of the author.

in its metaphysical communications. First published in 1894, the book features chapters that originated in a series of articles contributed to Unity publications from 1892 by Cady, a practicing physician. Exact records of how many copies have been published are not available, but the back cover of the 1967 edition offers one piece of evidence, announcing that the print order came to 60,000 copies per printing for many years and that this particular edition is the forty-fourth. Over thirty years later now, it is not unreasonable to estimate that some 3 million copies of the text have been printed.

This work stands out not only because of its classical status but also because its slightly old-fashioned title *Lessons in Truth* conjures, in an especially marked way, the sense of belief in a fixed order of the universe that evocations of metaphysics initially convey. In this reified ontology there is a realm of absolute truth and reality, substantial and unchanging. By contrast, there is a world of mirage and illusion in which humans lose sight of the eternal. And certainly some of Cady's language supports this analysis. For instance, she unequivocally affirms that God "as the underlying substance of all things, God as principle, is unchanging, and does remain forever uncognizant of and unmoved by the changing things of time and sense" (166).

Granted this and similar statements, though, as this essay will show, Cady and the entire metaphysical tradition—including its contemporary manifestation in the New Age movement—have always been drawn more to flow charts than to static entities. In fact, the preference for motion—for "flow"—is so ubiquitous in metaphysics that, if the meaning of spirituality is to be understood for the tradition, that meaning must be grasped in metaphors, descriptions, and cultural practices that, literally, go with the flow. In what follows, then, this article explores the metaphysical tradition—and especially its current manifestation in the New Age movement—against a contemporary vernacular religious horizon suffused with notions of "spirituality." What registers as spirituality for past- and present-day metaphysicians? the article asks. What continuities exist between the nineteenth-and early-twentieth-century tradition and the present metaphysical moment? And, likewise, what departures from the past can be noticed in contemporary metaphysics, dominated as it is by the New Age movement? Finally, how can we revise received notions of metaphysics in light of the contemporary popular discourse of the spiritual?

First, though, let it be clear what counts for the discussion as metaphysics. Some, like Charles Braden, have closely identified metaphysical religion with the New Thought, or mental-healing, tradition. Mind cure, as he explains, yielded denominations like Unity as well as Religious Science and Divine Science, and it also percolated into general culture in ideas like the "positive thinking" most classically articulated by Norman Vincent Peale.[1] But even given Braden's focus in his work, he makes it clear that he views the mental-healing tradition as but one expression of a much larger religious family that includes domestic as well as Asian and European esoteric representatives (4). Still more, J. Stillson Judah—while he acknowledges the provenance of the term "metaphysical movement" in late-nineteenth-century New Thought— employs it for studying a broad strand in American religious and cultural history. The metaphysical strand, for Judah, finds expression in Transcendental- ism as well as spiritualism and occultism, in theosophy as much as mind-cure manifestations (11–12). And if Braden and Judah were writing in the eighties and nineties, they would surely point, as this article already has, to the New Age movement as a late-twentieth-century incarnation of metaphysics.

It should be added too that the term "spirituality"—although it is surely *au courant* and although it has an old and venerable past—also has a recent and contemporary history that extends back, at least in Roman Catholic circles, for probably the last quarter century. Paulist Press was publishing its Classics of Western Spirituality series, with apparent success, from the late sev- enties.[2] By 1980, in a periodical significantly entitled *Spirituality Today,* Roman Catholic scholar Jon Alexander was asking in print "What do recent writers mean by spirituality?" and concluding that they meant something at once ex- periential, removed from particular religious traditions, and directed to con- nections made with ultimate meanings and values. And Alexander was quoting Catholic theologian Hans Urs von Balthazar to the effect that spirituality signi- fied "that basic practical or existential attitude of man which is the conse- quence and expression of the way in which he understands his religious—or more generally, his ethically committed—existence" (251).

These assessments are both broad and specific enough to serve as guidelines for exploring the meaning of spirituality for metaphysics. Moreover, their ori- gins in Roman Catholic intellectual neighborhoods are not inappropriate for the metaphysical tradition with its almost crypto-Catholic nuances of mysti- cism and its self-conscious searches for unity with the One. Moving out from here, metaphysics possesses its own set of markers and distinctives. In fact, it offers a chance to look at an American form of spirituality in which the ancient cosmology of correspondence organizes insight and experience for believers. Etymologically, metaphysics moves, literally, "beyond the physical," and the "beyond" that particularly concerns metaphysicians is the life of the mind. For metaphysicians, empowerment (arguably a goal or pay-off in all forms of spirituality) comes largely through the experience of mind, the creator and controller of one's destiny. Here what happens in the human world and mind replicates a larger, more holistic universe of life and mind.[3] There are connec- tions between individual minds and a divine one and, more broadly, organic links between the material world and a spiritual realm. As important, religious practice or ritual may be understood under the rubric of mental or material magic.

Another way to say this is that for metaphysical believers everything is linked to everything else—cut of the same cloth, as it were—and in metaphysics life becomes holographic. One piece of the universe can operate or act on any other piece of the universe, and, with the guiding power of Mind for steerage, seemingly miraculous change can become commonplace and ordinary. In a straightforward mental magic the central ritual is some form of meditation. In material magic the mind uses the body as tool in occult practice—which often involves rituals but differently oriented from those of the churches. Ideally, the result in both mental and material cases is the attainment of states of tranquility, with the model person an exemplar more than a missionary. More than that, the model person—the exemplar—privileges individualism, and, at least hypothetically, the community drops away.

So far the description here seems to conform at least in its cosmology of Mind to Cady's "God as the underlying substance of all things." And it appears to echo as well the words of a nameless metaphysical practitioner cited by Judah, a man who thought metaphysics the "practical application" of the "absolute Truth of Being in all the affairs of our daily and hourly living" (11). These expressions reflect the tradition and its spirituality so far as they go. But arguably they do not go far enough. What does not emerge from either rendition is a strong sense of what will here be called the subtle energies of spirit. And, for this revisionary reading of the tradition, it is these energies that are basic to what metaphysicians and New Agers have understood as spirituality. Any alert reading of the documents of the tradition supports this analysis, for the signs of a kinetic spirituality are prominent in Cady and elsewhere, and they are almost banal.[4]

The energy equivalence of spirit is, moreover, nothing new. It is a commonplace in religious-studies scholarship that the English term "spirit" translates the Hebrew *ruah* and its Greek counterpart *pneuma*, both of which signify wind or breath, a principle of vital activity, what moves (MacGregor:455–456). Closer, historically, to American metaphysics, however, are mid-nineteenth-century formative influences on the tradition. From Europe came mesmerism and Swedenborgianism, each of them affirming from its different perspective the energetic dimension of spirit. For mesmerism there was the legacy of Franz Anton Mesmer's "invisible tides," the subtle energies that moved through the universe and through humans as well, their blockage the cause of illness and their free flow, abetted by an animal magnetist, the source of the return of health (Mesmer; Fuller). For Swedenborgianism, there was the doctrine of divine influx, the news that "the life of every one, whether man, spirit or angel" flowed in "solely from the Lord," who diffused himself "through the universal heaven, and even hell," in both a general and a particular version of the influx (Synnestvedt:126–127). From America itself came the language of motion that pervaded the nature religion of the American Transcendentalists, among them Ralph Waldo Emerson and Henry David Thoreau, but also many others (Albanese 1977). And from America, still more pervasively, came both philosophical and practical forms of spiritualism that traded on beliefs about the continuous flow between matter and spirit (a refined form of matter) and about the ever-ready manifestations of spirit (Carroll; Moore).

With this background in mind, it is useful to look again at H. Emilie Cady's *Lessons in Truth*. Here the reader does not need to go far to stumble onto Cady's "Statement of Being," which in part announces that "God is Spirit, or the creative energy that is the cause of all visible things" and that "man is the last and highest manifestation of divine energy, the fullest and most complete expression (or pressing out) of God." Cady specifies further in a series of fountain metaphors that make God a "great reservoir," complete with channels issuing into small fountains. Each human fountain, she tells, "is not only being continually filled and replenished from the reservoir but is itself a radiating center whence it gives out in all directions that which it receives, so that all who come within its radius are refreshed and blessed." And, indeed, "the love, the life, and the power of God are ready and waiting with longing impulse to flow out through us in unlimited degree!" By contrast, Cady declares that "stagnation is death." "It is our business to keep both the inlet and outlet open, and God's business to keep the stream flowing in and through us" (20, 23, 39–40, 109).

Enter, then, the role of spirituality. Keeping the channel open, keeping the flow unimpeded, is—for the metaphysical tradition and its New Age manifestation—the essential spiritual task. This point can be underlined with a glance at another classic text for the tradition. Ralph Waldo Trine's *In Tune with the Infinite* is a second catechism that can be read with profit. First published in 1897, like Cady's work the small book went through numerous editions, with Trine himself renewing the copyright at least five times. The 1970 edition, for example, boasts on its back cover that "over 1,250,000 copies of this book have been sold."

Again, as for Cady, the reader does not need to go far to discover Trine's assessment of spirit. He acknowledges that the spirit is "that Spirit of Infinite Life and Power ... from which all is continually coming," that "the life of individual man ... must come by a divine inflow from this Infinite Source," and that "the degree that man opens himself to this divine inflow" is the degree that he approaches God. Trine announces that the results of such openings are "God men," those "in whom the powers of God are manifesting." Moreover, his rhetoric of relationship finds comfort in magnetic metaphor and water imagery. "We are continually attracting to us, from both the seen and the unseen side of life," he says, "forces and conditions most akin to those of our own thoughts." He calls Emanuel Swedenborg "the highly illumined seer," citing his teaching on "the divine influx and how we may open ourselves more fully to its operations," and he also hails the seer from Concord (Massachusetts) with a paraphrase of Emerson's statement: "We are all inlets to the great sea of life." As for Cady, God is a great reservoir, and it is the human job to be busy "opening the gate of the trough which conducts the water from the reservoir above into the field below" (15, 18, 20, 26, 150, 159).

In short, Cady and Trine point in a direction that gives large clues to the present. They carry across historic sources for metaphysical and New Age spirituality, bridging the century divider and showing us clearly what counts for the tradition. Surveying, however briefly, historic sources for contemporary metaphysical and New Age readings of spirituality leads to a horizon of meaning that includes the experiential and the sense of connection with ultimates, as with other forms of spirituality. It is also a horizon patterned to reflect a larger reality in correspondence with which the human world finds its truest form. But at the same time the horizon shows itself to be ever shifting, transforming itself from moment to extended moment. To be spiritual in a metaphysical universe is to unblock the door and to let the waters of life flow through. To put the matter in more contemporary language, it is to be sensitive to subtle energies and to respond to them.

II

Exploring the cultural narratives that convey the content of this metaphysical spirituality brings past and present together again, especially in the domain of these subtle energies. For the metaphysical tradition, however, it needs to be noticed that, manifestly, these narratives are not merely told or printed. They are enacted, and their favored location is in ritual practice, especially the ritual practice of healing, and in the ideational world that has supported practice. In the nineteenth century the ideational world of the energetic model conformed in general outline to scientific theories of the ether, a medium believed to permeate all space and to transmit waves that were transverse. In the late twentieth, it lined up for believers and practitioners with the world of quantum physics. Light—that convenient legacy of the mystical tradition in both Eastern and Western Christian versions—behaves for quantum scientists sometimes as a particle and sometimes as a wave. So from a quasi-scientific world there has seemed to be confirmation, of a sort, of metaphysical experience. "When viewed from the microcosmic level," one metaphysical physician (Gerber:59) exultantly announced in 1988, *"all matter is frozen light!"*[5] Thus, spirit and science have come together for New Agers and other metaphysicians to disclose a grand master plan of the universe, and in the master plan matter and spirit (or, in scientific parlance, energy) have been seen as in essence the same.

A classic case of the equation may be found in the central ritual of nineteenth-century American spiritualism, the séance. Bret Carroll has documented the pervasiveness of séance circles in major American cities and explored their ritual structure (120–151). What needs to be emphasized here, though, is the ways that they have functioned to bring the energies of spirit into a material realm to comfort and to heal. By the mid-twentieth century the National Spiritualist Association of Churches was teaching that spirits communicated by lowering their vibrational rate to synchronize with that of a medium's body and, after the inner, or astral, body of the medium was projected outward, using it as a scaffolding for the ectoplasm that enabled them to materialize. Where did the ectoplasm come from? It flowed, said spiritualists, from a medium's nose and ears (Judah:68).

In the New Age approximation the medium has become a channel, and the semantic world out of which the word arose is an important clue to the contemporary channeling movement's origins and its continuing energy concerns. The language of "channeling" (rather than "mediumship") comes from the technological shamanism of the UFO contactee movement. The human "channel" is seen as analogous to a radio or video channel, receiving waves of energy from out in space that are transformed into sound, sight, and meaning. Thus, in a relativistic quantum universe the human channel provides one conduit, one point of connection, between those who dwell within the limits of material human bodies and, hypothetically, those other "personalities"— sometimes individual, sometimes collective—who dwell beyond.[6] As important, these personalities offered to seekers a measure of healing for the hurts and wounds of the late twentieth century.

In his recent book, *The Channeling Zone*, Michael F. Brown identifies late-twentieth-century channels of two kinds, with some interconnection between them. There are conscious channels who function more or less as intuitive counsellors. But the more thoroughgoing channels are trance channels whose bodies and minds are possessed, as it were, by the entities who use them to get their therapeutic messages through (25). Trance channels do become, indeed, most like radio or video channels, with their own personalities and characteristic responses held, for the most part, in abeyance. So spirituality in the channeling zone means contacting spirit energy, either directly or through the aid of the human channel who allows in vibrational forces from beyond.

Another case of the energetic world of spirit-matter may be found in New Thought formulations and especially in New Thought healing practice. Mind, for New Thought, can bring matter into correspondence—not as one substance fixing the substance of another but as a constant source of in-streaming energy that catalyzes the subtle energies of the body with those of the spirit. The New Thought vehicle for so doing, since the nineteenth-century time of Warren Felt Evans, has been the affirmation. In *The Divine Law of Cure* (1881) Evans—the Methodist-turned-Swedenborgian minister who became a major New Thought theologian and practitioner—linked bodily condition to mental process. If we want to change our bodies for better, he declared, "let us *imag-*

ine, or *think* and *believe*, that the desired change is being effected, and it will do more than all other remedial agencies to bring about the wished for result" (174; as quoted in Braden:101 [emphasis in original]). Evans's "affirmative attitude of mind" took effective form in the practice of affirmation (Braden:122–123), and the New Thought movement turned the practice itself into a healing form of energy.

To gain an idea of what this means concretely today, one need only call the prayer line maintained by Silent Unity at its headquarters outside of Kansas City, Missouri. The voice on the other end of the line will pray with the caller in a rhetorical mix of spontaneity and formula that affirms the good that is desired—calling it out not dryly, as the formulaic might suggest, but with "heart" and with feeling. Thus the words become catalysts for a narrative that is already a form of action. Meanwhile, readers of Unity's small monthly pamphlet *Daily Word* must likewise take each day's printed affirmation to heart, i.e., speak or think it with feeling—as a prompt to inner or outer action. In similar fashion, New Agers evoke the energetic basis of their spirituality when they tell each other that they create their own reality, affirming the pliancy of matter and its plasticity before the moving force of spirit. Sickness, for *A Course in Miracles,* is a defense against truth, in other words, a blockage and point of fixity. By contrast, the *Course* says, "healing will flash across your open mind" ([Schucman]:250–252).

Narratives and practices of healing energy, however, need to be set in further contexts. For if metaphysically inclined Americans have arrived at their insights in considerable measure through an esoteric export-import trade with Europe, they have also traded with Asia, and the Asian trade has shaped kinetic spirituality in significant ways. The culture brokers who joined to produce, eventually, American metaphysics had been deeply impressed by Asia. Emerson and Henry David Thoreau among the Transcendentalists had eagerly read the Asian classics they found in Harvard's library and by the late 1830s were familiarly at home with an Asian religious vernacular.[7] Later, esoteric American Buddhists and Buddhist sympathizers blended Swedenborgian with Asian categories and combined Buddhism with American spiritualism. The results were most prominently displayed in the Theosophical Society, begun in 1875 as a spiritualist reform movement (Prothero 1993; Prothero 1996:44–51) but by 1878 decidedly turning to the East and especially to Buddhism. The cofounders of the Theosophical Society, Madame Helena Blavatsky and Colonel Henry Steel Olcott, formally professed Buddhism after they traveled to Ceylon (Sri Lanka). Moreover, Blavatsky's published writings bear heavy burdens from the East.[8] Blavatsky's theosophy made terms like karma and reincarnation household coinage for the metaphysical tradition, and they point, noticeably, to movement and change, to an eternal order not of fixity but of progress and evolution.

Even more germane to the practiced narratives of the metaphysical world, however, are the theosophical teachings of subtle bodies. In her huge synthesis that became a corpus of theosophical doctrine Helena Blavatsky bridged the gap between matter and spirit by claiming the existence of a series of seven bodies, beginning with the human physical body and ending with the highest human spirit body. In this "septenary constitution of man" the bodies that Blavatsky was talking about were for the most part *energy* bodies (Blavatsky 1972:55–59). As Bruce Campbell has summarized them, "The lower four are the physical body, life or the vital principle, the astral body, and the seat of animal desires and passions. These four elements are transitory. . . . The 'upper imperishable triad' is composed of mind or intelligence, the spiritual soul, and spirit" (66). It remained for British theosophist Charles W. Leadbeater to provide the final embellishment to the teaching, an embellishment that became perhaps even more fundamental to later metaphysical thought than the subtle-body doctrine itself. In his 1927 book, *The Chakras,* Leadbeater—who was widely admired among theosophists in the United States as a clairvoyant—combined South Asian and European mystical sources with his own visions. He called the chakras (Sanskrit for "wheels") "a series of wheel-like vortices which exist in the surface of the etheric double of man." Significantly, the chakras were "points of connection at which energy flows from one vehicle or body of a man to another" (1, 4).

Accompanied by these South Asian chakras, the theosophical bodies became part of the parlance of New Thought and the New Age. Ralph Waldo Trine could evoke them when he referred to the "thought forms" of those who had died, "now manifesting through the agency of bodies of a different nature" (28). For the New Age, the energies exuding from subtle bodies became auras, visible, it was said, to anyone who tried to see them after appropriate training. Moreover, the New Age auric light acquired a scientific pedigree. It was a "magnetic" field, and the academics who have studied it have received notice in New Age literature. There is, for example, Valerie Hunt of the University of California, Los Angeles, reported to have measured the "frequency and location" of the human "biofield" (Taylor). And there is William A. Tiller, professor for over thirty years in the Department of Materials Science at Stanford and author of a more or less popular-audience book reproducing a line drawing of multiple "auric sheaths" around the physical body and explaining the phenomenon. "Just as the physical body has major antenna systems associated with it, the etheric body and our more subtle bodies have special antenna systems associated with them," Tiller writes (128–129).

What is especially important about the aura in the context of metaphysical practical narration, however, is that it can be manipulated—and it can be healed. For if there is a prevailing mode in which the subtle energies of spirit have been narrated in the metaphysical tradition, it is the mode of healing.

This was as true for nineteenth-century spiritualists with their numerous newspaper advertisements by trance physicians and healers as it is today in the New Age. It was—and is—a continuing theme in the New Thought tradition, and it has certainly been part of the theosophical universe as well. Blavatsky's "chum" and co-founder of the Theosophical Society, Henry Steel Olcott, for instance, studied mesmerism in his youth, discovered that he could heal others "magnetically" and later achieved renown in South Asia as a spiritual healer (Prothero 1996: 107–110). At present, New Age energy healers like Barbara Brennan and Rosalyn Bruyere understand their work as spiritual healing to alter and assist broken and disfigured auras, and they predicate such healing on their announced perceptions of the theosophical subtle bodies and their energy formations. Brennan especially, with her credentials as a former National Aeronautics and Space Administration physicist (she studied the reflection of solar light from the earth), her Barbara Brennan School of Healing in East Hampton, New York, her widely selling textbook and her audiotapes, and her popular lecturing has brought science and spirit together in familiar New Age ways.

Meanwhile, others like medical intuitive Caroline Myss base their analysis and healing advice on extensive elaboration of the meaning of the chakras as key places of energy exchange on the body and as modes of simultaneous spirituality and physicality. In her recent book *Anatomy of the Spirit*, for example, Myss weaves together an intricate cosmology connecting each of the seven major chakras of the South Asian system with the seven Roman Catholic sacraments (her background is Catholic) and with the ten sefirot (or, as she says, "Tree of Life") of the medieval kabbalistic text of the *Zohar* (29–30). Her personal confession at the beginning of one of her book's chapters is instructive for all of the tradition: "Ever since I got my first medical intuitions, I have been aware that they are basically about the human spirit, even though they describe physical problems and even though I use energy terms to explain them to others. *Energy* is a neutral word that evokes no religious associations or deeply held fears about one's relationship to God. It is much easier for someone to be told 'Your energy is depleted' than 'Your spirit is toxic.' Yet most of the people who come to me have, in fact, been in spiritual crises. I have described their crises to them as energy disorders, but doing so was not as helpful as discussing them in spiritual terms, too, would have been" (63 [emphasis in original]).

III

Subtle energies almost by definition are changing energies, so that following the transformations of metaphysical spirituality at the present time is of a piece with following its history. Strong continuities exist, to be sure, and this article has been focusing on these up until now. It needs also to be added that it is hard not to notice other continuities that fall between the cracks in the questions addressed here. Such continuities include, for example, the prominence of women in the metaphysical tradition in the nineteenth century and now. They also include the then-and-now hostility and/or indifference to organized religion within much of the tradition—a hostility that is probably a large source of the distinction people today draw between spirituality (which they see as good) and religion (which they consider bad). Still, for all that, there are significant differences between past and present, and it is important to look at these, even if the summary is partial and incomplete.

First, though, let it be stated even more explicitly than earlier that much, if not most, of contemporary metaphysics flies under the banner of the New Age. Here, in postmodern context, metaphysical religion may be read as a response to the nihilism of a nonreligious world at a time when biblically based traditions have trouble persuading and comforting many. The pursuit of tranquility that is the spiritual goal of metaphysical practice appeals in times in which, more and more, religion functions as a form of therapy.

Beyond that, it can be noticed that with their openness to the more mystical aspects of new scientific paradigms metaphysicians have placed themselves strategically to sabotage a secular science by seeming to join it. Spiritualists of old welcomed scientific testing of the reality of their spirit visitors. Helena Blavatsky's huge work *The Secret Doctrine* was built in part on her fascination with the theory of evolution and with purported scientific evidence for the submerged continents of Atlantis and Lemuria (1888). Similarly, present-day New Agers celebrate quantum theory as they speak of hidden "energies" and explore connections between the matter of the human body and its energetic (read spiritual) equivalences (e.g., Brennan).

In this context, one marked transformation in metaphysical spirituality is the increasing hegemony of the language of science. The "tides" and "influxes," the open "reservoirs" and "fountains" of the late nineteenth century, seem decidedly antiquated in the discourse community of a century later. Now there is talk of "bioenergy" and "electromagnetic fields," of "biofields," "bioplasmic energy bodies," and "subtle energies." A case in point is William Collinge's book *Subtle Energy*. Its table of contents is a mélange of titles and subtitles that combine contemporary language of science-sounding provenance with older esoteric and Asian-inspired concepts. One chapter alludes to the "biofield" and "flowing rivers of energy," another to "paths of the dragon" and "man-made electromagnetic fields" (vii). Figures include one of the human aura, another of Chinese acupuncture points, still others of the earth's "geomagnetic field" and, again, the "solar radio flux vs. lunar cycle" (ix).

Moving glibly between science and spirit, Collinge tells readers that conventional physics acknowledges but four types of energy: "electromagnetism, gravity, and two subatomic forces called the strong force and the weak force" (16). He finds electromagnetism the most germane of the four but still seeks to "bridge the boundary between physics and metaphysics," citing human reality as "multidimensional," with humans experiencing "a whole *spectrum* of energies, some from the physical dimension and some from beyond" (23–24, 26, 16 [emphasis in original]). Collinge points to the "energy anatomy of the earth" and calls the human mind "energy" as well. The mind, he says, is "energy, but of a special, higher order—one that can influence other energies by our conscious intention." The mind's home, he declares, "is in a higher dimension, one that encapsulates our physical time-space dimension but is not confined to it. That higher dimension has been called by many names, such as 'the field of consciousness,' 'the higher mind,' 'the One Mind,' 'the Divine Mind,' and others" (54–55).

For Collinge and others, the "higher mind" may be accessed through forms of prayer, and recent talk in New Age circles has aimed to demonstrate that even prayer can be scientific. Holistic physician Larry Dossey has pioneered in books that claim the practical efficacy of prayer, seeing prayer as a species of "non-local medicine" that is the product of "non-local mind" (Collinge:265, 116). Others also design experiments on the scientific model to test the results of the energies of prayer. In one example, Randolph Byrd, a cardiologist from San Francisco General Hospital, was reported to have carried through a controlled study of 400 coronary patients, half of whom received standard care and half of whom were the focus of prayer by various Protestant and Catholic groups throughout the nation. The usual experimental protocols were observed with neither patients nor medical staff knowing to which group particular patients were assigned. Collinge, who summarizes, calls the outcomes "striking" and continues enthusiastically, citing for those prayed for "significantly less congestive heart failure, need for diuretics, cardiopulmonary arrest, or incidence of pneumonia. They were five times less likely to require antibiotics and three times less likely to develop pulmonary edema" (265).

Likewise, Collinge's sometime Asian allusions suggest another transformation in metaphysical spirituality. That is its increasing comfort with the "energy" vocabulary of East and South Asia. Talk of Chinese meridians and acupuncture points in the human body leads to questions about what travels these inner pathways and markers, and the answer in traditional Chinese medicine is *qi*. An elusive concept for Westerners, *qi* is something—but not altogether— like an *élan vital*; it is at once physical and spiritual or energetic, both body and what makes the body's becoming. It is what the practitioner seeks to raise in *qi gong*, to experience in *taiji*, and to cultivate in various East Asian methods of meditation as, for example, on the Taoist "microcosmic orbit" that has its beginning and end at the navel and extends from palate to perineum. Alternately, *qi* is considered to have its South Asian equivalent in *prana*, the breath power that is nurtured through yogic *pranayama,* or—in one form—in *kun-dalini* yoga, focusing on the serpent power at the base of the spine (the first chakra) that the practitioner aspires to move upward (Kaptchuk: 35–41; Olson; Chia; Eliade; Woodroffe).[9]

New Agers, especially, keep a ready, easy commerce between key Asian terms and a late-twentieth-century American energy argot. Consider, for example, the language of late-century macrobiotics, a movement that Gordon Melton calls "an important element within the larger New Age Movement" (333). Macrobiotics, which began to grow in the United States in the late sixties and early seventies, is of Japanese provenance, and George Ohsawa (Yukikazu Sakurazawa), its founder, built his system on an older Japanese tradition of food philosophy. Evoking the *yin* and *yang* energies of Chinese Taoist philosophy, Ohsawa and his Japanese students in America (most notably Michio Kushi and Herman Aihara) classified all foods on a continuum between *yin* and *yang* polarities, understanding them as mutually complementary and yet antagonistic. Balanced eating has meant eating that is centered between *yin* and *yang* forces. Such eating has been seen as the key not only to health and interpersonal harmony; it becomes the way to transform energy so that peace among nations will result.[10]

"To balance yin and yang, we need to learn how to create, transform, and modify energy," Aveline Kushi writes. "Our body, our food, and our environment are changing forms and patterns of energy." And again, "Changing the quality of food on a global level is the key to ending the spread of cancer, heart disease, mental illness, and infertility in the modern world, as well as reversing the breakdown of the family, social disorder, and mistrust between nations" (11, xi). What is wrong with conventional concepts in modern nutritional theory, argues macrobiotic counsellor Steve Gagné, is that they assume "that food is *matter.*" By contrast, he would teach the "energetics" of food, and he finds the word "entrainment" to be "a perfectly descriptive one for *Food Energetics*— because electrical events are exactly what we're discussing!" That electrical events glide off into spiritual events is also clear. The philosophy that inspires and informs his writing, he affirms, is one about "voiding our differences" (16, 22, 282, xv [emphasis in original]).

If matter shades off into spirit for macrobiotics and other forms of metaphysical practice, other transformations of metaphysical and New Age spirituality take their cue from psychology. The human potential movement of the sixties has exhibited numerous and intricate turns, and today permutations of Freudian, neo-Freudian, and Jungian thought color metaphysical spirituality. Even a glance at the advertisements in local pulp publications like the ubiquitous *Whole Life Times,* which appears in region-specific incarnations in various cities throughout the United States, suggests the prominence of psychological language in the energy world of metaphysics. Barbara Brennan's work is a good example. Building on the model of Sigmund Freud's break-away disciple Wilhelm Reich, Brennan has posited five character structures that employ six general types of energy blocks. In Brennan's characterology, schizoid, anal, psychopathic, masochistic, and rigid personality types each got their "wounding" at different stages in their development, the first, in fact, even at the prenatal stage. But the resolution of their problems is always an energy resolution, and energy for Brennan is always spiritual. Indeed, the highest energy is love, and the universal malady is "self-hatred," as people again and again fail to demonstrate unconditional love for the "Godself within" (101–107, 109–127, esp. 109–110).

Any number of other healers engage in relationship therapies that at once psychologize and spiritualize, always finding love as the resolution for human ills. Metaphysical teacher and minister Louise L. Hay, for example, in her ubiquitous pamphlet *Heal Your Body* and in her later *You Can Heal Your Life,* identifies "mental causes for physical illness." It is clear, though, from even a cursory reading of her work that the mental causes are, in fact, emotional. "Everyone suffers from self-hatred and guilt," Hay announces, and "when we really love ourselves, everything in our life works." For Hay, as for so many others in the present-day tradition, "self-approval and self-acceptance in the now are the key to positive changes." Indeed, specific ills in specific body parts can be correlated to particular emotional ills, as the charts produced in her book make manifest. Bronchitis is connected to an "inflamed family environment," a sore thumb to mental "worry," cancer to "longstanding resentment" and "grief eating away at the self" (Hay 1984a: 12–13, 17; Hay 1984b: 5, 158–159, 165). The cure is always mental, but it is always also psychological. Thinking differently, for Louise Hay and so many others, means *feeling* differently.

Nor, familiarly, do metaphysical healers and their clientele consider their efforts unscientific. The Institute of HeartMath, as one instance, has things all ways. Dedicated to studying the relationship between the heart's (the physical organ's) function and mental and emotional well-being, it also notices connections between the production of love and positive immune-system effects. "Love, in this context," explains William Tiller, "is defined as benevolent heart focus towards the well-being of others and it is found that the heart-focussed feeling . . . produces profound electrophysiological changes in heart rate variability" (213; Collinge:238–239, 293–294).

Love, however, for Brennan, Hay, the Institute of HeartMath, and the metaphysical movement in general, is not a free gift of the spirit. For what is especially noticeable in metaphysical/New Age spirituality in the late twentieth century is its commodification and its association with a new service industry of professionals who seek to produce it. The commerce of the spirit was surely part of the spiritualist movement of the nineteenth century, and the *Banner of Light* and other spiritualist newspapers regularly published the advertisements of spiritualist mediums of one or another sort. New Thought by the turn of the century was proclaiming its prosperity consciousness. And meanwhile theosophical ideas came into the New Age through a lineage of theosophical teachers and their students, including prominently Alice Bailey and her Arcane School and Guy and Edna Ballard and the I Am Movement, with a particularly strong infusion from the twenties to the forties through the readings of trance healer Edgar Cayce. All of these had their commercial aspects, and in the Ballard case the accusation of mail-order fraud, in fact, reached the United States Supreme Court (*United States v. Ballard*).[11]

Still, commercialization has become the hallmark of the New Age, and no metaphysical believers seem particularly apologetic about it. Writing specifically about the channeling phenomenon, Michael Brown observes that the market "fills much of the moral space created by the perceived bankruptcy of family, church, and government." This estimate hardly violates the energetic character of New Age metaphysical spirituality. "Money," Brown goes on to explain, "is viewed simply as an energy—'accumulated human and planetary creative energy,' to be precise—and therefore as a force of nature analogous to gravity, light, or sound waves." Brown cites the "new religious consumerism of our time," and he argues that channeling "mirrors . . . perfectly the society in which it has arisen"—even if, for most channels, riches are a far cry from reality (142, 145, 173).

Beyond that, increased commercialization goes hand in hand with increasing professionalism. Metaphysical service providers today come, often, with advanced degrees and specialized forms of training. To be sure, many, if not most, are products of alternative educational worlds, but this does not negate the differences between, say, a late-twentieth-century energy healer and a nineteenth-century spiritualist. Professionals in metaphysics, as elsewhere, locate themselves and what they do in terms of bodies of received theoretical understanding and practical savoir faire. They network with other professionals, attend meetings and conferences together, produce literature to support their work, and arrive at shared judgments regarding fee structures. They bring a new rationalization and bureaucratization to metaphysical service businesses that earlier healers did not know.

All the same, it is important to notice finally that what these professionals seek to produce transcends their pocketbooks and the solipsism of individual healing. It moves, in fact, toward issues of community and social consciousness. The pervasiveness of the language of "relationship" in metaphysical and New Age spirituality in our time suggests already the beginnings of the social turn. The wounds of the New Age and their resultant auric and energetic problems stand in the way of whole and harmonious human relationships; relationships shape the infrastructure for community; and community mediates the collective conscience that works to transform society for the good. The spiritualists of old had been social reformers, as R. Laurence Moore and Ann Braude both have emphasized. Moreover, after 1878 theosophists consciously promoted "universal brotherhood" as one of their three purposes (Campbell:28), and, as the work of Gary Ward Materra has made clear, New Thoughters in one of the movement's two major divisions were actively concerned with social transformation and, in fact, sometimes embraced socialism.

Over the years the causes have changed, and they have become more collective. Antislavery, women's rights, and socialism have yielded place to a feminism vastly more far-reaching and ambitious than the earlier movement, to an environmentalism that encompasses global thinking and trends, and to a peace activism that is likewise global in intent. It is important to notice this especially because the standard Protestant theological critique has uncritically faulted metaphysical spirituality for its lack of a social dimension (Albanese 1999). Although the lack was never true in the past, it is even less true now. Metaphysicians pray for the planet, and they seek to heal it. If they seem preoccupied with personal issues and private concerns, their own awareness is shaped by a sense of the collective. "Let there be peace on earth, and let it begin with me," begins one popular Unity hymn.

In sum, in the late twentieth century subtle energies are also transformed energies. Spirituality in the metaphysical movement, especially in its present-day New Age manifestation, means working with the energies of the moment, "going with the flow," and seeking, as earlier metaphysicians, to combine all of the cultural currents that act as catalysts in our time. Far from keeping their gaze focused unswervingly on a fixed order of verities, in practice metaphysicians are manifestly sensitive to movement and change. This means considerably more than stereotypical assessments regarding "health and wealth and metaphysics." Rather, in what could be described as constitutional ways, the metaphysical brand of contemplation ends ironically by situating believers in the midst of the very world that one side of metaphysical literature has displaced and exchanged for Truth. Metaphysicians, and among them New Agers, mostly trade in variation and difference.[12]

NOTES

1. For Norman Vincent Peale and positive thinking, the definitive source is George.

2. The first volume in the extensive and ambitious Paulist Press series was Julian of Norwich's *Showings.*

3. For an extended discussion of the worldview of correspondence, see Albanese 1977:4–21. I explore metaphysical spirituality in many of the same words but in a comparative context in Albanese 1999.

4. Their prominence makes all the more astounding Judah's long list of characteristics of metaphysical movements, which cites the energetic dimension nowhere (12–18).

5. Emphasis in original. Gerber's "M.D." is prominently displayed on the cover and title page of his book.

6. I borrow this analysis from conversations with J. Gordon Melton over the years and from my discussion in Albanese 1998:659.

7. The classic discussion is Christy. Significantly, the Transcendentalists themselves read the Asian classics in kinetic terms, if their own expressive language can be considered a clue (Albanese 1977).

8. For a discussion of esoteric Buddhism, see Tweed:50–60.

9. Woodroffe is the classic text hailed by theosophists.

10. Ohsawa, in fact, was a major force in the Japanese Shoku-Yo Kai (Food Cure Society) after 1916, an organization with a strong component of Japanese cultural nationalism and a political edge. By 1948, now interested in "World Federalism," he had begun a "World Government Center," in Yokohama (Kotzsch 1985:37–118; Kotzsch 1981).

11. After the death of Guy Ballard, a Federal Grand Jury indicted his wife, Edna, and her son Donald for mail fraud. Questions about the appropriateness of using estimates of the truth and sincerity of the Ballards' beliefs eventually brought the case before the Supreme Court (Chidester:231–233).

12. A version of this article was presented at a consultation on spirituality organized by my colleague Wade Clark Roof at the University of California, Santa Barbara, in February 1998.

References

Albanese, Catherine L.
1977
Corresponding Motion: Transcendental Religion and the New America. Philadelphia: Temple University Press.

1998
Review of Michael F. Brown, *The Channeling Zone: American Spirituality in an Anxious Age.* In *Journal of the American Academy of Religion* 66/3:658–660.

1999
"Narrating an Almost Nation: Contact, Combination, and Metaphysics in American Religious History." *Criterion* 38/1:2–15, 44.

Alexander, Jon
1980
"What Do Recent Writers Mean by Spirituality?" *Spirituality Today* 32/2:247–254.

Blavatsky, H[elen] P.
1888
The Secret Doctrine: The Synthesis of Science, Religion, and Philosophy. 2 vols. London: Theosophical Publishing et al.

1972
The Key to Theosophy: An Abridgement. Ed. by Joy Mills. Wheaton, IL: Theosophical Publishing House. Original complete edition 1889.

Braden, Charles S.
1963
Spirits in Rebellion: The Rise and Development of New Thought. Dallas: Southern Methodist University Press.

Braude, Ann   *Radical Spirits: Spiritualism and Women's Rights in*
1989   *Nineteenth-Century America.* Boston: Beacon Press.

Brennan, Barbara Ann   *Hands of Light: A Guide to Healing through the Human Energy*
1988   *Field.* New York: Bantam Books. Original edition 1987.

Brown, Michael F.   *The Channeling Zone: American Spirituality in an Anxious*
1997   *Age.* Cambridge, MA: Harvard University Press.

Bruyere, Rosalyn   *Wheels of Light: A Study of the Chakras.* Glendale, CA: Heal-
1987   ing Light Center.

Cady, H. Emilie   *Lessons in Truth.* Lee's Summit, MO: Unity Books. Original
[1967]   edition 1894.

Campbell, Bruce F.   *Ancient Wisdom Revived: A History of the Theosophical Move-*
1980   *ment.* Berkeley: University of California Press.

Carroll, Bret E.   *Spiritualism in Antebellum America.* Bloomington: Indiana
1997   University Press.

Chia, Mantak   *Awaken Healing Energy through the Tao: The Taoist Secret of*
1983   *Circulating Internal Power.* Santa Fe: Aurora Press.

Chidester, David   *Patterns of Power: Religion and Politics in American Culture.*
1988   Englewood Cliffs, NJ: Prentice Hall.

Christy, Arthur E.   *The Orient in American Transcendentalism: A Study of Emer-*
1978   *son, Thoreau, and Alcott.* New York: Octagon Books. Original
          edition 1932.

Collinge, William   *Subtle Energy: Awakening to the Unseen Forces in Our Lives.*
1998   New York: Warner Books.

Dossey, Larry   *Healing Words: The Power of Prayer and the Practice of Medi-*
1993   *cine.* San Francisco: Harper.

1996   *Prayer Is Good Medicine: How to Reap the Healing Benefits of*
          Prayer. San Francisco: Harper.

Eliade, Mircea   *Yoga: Immortality and Freedom.* Trans. by Willard R. Trask.
1969   2d ed. Princeton: Princeton University Press.

Evans, Warren Felt   *The Divine Law of Cure.* Boston: H. H. Carter.
1881

Fuller, Robert C.   *Mesmerism and the American Cure of Souls.* Philadelphia:
1982   University of Pennsylvania Press.

Gagné, Steve   *Energetics of Food.* Ed. by John David Mann. Santa Fe: Spi-
1990   ral Sciences.

George, Carol V. R.   *God's Salesman: Norman Vincent Peale and the Power of Posi-*
1993   *tive Thinking.* New York: Oxford University Press.

Gerber, Richard   *Vibrational Medicine: New Choices for Healing Ourselves.*
1988   Santa Fe: Bear.

Hay, Louise L.   *Heal Your Body: The Mental Causes for Physical Illness and the*
    1984a   *Metaphysical Way to Overcome Them.* Rev. ed. Santa Monica,
                    CA: Hay House. Original edition 1976.

    1984b   *You Can Heal Your Life.* Santa Monica, CA: Hay House.

Judah, J. Stillson *The History and Philosophy of the Metaphysical Movements in*
    1967   *America.* Philadelphia: Westminster Press.

Julian of Norwich   *Showings.* Trans. and intro. by Edmund Colledge and James
    1978   Walsh. New York: Paulist Press.

Kaptchuk, Ted. J.   *The Web That Has No Weaver: Understanding Chinese Medi-*
    1983   *cine.* New York: Congdon & Weed.

Kotzsch, Ronald E. "George Ohsawa and the Japanese Religious Tradition."
    1981   Ph.D. diss., Harvard University.

    1985   *Macrobiotics: Yesterday and Today.* New York: Japan Publica-
                    tions.

Kushi, Aveline,   *Aveline Kushi's Complete Guide to Macrobiotic Cooking: For*
  with Alex Jack   *Health, Harmony, and Peace.* New York: Warner Books.
    1985

Leadbeater,   *The Chakras.* Wheaton, IL: Theosophical Publishing. Origi-
  C[harles] W.   nal edition 1927.
    1980

MacGregor, Geddes   "Soul: Christian Concept." In *Encyclopedia of Religion*
    1987   13:455–460. Ed. by Mircea Eliade. New York: Macmillan.

Materra, Gary Ward "Women in Early New Thought: Lives and Theology in Tran-
    1997   sition, from the Civil War to World War I." Ph.D. diss., Uni-
                    versity of California, Santa Barbara.

Melton, J. Gordon   "Ohsawa, George." In *New Age Encyclopedia,* 332–334. Ed. by
    1990   J. Gordon Melton, Jerome Clark, and Aidan A. Kelly. Detroit:
                    Gale Research.

Mesmer, F[ranz] A. *Mesmerism: A Translation of the Original Scientific and Medi-*
    1980   *cal Writings of F. A. Mesmer.* Trans. and comp. by George
                    Bloch. Los Altos, CA: William Kaufmann.

Moore, R. Laurence *In Search of White Crows: Spiritualism, Parapsychology, and*
    1977   *American Culture.* New York: Oxford University Press.

Myss, Caroline   *Anatomy of the Spirit: The Seven Stages of Power and Healing.*
    1996   New York: Harmony Books.

Olson, Stuart Alve, *Cultivating the Ch'i.* 3d ed. St. Paul: Dragon Door Publica-
  comp. and trans. tions.
    1993

Prothero, Stephen
1993   "From Spiritualism to Theosophy: 'Uplifting' a Democratic Tradition." *Religion and American Culture: A Journal of Interpretation* 3/2:197–216.

1996   *The White Buddhist: The Asian Odyssey of Henry Steel Olcott.* Bloomington: Indiana University Press.

[Schucman, Helen Cohn]
1985   *A Course in Miracles: Workbook for Students.* Tiburon, CA: Foundation for Inner Peace.

Synnestvedt, Sig
1970   *The Essential Swedenborg: Basic Teachings of Emanuel Swedenborg, Scientist, Philosopher, and Theologian.* New York: Swedenborg Foundation, Twayne Publishers.

Taylor, Wanda Romer
1996   "Energy Field around the Human Body." *Compass.* May/June: 115.

Tiller, William A.
1997   *Science and Human Transformation: Subtle Energies, Intentionality, and Consciousness.* Walnut Creek, CA: Pavior Publishing.

Trine, Ralph Waldo
1970   *In Tune with the Infinite.* Indianapolis: Bobbs-Merrill. Original edition 1897.

Tweed, Thomas A.
1992   *The American Encounter with Buddhism, 1844–1912: Victorian Culture and the Limits of Dissent.* Bloomington: Indiana University Press.

United States v. Ballard
1944   332 U.S. 78.

Woodroffe, John, trans. and ed.
1972   *The Serpent Power; Being the* Sat-Dakra-Nirupana *and* Paduka-Pancaka. 8th ed. [reprint of 3d—1928—ed.]. Madras: Ganesh.

20

Fullness of Life—Bodily Health and Vigor

Ralph Waldo Trine

For the general American public, probably the best-known classic of metaphysical spirituality is Ralph Waldo Trine's *In Tune with the Infinite,* published originally in 1897 and still in print. By the mid-1980s, the book had sold at least a million and a half copies in English. The chapter from Trine's book reprinted below underlines a theme central to the New Thought tradition, in which the human mind—as it opens to the stream of life and wholeness from the divine Mind—brings health and healing to an ailing human body. In a more public context, shaped by his study of history and political science at the University of Wisconsin and Johns Hopkins University, Trine (1866–1954) became a convinced socialist, a stance that he connected to his "actual living belief in the . . . Fatherhood of God and the brotherhood of Man." Something of the socialist universe that lay behind Trine's vision may be grasped in the metaphors of flow and connection that pervade his chapter and his book. For Trine, the divine influx permeates our world; and when energy runs unimpeded through all living things, they experience health, wholeness, and blessing. Just as, in his socialist vision, a society bathed in the influx of spirit—unblocking all obstacles to allow spirit to enter—is a society in which mutual sharing brings the common good, so, too, ideas of sharing and interconnection shape his view of the well human body, in which free flow and linkage are everywhere. Trine's New Thought tradition continues to teach and practice these ideas in denominations like Unity, the Church of Divine Science, and the Church of Religious Science. Beyond the denominations, through ideas like positive thinking and creating one's own reality, these views have attracted a far larger following.

God is the Spirit of Infinite Life. If we are partakers of this life, and have the power of opening ourselves fully to its divine inflow, it means more, so far as even the physical life is concerned, than we may at first think. For very clearly, the life of this Infinite Spirit, from its very nature, can admit of no disease; and if this is true, no disease can exist in the body where it freely enters, through which it freely flows.

From *In Tune with the Infinite* [1897].

Let us recognize at the outset that, so far as the physical life is concerned, *all life is from within out.* There is an immutable law which says: "As within, so without; cause, effect." In other words, the thought forces, the various mental states and the emotions, all have in time their effects upon the physical body.

Some one says: "I hear a great deal said today in regard to the effects of the mind upon the body, but I don't know as I place very much confidence in this." Don't you? Some one brings you sudden news. You grow pale, you tremble, or perhaps you fall into a faint. It is, however, through the channel of your mind that the news is imparted to you. A friend says something to you, perhaps at the table, something that seems very unkind. You are hurt by it, as we say. You have been enjoying your dinner, but from this moment your appetite is gone. But what was said entered into and affected you through the channel of your mind.

Look! yonder goes a young man, dragging his feet, stumbling over the slightest obstruction in the path. Why is it? Simply that he is weak-minded, an idiot. In other words, *a falling state of mind is productive of a falling condition of the body.* To be sure minded is to be sure footed. To be uncertain in mind is to be uncertain in step.

Again, a sudden emergency arises. You stand trembling and weak with fear. Why are you powerless to move? Why do you tremble? And yet you believe that the mind has but little influence upon the body. You are for a moment dominated by a fit of anger. For a few hours afterwards you complain of a violent headache. And still you do not seem to realize that the thoughts and emotions have an effect upon the body.

A day or two ago, while conversing with a friend, we were speaking of worry. "My father is greatly given to worry," he said. "Your father is not a healthy man," I said. "He is not strong, vigorous, robust, and active." I then went on to describe to him more fully his father's condition and the troubles which afflicted him. He looked at me in surprise and said, "Why, you do not know my father?" "No," I replied. "How then can you describe so accurately the disease with which he is afflicted?" "You have just told me that your father is greatly given to worry. When you told me this you indicated to me cause. In describing your father's condition I simply connected with the cause its own peculiar effects."

Fear and worry have the effect of closing up the channels of the body, so that the life forces flow in a slow and sluggish manner. Hope and tranquillity open the channels of the body, so that the life forces go bounding through it in such a way that disease can rarely get a foothold.

Not long ago a lady was telling a friend of a serious physical trouble. My friend happened to know that between this lady and her sister the most kindly relations did not exist. He listened attentively to her delineation of her troubles, and then, looking her squarely in the face, in a firm but kindly tone said: "Forgive your sister." The woman looked at him in surprise and said: "I can't forgive my sister." "Very well, then," he replied, "keep the stiffness of your joints and your kindred rheumatic troubles."

A few weeks later he saw her again. With a light step she came toward him and said: "I took your advice. I saw my sister and forgave her. We have become good friends again, and I don't know how it is, but somehow or other from the very day, as I remember, that we became reconciled, my troubles seemed to grow less, and today there is not a trace of the old difficulties left; and really, my sister and I have become such good friends that now we can scarcely get along without one another." Again we have effect following cause.

We have several well-authenticated cases of the following nature: A mother has been dominated for a few moments by an intense passion of anger, and the child at her breast has died within an hour's time, so poisoned became the mother's milk by virtue of the poisonous secretions of the system while under the domination of this fit of anger. In other cases it has caused severe illness and convulsions.

The following experiment has been tried a number of times by a well-known scientist: Several men have been put into a heated room. Each man has been dominated for a moment by a particular passion of some kind; one by an intense passion of anger, and others by different other passions. The experimenter has taken a drop of perspiration from the body of each of these men, and by means of a careful chemical analysis he has been able to determine the particular passion by which each has been dominated. Practically the same results revealed themselves in the chemical analysis of the saliva of each of the men.

Says a noted American author, an able graduate of one of our greatest medical schools, and one who has studied deeply into the forces that build the body and the forces that tear it down: "The mind is the natural protector of the body. . . . Every thought tends to reproduce itself, and ghastly mental pictures of disease, sensuality, and vice of all sorts, produce scrofula and leprosy in the soul, which reproduces them in the body. Anger changes the chemical properties of the saliva to a poison dangerous to life. It is well known that sudden and violent emotions have not only weakened the heart in a few hours, but have caused death and insanity. It has been discovered by scientists that there is a chemical difference between that sudden cold exudation of a person under a deep sense of guilt and the ordinary perspiration; and the state of the mind can sometimes be determined by chemical analysis of the perspiration of a criminal, which, when brought into contact with selenic acid, produces a distinctive pink color. It is well known that fear has killed thousands of victims; while, on the other hand, *courage is a great invigorator.*

"Anger in the mother may poison a nursing child. Rarey, the celebrated horse-tamer, said that an angry word would sometimes raise the pulse of a horse ten beats in a minute. If this is true of a beast, what can we say of its power upon human beings, especially upon a child? Strong mental emotion often causes vomiting. Extreme anger or fright may produce jaundice. A violent paroxysm of rage has caused apoplexy and death. Indeed, in more than one instance, a single night of mental agony has wrecked a life. Grief, long-standing jealousy, constant care and corroding anxiety sometimes tend to develop insanity. Sick thoughts and discordant moods are the natural atmosphere of disease, and crime is engendered and thrives in the miasma of the mind."

From all this we get the great fact we are scientifically demonstrating to-day,—that the various mental states, emotions, and passions have their various peculiar effects upon the body, and each induces in turn, if indulged in to any great extent, its own peculiar forms of disease, and these in time become chronic.

Just a word or two in regard to their mode of operation. If a person is dominated for a moment by, say a passion of anger, there is set up in the physical organism what we might justly term a bodily thunder-storm, which has the effect of souring, or rather of corroding, the normal, healthy, and life-giving secretions of the body, so that instead of performing their natural functions they become poisonous and destructive. And if this goes on to any great extent, by virtue of their cumulative influences, they give rise to a partic-ular form of disease, which in turn becomes chronic. So the emotion opposite to this, that of kindliness, love, benevolence, good-will, tends to stimulate a healthy, purifying, and life-giving flow of all the bodily secretions. All the channels of the body seem free and open; the life forces go bounding through them. And these very forces, set into a bounding activity, will in time counter-act the poisonous and disease-giving effects of their opposites.

A physician goes to see a patient. He gives no medicine this morning. Yet the very fact of his going makes the patient better. He has carried with him the spirit of health; he has carried brightness of tone and disposition; he has carried hope into the sick chamber; he has left it there. In fact, the very hope and good cheer he has carried with him has taken hold of and has had a subtle but powerful influence upon the mind of the patient; and this mental condition imparted by the physician has in turn its effects upon the patient's body, and so through the instrumentality of this mental suggestion the healing goes on.

> "Know, then, whatever cheerful and serene
> Supports the mind, supports the body, too.
> Hence the most vital movement mortals feel
> Is *hope;* the balm and life-blood of the soul."

We sometimes hear a person in weak health say to another, "I always feel better when you come." There is a deep scientific reason underlying the statement. "The tongue of the wise is health." The power of suggestion so far as the human mind is concerned is a most wonderful and interesting field of study. Most wonderful and powerful forces can be set into operation through this agency. One of the world's most noted scientists, recognized everywhere as one of the most eminent anatomists living, tells us that he has proven from laboratory experiments that the entire human structure can be completely changed, made over, within a period of less than one year, and that some portions can be entirely remade within a period of a very few weeks.

"Do you mean to say," I hear it asked, "that the body can be changed from a diseased to a healthy condition through the operation of the interior forces?" Most certainly; and more, this is the natural method of cure. The method that has as its work the application of drugs, medicines and external agencies is the artificial method. The only thing that any drug or any medicine can do is to remove obstructions, that the life forces may have simply a better chance to do their work. *The real healing process must be performed by the operation of the life forces within.* A surgeon and physician of world-wide fame recently made to his medical associates the following declaration: "For generations past the most important influence that plays upon nutrition, the *life principle* itself, has remained an unconsidered element in the medical profession, and the almost exclusive drift of its studies and remedial paraphernalia has been confined to the action of matter over mind. This has seriously interfered with the evolutionary tendencies of the doctors themselves, and consequently the psychic factor in professional life is still in a rudimentary or comparatively undeveloped state. But the light of the nineteenth century has dawned, and so the march of mankind in general is taken in the direction of the hidden forces of nature. Doctors are now compelled to join the ranks of students in psychology and follow their patrons into the broader field of mental therapeutics. There is no time for lingering, no time for skepticism or doubt or hesitation. *He who lingers is lost, for the entire race is enlisted in the movement.*"

I am aware of the fact that in connection with the matter we are now considering there has been a great deal of foolishness during the past few years. Many absurd and foolish things have been claimed and done; but this says nothing against, and it has absolutely nothing to do with the great underlying laws themselves. The same has been true of the early days of practically every system of ethics or philosophy or religion the world has ever known. But as time has passed, these foolish, absurd things have fallen away, and the great eternal principles have stood out ever more and more clearly defined.

I know *personally* of many cases where an entire and permanent cure has been effected, in some within a remarkably short period of time, through the operation of these forces. Some of them are cases that had been entirely given up by the regular practice, *materia medica*. We have numerous accounts of such cases in all times and in connection with all religions. And why should not the power of effecting such cures exist among us today? The *power does exist*, and it will be actualized in just the degree that we recognize the same great laws that were recognized in times past.

One person may do a very great deal in connection with the healing of another, but this almost invariably implies co-operation on the part of the one who is thus treated. In the cures that Christ performed he most always needed the co-operation of the one who appealed to him. His question almost invariably was, "Dost thou believe?" He thus stimulated into activity the life-giving forces within the one cured. If one is in a very weak condition, or if his nervous system is exhausted, or if his mind through the influence of the disease is not so strong in its workings, it may be well for him for a time to seek the aid and co-operation of another. But it would be far better for such a one could he bring himself to a vital realization of the omnipotence of his own interior powers.

One may cure another, but to be *permanently healed* one must do it himself. In this way another may be most valuable as a teacher by bringing one to a clear realization of the power of the forces within, but in every case, in order to have a permanent cure, the work of the self is necessary. Christ's words were almost invariably,—Go and sin no more, or, thy sins are forgiven thee, thus pointing out the one eternal and never-changing fact,—that all disease and its consequent suffering is the direct or the indirect result of the violation of law, either consciously or unconsciously, either intentionally or unintentionally.

Suffering is designed to continue only so long as sin continues, sin not necessarily in the theological, but always in the philosophical sense, though many times in the sense of both. The moment the violation ceases, the moment one comes into perfect harmony with the law, the cause of the suffering ceases; and though there may be residing within the cumulative effects of past violation, the cause is removed, and consequently there can be no more effects in the form of additions, and even the diseased condition that has been induced from past violation will begin to disappear as soon as the right forces are set into activity.

There is nothing that will more quickly and more completely bring one into harmony with the laws under which he lives than this vital realization of his oneness with the Infinite Spirit, which is the life of all life. In this there can be no disease, and nothing will more readily remove from the organism the obstructions that have accumulated there, or in other words, the disease that resides there, than this full realization and the complete opening of one's self to this divine inflow. "I shall put My spirit in you, and ye shall live."

The moment a person realizes his oneness with the Infinite Spirit he recognizes himself as a spiritual being, and no longer as a mere physical, material being. He then no longer makes the mistake of regarding himself as body, subject to ills and diseases, but he realizes the fact that he is spirit, spirit now as much as he ever will or can be, and that he is the builder and so the master of the body, the house in which he lives; and the moment he thus recognizes his power as master he ceases in any way to allow it the mastery over him. He no longer fears the elements or any of the forces that he now in his ignorance allows to take hold of and affect the body. The moment he realizes his own supremacy, instead of fearing them as he did when he was out of harmony with them, he learns to love them. He thus comes into harmony with them; or rather, he so orders them that they come into harmony with him. He who formerly was the slave has now become the master. The moment we come to love a thing it no longer carries harm for us.

There are almost countless numbers today, weak and suffering in body, who would become strong and healthy if they would only give God an opportunity to do His work. To such I would say, *Don't shut out the divine inflow.* Do anything else rather than this. Open yourselves to it. Invite it. In the degree that you open yourselves to it, its inflowing tide will course through your bodies a force so vital that the old obstructions that are dominating them today will be driven out before it. "My words are life to them that find them, and health to all their flesh."

There is a trough through which a stream of muddy water has been flowing for many days. The dirt has gradually collected on its sides and bottom, and it continues to collect as long as the muddy water flows through it. Change this. Open the trough to a swift-flowing stream of clear, crystal water, and in a very little while even the very dirt that has collected on its sides and bottom will be carried away. The trough will be entirely cleansed. It will present an aspect of beauty and no longer an aspect of ugliness. And more, the water that now courses through it will be of value; it will be an agent of refreshment, of health and of strength to those who use it.

Yes, in just the degree that you realize your oneness with this Infinite Spirit of Life, and thus actualize your latent possibilities and powers, you will exchange dis-ease for ease, inharmony for harmony, suffering and pain for abounding health and strength. And in the degree that you realize this wholeness, this abounding health and strength in yourself, will you carry it to all with whom you come in contact; for *we must remember that health is contagious as well as disease.*

I hear it asked, What can be said in a concrete way in regard to the practical application of these truths, so that one can hold himself in the enjoyment of perfect bodily health; and more, that one may heal himself of any existing disease? In reply, let it be said that the chief thing that can be done is to point out the great underlying principle, and that each individual must make his own application; one person cannot well make this for another.

First let it be said, that the very fact of one's holding the thought of perfect health sets into operation vital forces which will in time be more or less productive of the effect,—perfect health. Then speaking more directly in regard to the great principle itself, from its very nature, it is clear that more can be accomplished through the process of realization than through the process of affirmation, though for some affirmation may be a help, an aid to realization.

In the degree, however, that you come into a vital realization of your oneness with the Infinite Spirit of Life, whence all life in individual form has come and is continually coming, and in the degree that through this realization you open yourself to its divine inflow, do you set into operation forces that will sooner or later bring even the physical body into a state of abounding health and strength. For to realize that this Infinite Spirit of Life can from its very nature admit of no disease, and to realize that this, then, is the life in you, by realizing your oneness with it, you can so open yourself to its more abundant entrance that the diseased bodily conditions—effects—will respond to the influences of its all-perfect power, this either quickly or more tardily, depending entirely upon yourself.

There have been those who have been able to open themselves so fully to this realization that the healing has been instantaneous and permanent. The degree of intensity always eliminates in like degree the element of time. *It must, however, be a calm, quiet, and expectant intensity, rather than an intensity that is fearing, disturbed, and non-expectant.* Then there are others who have come to this realization by degrees.

Many will receive great help, and many will be entirely healed by a practice somewhat after the following nature: With a mind at peace, and with a heart going out in love to all, go into the quiet of your own interior self, holding the thought,—I am one with the Infinite Spirit of Life, the life of my life. I then as spirit, I a spiritual being, can in my own real nature admit of no disease. I now open my body, in which disease has gotten a foothold, I open it fully to the inflowing tide of this Infinite Life, and it now, even now, is pouring in and coursing through my body, and the healing process is going on. Realize this so fully that you begin to feel a quickening and a warming glow imparted by the life forces to the body. Believe the healing process is going on. Believe it, and hold continually to it. Many people greatly desire a certain thing, but expect something else. They have greater faith in the power of evil than in the power of good, and hence remain ill.

If one will give himself to this meditation, realization, treatment, or whatever term it may seem best to use, at stated times, as often as he may choose, and then *continually hold himself in the same attitude of mind,* thus allowing the force to work continually, he will be surprised how rapidly the body will be exchanging conditions of disease and inharmony for health and harmony. There is no particular reason, however, for this surprise, for in this way he is simply allowing the Omnipotent Power to do the work, which will have to do it ultimately in any case.

If there is a local difficulty, and one wants to open this particular portion, in addition to the entire body, to this inflowing life, he can hold this particular portion in thought, for to fix the thought in this way upon any particular portion of the body stimulates or increases the flow of the life forces in that portion. It must always be borne in mind, however, that whatever healing may be thus accomplished, effects will not permanently cease until causes have been removed. In other words, *as long as there is the violation of law, so long disease and suffering will result.*

This realization that we are considering will have an influence not only where there is a diseased condition of the body, but even where there is not this condition it will give an increased bodily life, vigor, and power.

We have had many cases, in all times and in all countries, of healing through the operation of the interior forces, entirely independent of external agencies. Various have been the methods, or rather, various have been the names applied to them, but the great law underlying all is one and the same, and the same today. When the Master sent his followers forth, his injunction to them was to heal the sick and the afflicted, as well as to teach the people. The early church fathers had the power of healing, in short, it was a part of their work.

And why should we not have the power today, the same as they had it then? Are the laws at all different? Identically the same. Why, then? Simply because, with a few rare exceptions here and there, we are unable to get beyond the mere letter of the law into its real vital spirit and power. It is the letter that killeth, it is the spirit that giveth life and power. Every soul who becomes so individualized that he breaks through the mere letter and enters into the real vital spirit, *will have the power,* as have all who have gone before, and when he does, he will also be the means of imparting it to others, for he will be one who will move and who will speak with authority.

We are rapidly finding today, and we shall find even more and more, as time passes, that practically all disease, with its consequent suffering, has its origin in perverted mental and emotional states and conditions. *The mental attitude we take toward anything determines to a greater or less extent its effects upon us.* If we fear it, or if we antagonize it, the chances are that it will have detrimental or even disastrous effects upon us. If we come into harmony with it by quietly recognizing and inwardly asserting our superiority over it, in the degree that we are able successfully to do this, in that degree will it carry with it no injury for us.

No disease can enter into or take hold of our bodies unless it find therein something corresponding to itself which makes it possible. And in the same way, no evil or undesirable condition of any kind can come into our lives unless there is already in them that which invites it and so makes it possible for it to come. The sooner we begin to look within ourselves for the cause of whatever comes to us, the better it will be, for so much the sooner will we begin to make conditions within ourselves such that only *good* may enter.

We, who from our very natures should be masters of all conditions, by virtue of our ignorance are mastered by almost numberless conditions of every description.

Do I fear a draft? There is nothing in the draft—a little purifying current of God's pure air—to cause me trouble, to bring on a cold, perhaps an illness. The draft can affect me only in the degree that *I myself* make it possible, only in the degree that I allow it to affect me. We must distinguish between causes and mere occasions. The draft is not cause, nor does it carry cause with it.

Two persons are sitting in the same draft. The one is injuriously affected by it, the other experiences not even an inconvenience, but he rather enjoys it. The one is a creature of circumstances; he fears the draft, cringes before it, continually thinks of the harm it is doing him. In other words, he opens every avenue for it to enter and take hold of him, and so it—harmless and beneficent in itself—brings to him exactly what he has empowered it to bring. The other recognizes himself as the master over and not the creature of circumstances. He is not concerned about the draft. He puts himself into harmony with it, makes himself positive to it, and instead of experiencing any discomfort, he enjoys it, and in addition to its doing him a service by bringing the pure fresh air from without to him, it does him the additional service of hardening him even more to any future conditions of a like nature. But if the draft was cause, it would bring the same results to both. The fact that it does not, shows that it is not a cause, but a condition, and it brings to each, effects which correspond to the conditions it finds within each.

Poor draft! How many thousands, nay millions of times it is made the scapegoat by those who are too ignorant or too unfair to look their own weaknesses square in the face, and who instead of becoming imperial masters, remain cringing slaves. Think of it, what it means! A man created in the image of the eternal God, sharer of His life and power, born to have dominion, fearing, shaking, cringing before a little draft of pure life-giving air. But scapegoats are convenient things, even if the only thing they do for us is to aid us in our constant efforts at self-delusion.

The best way to disarm a draft of the bad effects it has been accustomed to bring one, is first to bring about a pure and healthy set of conditions within, then, to change one's mental attitude toward it. Recognize the fact that of itself it has no power, it has only the power you invest it with. Thus you will put yourself into harmony with it, and will no longer sit in fear of it. Then sit in a draft a few times and get hardened to it, as every one, by going at it judiciously, can readily do. "But suppose one is in delicate health, or especially subject to drafts?" Then be simply a little judicious at first; don't seek the strongest that can be found, especially if you do not as yet in your own mind feel equal to it, for if you do not, it signifies that you still fear it. That supreme regulator of all life, *good common sense,* must be used here, the same as elsewhere.

If we are born to have dominion, and that we are is demonstrated by the fact that some have attained to it,—and what one *has* done, soon or late all *can* do,—then it is not necessary that we live under the domination of any physical agent. In the degree that we recognize our own interior powers, then are we rulers and able to dictate; in the degree that we fail to recognize them, we are slaves, and are dictated to. We build whatever we find within us; we attract whatever comes to us, and all in accordance with spiritual law, for all natural law is spiritual law.

The whole of human life is cause and effect; there is no such thing in it as chance, nor is there even in all the wide universe. Are we not satisfied with whatever comes into our lives? The thing to do, then, is not to spend time in railing against the imaginary something we create and call fate, but to look to the within, and change the causes at work there, in order that things of a different nature may come, for there will come exactly what we cause to come. This is true not only of the physical body, but of all phases and conditions of life. We invite whatever comes, and did we not invite it, either consciously or unconsciously, it could not and it would not come. This may undoubtedly be hard for some to believe, or even to see, at first. But in the degree that one candidly and openmindedly looks at it, and then studies into the silent, but subtle and, so to speak, omnipotent workings of the thought forces, and as he traces their effects within him and about him, it becomes clearly evident, and easy to understand.

And then whatever does come to one depends for its effects entirely upon his mental attitude toward it. Does this or that occurrence or condition cause you annoyance? Very well; it causes you annoyance, and so disturbs your peace merely because you allow it to. You are born to have absolute control over your own dominion, but if you voluntarily hand over this power, even if for a little while, to some one or to some thing else, then you of course, become the creature, the one controlled.

To live undisturbed by passing occurrences you must first find your own centre. You must then be firm in your own centre, and so rule the world from within. He who does not himself condition circumstances allows the process to be reversed, and becomes a conditioned circumstance. Find your centre and live in it. Surrender it to no person, to no thing. In the degree that you do this will you find yourself growing stronger and stronger in it. And how can one find his centre? By realizing his oneness with the Infinite Power, and by living continually in this realization.

But if you do not rule from your own centre, if you invest this or that with the power of bringing you annoyance, or evil, or harm, then take what it brings, but cease your railings against the eternal goodness and beneficence of all things.

> "I swear the earth shall surely be complete
> To him or her who shall be complete;

The earth remains jagged and broken
Only to him who remains jagged and broken."

If the windows of your soul are dirty and streaked, covered with matter foreign to them, then the world as you look out of them will be to you dirty and streaked and out of order. Cease your complainings, however; keep your pessimism, your "poor, unfortunate me" to yourself, lest you betray the fact that your windows are badly in need of something. But know that your friend, who keeps his windows clean, that the Eternal Sun may illumine all within and make visible all without,—know that he lives in a different world from yours.

Then, go wash your windows, and instead of longing for some other world, you will discover the wonderful beauties of this world; and if you don't find transcendent beauties on every hand here, the chances are that you will never find them anywhere.

"The poem hangs on the berry-bush
When comes the poet's eye,
And the whole street is a masquerade
When Shakspeare passes by."

This same Shakspeare, whose mere passing causes all this commotion, is the one who put into the mouth of one of his creations the words: "The fault, dear Brutus, is not in our stars, but in ourselves, that we are underlings." And the great work of his own life is right good evidence that he realized full well the truth of the facts we are considering. And again he gave us a great truth in keeping with what we are considering when he said:

"Our doubts are traitors,
And make us lose the good we oft might win
By *fearing* to attempt."

There is probably no agent that brings us more undesirable conditions than fear. We should live in fear of nothing, nor will we when we come fully to know ourselves. An old French proverb runs:

"Some of your griefs you have cured,
And the sharpest you still have survived;
But what *torments of pain* you endured
From evils that never arrived."

Fear and lack of faith go hand in hand. The one is born of the other. Tell me how much one is given to fear, and I will tell you how much he lacks in faith. Fear is a most expensive guest to entertain, the same as worry is: so expensive are they that no one can afford to entertain them. *We invite what we fear, the same as, by a different attitude of mind, we invite and attract the influences and conditions we desire.* The mind dominated by fear opens the door for the entrance of the very things, for the actualization of the very conditions it fears.

"Where are you going?" asked an Eastern pilgrim on meeting the plague one day. "I am going to Bagdad to kill five thousand people," was the reply. A few days later the same pilgrim met the plague returning. "You told me you were going to Bagdad to kill five thousand people," said he, "but instead, you killed fifty thousand." "No," said the plague. "*I killed only five thousand,* as I told you I would; *the others died of fright.*"

Fear can paralyze every muscle in the body. Fear affects the flow of the blood, likewise the normal and healthy action of all the life forces. Fear can make the body rigid, motionless, and powerless to move.

Not only do we attract to ourselves the things we fear, but we also aid in attracting to others the conditions we in our own minds hold them in fear of. This we do in proportion to the strength of our own thought, and in the degree that they are sensitively organized and so influenced by our thought, and this, although it be unconscious both on their part and on ours.

Children, and especially when very young, are, generally speaking, more sensitive to their surrounding influences than grown people are. Some are veritable little sensitive plates, registering the influences about them, and embodying them as they grow. How careful in their prevailing mental states then should be those who have them in charge, and especially how careful should a mother be during the time she is carrying the child, and when every thought, every mental as well as emotional state has its direct influence upon the life of the unborn child. Let parents be careful how they hold a child, either younger or older, in the thought of fear. This is many times done, unwittingly on their part, through anxiety, and at times through what might well be termed over-care, which is fully as bad as under-care.

I know of a number of cases where a child has been so continually held in the thought of fear lest this or that condition come upon him, that the very things that were feared have been drawn to him, which probably otherwise never would have come at all. Many times there has been no adequate basis for the fear. In case there is a basis, then far wiser is it to take exactly the opposite attitude, so as to neutralize the force at work, and then to hold the child in the thought of wisdom and strength that it may be able to meet the condition and master it, instead of being mastered by it.

But a day or two ago a friend was telling me of an experience of his own life in this connection. At a period when he was having a terrific struggle with a certain habit, he was so continually held in the thought of fear by his mother and the young lady to whom he was engaged,—the engagement to be consummated at the end of a certain period, the time depending on his proving his mastery,—that he, very sensitively organized, *continually* felt the depressing and weakening effects of their negative thoughts. He could always tell exactly how they felt toward him; he was continually influenced and weakened by their fear, by their questionings, by their suspicions, all of which had the effect of lessening the sense of his own power, all of which had an endeavor-paralyzing influence upon him. And so instead of their begetting courage and strength in him, they brought him to a still greater realization of his own weakness and the almost worthless use of struggle.

Here were two who loved him dearly, and who would have done anything and everything to help him gain the mastery, but who, ignorant of the silent, subtle, ever-working and all-telling power of the thought forces, instead of imparting to him courage, instead of adding to his strength, disarmed him of this, and then added an additional weakness from without. In this way the battle for him was made harder in a three-fold degree.

Fear and worry and all kindred mental states are too expensive for any person, man, woman, or child, to entertain or indulge in. Fear paralyzes healthy action, worry corrodes and pulls down the organism, and will finally tear it to pieces. Nothing is to be gained by it, but everything to be lost. Long-continued grief at any loss will do the same. Each brings its own peculiar type of ailment. An inordinate love of gain, a close-fisted, hoarding disposition will have kindred effects. Anger, jealousy, malice, continual fault-finding, lust, has each its own peculiar corroding, weakening, tearing-down effects.

We shall find that not only are happiness and prosperity concomitants of righteousness,—living in harmony with the higher laws, but bodily health as well. The great Hebrew seer enunciated a wonderful chemistry of life when he said,—"As righteousness tendeth to life, so he that pursueth evil, pursueth it to his own death." On the other hand, "In the way of righteousness is life; and in the pathway thereof there is no death." The time will come when it will be seen that this means far more than most people dare *even to think as yet*. "It rests with man to say whether his soul shall be housed in a stately mansion of ever-growing splendor and beauty, or in a hovel of his own building,—a hovel at last ruined and abandoned to decay."

The bodies of almost untold numbers, living their one-sided, unbalanced lives, are every year, through these influences, weakening and falling by the wayside long before their time. Poor, poor houses! Intended to be beautiful temples, brought to desolation by their ignorant, reckless, deluded tenants. Poor houses!

A close observer, a careful student of the power of the thought forces, will soon be able to read in the voice, in the movements, in the features, the effects registered by the prevailing mental states and conditions. Or, if he is told the prevailing mental states and conditions, he can describe the voice, the movements, the features, as well as describe, in a general way, the peculiar physical ailments their possessor is heir to.

We are told by good authority that a study of the human body, its structure, and the length of time it takes it to come to maturity, in comparison with the time it takes the bodies of various animals and their corresponding longevity, reveals the fact that its natural age should be nearer a hundred and twenty years than what we commonly find it today. But think of the multitudes all about us whose bodies are aging, weakening, breaking, so that they have to abandon them long before they reach what ought to be a long period of strong, vigorous middle life.

Then, the natural length of life being thus shortened, it comes to be what we might term a race belief that this shortened period is the natural period. And as a consequence many, when they approach a certain age, seeing that as a rule people at this period of life begin to show signs of age, to break and go down hill as we say, they, thinking it a matter of course and that it must be the same with them, by taking this attitude of mind, many times bring upon themselves these very conditions long before it is necessary. Subtle and powerful are the influences of the mind in the building and rebuilding of the body. As we understand them better it may become the custom for people to look forward with pleasure to the teens of their second century.

There comes to mind at this moment a friend, a lady well on to eighty years of age. An old lady, some, most people in fact, would call her, especially those who measure age by the number of the seasons that have come and gone since one's birth. But to call our friend old, would be to call black white. She is no older than a girl of twenty-five, and indeed younger, I am glad to say, or I am sorry to say, depending upon the point of view, than *many* a girl of this age. Seeking for the good in all people and in all things, she has found the good everywhere. The brightness of disposition and of voice that is hers today, that attracts all people to her and that makes her so beautifully attractive to all people, has characterized her all through life. It has in turn carried brightness and hope and courage and strength to hundreds and thousands of people through all these years, and will continue to do so, apparently, for many years yet to come.

No fears, no worryings, no hatreds, no jealousies, no sorrowings, no grievings, no sordid graspings after inordinant gain, have found entrance into her realm of thought. As a consequence her mind, free from these abnormal states and conditions, has not externalized in her body the various physical ailments that the great majority of people are lugging about with them, thinking in their ignorance, that they are natural, and that it is all in accordance with the "eternal order of things" that they should have them. Her life has been one of varied experiences, so that all these things would have found ready entrance into the realm of her mind and so into her life were she ignorant enough to allow them entrance. On the contrary she has been wise enough to recognize the fact that in one kingdom at least she is ruler,—the kingdom of her mind, and that it is hers to dictate as to what shall and what shall not enter there. She knows, moreover, that in determining this she is determining all the conditions of her life. It is indeed a pleasure as well as an inspiration to see her as she goes here and there, to see her sunny disposition, her youthful step, to hear her joyous laughter. Indeed and in truth, Shakspeare knew whereof he spoke when he said,—"It is the mind that makes the body rich."

With great pleasure I watched her but recently as she was walking along the street, stopping to have a word and so a part in the lives of a group of children at play by the wayside, hastening her step a little to have a word with a washerwoman toting her bundle of clothes, stopping for a word with a laboring man returning with dinner pail in hand from his work, returning the recognition from the lady in her carriage, and so imparting some of her own rich life to all with whom she came in contact.

And as good fortune would have it, while still watching her, an old lady passed her,—really old, this one, though at least ten or fifteen years younger, so far as the count by the seasons is concerned. Nevertheless she was bent in form and apparently stiff in joint and muscle. Silent in mood, she wore a countenance of long-faced sadness, which was intensified surely several fold by a black, sombre headgear with an immense heavy veil still more sombre looking if possible. Her entire dress was of this description. By this relic-of-barbarism garb, combined with her own mood and expression, she continually proclaimed to the world two things,—her own personal sorrows and woes, which by this very method she kept continually fresh in her mind, and also her lack of faith in the eternal goodness of things, her lack of faith in the love and eternal goodness of the Infinite Father.

Wrapped only in the thoughts of her own ailments, and sorrows, and woes, she received and she gave nothing of joy, nothing of hope, nothing of courage, nothing of value to those whom she passed or with whom she came in contact. But on the contrary she suggested to all and helped to intensify in many, those mental states all too prevalent in our common human life. And as she passed our friend one could notice a slight turn of the head which, coupled with the expression in her face, seemed to indicate this as her thought,—Your dress and your conduct are not wholly in keeping with a lady of your years. Thank God, then, thank God they are not. And may He in His great goodness and love send us an innumerable company of the same rare type; and may they live a thousand years to bless mankind, to impart the life-giving influences of their own royal lives to the numerous ones all about us who stand so much in need of them.

Would you remain always young, and would you carry all the joyousness and buoyancy of youth into your maturer years? Then have care concerning but one thing,—how you live in your thought world. This will determine all. It was the inspired one, Gautama, the Buddha, who said,—"The mind is everything; what you think you become." And the same thing had Ruskin in mind when he said,—"Make yourself nests of pleasant thoughts. None of us as yet know, for none of us have been taught in early youth, what fairy palaces we may build of beautiful thought,—*proof against all adversity.*" And would you have in your body all the elasticity, all the strength, all the beauty of your younger years? Then live these in your mind, making no room for unclean thought, and you will externalize them in your body. In the degree that you keep young in thought will you remain young in body. And you will find that your body will in turn aid your mind, for body helps mind the same as mind builds body.

You are continually building, and so externalizing in your body conditions most akin to the thoughts and emotions you entertain. And not only are you so building from within, but you are also continually drawing from without, forces of a kindred nature. Your particular kind of thought connects you with a similar order of thought from without. If it is bright, hopeful, cheerful, you connect yourself with a current of thought of this nature. If it is sad, fearing, despondent, then this is the order of thought you connect yourself with.

If the latter is the order of your thought, then perhaps unconsciously and by degrees you have been connecting yourself with it. You need to go back and pick up again a part of your child nature, with its careless and cheerful type of thought. "The minds of the group of children at play are unconsciously concentrated in drawing to their bodies a current of playful thought. Place a child by itself, deprive it of its companions, and soon it will mope and become slow of movement. It is cut off from that peculiar thought current and is literally 'out of its element.'

"You need to bring again this current of playful thought to you which has gradually been turned off. You are too serious or sad, or absorbed in the serious affairs of life. You can be playful and cheerful without being puerile or silly. You can carry on business all the better for being in the playful mood when your mind is off your business. There is nothing but ill resulting from the permanent mood of sadness and seriousness,—the mood which by many so long maintained makes it actually difficult for them to smile at all.

"At eighteen or twenty you commenced growing out of the more playful tendency of early youth. You took hold of the more serious side of life. You went into some business. You became more or less involved in its cares, perplexities and responsibilities. Or, as man or woman, you entered on some phase of life involving care or trouble. Or you became absorbed in some game of business which, as you followed it, left no time for play. Then as you associated with older people you absorbed their old ideas, their mechanical methods of thinking, their acceptance of errors without question or thought of question. In all this you opened your mind to a heavy, care-laden current of thought. Into this you glided unconsciously. That thought is materialized in your blood and flesh. The seen of your body is a deposit or crystallization of the unseen element ever flowing to your body from your mind. Years pass on and you find that your movements are stiff and cumbrous,—that you can with difficulty climb a tree, as at fourteen. Your mind has all this time been sending to your body these heavy, inelastic elements, making your body what now it is. . . .

"Your change for the better must be gradual, and can only be accomplished by bringing the thought current of an all-round symmetrical strength to bear on it,—by demanding of the Supreme Power to be led in the best way, by diverting your mind from the many unhealthy thoughts which habitually have been flowing into it without your knowing it, to healthier ones. . . .

"Like the beast, the bodies of those of our race have in the past weakened and decayed. This will not always be. Increase of spiritual knowledge will show the cause of such decay, and will show, also, how to take advantage of a Law or Force to build us up, renew ever the body and give it greater and greater strength, instead of blindly using that Law or Force, as has been done in the past, to weaken our bodies and finally destroy them."

Full, rich, and abounding health is the normal and the natural condition of life. Anything else is an abnormal condition, and abnormal conditions as a rule come through perversions. God never created sickness, suffering, and disease; they are man's own creations. They come through his violating the laws under which he lives. So used are we to seeing them that we come gradually, if not to think of them as natural, then to look upon them as a matter of course.

The time will come when the work of the physician will not be to treat and attempt to heal the body, but to heal the mind, which in turn will heal the body. In other words, the true physician will be a teacher; his work will be to keep people well, instead of attempting to make them well after sickness and disease comes on; and still beyond this there will come a time when each will be his own physician. In the degree that we live in harmony with the higher laws of our being, and so, in the degree that we become better acquainted with the powers of the mind and spirit, will we give less attention to the body,—no less *care*, but less *attention*.

The bodies of thousands today would be much better cared for if their owners gave them less thought and attention. As a rule, those who think least of their bodies enjoy the best health. Many are kept in continual ill health by the abnormal thought and attention they give them.

Give the body the nourishment, the exercise, the fresh air, the sunlight it requires, keep it clean, and then think of it as little as possible. In your thoughts and in your conversation never dwell upon the negative side. Don't talk of sickness and disease. By talking of these you do yourself harm and you do harm to those who listen to you. Talk of those things that will make people the better for listening to you. Thus you will infect them with health and strength and not with weakness and disease.

To dwell upon the negative side is always destructive. This is true of the body the same as it is true of all other things. The following from one whose thorough training as a physician has been supplemented by extensive study and observations along the lines of the powers of the interior forces, are of special significance and value in this connection: "We can never gain health by contemplating disease, any more than we can reach perfection by dwelling upon imperfection, or harmony through discord. We should keep a high ideal of health and harmony constantly before the mind. . . .

"Never affirm or repeat about your health what you do not wish to be true. Do not dwell upon your ailments, nor study your symptoms. Never allow yourself to be convinced that you are not complete master of yourself. Stoutly affirm your superiority over bodily ills, and do not acknowledge yourself the slave of any inferior power. . . . I would teach children early to build a strong barrier between themselves and disease, by healthy habits of thought, high thinking, and purity of life. I would teach them to expel all thoughts of death, all images of disease, all discordant emotions, like hatred, malice, revenge, envy, and sensuality, as they would banish a temptation to do evil. I would teach them that bad food, bad drink, or bad air makes bad blood; that bad blood makes bad tissue, and bad flesh bad morals. I would teach them that healthy thoughts are as essential to healthy bodies as pure thoughts to a clean life. I would teach them to cultivate a strong will power, and to brace themselves against life's enemies in every possible way. I would teach the sick to have hope, confidence, cheer. Our thoughts and imaginations are the only real limits to our possibilities. No man's success or health will ever reach beyond his own confidence; as a rule, we erect our own barriers.

"Like produces like the universe through. Hatred, envy, malice, jealousy, and revenge all have children. Every bad thought breeds others, and each of these goes on and on, ever reproducing itself, until our world is peopled with their offspring. The true physician and parent of the future will not medicate the body with drugs so much as the mind with principles. The coming mother will teach her child to assuage the fever of anger, hatred, malice, with the great panacea of the world,—Love. The coming physician will teach the people to cultivate cheerfulness, good-will, and noble deeds for a health tonic as well as a heart tonic; and that a merry heart doeth good like a medicine."

The health of your body, the same as the health and strength of your mind, depends upon what you relate yourself with. This Infinite Spirit of Life, this

Source of all Life, can from its very nature, we have found, admit of no weakness, no disease. Come then into the full, conscious, vital realization of your oneness with this Infinite Life, open yourself to its more abundant entrance, and full and ever-renewing bodily health and strength will be yours.

> "And good may ever conquer ill,
>   Health walk where pain has trod;
> 'As a man thinketh, so is he,'
>   Rise, then, and think with God."

The whole matter may then be summed up in the one sentence, "God is well and so are you." You must awaken to the knowledge of your *real being*. When this awakening comes, you will have, and you will see that you have, the power to determine what conditions are externalized in your body. You must recognize, you must realize yourself as one with Infinite Spirit. God's will is then your will; your will is God's will, and "with God all things are possible." When we are able to do away with all sense of separateness by living continually in the realization of this oneness, not only will our bodily ills and weaknesses vanish, but all limitations along all lines.

Then "delight thyself in the Lord, and He shall give thee the desires of thine heart." Then will you feel like crying all the day long, "The lines are fallen unto me in pleasant places; yea, I have a goodly heritage." Drop out of mind your belief in good things and good events coming to you in the future. Come *now* into the real life, and coming, appropriate and actualize them *now*. Remember that only the best is good enough for one with a heritage so royal as yours.

> "We buy ashes for bread;
> We buy diluted wine;
> Give me the true,—
> Whose ample leaves and tendrils curled
> Among the silver hills of heaven,
> Draw everlasting dew."

21

The Gift of Understanding AND
The Night of the Senses

Thomas Merton

During the late 1940s and 1950s, Thomas Merton (1915–1968) was easily the most well-known representative of American Catholic metaphysical piety. Born in France of two artist parents—his mother from
Ohio and his father from New Zealand—Merton lost both before he
was seventeen (his mother while he was still a child). He lived in New
York City and a series of other places, studying in Bermuda, France,
and England as well as the United States. By 1938 he had become a
Roman Catholic convert, and by 1941 he entered the Trappist monastery at Gethsemani, Kentucky. Eventually some sixty books were to flow
from his pen, including eight volumes of poetry, and beyond these
probably six hundred articles. In the final phase of his career, he became
a public figure, protesting the Vietnam War, nuclearism, racism, and a
dehumanization that he linked to technology. His contemplative vision
was as broad and encompassing, and in the last years before his acci-
dental death by electrocution in Thailand he turned not only to Christian but also to Hindu and Buddhist—especially Zen Buddhist—spirituality, attracted by the Asian emphasis on direct experience. In the
chapters here, from his book *Seeds of Contemplation* (1949), a glimpse
may be gained of what knowing through the mind can mean in a Roman Catholic context. Against a background of Platonic and Neopla-
tonic spirituality carried forward through the Middle Ages into modern
times, the metaphysical spirituality of Merton teaches a contemplative
gaze on what is experienced as divine reality. Through prayer to a personal God, Merton testifies, the seeker comes to fulfillment in and
through the light of understanding—in an awakening that floods the
spirit with clarity and certitude.

The Gift of Understanding

Contemplation, by which we know and love God as He is in Himself, appre-
hending Him in a deep and vital experience which is beyond the reach of any

natural understanding, is the reason for our creation by God. And although it is absolutely above our nature, it is our proper element because it is the fulfillment of deep capacities in us that God has willed should never be fulfilled in any other way. All those who reach the end for which they were created will therefore be contemplatives in heaven: but many are also destined to enter this supernatural element and breathe this new atmosphere while they are still on earth.

Since contemplation has been planned for us by God as our true and proper element, the first taste of it strikes us at once as utterly new and yet strangely familiar.

Although you had an entirely different notion of what it would be like, (since no book can give an adequate idea of contemplation except to those who have experienced it) it turns out to be just what you seem to have known all along that it ought to be.

The utter simplicity and obviousness of the infused light which contemplation pours into our soul suddenly awakens us to a new world. We enter a region which we had never even suspected, and yet it is this new world which seems familiar and obvious. The old world of our senses is now the one that seems to us strange and remote and unbelievable—until the intense light of contemplation leaves us and we fall back to our own level.

Compared with the pure and peaceful comprehension of love in which the contemplative is permitted to see the truth not so much by seeing it as by being absorbed into it, ordinary ways of seeing and knowing are full of blindness and labor and uncertainty.

The sharpest of natural experience is like sleep compared with the awakening which is contemplation. The keenest and surest natural certitude is a dream compared to this serene comprehension.

Our souls rise up from our earth like Jacob waking from his dream.... God Himself becomes the only reality, in Whom all other reality takes its proper place—and falls into insignificance.

Although this light is absolutely above our nature, it now seems to us "normal" and "natural" to see, as we now see, without seeing, to possess clarity in darkness, to have pure certitude without any shred of discursive evidence, to be filled with an experience that transcends experience and to enter with serene confidence into depths that leave us utterly inarticulate....

A door opens in the center of our being and we seem to fall through it into immense depths which, although they are infinite, are all accessible to us; all eternity seems to have become ours in this one placid and breathless contact.

God touches us with a touch that is emptiness and empties us. He moves us with a simplicity that simplifies us. All variety, all complexity, all paradox, all multiplicity cease. Our mind swims in the air of an understanding, a reality that is dark and serene and includes in itself everything. Nothing more is desired. Nothing more is wanting. Our only sorrow, if sorrow be possible at all, is the awareness that we ourselves still have a separate existence.

For already a supernatural instinct teaches us that the function of this abyss of freedom that has opened out within our own midst, is to draw us utterly out of our own selfhood and into its own immensity of liberty and joy.

You seem to be the same person and you are the same person that you have always been: in fact you are more yourself than you have ever been before. You have only just begun to exist. You feel as if you were at last fully born. All that went before was a mistake, a fumbling preparation for birth. Now you have come out into your element. And yet now you have become nothing. You have sunk to the center of your own poverty, and there you have felt the doors fly open into infinite freedom, into a wealth which is perfect because none of it is yours and yet it all belongs to you.

And now you are free to go in and out of infinity.

It is useless to think of fathoming the depths of wide open darkness that have yawned inside you, full of liberty and exultation.

They are not a place, not an extent, they are a huge, smooth activity. These depths, they are Love. And in the midst of you they form a citadel.

There is nothing that can penetrate into the heart of that peace. Nothing from the outside can get in. There is even a whole sphere of your own activity that is excluded from that beautiful airy night. The five senses, the imagination, the discoursing mind, the hunger of desire do not belong in that starless sky.

And you, while you are free to come and go, yet as soon as you attempt to make words or thoughts about it you are excluded—you go back into your exterior in order to talk.

Yet you find that you can rest in this darkness and this unfathomable peace without trouble and without anxiety, even when the imagination and the mind remain in some way active outside the doors of it.

They may stand and chatter in the porch, as long as they are idle, waiting for the will their queen to return, upon whose orders they depend.

But it is better for them to be silent. However you now know that this does not depend on you. It is a gift that comes to you from the bosom of that serene darkness and depends entirely on the decision of Love.

Within the simplicity of this armed and walled and undivided interior peace is an infinite unction which, as soon as it is grasped, loses its savor. You must not try to reach out and possess it altogether. You must not touch it, or try to seize it. You must not try to make it sweeter or try to keep it from wasting away . . .

The situation of the soul in contemplation is something like the situation of Adam and Eve in Paradise. Everything is yours, but on one infinitely important condition: that it is all *given*.

There is nothing that you can claim, nothing that you can demand, nothing that you can *take*. And as soon as you try to take something as if it were your own—you lose your Eden.

The only difference is that you do not at once realize what you have lost. Therefore only the greatest humility can give us the instinctive delicacy and caution that will prevent us from reaching out for pleasures and satisfactions that we can understand and savor in this darkness. The moment we demand anything for ourselves or even trust in any action of our own to procure a deeper intensification of this pure and serene rest in God, we defile and dissipate the perfect gift that He desires to communicate to us in the silence and repose of our own powers.

If there is one thing we must do it is this: we must realize to the very depths of our being that this is a pure gift of God which no desire, no effort and no heroism of ours can do anything to deserve or obtain. There is nothing we can do directly either to procure it or to preserve it or to increase it. Our own activity is for the most part an obstacle to the infusion of this peaceful and pacifying light, with the exception that God may demand certain acts and works of us by charity or obedience, and maintain us in deep experimental union with Him through them all, by His own good pleasure, not by any fidelity of ours.

At best we can dispose ourselves for the reception of this great gift by resting in the heart of our own poverty, keeping our soul as far as possible empty of desires for all the things that please and preoccupy our nature, no matter how pure or sublime they may be in themselves.

And when God reveals Himself to us in contemplation we must accept Him as He comes to us, in His own obscurity, in His own silence, not interrupting Him with arguments or words or conceptions or activities that belong to the level of our own tedious and labored existence.

For all God's gifts there must be in us a response of thanksgiving and happiness and joy: but here we thank Him less by words than by the serene happiness of silent acceptance. . . . It is our emptiness in the presence of the abyss of His reality, our silence in the presence of His infinitely rich silence, our joy in the bosom of the serene darkness in which His Light holds us absorbed, it is all this that praises Him. It is this that causes love of God and wonder and adoration to swim up into us like tidal waves out of the depths of that peace, and break upon the shores of our consciousness in a vast, hushed surf of inarticulate praise, praise and glory!

This clear darkness of God is the purity of heart Christ spoke of in the sixth Beatitude. . . . It is created in us when the Holy Ghost infuses into our souls the

Gift of Understanding in a particularly strong degree, and usually not without its companion Gift, Wisdom. And this purity of heart brings at least a momentary deliverance from images and concepts, from the forms and shadows of all the things men desire with their human appetites. It brings deliverance even from the feeble and delusive analogies we ordinarily use to arrive at God—not that it denies them, for they are true as far as they go, but it makes them temporarily useless by fulfilling them all in the sure grasp of a deep and penetrating experience.

In the vivid darkness of God within us there sometimes come deep movements of love that deliver us entirely, for a moment, from our old burden of selfishness, and number us among those little children of whom is the kingdom of heaven.

And when God allows us to fall back into our own confusion of desires and judgments and temptations, we carry a scar over the place where that joy exulted for a moment in our hearts.

The scar burns us. The sore wound aches within us, and we remember that we have fallen back into what we are not, and are not yet allowed to remain where God would have us belong. And we long for the place He has destined for us and weep with desire for the time when this pure poverty will catch us and hold us in its liberty and never let us go, when we will never fall back from the paradise of the simple and the little children into the forum of prudence where the wise of this world go up and down in sorrow and set their traps for a happiness that cannot exist.

The Night of the Senses

The life of infused contemplation does not always begin with a definite experience of God in the strong inpouring of light that has been described. And in any case such moments of freedom and escape from the blindness and helplessness of the ordinary, laborious ways of the spirit will always be relatively rare. And it is not too hard to recognize these sudden, intense flashes of the gift of understanding, these vivid "rays of darkness" striking deep into the soul and changing the course of a man's whole life. They bring with them their own conviction. They strike blindness from our eyes like scales. They plant in us too deep and too calm and too new a certainty to be misunderstood or quickly forgotten.

But if a man had to wait for such experiences before he became a contemplative he might have to wait a long time—perhaps a whole lifetime. And perhaps his expectation would be vain.

It is more ordinary for the spirit to learn contemplation from God not in a sudden flash but imperceptibly, by very gradual steps. And as a matter of fact, without the groundwork of long and patient trial and slow progress in the darkness of pure faith, contemplation will never really be learned at all. For a few isolated, though intense, flashes of the spirit of understanding and wisdom will not make a man a contemplative in the full sense of the word; contemplative prayer is only truly what it is called when it becomes more or less habitual.

The ordinary way to contemplation lies through a desert without trees and without beauty and without water. The spirit enters a wilderness and travels blindly in directions that seem to lead away from vision, away from God, away from all fulfillment and joy. It may become almost impossible to believe that this road goes anywhere at all except to a desolation full of dry bones—the ruin of all our hopes and good intentions.

The prospect of this wilderness is something that so appalls most men that they refuse to enter upon its burning sands and travel among its rocks. They cannot believe that contemplation and sanctity are to be found in a desolation where there is no food and no shelter and no rest and no refreshment for their imagination and intellect and for the desires of their nature.

Convinced that perfection is to be measured by brilliant intuitions of God and fervent resolutions of a will on fire with love, persuaded that sanctity is a matter of sensible fervor and tangible results, they will have nothing to do with a contemplation that does not delight their reason and invest their minds and wills with consolations and sensible joy. They want to know where they are going and see what they are doing, and as soon as they enter into regions where their own activity becomes paralyzed and bears no visible fruit, they turn around and go back to the lush fields where they can be sure that they are doing something and getting somewhere. And if they cannot achieve the results they desire with such intense anxiety, at least they convince themselves that they have made great progress if they have said many prayers, performed many mortifications, preached many sermons, read (and perhaps also written) many books and articles, paged through many books of meditations, acquired hundreds of new and different devotions and girdled the earth with pilgrimages. Not that all of these things are not good in themselves: but there are times in the life of a man when they can become an escape, an anodyne, a refuge from the responsibility of suffering in darkness and obscurity and helplessness, and allowing God to strip us of our false selves and make us into the new men that we are really meant to be.

And so, when God begins to infuse His light of understanding into the spirit of a man drawn to contemplation, the experience is often not so much one of fulfillment as of defeat.

The mind finds itself entering uneasily into the shadows of a strange and silent night. The night is peaceful enough. But it is very strange. Thought becomes cramped and difficult. There is a peculiarly heavy sense of weariness and distaste for mental and spiritual activity. Yet at the same time the soul is haunted with a fear that this new impotence is a sin, or a sign of imperfection. It tries to force acts of thought and will. Sometimes it makes a mad effort to squeeze some feeling of fervor out of itself, which is, incidentally, the worst thing it could possibly do. All the pretty images and concepts of God that it once cherished have vanished or have turned into unpleasant and frightening distortions. God is nowhere to be found. The words of prayers return in a hollow echo from the walls of this dead cave.

If a man in this night lets his spirit get carried away with fear or impatience and anxiety, everything is lost. He will twist and turn and torture himself with attempts to see some light and feel some warmth and recapture the old consolations that are beyond recovery. And finally he will run away from darkness, and do the best he can to dope himself with the first light that comes along.

But there are others who, no matter how much they suffer perplexity and uneasiness in the wilderness where God begins to lead them, still feel drawn further and further on into the wasteland. They cannot think, they cannot meditate; their imagination tortures them with everything they do not want to see; their life of prayer is without light and without pleasure and without any feeling of devotion.

On the other hand they sense, by a kind of instinct, that peace lies in the heart of this darkness. Something prompts them to keep still, to trust in God, to be quiet and listen for His voice; to be patient and not to get excited. Soon they discover that all useless attempts to meditate only upset and disturb them; but at the same time, when they stay quiet in the muteness of naked faith, resting in a simple and open-eyed awareness, attentive to the darkness which baffles them, a subtle and indefinable peace begins to seep into their souls and occupies them with a deep and inexplicable satisfaction. This satisfaction is tenuous and dark. It cannot be grasped or identified. It slips out of focus and gets away. Yet it is there.

What is it? It is hard to say: but one feels that it is somehow summed up in "the will of God" or simply, "God."

The man who does not permit his spirit to be beaten down and upset by dryness and helplessness, but who lets God lead him peacefully through the wilderness, and desires no other support or guidance than that of pure faith and trust in God alone, will be brought to deep and peaceful union with Him.

The man who is not afraid to abandon all his spiritual progress into the hands of God, to put prayer, virtue, merit, grace, and all gifts in the keeping of Him from Whom they all must come, will quickly be led to peace in union with Him.

Just as the light of faith is darkness to the mind, so the supreme supernatural activity of the mind and will in contemplation and infused love at first seems to us like inaction. That is why our natural faculties are anxious and restless and refuse to keep still. They want to be the principles of their own acts. The thought that they cannot act according to their own pleasure brings them a suffering and humiliation which they find it hard to stand.

But contemplation lifts us beyond the sphere of our natural powers.

When you are travelling in a plane close to the ground you realize that you are going somewhere: but in the stratosphere, although you may be going seven times as fast, you lose all sense of speed.

And so, as soon as there is any reasonable indication that God is drawing the spirit into this way of contemplation, we ought to remain at peace in a prayer that is utterly simplified, stripped of acts and reflections and clean of images, waiting in emptiness and vigilant expectancy for the will of God to be done in us. This waiting should be without anxiety and without deliberate hunger for any experience that comes within the range of our knowledge or memory, because any experience that we can grasp or understand will be inadequate and unworthy of the state to which God wishes to bring our souls.

The most important practical question that people will ask at this point is: what are the signs that it is safe to abandon formal meditation and rest in this more or less passive expectancy?

In the first place, if meditation and affective prayer are easy and spontaneous and fruitful they should not be given up. But when they have become practically impossible, or if they simply deaden and exhaust the mind and will, and fill them with disgust, or if they involve them in many distractions, it would be harmful to force your mind to have special thoughts and your will to go through a routine of specified acts. For if you reflect on your state you will easily see that your mind is absorbed in one vast, obscure thought of God and your will is occupied, if not haunted, with a blind, groping, half-defined desire of God. These two combine to produce in you the anxiety and darkness and helplessness which make lucid and particular acts at once so hard and so futile.

And if you allow yourself to remain in silence and emptiness you may find that this thirst, this hunger that seeks God in blindness and darkness, will grow on you and at the same time, although you do not yet seem to find anything tangible, peace will establish itself in your soul.

This alone may be a good enough sign that you should no longer trouble yourself with methodical forms of meditation, except at rare moments when you feel positively drawn to return to them.

On the other hand, if giving up meditation simply means that your mind goes dead and your will gets petrified, and you lean against the wall and spend your half-hour of meditation wondering what you are going to get for supper, you had better keep yourself occupied with something. After all, there is always a possibility that laziness will dress itself up as "prayer of quiet" or "prayer of simplicity" and degenerate into torpor and sleep. The mere absence of activity does not *ipso facto* turn you into a contemplative.

This is where a book may sometimes help you. If you find some paragraph or sentence that interests you, stop reading and turn it over in your mind and absorb it and contemplate it and rest in the general, serene, effortless consideration of the thought, not in its details but as a whole, as something held and savored in its entirety: and so pass from this to rest in the quiet expectancy of God. If you find yourself getting distracted, go back to the book, to the same sentence or to another. You can do this with Scripture, or with pictures, or with a few snatches of vocal prayer, best of all in the presence of the Blessed Sacrament, but also out in the woods and under the trees. The sweep and serenity of a landscape, fields and hills, are enough to keep a contemplative riding the quiet interior tide of his peace and his desire for hours at a time.

The absence of activity in contemplative prayer is only apparent. Below the surface, the mind and will are drawn into the orbit of an activity that is deep and intense and supernatural, and which overflows into our whole being and brings forth incalculable fruits.

There is no such thing as a kind of prayer in which you do absolutely nothing. If you are doing nothing you are not praying. On the other hand if God dominates your interior activity and becomes its immediate principle, by the Gifts of the Holy Ghost, the work of your faculties may be entirely beyond conscious estimation, and its results may not be seen or understood.

Contemplative prayer is a deep and simplified spiritual activity in which the mind and will are fused into one. They rest in a unified and simple concentration upon God, turned to Him and intent upon Him and absorbed in His own light, with a simple gaze which is perfect adoration because it silently tells God that we have left everything else and desire even to leave our own selves for His sake, and that He alone is important to us, He alone is our desire and our life, and nothing else can give us any joy.

22

Seeing

Annie Dillard

Annie Dillard (b. 1945) grew up in Pittsburgh, Pennsylvania, with a Presbyterian legacy and four summers in church camp that provided grist for later memories. Her Calvinism, however, was transformed in a turn to the natural environment expressed in and through her literary work. Like a late-twentieth-century Henry David Thoreau, the mature Dillard asked searching questions about the relationship of God to nature even as she left the church of her childhood behind and—in contrast to Thoreau—moved increasingly toward Catholicism. More important here, like Thoreau, too, she structured her most celebrated book around a year spent in nature—in Dillard's case, the mountain valley of Tinker Creek in Virginia's Blue Ridge. *Pilgrim at Tinker Creek,* which won a Pulitzer Prize in 1975, emerged as a meditation on violence and beauty in nature amidst intense observation of small and larger life forms. The nature Dillard met seemingly everywhere was hardly benign and placid. Rather, like the Calvinist God from whom she had walked away, nature challenged with its mystery, inscrutability, and wildly cruel power. And Dillard met it by stalking. Like a native hunter after prey, Dillard was hot on the trail of nature, senses stretched taut in an all-alert for the divine presence therein. At the heart of her stalking was an act of observation and "seeing"—a "catch-it-if-you-can" that echoed Henry Thoreau's unfinished search for the hound, bay horse, and turtle-dove of his fleeting glimpse. Dillard had seen the "tree with the lights in it" in a mystical moment that colored later days. In the chapter from *Pilgrim at Tinker Creek* here, Dillard's act of seeing points to a knowing through the mind at once resonant with and different from the mindfulness of traditional contemplative practice.

When I was six or seven years old, growing up in Pittsburgh, I used to take a precious penny of my own and hide it for someone else to find. It was a curious compulsion; sadly, I've never been seized by it since. For some reason I always "hid" the penny along the same stretch of sidewalk up the street. I would cradle it at the roots of a sycamore, say, or in a hole left by a chipped-off piece of sidewalk. Then I would take a piece of chalk, and, starting at either end of the block, draw huge arrows leading up to the penny from both directions. After I learned to write I labeled the arrows: SURPRISE AHEAD or MONEY THIS WAY. I was greatly excited, during all this arrow-drawing, at the thought of the first lucky passer-by who would receive in this way, regardless of merit, a free gift from the universe. But I never lurked about. I would go straight home and not give the matter another thought, until, some months later, I would be gripped again by the impulse to hide another penny.

It is still the first week in January, and I've got great plans. I've been thinking about seeing. There are lots of things to see, unwrapped gifts and free surprises. The world is fairly studded and strewn with pennies cast broadside from a generous hand. But—and this is the point—who gets excited by a mere penny? If you follow one arrow, if you crouch motionless on a bank to watch a tremulous ripple thrill on the water and are rewarded by the sight of a muskrat kit paddling from its den, will you count that sight a chip of copper only, and go your rueful way? It is dire poverty indeed when a man is so malnourished and fatigued that he won't stoop to pick up a penny. But if you cultivate a healthy poverty and simplicity, so that finding a penny will literally make your day, then, since the world is in fact planted in pennies, you have with your poverty bought a lifetime of days. It is that simple. What you see is what you get.

I used to be able to see flying insects in the air. I'd look ahead and see, not the row of hemlocks across the road, but the air in front of it. My eyes would focus along that column of air, picking out flying insects. But I lost interest, I guess, for I dropped the habit. Now I can see birds. Probably some people can look at the grass at their feet and discover all the crawling creatures. I would like to know grasses and sedges—and care. Then my least journey into the world would be a field trip, a series of happy recognitions. Thoreau, in an expansive mood, exulted, "What a rich book might be made about buds, including, perhaps, sprouts!" It would be nice to think so. I cherish mental images I have of three perfectly happy people. One collects stones. Another—an Englishman, say—watches clouds. The third lives on a coast and collects drops of seawater which he examines microscopically and mounts. But I don't see what the specialist sees, and so I cut myself off, not only from the total picture, but from the various forms of happiness.

Unfortunately, nature is very much a now-you-see-it, now-you-don't affair. A fish flashes, then dissolves in the water before my eyes like so much salt. Deer apparently ascend bodily into heaven; the brightest oriole fades into leaves. These disappearances stun me into stillness and concentration; they say of nature that it conceals with a grand nonchalance, and they say of vision that it is a deliberate gift, the revelation of a dancer who for my eyes only flings away her seven veils. For nature does reveal as well as conceal: now-you-don't-see-it, now-you-do. For a week last September migrating red-winged black-birds were feeding heavily down by the creek at the back of the house. One day I went out to investigate the racket; I walked up to a tree, an Osage orange, and a hundred birds flew away. They simply materialized out of the tree. I saw a tree, then a whisk of color, then a tree again. I walked closer and another hundred blackbirds took flight. Not a branch, not a twig budged: the birds were apparently weightless as well as invisible. Or, it was as if the leaves of the Osage orange had been freed from a spell in the form of red-winged black-birds; they flew from the tree, caught my eye in the sky, and vanished. When I looked again at the tree the leaves had reassembled as if nothing had happened. Finally I walked directly to the trunk of the tree and a final hundred, the real diehards, appeared, spread, and vanished. How could so many hide in the tree without my seeing them? The Osage orange, unruffled, looked just as it had looked from the house, when three hundred red-winged blackbirds cried from its crown. I looked downstream where they flew, and they were gone. Search-ing, I couldn't spot one. I wandered downstream to force them to play their hand, but they'd crossed the creek and scattered. One show to a customer. These appearances catch at my throat; they are the free gifts, the bright coppers at the roots of trees.

It's all a matter of keeping my eyes open. Nature is like one of those line drawings of a tree that are puzzles for children: Can you find hidden in the leaves a duck, a house, a boy, a bucket, a zebra, and a boot? Specialists can find the most incredibly well-hidden things. A book I read when I was young recommended an easy way to find caterpillars to rear: you simply find some fresh caterpillar droppings, look up, and there's your caterpillar. More recently an author advised me to set my mind at ease about those piles of cut stems on the ground in grassy fields. Field mice make them; they cut the grass down by degrees to reach the seeds at the head. It seems that when the grass is tightly packed, as in a field of ripe grain, the blade won't topple at a single cut through the stem; instead, the cut stem simply drops vertically, held in the crush of grain. The mouse severs the bottom again and again, the stem keeps dropping an inch at a time, and finally the head is low enough for the mouse to reach the seeds. Meanwhile, the mouse is positively littering the field with its little piles of cut stems into which, presumably, the author of the book is con-stantly stumbling.

If I can't see these minutiae, I still try to keep my eyes open. I'm always on the lookout for antlion traps in sandy soil, monarch pupae near milkweed, skipper larvae in locust leaves. These things are utterly common, and I've not seen one. I bang on hollow trees near water, but so far no flying squirrels have appeared. In flat country I watch every sunset in hopes of seeing the green ray. The green ray is a seldom-seen streak of light that rises from the sun like a spurting fountain at the moment of sunset; it throbs into the sky for two seconds and disappears. One more reason to keep my eyes open. A photography professor at the University of Florida just happened to see a bird die in midflight; it jerked, died, dropped, and smashed on the ground. I squint at the wind because I read Stewart Edward White: "I have always maintained that if you looked closely enough you could *see* the wind—the dim, hardly-made-out, fine débris fleeing high in the air." White was an excellent observer, and devoted an entire chapter of *The Mountains* to the subject of seeing deer: "As soon as you can forget the naturally obvious and construct an artificial obvious, then you too will see deer."

But the artificial obvious is hard to see. My eyes account for less than one percent of the weight of my head; I'm bony and dense; I see what I expect. I once spent a full three minutes looking at a bullfrog that was so unexpectedly large I couldn't see it even though a dozen enthusiastic campers were shouting directions. Finally I asked, "What color am I looking for?" and a fellow said, "Green." When at last I picked out the frog, I saw what painters are up against: the thing wasn't green at all, but the color of wet hickory bark.

The lover can see, and the knowledgeable. I visited an aunt and uncle at a quarter-horse ranch in Cody, Wyoming. I couldn't do much of anything useful, but I could, I thought, draw. So, as we all sat around the kitchen table after supper, I produced a sheet of paper and drew a horse. "That's one lame horse," my aunt volunteered. The rest of the family joined in: "Only place to saddle that one is his neck"; "Looks like we better shoot the poor thing, on account of those terrible growths." Meekly, I slid the pencil and paper down the table. Everyone in that family, including my three young cousins, could draw a horse. Beautifully. When the paper came back it looked as though five shining, real quarter horses had been corralled by mistake with a papier-mâché moose; the real horses seemed to gaze at the monster with a steady, puzzled air. I stay away from horses now, but I can do a creditable goldfish. The point is that I just don't know what the lover knows; I just can't see the artificial obvious that those in the know construct. The herpetologist asks the native, "Are there snakes in that ravine?" "Nosir." And the herpetologist comes home with, yessir, three bags full. Are there butterflies on that mountain? Are the bluets in bloom, are there arrowheads here, or fossil shells in the shale?

Peeping through my keyhole I see within the range of only about thirty percent of the light that comes from the sun; the rest is infrared and some little ultraviolet, perfectly apparent to many animals, but invisible to me. A nightmare network of ganglia, charged and firing without my knowledge, cuts and splices what I do see, editing it for my brain. Donald E. Carr points out that the sense impressions of one-celled animals are *not* edited for the brain: "This is philosophically interesting in a rather mournful way, since it means that only the simplest animals perceive the universe as it is."

A fog that won't burn away drifts and flows across my field of vision. When you see fog move against a backdrop of deep pines, you don't see the fog itself, but streaks of clearness floating across the air in dark shreds. So I see only tatters of clearness through a pervading obscurity. I can't distinguish the fog from the overcast sky; I can't be sure if the light is direct or reflected. Everywhere darkness and the presence of the unseen appalls. We estimate now that only one atom dances alone in every cubic meter of intergalactic space. I blink and squint. What planet or power yanks Halley's Comet out of orbit? We haven't seen that force yet; it's a question of distance, density, and the pallor of reflected light. We rock, cradled in the swaddling band of darkness. Even the simple darkness of night whispers suggestions to the mind. Last summer, in August, I stayed at the creek too late.

* * *

Where Tinker Creek flows under the sycamore log bridge to the tear-shaped island, it is slow and shallow, fringed thinly in cattail marsh. At this spot an astonishing bloom of life supports vast breeding populations of insects, fish, reptiles, birds, and mammals. On windless summer evenings I stalk along the creek bank or straddle the sycamore log in absolute stillness, watching for muskrats. The night I stayed too late I was hunched on the log staring spellbound at spreading, reflected stains of lilac on the water. A cloud in the sky suddenly lighted as if turned on by a switch; its reflection just as suddenly materialized on the water upstream, flat and floating, so that I couldn't see the creek bottom, or life in the water under the cloud. Downstream, away from the cloud on the water, water turtles smooth as beans were gliding down with the current in a series of easy, weightless push-offs, as men bound on the moon. I didn't know whether to trace the progress of one turtle I was sure of, risking sticking my face in one of the bridge's spiderwebs made invisible by the gathering dark, or take a chance on seeing the carp, or scan the mud bank in hope of seeing a muskrat, or follow the last of the swallows who caught at my heart and trailed it after them like streamers as they appeared from directly below, under the log, flying upstream with their tails forked, so fast.

But shadows spread, and deepened, and stayed. After thousands of years we're still strangers to darkness, fearful aliens in an enemy camp with our arms crossed over our chests. I stirred. A land turtle on the bank, startled, hissed the air from its lungs and withdrew into its shell. An uneasy pink here, an unfathomable blue there, gave great suggestion of lurking beings. Things were going on. I couldn't see whether that sere rustle I heard was a distant rattlesnake, slit-eyed, or a nearby sparrow kicking in the dry flood debris slung at the foot of a willow. Tremendous action roiled the water everywhere I looked, big action, inexplicable. A tremor welled up beside a gaping muskrat burrow in the bank and I caught my breath, but no muskrat appeared. The ripples continued to fan upstream with a steady, powerful thrust. Night was knitting over my face an eyeless mask, and I still sat transfixed. A distant airplane, a delta wing out of nightmare, made a gliding shadow on the creek's bottom that looked like a stingray cruising upstream. At once a black fin slit the pink cloud on the water, shearing it in two. The two halves merged together and seemed to dissolve before my eyes. Darkness pooled in the cleft of the creek and rose, as water collects in a well. Untamed, dreaming lights flickered over the sky. I saw hints of hulking underwater shadows, two pale splashes out of the water, and round ripples rolling close together from a blackened center.

At last I stared upstream where only the deepest violet remained of the cloud, a cloud so high its underbelly still glowed feeble color reflected from a hidden sky lighted in turn by a sun halfway to China. And out of that violet, a sudden enormous black body arced over the water. I saw only a cylindrical sleekness. Head and tail, if there was a head and tail, were both submerged in cloud. I saw only one ebony fling, a headlong dive to darkness; then the waters closed, and the lights went out.

I walked home in a shivering daze, up hill and down. Later I lay open-mouthed in bed, my arms flung wide at my sides to steady the whirling darkness. At this latitude I'm spinning 836 miles an hour round the earth's axis; I often fancy I feel my sweeping fall as a breakneck arc like the dive of dolphins, and the hollow rushing of wind raises hair on my neck and the side of my face. In orbit around the sun I'm moving 64,800 miles an hour. The solar system as a whole, like a merry-go-round unhinged, spins, bobs, and blinks at the speed of 43,200 miles an hour along a course set east of Hercules. Someone has piped, and we are dancing a tarantella until the sweat pours. I open my eyes and I see dark, muscled forms curl out of water, with flapping gills and flattened eyes. I close my eyes and I see stars, deep stars giving way to deeper stars, deeper stars bowing to deepest stars at the crown of an infinite cone.

"Still," wrote van Gogh in a letter, "a great deal of light falls on everything." If we are blinded by darkness, we are also blinded by light. When too much light falls on everything, a special terror results. Peter Freuchen describes the notorious kayak sickness to which Greenland Eskimos are prone. "The Greenland fjords are peculiar for the spells of completely quiet weather, when there is not enough wind to blow out a match and the water is like a sheet of glass. The kayak hunter must sit in his boat without stirring a finger so as not to scare the shy seals away. . . . The sun, low in the sky, sends a glare into his eyes, and the landscape around moves into the realm of the unreal. The reflex from the mirrorlike water hypnotizes him, he seems to be unable to move, and all of a sudden it is as if he were floating in a bottomless void, sinking, sinking, and sinking. . . . Horror-stricken, he tries to stir, to cry out, but he cannot, he is completely paralyzed, he just falls and falls." Some hunters are especially cursed with this panic, and bring ruin and sometimes starvation to their families.

Sometimes here in Virginia at sunset low clouds on the southern or northern horizon are completely invisible in the lighted sky. I only know one is there because I can see its reflection in still water. The first time I discovered this mystery I looked from cloud to no-cloud in bewilderment, checking my bearings over and over, thinking maybe the ark of the covenant was just passing by south of Dead Man Mountain. Only much later did I read the explanation: polarized light from the sky is very much weakened by reflection, but the light in clouds isn't polarized. So invisible clouds pass among visible clouds, till all slide over the mountains; so a greater light extinguishes a lesser as though it didn't exist.

In the great meteor shower of August, the Perseid, I wail all day for the shooting stars I miss. They're out there showering down, committing hara-kiri in a flame of fatal attraction, and hissing perhaps at last into the ocean. But at dawn what looks like a blue dome clamps down over me like a lid on a pot. The stars and planets could smash and I'd never know. Only a piece of ashen moon occasionally climbs up or down the inside of the dome, and our local star without surcease explodes on our heads. We have really only that one light, one source for all power, and yet we must turn away from it by universal decree. Nobody here on the planet seems aware of this strange, powerful taboo, that we all walk about carefully averting our faces, this way and that, lest our eyes be blasted forever.

Darkness appalls and light dazzles; the scrap of visible light that doesn't hurt my eyes hurts my brain. What I see sets me swaying. Size and distance and the sudden swelling of meanings confuse me, bowl me over. I straddle the sycamore log bridge over Tinker Creek in the summer. I look at the lighted creek bottom: snail tracks tunnel the mud in quavering curves. A crayfish jerks, but by the time I absorb what has happened, he's gone in a billowing smokescreen of silt. I look at the water: minnows and shiners. If I'm thinking minnows, a carp will fill my brain till I scream. I look at the water's surface: skaters, bubbles, and leaves sliding down. Suddenly, my own face, reflected, startles me witless. Those snails have been tracking my face! Finally, with a shuddering wrench of the will, I see clouds, cirrus clouds. I'm dizzy, I fall in. This looking business is risky.

Once I stood on a humped rock on nearby Purgatory Mountain, watching through binoculars the great autumn hawk migration below, until I discovered that I was in danger of joining the hawks on a vertical migration of my own. I was used to binoculars, but not, apparently, to balancing on humped rocks while looking through them. I staggered. Everything advanced and receded by turns; the world was full of unexplained foreshortenings and depths. A distant huge tan object, a hawk the size of an elephant, turned out to be the browned bough of a nearby loblolly pine. I followed a sharp-shinned hawk against a featureless sky, rotating my head unawares as it flew, and when I lowered the glass a glimpse of my own looming shoulder sent me staggering. What prevents the men on Palomar from falling, voiceless and blinded, from their tiny, vaulted chairs?

I reel in confusion; I don't understand what I see. With the naked eye I can see two million light-years to the Andromeda galaxy. Often I slop some creek water in a jar and when I get home I dump it in a white china bowl. After the silt settles I return and see tracings of minute snails on the bottom, a planarian or two winding round the rim of water, roundworms shimmying frantically, and finally, when my eyes have adjusted to these dimensions, amoebae. At first the amoebae look like muscae volitantes, those curled moving spots you seem to see in your eyes when you stare at a distant wall. Then I see the amoebae as drops of water congealed, bluish, translucent, like chips of sky in the bowl. At length I choose one individual and give myself over to its idea of an evening. I see it dribble a grainy foot before it on its wet, unfathomable way. Do its unedited sense impressions include the fierce focus of my eyes? Shall I take it outside and show it Andromeda, and blow its little endoplasm? I stir the water with a finger, in case it's running out of oxygen. Maybe I should get a tropical aquarium with motorized bubblers and lights, and keep this one for a pet. Yes, it would tell its fissioned descendants, the universe is two feet by five, and if you listen closely you can hear the buzzing music of the spheres.

Oh, it's mysterious lamplit evenings, here in the galaxy, one after the other. It's one of those nights when I wander from window to window, looking for a sign. But I can't see. Terror and a beauty insoluble are a ribband of blue woven into the fringes of garments of things both great and small. No culture explains, no bivouac offers real haven or rest. But it could be that we are not seeing something. Galileo thought comets were an optical illusion. This is fertile ground: since we are certain that they're not, we can look at what our scientists have been saying with fresh hope. What if there are *really* gleaming, castellated cities hung upside-down over the desert sand? What limpid lakes and cool date palms have our caravans always passed untried? Until, one by one, by the blindest of leaps, we light on the road to these places, we must stumble in darkness and hunger. I turn from the window. I'm blind as a bat, sensing only from every direction the echo of my own thin cries.

I chanced on a wonderful book by Marius von Senden, called *Space and Sight.* When Western surgeons discovered how to perform safe cataract operations, they ranged across Europe and America operating on dozens of men and women of all ages who had been blinded by cataracts since birth. Von Senden collected accounts of such cases; the histories are fascinating. Many doctors had tested their patients' sense perceptions and ideas of space both before and after the operations. The vast majority of patients, of both sexes and all ages, had, in von Senden's opinion, no idea of space whatsoever. Form, distance, and size were so many meaningless syllables. A patient "had no idea of depth, confusing it with roundness." Before the operation a doctor would give a blind patient a cube and a sphere; the patient would tongue it or feel it with his hands, and name it correctly. After the operation the doctor would show the same objects to the patient without letting him touch them; now he had no clue whatsoever what he was seeing. One patient called lemonade "square" because it pricked on his tongue as a square shape pricked on the touch of his hands. Of another postoperative patient, the doctor writes, "I have found in her no notion of size, for example, not even within the narrow limits which she might have encompassed with the aid of touch. Thus when I asked her to show me how big her mother was, she did not stretch out her hands, but set her two index-fingers a few inches apart." Other doctors reported their patients' own statements to similar effect. "The room he was in . . . he knew to be but part of the house, yet he could not conceive that the whole house could look bigger"; "Those who are blind from birth . . . have no real conception of height or distance. A house that is a mile away is thought of as nearby, but requiring the taking of a lot of steps. . . . The elevator that whizzes him up and down gives no more sense of vertical distance than does the train of horizontal."

For the newly sighted, vision is pure sensation unencumbered by meaning: "The girl went through the experience that we all go through and forget, the moment we are born. She saw, but it did not mean anything but a lot of different kinds of brightness." Again, "I asked the patient what he could see; he answered that he saw an extensive field of light, in which everything appeared dull, confused, and in motion. He could not distinguish objects." Another patient saw "nothing but a confusion of forms and colors." When a newly sighted girl saw photographs and paintings, she asked, "'Why do they put those dark marks all over them?' 'Those aren't dark marks,' her mother explained, 'those are shadows. That is one of the ways the eye knows that things have shape. If it were not for shadows many things would look flat.' 'Well, that's how things do look,' Joan answered. 'Everything looks flat with dark patches.'"

But it is the patients' concepts of space that are most revealing. One patient, according to his doctor, "practiced his vision in a strange fashion; thus he takes off one of his boots, throws it some way off in front of him, and then attempts to gauge the distance at which it lies; he takes a few steps towards the boot and tries to grasp it; on failing to reach it, he moves on a step or two and gropes for the boot until he finally gets hold of it." "But even at this stage, after three weeks' experience of seeing," von Senden goes on, "'space,' as he conceives it, ends with visual space, i.e. with color-patches that happen to bound his view. He does not yet have the notion that a larger object (a chair) can mask a smaller one (a dog), or that the latter can still be present even though it is not directly seen."

In general the newly sighted see the world as a dazzle of color-patches. They are pleased by the sensation of color, and learn quickly to name the colors, but the rest of seeing is tormentingly difficult. Soon after his operation a patient "generally bumps into one of these color-patches and observes them to be substantial, since they resist him as tactual objects do. In walking about it also strikes him—or can if he pays attention—that he is continually passing in between the colors he sees, that he can go past a visual object, that a part of it then steadily disappears from view; and that in spite of this, however he twists and turns—whether entering the room from the door, for example, or returning back to it—he always has a visual space in front of him. Thus he gradually comes to realize that there is also a space behind him, which he does not see."

The mental effort involved in these reasonings proves overwhelming for many patients. It oppresses them to realize, if they ever do at all, the tremendous size of the world, which they had previously conceived of as something touchingly manageable. It oppresses them to realize that they have been visible to people all along, perhaps unattractively so, without their knowledge or consent. A disheartening number of them refuse to use their new vision, continuing to go over objects with their tongues, and lapsing into apathy and despair. "The child can see, but will not make use of his sight. Only when pressed can he with difficulty be brought to look at objects in his neighborhood; but more than a foot away it is impossible to bestir him to the necessary effort." Of a twenty-one-year-old girl, the doctor relates, "Her unfortunate father, who had hoped for so much from this operation, wrote that his daughter carefully shuts her eyes whenever she wishes to go about the house, especially when she comes to a staircase, and that she is never happier or more at ease than when, by closing her eyelids, she relapses into her former state of total blindness." A fifteen-year-old boy, who was also in love with a girl at the asylum for the blind, finally blurted out, "No, really, I can't stand it anymore; I want to be sent back to the asylum again. If things aren't altered, I'll tear my eyes out."

Some do learn to see, especially the young ones. But it changes their lives. One doctor comments on "the rapid and complete loss of that striking and wonderful serenity which is characteristic only of those who have never yet seen." A blind man who learns to see is ashamed of his old habits. He dresses up, grooms himself, and tries to make a good impression. While he was blind he was indifferent to objects unless they were edible; now, "a sifting of values sets in ... his thoughts and wishes are mightily stirred and some few of the patients are thereby led into dissimulation, envy, theft and fraud."

On the other hand, many newly sighted people speak well of the world, and teach us how dull is our own vision. To one patient, a human hand, unrecognized, is "something bright and then holes." Shown a bunch of grapes, a boy calls out, "It is dark, blue and shiny. . . . It isn't smooth, it has bumps and hollows." A little girl visits a garden. "She is greatly astonished, and can scarcely be persuaded to answer, stands speechless in front of the tree, which she only names on taking hold of it, and then as 'the tree with the lights in it.'" Some delight in their sight and give themselves over to the visual world. Of a patient just after her bandages were removed, her doctor writes, "The first things to attract her attention were her own hands; she looked at them very closely, moved them repeatedly to and fro, bent and stretched the fingers, and seemed greatly astonished at the sight." One girl was eager to tell her blind friend that "men do not really look like trees at all," and astounded to discover that her every visitor had an utterly different face. Finally, a twenty-two-year-old girl was dazzled by the world's brightness and kept her eyes shut for two weeks. When at the end of that time she opened her eyes again, she did not recognize any objects, but, "the more she now directed her gaze upon everything about her, the more it could be seen how an expression of gratification and astonishment overspread her features; she repeatedly exclaimed: 'Oh God! How beautiful!'"

I saw color-patches for weeks after I read this wonderful book. It was summer; the peaches were ripe in the valley orchards. When I woke in the morning, color-patches wrapped round my eyes, intricately, leaving not one unfilled spot. All day long I walked among shifting color-patches that parted before me like the Red Sea and closed again in silence, transfigured, wherever I looked back. Some patches swelled and loomed, while others vanished utterly, and dark marks flitted at random over the whole dazzling sweep. But I couldn't sustain the illusion of flatness. I've been around for too long. Form is condemned to an eternal danse macabre with meaning: I couldn't unpeach the peaches. Nor can I remember ever having seen without understanding; the color-patches of infancy are lost. My brain then must have been smooth as any balloon. I'm told I reached for the moon; many babies do. But the color-patches of infancy swelled as meaning filled them; they arrayed themselves in solemn ranks down distance which unrolled and stretched before me like a plain. The moon rocketed away. I live now in a world of shadows that shape and distance color, a world where space makes a kind of terrible sense. What gnosticism is this, and what physics? The fluttering patch I saw in my nursery window—silver and green and shape-shifting blue—is gone; a row of Lombardy poplars takes its place, mute, across the distant lawn. That humming oblong creature pale as light that stole along the walls of my room at night, stretching exhilaratingly around the corners, is gone, too, gone the night I ate of the bittersweet fruit, put two and two together and puckered forever my brain. Martin Buber tells this tale: "Rabbi Mendel once boasted to his teacher Rabbi Elimelekh that evenings he saw the angel who rolls away the light before the darkness, and mornings the angel who rolls away the darkness before the light. 'Yes,' said Rabbi Elimelekh, 'in my youth I saw that too. Later on you don't see these things anymore.'"

Why didn't someone hand those newly sighted people paints and brushes from the start, when they still didn't know what anything was? Then maybe we all could see color-patches too, the world unraveled from reason, Eden before Adam gave names. The scales would drop from my eyes; I'd see trees like men walking; I'd run down the road against all orders, hallooing and leaping.

* * *

Seeing is of course very much a matter of verbalization. Unless I call my attention to what passes before my eyes, I simply won't see it. It is, as Ruskin says, "not merely unnoticed, but in the full, clear sense of the word, unseen." My eyes alone can't solve analogy tests using figures, the ones which show, with increasing elaborations, a big square, then a small square in a big square, then a big triangle, and expect me to find a small triangle in a big triangle. I have to say the words, describe what I'm seeing. If Tinker Mountain erupted, I'd be likely to notice. But if I want to notice the lesser cataclysms of valley life, I have to maintain in my head a running description of the present. It's not that I'm observant; it's just that I talk too much. Otherwise, especially in a strange place, I'll never know what's happening. Like a blind man at the ball game, I need a radio.

When I see this way I analyze and pry. I hurl over logs and roll away stones; I study the bank a square foot at a time, probing and tilting my head. Some days when a mist covers the mountains, when the muskrats won't show and the microscope's mirror shatters, I want to climb up the blank blue dome as a man would storm the inside of a circus tent, wildly, dangling, and with a steel knife claw a rent in the top, peep, and, if I must, fall.

But there is another kind of seeing that involves a letting go. When I see this way I sway transfixed and emptied. The difference between the two ways of seeing is the difference between walking with and without a camera. When I walk with a camera I walk from shot to shot, reading the light on a calibrated meter. When I walk without a camera, my own shutter opens, and the moment's light prints on my own silver gut. When I see this second way I am above all an unscrupulous observer.

* * *

It was sunny one evening last summer at Tinker Creek; the sun was low in the sky, upstream. I was sitting on the sycamore log bridge with the sunset at my back, watching the shiners the size of minnows who were feeding over the muddy sand in skittery schools. Again and again, one fish, then another, turned for a split second across the current and flash! the sun shot out from its silver side. I couldn't watch for it. It was always just happening somewhere else, and it drew my vision just as it disappeared: flash, like a sudden dazzle of the thinnest blade, a sparking over a dun and olive ground at chance intervals from every direction. Then I noticed white specks, some sort of pale petals, small, floating from under my feet on the creek's surface, very slow and steady. So I blurred my eyes and gazed towards the brim of my hat and saw a new world. I saw the pale white circles roll up, roll up, like the world's turning, mute and perfect, and I saw the linear flashes, gleaming silver, like stars being born at random down a rolling scroll of time. Something broke and something opened. I filled up like a new wineskin. I breathed an air like light; I saw a light like water. I was the lip of a fountain the creek filled forever; I was ether, the leaf in the zephyr; I was flesh-flake, feather, bone.

When I see this way I see truly. As Thoreau says, I return to my senses. I am the man who watches the baseball game in silence in an empty stadium. I see the game purely; I'm abstracted and dazed. When it's all over and the white-suited players lope off the green field to their shadowed dugouts, I leap to my feet; I cheer and cheer.

But I can't go out and try to see this way. I'll fail, I'll go mad. All I can do is try to gag the commentator, to hush the noise of useless interior babble that keeps me from seeing just as surely as a newspaper dangled before my eyes. The effort is really a discipline requiring a lifetime of dedicated struggle; it marks the literature of saints and monks of every order East and West, under every rule and no rule, discalced and shod. The world's spiritual geniuses seem to discover universally that the mind's muddy river, this ceaseless flow of trivia and trash, cannot be dammed, and that trying to dam it is a waste of effort that might lead to madness. Instead you must allow the muddy river to flow unheeded in the dim channels of consciousness; you raise your sights; you look along it, mildly, acknowledging its presence without interest and gazing beyond it into the realm of the real where subjects and objects act and rest purely, without utterance. "Launch into the deep," says Jacques Ellul, "and you shall see."

The secret of seeing is, then, the pearl of great price. If I thought he could teach me to find it and keep it forever I would stagger barefoot across a hundred deserts after any lunatic at all. But although the pearl may be found, it may not be sought. The literature of illumination reveals this above all: although it comes to those who wait for it, it is always, even to the most practiced and adept, a gift and a total surprise. I return from one walk knowing where the killdeer nests in the field by the creek and the hour the laurel blooms. I return from the same walk a day later scarcely knowing my own name. Litanies hum in my ears; my tongue flaps in my mouth Ailinon, alleluia! I cannot cause light; the most I can do is try to put myself in the path of its beam. It is possible, in deep space, to sail on solar wind. Light, be it particle or wave, has force: you rig a giant sail and go. The secret of seeing is to sail on solar wind. Hone and spread your spirit till you yourself are a sail, whetted, translucent, broadside to the merest puff.

When her doctor took her bandages off and led her into the garden, the girl who was no longer blind saw "the tree with the lights in it." It was for this tree I searched through the peach orchards of summer, in the forests of fall and down winter and spring for years. Then one day I was walking along Tinker Creek thinking of nothing at all and I saw the tree with the lights in it. I saw the backyard cedar where the mourning doves roost charged and transfigured, each cell buzzing with flame. I stood on the grass with the lights in it, grass that was wholly fire, utterly focused and utterly dreamed. It was less like seeing than like being for the first time seen, knocked breathless by a powerful glance. The flood of fire abated, but I'm still spending the power. Gradually the lights went out in the cedar, the colors died, the cells unflamed and disappeared. I was still ringing. I had been my whole life a bell, and never knew it until at that moment I was lifted and struck. I have since only very rarely seen the tree with the lights in it. The vision comes and goes, mostly goes, but I live for it, for the moment when the mountains open and a new light roars in spate through the crack, and the mountains slam.

23

Four Applications of Mindfulness

B. Alan Wallace with Steven Wilhelm

From the mid-nineteenth century, Buddhism began to attract a small but dedicated number of Americans. They turned to Buddhism not because of the ritual practices of its huge Asian lay following, but for the meditation practices of its monks in the context of searching questions about ephemerality, suffering, and death. With its founder Siddhartha Gautama (563?–483? B.C.E.) understood as an "enlightened" or "awakened" one, Buddhism taught that spiritual insight was central. In time three major Buddhist schools developed, each of them incorporating meditative forms in different spiritualities. Among them, Theravada Buddhism—the Buddhism of Southeast Asia—stands out for its development of meditation techniques that have inspired a number of American Buddhist practitioners. Theravada vipassana (*vipasyana* or *vipashyana*) meditation has prompted an articulate American response to its themes of mindfulness and insight. Here insight means something like precise knowledge of the way things are, and mindfulness, in practice, means an intense and focused observation of the meditator's present state of being in all its aspects, including the physical and psychological. Such mindfulness pushes the meditator toward clearer and clearer insight into moments and processes that usually pass too quickly to be noticed. In the chapter reprinted here, B. Alan Wallace describes vipassana in more detail, pointing to its intended result of healing the individual and bringing greater sanity. Wallace himself represents a different Buddhist tradition from vipassana, but he presents it with grace and clarity. A Buddhist scholar and teacher, he lived as an ordained Tibetan monk for fourteen years and today is often asked by His Holiness the Dalai Lama to translate from Tibetan into English.

The Role of Insight

To uproot ignorance, the fundamental affliction of the mind, one needs insight into the nature of reality. In Sanskrit this is called *vipaśyanā*. Its basis is a stable mind, and the basis of that is moral discipline.

There are many forms of vipaśyanā, or insight meditation. Here we will explore a discipline known as the close application of mindfulness (known as *satipaṭṭhāna* in the Pali language). One can fruitfully engage in this practice without having attained meditative quiescence, but in order for this practice to be fully effective, one does need to have a stable mind. Without a stable mind one may gain some flashes of insight from one's satipaṭṭhāna practice, but these will not have the full transformative effect that occurs with meditative quiescence.

If we are to overcome the ignorance that lies at the root of other mental distortions, we need to enter into the experience of insight again and again, saturating the mind. As we become more experienced with insight into the true nature of reality, our ignorance will be swept away just as darkness is swept away by light.

Mindfulness of the Body

The path of satipaṭṭhāna, or close application of mindfulness, is one of the great paths to enlightenment. But unhappily, some adherents of this path believe it is the only way, and present it as if it were so. But in fact, that is not what the Buddha said. The word he used to describe this mindfulness training is *ekayāna; eka* means "one," *yāna* means "way." Consequently, ekayāna means "one way," not that it is "the only way."

This question is discussed in early Theravāda commentaries to the Buddha's discourse on the close application of mindfulness. Various interpretations of the word ekayāna are given. One interpretation is that it goes "only to nirvāṇa." Another interpretation is that it is a "solitary path" that must be trodden by oneself, not by anyone else. Neither the Buddha, nor these authoritative commentaries, indicate it is the "sole way" to liberation.[1]

The four applications of mindfulness concern mindfulness directed to four types of phenomena: the body, feelings, the mind, and other events, both mental and physical. Like most Buddhist practices, mindfulness training starts with the grossest, easiest object of practice, and then progresses to the most subtle, which is also the most difficult. In this case among the four objects we are going to consider—the body, the feelings, the mind, and other events—the body is the grossest. It makes good sense to start out with practices that are more basic, and objects of meditation that are relatively gross, for when we begin practice our minds are at their grossest. As we progress our minds become more refined, more subtle, and we are in a position to attend to objects that are more subtle.

The major theme in all four mindfulness practices is to distinguish more and more clearly between our conceptual projections upon reality, and what reality itself presents to us. This turns out to be a very formidable project. As we start, we find the role of our conceptual projection is deeply ingrained, much of it occurring either unconsciously or only semiconsciously.

Because conceptualization is largely semiconscious, we usually are not aware that this compulsive and semiconscious interpretation is taking place. Instead, we tend to assume we are not projecting anything on reality at all, and that our basic sense of things is valid. There can be a lot of delusion in that. The application of mindfulness takes a mental scalpel created by quieting the mind, and uses this scalpel to slice through conceptual projections. In doing so we penetrate into the essential reality that is present in the absence of conceptual projections.

As the Buddha taught this practice, he said to first sit down and simply follow the breath. One first gets into a comfortable position, brings one's awareness into the present, and stabilizes it by following the in-breath and the out-breath. The emphasis here, as it often is in Buddhism, is on developing a fine tool. Just as in science one must develop finely honed tools to make reliable, precise measurements, so in contemplative practice one must hone the tool of one's awareness to understand the nature of reality.

The practice starts quite simply, with posture. The Buddha spoke of four simple postures we already engage in: sitting, standing, walking and lying down. The point of applying mindfulness to these is to engage our awareness and direct it toward our posture. It is often the case that whatever we are doing, be it sitting, walking, standing, or lying, the mind is frequently disengaged from the immediate reality and is instead absorbed in compulsive conceptualization about the future or past. While we are walking, we think about arriving, and when we arrive, we think about leaving. When we are eating, we think about the dishes, and as we do the dishes, we think about watching television.

This is a weird way to run a mind. We are not connected with the present situation, but we are always thinking about something else. Too often we are consumed with anxiety and cravings, regrets about the past and anticipation for the future, completely missing the crisp simplicity of the moment.

A very important mindfulness practice is based on one of the most fundamental human activities: walking. We are accustomed to walking along busily, thinking ahead to where we are going and forgetting where we are. Our eyes wander everywhere, and our minds are like eggs being scrambled, flipping from one thing to another. But another possibility is to pull our awareness out of this mesh of compulsive, exhausting ideation, and instead bring it to the soles of our feet. This allows us to be aware of the feet rising and falling, to be aware of the contact with the earth.

It can help to slow the walking down. In this practice one walks very slowly and deliberately, paying close attention to each moment. First the foot is rising, rising, rising; then, ever so slowly, it is placing, placing, placing. One is aware of the tactile sensations of the body, and the sensations of the soles of the feet on the ground. It grounds one, literally and metaphorically. It brings one's awareness into the present.

This may sound boring, but that is only because we are so used to not being in the present. If we start doing this well, if we really start calming the mind and bringing it into the body, we find it turns out to be fascinating.

Imagine you are sitting totally motionless, and then, when you are firmly in the present, you do something that is quite extraordinary—you raise your hand! As you learn to do this mindfully, you find this simple activity has many parts. There is an intention, a mental event, and somehow this results in the hand moving, a physical event. How do they connect? How did this happen? It becomes an absorbing process.

One central aspect of this practice is mindfulness, which in this context means maintaining a continuity of awareness of one's chosen object. Another is vigilance, which refers here to a keen and intelligent examination of events.

The Nature of the Self

Now let us consider how this finely honed tool, this mindfulness, can generate insight into the essential question of the spiritual path: What is the nature of the self?

A famous commentary by Buddhaghosa sheds light on this. Speaking of physical motion, he says:

> A living being goes, a living being stands ... but truly, there is no living being going or standing. This talk of a living being going and standing is similar to speech in the following way: A cart goes, a cart stands.[2]

The point he is raising here is exactly what makes the cart go or not go, the living being go or not go. What is the source of their motion, or, looked at on a deeper level, what is the source of the volition that makes them move? What is this self from which motion apparently comes?

It is evidently true that the cart is moved by something, perhaps a bull, a harness attaching the bull to the cart, maybe a driver to direct the bull. On a subtler level, the event of a living being standing and going also has causes and conditions. In fact, movement takes place as a result of complex interactions of external and internal events. Nowhere does one find an autonomous self that takes charge and says, "I am going to move the hand," and then it moves. This, of course, is counter to our gut sense of things, our inherent sense that each of us is a self-sufficient "I" who is in charge of our behavior. However, through mindfulness practice we can develop great insight into the nature of selflessness or the noninherent existence of the "I."

To do this, we simply start to investigate. Starting from the gross and moving to the subtle, we focus the finely tuned tool of awareness on the components of action, and analyze them. Gazing upon the physical and mental causes of motion, we find that nowhere is there any evidence of an inherent "my-ness," or of an essential self, anywhere in the body, the flesh, the bones, or the marrow.

Mindfulness of Feelings

The feelings are the second object for the application of mindfulness. A step more subtle than identification with the body, identification with feelings can take us on a roller coaster of feeling good and feeling bad that can be very difficult to penetrate.

While the word "feelings" is used in many ways in English, referring to emotions as well as tactile sensations, in Buddhism it has a more restricted meaning, captured in the Sanskrit word *vedanā*. This word refers simply to the feelings of pleasure, pain, and indifference, with which we can so easily identify ourselves. This is a very powerful point, because if we identify with our body, certainly it is equally true we identify with our feelings.

When unhappiness arises, we respond with the thoughts, "I am unhappy, I am depressed, I am so discouraged." And when happiness arises it is much the same: "I am happy! I'm feeling great!" The key is that none of these feelings are in fact "I." Like the movements of the body they arise from causes and conditions, and these are ever-changing.

The feelings we identify with are rooted in propensities unique to ourselves. If someone praises me in a way that fits my propensities I will feel happy, while someone else's praise might cause me to react indifferently. On the negative side, the same goes for blame and feelings of sadness. In either case, the feelings are simply one instant within a causal matrix of events.

The problem with feelings is that we identify with them so strongly. We almost never cut through the conceptual overlay that causes us to regard certain feelings as inherently "our feelings." In fact, feelings are inherently no one's. All that is taking place is the arising and passing of feelings, brought about by causes and conditions.

The Buddha spoke of several qualities of feelings, one of the most important being their impermanence. Despair, for example, which can seem so leaden, is in fact an emotion that is in constant flux. Even the heaviest feelings are constantly changing, but this is very difficult to recognize. Identification with depression obscures the fluctuations that are taking place from one moment to the next, replacing them instead with a sense of a homogeneous continuity.

Sometimes things go well, we feel great, and we think, "Now my troubles are over, that was the last hurdle." Our conceptual mind plays another trick on us, and we think, "As it is now, so it must be forever." The same applies to the downside, of course. Sorrow sets in, and the mind becomes negative: "I am really a failure, I will be a failure next year, in fact my whole life is a failure." Again, these feelings are arising in the moment, and the mind is fixing on that moment in a deluded way.

The problem with attachment to feelings, especially if they are hinged upon pleasurable external stimuli, is that everything around us is constantly changing, most of it out of our control. We try to manipulate and control our immediate environment, but even our own body is to a significant degree beyond our control. Our mind, too, is often out of our control.

Grasping onto pleasurable feelings is not bad in the sense of being evil, but rather in the sense that it is not effective. As the well-known Burmese Buddhist teacher Goenka once said, "Grasping at things can yield only one of two results: either the thing you are grasping at disappears, or you yourself disappear. It is only a matter of which occurs first."

Mindfulness of the Mind

Mindfulness of the mind is quite different from the practice of meditative quiescence focused on the mind. . . . That practice is a penetrating and focused look at pure awareness, but this mindfulness practice is instead a meditation on the ways in which the mind works.

Mindfulness of the mind is not a practice to develop stability, but is instead an insight practice. The object of meditation here is the mental states rather than awareness itself.

An important part of this practice is investigating the mind dominated by the three poisons . . . ignorance, hatred, and attachment. In this practice the meditator notes and investigates these mind states, with special emphasis on the "tone" of the mind as these states arise.

In normal life, we tend to do quite the opposite. When the mind manifests anger, for instance, we immediately identify with it. I spill a glass of water on my trousers, and without thinking I focus out there on an object, either the glass itself or the person who bumped my elbow and made me spill it, and I become angry. I am identifying with the anger. And if someone should ask me how I am doing, I will say, "I am angry." I have identified with a mental event that is not I.

Mental events like anger arise out of our own propensities for anger, which are activated by external events. On that level we have no choice, because if we have those propensities and the necessary conditions arise, we will experience anger. We may forget everything we have heard about mindfulness, and the next time anger arises we will simply identify with it. We focus on the object of anger, we think about it, and we act upon it. Everything is predictable and mechanical.

By introducing mindfulness, however, the possibility of choice is presented. We do not identify with the event, but we attend to it mindfully. Considering anger again, we are now faced with a meaningful choice. Being aware, "Aha, the event of anger has arisen again," we can choose between identifying with the event or being mindful. Do we want to act upon the anger, or do we simply want to observe it? If we have mindfulness we are presented with the choice. We have an option.

Recall Śāntideva's suggestion that when our minds are dominated by the mental distortions, such as jealousy, contempt, resentment, and sarcasm, we should remain as a block of wood. This does not mean that we should unintelligently suppress or repress those negative feelings. This will only make us sick; it is bad for the heart, for the digestion, for the blood pressure.

The Buddhist alternative is mindfulness. By exercising mindfulness, we may become clearly aware in the presence of harmful mental events taking place. And by being mindful of them, we are not perpetuating them. Anger and other negativities must be "fed" to survive. Let us say I am angry at Harry, and I want to feed that anger, so I think of all the nasty things he has done. And if this is not enough, I can think of all the nasty things he would do if he had a chance. This keeps the anger going; it can feed the anger for decades.

When Śāntideva suggested we remain as a block of wood when afflictions arise, what he meant was not to feed the anger. Rather than feeding it, we may direct our awareness to the anger itself and be mindful of it so that we do not allow it to dominate our speech or physical behavior.

When the mind is swayed by a mental distortion it is dysfunctional, like a sprained wrist. When the mind is dysfunctional, we can let it heal a bit, and then act. This can prevent a lot of problems, and can solve others that need not have arisen in the first place.

Mindfulness of Events

The most subtle of these practices, mindfulness of events, encompasses all we have discussed above. We have proceeded here from the gross to the subtle, from mindfulness of the body, to mindfulness of feelings, to mindfulness of mind states. In each of these practices the emphasis has been on close inspection, a direct application of attention on the theme we started out with.

That theme, you may recall, is whether or not there is a substantial self, or ego, to be found within the body, feelings, or mind states. We start with the body, trying to see if there is a substantial ego, a self, hidden in there somewhere. Then we move on to the feelings, because we do tend to identify with them at least as strongly. As we inspect the feelings moment by moment, the questions are much the same: Is there an "I" in there? Is there an agent? Is there an entity that feels, apart from the feelings themselves? We investigate and we investigate, and all we see are mere events, arising and passing.

Close inspection of the third stage, the mind, yields a similar result. By directing the awareness to the nature of the mind itself, the mental events, and the mind with its mental distortions, we find the same thing; that is, mental events arising and passing. Even awareness itself is arising and passing, without any personal identity. Awareness has no intrinsic identity. It is just awareness. And mental distortions have no identity either; they are just mental distortions.

At this point a critical observer may protest, saying, "If you want to find the self, investigate who is doing the looking. It is futile to look for a flashlight in a pitch-black room with that same flashlight, and in the same way, the fact that you cannot find the self in the body, feelings, or mind does not mean it is not there. There is a self and that self is doing the looking and the meditating."

Buddhism responds to this by asserting that while we are born with a natural, unlearned sense of intrinsic self, that does not mean such a self actually exists. We think, "I will, therefore I am. I intend, therefore I am. I meditate, therefore I am." This sense that things flow from me, that thoughts flow from me, is associated with this inborn sense of personal identity.

We look at someone who is repugnant, and we somehow feel it is the person himself gushing forth repugnance. We feel there is a source for all the qualities we identify a person with, and that the source is the person behind the scene, the self, the "I" that is in charge.

We have an inborn sense there is an autonomous self in control. This self, we believe, is the one making things coherent, making any one of us a human being. And without this self, one might think, everything would fall apart and there would be no person at all.

This can be checked, not by looking for the self, but by observing the interactions of the body, feelings, mental states, and other events. It is like a company where the workers are told the factory would shut down if there were no outside owner overseeing them. As a worker one might believe that, until one starts analyzing the individual connections. And then one can see that the interrelationships among the workers continue to function without the owner, and the company continues to operate. The workers, acting together, manage themselves.

When the mind is stabilized, it is possible to withdraw the sense of an ego controlling the body and mind, and simply enter a witnessing mode of awareness. And in that state we find that mental and physical behavior occurs only in relation to other events; it does not need a controlling ego. All the elements of the body-mind system interact as coherent dependently related events and, in fact, there is no room for an autonomous ego at all.

Mindfulness covers a wide range of events, generating insight about how all of them interrelate. The events we investigate include all the physical events of the body and things external to the body; all the feelings and mental formations, and finally, awareness itself. And the revelation from all of this is that there is no autonomous self coordinating these events, but rather a complex set of interrelationships that operate on their own, without a single, external manager.

Again and again the Buddha said, when discussing this, that we should check this out with our own experience. We should gain insight, and then apply this in our experience with others. Sometimes we can do this perceptually, by observing other people's behavior. But when we are considering mind states this is not normally possible, and so we must inferentially extrapolate from our own experience. This is done by reflecting, "As this arises in my experience, so it likely occurs in the experience of others." The process is similar to the one we explored in the practice of loving kindness, where we started by generating loving kindness toward ourselves, then extended that to other beings.

Three Themes

There are three themes the Buddha emphasized strongly for these insight practices: impermanence, dissatisfaction (suffering), and identitylessness.

Impermanence is understood only when we saturate our minds with the fluctuating, transient nature of all conditioned phenomena. Why is this so important? It is crucial because so much of what we do and think in life is founded on quite the opposite premise: that things are static, and can be made to stay the way we want them to be.

A key problem in life is that we tend to reify things, making them seem permanent and stable when in fact they are not. We enter into relationships, we acquire things, and we say, "Ah, here lies my happiness." In doing this, we suppress the transient nature of the experienced world. It is one thing to know this intellectually, but quite another to experience it moment by moment, and to adapt our way of life accordingly. By recognizing our attachments to these events, to these people, we can cut through this false sense of permanence and replace it with a deeper insight into reality.

Dissatisfaction (suffering) is the second theme, also called *duhkha*. The emphasis here, as discussed previously, is to recognize the reality of our lives. A common mistake is to hinge our entire well-being on pleasant stimuli from the outside—on a house, a family, a spouse, a child—all situations that are subject to change at every moment. We grasp at these things urgently as if they will support us, but they will not. Instead they will inevitably change, and if we invest our well-being in them with attachment, we will experience nothing but anxiety as those changes affect us. That is suffering, not because the situation is wrong, but because we seek an enduring basis for well-being in events that do not endure.

The last is identitylessness, the lack of an intrinsic self. This is crucial because the opposite, grasping at an intrinsic self, is the confusion posited as the fundamental mental distortion, the root from which all other afflictions arise.

All of the above are fundamental Buddhist teachings. Their major emphasis is on healing the individual, on bringing about greater sanity for the individual. . . .

NOTES

1. See Soma Thera's *The Way of Mindfulness* (Kandy: Buddhist Publication Society, 1975).

2. Buddhaghosa Thera, The Satipaṭṭhāna Sutta Vannana of the Papañcasudani, in The Way of Mindfulness: The Satipaṭṭhāna Sutta and Commentary, trans. by Soma Thera (Kandy: Buddhist Publication Society, 1975), pp. 80–81.

24

Renewing the Sacred Hoop

Dhyani Ywahoo

In 1983, Dhyani Ywahoo founded the Sunray Meditation Society in
Bristol, Vermont, an international society dedicated to planetary peace
with a practical program of education and training known as the
Peacekeeper Mission. By the late 1980s, training meetings were being
held in North America and Europe, and Sunray meditation groups
that hinted of the New Age had sprung up in cities in the United States
and Canada. Ywahoo came from a traditional Native American background. A member of the Etowah Band of the Eastern Tsalagi (Cherokee) Nation, she pointed to twenty-seven generations of the Ywahoo
lineage through which her teachings had been maintained. In 1969, she
said, long years of Tsalagi secrecy ended, and the decision was made to
go public—to share cherished spiritual teachings with nonnative
people as a way of strengthening communities and nations and foster-
ing right relationships, too, with the land. She called the teachings she
was sharing "foundational"—appropriate for people whatever their religion or nationality and not in violation of other, sacrosanct forms of
wisdom kept from whites in accord with clan laws. In her book *Voices of
Our Ancestors* (1987), from which the present excerpt is taken, Ywahoo
systematically explains the foundational teachings in ways that point to
metaphysical spirituality. She emphasizes being present to the moment
with a clear mind and in right relationship, and she is keenly sensitive
to the manifestation of energy in nature and in the human body—and
its role therein in meditation. Ywahoo herself had been in conversation
with His Holiness the Dalai Lama of Tibet, and she resonated to his
spirituality and to his Buddhist teachings. Still, she was clear on her
Tsalagi identity and her commitment to her Native American heritage.

Without spiritual foundation there can be no society. Without spiritual practice confusion reigns. Even the softest prayer sends vibrations of prayer moving through the air, just as the guitar strings stir the piano's song. To call forth
the voice and to sing in joy and harmony, to let the beauty flow in our hearts,
is something all of our elders have talked about, saying to us, "Let us pray
together, let us do things together." People come together to pray not only for

social reasons; there is a real power in joined voices. It is the power of human nature reweaving the sacred web of light, acknowledging the whole community. All that we see is a reflection of consciousness, and to see requires pulling the veils from the eyes, pulling away the illusions that limit us in time and space, the illusions that say we are separate. We are not separate. We are all together. When we join our hearts in prayer, in singing, in sacred dancing, in planting things together, we are returning something to the Earth, planting seeds of good cause.

The qualities of laughter, joy, and sorrow and our thoughts and actions weave the tapestry of life. Spiritual practice transforms ideas of conflict and develops perception of ourselves and the universe as energies, tones, complementary aspects seeking balance and resolution. There is a song arising in our hearts as a community of human beings sharing and co-creating an environment. The song is of planetary peace, planetary cooperation. It is calling each of us to transform conflicting emotions, to reveal the inherent beatitude. Speak the best of yourself and others, recognize process and change, and affirm the healing power of peaceful thought. Hold the form of peace. Realize that our thought and action shape tomorrow. Each one contributes to the outcome of peaceful resolution. Our hearts and the heart of the Earth are one.

Ideas float through the atmosphere, become trends. Ideas of "Buy this, buy that" float about as advertisements on the waves of the media age. Such thoughts fuel patterns of behavior and cultural belief systems such as "This is good" or "More is better." One chooses which of the trends to flow with. Will you flow with the trend of "holistic health" and become a healer? Do you flow with the trend of "M.B.A." and become a banker? Each person needs to choose carefully his or her response to cultural expectations. The media wave may espouse "Thin is in" while your genes sing "Round survives." The wise practitioner chooses to actualize those thoughts which clarify and ennoble all our relations. As the melodies of life thread through our actions, each person is weaving the tapestry that becomes our tomorrow. Affirm the sounds and overtones in harmonious resolution.

Habitual thought patterns become your reality. While the thoughts may be expressed internally, they still create a force seeking fruition. Prayers and sacred mantras tame the mind by replacing destructive or limiting thought patterns with those that pacify negative traits and affirm the inherent good. One who is consistently thinking "I can't" is really chanting the mantra of failure. One who tames the mind with a prayer mantra—such as prayers to assist one's family and the Earth—creates a new reality. Thus the light of clear understanding transforms patterns of conflict, through developing equanimity, nonreaction to this or that, for reaction creates charge of attraction and repulsion, ripples on the still pool of mind.

Know that all of our relationships are aspects of mind and that our thoughts are always contributing to the forms around us. Within every being there is the seed of our family's full unity; the opening of that great flower of the heart's wisdom is a moment of capitulation into the vastness of mind. When we affirm love and forgiveness as a stream within our hearts, we release in our bodies a great energy, and the sacred flow within us flows more readily, more fully. In that stream of forgiveness we see that we continue on in a process and that we have choice. Our words, our actions, our very breath shape the fiber of our reality. The rocks in the stream are part of the dream.

Everything in form is vibration. Energy moves along an axis, a line of energy of greatest flow and of least resistance. Energy within crystal structure flows as a generator; to manifest the initial form it chooses a path of least resistance through the spiral. Our thoughts sing into the atmosphere. Our very life is application; no separation of the theory and the practice. As you look at yourself, you are recognizing a vibration of life. Removing some of the obstructing thought forms is a result of meditation. See the effect of your consciousness on the stream of life. Choose to manifest wholesome thoughts.

The shape, the movement of the atomic structure within the crystal is consciousness, and the consciousness atoms are moving within us. We are in relationship to all that goes on in this universe. One may commit oneself to holding the song, the vibration, that the current of enlightenment may stir in all being. Choice is very significant. The crystal in its growth process chooses at certain points whether to elongate or truncate its form; the octahedron can also become a cube. The way in which the crystal aligns itself determines how the light will move through. So it is with us.

Thus the Peacemaker must understand vibration and realize that life is a cycle, a process. Attunement to the intersection of the individual cycles with the larger cycles in the Medicine Wheel brings harmony. There is harmony in your heart; it is a gift to share with all the universe. Wisdom arises in observing repeated patterns of mind and action and casting out what is inappropriate. Wisdom develops like the pearl: it develops within the oyster or the mussel as an irritation, and it surrounds that with a very beautiful layered crystalline structure.

To understand process, cycles, patterns is to recognize the beauty of the moment unfolding. It is to be present. What is the thought that stands beyond the present, that builds fortifications of mind and heart? Basically, it is a thought of fear. Yet in our true nature there are only two real fears: fear of sudden noises and fear of falling. All other fears are fed by the mind.

We have come beyond the beliefs of childhood to a stage in our lives where it is time to know who we are and how we are in relation to other things—and to be aware of our choice. Destiny is a matter of our thinking. Life unfolds in the world around us, and our interaction is a part of its unfolding. So the world situation is not happening *to* us; situations are the results of our collective thought and action.

It is important to understand the process of balancing ourselves. The first stage is to know the mother and the father in our hearts, because everything in form, to maintain its pattern, seeks the balance of mother and father. And then there is a third quality generated that people often refer to as the Child, or wisdom nature. What is important is that we be aware of wisdom energy and its flow in our own consciousness, that we make peace with ourselves, accept the wisdom of the past and know that the future exists in our hearts in this moment. Many of us have great secrets stored in our hearts, in our muscles, in our minds. It is time to let those secrets free, to be all that we are. Some secrets may obscure awareness of your life purpose.

It is a common concept in Native American philosophy that we all have a purpose, a spiritual duty. The religion of the indigenous peoples teaches that we have a spiritual relationship and a responsibility with our entire environment. Spiritual relationship perceives a thought of clear action, of people communicating, acting together in harmony. To create the means whereby that may happen, a whole system of ceremonies and seasonal cycles of relationship was carried on for generations. My relatives say it is over 133,000 years that we have been here, the time period of human mind development upon this land. There have been four creations before this, and now we are in the Fifth Creation, the Fifth World. The Fifth Creation, like the fifth tone in music, is the opportunity to go into yet another realm. We can come now to the Beauty Path, the path of right action, of good relationship, of clear intention. That is a choice we make as this fifth cycle ends.

To make that choice is to honor yourself and to honor and respect all aspects of this world we live in, because through this world we are given the opportunity to realize the Great Mystery, the One from which we all descend. To recognize that Mystery is to recognize oneself in step with the seasons, attuned with the voice of the sun and the cycles of the moon. These days these rhythms are called biorhythms; through them we are interacting with the Earth and the entire universe.

Through the energy centers within our own bodies and the meridians that carry elemental energy, we are in communion with Earth and stars. Our thoughts, our actions are contributing creative vitality, or perhaps holding something back by not fully connecting with Earth, due to selfishness. So one goes on a vision quest to be sure one is truly doing the work one has come here for; to understand the seed that planted one in this time and place; to understand the sacred energy and the angelic guide that stands beside one, the protecting forces of life, the protecting angels of life. They, too, are elements of the mind fire.

Cornmeal is the gift of life. It comes from the Corn Mother, we say. The corn grows according to our thinking and our actions. If we do not tend it, if we do not thin it out and water it at the right times, then it grows not so well. So, too, with our relationships as individuals in a family, with our co-workers, our friends. Each of us must sow good seeds. We must plant a garden where we are able to honor and respect one another and recognize ourselves moving in step with the very rhythm of this Earth. This we all know. It is the ideal.

We call that ideal realm Galunlati. In this time of purification we sometimes forget the how, the means to manifest the ideal. First, affirm that there is a path of beauty, very diligently put your feet upon that path, and with great energy, through the practice of good voice, speak of what is good, recognize what is and what may be in the process of change. When speaking of something that needs correction, let the energy you place upon it with your voice be without charge, that things may come to balance and resolution. This is a practice, this is something each of us can do. By practicing a voice of compassion, by activating the wisdom that discriminates, we can speak to one another in the moment and realize how to work together. Basically, as human beings we wish to survive and we wish to communicate with one another. We are all coming to know in a deeper way the nature of true communication. It is said that there will be a time when all upon this planet will speak one language and that language will be few words, many visions. That is a seed germinating in our hearts even now.

The cosmology, the system of understanding from which these teachings spring, it is very old. In this time many are stirred with curiosity to understand these things. And it is good that after the fifth generation of much obscuration and bitterness and separation from ourselves as a people upon the land, we come together again as dignified human beings and look to the means by which we can manifest peace in this great land. We live in North America together. We live on planet Earth together. We live in this galaxy together.

What is the purpose of our being here? The old people say it is to experience and to realize the Great Mystery. That is the purpose. And the seed of that Mystery and that wisdom is ever in us. Mystery carries us around the circle, the Medicine Wheel. In the North we see the special lesson of our actions. We become still, as the lakes become frozen; we understand a certain balance of mind, gentle balance. As we move to the East there is the sunlight of our illumination, the realization, "Oh, I am a person thinking, sitting here now." In the South we find the seeds of our actions, we see the gentle sprouts of their coming to fruition. And we also realize that we carry upon our backs tradition, the thoughts of our ancestors, things that again and again have given a cohesiveness to the very world we live in. As the water drips and makes a canyon, so do the patterns of a people. In the West burns the transforming fire, gateway to the clear light—or to your choice to come again until all the people realize the Mystery. And as we grow wiser, we come again in our sacred meanderings back to the center.

Whatever your tradition is, whatever your practice has been to see the clarity of your mind, whatever has stilled you, trace the roots of that—because as you trace those roots you see there is but one truth, one wisdom. And here the people of Turtle Island say, "Together, by tracing our roots to the Great Tree of Peace, we make whole the sacred hoop, and the sacred fire will be alight in every heart again." To see that happen is an idea, and that idea becomes manifest as each of us makes an offering of our ignorance upon that fire of transformation. Ignorance is heavy—why be attached to it? It can be cast into the flame.

> Be gone, be gone, O thoughts of doubt!
> Be gone, be gone! Let there be peace throughout.

How to make strong the voice and how to maintain it as you walk into the world with many things to do? Perhaps there is a traffic jam, a certain clear reminder of obscuration. "Have to stay cool, watch it. Did I make this happen, did I cause this traffic jam? Well, here I am on this road. Can I blame the street lights? Can I blame the road repair crews? No, here I am sitting on this road. So better I see and think as I drive and look ahead. And better that I remember that I'm on the road because I choose to be." That is a big step; then you are no longer abdicating responsibility for manifesting in your own life what is correct, what is good for you and for the people with you.

So here we are, sitting in the world; we see people playing lots of games with very big missiles, and we are thinking about peace in our hearts. How does it all meet? The ideal of our living as planetary human beings, how are we to manifest that in this time of great arms buildups along borders here and there? It is for us to look at the borders of our minds. It is for us to speak out about those deeds which are unkind. It is for us to stand very firm and strong and say that we will not accept fear or aggression. To be a Peacekeeper is not to be a sissy or a wimp. It is to speak very clearly and to stand up for what you know is correct. To hold the form. If we are anti-anything, then we are still arguing. When we recognize ourselves as making peace, we are keeping peace in our hearts and looking for ways to communicate that in a group process.

Why do we come to war? Because someone thinks there is not enough, not enough. It is the illusion of scarcity. "Not enough oil"—that is not so. We don't need to take it from the Earth, and we know that. So you know you don't want to take any more oil from the Earth and you don't wish to be caught in the game-playing that has become wars around oil. What do you do as an individual? You chop wood. There is always something we can do. As a human family, what are we to do? We meet in groups, we pray, we call people to right action, and we examine very carefully the possible futures being generated by such actions. Have we come to resolution? Do we know ourselves as a planetary family? Your voice makes a difference. It is for each of us to send forth light and a strong voice to say, "We can live in peace, we are strong in our awareness of an abundant universe." As the abundance is known, then what is there to argue about?

To have the gift of a body, to be alive in this time is indeed an opportunity to co-create, to bring forth a family of dignified human beings. Through right relationship with one another, through actions that bring forth good for the people, through clear intelligence we see what is open before us and we choose wisely what is the best course—peace. We come again to the Beauty Path by walking in beauty within ourselves and by honoring and respecting that seed of beauty within one another. Thus we bring forth the wisdom of the planetary family. So it is now, in this moment. When my grandfather used to speak these things to me, I would wonder, "Does that mean we were here before?" And he would say, "We were here before, but we are here now and before and after; everything is happening now." To be attentive here and now, that is what is called for. That is to be upon the Beauty Path.

So let us walk clearly upon the Beauty Path. There are many signposts along the way. What do they say? "Quagmire of doubtful thought." Don't walk down that way. See it for what it is, and know that it is woven by the thought. If feeling doubt, just know that as you sit you are breathing, in and out. You can be sure of that. Have some certainty. Realize your voice as a treasure and a powerful co-creator. Let us learn to speak rightly of one another; let us call forth the beauty of one another. Affirm the creative life force within ourselves. Have courage to speak truth.

In this family of human beings many have made a clear voice. Many are finding ways to share skills, planting gardens together, of good will and good seed, respect for ourselves and one another. Many have recalled the wisdom of the elders and know that old truth, new truth, truth is something to be perceived within. Together we can experience moving through thoughts, moving through doubt, coming to know ourselves as human beings. Those who practice and pray together become relatives of one mind. Thus we set into motion a common song, a hope, a dream within this great dream of life. The dream of the Peacekeeper, bringing forth the light that is always there, rekindling the sacred fire. One of the other names for the Tsalagi, the Cherokee people, is People of One Fire. One fire brought forth all, and that fire was a light, it was a sound. So from those sounds, we say, it all happens, from those sounds, through the blue fire of will. And we can meditate and contemplate and communicate with these energies within ourselves. It is not just an idea; it is truly living. As the air is moving in our chest, as the blood is moving through our body, so, too, is the sacred fire of will. The will to be unites us in the dream of humanity. We have come here together, and always that will to continue is strong until we have learned fully the lessons of uncovering peace.

To come to the shores of our knowing, we say you need a canoe to get to the other side. It is good to have a conveyance, to have a means of travel, and that conveyance is a spiritual practice that we share. It is affirming the power of our voice, of our action. It is recognizing that what is happening is simply happening as it is, and our thinking is in relationship to it and calling it forth. We rekindle and relight the wisdom of peaceful relationship, of right relationship, in our hearts, with one another, that right relationship may resonate as a form all around this planet.

What is a thought form? It is an idea. Yesterday I thought of the people needing food; today I plant a garden. There are realms of ideas; Galunlati is the realm of ideal form where our potentials are dancing in the light. We begin to manifest these ideals through inspiration, the inhalation of the Earth's and heaven's flow, meeting in our hearts.

So often our movement through life is based upon someone else's expectations, someone else's vision. Yet there is an innate purpose and pattern for one's birth, a particular harmony maintained by each individual so that the family may manifest its unity. And Earth is asking that human beings realize that the bears, the whales, the coyotes, the trees, the ants, all of these creatures are our relatives. We have a duty to ourselves and to the future to live correctly with all our relatives, to preserve life rather than push to extinction. The environment responds to our thought and feeling. It is for humans to be aware of how our thought, word, and deed affect the environment. One person filled with doubt and anger may wilt the flowers; another person's enthusiasm is such that cut flowers last for weeks.

Just as the seed follows sacred laws to grow, so it is with the sacred fire of clear mind. We come here as infants, whole and knowing. The body is sensing, vibrating to the note of our purpose. Then as children we listen and hear people saying, "You can't, you're too small." So one may shut down a little; that sacred tube that connects us with all that is becomes smaller, dammed by the heart that fears and refuses to see the beauty of one's own nature. Where does the damming come from? Shame: "Oh, was I born with sin?" I don't think so. Blame: "Oh, Mother hurt herself; I must have done it." You would be surprised how many of these old tunes are still running around in your mind even though you are fully grown. Perhaps the names are changed; perhaps now it is a husband or a boss or someone else. But you are still feeling shame, blame, and guilt. These feelings arise from conflicting emotions; they do not reflect the purity that is you. Ember of the true light still glows, awaits rekindling.

Magnetizing, Realizing the Vision of Peace

To understand Mystery,
observe mind.
Stilling fear, mind moves clear.
Sing a song of equanimity
awake within serenity.
Affirm your voice
and choice.
Magnetize a potent dream:
World alight,
illumined peace.

The confused mind is pacified through regular practice to clarify emotions and stabilize the mind. The energy of purification is the power of sound and the chant and the bringing forth of rainbow light into the body from the stars above. By the energy of smudging, prayer offerings of sacred cedar or sage, we purify our environment and atmosphere of habitual thoughts of conflict and lethargy. In the Tsalagi tradition the concepts of pacifying, purifying, magnetizing, and actualizing are the four posts of the medicine cabin. In these pages much has been said of the energies of pacification and purification. We look now to the fourth pillar of manifestation—magnetizing the vision of peace—that we may manifest the body of enlightened action through affirmation and harmony with the sacred law and with one's individual purpose.

To manifest right relationship we energize the vision and attract positive outcome through magnetization. This is the principle of vivifying a sacred vision for the benefit of all beings through chanting, clear envisioning, and right action. Your body, it is an alchemical retort. Encoded within, genetic patterns determine your form and predispose you to certain patterns of attitude, belief, and behavior as shaped by your family of origin. The wise practitioner on the road to enlightened action creates harmony through disciplined practice.

Magnetization is a principle of attraction: by our patterns of thought we attract to our life circle that which appears. Through the generation of sound power, prayer power, and harmonious relationship with the sacred law, we can attract what will benefit all. Our days arise out of our mind's actions, whether we are conscious of the patterns of attraction and repulsion or not. So it is incumbent upon each human being who wishes to live in a sacred manner to maintain a spiritual practice and a moral and ethical framework of living.

All physical form—the table that we see, the tree, the mountain—was first a thought. Some thoughts originate in the mind of God, some originate in the minds of people. All thought is united in the sacred hoop, in that we are one in creation. Whether we refer to the inclusiveness of mind as Great Spirit,

Buddha-mind, Christ-mind, Allah, or by another name, essentially there is one truth underlying our attempts to describe what is indescribable. The telephone was an idea; an inventor manifested it as form, and today we call one another around the world. That same thought that brings the communication of the telephone, the mind itself, is the means whereby we may discover the clear light.

Magnetization is a principle by which one conscientiously cultivates thoughts of peace, harmony, good relationship for self, family, clan, nation, the entire planet. Magnetizing appears in many forms. Whether one is aware of it or not, the ways in which we think and speak about ourselves attract results and become self-fulfilling prophecies.

It is said in the Tsalagi tradition that in the first six years of life the child is completely formed and will show you the person she or he will become. Many adults may still be motivated by those early patterns set down in childhood. It is a wise practitioner who carefully changes the thought form of habit and sets a path for certainty through understanding his or her own nature, pulling threads of early patterns and reweaving them into a beauteous garment.

The means of perceiving the nature of your own mind is to observe your thoughts and actions and to set the intention to be the best person you can possibly be, to benefit all. Thus you establish a mind dedicated to the apperception of truth. Dedication is required, for often there are unconscious levers that you tip when faced with the opportunity of leaving behind your security blanket, some old attachment. Sometimes the security blanket is the phrase "I can't," or it may be, "Well, nobody likes me anyway." Invariably everyone writes his or her own script—with the help of family members! Therefore, strong determination and faith reveal energy to accomplish.

Meditation practice with visualization and chanting creates a still pool upon which your nature is reflected. As you begin to practice, many thoughts and emotions race across the pool. As you continue, the emotions race less and less, the mind becomes more transparent, patterns of behavior become apparent. As the thought arises, watch. You need not react. The watching of your mental process is the beginning of understanding. Continue visualizing and chanting. Then begin to clarify channels within the body, that the sacred wisdom fire may manifest in your actions. (The visualizations and the meditation of the Sunray practice, based on the teachings of the Ywahoo lineage, also have a physiological effect in that they release hormones to ease stress and pain, lower blood pressure, and provide other healthy benefits.) Patterns of thought, word, and deed become apparent as you continue to practice chanting and visualization. With diligence and certainty, there is an unraveling of discordant habits.

Speaking to one another clearly of intent and purpose and developing the voice of conciliation prepares us for the great work of magnetizing a vision of peace. Sound also purifies, the inflowing light purifies, making apparent and transforming thoughts and patterns that had been obstacles. Praying out loud, giving thanks and affirming the gifts received, renews body and mind. To take the staff of your destiny into your hands is to align the spine and the breath with the pulses of heaven and Earth: inhaling and exhaling, giving and receiving the mind of appreciation and generosity.

A foundation practice of principles of magnetization includes affirmation and altruism, the desire to help self and others overcome suffering. We may take a negativity fast, observing the ways in which we speak about ourselves and others. When you hear yourself say, "I'm dying to do that," correct to the positive statement, "I'm living to do that." Consider carefully the choice of words in describing self and others. In that words become realities, speak not of another's perceived shortcomings; instead consider that you and others are in a process of becoming enlightened beings, and affirm that the seeds of enlightenment are there.

To begin the process of positive affirmation, give thanks for the gift of life in the human body. When it is clear to you that it is time to change a certain pattern, after giving thanks look at your face in the mirror and affirmatively state, "I shall manifest peaceful mind today." Repeat this three times, and also affirm that you will accomplish three specific tasks in that day. By actually accomplishing those tasks, you create a charge of light energy to illumine the recesses of your own mind. The more you practice, and the greater the effort, the stronger this force. As you become a committed caretaker for the Earth and for others, your affirmation to benefit people and the land unto future generations becomes a storehouse of energy that even shakes loose the energies of aggression, avarice, lust, and envy. When you create this force of prayer energy, always remembering to give thanks and to call forth in yourself and others what is beneficial, this energy transforms thought forms of confusion even in the environment. It is said in the Tsalagi tradition that just a small number of people of one mind, one purpose, fully attuned to the sacred principles, can transform the world and precipitate and manifest what is needed to relieve suffering and benefit all beings.

Heart-to-heart, mind-to-mind communication, acknowledging the sacred fiber that unites us all in this stream, is yet another foundation practice of magnetization. The gardener who cares for and respects the plants has the greatest harvest. The nation that casts aside its farmers manifests drought and scarcity. Our actions individually and collectively manifest in our environment.

In short, magnetization requires clear intention, a clear vision aligned with the sacred will, the Law of the universe, compassionate wisdom, voice of affirmation. Diligence of practice creates the force, attracting and manifesting a goal of enlightened action.

Some people have been severely hurt in childhood, while others have had the good fortune of a very happy childhood. The ease or hardness of early years can set a habit. One person may develop scar tissue and be afraid to love; another, because of early years of ease, may not feel motivation to expand awareness of generosity. Some people feel that they have closed off access to the pure light within themselves when they entered school or when specific events occurred in their lives. One can transform and re-form ideas of self and patterns of relationship. For example, perhaps someone went from foster home to foster home and never felt quite part of the life circle. That pattern may be acted out in adult life as inability to make committed relationships or to actualize creative potential. The antidote is to communicate with the stored memories of the child within, to acknowledge the strength and ability of having survived and come through, and to set open a gateway for loving relationships in the present.

The energy of the loving heart, the energy of the generous heart, attracts into its field what is good. Through the currents of energy moving around the heart, the principle of the life force enables us to incarnate. The thoughts, the feelings that we manifest in this life are a collected pattern with qualities of attraction and repulsion. We attract to ourselves those people and situations which enable us to fulfill our vision and life expectations. Upon awakening commitment to living in a sacred manner, we attract to ourselves the information, the understanding, the teachings that will help us realize our gifts to benefit all.

In the past one found redemption through a savior, through a great teacher. These times call each one of us to manifest fully in alignment with the concept of savior, redeemer. Let us redeem through clarity of speech, purpose, and action, through harmonious living with respect for future generations.

The sacred traditions of each age, of each nation, of each group, arise from society's desire to understand, to codify the mystery of life. The sacred teachings of the Native way, the Buddhist way, the Christian way, the Jewish way, the Islamic way, ultimately trace their form to direct experience of the Mystery. The Pale One, the Buddha, Christ, Moses, Muhammad—each directly experienced truths, and their teachings met the evolving consciousness of the societies in which they grew. The family into which we are born and its religion reflect a star in the mysterious sky. Different people have different spiritual needs, and we can coexist as we are attentive to basic ethics, manners, and morality, codes evolved from people's experience of the Mystery and desire for beauteous relationship.

One can approach study with the zealousness of a convert and then quickly toss it aside. Wise practitioners test and evaluate the teachings of the times and look to understand the nature of their *own* mind, to carefully ascertain their potent spiritual practice. These teachings are to enable you to be the best human being you can possibly be and to help you understand the causes of your birth and retrieve the jewels of your family.

When Native American people sing for the rain, the rain comes—because those singers have made a decision that they and the water and the air and the Earth are one. The song is sung that all beings may benefit from the gentle rains. One's small song—"I like, I dislike," habits of thought—creates dissonance with the large song. Today we are called to sing a unity song. The song of cosmic jubilation renews all beings.

What is creation? Is it something outside you, or are you a part of creation? Creation, the Mystery—in Algonquin, the root language of Tsalagi, it is Ywahoo, the "Great Mystery," beyond the form of words. There is no word for "God"; we call it a Great Mystery, because of its formlessness. And we recognize that there is a creative building that has occurred. The three Elder Fires Above express this Mystery in form, and we ourselves are an expression of the Mystery. In some of the old Tsalagi hymns the Creator is referred to as the One Who Makes the Breath; in other hymns as the Master of Life and Death. Yet as children, when we asked our elders, "What is God? Is it different from the Christian God?" they said, "That which is called God is Aqteshna Ana, which means 'the dew is on the grass.' And there is but One Mind that underlies the dream."

Look carefully at the nature of your mind; look carefully into your heart. Can you perceive in your thoughts the seeds of your reality? Consider carefully the future harvest, your tomorrow, your children's tomorrow, and think of beauty. All of our people are saying we cannot go on this way; all the old people around the planet are saying the Earth is hurting because we have forgotten to take responsibility for life. We think somebody else is to blame, somebody else is the aggressor, somebody else is the victim. It is not so. In the mind it arises, and in the mind it is resolved. In the mind we are related to everything.

When we abdicate our creative energy, then whatever our nightmare is, that will become our reality. Our human nature knows what is true. All of us have felt the sacred fire of truth and at some point in our lives have made commitments to upholding it. We are all being asked, "Yes or no? Are you in the stream, or are you trying to hug the rocks?" We can't say "Maybe" or "I'm working on it, and tomorrow it will be all right." In *this* moment it is all right, when we cultivate seeds of good cause, when we remember the beauty in one another, when we remember that life is inhalation and exhalation. Everything is going and it is also coming; we are dreaming this dream together, and it has no beginning and no end.

Through the vibrancy of mind seeking to know, our lives have been sparked. Every aspect of our life is following this same principle. Whatever we see around us, be it joyous or sad, somehow the seeds of its manifestation have been cast upon the sea of experience by one's own feelings, actions, and thoughts.

Let us remember the prayers that have come to us through our families. If you think your family religion is unimportant, it is only because you have not yet really looked to the essence of the truth within it. We can all trace our roots to the Great Tree of Peace. Many roots, many nations, many religions, all on one Earth. And the root of that sacred Tree of Peace is also within our brain; the Tree of Life and the spiral of the DNA are symbols to remind us of continuity. By your thinking and desire you will be brought here again and again until you awaken to the sacred light within yourself and every being.

So it is not just for ourselves that we pray. What we pray is that all may recall enlightened mind; we pray that all may come again to perceive the beauty of what is. It is not something out there, far away. It is in the heart. In the Tsalagi way of praying we are not asking for something; all we need is already here in abundance. When we pray we are giving thanks for what is and affirming our intention to manifest what is good for all people. So in the prayer there is a reminder for the action; prayer and action are the same. What is the use of understanding how to grow corn when your neighbors are starving and you don't share that knowledge? What is it to receive the gift of your grandmother without living it and sharing it?

May we begin again to honor the sacred practices of our ancestors. Candles, fireplace, fire, altar, cross, star, half moon, triangle; sacred symbols, all are doorways to clear mind. There is a secret message given in the prayer. When you recite the Twenty-third Psalm you are connecting with all who have understood reality through the tradition that psalm expresses; when someone sings a sacred song, that is your grandmother reminding you of what is. The coming-of-age ceremony, the song rising from the young person's heart, connects one to all one's ancestors.

To understand is not as important as to be, because understanding in itself implies a separation, someone to understand and something to be understood. The knowing is within you, the flow of breath. All the old people have given us this message. It may have become codified and dogmatic, but still the kernel of the one truth is there.

People praying together is a beginning—and still the Earth is asking more of us. She is asking that we take one another's hands and that we grow gardens together, that we put aside the idea of "my" garden and "your" garden. It is "our" garden. Look at some of the old people living around you. Whatever they are doing or not doing, they have done more than you—and they have something to say. When society falls flat, when the culture is dying, the elders are disrespected and we forget how to give or receive. There are things that one can *live*, not just pray and think about. Chop wood for some old man and take it to him. And the lady who lives by herself, who can't get around without her walker, go and visit her once in a while, ask if she needs something from the store. These things we have forgotten, and that forgetting is the sickness of the time. We have all been given clear direction as to what right life, right action is, and yet it has come to the point now where many even doubt that the family is something to be preserved. Family is the circle of humanity. Everything is our relative. We cannot put aside the idea of mother and father and extended family because that one note becomes two, becomes three, becomes four. The family becomes the clan and the nation and the whole planet.

There are beings all around who are watching the Earth to see if we can fulfill the plan of love and peace on this planet. The medicine people, the holy people, are asking for time for the good seeds to sprout. "We are working on it," they are saying. "The people are waking up. We promise to come correct." The Mother is saying, "I don't know, you have had so many warnings, so many opportunities. When will you see?" And the people are saying, "We are still trying." So let us see now. Will people really live in peace and respect one another? Are you willing to put aside a little time each week to share with other people? Are you willing to put aside some time where you meditate and pray together? That is the basis of community. Everything is related. Mother Earth cannot be renewed without our renewal; the pollution in the atmosphere will not be transmuted until the pollution of the mind is transformed. And the transformation comes from putting aside the idea of "them" and "us" and understanding that we are all human beings here together. It is we who have the capability and the responsibility to renew life here on Earth.

It is not so easy to be a human being. Many walk and run, think and talk, have the body of a human being—but there is still a hungry echo, a confused being. What is that? It is wanting. It is living for tomorrow. "Tomorrow it will get better, tomorrow I will know more." But *now* is what is happening. Here we are in the moment. Be present. Understand the patterns of discord. Purify, reform the thought and action by contemplating what has been accomplished. Transformation is a subtle process. It is easy to slip, easy to think, "It's getting better." That is the hungry spirit again; it always talks in terms of more or less. That is confusion, taking us out of the moment. Just see what is. Commit to right action.

All that is to be learned is in the heart. All of creation is a thought of which you are part. Wisdom is in your heart; look within. My family taught me that we came from the stars. Earth and stars: the spiral has neither up nor down, neither in nor out. The energies of Earth and heavens are coming together within us all the time, continually in motion, and within that motion is utter stillness. My grandfather said, "Go sit, listen to the stars. Feel the stars above your head. What are they? Explore them. Listen."

I invite you to now to explore and in that exploration to recognize clarity of mind. Reweave with the light those spaces where emotion and mind may have been torn asunder, reweave where some subtle distortion may have obscured your view of wisdom's fire in your own nature. Come again to the circle of your knowing. Let us explore the many realms of the One.

Meditation[1]

Sitting easily, spine erect, breathing naturally, fully, let mind become still. Breathe in, breathe out. Sense or visualize a spiral of light descending from heaven through crown of head, a second spiral ascending from Earth through base of spine. Two spirals of sacred light, mother and father, heaven and Earth, meeting in your heart, dancing in your spine. Sense in *sacrum,* base of spine, a golden triangle within which burn the Elder Fires Above, three sacred fires of manifestation: blue fire of will, red fire of compassion, yellow fire of active intelligence. Energy spirals up from Earth through sacrum to *navel* center, deep forest-green ring just below umbilicus, receiving from Earth five rivers of color and sound feeding five organ systems. A-E-I-O-U chant arises from navel, resonating deep within your spine, aligning your intention to be and your being here on Earth in this time. Rising light illumines *solar plexus* center, blue square filled with brilliant orange sun of solar consciousness. Chant *Ha-ha-ha-haa,* diaphragm expelling fear, anger, shame, blame, one with stream of clear light. In *heart* center, see two triangles, one pointing up and one down, apexes meeting. At their joining a deep rose light arises, filling your body, surrounding you with its glow of compassionate wisdom. Breathe in, breathe out, perceive energy of equanimity. Chant the *Ah* sound, radiate the rosy light of love-wisdom. *Throat* center receives ascending spiral light, deep indigo blue tunnel illumined by a single star, center of expression and manifestation. Let the sound *Ooo* become one with blue vortex of Creation's song. Ever moving, light enters golden triangle in center of *forehead,* wisdom eye of awakened mind. Chant *Eee* as crown of head opens to receive light from the stars above.

Above the head seven stars, one above the other, doorways of consciousness. From the stars, cascading rainbow light fills your mind and body, infusing you with vibrancy and purity. Breathe in, breathe out, draw in luminosity through every atom.

Now from your heart send out waves of rose light to touch your family, friends, co-workers, community, bathing all relations in the gentle glow of compassionate care. Breathe in, draw that rose light back into your heart. Rest in the stillness.

In completing the meditation, draw the light energy back within your spine;

ascending and descending spirals merge. Arise, peaceful and vibrant with the light, giving thanks for the gift of pure mind, the wisdom fire within. It is well.

NOTES

1. This meditation derives from the meditation practice of the Ywahoo lineage as taught by Eli Ywahoo, which is the foundation practice of Sunray Meditation Society and Sunray Peacekeepers throughout the world. The Basic Meditation is also available on tape and video cassette, with instruction by Dhyani Ywahoo.

25

The New Age and Rational Thought
AND A Rainbow of Expression

Shirley MacLaine

Film star and political activist Shirley MacLaine (b. 1934) received additional notice during the 1980s as an outspoken representative of the New Age movement. MacLaine's autobiographical narrative *Out on a Limb* (1983) told of her search for spiritual answers through the phenomenon of channeling and through UFO experiences in the Peruvian Andes. When a film version of the book appeared in 1987 and aired on national television, MacLaine achieved a reputation seemingly overnight as a leading New Age teacher. She began to conduct weekend seminars in various cities throughout the United States and to offer self-help guidance for other spiritual seekers. In her *Going Within* (1989), MacLaine built on seminar content to share her ideas with a larger public. At the core of her message and her book was the South Asian, and then theosophical, understanding of the physical energies of the body in terms of chakras. Named for the Sanskrit term for "wheel," these are conceived as energy vortices that appear at seven major body sites and at numerous smaller ones—exchange systems that bring the energetic universe of the outside in and of the inside out. According to this view, when the chakras turn properly—in the right direction and with the right amount of energy—health, wholeness, and spiritual luminosity result. When they are blocked, the individual is in trouble. In the chapters reprinted here from MacLaine's book, she offers a brief theoretical synthesis for the New Age through quantum physics and a journey through the seven major chakras of the body as she understands them. In so doing, she demonstrates that the knowing of knowing through the mind can be knowledge of the physical body itself and that the goal of balancing human energies needs to be acknowledged as metaphysical.

The New Age and Rational Thought

It is as vital to be physical
as it is to be spiritual.

To find God within oneself it would seem necessary at least to acknowledge his existence. The knotty question of whether God exists, and if so, where, points up a basic difference between Eastern and Western systems of consciousness. The Eastern search for God is directed within the individual; the Western search, without. The Eastern sage believes God is within and integral to human existence. The consciousness of Western religion says God is separate from man, superior to him, and that the deity's existence must be accepted on faith.

But now we have an astounding and marvelous thing happening. Science, which traditionally has had to maintain a position of "no proof, hence no God" (and no one is more hidebound than your average scientist), now finds itself in the rather delicate condition of having to admit that, yes, there *is* something, neither energy nor matter, but *some*thing whose existence we have proved but which we cannot really measure, or weigh, or see. Because if we try to observe it, it changes. If we even think about it, it changes! And this non-energy, non-matter, non-solid something is the stuff of which the universe is made. What a dilemma! Because nobody has yet figured out how this chameleon "something" has the knowledge to make itself into a planet or a poodle.

The Eastern system of thought tends toward going within for the answer. It is right-brained: intuitive, open, capable of holding contradictory concepts without confusion. The traditional Western system of thinking is more left-brained: linear, logical, and rational.

New Age thinking is an attempt to balance the two by pressing past the linear thinking of the rational to include the depth and dimension of the intuitive. I have found that meditation and the solitude of going within opens up my internal universe, whereupon my previous concepts of time, of life and death, of God himself seem quite limited. It is a liberating and adventurous experience.

Similarly, from the scientific books I have been reading, I've learned that the field of subatomic quantum physics has opened up a whole new world for modern scientists to explore. Michael Talbot's masterly work *Beyond the Quantum* is a particularly clear and fascinating presentation of complex theories and experiments of several New Age scientists. Some of their conclusions have given rise to speculation about the "realness" of reality and highly controversial views (in scientific circles at least) on what can only be described as mysticism. Science and spirituality seem to be converging. Alain Aspect, for instance, in his 1982 experiment, proved that at least one of two conclusions had to be true—either reality as we define it does not exist, i.e., *we* create reality to be what we think it is, *or* communication with the past *and with our future* does exist.

Rupert Sheldrake, a biochemist, has postulated a superimposed *field* (web of information) which he calls a "morphogenetic field," or M-field, to account for the conveyance of information within like species. He calls this informational movement "morphic resonance." On an experimental basis his theory gains support from a thirty-four-year study by William McDougall in which rats from totally different, widely separated genetic lines, nevertheless learned the new useful habits that only one group was working with—except that "learn" is slightly misleading as this information appears to have become universally available once a certain number of rats had acquired it. In other words, the information had entered the rat M-field.

Again, there is the famous "hundredth monkey effect"—not really a controlled experiment, but an observed event that occurred in the 1950's on the island of Koshima. Researchers performing various studies of the local population of monkeys dumped sweet potatoes on the beach. This particular species of monkey had never encountered sweet potatoes before, and while they liked the vegetable they clearly did not like its sandy coating. Then one monkey genius discovered she could clean the potatoes by washing them in the sea. First a few other monkeys, observing this, did the same, later followed by several more busy potato washers. Then quite suddenly, all at once, the entire troop took to washing their potatoes. At this point, other researchers, *on islands far removed from the original,* reported that all *their* monkeys started to utilize the same washing technique!

The conclusion is that information acquired by a certain number of any given species acts like a flashpoint—from that point forward the species as a whole is equipped with that information. The new knowledge has entered their M-field via morphic resonance. Moreover, since the species can be widely separated geographically but all its descendants everywhere will also be born with that information, when Sheldrake talks about an M-field he is talking about a subatomic informational web that operates across both space and time. In addition, the M-field may well be connected to the subatomic particle behavior that always expresses itself as a movement toward *wholeness,* a movement that is true for all forms and species, including crystals. . . . And, in further addition, the M-field may account for the ability of undifferentiated cells to decide which ones will grow into a hand, or a head, or whatever; or, when a group of generalized cells is divided in half, to create twins—that is, two *wholes.*

And as recently as 1984, Nobel Prize-winning neurophysiologist Sir John Eccles announced the discovery of what he believes to be biochemical evidence supporting the existence of the human soul.

Perhaps I should take back my remark about "hidebound scientists." . . .

Many, many men and women in the worlds of science are now opening their minds to new ways of thinking. In the past ten years, extraordinary experimentation has shattered long-held beliefs and opened up whole new areas for exploration and speculation. Science still shies away from words like *God* and *soul* (despite Sir John), using more comfortable phraseology such as *information,* or even *universal information bank* (scientists do not, of course, acknowledge any coincidence between this concept and the system of information known as "Akashic Records" in the East). What is happening, in fact, is that Eastern mysticism, which intuitively accepts so much, and Western pragmatism, which insists on scientifically proving so much, are coming together. In my opinion, this New Age is the time when the intuitive beliefs of the East and the scientific thinking of the West could meet and join—the twain wed at last. For me, both are necessary, and both are desirable.

With this understanding I can more easily appreciate how people (including myself) can remember past existences and "clairvoyantly" see future times.

I found in my travels that such experiences are well accepted in the East, while here at home in the West these ideas still disturb our linear concepts of rationality. But rationality itself is a tenuous concept. We "stack" information to conform to our reality—that is, we see what we want to see, influenced by what we already know. The question of reality then becomes a question of perception, conditioning, and beliefs.

How to sort out the multilayered levels of belief and perception is what is motivating new approaches to truth in science.

Basic to New Age subatomic discoveries is the concept that in the subatomic world—the stuff of the universe—everything, every last thing, is linked. The universe is a gigantic, multidimensional web of influences, or information, light particles, energy patterns, and electromagnetic "fields of reality." Everything it is, everything we are, everything we do, is linked to everything else. There is no separateness.

This understanding brings us to the most controversial concept of the New Age philosophy: the belief that God lies within, and therefore *we* are each part of God. Since there is no separateness, we are each Godlike, and God is in each of us. We experience God and God experiences through us. We are literally made up of God energy, therefore we can create whatever we want in life because we are each co-creating with the energy of God—the energy that makes the universe itself.

Science itself is attempting to establish, in the exploration of subatomic-particle behavior, whether mankind is creating its own reality with the God Source energy, or with *some* form of universal energy of "information." Life itself is a creation from this energy. What is it, then? If the pattern of that energy has order, and balance, and grace (which science claims it does), if it has meaning in terms of all life, what is to distinguish it from what the New Age calls God?

In my reading on the relationship between mysticism and quantum physics I was fascinated to learn that each organ of the human body has a harmonious energy pattern that science can now identify. The organs are matter within an electromagnetic energy field, which William Burr described as "the blueprint for life." In the spatial relationship between the molecules in that energy field, the molecules are, relatively speaking, farther apart than the planets in our perceived universe are to each other. The universe within, then, is more vast than the universe without! Furthermore, according to science the solidity of matter is actually an illusion. The grand illusion, as a matter of fact, is that our physical world is solid. It is not. It is a molecular structure of subatomic particles that *appears* to be solid. Is this science or is this mysticism?

Science says there are three basic components to the event of an experience: time, space, and matter. When there is a consensus that each of those component parts exists, we have what we term reality. So it only takes an agreement of perception for anything to exist as real. According to science, the physical dimension becomes real only through the consciousness of our intentions. Reality is then actually an intention that becomes an illusion of consciousness.

The molecules that create the illusion of physical reality are organized by electromagnetic fields of energy. If through our "intentional consciousness" we alter the frequency of those electromagnetic fields, we "defy" (or alter) reality. Examples of that are feats by yogis who stop their heartbeats by will (i.e., intention of consciousness), fire-walking, levitation (reversing the polarities of the body relating to gravity), and so on.

So each of us is a living, walking electrical field of energy. Our field of energy organizes the molecular structure that we *perceive*, both within and without, as physical reality.

One of the most extraordinary and beautiful truths about subatomic worlds is that they tend to "move" toward order. Each of us is an amalgamation of frequencies that *needs* to be harmonious and compatible, whose natural order is to move toward harmony. This harmony, this order, is impeded and distorted by feelings of fear, anger, hatred, et cetera. Here, right here, is the interface between who we think we are and the subatomic world from which we have created ourselves.

Conscious awareness of these dynamics within can help to bring our frequencies into balance. When that occurs, "reality" itself goes beyond our customary comprehension of it—the form of reality takes on a dimension we do not normally perceive.

Highly self-realized and disciplined people with total self-awareness can create antibodies that cure disease. Of course, that is a contradiction in itself because totally self-realized people rarely become dis-eased. They are in total "easement" within themselves. They will be more, or less, dis-eased depending on the degree of their spiritual awareness. Disease in the body, as I have learned from experience, begins first with a blockage of energy in the spirit. For me, *all* of my physical problems begin in my *consciousness*. And when I stop to meditate, when I go within and literally "ask" my Higher Self why I am manifesting a particular physical problem, I usually get an answer and always it relates to some fear, rejection, or feeling of "nonworthiness." I try to reconnect with spiritual harmony and God. If I'm successful, I get well. This particular aspect of New Age thinking—self-healing—is a highly developed stage, obviously a long way down the road to full self-awareness.

It requires patience and a full confrontation of one's own consciousness, which can sometimes be extremely painful, because it involves the most difficult of all human feelings: *self*-forgiveness. I have found that I first have to *admit* that I am afraid, or angry, or rejected, or feeling undeserving. *Then* I can forgive myself for allowing myself such disharmony. When I forgive myself, healing begins.

So, since both scientists *and* mystics claim that harmony is the natural order of life, I try continually to remind myself that I have the right and indeed the Divine inheritance to reflect that harmony in myself. It's not easy in a world full of suffering and anger and anguish, but I am learning that if I work on myself to attempt to achieve an internal reality of harmony, it alters my physical reality.

It is now possible to monitor and correlate how a change of consciousness affects physical reality. An individual capable of this is manipulating his or her physical reality by manipulating his own electromagnetic fields of energy. And he does that by consciously orchestrating his patterns of thought. The resulting manifestation of the thought patterns alters the physical reality. Thus, we begin to see how it is possible to create one's own physical reality with the use of thought and higher conscious awareness.

Instrumentation now makes it possible to quantify these phenomena and therefore observe the biological and psychological effects. As a result of these observations, some members of the scientific community are now saying we need to factor in consciousness in our scientific studies. The behavior of that which is being observed is directly altered by the consciousness of the observer. There is no separateness. We each have an inextricable effect on everyone and every thing around and beyond us. Each and every cell in our bodies is reacting to electromagnetic information from the universe at every moment. *We are all, everything is, connected.*

This was a truly profound understanding for me, particularly in a sociopolitical sense. If our bodies, made up of vibratory patterns, resonate to the "information," or the "field," of the entire subatomic world, and each individual vibratory pattern moves toward harmony, then when we are in touch with that harmony we are more peaceful. Suddenly I could understand how spiritual awareness included relevance to politics and society as a whole. The more aware we made ourselves of our own electromagnetic fields, the more integrity of harmony we would have within ourselves and with the rest of the world in the harmonious universe. The more unaware we remained, the more randomly chaotic our lives would continue to be. Each one of us is different because we each have accumulated different libraries of stored information in our experience. But we can become more aware of our personal libraries with techniques of breathing, meditation, exercise, and visualization. In the solitude of these practices we not only become more in touch with our own accumulated information, but in doing so we can more easily exchange and share with others and their experiences, making it very much simpler to relate to and understand the differences in reality that we each perceive. Thus, we would more readily understand ways to achieve peace with those who perceived reality differently than we do. Spiritual technology and Soul Physics were becoming politically and socially pragmatic to me.

Science now says that the DNA molecule is in effect an antenna and that each coding has its own electromagnetic wavelength. It is believed that the DNA code carries within it racial memories of the collective unconscious and that we create the physical dimension with DNA codes. If this is so, then I can understand why past-life recall is possible. Again, I realize how the Eastern systems of thought have gone within to find the source of our human truth, while the Western systems of thought have pursued the puzzle of origins through the sciences of technology. *Both systems are valid.*

Science makes a set of hypotheses, makes its observations, then experiments to prove or disprove. When there is a large enough consensus on the result, it becomes scientific fact. The Eastern mind would say the scientist is creating what he is observing and therefore what he wants to believe anyway. The Western scientist has to concede that the electromagnetic patterns of his thoughts are a field of energy that directly affects what he is observing.

Each warrior of truth has a separate path. Scientists and mystics are inseparable, though, each motivated by the search for the creator of the grand design of which we are a part and to which each of us is a contributor. For simplicity's sake, some of us call that grand design God.

When I change my consciousness to include myself in that God-creator, I change my external reality. And I find that the more harmonious I am in my spiritual consciousness, the more I can be tolerant of others, peaceful with myself, and capable of allowing myself to feel the natural principles of integration and harmony with everything in creation. If I'm out of alignment with my spiritual nature, nothing much goes well for me and I am unhappy and frustrated to boot.

As soon as I understood the positive logic in accepting the God energy within myself, it didn't seem so blasphemous to me, so outrageously ridiculous to others. My limiting education and narrow systems of thought had actually prevented me from understanding the deeper and more real possibility of harmony and peace. I don't mean to say that now I feel peacefully harmonious all the time. Far from it. But whenever I really get out of balance I look for silence. Silence is necessary to perceive the truth of our God-selves inwardly. We could take the mystery out of mysticism *and* out of technology if we allowed ourselves to find the time and the silence necessary to access that eternal God energy within.

This is not what I would call a "cult of self," nor is it selfish, self-indulgent, self-centered, or self-aggrandizing. It is what I call survival. It is evolution. It is basic pragmatic functionalism. It is necessary to growth, progress, and a more humane technology. It would help us clarify our intent and galvanize our purpose. It would more fully enrich our lives and inspire our work. The more peaceful and happy we are individually, the better work we produce. The more angry, chaotic, and out of touch with ourselves, the more the work reflects that state of mind, that negativity.

And all of it comes down to the belief that we each contain and hold the God-spark within us. Our humanity toward one another directly reflects the humanity we feel for ourselves. And that humanity is directly related to self-love. If God is love and each of us possesses God within us, then all of us would be happier and more peaceful with one another, recognizing that the more we try to *express* as God, the more harmony there will be in the world.

That is the basic principle of the New Age. And science agrees that harmony is the natural order of the universe.

Begin with self; recognize the God within, and the result will be the recognition, with tolerance and love, that everyone else possesses God within as well. In other words, we are each part of God experiencing the adventure of life.

A Rainbow of Expression

We do not have a soul. We are a soul that has
a body, with functions, needs, and
feelings. We have a body to experience and we gain
experience for the soul.

In the course of my spiritual investigations I learned about a specific power of aligning with certain energies within, which has altered and improved my concept of internal harmony ever since. A consistent and ancient belief held by man down through the ages is that the physical body is but the reflection of a series of more subtle bodies of energy within, and that these subtle bodies of energy reflect the vibration of the God Source. *That* vibration is the vast energy at our disposal if we know how to access it.

The Egyptians, the Chinese, the Greeks, the North American Indian and African tribes, the Incas, the early Christians, the Hindus of India, the Buddhists of Asia, and today's metaphysicists and mystics everywhere in the world share, to some degree, a common belief: that the body is only a physical manifestation of energies that together create an entity beyond that which can be seen only with the naked eye, and that those levels of existence, those energies, that entity, reflect the nature of God and the universe.

The correlation between man and God has been the subject of the most profound of all wonderings. The ancient schools of study focused this correlation on esoteric systems of energy located in seven centers of the human body. These centers are called *chakras,* translated from the Hindi to mean "wheels of energy."

Just as there are seven levels of consciousness, seven ages of man, seven colors in the rainbow color spectrum, and seven notes on the Western musical scale, there are seven primary chakras in the human body. We cannot see the soul or measure the aura of human energy; nor can we measure these centers. But we know they exist.

The chakras represent the subtle anatomy of human beings just as the physical organs represent the gross anatomy. The subtle and the gross are connected. There are seven endocrine glands, which correspond to the seven chakras. Therefore, our bodies (the vehicles through which we express ourselves) reflect the balance or the imbalance of subtle and gross anatomy. As I was learning I was continually reminded that when and if the spiritual is out of kilter, ignored, or misused, it will show up in the physical—*not* the other way around! The physical (gross) is a reflection of the spiritual (subtle).

Western systems of thought, dedicated to "rational" provability, to the measurement of progress by the wonders of technological development, have lost recognition of the chakra wheels of energy. In fact, I don't know if we were ever aware of them. But the ancient Oriental masters were adept at this spiritual technology. Happily, this knowledge and understanding are finding new recognition in the West. Here is a summary of what I learned in my travels through India, the Far East, and the Himalayas.

* * *

According to the masters, the soul creates the body in accordance with the laws of the earth plane, in order to provide a "house" for itself in this physical dimension. The physical body thus gives the soul the opportunity to be focused in time and space. The chakras govern this physical reality because the seven centers of consciousness are the areas through which the human personality experiences itself. The chakras, then, are both a communicative, and a controlling link, connecting the soul entity (the Higher Self), the personality, and the body that the soul has created through which to express itself.

Since this human personality is the medium through which we communicate with one another, recognition of the chakras and the various energies they hold and connect to is essential to an understanding of what human expression in the physical is all about.

It was helpful for me to think of my body as a musical instrument inside of which were seven notes, seven different rates of vibration, and a spectrum of seven colors. If I played only one note or focused on one color all the time, my instrument would be monotonous and boring. But learning to work with all of the notes, colors, and vibrations created a harmonious, kaleidoscopic work of art. I learned I could work with my musical instrument and play harmonious music for myself.

The seven chakras of energy are not in need of opening. They are always open, spinning, and in complete harmony. It is our minds that are closed and don't recognize their harmonious importance and existence. Therefore, we don't work to open the chakras, we work to open the mind to recognize the chakras. That is why the basic steps of meditation are so important.

Our personalities become a product of the recognition allowed by our minds of chakra "language," or energy, and are rich or limited, open or closed, to the degree of that recognition. The more we work with the spiritual dimensions of our beings, the more we are conscious of the chakras, the more attuned and centered as human beings we become. When we attune the conscious mind to the spiritual energies of the chakras, the mind itself begins to expand with an awareness of its own higher consciousness. So it is through the chakras that we fully integrate mind, body, and spirit.

Our physical sciences look to biological and physiological patterns of data as the source of the human personality, but when we align our chakras we are integrating a memory of our soul's experience, which allows our personality to manifest—make visible—the aspects that make it unique. The human personality then emerges as an expression of the soul: the body is merely the vehicle, or temple through which the soul incarnates and expresses itself.

Since the chakras are created with soul energy, when we attune to them we are attuning to the specialized centers that have shaped our characters and our natures each time we have entered the physical plane to learn and experience. The more we are attuned to the unique energies within our bodies, the more we can open our consciousness to the higher resource to which they are connected and of which we, and they, are a part.

The more we are connected to higher resources, the more infinite we become as human beings. Carl G. Jung claimed that the chakras were the gateways of consciousness in man, receptive points for the inflow of energies from the cosmos and the spirit and soul of man; that the chakras are always aligned with the Divine God energy because they are the creation of the soul.

The ancient masters claimed that good health depends upon the correct alignment and functioning of these seven etheric energy centers: that the union of spirit and matter manifests as consciousness in the physical, and the seven chakras govern how our consciousness is experienced in the physical body. How then to open the mind to the energies of the chakras?

In order to understand the meaning of aligning the chakras it is necessary to understand the area of physical consciousness that each one represents.

* * *

For me, the seven chakras can best be identified by using key words that represent the emotional issues associated with each chakra. The function of the physical glands associated with the emotional issues of each chakra then becomes clear.

The first chakra, also known as the base chakra or root chakra, is located at the base of the spine and is defined as the chakra that governs one's understanding of the physical dimension. It is the grounding chakra—that is, it grounds one in the Earth, it puts both feet on the ground: it is pragmatic, ultrarealistic, the "survival" chakra responsible for our balance and our attitudes toward fight or flight. It is therefore the chakra that externalizes as the adrenal gland, and it also governs the functioning of the kidneys and the spinal column. It is esoterically perceived as *red.*

Indian Hindu Vedic seers claim that the base chakra also channels the energy of the human will and that the entire human system balances itself on this base support. It is the seat of insecurity, where survival, possessiveness, and materialism lie. It is referred to as the survival chakra because it is through this center that we feel fear or anger when threatened.

These negative aspects to survival lead to an interesting anomaly. Because the root chakra is ground-based, its fundamental nature is secure. But the personality, conditioned by the process of evolution, has learned to fire off alarm signals, triggered by *perceived* threat, so that the adrenals will start pumping adrenaline.

The intriguing thing that explorers have learned about animals living in an environment previously devoid of mankind is that *they do not perceive humans as a threat.* Even now, animals in the wild react to their natural predators only while an actual hunt is in progress. The rest of the time they get along peacefully, allowing quiet coexistence at a respectful distance.

Is it conceivable that when humans first became hunters and eaters of flesh, the glandular tie to the security chakra evolved in a distorted fashion? I wonder how far back we would have to go to learn when people first became afraid of people. This would be an interesting area for exploration as greater skills develop in working with the chakras, and might help to explain some of the basic insecurities that we as individuals may feel.

As I learned how to work with my chakras, it was with this first chakra—the red chakra, the root and base of the human chakra system—that I worked with first. In the meantime, though, I needed to learn where and what the other six chakras were.

The second chakra is the sexual chakra, the chakra of creativity, located in the reproductive organs (the ovaries in the female and the testes in the male). It is the color *orange* and governs one's creative attitudes in relationships, sex, and reproduction.

The third chakra is located in the solar plexus. Its glandular externalization manifests in the pancreas and it governs the action of the liver, stomach, gallbladder, spleen, and certain aspects of the nervous system. This chakra is the clearinghouse for emotional sensitivities and issues of personal power. Its color is seen as *yellow*.

Sensitives often comment that they see most people who have emotional attachments to children and loved ones "leaking" from the third chakra. The yellow color spills out of its center and depletes the energy of the individual experiencing concern, possessiveness, and proprietary interest in the lives of those they love. This does not mean one should not be concerned, for instance, about one's children. But the concern should be in terms of the child's well-being, not for the relief of one's own possessive anxiety.

This third chakra gives all of us more problems than any other because it is essentially the "seat of emotional living." Out of unbalanced emotions come ulcers, digestive problems, and liver, spleen, and pancreatic troubles. The positive and negative energy polarities are located in the solar plexus chakra, which, when balanced, is bi-polar, meaning that the positive (masculine-yang) and negative (female-yin) are perfectly harmonious. When a person crosses his arms in front of his solar plexus, he is blocking off the energy of that potential balance by adopting a defensive posture; or to put it another way, he is protecting his feelings by crossing his arms.

When a person is overwhelmed with emotion there is an automatic triggering of an almost involuntary act called crying. When tears well up, if allowed to proceed, they often lead to sobbing. The physical act of sobbing produces a gentle—or sometimes not so gentle—massage of the solar plexus. The deep and heavy sob caresses the solar plexus, which can then relax, releasing the pent-up emotion that it was unable to process in the first place. "Having a good cry" enables the third, yellow, chakra at the solar plexus center to reestablish its balance and release itself from emotional overload.

If the sobbing doesn't bring this about, sometimes a person will vomit. The act of vomiting activates the diaphragm muscles. The diaphragm itself is a dome-shaped muscle that separates the lower three chakras from the upper four chakras. Vomiting actually clears out the physical manifestation of what is causing the emotional overload. That is why we feel so "spacey" and mellow after a good cry or a purging vomit! It is the body's defense mechanism against feeling more of an emotional overload than it is able to handle.

The fourth chakra is called the heart chakra. Its glandular externalization manifests in the thymus. The fourth chakra governs the heart, blood, and circulatory system. It has a strong influence on the vagus nerve, located in the brain, and also governs the immune and endocrine systems. Its color, usually seen as *green,* depends on the level of clairvoyant perspective from which it is viewed.

When I began meditating on the heart chakra, I soon realized that the key word was *acceptance*—acceptance of others, and acceptance of the love within self. It is often said that when we pray we speak to God. Meditation is when God speaks to us through the God within via the communicative centers of energy. Achieving true meditation on all the chakras is a path to complete inner peace.

The Sanskrit word for the heart center is *anahata.* It means "that which is ever new, that which is self-sustaining." Through the heart chakra we "fall in love." Instinctively, when we recognize the attraction in another we move from the heart chakra down to the yellow solar plexus chakra of emotional integration, to the bright orange sexual chakra, which is motivated by love, and finally to the root chakra, the warm red energy that inspires us to settle down, to ground ourselves in the Earth with this person.

The Eastern mystics say we define our personalities through the heart chakra, which they believe is the core of the soul. The soul manufactures the "forever hormone," which, when experienced, keeps us feeling forever young through love.

The "forever hormone" is said by the masters to emanate as energy from the heart when one is in a state of love. This energy hormone nourishes all of the lower chakras, where we feel insecurity, survival needs, and fear.

It is amusing to me that we never "go (up) in love"—we always "fall (down) in love." To me that is the intuitive recognition of the soul attraction first experienced in the heart chakra, which then spills down through the energy systems of emotion (third chakra) and sexuality (second chakra) until it becomes anchored in the Earth (first chakra).

The fifth chakra is the throat chakra. Its focal point of activity is the thyroid gland and it governs the lungs, the vocal cords, the bronchial apparatus, and metabolism. This chakra is usually seen as *blue.* It is the center not only of expression and communication but of judgment.

I find that it is extremely important to work with the fifth chakra these days because individual self-expression *without* judgment is the task of balancing a free democracy. We feel the urge to tell the truth as we see it. But we should try to accomplish this without judgmental condemnations that hurt others. Again, when we remember that what we perceive in another is a reflection of ourselves, we become less judgmental. So when we freely express harsh judgment of another, we are in effect talking about those aspects of ourselves that trouble *us* the most. I find that when I feel negatively judgmental about someone, by examining that feeling in meditation on the fifth, blue, chakra, I usually achieve better understanding of my own communicative dynamics and better judgment of what to say and what not to say to others.

The sixth chakra is located in the center of the forehead. It is better known as the third eye and externalizes as the pituitary gland. Its color is usually seen as *indigo*—a deep, vibrant color composed of red and blue. Primarily it governs the lower brain and nervous system, the ears, the nose, and the left eye, which is the eye of the personality.

Idealism and imagination center in the sixth chakra, which also reflects inner vision and governs the outer expression of that inner vision. The mystics say that to access a limitless potential of thought it is necessary to "tickle" the pituitary. They accomplish this through visualization in meditation. They focus on the third eye and allow their inner vision to be limitless.

The seventh chakra, or crown chakra, is located at the top of the head. Its color is seen as *violet* or sometimes *white*. It externalizes as the pineal gland and governs the upper brain and right eye. Within the crown chakra are the counterparts of all the other chakras. It is the chakra that speaks, in combination with other chakras, to unlimited consciousness and Divine purpose. It is through this chakra, they say, that one reaches, ultimately, the feeling of integration with God.

The upper three chakras form what is known as the Golden Triangle, which represents a triad of energy reflecting the perfection of cosmic harmony in a balanced way, which then infuses the neurological, or nervous system, within the physical body. A kind of esoteric pumping effect occurs whereby three harmonious cosmic energies are "milked down" through the entire chakra system to the root chakra, which grounds the harmony and thus provides a feeling of security. Thus reinforced, the cosmic energy travels back up the chakra system until it reaches the crown chakra again and the cycle is complete, whole. The energy is, as it were, plugged in, the circuit connected.

Unfortunately, in most of us the return of cosmic energy back up the chakra system is blocked in either the sexual chakra or the solar plexus, in our strong feelings of attraction/deprivation, or love/possession, need/power, et cetera. The problem does not lie in whether or not we are infusing the cosmic energies. We are. But we tend to prevent their completing the circuit of power by allowing them to become stuck in the second and third chakras. Meditating on those chakra energy centers will help free the blockage. The results are often astonishing. Again, we will explore this form of meditative technique more fully later.

When all the chakras are recognized and aligned with the conscious mind, the consciousness of the individual is expanded and made more aware of the energy sources available for good health and happiness. An imbalance in the chakras (or, more precisely, imbalance in recognition of the chakras) disturbs and blocks the flow of energy within the consciousness and properly functioning physical health becomes distorted.

*   *   *

Meditating on the chakras was extremely important to me, because anything I could learn about how they related to my physical body was helpful in working with these energy centers. In learning how the chakras affected my body, I also learned something about how they contribute to emotional growth and development.

The philosophy surrounding the knowledge of the chakra energy centers included cycles of growth in terms of years. I learned that the development of the physical human body in relation to its soul is divided into cycles of seven. Each cycle deals with the emotional issues of the corresponding chakras.

The first seven years of a human being's life revolve around survival and instincts of adjusting to the physical earth-plane experience. One learns to crawl, walk, run, eat, and accept the physical expression of embracing, being loved and caressed, and so on. We develop our sense of balance until the physical form securely anchors itself to the Earth, according to how effectively these emotional experiences occur, and then prepares for its process of learning—the red, root chakra controls the assimilating of these processes.

In the second seven years (eight to fourteen years of age) sexuality develops and produces crises of various kinds so that the human being can develop the subjective mind, the capacity for creativity and for fuller consciousness of self-identity—sex and identity are controlled through the orange, genital chakra.

The third seven years (adolescence to age twenty-one) deal with issues of emotionality relating to other people, the assessment of personal power, and the practice of free will—all of the problems of adolescence are felt through the yellow, solar plexus chakra.

The fourth seven years (ages twenty-two to twenty-eight) develop a human's relationship to love—self-love and mature love of others—and abilities of evaluation and decision in terms of lifestyle. Through the green, heart chakra the individual decides during these years how harmonious he desires to be in life.

The fifth seven years (ages twenty-nine to thirty-five) are the years when a human questions and/or reaffirms the wisdom of his or her self-expression and is dealing heavily with the consequences of judgment in others. This is the time when we become profoundly aware that how we express ourselves is how we live with others.

In the sixth seven-year period (ages thirty-six to forty-two) we begin seriously to question our spiritual nature as it relates to the lifestyle we have created. All the knowledge we have gained begins to transmute to a kind of wisdom, and during these years we decide to develop our spiritual nature or we affirm the consequences of avoiding this growth.

In the seventh seven years (ages forty-three to forty-nine, or late forties and fifties) we actively attempt to integrate ourselves with the understanding of God—that is, to bring our exterior and interior lives together into a harmonious whole with the Source. That goes on for the rest of our lives.

We can become emotionally stuck, blocked, or damaged at any point along the line, and/or at differing points with respect to differing aspects of growth. We have all heard, for instance, of the infantilized male, or the child-woman. The task then is to free ourselves from those blockages of consciousness, which will automatically free up the blockages in our physical experience. Again, the body reflects the disorders of the soul.

Body Language

Body language—that is, the physical expression of interior blockage (or not, of course)—is an entire study in itself.

Dr. Anne Marie Bennstrom of the Ashram in Calabasas, California, has been studying what she calls "body types" for years. Since she is an expert physical culturist herself, she began to document the correlation between the language of the body and the blockages in consciousness of individuals whom she met and ultimately came to know. She says that in all her experience she never encountered a body that did not express, in physical terms, the internal attitudes of the consciousness it housed.

For example, a man with a short, squat body is predominantly interested in survival and in how his individual identity relates to home and hearth and material security. He is apt to be aggressive. Self-expression in a tall man, however, tends to appear as an overview tied to the future. "The short people are self-starters," says Bennstrom. "The tall men come in and take over to finish off the idea."

People with splayed, turned-out feet have energy that moves outward. They are outwardly motivated, always on the move, ready to travel, and often don't stop to think about what they are leaving behind. The splay-footed person throws caution to the winds and promises many things without thought of how to conserve the energy to accomplish any of them.

On the other hand (so to speak), pigeon-toed people tend to withhold their energy, sometimes tripping over their own best intentions. Such people tend also to be stubborn, defensive, and inflexible.

Anne Marie believes that the point of making these correlations is that changing the body attitude can assist in changing the emotional attitude. In working with people, if she reminds a pigeon-toed person to consciously turn the feet out more, the act itself affects the inner consciousness to be more outgoing.

The purpose, then, of altering the habits of a body type is to help an individual find "the middle way" and achieve more balance in life, to become more centered. If one can establish where the blockages lie, it is easier to offer advice on where that person should look for his own weakness.

The more balance we hold between the masculine and feminine (or yang and yin) in ourselves, the more streamlined our bodies become, because our bodies reflect our consciousness. Fat in any area equals emotion unexpressed. The more androgynously balanced we become, the less fat we hold. I do not mean androgynous in the sense of bisexuality, but androgynous as it relates to feeling equally balanced with the male and female aspects in ourselves.

There is an obvious link between human physicality and human consciousness. When the consciousness is expanded to include recognition of the esoteric and spiritual nature of man, the physical body reflects that recognition. Since physicality follows consciousness, we would do well to go to the source of our physical problems rather than to treat symptoms, although treating symptoms can free us to focus on the source.

Despite the dominance of traditional methods of medicine, there is an ever-increasing interest in exploring the roots of consciousness as a guide to a solution for physical suffering. And the roots of consciousness speak directly through the seven chakras of which the physical body is an expression.

To me, what is most attractive about this holistic approach is that it recognizes and honors the balancing of man's energies by means which acknowledge that we are more than simply physical beings.

26

The Tree and Its Parts

B. K. S. Iyengar

B. K. S. Iyengar (b. 1918) has spent a lifetime in India and other nations teaching his distinctive interpretation of hatha yoga. The most well-known yogic form in the West, hatha yoga is the physical discipline of postures and poses ('*āsanas*) designed to build flexibility, strength, and endurance and so to prepare the body for extended periods of meditation as well as to reverse processes of aging. The term *yoga* itself comes from a Sanskrit root meaning to "yoke" or "join"; and Iyengar and numerous other hatha yoga teachers understand their discipline as the yoking, or union, of the individual self or soul to the Universal Spirit. The Indian yogic system that Iyengar teaches, he and his followers say, is based on the classic *Yoga Sutras* of Patanjali (most likely actually a collective work produced between the second century B.C.E. and the third to fifth centuries C.E.). The Iyengar teachings have resulted in a codification of yogic postures and procedures and a worldwide certification process for yoga teachers, with Iyengar's large and authoritative *Light on Yoga* (1966) the bible of the movement. Characteristic of the Iyengar tradition is the achievement of a concentrated stillness. Iyengar students hold their postures, and the further they progress the longer they hold them. In the excerpt here, from Iyengar's *Tree of Yoga*—itself based on his lectures and discussions with students—it is clear that a posture should be held for an extended moment in time, in which the student becomes totally aware—totally conscious—of muscular groups and movement and, through that total mental and cellular awareness, involved in a profound act of meditation. For B. K. S. Iyengar's numerous American students, then, knowing through the mind becomes an intense knowing of the spirit residing in cells and bones and muscles.

Effort, Awareness, and Joy

When you are practising a pose in yoga, can you find the delicate balance between taking the pose to its maximum extent, and taking it beyond that point so that there is too much effort creating wrong tension in the body?

When you are overstretching somewhere to get the optimum movement, have you ever noticed that you are also giving too little attention to other parts of the body? That disturbs the body and makes it shake. If the root of a tree is weak, the tree itself cannot be strong. Suppose you are doing a head-balance. What happens if you stretch your legs in order to get a good pose and let your neck muscles become loose, or if your elbows do not grip the floor, so the fear comes that you are falling or swaying from side to side? Because the strong muscles try to control the pose, the weak muscles give way. When doing the pose, therefore, you have to maintain a single stretch from the floor to the top without letting any part drop. When you are stretching the legs, you have to send an alarm signal to your arms: 'I am stretching a leg, so don't lose your attention!' That is awareness. Because we lose our awareness and our attention is partial, we don't know whether we are holding the grip or not.

You can lose the benefits of what you are doing because of focusing too much partial attention on trying to perfect the pose. What are you focusing on? You are trying to perfect the pose, but from where to where? That is where things become difficult. Focusing on one point is concentration. Focusing on all points at the same time is meditation. Meditation is centrifugal as well as centripetal. In concentration, you want to focus on one point, and the other points lose their potential. But if you spread the concentration from the extended part to all the other parts of the body, without losing the concentration on the extended part, then you will not lose the inner action or the outer expression of the pose, and that teaches you what meditation is. Concentration has a point of focus; meditation has no points. That is the secret.

In concentration, you are likely to forget some parts of the body as you focus your attention on other parts. That is why you get pain in certain parts of the body. It is because the unattended muscles lose their power and are dropped. But you will not know that you are dropping them, because they are precisely the muscles in which you have momentarily lost your awareness. In yoga there is one thing you should all know: the weakest part is the source of action.

In any yoga pose, two things are required: sense of direction and centre of gravity. Many of us do not think of the sense of direction, yet in each pose, both the sense of direction and the centre of gravity need to be maintained. To maintain the centre of gravity, the muscles all have to be aligned with each other.

If there is an overstretch in certain muscles, the centre of gravity also shifts. Perhaps through insensitivity you are not aware that you are doing this. Insensitivity means that part of the body is dull—that it has no awareness—and this is the part where pain will develop. You may have the impression that there was no pain while you were performing the pose, but the pain comes later. How is it that you didn't feel any pain at the time?

Take the example of a pain in the back at the top of the buttock bone when you have been performing a forward bend such as paśchimottānāsana. If you have this problem, observe next time you perform the pose that one leg will be touching the floor and the other buttock slightly off the floor, and one sacro-iliac muscle will be stretching on the outside while on the other side, the inner part of the muscle stretches. That is due to one muscle being sensitive and the other insensitive. They each move according to their own developed memories and intelligence.

Are you aware of all these things? Perhaps you are not, because you don't meditate in the poses. You do the pose, but you don't reflect in it. You are focusing, trying to do the pose well. You want to do the optimum, but you are doing the optimum only on one side. That is known as concentration, not meditation. You must shift the light of awareness from that side to cover the other side as well; that is what is required for practice.

If you have any kind of problem, you have to observe what is happening in the pose. Is there alignment, or is there non-alignment? Perhaps your liver is extending, but your stomach is contracting, or perhaps it is the other way round. Your teacher can also observe this and touch the relevant part to help you extend the stomach or the liver, so that they are on a par with each other and you find the right adjustment and placement of the physical organs.

In your practice you will find within your own body that one part is violent and another part non-violent. On one side is deliberate violence because the cells are overworking. And on the so-called non-violent side there is non-deliberate violence, because there the cells are dying, like still-born children. I give a touch to the part where the cells are still-born, so that there can be a little germination—so that the cells can have new life. I create life in those cells by this adjustment which I make by touching my pupils. But this creative adjustment is seen by some people as violence, and I am described as a violent or aggressive teacher!

This touch of the teacher on the body is not like the touch of massage. It is more than massage—it is auto-adjustment which massage cannot produce at all. The effect of this touch in yoga is permanent because we make the person understand subjectively the process which is taking place in his or her body. In massage you cannot do this. You use strength and the effect is only momentary. The principle is the same but the effect will not be there.

You should not mix massage with yoga. If you do some good yoga, then take a massage, just see what will happen to you the next day. You will be half dead! Massage is relaxing, but it is forced relaxation, coming from external manipulation. Yoga is extension—extension giving freedom for the body to relax by itself. This is a natural relaxation.

Let us return to the question of effort. If you observe the effort involved in doing the pose as a beginner, and then continue to observe the effort as you make progress, the effort becomes less and less, but the level of performance of the āsana improves. The degree of physical effort decreases and the achievement increases.

As you work, you may experience discomfort because of the inaccuracy of your posture. Then you have to learn and digest it. You have to make an effort of understanding and observation: 'Why am I getting pain at this moment? Why do I not get the pain at another moment or with another movement? What have I to do with this part of my body? What have I to do with that part? How can I get rid of the pain? Why am I feeling this pressure? Why is this side painful? How are the muscles behaving on this side and how are they behaving on the other side?'

You should go on analysing, and by analysis you will come to understand. Analysis in action is required in yoga. Consider again the example of pain after performing paśchimottānāsana. After finishing the pose you experience pain, but the muscles were sending messages while you were in the pose. How is it that you did not feel them then? You have to see what messages come from the fibres, the muscles, the nerves and the skin of the body while you are doing the pose. Then you can learn. It is not good enough to experience today and analyse tomorrow. That way you have no chance.

Analysis and experimentation have to go together, and in tomorrow's practice you have to think again, 'Am I doing the old pose, or is there a new feeling? Can I extend this new feeling a little more? If I cannot extend it, what is missing?'

Analysis in action is the only guide. You proceed by trial and error. As the trials increase, the errors become less. Then doubts become less, and when the doubts lessen, the effort also becomes less. As long as doubts are there, the efforts are more because you go on oscillating, saying, 'Let me try this. Let me try that. Let me do it this way. Let me do it that way.' But when you find the right method, the effort becomes less because the energy which dissipates into various areas is controlled and not dissipated further.

It is true that in analysis you dissipate energy at first. Later you will not. That is why effort will become less. Direction will come, and when you go in the right direction, wisdom begins. When wise action comes, you no longer feel the effort as effort—you feel the effort as joy. In perfection, your experience and expression find balance and concord.

The Depth of Āsana

The body cannot be separated from the mind, nor can the mind be separated from the soul. No-one can define the boundaries between them. In India, āsana was never considered to be a merely physical practice as it is in the West. But even in India nowadays many people are beginning to think in this way

because they have picked it up from people in the West whose ideas are reflected back to the East.

When Mahātmā Gandhi died, George Bernard Shaw said that it may be
another thousand years before we see another Mahātmā Gandhi on this earth.
Mahātmā Gandhi did not practise all the aspects of yoga. He only followed
two of its principles—non-violence and truth, yet through these two aspects
of yoga, he mastered his own nature and gained independence for India. If a
part of yama could make Mahātmā Gandhi so great, so pure, so honest and so
divine, should it not be possible to take another limb of yoga—āsana—and
through it reach the highest level of spiritual development? Many of you may
say that performing an āsana is a physical discipline, but if you speak in this
way without knowing the depth of āsana, you have already fallen from the
grace of yoga.

Within the one discipline of āsana all the eight levels of yoga are involved,
from yama and niyama through to samādhi. I deliberately pursue in depth the
various levels involved in the performance of āsana, because in the West this
practice is too often considered to be only physical.

When we start working on the performance of āsanas, we all begin by just
scratching the surface of the pose: our work on the pose is peripheral, and this
is known as conative action. The word 'conatus' means an effort or impulse,
and conation is the active aspect of mind, including desire and volition. Conative action is simply physical action at its most direct level.

Then, when we are physically doing the pose, all of a sudden the skin, eyes,
ears, nose and tongue—all our organs of perception—feel what is happening
in the flesh. This is known as cognitive action: the skin cognises, recognises
the action of the flesh.

The third stage, which I call communication or communion, is when the
mind observes the contact of the cognition of the skin with the conative action
of the flesh, and we arrive at mental action in the āsana. At this stage, the mind
comes into play and is drawn by the organs of perception towards the organs
of action, to see exactly what is happening. The mind acts as a bridge between
the muscular movement and the organs of perception, introduces the intellect
and connects it to every part of the body—fibres, tissues, and cells, right
through to the outer pores of the skin. When the mind has come into play, a
new thought arises in us. We see with attention and remember the feeling of
the action. We feel what is happening in our body and our recollection says,
'What is this that I feel now which I did not feel before?' We discriminate with
the mind. The discriminative mind observes and analyses the feeling of the
front, the back, the inside and the outside of the body. This stage is known as
reflective action.

Finally, when there is a total feeling in the action without any fluctuations
in the stretch, then conative action, cognitive action, mental action and reflec-

tive action all meet together to form a total awareness from the self to the skin and from the skin to the self. This is spiritual practice in yoga.

The body comprises three tiers, which are themselves composed of several sheaths. The gross body, called the sthūlaśarīra, corresponds to the physical or anatomical sheath (annamaya-kośa). The subtle body, or sūkṣma-śarīra, is made up of the physiological sheath (prāṇamaya-kośa), the mental sheath (manomaya-kośa) and the intellectual sheath (vijñānamaya-kośa). The innermost body, on which all the others depend, is known as the causal body, or kāraṇa-śarīra. This is the spiritual sheath of joy (ānandamaya-kośa). When all these sheaths come together in each and every one of our trillions of cells—when there is oneness from the cell to the self, from the physical body to the core of the being—then the pose is a contemplative pose and we have reached the highest state of contemplation in the āsana.

That is known as integration, which Patañjali describes in the third chapter of the *Yoga Sūtras,* and which involves integration of the body (śarīra-saṁyama), integration of the breath (prāṇa-saṁyama), integration of the senses (indriya-saṁyama), integration of the mind (manaḥ-saṁyama), integration of the intelligence or of knowledge (buddhi-saṁyama or jñāna-saṁyama) and, finally, integration of the self with all existence (ātma-saṁyama).

This is how the āsanas have to be performed. It cannot come in a day and it cannot come in years. It is a lifelong process, provided that the practitioner has the yogic vitamins of faith, memory, courage, absorption, and uninterrupted awareness of attention. These are the five vitamins required for the practice of yoga. With these five vitamins you can conquer the five sheaths of the body and become one with the Universal Self.

Since yoga means integration, bringing together, it follows that bringing body and mind together, bringing nature and the seer together, is yoga. Beyond that there is nothing—and everything! In a yogī who is perfect, the potency of nature flows abundantly.

27

Discourse on Mind-Intent and Ch'i

Chen Kung

Chen Kung (b. 1906) is the pen name for Chen Yen-lin, also known to Westerners as Yearning K. Chen—a wealthy Chinese merchant and student of Yang Cheng-fu (1883–1936), who transmitted the Yang family tradition of t'ai-chi ch'uan (*taijiquan*) to twentieth-century students. According to the account given by American Stuart Alve Olson, who compiled and translated Chen Kung's writings, Chen Yen-lin, in effect, stole Yang family teachings by borrowing transcripts one evening and hiring seven transcribers to work through the night to reproduce them, publishing these notes in Chinese in 1932. Whatever the accuracy of the tale, Olson's translation of the material resulted in the five-volume English-language Chen Kung Series, with the first volume *Cultivating the Ch'i,* from which the present excerpt is taken. T'ai-chi chuan is a "soft" Chinese martial arts system synthesized in South China early in the seventeenth century. Although the original style was the so-called Chen style, today the Yang family style is the most prevalent. In whatever style or variation, t'ai-chi became increasingly public with time, and its holistic health benefits came to be emphasized, even as its fluid dance-like forms made of it a meditation in motion. Philosophically, t'ai-chi is Taoist in orientation, with the term itself meaning Great Ultimate Principle. But the "ch'i" or *qi* that is cultivated in Olson's translation is different. Ch'i here is a kind of vital energy that travels mysterious body pathways called meridians—it is a middle "substance," as it were, between matter and energy. Living people are said to have ch'i; the dead do not. And in living people, Chen Kung tells, it is the mind's intent, ultimately, that moves the ch'i. Knowing through the mind comes full circle here and leads back to the spirituality of the body.

Within each person there is *mind-intent*[1] and ch'i,[2] both of which are invisible and formless.

It is essential to know that the ch'i is produced within the body. To harness this energy is extremely important as the ch'i and the body must satisfy each other's needs.

In application, the ch'i stimulates the blood and nourishes it. This is the process of perfecting the ch'i. The heat from the ch'i rises up from the *"gate of life."*[3] The *ching*[4] should then be cherished and nourished. Both of these (the ch'i and ching) should be repeatedly stimulated and perfected. The Taoist schools call this, *"perfecting the fire and water,"*[5] or the *"internal elixir."* They seek to retain the ch'i and store it in the *tan-tien.*[6] The Taoists regard the ch'i as being an exceptionally precious possession.

Blood or ch'i, what is to be most prized? Most people are unaware that the ch'i is more substantial than the blood. The ch'i acts as the master to the blood; the blood is like the assistant.

The ch'i is like the troops and the blood like the camp. During a man's entire lifetime he must depend completely upon both the troops and the camp. Supposing an army had a camp and no troops; there would then be no convoys. Likewise, having troops and no camp, there would be nowhere to unite.

In other words, the ch'i is most important and the blood is secondary. If the blood is insufficient, it is still possible to maintain life for a short period, but if the ch'i is lacking, there will arise an immediate crisis, resulting in death.

Therefore, when nourishing the ch'i, what is the most important condition? Specifically you must practice T'ai Chi Ch'uan. Get rid of the external gymnastics. Moreover, master the production and nourishment of ch'i. As the proverb says, "Externally exercise the muscles, bones and skin; internally train the one breath."[7] So in general this means to practice T'ai Chi Ch'uan.

It becomes immaterial later on whether you practice the circular motions of the solo forms, the *tui-shou*[8] or the *ta-lu*[9] exercises. All that really matters is that while performing these exercises you are conscious of breathing naturally. Likewise, your facial expression should be unchanging.

The ch'i should circulate throughout the inner areas of the body. Previous to stretching and before actually having set the exercise into motion, you will already be well aware of how to nourish the ch'i through the exercises. The efficacy of the T'ai Chi Ch'uan exercises is very great. So on no account corrupt your practice by training in too hasty, laborious or fatiguing a manner. This cannot be stressed enough.

When the blood has been completely purified, the body will become extremely strong. When the body is strong the mind is strengthened and rendered more determined. With this the spirit (*p'o*)[10] is made strong and brave. With a strong spirit you can increase your life span and benefit greatly from this longer life.

Students should know that the only gateway to acquiring the skills of T'ai Chi Ch'uan is by constant cultivation of ch'i.

Some have said that mind-intent is no other than the mind (rational thinking), or that the mind is no other than the mind-intent. But truly there is both a mind and mind-intent; they are two separate things and should be thought of as such.

The master of the mind is the mind-intent. The mind acts as only an assistant to the mind-intent. When the mind moves, it does so because of the mind-intent; when the mind-intent arises the ch'i will follow.

In other words: mind, mind-intent and ch'i are all interconnected and work in a rotational manner. When the mind is confused the mind-intent will disperse. When the mind-intent is dispersed the ch'i will become insubstantial (weak).

So it is said, "*When the ch'i sinks into the tan-tien, the mind-intent is made strong and vital; with a strong and vital mind-intent, the mind then becomes tranquil.*" Therefore, these three mutually employ each other, and in truth they must be united and not allowed to become separate.

The application of ch'i will expedite the blood circulation and stimulate the spirit. When the spirit and ch'i circulation are active, they can then be put into use; otherwise, neither the ch'i nor the mind-intent can be regulated properly.

The way of the ch'uan (internal boxing) art is to have regulation without method, or principles without techniques. At some point this will be clear to the ch'uan-*ist*.

Having only techniques without principles amounts to nothing more than giving up one's capital in order to follow an inferior scheme (to invest in a losing business venture).

So, in the ch'uan arts, the regulation of ch'i and mind-intent is based on mutual dependence. But to actually employ mind-intent and the ch'i within your T'ai Chi Ch'uan practice is very, very difficult, especially for beginning students. Yet, there really is no beginning method other than practicing the thirteen postures of the solo movements.

What is absolutely necessary in the beginning, however, is to follow the imagination. For instance: when the two hands perform the *Press* gesture, there is an imagined intent to the front, as if an opponent was really there. At this time, within the palms of the hands there is no ch'i which can be issued. The practitioner must then imagine the ch'i rising up from the tan-tien into the spine, through the arms and into the wrists and palms. Thus, accordingly, the ch'i is imagined to have penetrated outwards onto the opponent's body.

This use of imagination during initial study and practice will be difficult to trust and will not be susceptible to proof. Only after a long period of training will you be able to apply it in a natural manner, which is when the ch'i penetrates the inner regions of the body. This occurs when the gestures maintain two circuits of the ch'i; then the ch'i flows into the limbs of the body. When control of the mind-intent is achieved, the ch'i will follow. At what point this occurs is immaterial as long as it is mobilized.

In T'ai Chi Ch'uan there are the fundamental principles of "*opening* and *closing*," "*fullness* and *emptiness*," "*inhaling* and *exhaling*" and "*advancing* and *withdrawing*." These are the training methods for circulating the ch'i throughout the entire body. From these the body will become quite sensitive and alert, as will the muscles and tendons. The sense of touch will also become increasingly more acute. Thus, the spirit will be made active and alert.

Within the text of *The Mental Elucidation of the Thirteen Kinetic Postures* there is a verse which states, "*If the ch'i is not present the spirit of vitality of the entire body and mind will be obstructed. When the ch'i is present there is no need to exert muscular force, and without the ch'i it is simply hardness.*"

In summary, the ch'i will be useless unless it is dutifully regulated in an unconscious manner. Otherwise, the ch'i will cause obstructions in your body, become unstable or fleeting, or abruptly produce a state of anger. At the time of having to issue the ch'i, obstructive ch'i, unstable ch'i and anger ch'i will cause the feet to float and make the center of balance unsteady. This is what is meant by to "be without strength."

T'ai Chi Ch'uan is said to center around the ch'i of the tan-tien, (positive ch'i). This ch'i is very pure and tranquil. This tranquility makes it possible to be harmonious; this harmony makes it lucid; and lucidity makes the ch'i safe and unobstructed. This prevents the ch'i from producing scorching heat. In no way is this type of ch'i similar to the above three negative kinds of ch'i.

The discussion on ch'i within the text of *The Mental Elucidation of the Thirteen Kinetic Postures* is of great importance. For example:

The mind moves the ch'i so that it may sink
deeply and penetrate the bones. When the ch'i circulates freely and
unhindered throughout the body,
then it can easily follow the intentions of the mind.

The mind-intent and ch'i must interact in a lively manner in order
to achieve both smoothness and circularity.

The ch'i is mobilized as though it were threading a pearl with nine
crooked pathways; no hollow or corner is left unreached.

The ch'i should be nourished naturally so as
not to have any injurious effects.

Relax (sung) *the abdomen, to allow the ch'i to*
penetrate into the bones.

Whether moving 'to or fro' the ch'i is to adhere
to the spine.

Within *The Song of Thirteen Postures* it is said:

The ch'i should be circulated throughout the
entire body without the slightest obstruction.

When the mind-intent and ch'i are the rulers
the bones and flesh follow their dictates.

When the mind-intent and ch'i are regulated,
it follows that the bones and flesh will become
heavier.

These verses concerning the ch'i are all of great importance. When learning these it is difficult to distinguish all of them from one another, especially when differentiating bright (*positive*) ch'i from the scorching heat of the obstructive (*negative*) ch'i.

The relationship between the mind-intent and ch'i is like that of an automobile; inside is the driver and an engine. The mind-intent is the driver and the ch'i, the engine. Either of these would be seriously lacking without the other.

NOTES

1. I: (pronounced *yi*) In the practice of T'ai Chi Ch'uan the function of the *mind-intent*, or will, is both transcendental and intrinsically connected with ch'i. Mind-intent is neither a conditioned response nor an unconscious reaction. It is a reaction founded in awareness, intuition and sensitivity. However, mind-intent is *"conditioned"* in that it is developed over a long period of time through practice of the various T'ai Chi Ch'uan exercises. The mind-intent is also *"unconscious"* in that the rational thinking mind is not used.

The problem in defining the mind-intent is an empirical one in that you must first be truly capable of sinking the ch'i into tan-tien, which then strengthens the vitality of mind-intent, which in turn will affect the mind, producing tranquility. So without initiating the use of mind-intent, however vague at first, in order to sink the ch'i into the tan-tien, the mind-intent cannot be made strong enough for you to truly realize the difference between mind-intent and mind.

2. **CH'I:** *Vital Life Energy and/or Breath.* There are many explanations of what ch'i is, such as: an inherent oxygen in the blood for stamina and vitality; or a subtle cosmic energy which constitutes life, growth and motion in all things. Both these, and all the explanations, are true. Most teachings and teachers however prefer to explain its stimulation, nourishment, accumulation and/or circulation, than to attempt the difficult task of defining it.

In T'ai Chi Ch'uan and seated meditation you experience the sensations of ch'i when 1) mind-intent sinks the ch'i into the tan-tien, 2) when mind-intent becomes vital, and 3) the mind is tranquil—then ch'i will not only be sensed, but will circulate freely throughout the entire body.

3. **MING-MEN:** *The Gate of Life.* This is a ch'i cavity associated with the kidneys, located over the kidneys along the spine.

4. **CHING:** *Regenerative Force or Energy.* Ching is usually translated as sperm (for the male) and sexual fluids (for women). However ching is not necessarily just a substance, but rather the subtle energy which produces it, i.e., sexual force or the force that gives all things form. All Taoist practices call for the conservation of ching, which stimulates the ch'i, which stimulates shen (spirit). (For more information on this subject see *The Jade Emperor's Mind Seal Classic: A Discourse on Refining the Three Treasures (Ching, Ch'i, Shen),* translation and commentary by Stuart Alve Olson. Dragon Door Publications, 1992).

5. **HUO SHUI:** *Fire and Water.* A symbolic expression representing the interaction of ching and ch'i. The idea is that the ch'i heats the ching, which then causes the ch'i

to move; once the ch'i moves and can be circulated this is then "perfecting the fire and water."

6. **TAN-TIEN:** *Field of Elixir.* This is the central and most important ch'i center of all Chinese spiritual practices. This center, or cavity, is the source from which the ch'i is stimulated and accumulated. In T'ai Chi Ch'uan all movement finds its source originating from the tan-tien. It is called the "field of elixir" because the Three Treasures (ching, ch'i and shen) are all united, forming a mixture in the central point (Taoist analogies: *pot, stove, furnace, caldron*) and are refined forming an elixir, which then confers health, longevity, immortality or enlightenment, depending upon the degree to which the essences (ching, ch'i and shen) have been refined.

The process with the tan-tien in T'ai Chi Ch'uan is as follows:

The mind-intent leads the ch'i down into the tan-tien; when this is accomplished the ch'i strengthens the mind-intent; the more vital the mind-intent, the greater the mobilization of ch'i and the greater the tranquility of the mind. At this point the entire body moves in accordance with the movement of ch'i guided by mind-intent. This is true spontaneity and *sung* (relaxation, alertness and sensitivity). This is why the T'ai Chi Ch'uan classics insist on *"abiding by the tan-tien."*

If one were to strip Taoism to its bare essentials there would be nothing left except "abiding by the tan-tien" in order to concentrate the ching, ch'i and shen in *one* center. This is the root of all Taoist philosophy and practices; everything else is but branches and leaves. Lao Tzu (*Tao Te Ching*) says: "Embrace the One (*Pao-I*) and return to the source (*Kuei Yuan*)," which means abide by the tan-tien.

7. **I K'OU CH'I:** *In One Breath.* This means: with one mind focus and concentrate on the internal. The term carries various meanings, ranging from: connecting the inhalation and exhalation without pause, one flowing into the next; developing the mind and body unceasingly so that both function as one unit; and completion (internal attainment), which is the result of continuous repetition of practice. Sometimes this term is given as *i-ch'i* (*one breath; one action; one energy*). Here, i k'ou chi, literally translates as "one mouthful of ch'i," which in the higher practices of Taoist alchemy is a reference to the ingesting of breath or swallowing ch'i.

8. **TUI-SHOU:** *Pushing-Hands.* This is one of the three main two-person training exercises of T'ai Chi Ch'uan concerning development of chin (intrinsic energy) and its application, both in fixed form and free-sparring. The other two are *san-shou* and *ta-lu.* Tui-shou is generally associated with the movements of the four initial postures of of *Ward-Off, Roll-Back, Press* and *Push.* (San-shou, *dispersing-hands,* is exclusive to Yang style T'ai Chi Ch'uan. San-shou is a two-person exercise dealing with the applications, in active stepping, of the postures of T'ai Chi Ch'uan. See following note for explanation of ta-lu).

9. **TA-LU:** *Great Roll-Back.* This exercise is associated with the movements of the four diagonal directions and the *Four Primary Postures* of Pull, Split, Elbow-Stroke and

Shoulder-Stroke, which are neutralized by the postures of Ward-Off, Roll-Back, Push and Press. However, there are other variations of ta-lu besides this one.

10. **P'O:** *Earth Bound Spirit or Sentient Spirit.* In brief, Taoism professes that a person obtains two spirit energies at birth, the *p'o* and *h'un* (heavenly and earthly bound spirit). P'o represents the physical body; h'un the spiritual body. Now, at the time of death, if the Three Treasures are not cultivated the p'o descends to earth with the *yuan shen* (original spirit) to become a ghost, which dies off relatively quickly. If, on the other hand, the Three Treasures are cultivated, then the yuan shen ascends to heaven with the h'un, thus becoming one of three stages of immortals: *Ti Hsien* (Earthly Immortal), *T'ien Hsien* (Heavenly Immortal) and *Yang Hsien* (Pure Immortal).

The reason for referring here to p'o rather than shen is that while alive the p'o benefits from the vitality and strength of ch'i, thereby increasing the life span and enhancing the health. In Taoist alchemy there is a saying, *"Replenish the Yang with Yin."* The p'o is yin, the h'un yang. Through T'ai Chi Ch'uan practices this is exactly what occurs, yang is made strong through yin.

In the T'ai Chi Ch'uan classics it says, *"From the flexible and most yielding one can become the most powerful and unyielding."* So the use of p'o here is a symbolism for how softness and yielding can overcome the hard and unyeilding, such as water wearing away at a rock, or in Lao Tzu's analogy, *"The tongue lasts a long time because it is soft. Because they are hard, the teeth cannot outlast the tongue."*

Suggestions for Further Reading

The books listed below have been limited to a few introductory selections and were chosen according to the themes emphasized in this reader. The number of titles on spirituality is vast and continues to grow in today's cultural climate.

General Spirituality

Alexander, Jon. "What Do Recent Writers Mean by Spirituality?" *Spirituality Today* 32 (September 1980): 247–54.

Beaudoin, Tom. *Virtual Faith: The Irreverent Spiritual Quest of Generation X.* San Francisco: Jossey-Bass, 1998.

Cousins, Ewert. "Spirituality in Today's World." In *Religion in Today's World: The Religious Situation in the World from 1945 to the Present Day.* Edited by Frank Whaling. Edinburgh: T. & T. Clark, 1987.

Ellwood, Robert S. *The Fifties Spiritual Marketplace: American Religion in a Decade of Conflict.* New Brunswick: Rutgers University Press, 1997.

———. *The Sixties Spiritual Awakening: American Religion Moving from Modern to Postmodern.* New Brunswick: Rutgers University Press, 1994.

James, William. *The Varieties of Religious Experience: A Study in Human Nature.* 1902. Reprint, Cambridge: Harvard University Press, 1985.

Lesser, Elizabeth. *The New American Spirituality: A Seeker's Guide.* New York: Random House, 1999.

Roof, Wade Clark. *A Generation of Seekers: The Spiritual Journeys of the Baby Boom Generation.* San Francisco: Harper, 1993.

———. *Spiritual Marketplace: Baby Boomers and the Remaking of American Religion.* Princeton: Princeton University Press, 1999.

———, et al. "Forum: American Spirituality." *Religion and American Culture: A Journal of Interpretation* 9 (Summer 1999): 131–57.

Taves, Ann. *Fits, Trances, and Visions: Experiencing Religion and Explaining Experience from Wesley to James.* Princeton: Princeton University Press, 1999.

Tickle, Phyllis. *Rediscovering the Sacred: Spirituality in America.* New York: Crossroads, 1995.

Torrance, Robert. *The Spiritual Quest: Transcendence in Myth, Religion, and Science.* Berkeley: University of California Press, 1994.

Wuthnow, Robert. *After Heaven: Spirituality in America since the 1950s.* Berkeley: University of California Press, 1998.

Zinnbauer, Brian J., et al. "Religion and Spirituality: Unfuzzing the Fuzzy." *Journal for the Scientific Study of Religion* 36 (December 1997): 549–64.

Knowing through the Body: The Path of Ritual

Bell, Catherine. *Ritual Theory, Ritual Practice.* New York: Oxford University Press, 1992.

Geertz, Clifford. "Religion as a Cultural System." In *The Interpretation of Cultures.* New York: Basic Books, 1973.

Grimes, Ronald L. *Beginnings in Ritual Studies.* Rev. ed. Columbia: University of South Carolina Press, 1995.

Hambrick-Stowe, Charles E. *The Practice of Piety: Puritan Devotional Disciplines in Seventeenth-Century New England.* Chapel Hill: University of North Carolina Press, 1982.

Heilman, Samuel C. *Synagogue Life: A Study in Symbolic Interaction.* Chicago: University of Chicago Press, 1976.

Smith, Jonathan Z. *To Take Place: Toward Theory in Ritual.* Chicago: University of Chicago Press, 1987.

Taves, Ann. *The Household of Faith: Roman Catholic Devotions in Mid-Nineteenth-Century America.* Notre Dame: University of Notre Dame Press, 1986.

Turner, Victor. *The Ritual Process.* Chicago: Aldine, 1969.

Knowing through the Heart: The Path of Feeling and Emotion

Alexander, Jon, ed. *American Personal Religious Accounts, 1600–1980: Toward an Inner History of America's Faiths.* New York: Edwin Mellen Press, 1983.

Balmer, Randall. *Mine Eyes Have Seen the Glory: A Journey into the Evangelical Subculture in America.* Expanded ed. New York: Oxford University Press, 1993.

Cox, Harvey. *Fire from Heaven: The Rise of Pentecostal Spirituality and the Reshaping of Religion in the Twenty-first Century.* Reading, Mass.: Addison-Wesley, 1995.

Datta, A. K. *Bhaktiyoga.* Bombay: Bharatiya Vidya Bhavan, 1959.

Johnson, Curtis D. *Redeeming America: Evangelicals and the Road to Civil War.* Chicago: Ivan R. Dee, 1993.

McLoughlin, William G., Jr. *Modern Revivalism: Charles Grandison Finney to Billy Graham.* New York: Ronald Press, 1959.

Otto, Rudolf. *The Idea of the Holy: An Inquiry into the Non-Rational Factor in the Idea of the Divine and Its Relation to the Rational.* Trans. John W. Harvey. 2d (1950) ed. Reprint; New York: Oxford University Press, 1958.

Streng, Frederick J. "Personal Apprehension of a Holy Presence." In *Understanding Religious Life.* 3d ed. Belmont, Calif.: Wadsworth, 1985.

Knowing through the Will: The Path of Prophecy and Social Action

McLoughlin, William G. *Revivals, Awakenings, and Reform: An Essay on Religion and Social Change in America, 1607–1977.* Chicago: University of Chicago Press, 1978.

Meconis, Charles A. *With Clumsy Grace: The American Catholic Left, 1961–1975.* New York: Seabury Press, Continuum, 1979.

Niebuhr, H. Richard. "Christ against Culture." In *Christ and Culture.* New York: Harper, 1951.

Quinley, Harold E. *The Prophetic Clergy: Social Activism among Protestant Ministers.* New York: Wiley, 1974.

Sorin, Gerald. *The Prophetic Minority: American Jewish Immigrant Radicals, 1880–1920.* Bloomington: Indiana University Press, 1985.

Streng, Frederick J. "The Religious Significance of Social Responsibility." In *Understanding Religious Life*. 3d ed. Belmont, Calif.: Wadsworth, 1985.

Tyler, Alice Felt. *Freedom's Ferment: Phases of American Social History from the Colonial Period to the Outbreak of the Civil War*. 1944. Reprint, New York: Harper & Row, Harper Torchbooks, 1962.

Weber, Max. "The Prophet." *The Sociology of Religion*. Translated from the 4th (1956) ed. by Ephraim Fischoff (1st ed. published in German in 1922). Boston: Beacon Press, 1963.

Wilmore, Gayraud S. *Black Religion and Black Radicalism: An Interpretation of the Religious History of Afro-American People*. 2d ed. Maryknoll, N.Y.: Orbis Books, 1983.

Knowing through the Mind: The Path of Metaphysics

Albanese, Catherine L. "Child of the Universe." In *Corresponding Motion: Transcendental Religion and the New America*. Philadelphia: Temple University Press, 1977.

———. "Homesteads of the Mind: Belief and Practice in Metaphysics." In *America: Religions and Religion*. 3d ed. Belmont, Calif.: Wadsworth, 1999.

———. *Nature Religion in America: From the Algonkian Indians to the New Age*. Chicago: University of Chicago Press, 1990.

Campbell, Bruce F. *Ancient Wisdom Revived: A History of the Theosophical Movement*. Berkeley: University of California Press, 1980.

Carroll, Bret E. *Spiritualism in Antebellum America*. Bloomington: Indiana University Press, 1997.

Ellwood, Robert S., Jr. *Alternative Altars: Unconventional and Eastern Spirituality in America*. Chicago: University of Chicago Press, 1979.

Hanegraaf, Wouter J. *New Age Religion and Western Culture: Esotericism in the Mirror of Secular Thought*. Albany: State University of New York Press, 1998.

Heelas, Paul. *The New Age Movement: The Celebration of Self and the Sacralization of Modernity*. Oxford: Blackwell Publishers, 1996.

Judah, J. Stillson. *The History and Philosophy of the Metaphysical Movements in America*. Philadelphia: Westminster Press, 1967.

Streng, Frederick J. "Attaining Freedom through Spiritual Discipline" and "Living in Harmony with Cosmic Law." In *Understanding Religious Life*. 3d ed. Belmont, Calif.: Wadsworth, 1985.

INDEX

CATHERINE L. ALBANESE is Professor of Religious Studies at the University of California, Santa Barbara. She is the author of the widely used textbook *America: Religions and Religion* (Wadsworth), now in its third edition (1999), and of numerous other articles and books, including *Nature Religion in America: From the Algonkian Indians to the New Age* (University of Chicago Press). Albanese is a former president of the American Academy of Religion.